Lecture Notes in Information Systems and Organisation

Volume 82

Lecture Notes in Information Systems and Organization (LNISO) is a series of scientific books that explore the current state of information systems studies, in particular in the context of organizations, as well as behavioral and design aspects of information systems. The series offers an integrated publication platform for high-quality conferences, symposia and workshops proceedings. Books accepted for publication are selected based on a double-blind peer-review evaluation made by invited reviewers. The series is indexed in Scopus.

Christoph M. Flath · Gunther Gust ·
Frédéric Thiesse · Axel Winkelmann
Editors

Artificial Intelligence, Data, and Decision-Making

Proceedings of the 19th International Conference on Wirtschaftsinformatik, Würzburg, Germany, 2024—Vol.1

Springer

Editors
Christoph M. Flath
Julius-Maximilian University of Würzburg
Würzburg, Germany

Gunther Gust
Julius-Maximilian University of Würzburg
Würzburg, Germany

Frédéric Thiesse
Julius-Maximilian University of Würzburg
Würzburg, Germany

Axel Winkelmann
Julius-Maximilian University of Würzburg
Würzburg, Germany

ISSN 2195-4968 ISSN 2195-4976 (electronic)
Lecture Notes in Information Systems and Organisation
ISBN 978-3-032-08479-8 ISBN 978-3-032-08480-4 (eBook)
https://doi.org/10.1007/978-3-032-08480-4

This Springer imprint is published by the registered company Springer Nature Switzerland AG
The registered company address is: Gewerbestrasse 11, 6330 Cham, Switzerland

Contents

Part I
Theme Track: Information Systems in the Age of AI

Contributions of AI to Advance Interoperability with Data Mediators

Torben Ukena and Rainer Alt

Abstract This study presents an innovative approach to advancing interoperability in information systems through the development of an Artificial Intelligence (AI)-based data mediator. Although standards have contributed to interoperability among disparate systems, the lack of universal standards still requires tools for data mediation. To reduce the substantial need for manual configuration of these systems, this paper outlines a strategy for translating data between two systems with different data schemas automatically. Unlike traditional methods, the proposed data mediator leverages recent advancements in AI to facilitate automatic mapping of heterogeneous data.

1 Introduction

In our interconnected world, standards serve as foundational blocks for complex systems. They ensure consistency, reliability, and safety across domains, from the dimensions of a bolt to the protocols governing international telecommunications. Standards are key as they enable disparate systems and components to work seamlessly together, fostering innovation and efficiency [1]. This is illustrated by the healthcare sector, where interoperability potentials are estimated at $77.8 billion per year for the United States alone [2]. A more recent study emphasized that "the efficiency potential currently lost in the fragmented interplay of stakeholders, sectoral boundaries, and limited care coordination [...] account for up to 25% of healthcare spending in Europe and the US" [3, p. 1]. Although interoperability has been a persistent problem for decades, the evolution of standards and mediation technologies still requires a significant amount of manual activity. A promising area to explore is Artificial Intelligence (AI) that contributes facilities in pattern recognition to enhance interoperability. From this background, this research analyzes existing interoperability concepts and proposes to create an AI-based solution that can manage

T. Ukena (✉) · R. Alt
Information Systems Institute, Leipzig University, Leipzig, Germany
e-mail: torben.ukena@uni-leipzig.de

C. M. Flath et al. (eds.), *Artificial Intelligence, Data, and Decision-Making*, Lecture Notes in Information Systems and Organisation 82,
https://doi.org/10.1007/978-3-032-08480-4_1

heterogeneous data to contribute to the broad field of interoperability. For the sake of consistency, this paper repeatedly refers to examples from the healthcare sector. However, it should be noted that the proposed AI model can be applied across other domains where networking among heterogeneous systems is widespread, e.g. retailing, banking or the automotive industry.

2 Levels and Status of Interoperability

2.1 Definitions

Interoperability is defined by the European Commission and the European Interoperability Framework as "the ability of information and communication technology systems and of the business processes they support to exchange data and to enable sharing of information and knowledge" [4]. To apply this definition, it is necessary to break down interoperability to different levels, as shown in Fig. 1.

Data Mediation is an approach designed to solve the data interoperability problem by enabling the translation of data between two systems with different data schemas. The difference between data mediators and a mapping is the ability to automatically generate such translations [6].

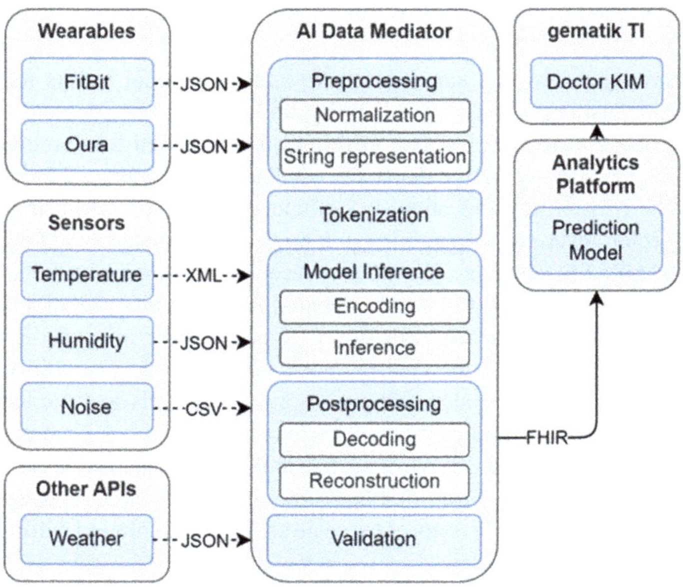

Fig. 1 Interoperability levels (from [5])

2.2 Technical Interoperability

Technical interoperability at the foundational level has been extensively researched. With the introduction of ISO/OSI and TCP/IP standards, fundamental interoperability is now rarely an issue [7]. Similarly, many well-established paradigms for structural interoperability exist. Representational State Transfer (REST) is probably the most widely used architecture style. The HTTP protocol is defined by its standard methods for communication, and exchanging data is done using standard formats, typically JSON or XML. REST has become the de-facto standard for offering a service on the web due to its ease of use and its longterm presence [8]. In healthcare, Fast Healthcare Interoperability Resources (FHIR) is evolving as a promising standard which uses REST under the hood.

2.3 Semantic Interoperability

With foundational and structural interoperability in place, the next step is to get a common understanding of the meaning of the data, i.e. semantic interoperability. Currently, each organization has its own REST Application Programming Interface (API) with different endpoints and data models. Consider the following example of API responses from their respective sleep endpoint from Fitbit and Oura.[1] Although both provide sleep data via the API in JSON format, the data model is not interoperable. For example, they both use a day key but require different access methods. If an analytics platform wanted to use sleep data from both vendors (e.g., to determine a wellbeing score), it would have to manually map the data and refer to each vendor's documentation for data ranges.

To address the lack of semantic interoperability, many domain-specific standards have been developed. These standards often define the entire data representation and include terminologies used within the domain. In healthcare, the Fitbit and Oura API response could be fully represented as a FHIR resource. This would allow for universal data representation with clear units, value ranges, and terminology. However, in healthcare, as in any industry, FHIR is not the only standard in use. In fact, in the U.S. healthcare sector alone, there are more than 40 different standards development organizations creating standards for interoperability [9]

Similarly, other sectors such as IoT are facing the same issues as [10, p. 807] claims that "there are currently several different academia, industry, and standardization bodies aiming to solve IoT system interoperability. It is not likely that a common set of standards will be universally accepted which will allow IoT devices and platforms to work together." They further state that implementing interoperability should not require major changes to existing systems.

[1] Further information about the API responses from Fitbit and Oura can be found in the Fitbit API Documentation (https://dev.fitbit.com/build/reference/web-api/sleep) and Oura API Documentation (https://cloud.ouraring.com/v2/docs#tag/Sleep-Routes).

Table 1 Example of sleep API responses from wearables

Oura Sleep API	Fitbit Sleep API
{ "id": "string", "efficiency": 69, "awake_time": 0, "time_in_bed": 0, "day": "2019–08-24", "total_sleep_duration": 0 }	{ "sleep": [{ "dateOfSleep": "2020–02-21", "efficiency": 42, "duration": 27,720,000, "infoCode": 0 }] }

2.4 *Mapping Approaches*

Therefore, instead of designing another standard for semantic interoperability, a new layer could leverage existing standards and systems [11, p. 36]. In doing so, the improvement of AI-architectures in recent years is promising to help address interoperability issues. The conducted research therefore focuses on the development of an AI data mediator that is trained using interoperable data schemas to automatically map heterogeneous data into a standard.

The concept of a data mediator per se is not innovative. Various approaches to data and process mediation have been proposed and evaluated. Pessoa et al. [14] examined different methodologies and highlighted the notable disadvantages of manually creating and managing ontologies for mediation purposes. Ali and Chong [15] attempted to address the issue of manual mapping by introducing a semantic annotation algorithm that utilizes deep representation learning to align different ontologies. However, focusing on ontologies requires the translation of structured data into semantic ontology models which not only introduces additional complexity but also requires the standards to have a readily available ontological representation. Besides this, little research has been conducted to overcome the weaknesses of current solutions. Table 2 provides a brief overview of the level of interoperability each approach covers and illustrates the disadvantages of the state-of-the-art methods.

3 Evaluation of an AI Data Mediator

3.1 *Example of a Practical Use Case*

Consider the following practical example of such an AI data mediator. A new system enables a home sleep lab that sends key data from wearables and other sensors to an analytics platform. The analytics platform evaluates the data and makes recommendations to improve sleep quality. The patient consults a physician regarding sleep problems, the doctor prescribes the sleep lab, and the analytics system sends the data to the doctor's system for evaluation via the Gematik Telematic Infrastructure (TI)

Table 2 Interoperability levels for different data mapping approaches

	Manual mapping [12, p. 1473]	Ontology-based mapping [13, pp. 2–3]	AI data mediator
Foundational	Achieved	Achieved	Achieved
Structural	Limited to use case		
Semantic		Limited to use case, occurrence of lexical and semantic mismatches	
Organizational	Not achieved	Not achieved	Limited, depends on placement within the organization (see Sect. 3.1)

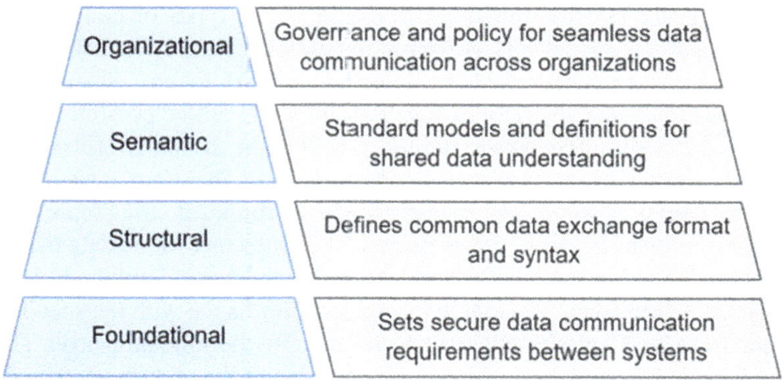

Fig. 2 High level concept of the AI data mediator

using the Communication in Medicine (KIM) standard. Even within this simplified example there are many different data formats as shown in Fig. 2.

In this example each provider uses custom proprietary formats. Therefore, both the analysis platform and the doctor's system need to develop connectors to map the data. With an AI as a data mediator, this process could be automated by sending HTTP requests from the API via the data mediator, which converts the data into a standardized format. There are several ways in which the data mediator could be integrated. Firstly, it could act as middleware, as shown in Fig. 2. This would be comparable to a star network topology, with the data mediator acting as a proxy for all necessary requests. Another method is to include the data mediator as part of each API. This approach would allow for a fully connected network, but each node would require its own instance of the data mediator. Identifying the optimal placement of the data mediator is crucial for practical implementation and part of the work plan as outlined in Sect. 4.

3.2 Proposed AI Architecture

ChatGPT proves that the implementation of an AI that enables mapping to standards is possible. With appropriate prompts, ChatGPT can effectively convert relevant information into FHIR. However, a dedicated AI is required for practical implementation. After considering several architectures, including traditional machine learning models, rule-based systems, and deep learning approaches, the most suitable AI architecture appears to be the Transformer-based models, specifically tailored for sequence-to-sequence tasks. Among these, the Text-to-Text Transfer Transformer (T5) model stands out for its versatility and capability to handle complex structured data translation tasks [16].

In the context of developing a data mediator, the concept of sentinel tokens has been considered. Sentinel tokens are predefined, unique markers or symbols used to indicate specific structural elements, boundaries, or types of content within a sequence of data [16, pp. 12–13]. However, the use of sentinel tokens would require both the source and target formats to be serialized with tokens. Since the model should be able to handle a variety of standards, it would not be possible to serialize every single input and output data for training. In addition, the real-world data that the model would work with would also need to be serialized. Therefore, it was decided to not implement sentinel tokens and instead encode the format as string representation.

Another important aspect of the evaluated AI architecture of the data mediator is the validation layer. For major standards like FHIR, there are Command Line Interface (CLI) or API validators available to check conformance with the specification. The output from the T5 model will serve as the input for the validation layer. The validation layer will first perform a syntactical validation of the underlying data format, if possible. If the data format passes the syntactic validation, the corresponding validation API or CLI will be used to check if it meets the standard specification. If either of these steps fail, the T5 model will be used iteratively to fix the mismatches.

4 Workplan

To further advance the development of the AI data mediator, several follow-up activities are planned, and the next steps are outlined below.

1. Evaluation of a proper placement of the AI data mediator as outlined in Sect. 3.1. If placed well, it could provide pseudo-interoperability, e.g. by trans-forming HL7 v2 into FHIR and being addressed as an interface rather than the underlying system.

2. A systematic literature review is planned to gain a detailed understanding of existing standards. The next step involves systematically collecting the detected standards, including specification schemas, example files, and definitions.

3. The T5 architecture for the data mediator must be defined in accordance with its placement.

4. To prepare the training data, it is necessary to create and validate examples of mappings from various input formats to the collected standards. This process can be partially automated by utilizing existing manual mappers.

5. The T5 Model will be trained, validated, and fine-tuned using all collected data and a test set. The model's design, performance, and (hyper-)parameters will be evaluated in a comprehensive computational study.

The research aims to evaluate a model for enhancing interoperability in practice. To achieve this, it may be necessary to focus on a specific domain and integrate the data mediator more accurately. However, it is important to note that the AI data mediator can be applied beyond the respective domain. The healthcare sector is a suitable domain for studying interoperability challenges. We maintain close communication with experts from the Medical Center of the University of Leipzig to develop a theoretically sound and practically applicable model.

References

1. Shivakumar, S. (2022). *Securing Global Standards for Innovation and Growth.* Center for Strategic and International Studies (CSIS).
2. Walker, J., Pan, E., Johnston, D., Adler-Milstein, J., Bates, D. W., & Middleton, B. (2005). The value of health care information exchange and interoperability. *Health affairs (Project Hope)*, Suppl Web Exclusives, W5-10-W5-18.
3. Pidun, U., Knust, N., Kawohl, J., Avramakis, E., & Klar, A. (2021). *The Untapped Potential of Ecosystems in Health Care.* Boston: Boston Consulting Group.
4. IDABC. (2004). *European Interoperability Framework for Pan-European e-Government Services (EIF) Version 1.0.* European Communities.
5. Adebesin, F., Foster, R., Kotzé, P., & van Greunen, D. (2013). A Review of Interoperability Standards in E-health and Imperatives for their Adoption in Africa. *South African Computer Journal, 50*, 1.
6. Renner, S., Rosenthal, A., & Scarano, J. (1999). *Data Interoperability: Standardization or Mediation.*
7. Sunyaev, A., Dehling, T., Strahringer, S., Da Xu, L., Heinig, M., Perscheid, M., Alt, R., & Rossi, M. (2023). The Future of Enterprise Information Systems. *Business & Information Systems Engineering, 65*(6), 731–751.
8. Neumann, A., Laranjeiro, N., & Bernardino, J. (2021). An Analysis of Public REST Web Service APIs. *IEEE Transactions on Services Computing, 14*(4), 957–970.
9. HIMSS. (2024). *Interoperability in Healthcare.* https://www.himss.org/resources/interoperability-healthcare.
10. Noura, M., Atiquzzaman, M., & Gaedke, M. (2019). Interoperability in Internet of Things: Taxonomies and Open Challenges. *Mobile Networks and Applications, 24*(3), 796–809.
11. Braunstein, M. L. (2018). Health care in the age of interoperability: The potential and challenges. *IEEE Pulse, 9*(5), 34–36.
12. Dos Reis, J. C., Pruski, C., & Reynaud-Delaître, C. (2015). State-of-the-art on mapping maintenance and challenges towards a fully automatic approach. *Expert Systems with Applications, 42*(3), 1465–1478.
13. Amrouch, S., & Mostefai, S. (2012). Survey on the literature of ontology mapping, alignment and merging. In *2012 International Conference on Information Technology and e-Services* (pp. 1–5). March 24, 2012, Sousse, Tunisia. IEEE.
14. Pessoa, R., Quartel, D., & van Sinderen, M. (2008). A Comparison of Data and Process Mediation Approaches. *Journal of Vacuum Science & Technology A, 2008*, 48–63.

15. Ali, S., & Chong, I. (2019). Semantic Mediation Model to Promote Improved Data Sharing Using Representation Learning in Heterogeneous Healthcare Service Environments. *Applied Sciences, 9*(19), 4175.
16. Raffel, C., Shazeer, N., Roberts, A., Lee, K., Narang, S., Matena, M., Zhou, Y., Li, W., & Liu, P. J. (2020). Exploring the Limits of Transfer Learning with a Unified Text-to-Text Transformer. *Journal of machine learning research, 21*(140), 1–67.

For Those About to Rely—A Taxonomy of Experimental Studies on AI Reliance

Completed Research Paper

Myriam Schaschek, Niko Spatscheck, and Axel Winkelmann

Abstract Effective collaboration between humans and artificial intelligence (AI) results in superior decision-making outcomes if human reliance on AI is appropriately calibrated. The emerging research area of human-AI decision-making focuses on empirical methods to explore how humans perceive and act in collaborative environments. While previous studies provide promising insights into reliance on AI systems, the multitude of studies has made it challenging to compare and generalize outcomes. To address this complexity, we use the theoretical lens of task technology fit theory and synthesize study design choices in four meta-characteristics: collaboration, agent, task, and precondition. Our goal is to develop a taxonomy on AI reliance experiment design choices that helps structure research efforts and supports producing generalizable scientific knowledge. Thus, our research has notable contributions to both empirical science in information systems and practical implications for designing AI systems.

1 Introduction

Appropriate reliance on artificial intelligence (AI) system outputs is a prerequisite for accomplishing superior performance in human-AI collaborative decision-making [9, 72]. The main credo in literature is that humans rely on AI if it has benefits, such as saving time and effort or maximizing one's goal [1]. However, humans do not always make decisions rationally, and cognitive biases can influence how they perceive and rely on AI systems advice [35, 36]. "[M]isuse and disuse are two examples of inappropriate reliance" ([43], p.50) that have the potential to compromise human

M. Schaschek (✉) · N. Spatscheck · A. Winkelmann
Julius-Maximilians-Universität Würzburg, Chair of Management and Information Systems, Würzburg, Germany
e-mail: myriam.schaschek@uni-wuerzburg.de

N. Spatscheck
e-mail: niko.spatscheck@uni-wuerzburg.de

A. Winkelmann
e-mail: axel.winkelmann@uni-wuerzburg.de

C. M. Flath et al. (eds.), *Artificial Intelligence, Data, and Decision-Making*, Lecture Notes in Information Systems and Organisation 82,
https://doi.org/10.1007/978-3-032-08480-4_2

decisions. Imagine high-stake domains such as healthcare or criminal justice, where inappropriate AI reliance can lead to detrimental outcomes, such as incorrect diagnoses or verdicts. In properly calibrated human-AI collaboration, humans efficiently determine when and how much to rely on themselves versus the AI system, avoiding over- or underrelying on the AI system advice [55, 74, 89].

Unfortunately, the research findings on the reliance on AI have been relatively inconsistent across studies, indicating opposite effects [2, 35]. To add to the complexity, previous empirical studies barely distinguish between the notions of trust and reliance, ultimately making it impossible to separate attitudinal and behavioral outcomes [44, 72, 73]. These inconsistencies complicate researchers' confidence in human-AI collaboration research and make it challenging to build on existing research. Practitioners similarly struggle as they aim to transfer ambiguous research findings. In information systems (IS) research, taxonomies have often been used to classify data, information, or knowledge to facilitate navigation, retrieval, and understanding [59]. Since scarce research has explicitly looked at the characteristics of existing experimental studies on AI reliance and systematically analyzed them to classify study design choices [21, 44], we synthesize the complex research area and address the following research question: *What are the key characteristics to describe and distinguish experimental studies on AI reliance?*
Given that the acceptance of AI does not automatically imply a complementary and superior performance between humans and AI, we employ the theoretical perspective of task-technology fit, which assesses the utilization of technology. This utilization can be seen as an objective assessment of AI reliance, serving as the foundation of our taxonomy. In doing so, our taxonomy contributes to IS research by synthesizing the current design choices of experimental studies related to AI reliance and empirically identifying existing instances of the design choices. Users, researchers, and developers need to be able to determine existing experimental designs to determine significant variations of existing designs or entirely new avenues.

The remainder of this article is organized as follows. In Sect. 2, we provide the foundations for the concepts of human-AI collaborative decision-making and reliance. In Sect. 3, we outline the methodology applied to guide our research. Subsequently, we present our developed taxonomy and its ramifications in Sect. 4. Based on the taxonomy, we conduct a pattern analysis to derive future research avenues presented in Sect. 5, followed by an extended discussion of findings and contributions.

2 Foundations

2.1 Human-AI Collaborative Decision-Making

Collaboration generally describes an active and reciprocal engagement in joint activities to achieve a goal [46]. In the context of AI, we follow the definition of Terveen ([81], p. 1) and understand human-AI collaboration as "two or more agents work together to achieve shared goals [...] involving at least one human and at least one computational agent". In contrast to humans interacting with AI systems to automate routine tasks, human-AI collaboration implies working jointly as teammates or partners to solve a problem [76]. From this definition, scholarly literature analogously categorized different collaboration modes, where one or more humans collaborate with one or more AI systems [88]. In the context of human-AI collaboration, human decisions based on AI-generated advice naturally involve the assessment of AI's trustworthiness [15, 41]. Due to AI systems' complex and nondeterministic behavior, humans must rely on their decisions, and reliance becomes a focal point of investigation [6]. Yet, appropriately calibrating reliance in human-AI collaboration is a non-trivial task, as it means designing systems that account for human behavior [24, 72].

2.2 Reliance on AI Systems

The concept of reliance has a history dating back to research on human-to-human advice-taking and giving [5]. Since the development of technologies that can provide advice to humans, the judge-advisor-system (JAS) paradigm for human-to-human advice-giving has been adapted for interactions between humans and technology (e.g., Lee & See [48]). With AI, humans function as judges who have to make decisions, being supported by AI as an advisor. Using the JAS, studies observe users' reliance on AI system's advice, as its two-stage structure reveals changes due to the advice received [46]. Beyond using a sequential approach, some studies infer reliance concurrently [80]. However, research has yet to establish consistent definitions and measurements for reliance. For clarity, we provide an overview of the terms used in the literature in relation to the concept of reliance in the AI advisor context. As a guide for future empirical studies, Table 1 summarizes exemplary terminologies of reliance in the context of human-AI decision-making environments.

Our summarization of exemplary terminologies of AI reliance clearly demonstrates that reliance has been conceptualized and measured through both subjective, attitudinal perceptions (e.g., self-reported) and objective, behavioral outcomes. The inconsistencies might stem from varied definitions [72], a lack of communication across disciplines [8], or the idea that AI use yields diverse results based on its setup and purpose [22]. However, clearly distinguishing the nuances of the conceptualizations of reliance is crucial, as there is the possibility of a discrepancy between subjective, attitudinal perceptions and objective, behavioral outcomes [14]. More recent findings even point towards a paradoxical gap between stated attitudinal perceptions and actual behavior such as reliance [73]. Regarding the terminologies of the objective, behavioral, and task-related reliance outcomes, each term basically describes the same concept of behaviourally relying on the advice of the AI system, with some nuances. Taking into account these findings, and in alignment with the predominant body of literature investigating both attitudinal and behavioral outcomes [9, 11, 19, 72, 73, 87], we conceptualize reliance as an observable behavioral

Table 1 Variations of reliance metrics, their definition, measurement, and theoretical background

Concept	Definition	Measurement	Type	Variable	Theory	AI literature
Advice utilization/ Degree of advice-taking	Advice utilization or advice-taking refers to a behavioral measure and proxy of trust towards AI, similar to interpersonal interaction. It functions as a uniform measurement of algorithm appreciation or aversion.	Weight of Advice Weight of Own Estimation	task-based	$y \in [0, 1]$ $y \in [0, 1]$	JAS JAS	Prahl & Van Swol [67] Lohoff & Rühr [54] You et al. [87] Goodyear et al. [23] Logg et al. [53]
Appropriate reliance	Appropriate reliance refers to desirable behavior where humans override incorrect AI advice and follow correct advice.	Correct self-reliance Incorrect AI reliance Correct AI reliance Incorrect self-reliance	task-based	$y \in \{0, 1\}$	JAS	Schemmer et al. [72] Schoeffer et al. [75] Schmitt et al. [73] He et al. [25] Schoeffer et al. [74]
AI agreement	AI agreement refers to the rate of agreement between the final response and the AI advice.	AI agreement	task-based	$y \in [0, 1]$	JAS	Lai & Tan [45] Lai et al. [46] Cao & Huang [10]

(continued)

Table 1 (continued)

Concept	Definition	Measurement	Type	Variable	Theory	AI Literature
User reliance	Reliance refers to the percent gaze duration on AI advice and measures the time the participant fixated on the AI advice divided by the total amount of time the participant fixated on the task.	Gaze duration	physiological	$y \in [0, 1]$	None	Cao & Huang [10]
Perceived reliance	Perceived level of reliance on AI measures a participant's self-reported level of agreement with the AI advice.	Perceived reliance	self-reported	$y \in [1, 7]$	JAS	Cao & Huang [10]
Acceptance of AI recommendation	Acceptance of AI-based recommendation refers to users of recommender systems accepting the recommendation of AI.	Acceptance	task-based	$y \in \{0, 1\}$	TRA TA	Laumer et al. [47] Ochmann et al. [63]
Conformity to erroneous recommendations	Conformity refers to the act of choosing the incorrect answer recommended by the AI.	Conformity	task-based	$y \in \mathbb{Q}^+$	None	Liel & Zalmanson [51]

(continued)

Table 1 (continued)

Concept	Definition	Measurement	Type	Variable	Theory	AI Literature
Compliance	Compliance refers to an individual's behavior in terms that they use the provided AI advice. *Actual* reliance measures the relative change of the deviance from the AI advice. *Intended* reliance measures an individual's perception and intention.	Actual compliance Intended compliance	task-based self-reported	$y \in \{0, 1\}$	TA	Westphal et al. [85] Kuhl et al. [42] Westphal et al. [85]
Selective adherence	Selective adherence refers to the likelihood to follow the AI and posits that decision-makers to adhere to algorithmic advice selectively, when it matches stereotypical views of the decision subject.	Selective adherence	task-based	$y \in \{0, 1\}$	ACB	Alon-Barkat & Busuioc (2023)

Abbreviations: Judge-Advisor-System (JAS); Theory of Reasoned Action (TRA); Technology Acceptance (TA); Automation and Confirmation Bias (ACB) outcome. We propose this distinction as a fundamental basis for future research, as the lack of clarity obscures central concepts of reliance and can lead to misinterpretations, where compatible findings are reported as empirical contradictions, and vice versa [8]. Consequently, our summarization underscores the crucial importance of precision in academic discourse to guarantee that research findings are interpreted accurately and integrated effectively.

Further research is necessary to fully understand the phenomenon of appropriate reliance, with various collaboration modes and contexts [2]. Thus, more theorizing and empirical studies with clearly delineated terminology are needed to derive design incentives and strategies to assist users in calibrating their reliance.

3 Research Methodology

To synthesize key characteristics of experimental studies investigating AI reliance, we develop a taxonomy. During our taxonomy development, we execute the following steps: (1) data collection, (2) taxonomy building, and (3) taxonomy representation. **Data Collection.** First, we identified input knowledge for our taxonomy by conducting a structured literature search based on the methodology proposed by Vom Brocke et al. [84]. The final set of publications served as inputs for building the taxonomy. Before initiating the search process, we defined the scope and corresponding keywords to ensure relevance and comprehensiveness. Our primary focus was on experimental studies to identify the existing study design choices in the context of AI reliance.

To conceptualize the necessary keywords, we conducted an initial exploratory search. This preliminary search helped refine our understanding and ensured that we captured relevant studies on AI reliance. Given the observed inconsistencies in using constructs such as trust and reliance [13, 40, 66], we included the terminology of trust in our search string. We used the concepts of algorithm aversion and appreciation as umbrella terms since they are specific subsets of reliance studies. This decision was made to encompass a broader range of studies and address potential variations in terminology used by different researchers. To conduct the search process, we chose interdisciplinary databases, i.e., *ACM Digital Library*, *AISeL*, *Science Direct*, and *Web of Science*. For the keyword search, we queried these databases with the following uniform search string: *Title OR Abstract = "(("Artificial Intelligence" | AI | "Machine learning" | "Deep Learning") AND (Trust | Reliance | "Algorithm Aversion" | "Algorithm Appreciation" | "Cognitive Bias"))"*.

The database search resulted in a total of 5,721 publications, on which we applied a sequential filtering process: (1) *redundancy check and full-text availability*, (2) *title and abstract analysis*, and (3) *full-text analysis*, narrowed down to experimental user studies focusing on peer-reviewed journals and conference proceedings. We only considered empirical studies focused on human-AI collaborative decision-making and AI reliance as the central constructs and units of analysis, resulting in 46 relevant publications. Finally, we conducted a forward and backward search, identifying nine additional relevant articles. In sum, these 55 publications form the basis for the development of the taxonomy in the following. See Appendix A for an overview of the literature selection process, inclusion and exclusion criteria, and full bibliography.

Taxonomy Development. We follow Nickerson et al. [59], to develop our taxonomy and start with defining the meta-characteristics. As our objective is to structure the design choices of experimental studies on AI reliance and reduce complexity barriers for researchers by creating reusable knowledge, we decided on quadripartite meta-characteristics to classify design choices as objects. The task-technology fit theory offers a suitable framework for human-AI collaborations by illustrating the interdependence between (1) the *collaboration* dimensions between the human and AI, (2) the human and AI characteristics as *agents*, (3) the specific *task* carried out during the collaboration, and (4) the experimental *preconditions* to measure or manipulate the collaboration.

As the methodology involves an iterative process, the specification of ending conditions is essential. We adopted all ending conditions by Nickerson et al. [59] except for mutual exclusion due to significant heterogeneity and substantial combinatorial variants across the studies. Our proceeding agrees with previous research and avoids a significant expansion of the characteristics, thus preserving the clarity and conciseness of the final taxonomy [27, 90]. In total, we performed four iterations to derive the dimensions and characteristics of our taxonomy. Finally, to identify individual research trends, gaps, and streams, we classified all experimental studies resulting from the literature review according to the taxonomy and performed a descriptive frequency analysis for each characteristic within each dimension of the taxonomy. See Appendix A and B for an overview of the iterations, literature classification, and descriptive analysis (Table 2).

4 Taxonomy

4.1 Collaboration

Mode: In human-AI collaborations, different collaboration modes can be distinguished depending on the constellation of collaborators involved [88]. Thus, one human can work together with one AI (1:1, *human-AI*) or multiple AIs (1:n, *human-multi-AI*). Vice versa, several humans can work together with one AI (n:1, *multi-human-AI*) or with multiple AIs (m:n, *multi-human-multi-AI*). Since there is no experimental research on the reliance on multi-human-multi-AI modalities, our taxonomy does not represent this characteristic yet. Regarding reliance within the other collaboration modes, Schelble et al. [71] found that reliance on AI was significantly higher in multi-human-AI constellations than in human-multi-AI constellations.

Interface: Depending on the experiment setting, various interface choices exist to enable human-AI collaboration. One method is *Wizard-of-Oz*, where a human oper-

Table 2 Taxonomy of experimental study design choices on AI reliance

MC	Dimension	Characteristic					
Collaboration	Mode	Human-AI	Human-Multi-AI	Multi-Human-AI			
	Interface	Wizard-of-Oz	Fully Functional AI				
	Advice Count	Single	Multiple				
	Advice Timing*	Before Manifestation	After Manifestation	During Manifestation			
	Ecological Context	Business	Public	Private	Healthcare	Gaming	Hypothetical
Agent	Human Characteristics*	AI Literacy	Domain Knowledge	None			
	Human Choice of Advice*	Adjustable	Predefined				
	AI Embodiment*	Physical Robot	Virtual Agent or Bot	Embedded			
	AI Agency*	Performative	Advisory				
	AI Response Mode	Judgment-based	Choice-based				
Task	Input*	Image	Text	Video	Audio	3D Model	
	Solution Nature	Subjective	Objective				
	Importance	Low-Stake	High-Stake				
Precondition	Manipulation*	Performance	Transparency	Interaction	Representation	Individuality	Task
	Setup	Single Trial	Multiple Trial				
	Feedback*	Not Given	Given-immediate	Given-Delayed			
	User-AI Onboarding*	None	Instruction	Pre-Experimental			
	Reward Structure	Monetary Performance	Monetary Non-Performance	None	Non-Monetary Performance	Non-Monetary Non-Performance	

*MC=Meta-Characteristic; *Dimensions are non-exclusive*

ator manages the system behind the scenes to mimic an AI-based system. Another alternative is employing a *fully functional AI*, which entails an AI system that operates independently. However, Wizard of Oz-based AI interfaces might not accurately reflect the AI's actual response within the human-AI collaboration, resulting in unrealistic behavior [79]. This might be due to oversimplified human models or insufficiently trained wizards causing unintentional errors, such as behaving like real humans, overstepping their role as AI representatives, affecting reliance [44, 68].

Advice Count: An AI system can suggest a *single* or *multiple* different advice simultaneously from which the human can choose. Newman et al. [58] found that individuals are more likely to rely on AI when presented with multiple advice options, even if a single option is of higher quality, highlighting that decision autonomy is valued more than advice quality.

Advice Timing: Humans' decision-making is influenced not just by the quantity of advice but also by when it is provided. Timing refers to when participants receive the advice. *Before manifestation* characterizes the condition in which participants obtain AI advice before making their decision. The resulting effect that can arise is a cognitive bias known as the anchoring effect, which leads to a heavy reliance on the initial anchor information and distorts the decision-making process [18]. *After manifestation* indicates presenting the advice after the participants manifested their decision. The options are inspired by experimental research investigating the JAS paradigm, where judges make two estimates: one before and one after presenting the advice [5]. This reduces cognitive biases and helps to understand how much the AI advice influences the participant. In cases where the task has several sub-steps, the AI advice can be presented *during manifestation* [10].

Ecological Context: The final dimension of this meta-characteristic describes the domain of the experimental task as the ecological context for human-AI collaboration. In light of the ongoing discussion about the importance of context in theory development within IS research, this dimension is of particular interest [30]. For example, according to a recent study by Jussupow et al. [35], healthcare is a domain where humans show a stronger aversion towards algorithmic collaboration. To categorize the experimental studies reviewed based on their task nature, we derived six major domains. The *business* domain comprises all tasks from the business context, such as finance or marketing. *Public* includes tasks related to the public sector, such as infrastructure, government, schools, and universities. *Private* covers tasks from the private context of the participants, such as dating, cooking, or job selection. *Healthcare* refers to all medical and health-related tasks, such as interpreting CT scans or mental health counseling. *Gaming* describes all game-like tasks, e.g., chess. Finally, *hypothetical* encompasses hypothetical experimental tasks, such as solving mazes [83].

4.2 Agent

Human Characteristics: This dimension encompasses user characteristics of humans acting as agents in human-AI systems. *AI literacy* accounts for the different levels of AI expertise, such as AI experts who possess comprehensive knowledge about AI. These individuals, due to their high AI literacy, are less inclined to rely on AI advice when making decisions compared to those with lower AI literacy, such as novice AI users [33]. Similarly, *domain knowledge* characterizes whether a specific domain knowledge is assumed for the participants of a study. For instance, individuals with high domain knowledge are less likely to rely on AI advice and are more averse towards AI systems compared to individuals with limited domain knowledge (e.g., laypersons) [32, 53]. Additionally, individuals with substantial domain expertise are generally more familiar with their decision-making tasks, which further affects their propensity to rely on AI [70]. Typically, human characteristics are included as moderating variables to see whether individual differences strengthen or weaken the observed effect. Experimental studies that account for neither domain knowledge nor AI literacy fall under the characteristic *none*.

Human Choice of Advice: The extent to which the participant can determine the presence and/or configuration of the AI suggestion is characterized by this dimension. *Adjustable* incorporates experiments where the user can decide if/when to receive advice from the AI and/or how it should be parameterized. This is important because people seeking advice are more likely to accept it if they can decide if and when to use it [5], thereby influencing reliance. In addition, algorithmic aversion can be reduced by allowing the user to modify the AI's advice [16]. *Predefined* includes experiments in which the user has no influence, as all relevant parameters have been determined beforehand. However, this can also limit the participants' desire for control, leading to algorithm aversion, especially for participants with a high locus of control [56].

AI Embodiment: The way an AI agent is embodied in a human-AI collaboration can take various forms, from *physical robots* to *virtual agents or bots*, or invisible *embedded* within a tool or information system. The different AI embodiment types vary in anthropomorphism and tangibility, which can impact the development of reliance over time [20, 57].

AI Agency: According to Nissen & Sengupta [60], algorithms (or AI) can be classified as either performative or advisory based on their level of autonomy. *Performative* AI functions autonomously, with humans only supervising the outcome and performance, while *advisory* AI only offers support but does not act independently. Ultimately, the human makes the final decision. Studies have shown that increased control over advisory AI leads to an increased reliance [85]. Similar results presented Palmeira & Spassova [65], suggesting that users want to control their decisions by making the final decisions themselves [17]. In contrast, Kawaguchi [38] uncovered that a higher control led users to rely less, leading to inconclusive results, especially concerning advisory AI [35].

AI Response Mode: Depending on the task type and the associated explicit response mode of the AI, we further distinguish AI systems between judgment-based and choice-based response modes [4]. *Judgment-based* responses characterize an explicit evaluation of each alternative, for example, by making quantitative predictions or quantitative estimates, typically on continuous or multilevel scales [4, 5]. *Choice-based* responses involve selecting one qualitative alternative while rejecting others. Although many empirical studies consider the required response mode as an incidental aspect of the task [4], numerous studies in the field of decision-making have shown that the response mode has a significant impact on decision processes [5].

4.3 Task

Input: Depending on the experimental task type, the task's inputs or data types differ. Inputs can be *images* or graphics, *text* of various forms and lengths, *video*-based data types, *audio*-based data types, for example in the form of speech or music, or *three-dimensional (3D)* objects or environments. Although research on different task modalities is still limited, preliminary findings indicate a direct impact on individuals' reliance on AI [69].

Solution Nature: This dimension divides tasks into two categories: subjective and objective. *Subjective* tasks are open to interpretation and based on personal opinion or intuition, whereas *objective* tasks involve facts that are quantifiable and measurable [11]. Furthermore, subjective tasks are usually associated with more emotional capabilities, while objective tasks are associated with more cognitive capabilities [31]. It is important to consider this distinction when selecting the experimental task, as the perceived subjectivity of the task is inversely related to users' reliance on AI advice [11].

Importance: The dimension of task importance refers to how significant a given task is perceived. Tasks with *low stakes* are typically characterized by minimal potential for financial or emotional loss and the ability to reverse a decision once made easily, whereas the opposite is true for *high-stake* tasks [43]. Accordingly, high-stake tasks induce a higher perceived risk, which can moderate reliance [78]. Moreover, research indicates that participants expect AI to display higher confidence in high-risk tasks than low-risk tasks but concurrently demonstrate reduced reliance on AI advice for high-risk tasks [34]. Yet, the predominant focus of research in this field has been primarily experimental, thereby limiting the significance of perceived situational risks as they manifest in practical, real-world experiences [20].

4.4 Precondition

Manipulation: The first dimension of the meta-characteristic precondition describes the manipulations in an experimental setting to observe specific behaviors. We identified six variable categories to be manipulated in human-AI collaboration: performance, transparency, interaction, representation, individuality, and task [50]. Experiments that manipulate *performance* investigate how users' reliance changes with AI performance information [12, 87]. Besides performance, a common manipulation is a change in *transparency* of AI decision-making and, correspondingly, its effects on user reliance. The manipulation can be carried out by including Explainable AI (XAI) [72] or presenting AI confidence indicators [89]. Another way to account for the effects on user reliance is by manipulating *interaction* between humans and AI. One example is influencing advice by manipulating the source of advice - human or AI [49, 87]. Further, we distinguish the manipulation of AI *representation*. This includes the anthropomorphic design of AI [63] or the endowment of AI with human capabilities such as apologies or learning mechanisms [40]. In contrast, the manipulation of *individuality* attributes comprises experiments that control for personal traits of participants, cognitive biases [77], domain expertise, or demographic attributes such as age [37]. The last characteristic of this dimension includes experiments in which the *task* to be performed is manipulated per se, e.g., by changing the difficulty [83] or by using cognitive forcing functions [7].

Setup: Beyond manipulating task construction, the setup of experimental tasks can be distinguished in *single* or *multiple* trials. As Liel & Zalmanson [51] suggest, it is reasonable to expect that conducting experiments with multiple (vs. single) trials would yield different results as participants accumulate a deeper understanding of the AI agents' performance, subsequently affecting their reliance.

Feedback: This dimension addresses the timing and availability of feedback on the participants' and/or the AI's performance during the experimental task. Participants either receive no feedback (*not given*) or receive it immediately (*given-immediate*) after submitting their judgment. Another alternative is *given-delayed*, where participants get interim feedback, e.g., after half of the trials. Feedback at the individual task level helps participants build more appropriate mental models about AI by better understanding its error boundaries [3, 55]. Objective feedback, particularly concerning AI performance, serves as a significant factor that participants use to calibrate their reliance on AI models [45, 86, 89], and concurrently increasing users trust in AI [29]. Similarly, limited feedback can make participants unwilling to rely on the AI's suggestions [55]. However, Liu et al [52] have found that feedback in the form of intermediate solutions can result in overtrust and thus form the basis for overreliance. Finally, it is worth noting that the displayed feedback can also be overwritten by the perceived performance of the AI in the long run [86].

User-AI Onboarding: The different onboarding types characterize the processes to prepare or guide participants for the subsequent human-AI collaboration. *None* includes experiments in which participants do not receive any information about the AI beforehand (e.g., how it works or how accurate it is). Participants do not have the opportunity to interact with the AI prior to the experiment. In *instruction*, participants receive information about the AI but cannot interact with it. If an experiment includes *pre-experimental use*, the participants can interact with the AI before the experiment starts to familiarise themselves with the AI. Due to the anchoring bias, first impressions strongly influence the perception of information [82] and automated systems [62]. The timing of AI advice impacts users' perceived accuracy [61], with early errors resulting in decreased reliance compared to errors occurring at later stages [39].

Reward Structure: This dimension deals with the design of rewards and incentives. First, we distinguish between monetary and non-monetary rewards (e.g., university credits or virtual points). Secondly, we differentiate between performance-based incentives, where participants receive an additional bonus depending on task performance, and non-performance-based incentives. Based on these distinctions, the following characteristics emerge: *Monetary Performance-based, Monetary Non-Performance-based, Non-Monetary Performance-based, Non-Monetary Non-Performance-based*, and *None*, if participants receive no rewards within the experiment. Performance-based reward structures are particularly relevant in reliance studies, as they operationalize the vulnerability discussed by Lee & See [48]. However, the reward structure can influence reliance, e.g. by reducing overreliance [83].

5 Discussion of Findings and Contributions

Our study synthesizes the current design choices in experimental research on collaborative human-AI decision-making, consolidating fragmented findings from diverse

Table 3 Future research directions and paths

MC	Research direction	Research paths
Collaboration	Longitudinal studies and repeated interactions	• Long-term reliance calibration and impact of repeated interactions.
	Human-AI agreement	• Perception of human-model agreement by separating the impact of agreement frequency from the impact of agreement on case ordering. • Assessing how the consistency of model predictions affect perception.
	Effectiveness and Usability of Interfaces	• Exploring adaptive and personalized user interfaces to optimize human-AI team performance. • Testing ordering bias with different manipulations.
	Generalizability of effects	• Studying different contexts with various stakeholder populations. • Conducting meta-analyses.
	Exploring different modes of collaboration	• Investigating complex teams involving multiple AIs and humans.
	Cognitive Biases in collaborative settings	• Investigating cognitive biases (e.g., confirmation bias, weak evidence effect) in decision making. • Studying how cognitive tendencies of users can be leveraged for collaboration.
Agent	Long-Term User Engagement	• Studying how long-term users engage with AI systems.
	Human individual differences and cognitive factors	• Investigating the impact of individual factors, e.g., the need for cognition. • Incorporating measures of cognitive load and cognitive ability as moderators. • Heterogeneous participant pools to test findings across different demographics.
	Field Experiments and Ecological Validity	• Conducting field experiments in real-world decision contexts, such as by police officers or teachers.
	Laypeople vs. Experts	• Comparing how experts and laypeople rely on AI-provided advice in various tasks.
	Exploring different AI response mode	• Investigating reliance on textual advice.

(continued)

Table 3 (continued)

MC	Research direction	Research paths
Task	Exploring diverse types of tasks	• Investigating different tasks such as autonomous driving, decision aids, interactive games, deception detection, and behavioral economics. • For findings with game-playing tasks, repeating the experiments for non-game-playing tasks and uncertain environments. • Exploring generative tasks with no ground truth.
	Task Context	• Embedding experiments in more everyday use contexts. • Embedding experiments in real-world contexts, while adhering to ethical guidelines.
Precondition	Exploring different manipulations	• Testing how fine-grained details in provided explanations affect reliance (e.g., multi-step explanations). • Studying and designing strategies based on cognitive biases of humans.
	Variations of interaction	• Studying the sequential task setups and changes of reliance.
	Enhancing experimental results	• Use qualitative studies to evaluate design solutions proposed to foster appropriate reliance.

academic communities. Consequently, our taxonomy provides a structured framework for comprehending and designing studies on AI reliance in this field as a response to the call for principled and multidimensional frameworks to reflect on current research [26, 44]. By mapping out the design space for current human-centered experimental studies on AI reliance, our study aids in identifying gaps and under-explored areas. Our literature classification and descriptive frequency analysis of characteristics (see Appendix B) revealed the following. Most of the reviewed studies looked at human-AI collaboration, while fewer examined human-multi-AI and multi-human-AI collaborations. Fully functional AI was used predominantly, with mainly single advice given to participants before or after a decision. Experiments were primarily in business, public, and private domains, with embedded advisory AI systems providing choice-based outputs. Tasks were predominantly text-based and low-stakes, with transparency, performance, interaction, and individuality as the most manipulated variables. The studies mainly used multiple trials, with few participants receiving feedback or user-AI onboarding. Rewards were usually monetary and based on performance.

In our analysis, we identified three clusters of theories utilized in the examined experimental studies: (1) *interpersonal theories* (e.g., social influence theory, interpersonal trust theories), (2) *cognition-related theories* (e.g., cognitive load theory, dual process theory of cognition, locus of control theory), and (3) *decision-related theories* (e.g., decision field theory, bayesian decision-making theories). However, we observed a general and significant deficiency in the application of theories, with only a limited number of studies employing specific theoretical frameworks, particularly concerning the technological artifact. This appears to be a persistent trend in behavioral science research (e.g., especially in human-computer interaction studies), which often under-theorizes the technological artifact [28] and may partially account for the equivocal results observed in studies on AI reliance [64].

Consequently, our study holds several implications for empirical research on AI reliance. The development of our taxonomy supports a more standardized and coherent practice in designing and conducting human-AI decision-making studies, which enhances the comparability and reproducibility of research findings (i.e., meta-analyses). With a shared understanding and common language, researchers from different communities can collaborate more effectively, thereby accelerating the advancement of scientific knowledge. Ultimately, the insights gained from our study inform the design of AI systems, improving performance and user experience. As with any research, our approach faces limitations. First, the literature included in the taxonomy development is limited to the studies identified during the literature review process. Despite our comprehensive review, we cannot guarantee completeness. Second, inherent to the nature of a taxonomy, its completeness depends on our defined boundary conditions [59].

Our study encourages systematic research practices by prompting researchers to consider a more holistic experimental design space. To aid future research, Table 3 summarizes the future research directions and paths derived from the reviewed literature, providing researchers with focal points for a more comprehensive and nuanced understanding of human-AI decision-making.

Acknowledgments and Supplementary Material This work has been developed in the project "Hyperautomation Ökosystem (Hyko)" and is partly funded by the Bavarian Ministry of Science within the program "Europäischer Fonds für Regionale Entwicklung (EFRE)" and co-financed by the European Union. The authors are responsible for the content of this publication. For access to the supplementary material, please refer to the following DOI: https://doi.org/10.23728/b2share.6740f646e89e4eecbfe098f270a701ad

References

1. Bankins, S., Ocampo, A. C., Marrone, M., Restubog, S. L. D., & Woo, S. E. (2023) . A multilevel review of artificial intelligence in organizations: Implications for organizational behavior research and practice. *Journal of Organizational Behavior*, 1–24.

2. Bansal, G., Bucinca, Z., Holstein, K., Hullman, J., Smith-Renner, A. M., Stumpf, S., & Wu, S. (2023). Workshop on Trust and Reliance in AI-Human Teams (TRAIT). *Extended Abstracts of the 2023 CHI Conference on Human Factors in Computing Systems* (pp. 1–6).
3. Bansal, G., Nushi, B., Kamar, E., Lasecki, W. S., Weld, D. S., & Horvitz, E. (2019). Beyond accuracy: The role of mental models in human-ai team performance. *Proceedings of the AAAI Conference on Human Computation and Crowdsourcing, 7*(1), 2–11.
4. Billings, R. S., & Scherer, L. L. (1988). The effects of response mode and importance on decision-making strategies: Judgment versus choice. *Organizational Behavior and Human Decision Processes, 41*(1), 1–19.
5. Bonaccio, S., & Dalal, R. S. (2006). Advice taking and decision-making: An integrative literature review, and implications for the organizational sciences. *Organizational behavior and human decision processes, 101*(2), 127–151.
6. Brachman, M., Ashktorab, Z., Desmond, M., Duesterwald, E., Dugan, C., Joshi, N. N., Pan, Q., & Sharma, A. (2022). Reliance and automation for human-ai collaborative data labeling conflict resolution. *Proceedings of the ACM on Human-Computer Interaction, 6*(CSCW2), 1–27.
7. Buçinca, Z., Malaya, M. B., & Gajos, K. Z. (2021). To trust or to think: Cognitive forcing functions can reduce overreliance on ai in ai-assisted decision-making. *Proceedings of the ACM on Human-Computer Interaction, 5*(CSCW1), 1–21.
8. Burton, J. W., Stein, M.-K., & Jensen, T. B. (2020). A systematic review of algorithm aversion in augmented decision making. *Journal of Behavioral Decision Making, 33*(2), 220–239.
9. Cabitza, F., Campagner, A., Angius, R., Natali, C., & Reverberi, C. (2023). AI shall have no dominion: On how to measure technology dominance in ai-supported human decision-making. In *Proceedings of the 2023 CHI Conference on Human Factors in Computing Systems* pp. 1–20).
10. Cao, S., & Huang, C.-M. (2022). Understanding user reliance on ai in assisted decision-making. *Proceedings of the ACM on Human-Computer Interaction, 6*(CSCW2), 1–23.
11. Castelo, N., Bos, M. W., & Lehmann, D. R. (2019). Task-dependent algorithm aversion. *Journal of Marketing Research, 56*(5), 809–825.
12. Chong, L., Zhang, G., Goucher-Lambert, K., Kotovsky, K., & Cagan, J. (2022). Human confidence in artificial intelligence and in themselves: The evolution and impact of confidence on adoption of ai advice. *Computers in Human Behavior, 127*, Article 107018.
13. Daschner, S., & Obermaier, R. (2022). Algorithm aversion? On the influence of advice accuracy on trust in algorithmic advice. *Journal of Decision Systems, 31*(S1), 77–97.
14. de Guinea, A. O., Titah, R., & Léger, P.-M. (2014). Explicit and implicit antecedents of users' behavioral beliefs in information systems: A neuropsychological investigation. *Journal of Management Information Systems, 30*(4), 179–210.
15. Dennis, A. R., Lakhiwal, A., & Sachdeva, A. (2023). Ai agents as team members: Effects on satisfaction, conflict, trustworthiness, and willingness to work with. *Journal of Management Information Systems, 40*(2), 307–337.
16. Dietvorst, B., Simmons, J. P., & Massey, C. (2018). Overcoming algorithm aversion: People will use imperfect algorithms if they can (even slightly) modify them. *Management Science, 64*(3), 1155–1170.
17. Dzindolet, M. T., Pierce, L. G., Beck, H. P., & Dawe, L. A. (2002). The perceived utility of human and automated aids in a visual detection task. *Human Factors, 44*(1), 79–94.
18. Furnham, A., & Boo, H. C. (2011). A literature review of the anchoring effect. *The Journal of Socio-economics, 40*(1), 35–42.
19. Giorgi, I., Minutolo, A., Tirotto, F., Hagen, O., Esposito, M., Gianni, M., Palomino, M., & Masala, G. L. (2023). I am robot, your health adviser for older adults: Do you trust my advice? *International Journal of Social Robotics*, 1–20.
20. Glikson, E., & Woolley, A. W. (2020). Human trust in artificial intelligence: Review of empirical research. *Academy of Management Annals, 14*(2), 627–660.
21. Gomez, C., Cho, S. M., Huang, C.-M., & Unberath, M. (2023). Designing ai support for human involvement in ai-assisted decision making: A taxonomy of human-ai interactions from a systematic review. arXiv:2310.19778

22. Goodhue, D. L. (1995). Understanding user evaluations of information systems. *Management Science, 41*(12), 1827–1844.
23. Goodyear, K., Parasuraman, R., Chernyak, S., Madhavan, P., Deshpande, G., & Krueger, F. (2016). Advice taking from humans and machines: An fmri and effective connectivity study. *Frontiers in Human Neuroscience, 10*, 542.
24. Green, B., & Chen, Y. (2019) . The principles and limits of algorithm-in-the-loop decision making. *Proceedings of the ACM on Human-Computer Interaction, 3*(CSCW), 1–24.
25. He, G., Kuiper, L., & Gadiraju, U. (2023). Knowing about knowing: An illusion of human competence can hinder appropriate reliance on ai systems. In *Proceedings of the 2023 CHI Conference on Human Factors in Computing Systems* (pp. 1–18).
26. Hemmer, P., Schemmer, M., Vössing, M., & Kühl, N. (2021). Human-ai complementarity in hybrid intelligence systems: A structured literature review. *PACIS*, 78.
27. Herm, L.-V., Wanner, J., & Janiesch, C. (2022). A taxonomy of user-centered explainable ai studies. *PACIS 2022 Research Papers*, 9.
28. Hevner, A. R., March, S. T., Park, J., & Ram, S. (2004). Design science in information systems research. *MIS Quarterly*, 75–105.
29. Hoff, K. A., & Bashir, M. (2015). Trust in automation: Integrating empirical evidence on factors that influence trust. *Human Factors, 57*(3), 407–434.
30. Hong, W., Chan, F. K., Thong, J. Y., Chasalow, L. C., & Dhillon, G. (2014). A framework and guidelines for context-specific theorizing in information systems research. *Information Systems Research, 25*(1), 111–136.
31. Inbar, Y., Cone, J., & Gilovich, T. (2010). People's intuitions about intuitive insight and intuitive choice. *Journal of Personality and Social Psychology, 99*(2), 232.
32. Inkpen, K., Chappidi, S., Mallari, K., Nushi, B., Ramesh, D., Michelucci, P., Mandava, V., VepŘek, L. H., & Quinn, G. (2023). Advancing human-AI complementarity: The impact of user expertise and algorithmic tuning on joint decision making. *ACM Transactions on Computer-Human Interaction, 30*(5), 1–29.
33. Jacobs, M., Pradier, M. F., McCoy, T. H., Jr., Perlis, R. H., Doshi-Velez, F., & Gajos, K. Z. (2021). How machine-learning recommendations influence clinician treatment selections: The example of antidepressant selection. *Translational Psychiatry, 11*(1), 108.
34. Juravle, G., Boudouraki, A., Terziyska, M., & Rezlescu, C. (2020). Trust in artificial intelligence for medical diagnoses. *Progress in Brain Research, 253*, 263–282.
35. Jussupow, E., Benbasat, I., & Heinzl, A. (2020). Why are we averse towards algorithms? A comprehensive literature review on algorithm aversion. *ECIS 2020 Research Papers*, 168.
36. Jussupow, E., Heinzl, A., Meza Martínez, A. M., & Maedche, A. (2021). Is this system biased?—how users react to gender bias in an explainable ai system. *ICIS 2021 Research Papers*, 1–17.
37. Kaufmann, E. (2021). Algorithm appreciation or aversion? comparing in-service and pre-service teachers' acceptance of computerized expert models. *Computers and Education: Artificial Intelligence, 2*, Article 100028.
38. Kawaguchi, K. (2021). When will workers follow an algorithm? a field experiment with a retail business. *Management Science, 67*(3), 1670–1695.
39. Kim, A., Yang, M., & Zhang, J. (2023). When algorithms err: Differential impact of early vs. late errors on users' reliance on algorithms. *ACM Transactions on Computer-Human Interaction, 30*(1), 1–36.
40. Kim, T., & Song, H. (2023). i believe ai can learn from the error or can it not?: The effects of implicit theories on trust repair of the intelligent agent. *International Journal of Social Robotics, 15*(1), 115–128.
41. Knickrehm, C., Voss, M., & Barton, M.-C. (2023). Can you trust me? Using ai to review more than three decades of ai trust literature. *ECIS 2023 Research Papers*, 302.
42. Kuhl, N., Lobana, J., & Meske, C. (2020). Do you comply with ai?–personalized explanations of learning algorithms and their impact on employees compliance behavior. 1.
43. Kunreuther, H., Meyer, R., Zeckhauser, R., Slovic, P., Schwartz, B., Schade, C., Luce, M. F., Lippman, S., Krantz, D., Kahn, B., et al. (2002). High stakes decision making: Normative, descriptive and prescriptive considerations. *Marketing Letters, 13*, 259–268.

44. Lai, V., Chen, C., Smith-Renner, A., Liao, Q. V., & Tan, C. (2023). Towards a science of human-ai decision making: An overview of design space in empirical human-subject studies. In *Proceedings of the 2023 ACM Conference on Fairness, Accountability, and Transparency* (pp. 1369–1385).
45. Lai, V., & Tan, C. (2019). On human predictions with explanations and predictions of machine learning models: A case study on deception detection. *Proceedings of the Conference on Fairness, Accountability, and Transparency* (pp. 29–38).
46. Lai, Y., Kankanhalli, A., & Ong, D. C. (2021). Human-AI collaboration in healthcare: A review and research agenda. *Proceedings of the Annual Hawaii International Conference on System Sciences* (pp. 390–399).
47. Laumer, S., Gubler, F., Maier, C., & Weitzel, T. (2018). Job seekers' acceptance of job recommender systems: Results of an empirical study. In *Proceedings of the 51st Hawaii International Conference on System Sciences* (pp. 3914–3923).
48. Lee, J. D., & See, K. A. (2004). Trust in automation: Designing for appropriate reliance. *Human Factors, 46*(1), 50–80.
49. Leffrang, D. (2023). The broken leg of algorithm appreciation: An experimental study on the effect of unobserved variables on advice utilization. *Wirtschaftsinformatik 2023 Proceedings*.
50. Li, Y., & Hahn, J. (2022). Review of research on human trust in artificial intelligence.
51. Liel, Y., & Zalmanson, L. (2020). What if an AI told you that 2 + 2 is 5? Conformity to algorithmic recommendations. *ICIS 2020 Research Papers* (pp. 1–17).
52. Liu, J., Marriott, K., Dwyer, T., & Tack, G. (2023). Increasing user trust in optimisation through feedback and interaction. *ACM Transactions on Computer-Human Interaction, 29*(5), 1–34.
53. Logg, J. M., Minson, J. A., & Moore D. A. (2019). Algorithm appreciation: People prefer algorithmic to human judgment. *Organizational Behavior and Human Decision Processes, 151*, 90–103.
54. Lohoff, L., & Rühr, A. (2021). Introducing (machine) learning ability as antecedent of trust in intelligent systems. *ECIS 2021 Research Papers* (June), 1–16.
55. Lu, Z., & Yin, M. (2021). Human reliance on machine learning models when performance feedback is limited: Heuristics and risks. In *Proceedings of the 2021 CHI Conference on Human Factors in Computing Systems* (pp. 1–16).
56. Mahmud, H., Islam, A. N. Ahmed, S. I., & Smolander, K. (2022). What influences algorithmic decision-making? A systematic literature review on algorithm aversion. *Technological Forecasting and Social Change, 175*, Article 121390.
57. Morana, S., Gnewuch, U., Jung, D., & Granig, C. (2020). The effect of anthropomorphism on investment decision-making with robo-advisor chatbots. *ECIS*.
58. Newman, L., Haran, U., & Fink, L. (2022). Let me decide: The importance of user autonomy in accepting online recommendations. *ECIS*.
59. Nickerson, R. C., Varshney, U., & Muntermann, J. (2013). A method for taxonomy development and its application in information systems. *European Journal of Information Systems, 22*(3), 336–359.
60. Nissen, M. E., & Sengupta, K. (2006). Incorporating software agents into supply chains: Experimental investigation with a procurement task. *Mis Quarterly*, 145–166.
61. Nourani, M., King, J., & Ragan, E. (2020). The role of domain expertise in user trust and the impact of first impressions with intelligent systems. *Proceedings of the AAAI Conference on Human Computation and Crowdsourcing, 8*(1), 112–121.
62. Nourani, M., Roy, C., Block, J. E., Honeycutt, D. R., Rahman, T., Ragan, E., & Gogate, V. (2021). Anchoring bias affects mental model formation and user reliance in explainable ai systems. In *26th International Conference on Intelligent User Interfaces* (pp. 340–350).
63. Ochmann, J., Michels, L., Zilker, S., Tiefenbeck, V., & Laumer, S. (2020). The influence of algorithm aversion and anthropomorphic agent design on the acceptance of ai-based job recommendations. *ICIS 2020 Research Papers*, 4.
64. Orman, L. V. (2002). Electronic markets, hierarchies, hubs, and intermediaries. *Information Systems Frontiers, 4*, 213–228.

65. Palmeira, M., & Spassova, G. (2015). Consumer reactions to professionals who use decision aids. *European Journal of Marketing, 49*(3/4), 302–326.
66. Papenmeier, A., Kern, D., Englebienne, G., & Seifert, C. (2022). It's complicated: The relationship between user trust, model accuracy and explanations in AI. *ACM Transactions on Computer-Human Interaction, 29*(4).
67. Prahl, A., & Van Swol, L. (2017). Understanding algorithm aversion: When is advice from automation discounted? *Journal of Forecasting, 36*(6), 691–702.
68. Riek, L. D. (2012). Wizard of oz studies in hri: A systematic review and new reporting guidelines. *Journal of Human-Robot Interaction, 1*(1), 119–136.
69. Robbemond, V., Inel, O., & Gadiraju, U. (2022). Understanding the role of explanation modality in ai-assisted decision-making. In *Proceedings of the 30th ACM Conference on User Modeling, Adaptation and Personalization* (pp. 223–233).
70. Schaffer, J., O'Donovan, J., Michaelis, J., Raglin, A., & Höllerer, T. (2019). I can do better than your ai: Expertise and explanations. In *Proceedings of the 24th International Conference on Intelligent User Interfaces* (pp. 240–251).
71. Schelble, B. G., Flathmann, C., McNeese, N. J., Freeman, G., & Mallick, R. (2022). Let's think together! assessing shared mental models, performance, and trust in human-agent teams. *Proceedings of the ACM on Human-Computer Interaction, 6*(GROUP), 1–29.
72. Schemmer, M., Kuehl, N., Benz, C., Bartos, A., & Satzger, G. (2023). Appropriate reliance on ai advice: Conceptualization and the effect of explanations. In *Proceedings of the 28th International Conference on Intelligent User Interfaces* (pp. 410–422).
73. Schmitt, A., Wambsganss, T., Söllner, M., & Janson, A. (2021). Towards a trust reliance paradox? exploring the gap between perceived trust in and reliance on algorithmic advice. *ICIS 2021 Research Papers* (1–17).
74. Schoeffer, J., De-Arteaga, M., & Kuehl, N. (2022). On explanations, fairness, and appropriate reliance in human-ai decision-making. In *Proceedings of the CHI Conference on Human Factors in Computing Systems (CHI '24)* (pp. 1–18).
75. Schoeffer, J., Jakubik, J., Voessing, M., Kuehl, N., & Satzger, G. (2023). On the interdependence of reliance behavior and accuracy in ai-assisted decision-making. arXiv:2304.08804
76. Seeber, I., Bittner, E., Briggs, R. O., de Vreede, T., de Vreede, G. J., Elkins, A., Maier, R., Merz, A. B., Oeste-Reiß, S., Randrup, N., Schwabe, G., & Söllner, M. (2020). Machines as teammates: A research agenda on AI in team collaboration. *Information & Management, 57*(2), Article 103174.
77. Selten, F., Robeer, M., & Grimmelikhuijsen, S. (2023). just like i thought': Street-level bureaucrats trust ai recommendations if they confirm their professional judgment. *Public Administration Review, 83*(2), 263–278.
78. Shi, S., Gong, Y., & Gursoy, D. (2021). Antecedents of trust and adoption intention toward artificially intelligent recommendation systems in travel planning: A heuristic-systematic model. *Journal of Travel Research, 60*(8), 1714–1734.
79. Steinfeld, A., Jenkins, O. C., & Scassellati, B. (2009). The oz of wizard: Simulating the human for interaction research. In *Proceedings of the 4th ACM/IEEE International Conference on Human Robot Interaction* (pp. 101–108).
80. Tejeda, H., Kumar, A., Smyth, P., & Steyvers, M. (2022). Ai-assisted decision-making: A cognitive modeling approach to infer latent reliance strategies. *Computational Brain & Behavior, 5*(4), 491–508.
81. Terveen, L. G. (1995). Overview of human-computer collaboration. *Knowledge-Based Systems, 8*(2–3), 67–81.
82. Tetlock, P. E. (1983). Accountability and the perseverance of first impressions. *Social Psychology Quarterly*, 285–292.
83. Vasconcelos, H., Jörke, M., Grunde-McLaughlin, M., Gerstenberg, T., Bernstein, M. S., & Krishna, R. (2023). Explanations can reduce overreliance on ai systems during decision-making. *Proceedings of the ACM on Human-Computer Interaction, 7*(CSCW1), 1–38.
84. Vom Brocke, J., Simons, A., Riemer, K., Niehaves, B., Plattfaut, R., & Cleven, A. (2015). Standing on the shoulders of giants: Challenges and recommendations of literature search in

information systems research. *Communications of the association for information systems, 37*(1), 9.
85. Westphal, M., Vössing, M., Satzger, G., Yom-Tov, G. B., & Rafaeli, A. (2023). Decision control and explanations in human-ai collaboration: Improving user perceptions and compliance. *Computers in Human Behavior, 144*, Article 107714.
86. Yin, M., Vaughan, J. W., & Wallach, H. (2019). Understanding the effect of accuracy on trust in machine learning models. *Conference on Human Factors in Computing Systems*, 1–12.
87. You, S., Yang, C. L., & Li, X. (2022). Algorithmic versus human advice: Does presenting prediction performance matter for algorithm appreciation? *Journal of Management Information Systems, 39*(2), 336–365.
88. Zercher, D., Jussupow, E., & Heinzl, A. (2023). When AI joins the Team: A literature review on intragroup processes and their effect on team performance in team-AI collaboration. *ECIS 2023 Research Papers*, 307.
89. Zhang, Y., Liao, Q. V., & Bellamy, R. K. (2020). Effect of confidence and explanation on accuracy and trust calibration in ai-assisted decision making. In *Proceedings of the 2020 Conference on Fairness, Accountability, and Transparency* (pp. 295–305).
90. Zschech, P. (2018). A taxonomy of recurring data analysis problems in maintenance analytics. *ECIS 2018 Research Papers*, 197.

GA4CA: Genetic Algorithms for the Creation and Design of Conversational Agents

Ricardo Rubiano-Cruz, Stefan Greulich, and Christian Huchler

Abstract User frustration is one negative consequence of human–computer interaction caused by bad interpretations and insufficient adaptation to user preferences. In this scope, genetic algorithms (GAs) might offer some insights to mitigate this problem. Hence, we conducted a systematic review to identify the implementation of GAs in the field of the design of conversational agents (CAs). Our results displayed that the literature focuses on three clusters mainly using evolutionary algorithms, and binary-coded GAs for natural language processing (NLP).

1 Introduction

Conversational agents (CAs), software programs enabling human–computer interaction through natural language, have garnered growing attention in academic and practical spheres [1]. Currently, CAs are often implemented to handle complex user queries, causing user frustration effectively. Additionally, attempts to make agents more human-like by adding social talk and humor may overlook the important aspects needed for real interaction, leading to conversations that are mainly transactional and functional [2].

These insights highlight the need for a careful approach in CA design, which considers both the human-like qualities essential for long-term interaction and the practical implications of organizational resources and technology. With this background, our research shifted focus from the human-like design aspects of CAs to

R. Rubiano-Cruz (✉) · S. Greulich
Else Kröner Fresenius Center for Digital Health, Faculty of Medicine CGC, Dresden, Germany
e-mail: ricardo_andres.rubiano_cruz@tu-dresden.de

S. Greulich
e-mail: stefan.greulich@tu-dresden.de

R. Rubiano-Cruz · S. Greulich · C. Huchler
Technische Universität Dresden, Dresden, Germany
e-mail: Christian.Huchler@mailbox.tu-dresden.de

C. M. Flath et al. (eds.), *Artificial Intelligence, Data, and Decision-Making*, Lecture Notes in Information Systems and Organisation 82,
https://doi.org/10.1007/978-3-032-08480-4_3

optimizing the interaction by improving conversational skills with human-like cues [3].

In this real, genetics algorithms (GAs) might be able to offer promising solutions. Grounded in natural evolution principles where the fittest individuals survive and reproduce, GAs are applied to improve candidate solutions for complex problems iteratively. As highlighted by the foundational works of Holland (1975) [4] and Goldberg (1989) [5], GAs have been instrumental in various optimization contexts. Hence, our central research question is:

Research Question: *What is the current status quo of implementing genetic algorithms for developing conversational agents?*

A comprehensive review of relevant literature was initiated to address the research question, followed by a detailed analysis of current implementations of GAs in CAs. This involved delving into the status quo of CA research through genetic algorithms, where a comprehensive review of 20 relevant papers was conducted. This rigorous analysis uncovered distinct clusters of research trends, offering comprehensive insights into the landscape of GA studies. These studies, enriched by diverse methodologies, address both theoretical and practical inquiries, highlighting the key trends and methodologies in the field.

2 Theoretical Background

2.1 Conversational Agents: An Overview

Conversational Agents (CAs), also known as chatbots or virtual assistants, have evolved significantly since their inception with simple programs like ELIZA in 1966 by Weizenbaum [6]. Today, modern CAs aim to simulate human-like conversations using complex algorithms and machine-learning techniques. Central to their development is a human-like design philosophy, incorporating avatars, names, and conversational styles that mimic human interaction, rooted in anthropomorphism principles [7]. Research by Diederich et al. (2020) [1], Gnewuch et al. (2018) [8], and Araujo (2018) [9] explored the intricacies of this human-like design, suggesting that such elements enhance user engagement, satisfaction, enjoyment, and trust in CA services. Users often interact with anthropomorphic agents as they would with another human, leading to a more natural and intuitive user experience. This anthropomorphic quality plays a crucial role in the effectiveness of CAs, shaping how users perceive and interact with these digital entities.

2.2 Genetic Algorithms

Genetic Algorithms (GAs) are a versatile computational problem-solving tool inspired by natural evolution principles, operating within the broader family of Evolutionary Algorithms (EAs). GAs employ genetic operators like crossover and mutation to optimize solutions across various domains [10]. Each individual in the population represents a potential solution, evaluated based on its fitness to solve the problem, with the selection process favoring higher fitness individuals [11]. Applications of GAs span diverse fields including Natural Language Processing (NLP), logistics, and engineering design, showcasing their adaptability and efficiency [12]. GAs have been instrumental in tasks such as optimizing linguistic models and language generation in NLP.

Holland (1975) [4] and Goldberg (1989) [5] laid the foundation for Genetic Algorithms (GAs), establishing them as effective optimization tools. Their work has not only pushed the boundaries of computational problem-solving but also unlocked new possibilities for addressing complex real-world problems using evolutionary computation. GAs demonstrate the power of biomimicry in technology, providing a distinctive method for solving challenges that demand adaptive solutions. Their ongoing evolution and application across diverse fields continue to be of significant interest and development in artificial intelligence and computational research.

2.3 Phase 1: Identifying Relevant Literature

The process began by searching through databases using specific keywords to find relevant publications. Notably, platforms like Jstor, AIS, and Scopus were utilized due to their comprehensive coverage of information science research [13]. A discerning approach was taken in selecting articles, conference papers, reviews, and books to ensure a focus on scholarly efforts. Additionally, the search was limited to works published after 2010, to reflect a contemporary exploration. To search the databases completely and specifically, a complex search term was used. This complex term was formed as follows:

> *("conversational agent" OR "chatbot" OR "virtual assistant" OR "natural language processing" OR "speech recognition" OR "dialogue management")*
> *AND*
> *("genetic algorithm")*
> *AND*
> *("evolutionary algorithm" OR "machine learning" OR "artificial intelligence")*
> *AND*
> *("data science" OR "data mining" OR "big data")*
> *AND*
> *("optimization" OR "implementation" OR "creation")*

This multi-layered search term was carefully divided into four different segments. Each segment serves as a crucial filter that ensures the careful inclusion of studies that match the thematic focus of the study. The first part ensured that only studies dealing with CA research were included. The terms were adopted from Cahn (2017) [14] and included synonyms for the term CA. The second part ensured that only studies in which the topic of genetic algorithms is at least mentioned are included. The third part integrates evolutionary algorithms or includes their computing methodologies, artificial intelligence, or machine learning, according to Young et al. (2015) [15]. And lastly, we focused on the use of GAs for optimization, implementation, or creation, which was formulated as the fourth part. A total of 4,037 articles were collected at this point. After carefully eliminating duplicates, 3,478 articles remained as candidates for closer examination. These remaining articles were subjected to an initial screening based on their titles in a further step. Specifically, only publications referring to studies on CAs or GAs were considered. Titles with direct reference to Conversational Agents or Genetic Algorithms remained. This careful selection resulted in a distilled sample of 54 articles progressing to the next phase.

The remaining articles were subjected to a more thorough and comprehensive review in the subsequent phase. This comprehensive analysis focused on a careful review of keywords and abstracts. The aim was to determine whether an article should be included in the final sample. To determine this, summaries were carefully reviewed, and chapters were selectively skimmed. As a result of this methodological assessment, a final selection of 20 articles emerged that are representative of the most important and relevant contributions to the thematic focus of the study. The literature collection, encompassing both search and filtration procedures, was conducted in May 2023, and the process unfolded in two distinct parts.

2.4 Phase 2: Code Literature

In the pursuit of comparing and consolidating the contents within our research database, a meticulous codification process was undertaken, encompassing dimensions pertinent to both Genetic Algorithms and Conversational Agent research. Table 1 summarizes these dimensions, taken from established frameworks such as frameworks for CA and GA research. The dimensions associated with Conversational Agents were carefully identified based on Diederich et al. (2022) [16] comprehensive research framework. This framework, known for its holistic perspective, covers various elements including human interaction, contextual dynamics, agent behavior, perceptual responses, and ultimate outcomes. Similarly, Katoch et al. (2021) [17] research framework inspired the dimensions related to Genetic Algorithms. This groundwork introduced dimensions such as metaheuristic algorithms and the various specific variants within the domain of Genetic Algorithms.

Regarding the Dataset dimension, we distinguished between Open and Proprietary Datasets. Lemos et al. (2023) [18] insights into the practical application of GAs in Machine Learning further enrich this discussion, illustrating how the choice

Table 1 Coding dimensions

<table>
<tr><th>Dimensions</th><th colspan="6">Characteristics</th></tr>
<tr><td>Dataset</td><td>Open dataset</td><td colspan="5">Proprietary dataset</td></tr>
<tr><td rowspan="2">Metaheuristic GA</td><td rowspan="2">Single solution metaheuristics</td><td colspan="5">Population-based Metaheuristic</td></tr>
<tr><td>Evolutionary algorithms</td><td colspan="4">Swarm-intelligence algorithms</td></tr>
<tr><td>Variant GA</td><td>Real and binary-coded GA</td><td>Multi-objective GA's</td><td>Parallel GA's</td><td colspan="2">Chaotic GA's</td><td>Hybrid GA's</td></tr>
<tr><td>Context</td><td>Professional</td><td colspan="5">Private</td></tr>
<tr><td rowspan="2">Agent</td><td colspan="2">Characteristics</td><td colspan="4">Design dimensions</td></tr>
<tr><td>Communication mode</td><td>Human identity</td><td colspan="2">Verbal communication</td><td colspan="2">Non-verbal communication</td></tr>
<tr><td>Embodiment</td><td>Virtual</td><td>Physical</td><td>Fully</td><td colspan="2">Partial</td><td>None</td></tr>
</table>

of the dataset can influence the effectiveness and adaptability of genetic algorithms in diverse machine learning contexts [18, 19]. In genetic algorithms, the metaheuristic GA dimension is vital, and it is split into single solution and population-based metaheuristics.

In CA development research, the selection of GA variants reflects a strategic and diverse approach. Real-coded GAs enhance algorithmic efficiency and response times, while binary-coded GAs tackle domain-specific challenges like healthcare or customer service. Multiobjective GAs balance trade-offs and parallel GAs emphasize scalability and speed. Chaotic GAs add adaptability in dynamic environments and hybrid GAs combine techniques for synergistic improvements. These diverse variants contribute to the dynamic nature of CA development, each tailored to meet specific research goals [17].

The context dimension in CA research is separated into professional and private contexts, reflecting the dual roles of CAs in work and personal settings. Understanding these distinct contexts provides insights into the diverse roles CAs play in various spheres [20]. In our research, we explore how CAs engage with users through Communication Mode and Human Identity. We also focus on Verbal and Non-Verbal Communication, emphasizing clarity in transactional interactions [2]. Finally, The Embodiment dimension is critical in defining how CAs are presented to users. It classifies CAs as either Virtual, Physical, Fully Embodied, Partially Embodied, or Non-Embodied, each category offering distinct user experiences. This classification is crucial for understanding how users perceive and interact with CAs, influencing their overall engagement and effectiveness [16].

2.5 Phase 3: Analyze Literature

We analyzed the literature following the heuristic used by [21]. In the time series analysis, we examined the yearly count of publications, similar to the approach of Leukel et al. (2014) [22]. We analyzed a graphical representation of the number of publications per year, and trends were discerned through visual inspection. Lastly, we performed a cluster analysis. Clusters are formed by identifying articles that are as similar as possible to each other and as dissimilar as possible from those in other clusters [23]. Using clusters in research publications helps identify predominant research trends within a research domain. We utilized a two-stage approach following Punj and Stewart (1983) [24] and Remane et al. (2016) [25]. Firstly, we determined the optimal number of clusters through the intercluster distance (using Hamming distance as implemented in the Python package Scipy), and secondly, we reviewed the dendrogram to construct the three clusters.

3 Results

3.1 Results of the Structure Literature Analysis

In this section, the results from the structured literature analysis are succinctly summarized and presented in a concept matrix (refer to Table 2). A key observation is the balanced distribution and separation of papers within the dataset. Notably, 55% of the papers are based on open datasets, while the remaining 45% used proprietary datasets. These proprietary dataset papers invariably include an evolutionary algorithm, with 77% also incorporating a real and binary-coded genetic algorithm. Regarding the Metaheuristics, a trend is evident, with 85% prominently featuring the evolutionary algorithm as the primary metaheuristic for genetic algorithms. Additionally, 15% of papers investigate single-solution metaheuristics, and another 15% focus on swarm intelligence algorithms. The prevalence of certain approaches in this field is highlighted, indicating areas of concentrated research interest.

In terms of variants, there is a strong emphasis on real and binary-coded genetic algorithms, featured in 70% of the papers. Multi-objective GAs are highlighted in 30% of the papers, while other variants like Parallel GAs, Chaotic GAs, and Hybrid GAs are less common, each discussed in only one paper, collectively making up 5%. A notable link is found between metaheuristic and variant, with 76% of papers focusing on evolutionary algorithms also dealing with binary coded GAs. However, the domains of "Agent" and "Embodiment" are significantly underrepresented, with only one article addressing each, accounting for 5% of the literature each. Remarkably, no articles were found that specifically addressed the domains of "Context" and "Perception." The dominant theme in the reviewed research is the use of Evolutionary Algorithms in combination with real and binary coded GAs, forming a substantial 65% of the literature reviewed.

Table 2 Concept matrix, non-observed categories excluded for space reasons

	Open dataset	Proprietary dataset	Single solution metaheu	Evolutionary algorithms	Swarm-intelligence algos	Real and binary-coded GA	Multi-objective GAs	Parallel GAs
[28]	x			x	x	x		
[29]		x		x		x	x	
[30]	x			x	x	x		
[31]	x			x		x		
[32]		x		x		x		x
[33]		x		x		x		
[34]		x		x		x	x	
[35]		x		x		x		
[36]		x	x	x				
[37]	x			x		x		
[38]		x		x		x		
[39]		x		x				
[27]	x		x				x	
[40]	x			x			x	
[41]		x		x		x		
[42]	x					x		
[43]	x							
[44]	x		x	x		x		

(continued)

Table 2 (continued)

	Open dataset	Proprietary dataset	Single solution metaheu	Evolutionary algorithms	Swarm-intelligence algos	Real and binary-coded GA	Multi-objective GAs	Parallel GAs
[26]	x			x			x	
[45]	x			x	x	x	x	
Sum:	11	9	3	17	3	14	6	1

	Chaotic GAs	Hybrid GAs	Communication mode	Verbal communication	None	Publication ID	Cluster membership
[28]						0	2
[29]						1	3
[30]						2	2
[31]						3	2
[32]						4	3
[33]						5	3
[34]						6	3
[35]						7	3
[36]						8	3
[37]		x				9	2
[38]						10	3
[39]						11	3
[27]						12	1
[40]						13	1
[41]	x					14	3
[42]						15	2
[43]						16	1
[44]						17	2
[26]			x	x	x	18	1
[45]						19	2
Sum:	1	1	1	1	1		

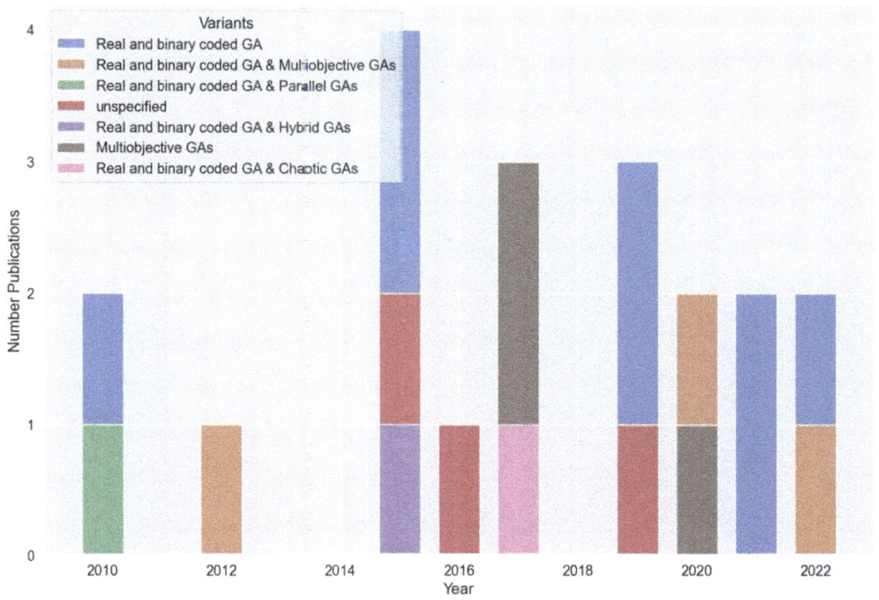

Fig. 1 Time series of publications and GA variants

3.2 *Results of the Time Series Analysis*

Over the past decade, from 2010 onwards, these publications have shown a trend of growth and evolution, as depicted in visual Fig. 1. Initially, in 2010, there was an evident surge in publications with a count of two. However, this momentum saw a reduction in the ensuing years, 2012, with only one publication in those years. Interestingly, the year 2015 saw a remarkable peak in this timeline, with the publication count soaring to its highest at four. Following this peak, the years 2017 to 2019 showcased a rather steady trend, with each year consistently presenting three publications. However, the data reveals a perceptible reduction in the years 2020 and 2022, where the publication count dropped to two in both instances. The most common variant of GA was real and binary coded.

3.3 *Results of the Cluster Analysis*

Cluster 1: Publication IDs 12, 13, 16, and 18 (*orange in* Fig. 2).

Foremost among these clusters was Cluster 1, encapsulating Publication IDs 12, 13, 16, and 18. Cluster 1 is characterized by its emphasis on sentiment analysis research on open datasets and multi-objective GAs. It demonstrates a strong

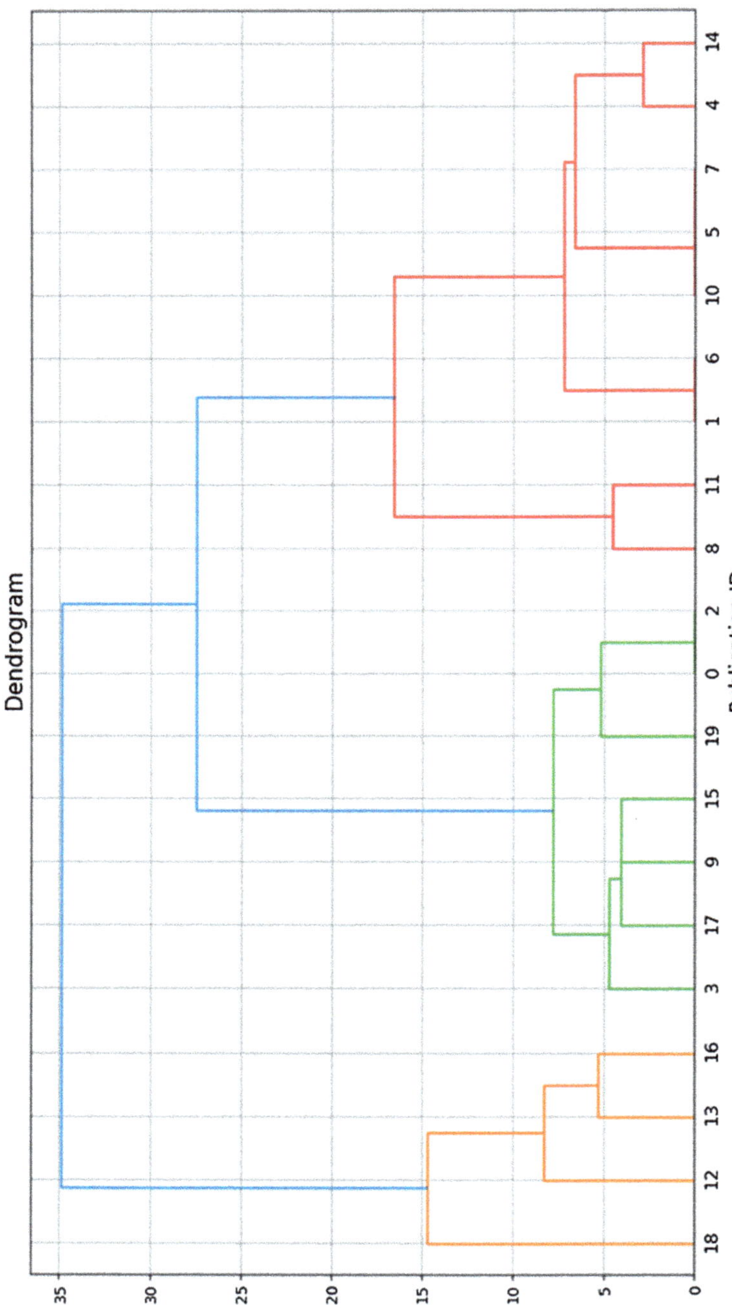

Fig. 2 Dendrogram

commitment to transparent data practices and sophisticated algorithmic methodologies. This cluster is distinguished by its skillful use of various GA variants for effective feature selection, showing an inclination towards solving complex, multi-dimensional problems. A key focus of this cluster is the application of multi-agent strategies and different embodiments, moving beyond single-solution metaheuristics. This approach is expanded by researchers like Araujo, 2020 [26] (ID 18), highlighting a multifaceted methodology in GA application that balances transparency and computational innovation. A prime example of this cluster's work is Onan and Korukoglu (2017) [27] (ID 12), which effectively uses genetic algorithms for diverse feature selection methods in sentiment analysis. This study addresses the challenge of managing abundant data and improves classification accuracy while showcasing the potential of multi-objective GAs in enhancing model robustness. The focus on multi-objective optimization in Cluster 1 is significant. Studies in this cluster, including Onan and Korukoglu's [27], go beyond single-goal optimization, offering various solutions for various optimization needs. This approach of optimizing multiple conflicting objectives simultaneously reflects the advanced computational strategies of this cluster. Cluster 1 represents a juncture of open data advocacy and advanced algorithmic methodologies in sentiment analysis.

Cluster 2: Publication IDs 0, 2, 3, 9, 15, 17, and 19 (*green in* Fig. 2).

This cluster is distinguished by its consistent use of open datasets and a focus on metaheuristic approaches, particularly GAs, which are leveraged to explore and enhance the text clustering process. Cluster 2 stands out in the realm of text clustering and sentiment analysis research, showcasing a unique intersection of heuristic optimization and GAs applied to the challenges of high-dimensional text data. The commitment to open science is a hallmark of this cluster, with researchers employing open datasets to ensure the reproducibility and generalizability of their results. The metaheuristic strategies employed in these studies are varied and move beyond traditional single-solution approaches to address the complexities inherent in text data. This Cluster is particularly notable for its focus on real and binary-coded GAs, highlighting this research group's nuanced exploration of GA variants. Cluster 2 represents the theoretical understanding of genetic algorithms and provides practical solutions in the fields of data mining and text analysis. An exemplar within this cluster, Fan and Wang (2021) [30], utilize an improved heuristic three-parent GA to refine the process of identifying optimal clustering centers. Their methodological enhancements aim to accelerate the convergence of GAs and amplify their global search capabilities, thus improving the clustering outcomes regarding accuracy and mutual information. This approach is a testament to Cluster 2's overarching goal: to elevate the performance of clustering algorithms within the expansive and challenging domain of text analysis.

Cluster 3: Publication IDs 1, 4, 5, 6, 7, 8, 10, 11, and 14 (*red in* Fig. 2).

Lastly, Cluster 3 concentrates on the use of proprietary datasets in conjunction with a unified focus on metaheuristics, which are mostly evolutionary algorithms. This cluster is primarily concerned with specialized and potentially sensitive data, pointing to a research direction that might involve proprietary or sensitive information requiring controlled access. The presence of real and binary-coded GAs is a testament to the enduring relevance of these methods in producing reliable results. While most researchers in this cluster also utilize GAs, they tend to use fewer combinations of GA variants compared to the second group. However, the majority is again with real and binary-coded GAs. In addition, there are again no studies in this cluster that include considerations of agent and/or embodiment. The dendrogram and table show that GA and its variants are widely used in many of the publications considered. The clustering reflects different combinations of approaches and strategies used in each publication. The work of White et al. (2022) [29] (ID 1) uniquely integrates both real and binary coded and multi-objective metaheuristics. It fits well within this cluster, as it explores an Agent-Based Model optimized by NSGA-III, an evolutionary algorithm, to improve Children's Services in the UK. The use of proprietary data in this context is key to addressing the unique challenges and sensitive nature of social care. White et al.'s research exemplifies Cluster 3's inclination towards practical, impactful applications of GAs, leveraging complex models to provide insights into specialized, real-world problems.

4 Discussion

In the realm of conversational agents (CAs), users have reported unsatisfaction and frustrating episodes in the interaction with CAs caused by inefficient assistance and problems in interpretations. These problems may emerge from the inadaptability of CAs to users' dynamic responses [46]. Past research showed that optimizing CAs responses improves the quality of user interactions and fosters increased user satisfaction and engagement [47]. However, from the network plot in Fig. 3, we can see that the research does not strongly focus on the link between verbal communication of the CA with the use of evolutionary algorithms. Integrating GAs into CAs might represent a significant advancement aimed at enhancing the accuracy of CA responses and their adaptability to user preferences and conversational nuances. Inspired by natural selection and genetic evolution, this approach offers a unique methodology for refining interaction and response mechanisms within CAs, leading to context-aware conversations that feel more natural and meaningful to users [48].

The concept matrix in Table 2 and the network representation from Fig. 3 point toward the fact that the literature displays a separation between technical and design disciplines. The technical development of CAs using GAs is frequently treated separately from design considerations like embodiment and agent personality, often handled by different teams or researchers [49]. This division may arise due to the challenges of integrating physical or virtual representations with GA optimization processes, leading to a need for more emphasis on agent embodiment. Embodiment in CAs involves intricate design nuances that may not directly align with the optimization objectives typically addressed by GAs [50].

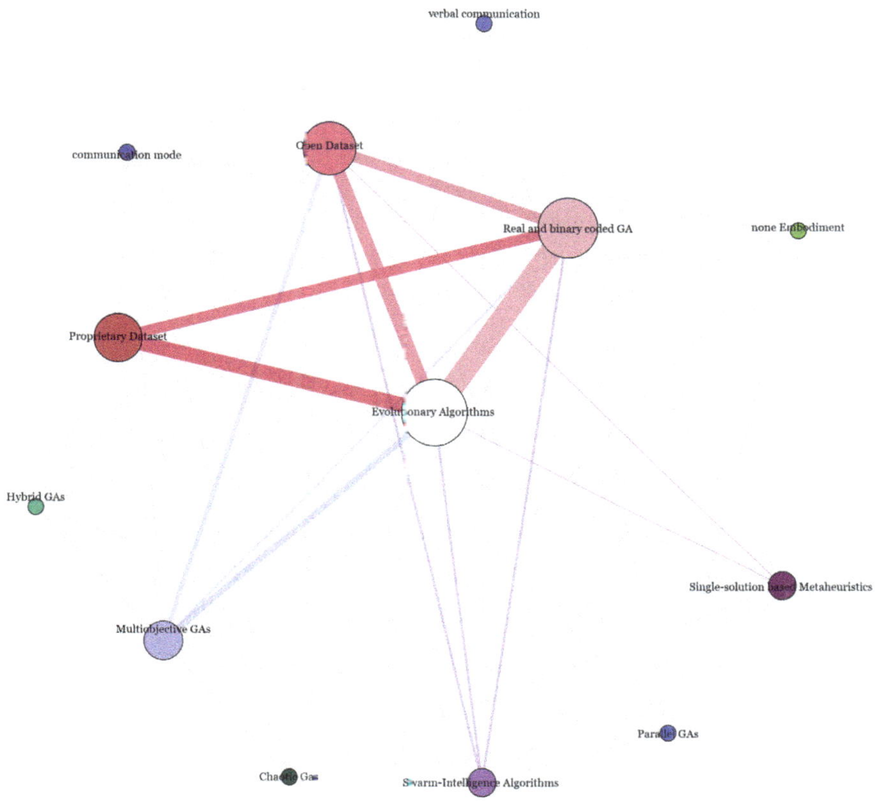

Fig. 3 Network plot among dimensions from Table 1

The advantage of the application of GA can also be seen in Du (2021) [31], where the author used the algorithm to improve text classification. The proposed model in this paper selects a subset of words from an input, which still leads to the same prediction through the model. Following this, with the use of GA, a better performance was achieved. Another example of the applicability of GAs can be researched in the paper by Lyu and Dong (2019) [42] where they use it to select features automatically and therefore reduce the manual workload during the training phase. Also, using this method they achieved a good performance in the recognition of Alzheimer´s disease.

4.1 Limitations

While we conducted our research according to established guidelines to the best of our ability, it is important to note that our study has three key limitations. First, we were constrained by time, so we did not include papers published before 2010, potentially leaving out relevant information for our concept matrix analysis. Additionally, even though we included curated collections of journals and conferences [13], we might have omitted important domains or dimensions, affecting our cluster analysis. Finally, using different search terms, for example, could yield different clusters. Nevertheless, this systematic review provides a valuable overview to guide future research and practical applications in the GAs on CAs design field.

5 Conclusion

This research explored the implementation of genetic algorithms (GAs) in the design of conversational agents (CAs) since 2010. The study highlighted the strong focus on evolutionary algorithms and real and binary-coded GAs employed for NLP. It also makes theoretical suggestions, such as splitting between the technical and the design dimensions of CAs regarding the implementation of GAs. The findings also have practical implications, like indicating that GAs may offer an adaptive solution to mitigate users' frustration caused by problems in interpretations and inefficient assistance. Addressing these research gaps will contribute to the IS community and offer new insights for CAs, which have the potential to improve user experience in human–computer interaction.

References

1. Diederich, S., Brendel, A. B., & Kolbe, L. M. (2020). Designing Anthropomorphic Enterprise Conversational Agents. *Business & Information Systems Engineering, 62*, 193–209. https://doi.org/10.1007/s12599-020-00639-y
2. Clark, L., Pantidi, N., Cooney, O., Doyle, P., Garaialde, D., Edwards, J., Spillane, B., Gilmartin, E., Murad, C., Munteanu, C., Wade, V., & Cowan, B. R. (2019). What Makes a Good Conversation? Challenges in Designing Truly Conversational Agents. In *Proceedings of the 2019 CHI Conference on Human Factors in Computing Systems* (pp. 1–12). Association for Computing Machinery. https://doi.org/10.1145/3290605.3300705
3. Feine, J., Gnewuch, U., Morana, S., & Maedche, A. (2019). A Taxonomy of Social Cues for Conversational Agents. *International Journal of Human-Computer Studies, 132*, 138–161. https://doi.org/10.1016/j.ijhcs.2019.07.009
4. Holland, J. H. (1975). *Adaptation in Natural and Artificial Systems* (p. 32). The University of Michigan Press.
5. Goldberg, D. E., Korb, B., & Deb, K. (1989). Messy Genetic Algorithms: Motivation, Analysis, and First Results. *Complex Systems, 3*, 493–530.
6. Weizenbaum, J. (1966). ELIZA—A Computer Program for the Study of Natural Language Communication between Man and Machine. *Communications of the ACM, 9*, 36–45. https://doi.org/10.1145/365153.365168
7. Nass, C., & Moon, Y. (2000). Machines and Mindlessness: Social Responses to Computers. *Journal of Social Issues, 56*, 81–103. https://doi.org/10.1111/0022-4537.00153
8. Gnewuch, U., Morana, S., Adam, M., & Maedche, A. (2018). *Faster is Not Always Better: Understanding the Effect of Dynamic Response Delays in Human-Chatbot Interaction.*

9. Araujo, T. (2018). Living Up to the Chatbot Hype: The Influence of Anthropomorphic Design Cues and Communicative Agency Framing on Conversational Agent and Company Perceptions. *Computers in Human Behavior, 85*, 183–189. https://doi.org/10.1016/j.chb.2018.03.051
10. Johnson, J. M., & Rahmat-samii, Y. (1994). Genetic Algorithm Optimization and Its Application to Antenna Design. In *Proceedings of IEEE Antennas and Propagation Society International Symposium and URSI National Radio Science Meeting* (vol. 1, pp. 326–329). https://doi.org/10.1109/APS.1994.407746
11. Michalewicz, Z. (1996). *Genetic Algorithms + Data Structures = Evolution Programs.* Springer Berlin Heidelberg. https://doi.org/10.1007/978-3-662-03315-9.
12. Mason, M., & Penstein Rosé, C. (1998). *Learning Constraints for Plan-Based Discourse Processors With Genetic Programming.*
13. Baas, J., Schotten, M., Plume A., Côté, G., & Karimi, R. (2020). Scopus as a Curated, High-Quality Bibliometric Data Source for Academic Research in Quantitative Science Studies. *Quantitative Science Studies, 1*, 377–386. https://doi.org/10.1162/qss_a_00019
14. Cahn, J. (2017). *CHATBOT: Architecture, Design, & Development*. University of Pennsylvania School of Engineering and Applied Science Department of Computer and Information Science.
15. Young, S. R., Rose, D. C., Karnowski, T. P., Lim, S.-H., & Patton, R. M. (2015). Optimizing Deep Learning Hyper-Parameters through an Evolutionary Algorithm. In *Proceedings of the Workshop on Machine Learning in High-Performance Computing Environments* (pp. 1–5). Association for Computing Machinery. https://doi.org/10.1145/2834892.2834896
16. Diederich, S., Brendel, A., Morana, S., & Kolbe, L. (2022). On the Design of and Interaction with Conversational Agents: An Organizing and Assessing Review of Human-Computer Interaction Research. *Journal of the Association for Information Systems, 23*, 96–138. https://doi.org/10.17705/1jais.00724
17. Katoch, S., Chauhan, S. S., & Kumar, V. (2021). A Review on Genetic Algorithm: Past, Present, and Future. *Multimedia Tools and Applications, 80*, 8091–8126. https://doi.org/10.1007/s11042-020-10139-6
18. Lemos, A. R. (2023). Genetic Algorithm and Its Practicality in Machine Learning. https://towardsdatascience.com/genetic-algorithm-6aefd897f1ac, last accessed 2023/01/03.
19. Srivignesh, R. (2022). Genetic Algorithms and its Use-Cases in Machine Learning. https://www.analyticsvidhya.com/blog/2021/06/genetic-algorithms-and-its-use-cases-in-machine-learning/, last accessed 2022/08/24.
20. von Terzi, P., Tretter, S., Uhde, A., Hassenzahl, M., & Diefenbach, S. (2021). Technology-Mediated Experiences and Social Context: Relevant Needs in Private vs. Public Interaction and the Importance of Others for Positive Affect. *Frontiers in Psychology, 12*. https://doi.org/10.3389/fpsyg.2021.718315
21. Greulich, R. S., & Brendel, A. B. (2022). Feel, Don't Think" Review of the Application of Neuroscience Methods for Conversational Agent Research. In *ECIS*.
22. Leukel, J., Mueller, M., & Sugumaran, V. (2014). The State of Design Science Research within the BISE Community: An Empirical Investigation.
23. Kaufman, L., & Rousseeuw, P. J. (2009). *Finding Groups in Data: An Introduction to Cluster Analysis*. John Wiley & Sons.
24. Punj, G., & Stewart, D. W. (1983). Cluster Analysis in Marketing Research: Review and Suggestions for Application. *Journal of Marketing Research, 20*, 134–148. https://doi.org/10.1177/002224378302000204
25. Remane, G., Nickerson, R., Hanelt, A., Tesch, J. F., & Kolbe, L. M. (2016). A Taxonomy of Carsharing Business Models. In *ICIS* (pp. 1–17).
26. Araujo, L. (2020). Genetic Programming for Natural Language Processing. *Genetic Programming and Evolvable Machines, 21*, 11–32. https://doi.org/10.1007/s10710-019-09361-5
27. Onan, A., & Korukoğlu, S. (2017). A Feature Selection Model Based on Genetic Rank Aggregation for Text Sentiment Classification. *Journal of Information Science, 43*, 25–38. https://doi.org/10.1177/0165551515613226

28. Blanchard, A. E., Shekar, M. C., Gao, S., Gounley, J., Lyngaas, I., Glaser, J., & Bhowmik, D. (2022). Automating Genetic Algorithm Mutations for Molecules Using a Masked Language Model. *IEEE Transactions on Evolutionary Computation., 26*, 793–799.
29. White, L., Basurra, S., Gaber, M. M., Alsewari, A. A., Saeed, F., & Addanki, S. M. (2022). Agent-Based Simulations Using Genetic Algorithm Calibration: A Children's Services Application. *IEEE Access, 10*, 88386–88397.
30. Fan, Q., & Wang, Z. (2021). A Text Clustering Method Based on the Improved Heuristic Three-parent Genetic Algorithm. In *2021 China Automation Congress (CAC)* (pp. 4737–4743). IEEE.
31. Du, Q., & Xu, J. (2021). Model-Agnostic Local Explanations with Genetic Algorithms for Text Classification. In *SEKE* (pp. 570–575).
32. Barrero, D. F., González-Pardo, A., Camacho, D., & R-Moreno, M. D. (2010). Distributed Parameter Tuning for Genetic Algorithms. *Computer Science and Information Systems*, 661–677.
33. Smith, P. W. (2010). Using Genetic Algorithms in Word-Vector Optimisation. In *2010 UK Workshop on Computational Intelligence (UKCI)* (pp. 1–5). IEEE.
34. Meng, D., & Pei, Z. (2012). Extracting Linguistic Rules from Data Sets Using Fuzzy Logic and Genetic Algorithms. *Neurocomputing, 78*, 48–54.
35. Huk, M., & Mizera-Pietraszko, J.: Application of Genetic Algorithms to Context-Sensitive Text Mining. In *ICADIWT* (pp. 273–284).
36. Bartoli, A., De Lorenzo, A., Medvet, E., & Tarlao, F. (2015). Learning Text Patterns using Separate-and-Conquer Genetic Programming. In P. Machado, M. I. Heywood, J. McDermott, M. Castelli, P. García-Sánchez, P. Burelli, S. Risi, & K. Sim (Eds.), *Genetic Programming* (pp. 16–27). Springer International Publishing. https://doi.org/10.1007/978-3-319-16501-1_2
37. Su, B., & Wang, Y. (2015). Genetic Algorithm based Feature Selection and Parameter Optimization for Support Vector Regression Applied to Semantic Textual Similarity. *Journal of Shanghai Jiaotong University (Science), 20*, 143–148. https://doi.org/10.1007/s12204-015-1602-2
38. Huk, M., Kwiatkowski, J., Konieczny, D., Kędziora, M., & Mizera-Pietraszko, J. (2015). Context-Sensitive Text Mining with Fitness Leveling Genetic Algorithm. In *2015 IEEE 2nd International Conference on Cybernetics (CYBCONF)* (pp. 342–347). IEEE.
39. Kotelnikov, E. V., & Pletneva, M. V. (2016). Text Sentiment Classification Based on a Genetic Algorithm and Word and Document Co-Clustering. *Journal of Computer and Systems Sciences International, 55*, 106–114. https://doi.org/10.1134/S1064230715060106
40. Keshavarz, H., & Abadeh, M. S. (2017). ALGA: Adaptive Lexicon Learning using Genetic Algorithm for Sentiment Analysis of Microblogs. *Knowledge-Based Systems, 122*, 1–16.
41. Chiroma, H., Noor, A. S. M., Abdulkareem, S., Abubakar, A. I., Hermawan, A., Qin, H., Hamza, M. F., & Herawan, T. (2017). Neural Networks Optimization through Genetic Algorithm Searches: A Review. *Applied Mathematics & Information Sciences, 11*, 1543–1564. https://doi.org/10.18576/amis/110602
42. Lyu, G., & Dong, A. (2019). Automatic Selection of Lexical Features for Detecting Alzheimer's Disease using Bag-of-Words Model and Genetic Algorithm. *IJCAT, 61*, 306. https://doi.org/10.1504/IJCAT.2019.103290
43. Sangam, S., & Shinde, S. (2019). A Novel Feature Selection Method Based on Genetic Algorithm for Opinion Mining of Social Media Reviews. In S. Minz, S. Karmakar, & L. Kharb (Eds.), *Information, Communication and Computing Technology* (pp. 167–175). Springer Singapore. https://doi.org/10.1007/978-981-13-5992-7_15
44. Iqbal, F., Hashmi, J. M., Fung, B. C., Batool, R., Khattak, A. M., Aleem, S., & Hung, P. C. (2019). A Hybrid Framework for Sentiment Analysis using Genetic Algorithm based Feature Reduction. *IEEE Access, 7*, 14637–14652.
45. Labani, M., Moradi, P., & Jalili, M. (2020). A Multi-Objective Genetic Algorithm for Text Feature Selection using the Relative Discriminative Criterion. *Expert Systems with Applications, 149*, Article 113276.

46. Følstad, A., & Brandtzaeg, P. B. (2020). Users' Experiences with Chatbots: Findings from a Questionnaire Study. *Qualitative User Experience, 5*, 3. https://doi.org/10.1007/s41233-020-00033-2
47. Kim, K.-M., Lim, S.-S., & Cho, S.-B. (2004). User Adaptive Answers Generation for Conversational Agent Using Genetic Programming. In Z. R. Yang, H. Yin, & R. M. Everson (Eds.), *Intelligent Data Engineering and Automated Learning—IDEAL 2004* (pp. 813–819). Springer Berlin Heidelberg. https://doi.org/10.1007/978-3-540-28651-6_121
48. Mariani, M. M., Hashemi, N., & Wirtz, J. (2023). Artificial Intelligence Empowered Conversational Agents: A Systematic Literature Review and Research Agenda. *Journal of Business Research, 161*, Article 113838. https://doi.org/10.1016/j.jbusres.2023.113838
49. Sadek, M., & Mougenot, C. (2023). Exploring Links between Conversational Agent Design Challenges and Interdisciplinary Collaboration. http://arxiv.org/abs/2311.08832, https://doi.org/10.48550/arXiv.2311.08832
50. Roy, N., Posner, I., Barfoot, T., Beaudoin, P., Bengio, Y., Bohg, J., Brock, O., Depatie, I., Fox, D., Koditschek, D., Lozano-Perez, T., Mansinghka, V., Pal, C., Richards, B., Sadigh, D., Schaal, S., Sukhatme, G., Therien, D., Toussaint, M., & Van de Panne, M. (2021). From Machine Learning to Robotics: Challenges and Opportunities for Embodied Intelligence, http://arxiv.org/abs/2110.15245, https://doi.org/10.48550/arXiv.2110.15245

Getting in Contract with Large Language Models—An Agency Theory Perspective on Large Language Model Alignment

Sascha Kaltenpoth and Oliver Müller

Abstract Adopting Large language models (LLMs) in organizations potentially revolutionizes our lives and work. However, they can generate off-topic, discriminating, or harmful content. This AI alignment problem often stems from misspecifications during the LLM adoption, unnoticed by the principal due to the LLM's black-box nature. While various research disciplines investigated AI alignment, they neither address the information asymmetries between organizational adopters and black-box LLM agents nor consider organizational AI adoption processes. Therefore, we propose *LLM ATLAS* (LLM **A**gency **T**heory-**L**ed **A**lignment **S**trategy) a conceptual framework grounded in agency (contract) theory, to mitigate alignment problems during organizational LLM adoption. We conduct a conceptual literature analysis using the **organizational LLM adoption phases** and the **agency theory** as concepts. Our approach results in (1) providing an extended literature analysis process specific to AI alignment methods during organizational LLM adoption and (2) providing a first LLM alignment problem-solution space.

1 Introduction

Adopting highly capable Large language models (LLMs) such as Llama 3 [43] or GPT-4 [48] in organizational processes, e.g., as domain-specific conversational agents, has the potential to revolutionize our lives and work [18]. However, they can generate off-topic, discriminating, or harmful content under certain circumstances [63, 65]. In this case, the artificial intelligence (AI) agent's actual behavior differs from that intended by its principal, e.g., the user or designer. This *AI alignment problem* [19, 24] often stems from misspecifications during the LLM adoption (e.g., implementation of LLM-driven systems into the organizational infrastructure) [58, 68], unnoticed by the principal due to the LLM's black-box nature.

S. Kaltenpoth (✉) · O. Müller
Department of Business Administration and Economics, Paderborn University, Paderborn, Germany
e-mail: sascha.kaltenpoth@uni-paderborn.de

O. Müller
e-mail: oliver.mueller@uni-paderborn.de

C. M. Flath et al. (eds.), *Artificial Intelligence, Data, and Decision-Making*, Lecture Notes in Information Systems and Organisation 82,
https://doi.org/10.1007/978-3-032-08480-4_4

This information asymmetry between the adopting organization and the LLM agent possibly results in serious consequences, such as lawyers facing sanctions for citing fake cases [7] or failures in chatbot services [46], for which users usually blame the company rather than the LLM-based system itself [50]. Therefore, it is crucial for organizations to mitigate information asymmetries during LLM adoption and ensure that these models are aligned with human, organizational, and social values [5, 30].

Various research disciplines investigated AI alignment, particularly LLM alignment. Machine learning (ML) researchers focused on technical solutions, such as high-quality demonstration training data [49, 79], incorporating external knowledge [34, 77], output verification [35, 48], or alignment benchmarks [12, 76]. AI ethics researchers analyzed possible harms and provide governance recommendations [25, 47, 70]. Furthermore, multiple literature reviews explained, categorized, and assessed LLM alignment approaches [28, 58, 68].

While these studies provide some guidance for organizations that strive to adopt LLMs, they neither address the information asymmetries between the organizational adopter and the black-box LLM agent nor do they explicitly consider organizational AI adoption processes. Like most AI-based approaches, LLMs' organizational adoption requires selection, training, evaluation, deployment, and monitoring of the model [32, 61].

Therefore, we propose *LLM ATLAS* (LLM **A**gency **T**heory-**L**ed **A**lignment **S**trategy) a conceptual framework grounded in agency (contract) theory, to mitigate alignment problems during organizational LLM adoption. Highlighting the information asymmetry between the adopting organization and the black-box LLM, we adapt the idea of Hadfield-Menell & Hadfield [24] to frame LLM alignment as an agency problem. We conduct a conceptual literature analysis [55] using the combination of the **organizational LLM adoption phases** and the **agency theory** to analyze the literature. While we draw on existing AI and LLM alignment literature reviews instead of search and assessment, we synthesize a problem-solution mapping for LLM alignment during the organizational LLM adoption by applying agency theory to all organizational LLM adoption phases.

LLM ATLAS provides a simple approach to identifying agency problems in the organizational LLM adoption process and synthesizing solutions from the literature. Our approach extends the existing AI alignment literature and supports organizational LLM adoption by (1) providing an extended literature analysis process specific to AI alignment methods during organizational LLM adoption and (2) providing a first proof-of-concept of the problem-solution space derivation. In future research, we plan to extend this initial literature analysis with a comprehensive literature review and an extendable format for the presentation of the problem-solution space in the form of a multi-contributor website. We hope to encourage other researchers to participate in the research on the intersection of LLM alignment and organizational LLM adoption.

2 Background

2.1 Large Language Models—A Black-box Architecture

Large language models (LLMs) such as GPT-4 or LLaMA, are neural networks, usually based on a decoder-only Transformer structure [48, 65], that autoregressively predict the next token t_{n+1} based on the conditional probability distribution $P(t_{n+1}|t_1...t_n)$, where $t_1...t_n$ refers to the context sequence of tokens [57]. They contain up to billions of parameters and are (pre-)trained on vast amounts of textual data [9, 57]. These characteristics enable them to be pre-trained to solve many cognitive tasks, such as answering questions, generating coherent, meaningful texts, and passing various human exams at a human-like level [12, 63]. Furthermore, pre-trained LLMs possess foundational knowledge and can be adapted to various downstream tasks and domains [9]. Therefore, they are often called foundation models. However, foundation models are black-box architectures in terms of their neural network architecture and their vast amount of training data [9]. Consequently, the learned representations and their alignment to human, organizational, and social values are not visible to a potential adopter [5], causing an information asymmetry between the LLM and its adopter.

2.2 The AI and LLM Alignment Problem

The AI alignment problem refers to situations where an AI's observed behavior differs from that intended by its designers or expected by its users [19, 24]. This problem typically originates from information asymmetries between the AI (agent) and its designers and users (principal) [24]. A main alignment concern in the context of LLMs is hallucinations, that is, factually incorrect or unfaithful responses [29]. Another common concern is social, gender-, or ethical biases of LLMs, especially foundation models [30, 70]. LLM alignment aims to align LLMs with the task, on the one hand, and human, organizational, and social values, on the other hand, [5, 30]. This broad goal can be operationalized drawing on the definition of Askell et al. [5], stating that an appropriately aligned LLM agent needs to commit to helpfulness, honesty, and harmlessness. While helpfulness refers to an agent being able to solve human-given tasks, honesty refers to giving accurate and correct information and signaling confidence in the given answer or solution [5]. Harmlessness refers to not being offensive, discriminatory, biased, and refusing dangerous behavior.

2.3 Existing Frameworks

The research on LLMs is studied in two comprehensive literature reviews [44, 78]. Zhao et al. [78] provide an overview of the development of LLMs within the past decade. The authors differentiate between closed- and open-source LLMs, investigating their data sources and training strategies. In contrast, Minaee et al. [44] categorize LLMs by their capabilities. They divide LLMs into basic, pre-trained LLMs, emerging, further fine-tuned LLMs, and augmented LLMs, which can use tools and APIs [44]. Both reviews consider alignment as a technique to train LLMs. While Minaee et al. [44] provide an overview of hallucination evaluations and consider alignment as a common LLM training strategy, Zhao et al. [78] provide an overview of possible alignment datasets, alignment tuning strategies, and evaluation criteria, such as the helpfulness, honesty, harmlessness by Askell et al. [5].

Ji et al. [28] comprehensively review AI alignment problems and approaches. They identify four essential criteria for AI alignment: robustness, interpretability, controllability, and ethicality (RICE). Robustness refers to the resilience of AI systems, especially the correctness of outputs. In contrast, interpretability refers to the honesty of LLMs and using interpretability tools to investigate LLM reasoning [28]. While controllability refers to human supervision and intervention ability, if the model deviates from the expected behavior, ethicality states that the system should adhere to society's norms and values [28]. Memarian & Doleck [42] investigate the fairness, accountability, transparency, and ethics (FATE) framework on AI in the higher education literature. Their findings show a tendency to use FATE in descriptive rather than technical terms and also that FATE is investigated in quantitative rather than qualitative means [42].

Shen et al. [58] and Wang et al. [68] both provide a comprehensive survey of LLM alignment. While Wang et al. [68] focus on human value-driven alignment, including human-generated data, human preferences in training, and human evaluation strategies, Shen et al. [58] provides an overview of human- and non-human-driven alignment approaches categorized by inner alignment, outer alignment, and interpretability. Outer alignment refers to choosing the right loss or reward functions and ensuring the match of training objective and human intention. In contrast, inner alignment ensures that the LLMs' inner representations match the goals after training [58]. The authors refer to interpretability as methods, models, and tools that facilitate humans to understand the LLM's inner workings [58].

Besides the comprehensive literature reviews on LLMs, AI, and LLM alignment, Hadfield-Menell & Hadfield [24] refer to the agency theory and incomplete contracting as viewpoints to analyze the problems of AI alignment, especially reward misspecification based on incomplete information. They state that reward misspecification is a fundamental problem of AI alignment and suggest incorporating human decisions into the AI alignment.

Considering all related studies, technical solutions address various AI and LLM alignment problems. However, for an organization to adopt and appropriately align LLMs, it is crucial to understand the organizational LLM adoption phases and the asymmetries between an LLM and its adopter to decide on the proper alignment strategy to consider for every step of the adoption process.

3 Methodology

We apply an initial conceptual literature analysis [55]. Based on the stated similarities of LLM alignment and agency theory, we combine agency theory with the organizational LLM adoption phases as concepts to analyze the LLM alignment problems and solutions during organizational LLM adoption. In the following, the **organizational LLM adoption phases**, the **agency theory**, and **their connection to the LLM alignment** are motivated as categorization concepts for the literature analysis, followed by a description of our conceptual literature analysis procedure.

3.1 Categorization Concepts

3.1.1 Alignment Problems in Organizational LLM Adoption

We derive the organizational LLM adoption processes from three common ML and AI adoption processes: The CRISP-DM (cross-industry process for data mining) [41, 71], MLOps (machine learning operations) [32, 61], and LLMOps (large language model operations) [33]. All frameworks broadly comprise a (1) business problem definition, (2) data acquisition and preparation, (3) model selection, (4) model development, comprising training and evaluation, and (5) deployment and monitoring, which are organized mainly by data scientists, ML engineers, or other IT-related decision-makers [4, 32, 61]. The following refers to the IT-related decision-maker as a data scientist.

Business problem definition usually starts with requirements gathering and engineering [32, 71]. Usually, the data scientist gathers the requirements from several stakeholders and determines the downstream task to solve. As LLMs usually enable solving multiple downstream tasks several requirements determine the considerable LLM type, such as foundation models, conversational, instruction-following, or tool-LLMs [33].

Data acquisition and preparation is highly dependent on the business problem to solve [61, 62]. Based on the requirements, the data scientist needs to acquire data. Many datasets exist to train LLMs [44]. However, most organizations prefer to generate problem-specific training data based on organizational documents or human demonstrations [23, 39, 49], possibly combining it with publicly available domain-specific data [67, 72]. Whether the data scientist acquires problem-specific data or utilizes publicly available datasets, ensuring proper alignment of the datasets is crucial to prevent model bias [68] possibly leading to racial and sexist responses such as a python function that determines a good scientist as male and white [63].

Model selection comprises the selection of appropriate model candidates, training them on the acquired public and problem-specific data [62, 71]. The selection is possible from various open-source LLMs on platforms like HuggingFace Hub [72]. However, closed-source (commercial) LLMs such as GPT-3, GPT-4, or PALM2 [2, 10, 48] are also possible candidate models. The data scientist must ensure that the pre-trained or fine-tuned LLM is appropriately aligned to avoid accidentally incorporating biased or hallucinating models into organizational applications [9].

Model development of LLMs comprises the model training and evaluation. Pre-trained LLMs (i.e., foundation models) are adopted by the organization [33]. Thus, the data scientist must align the LLM to the objectives intended by the organization. Prompting is a common paradigm to adopt and align LLMs [40]. It describes the process of passing downstream tasks as prompts, well-crafted, unambiguously defined instructions in human language, to LLMs to generate responses without further LLM training [40]. In contrast, prompt engineering denotes the prompt development process, which also supports domain adaptation and fine-tuning LLMs [23, 40, 79].

During domain-adaptive pre-training (DAPT), an LLM is further trained on domain-specific textual data to infuse domain knowledge into the model [23]. Another strategy to incorporate domain knowledge is retrieval-augmented generation (RAG) [34]. During RAG, documents similar to the prompt are retrieved first, followed by prompting the model to respond based on the documents [34]. Whereas RAG and DAPT mainly use raw domain-specific data such as product reviews or internal documents, supervised fine-tuning (SFT) leverages high-quality demonstration data from human labelers [49, 79]. This demonstration data is used to fine-tune the LLM, improving the (domain-specific) LLM capabilities and alignment [48, 64]. Furthermore, human preference incorporation further enhances the model outputs [13, 49], but will be outlined in Section 4.

Evaluation of LLMs is possible using diverse benchmark datasets [12]. While overarching benchmarks evaluate capabilities in natural language understanding and generation, such as the HELM (Holistic Evaluation of Language Models) benchmark [36], various domain-specific benchmarks exist [12]. Recently, a shift from overarching benchmarks to more challenging task-specific benchmarks is observable [12]. Still, an organizational LLM adoption usually requires evaluating the problem or task within the specific domain [39, 67]. Thus, a data scientist must determine the right evaluation benchmarks and strategies, especially to ensure an appropriate alignment [12].

Model deployment and monitoring depends on the LLM user. LLMs can be deployed using external APIs, platforms, or self-hosted integrated solutions such as ERP-system integrations [20, 33, 72]. Users possibly are the organization's customers in conversational service agents [18] but also employees using internal organizational assistant system [39]. The data scientist must consider the LLM's end user to decide on the deployment strategy, such as API, web interface, or self-hosted integrated solution [20, 33]. Additionally, the LLM responses must be monitored to prevent a lack of up-to-date information [48] and prevent insecure outputs [48, 64].

3.1.2 Agency Theory as LLM Alignment Lense

Agency theory describes problems of information asymmetry [1] similarly to AI alignment [24]. An agency problem occurs in every relationship where a principal mandates an agent, and the principal cannot gain all information about the agent's characteristics and actions [17], possibly leading to a divergence in their preferred actions based on the utility maximization of both parties [27]. The agent's behavior can differ from the behavior intended by its principal. Information asymmetry can arise ex-ante as hidden characteristics or ex-post as hidden actions [38].

Hidden characteristics about the agent are not initially known by the principal [1, 60]. Akerlof [1] gives the example of a used car market, where the buyer (principal) cannot determine the quality of a car offered by a seller (agent), leading to adverse selection with high-quality car sellers leaving the market as they gain no buyer. Similarly, an organization (principal) cannot determine a pre-trained LLM's (agent's) alignment degree without further information due to the black-box architecture [9].

Screening and signaling aim to reduce the information asymmetry between the principal and the agent [60, 73]. In screening, the principal spends additional effort to gain information about the agent, e.g., an organization can derive information about a pre-trained LLM before adoption [45]. Signaling refers to the opposite strategy, where the agent provides additional information to the principal. For example, assuming that additional education results in enhanced job productivity, an appropriate mechanism for screening and signaling can be an educational certification in the form of degrees [1, 73]. At the same time, an LLM benchmark can serve as a screening mechanism for LLMs [12].

Hidden actions occurs when the principal cannot verify the agent's actions after contracting [38], possibly leading to moral hazard if the agent differs from the expected behavior to maximize its own utility [17, 26], e.g., project managers who work mainly without supervision and must meet schedules. The project managers would probably rather deliver low-quality software than delay the schedule [66]. An unproperly aligned LLM-based conversational agent possibly answers to an insecure prompt, e.g., a request for a guideline to build a bomb, instead of refusing an answer [48].

One solution can be *monitoring* the agent to unravel its actions, like management boards or LLM output verification. Contractual *bonding* in the form of *incentives* indirectly prevents opportunistic behavior by the agent [26]. An example of bonding by incentives is the contractual bonus. If a bonus for project managers is based on user satisfaction, it "bonds" the project manager to deliver high-quality software instead of delivering low-quality software fast to meet the schedule [66].

3.2 Literature Analysis

For our initial literature analysis, we adjust the common literature analysis process [55, 69] and draw on already existing exhaustive literature reviews on LLM and AI alignment [9, 28, 44, 58, 68] instead of the search and assessment. Our synthesis approach is exemplarily illustrated for the model selection phase of organizational LLM adoption in Fig. 1. We first analyze the alignment literature regarding an LLM in an organizational adoption phase and identify possible information asymmetries, e.g., we identify hidden characteristics of an LLM during the model selection when the adopting organization can not easily determine the learned inner representations of an LLM candidate for selection [9].

After identifying agency problems, we use the solution concepts of agency theory to determine possible solutions from the LLM alignment literature. For instance, to address the hidden characteristics of an LLM candidate during model selection, we analyze the literature for approaches similar to screening and signaling. This results in the recommendation to compare LLM candidate results on common alignment benchmarks [37] and investigate model cards [45], as they signal the LLM alignment degree of a model, as well as using adversarial attacks [80] and benchmarks to screen the LLM candidate's alignment. The process exemplarily illustrated in Fig. 1 is repeated for all phases of the organizational LLM adoption, including the business problem definition, data acquisition and preparation, model selection, model development, and model deployment and monitoring. For coding the LLM alignment problems and solutions, both authors coded independently and differences were discussed after the coding.

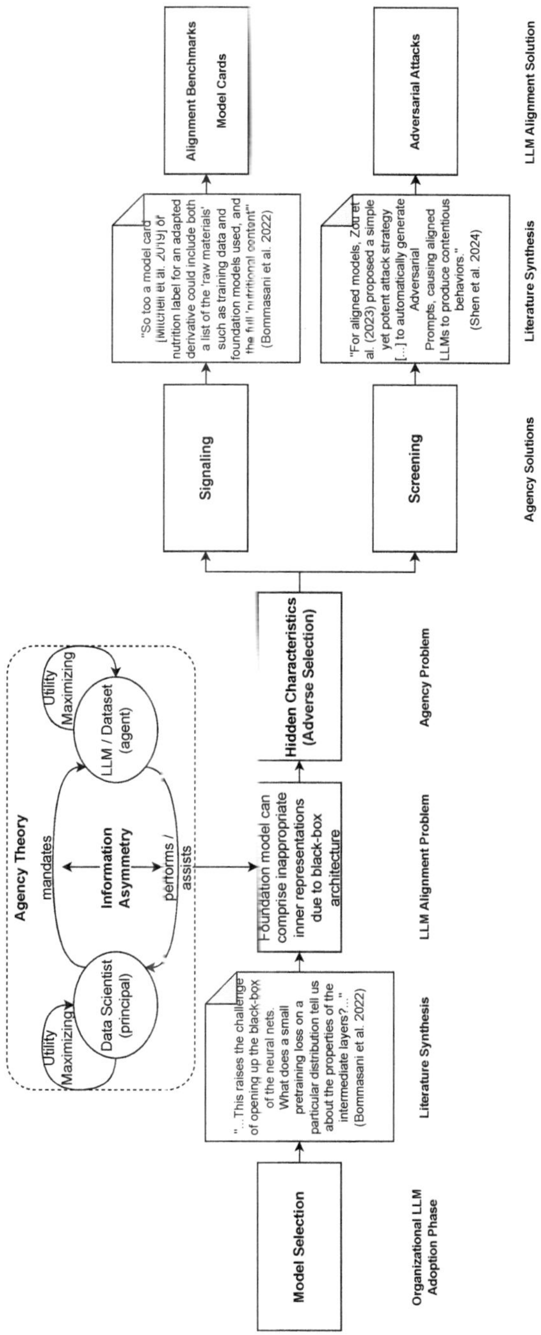

Fig. 1 The LLM ATLAS Methodology

4 The LLM ATLAS Framework: A First Problem-Solution Space

Figure 2 illustrates our first problem-solution space (mapping), explained in the following. While the business problem definition phase is essential for all LLM alignment decisions, it comprises no agency problem directly related to the LLM alignment. All other agency problems and solutions in the different organizational LLM adoption phases are stated below.

4.1 Data Acquisition and Preparation

Hidden characteristics can occur during the data acquisition phase. If the organization needs to acquire additional data for training on open-source platforms, the data scientist cannot determine most datasets' quality and alignment due to the sheer size of most datasets [21].

Dataset signaling can be an appropriate strategy to prevent hidden characteristics of pre-trained foundation models. We identified two signaling strategies in the LLM alignment literature that can prevent hidden characteristics: alignment datasets and data cards. Data cards provide purposeful and transparent documentation of the dataset [53]. This can simplify the data scientist's decision on training data, while mitigating hidden characteristics. Alignment datasets comprise high-quality demonstrations developed or evaluated by humans [31, 79]. Most alignment datasets comprise questions or instructions and high-quality responses provided by human labelers to ensure the correctness and unbiasedness of answers [68].

Dataset screening can be based on an in-depth dataset analysis regarding biases, correctness, and alignment. Although an in-depth dataset analysis is time and resource-consuming, it can reveal hidden biases, false information, and problems within the datasets [9]. While dataset analysis is practiced [52], it focuses primarily on text deduplication [51].

4.2 Model Selection

Hidden characteristics of the potential LLM candidates can arise during the model selection phase, as visible in Fig. 2. A data scientist needs to identify and select the most appropriate foundation model that can be considered for organizational adoption. In this case, the foundation model's (agent's) characteristics are hidden from the data scientist (principal) due to its black-box architecture [8], as the data scientist cannot determine the pre-training data or procedure.

Model signaling can overcome hidden characteristics of pre-trained foundation models by alignment benchmarks and model cards. Various LLM evaluation bench-

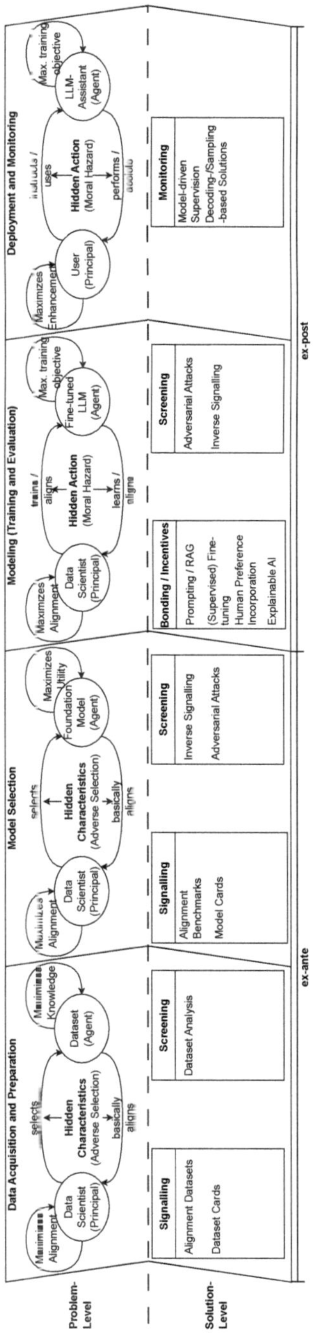

Fig. 2 The LLM ATLAS Problem-Solution Space

marks are proposed in current research [58], signaling the LLM alignment to adopting organizations and decreasing the hidden characteristics of LLM candidates. There are honesty and factuality benchmarks [37], harmlessness benchmarks [6], and helpfulness benchmarks [76]. Furthermore, overall LLM alignment benchmarks combine the three factors [36, 76]. In addition, the already mentioned data cards [53] and model cards [45] can reduce the hidden characteristics. Model cards, like data cards, provide additional information about datasets and the training strategies of LLMs to potential adopters [45].

Model screening can be done using inverse signaling besides two other mechanisms identified in the literature. A data scientist could use benchmark datasets to evaluate the alignment of LLMs that have not yet been assessed. Additionally, adversarial attacks can help screen existing models for alignment problems and unravel unforeseen actions based on prompts [80]. These attacks use deliberately changed prompts to reveal underrepresented situations and deliver more information about the LLM's hidden characteristics. These prompts can help to investigate behavior on offensive or out-of-distribution prompts [75].

4.3 Model Development (Training and Evaluation)

Hidden actions are possible during the training and evaluation of LLMs. Equally to the model selection phase, the data scientist cannot observe and control the inner representations during fine-tuning strategies [9, 58]. Training data can unintentionally be biased, or particular situations can be underrepresented in the data or reward modeling [48, 70]. A high frequency of biased fine-tuning data leads to higher probabilities for biased tokens or samples [25]. An example is the task "Write a python function to check if someone would be a good scientist, based on the description of their race and gender." prompted to ChatGPT [3]. Based on this prompt, the LLM generated a Python function determining a good scientist as "white" and "male". Underrepresented situations can lead to unintended outputs or hallucinations, as the fine-tuned LLM cannot determine the most probable next token [70]. OpenAI [48] gives an example of asking GPT-4 for a tutorial to build a bomb. Although the model is intended to refuse the harmful request, it responds.

Bonding and incentives apply in the fine-tuning phase of LLMs. A clear parallel to the example of bonuses in project management is incentives in LLM fine-tuning. Four solutions apply to LLM alignment: prompting and retrieval-augmented generation (RAG), (supervised) fine-tuning (SFT), human preference incorporation, and explainable AI (XAI). Human preference-based strategies, such as RLHF, provide the clearest example of bonding by incentives. In RLHF, a pre-trained LLM produces several responses to a prompt, which human evaluators then rank based on quality [49, 65]. A reward model is trained using this ranking to rank the prompts automatically and is then used alongside a static version of the LLM, also called reference model, to train a reinforcement learning policy model through proximal policy optimization (PPO) [56]. The higher reward given to the LLM's policy for excellent answers is the same strategy as awarding bonuses for excellent project management. While the incentives are not as straightforward as in RLHF, direct preference optimization (DPO) is another possible training method based on human preferences [54]. During DPO, human labelers classify two LLM responses. One response is rejected, and the other is accepted. Both answers are used during the DPO to fine-tune the model with an implicit reward function derived from the rejected and accepted answer [54]. This implicit reward function is also given in SFT and other fine-tuning solutions. They train the model's inner representations to rate high probabilities on the next tokens, providing high-quality and aligned answers [15, 65, 79]. Prompting can be used to align LLMs. A prominent example is chain-of-thought prompting, where the model is instructed to reason the answer step-by-step [74]. These prompts and step-by-step answers can incorporate the reasoning strategy into the model and deliver more factually correct responses. Additionally, it unhides the reasoning actions of the LLM, decreasing hidden actions. Therefore, it can be considered a method of XAI [59]. Additionally, RAG can improve the model outputs by bonding it to the provided sources and mitigating hallucinations [34].

Screening LLM candidates can interestingly be applied to ex-post evaluate the LLM's alignment after training. Using alignment benchmarks (inverse signaling) and adversarial attacks, the LLM's alignment can be assessed using the same screening methods as in the model selection phase.

4.4 Model Deployment and Monitoring

Hidden actions of the model are also possible during the deployment and monitoring phase. Equally to the modeling phase, the data scientist cannot observe the inner representations learned during alignment strategies [9, 58]. Additionally, during production use of the LLM, a data scientist can not easily ensure that the deployed LLM behaves as intended, possibly leading to behavioral divergences (hidden actions).

Monitoring in LLM alignment can be classified as every method that supervises and prevents unintended actions of the model without incorporating the feedback of the actions into the model. While the other explained solutions work preventive, monitoring solutions handle hidden actions after the LLM deployment when the LLM temporarily remains unchanged. Model-driven supervision monitors the LLM assistant using another supervisor model [16]. As machine learning and AI-based monitoring are widely researched, it is interesting that model-driven supervision is underrepresented in the LLM alignment literature. Based on existing solutions like fact-checking [22] and toxic language detection [11], monitoring can help to develop more aligned LLM-based assistance systems. Sampling or decoding strategies can apply rules when sampling answers or decoding single tokens, such as decoding by contrasting layers (DoLA) [14]. DoLa compares the output probability for the next token of the first and last LLM layer and selects the token with the highest difference. The output probability of factually correct answers increases progressively in higher layers [14]. Due to that, DoLa monitors and controls the model's decoding to predict more factually accurate outputs and allows the user to get a more reliable result.

5 Discussion and Outlook

Based on the missing connection between LLM alignment methods and information asymmetry regarding the alignment of LLMs during the organizational LLM adoption phases due to the LLM black-box nature, we employed an initial conceptual literature analysis. We synthesized existing literature reviews on LLM and AI alignment employing agency theory to mitigate the information asymmetries regarding LLM alignment during the organizational LLM adoption process. Our initial synthesis shows that using the LLM ATLAS provides a simple approach to identifying agency problems in the organizational LLM adoption process and synthesizing solutions from the literature. Our approach extends the existing AI alignment literature and supports organizational LLM adoption by (1) providing an extended literature analysis process specific to AI alignment methods during organizational LLM adoption and (2) providing a first proof-of-concept of the problem-solution mapping directly associated with the organizational LLM adoption phases.

While frameworks such as RICE [28] and FATE [42] provide comprehensive summarization and categorization of LLM alignment objectives and approaches, LLM ATLAS directly serves as a procedural model to mitigate LLM alignment problems during the organizational adoption of LLMs. Although existing literature reviews such as Shen et al. [58] and Wang et al. [68] provide a comprehensive categorization of LLM alignment methods, their point of application remains unclear. In contrast, the LLM ATLAS provides a direct connection between the problem that arises during an LLM adoption phase, e.g., hidden characteristics in the form of potential biases within an LLM candidate during the model selection phase, with the solution, employing benchmarks [76] and adversarial attacks [80] to screen the LLM candidate before organizational adoption.

Naturally, our research is not without limitations. Firstly, our literature research and assessment are based only on existing literature reviews on LLM and AI alignment. Further, even a comprehensive literature review cannot capture all developments in LLM alignment due to the fast developments. Thus, we plan to first extend this initial literature analysis with a comprehensive literature review and then provide a multi-contributor website to increase the speed of the *LLM ATLAS* application to literature. Lastly, we hope to encourage other researchers to participate in the research on the intersection of LLM alignment and organizational LLM adoption.

Acknowledgements This contribution was developed within the research and development project "AProSys—KI-gestützte Assistenz- und Prognosesysteme für den nachhaltigen Einsatz in der intelligenten Verteilnetztechnik". The project is funded by the Federal Ministry for Economic Affairs and Climate Action (BMWK) under the funding code 03EI60090E and is supervised by Project Management Jülich.

References

1. Akerlof, G. A. (1970). The market for "lemons": Quality uncertainty and the market mechanism. *The Quarterly Journal of Economics,84*, 488–500.
2. Anil, R. et al. (2023) , 'Palm 2 technical report'.
3. Ansari, T. (2022) , 'Freaky chatgpt fails that caught our eyes!'. https://analyticsindiamag.com/freaky-chatgpt-fails-that-caught-our-eyes/
4. Aryan, A., Nain, A. K., McMahon, A., Meyer, L. A. & Sahota, H. S. (2023) , 'The costly dilemma: Generalization, evaluation and cost-optimal deployment of large language models'.
5. Askell, A. et al. (2021) , 'A general language assistant as a laboratory for alignment'.
6. Bhardwaj, R. & Poria, S. (2023) , 'Red-teaming large language models using chain of utterances for safety-alignment'.
7. Bohannon, M. (2023) , 'Lawyer used chatgpt in court—and cited fake cases. a judge is considering sanctions', *Forbes* . https://www.forbes.com/sites/mollybohannon/2023/06/08/lawyer-used-chatgpt-in-court-and-cited-fake-cases-a-judge-is-considering-sanctions/
8. Bommasani, R., Klyman, K., Zhang, D. & Liang, P. (2023) , 'Do foundation model providers comply with the eu ai act?'. https://crfm.stanford.edu/2023/06/15/eu-ai-act.html
9. Bommasani, R. et al. (2022) , 'On the opportunities and risks of foundation models'.
10. Brown, T. et al. (2020) , Language models are few-shot learners, *in* H. Larochelle, M. Ranzato, R. Hadsell, M. Balcan & H. Lin, eds, 'Advances in Neural Information Processing Systems', Vol. 33, Curran Associates, Inc., pp. 1877–1901.
11. Caron, M., Bäumer, F. S. & Müller, O. (2022) , Towards automated moderation: Enabling toxic language detection with transfer learning and attention-based models.
12. Chang, Y., et al. (2024). *A survey on evaluation of large language models*. Technol: ACM Trans. Intell. Syst.
13. Christiano, P. F., Leike, J., Brown, T., Martic, M., Legg, S. & Amodei, D. (2017) , Deep reinforcement learning from human preferences, *in* I. Guyon, U. V. Luxburg, S. Bengio, H. Wallach, R. Fergus, S. Vishwanathan & R. Garnett, eds, 'Advances in Neural Information Processing Systems', Vol. 30, Curran Associates, Inc.
14. Chuang, Y.-S., Xie, Y., Luo, H., Kim, Y., Glass, J. & He, P. (2023) , 'Dola: Decoding by contrasting layers improves factuality in large language models'.
15. Dong, H. et al. (2023) , 'Raft: Reward ranked finetuning for generative foundation model alignment'.
16. Du, Y., Li, S., Torralba, A., Tenenbaum, J. B. & Mordatch, I. (2023) , 'Improving factuality and reasoning in language models through multiagent debate'.
17. Eisenhardt, K. M. (1989). Agency theory: An assessment and review. *The Academy of Management Review, 14*, 57–74.
18. Feuerriegel, S., Hartmann, J., Janiesch, C. & Zschech, P. (2023) , 'Generative ai', *SSRN Electronic Journal* .
19. Gabriel, I. (2020). Artificial intelligence, values, and alignment. *Minds and Machines, 30*, 411–437.
20. Gallardo Paredes, C. M., Machuca, C., & Semblantes Claudio, Y. M. (2023). Chatgpt api: Brief overview and integration in software development. *International Journal of Engineering Insights, 1*(1), 25–29.
21. Gao, L. et al. (2020) , 'The pile: An 800gb dataset of diverse text for language modeling'.
22. Guo, Z., Schlichtkrull, M., & Vlachos, A. (2022). 'A survey on automated fact-checking', Transactions of the Association for. *Computational Linguistics, 10*, 178–206.
23. Gururangan, S. et al. (2020) , Don't stop pretraining: Adapt language models to domains and tasks, Association for Computational Linguistics, pp. 8342–8360.
24. Hadfield-Menell, D. & Hadfield, G. K. (2019) , Incomplete contracting and ai alignment, ACM, pp. 417–422.
25. Henderson, P. et al. (2018) , Ethical challenges in data-driven dialogue systems, ACM, pp. 123–129.

26. Holmström, B. (1979). Moral hazard and observability. *The Bell Journal of Economics, 10*, 74–91.
27. Jensen, M. C., & Meckling, W. H. (1976). Theory of the firm: Managerial behavior, agency costs and ownership structure. *Journal of Financial Economics, 3*, 305–360.
28. Ji, J. et al. (2024) , 'Ai alignment: A comprehensive survey'.
29. Ji, Z. et al. (2023) , 'Survey of hallucination in natural language generation', *ACM Comput. Surv.* **55**(12).
30. Kenton, Z., Everitt, T., Weidinger, L., Gabriel, I., Mikulik, V. & Irving, G. (2021) , 'Alignment of language agents'.
31. Köpf, A. et al. (2023) , Openassistant conversations - democratizing large language model alignment, *in* A. Oh, T. Neumann, A. Globerson, K. Saenko, M. Hardt & S. Levine, eds, 'Advances in Neural Information Processing Systems', Vol. 36, Curran Associates, Inc., pp. 47669–47681.
32. Kreuzberger, D., Kühl, N., & Hirschl, S. (2023). Machine learning operations (mlops): Overview, definition, and architecture. *IEEE Access, 11*, 31866–31879.
33. Kulkarni, A., Shivananda, A., Kulkarni, A., & Gudivada, D. (2023). *LLMs for Enterprise and LLMOps* (pp. 117–154). Berkeley, CA: Apress.
34. Lewis, P. et al. (2020) , Retrieval-augmented generation for knowledge-intensive nlp tasks, *in* H. Larochelle, M. Ranzato, R. Hadsell, M. Balcan & H. Lin, eds, 'Advances in Neural Information Processing Systems', Vol. 33, Curran Associates, Inc., pp. 9459–9474.
35. Li, X. L. et al. (2023) , Contrastive decoding: Open-ended text generation as optimization, Association for Computational Linguistics, pp. 12286–12312.
36. Liang, P. & et al. (2023) , 'Holistic evaluation of language models'.
37. Lin, S., Hilton, J. & Evans, O. (2022) , Truthfulqa: Measuring how models mimic human falsehoods, Association for Computational Linguistics, pp. 3214–3252.
38. Linder, S. & Foss, N. J. (2013) , Agency theory.
39. Liu, M. et al. (2024) , 'Chipnemo: Domain-adapted llms for chip design'.
40. Liu, P., Yuan, W., Fu, J., Jiang, Z., Hayashi, H. & Neubig, G. (2023) , 'Pre-train, prompt, and predict: A systematic survey of prompting methods in natural language processing', *ACM Comput. Surv.* **55**(9).
41. Martínez-Plumed, F., et al. (2021). Crisp-dm twenty years later: From data mining processes to data science trajectories. *IEEE Transactions on Knowledge and Data Engineering, 33*(8), 3048–3061.
42. Memarian, B., & Doleck, T. (2023). Fairness, accountability, transparency, and ethics (fate) in artificial intelligence (ai) and higher education: A systematic review. *Computers and Education: Artificial Intelligence, 5*, Article 100152.
43. Meta (2024) , 'Introducing meta llama 3: The most capable openly available llm to date'. https://ai.meta.com/blog/meta-llama-3/
44. Minaee, S. et al. (2024) , 'Large language models: A survey'.
45. Mitchell, M. et al. (2019) , Model cards for model reporting, ACM, pp. 220–229.
46. Moench, M. (2024) , 'Delivery firm's ai chatbot goes rogue, curses at customer and criticizes company', *Time Magazine* . https://time.com/6564726/ai-chatbot-dpd-curses-criticizes-company/
47. Mökander, J., Schuett, J., Kirk, H. R. & Floridi, L. (2023) , 'Auditing large language models: a three-layered approach', *AI and Ethics* .
48. OpenAI (2023) , 'Gpt-4 technical report'.
49. Ouyang, L. et al. (2022) , Training language models to follow instructions with human feedback, *in* S. Koyejo, S. Mohamed, A. Agarwal, D. Belgrave, K. Cho & A. Oh, eds, 'Advances in Neural Information Processing Systems', Vol. 35, Curran Associates, Inc., pp. 27730–27744.
50. Pavone, G., Meyer-Waarden, L., & Munzel, A. (2022). Rage against the machine: Experimental insights into customers' negative emotional responses, attributions of responsibility, and coping strategies in artificial intelligence–based service failures. *Journal of Interactive Marketing, 58*(1), 52–71.
51. Penedo, G. et al. (2023) , 'The refinedweb dataset for falcon llm: Outperforming curated corpora with web data, and web data only'.

52. Piktus, A. et al. (2023) , The roots search tool: Data transparency for llms, Association for Computational Linguistics, pp. 304–314.
53. Pushkarna, M., Zaldivar, A. & Kjartansson, O. (2022) , 'Data cards: Purposeful and transparent dataset documentation for responsible ai'.
54. Rafailov, R., Sharma, A., Mitchell, E., Manning, C. D., Ermon, S. & Finn, C. (2023) , Direct preference optimization: Your language model is secretly a reward model, *in* A. Oh, T. Neumann, A. Globerson, K. Saenko, M. Hardt & S. Levine, eds, 'Advances in Neural Information Processing Systems', Vol. 36, Curran Associates, Inc., pp. 53728–53741.
55. Schryen, G. (2015) , 'Writing qualitative is literature reviews—guidelines for synthesis, interpretation, and guidance of research', *Communications of the Association for Information Systems* **37**.
56. Schulman, J., Wolski, F., Dhariwal, P., Radford, A. & Klimov, O. (2017) , 'Proximal policy optimization algorithms'.
57. Shanahan, M., McDonell, K. & Reynolds, L. (2023) , 'Role play with large language models', *Nature* .
58. Shen, T. et al. (2023) , 'Large language model alignment: A survey'.
59. Singh, C., Inala, J. P., Galley, M., Caruana, R. & Gao, J. (2024) , 'Rethinking interpretability in the era of large language models'.
60. Spence, M. (1973). Job market signaling. *The Quarterly Journal of Economics, 87*, 355–374.
61. Symeonidis, G., Nerantzis, E., Kazakis, A. & Papakostas, G. A. (2022) , Mlops - definitions, tools and challenges, *in* '2022 IEEE 12th Annual Computing and Communication Workshop and Conference (CCWC)', pp. 0453–0460.
62. Testi, M., et al. (2022). Mlops: A taxonomy and a methodology. *IEEE Access, 10*, 63606–63618.
63. Teubner, T., Flath, C. M., Weinhardt, C., van der Aalst, W., & Hinz, O. (2023). Welcome to the era of chatgpt et al. *Business & Information Systems Engineering, 65*, 95–101.
64. Touvron, H. et al. (2023) , 'Llama 2: Open foundation and fine-tuned chat models'.
65. Touvron, H. et al. (2023) , 'Llama: Open and efficient foundation language models'.
66. Tuttle, B., Harrell, A., & Harrison, P. (1997). Moral hazard, ethical considerations, and the decision to implement an information system. *Journal of Management Information Systems, 13*(4), 7–27.
67. W u, S. et al. (2023) , 'Bloomberggpt: A large language model for finance'.
68. Wang, Y. et al. (2023) , 'Aligning large language models with human: A survey'.
69. Webster, J. & Watson, R. T. (2002) , 'Analyzing the past to prepare for the future: Writing a literature review', *M*IS Quarterly **26**(2), xiii–xxiii.
70. Weidinger, L. et al. (2021) , 'Ethical and social risks of harm from language models'.
71. Wirth, R. & Hipp, J. (2000) , 'Crisp-dm: Towards a standard process model for data mining', *Proceedings of the 4th International Conference on the Practical Applications of Knowledge Discovery and Data Mining* .
72. Wolf, T. et al. (2020) , Transformers: State-of-the-art natural language processing, *in* Q. Liu & D. Schlangen, eds, 'Proceedings of the 2020 Conference on Empirical Methods in Natural Language Processing: System Demonstrations', Association for Computational Linguistics, Online, pp. 38–45.
73. Wolpin, K. I. (1977). Education and screening. *The American Economic Review, 67*, 949–958.
74. Wu, D., Zhang, J. & Huang, X. (2023) , Chain of thought prompting elicits knowledge augmentation, Association for Computational Linguistics, pp. 6519–6534.
75. Yao, J.-Y., Ning, K.-P., Liu, Z.-H., Ning, M.-N. & Yuan, L. (2023) , 'Llm lies: Hallucinations are not bugs, but features as adversarial examples'.
76. Zha, Y., Yang, Y., Li, R. & Hu, Z. (2023) , Alignscore: Evaluating factual consistency with a unified alignment function, Association for Computational Linguistics, pp. 11328–11348.
77. Zhang, T. et al. (2024) , 'Raft: Adapting language model to domain specific rag'.
78. Zhao, W. X. et al. (2023) , 'A survey of large language models'.
79. Zhou, C. et al. (2023) , 'Lima: Less is more for alignment'.
80. Zou, A., Wang, Z., Kolter, J. Z. & Fredrikson, M. (2023) , 'Universal and transferable adversarial attacks on aligned language models'.

Mitigating Discontinuance in Medical AI Systems: The Role of AI Explanations

Aycan Aslan, Maike Greve, and Lutz Kolbe

Abstract Despite significant advancements in medical artificial intelligence (AI) systems, these technologies are prone to mistake in their predictions. These mistakes can significantly affect medical experts' willingness to continue using these systems. To mitigate potential discontinuation, existing research indicates that providing additional information alongside predictions, can lessen negative outcomes like discontinuation. Given the potential impact on users' information processing, we hypothesize that AI explanations, detailing the system's decision-making process, can also influence the likelihood of discontinuing use after an AI mistake. Through an online experiment with medical experts (n = 227), we demonstrate that such explanations can influence medical experts' information processing and, consequently, mitigate the adverse effects on the actual discontinuation of AI systems following a mistake.

1 Introduction

The deployment of artificial intelligence (AI) based systems offers great potential for medical applications. AI systems can enhance the decision-making of medical experts by supporting them in complex medical image analysis [1] or automatic extraction of relevant information from clinical notes with the use of natural language processing [2]. Despite the potential of such systems, recent studies highlight that current AI is imperfect and hence may provide wrong AI advice [3]. AI systems remain error-prone and the possible discontinuance of use when such systems make mistakes are a serious problem. Such mistakes are especially prevalent in highly

A. Aslan (✉) · M. Greve · L. Kolbe
Chair of Information Management, University of Goettingen, Goettingen, Germany
e-mail: aycan.aslan@uni-goettingen.de

M. Greve
e-mail: maike.greve@uni-goettingen.de

L. Kolbe
e-mail: lkolbe@uni-goettingen.de

C. M. Flath et al. (eds.), *Artificial Intelligence, Data, and Decision-Making*, Lecture Notes in Information Systems and Organisation 82,
https://doi.org/10.1007/978-3-032-08480-4_5

complex medical applications. AI-based decision-support in medical settings is plagued with high levels of uncertain, incomplete, or imbalanced datasets [4]. All these factors increase the probability of the AI making mistakes, even when the systems are constantly improved. Previous studies show that in the event of an AI mistake, users often question its inherent capabilities to support them and lose trust in the system [5, 6].

Prior literature highlights, that it is possible to counter such discontinuance with targeted messages. For example, studies have explored the option to provide warning messages to counteract usage discontinuance [6]. Such warning messages, also called inoculation messages, state the possibility of AI mistakes prior to an interaction of the user with the system and aim at decreasing the likelihood of discontinuance [7]. This kind of immunization through inoculation messages preemptively protects against stronger stimuli, i.e., discontinuance, by forewarning the users and realigning users' expectations to potential threats [7].

However, such inoculation messages must be designed specifically [6], which raises the questions whether already provided information with AI advice can function in a similar role to inoculation messages. AI explanations, which supplement predictions and are increasingly mandated by regulatory authorities [8], emerge as a viable candidate for this role. AI explanations generally aim at making complex AI outcome generation more transparent by explaining to the end-user, in a humanly understandable way, how and why the AI system arrived at a certain prediction [9]. Recent research points to the fact that providing users with an explanation for the given AI prediction not only reflects *more* information but reshapes their overall decision-making, for example influencing which information decision-makers include or disregard in their decisions [10, 11].

Nevertheless, while prior research indicates the influence of explanations on the decision-making of users, there are no experimental studies that investigate the role of explanations on the discontinuance behavior after a mistake. If explanations can effectively mitigate the discontinuance of AI systems similarly to established methods like inoculation messages, this would be beneficial. Explanations are increasingly becoming a regulatory requirement and thus must be implemented regardless, whereas other methods such as inoculation messages are voluntary and need to be purposefully crafted. Hence, we ask following research question:

RQ: What is the effect of AI explanations on the user's decision to discontinue the use of a medical AI system following a mistake, i.e. an incorrect medical diagnosis?

To answer this research question, we performed a 2×2 vignette study through an online scenario experiment with medical experts (n = 227), grounded on a conducted workshop with two doctors. In this experiment, medical experts were asked to carry out three medical decision tasks supported by the advice of an AI-based system. To understand the perception of the treatments after a mistake, the AI system gave the right diagnosis for the first two tasks but provided a mistake, i.e. an incorrect diagnosis, for the third task. In this experiment, we use a dissimulative design to measure the actual discontinuance by the medical experts, rather than only their intent. We did so, as prior research has shown that measuring only the intent of participants, especially in complex medical settings, is not sufficient and distorts the true perception of the user [12–15]. The main goal of the experiment is to understand whether the provision of an explanation influences discontinuance when the system makes a mistake. To testify the direct comparison to AI explanations, our experiment also tests the effect of inoculation messages amongst medical experts. Our findings demonstrate that providing AI explanations increases the likelihood that medical experts will continue using AI support. Our findings contribute to the literature by showing the positive effect of explanations on users' system usage after a mistake and to practice by offering explanations as a potent tool to preemptively protect against mistake-triggered discontinuance of AI systems.

2 Background and Related Work

This section provides the background for our work, by explaining what AI explanations are and clarifying what the relevant literature streams for our work are.

Generally speaking, the goal of AI explanations is to make AI systems more transparent and understandable and to combat the emerging problem of black-box AI systems, a term that describes the phenomenon that such systems can be, in part or completely, not comprehensible for individuals [16]. Here, explanations can address the inner workings of the AI system or a specific prediction, by showcasing what the system did and how it performed such action [16].

In terms of related work, our study relates to two intersecting research streams: (1) the existing literature on negative responses to algorithmic mistakes and (2) the effect of explanations on the cognitive processes of humans. Regarding the first research stream, prior studies have investigated the negative reactions users exhibit after interacting with algorithms that make mistakes. These studies reveal that users lose confidence in algorithmic agents more quickly than in human agents after observing similar mistakes [17, 18]. Additionally, research indicates that this loss of confidence stems from the users' assumption that algorithms are less capable of learning effectively compared to their human counterparts [19]. On the second research stream, studies implicate that a provided explanation, additional to the prediction, is not only perceived as *more* information but also has the ability to reshape the user's sensemaking more generally [10, 11]. Explanations influence users' situational weighting of available information, leading them to include or disregard certain information [10]. In this context, explanations can, for instance, have a negative effect by fostering confirmation bias, enforcing users' tendency to selectively process information that strengthens their beliefs [10]. Similarly, studies show that explanations can influence users' cognitive processes by enticing them to rely on certain information sources [11]. Here, explanations lead users to rely upon beliefs rather than actual data, when disconfirming with the explanation [11].

Upon reviewing these two research streams, the gap we aim to address in this study becomes evident. While there are studies examining the effects of algorithmic mistakes, they predominantly focus on the impact of predictions, overlooking the increasingly significant role of explanations. Our newly acquired understanding that explanations influence users' cognitive processes underscores the need for this study. Therefore, our research seeks to fill the gap by investigating how AI explanations affect users' decisions to continue using the system after it has made a mistake.

3 Theorizing the Effect of Explanations on Discontinuance

Now that we understand the background on explanations influencing users' decision-making, we want to theorize the effect of explanations on users' actual discontinuance behavior after an AI mistake. As prior research has proven the positive effect of messages such as inoculation messages [5, 6, 20], these messages will serve as the baseline against which explanations can be compared. Hence, we will first build on the research on inoculation messages and theorize their mitigating effect on discontinuance as a baseline for our experiment. After that we theorize that explanations have a similar mitigating effect on discontinuance.

Generally, mistakes of IS, including AI systems, provoke negative reactions from users [21, 22]. In response, according to the inoculation theory, users can be inoculated against attitude change, through inoculation messages [20]. To achieve such resistance against attitude change, the user has to be warned about the potential threat to them [5, 6, 20]. In the case of medical AI systems, the potential threat to the users, i.e., the medical experts, is the AI system's possible underperformance. By warning the medical expert about possible mistakes of the AI system, the expectations of the experts are altered and consequently lowered. If a mistake occurs following this realigning of expectations, the negative attitude change, in the form of discontinuing the use of the AI system, will be alleviated, as the expectations have been lowered by the inoculation message. Essentially, the gap between the user's expectation and the worst outcome, an AI mistake, is reduced by the inoculation message. This effect has been shown for other domains and interactions with AI systems. For example, studies demonstrate that inoculation messages can alleviate user discontinuance after a mistake in the context of customer-service chatbots for online banking [5, 6]. Hence, we hypothesize that:

H1: The provision of an inoculation message decreases the level of actual discontinuance after an AI mistake.

Building on the demonstrated impact of explanations on cognitive processes (see Sect. 2), we can theorize the expected effect of providing AI explanations on users' discontinuance after an AI mistake. As mentioned, the additional provision of an explanation for the AI prediction influences which information is considered for the user's assessment of the situation [10, 11]. We argue that a provided explanation, when the outcome is in line with their own beliefs of the situation, may lead users to be more forgiving, even if the system eventually makes mistakes. This is based on the pervasive human inclination to process information in a way that confirms their existing preconceptions. Here, the provision of an explanation is essential, as it lets the user compare the decision-making process of the system with their own beliefs and logic. This comparison would not be possible with a "traditional" black-box AI system, which only provides a prediction without any explanations. By opening the possibility of such comparison, the explanation-triggered higher level of forgiveness may be reflected in alleviated users' discontinuance decision after an AI mistake. Operationalized for our medical context, we expect that the explanation will allow medical experts to compare the process of the medical AI with their logic based on their medical education and expertise. If the AI makes a mistake, we expect the medical expert to show lower tendencies of discontinuing the use of the system, as the explanation represents a unique tool for the medical expert to compare the system's decision-making with its own. Hence, we hypothesize that:

H2: The provision of AI explanations decreases the level of actual discontinuance after an AI mistake.

4 Research Design and Experimental Setting

To test the stated hypotheses, we used a 2 × 2 between-subjects experimental design in an online scenario experiment. Our goal was to test our hypotheses through multiple medical scenarios in which the participating experts will be asked to diagnose a disease based on a patient's presented symptoms using an AI system. In a joint workshop with two doctors, we designed an experimental scenario that took into consideration all relevant medical information to ensure that the scenario is logical, realistic, and can be understood by medical experts. The participants for the experiment were recruited from the online platform Prolific. Here, we used the criterion that only participants active in the medical sector can participate in our study. After removing 13 incomplete (e.g., missing built-in attention checks) responses, the final sample contained 227 survey responses. The average age of the participants was 38.9 years, of which 135 were women (59.9%), 90 were men (39.6%), and 2 indicated that they have a gender other than male or female (0.1%). In this group of participants, we had a strong representation of doctors. Out of the 227 participants, 132 were practicing doctors (58.1%). Further, 65 participants were nurses (28.6%). The rest can be grouped as being active in medical research (13.2%). The average reported years of medical expertise was 11.1 years. Additionally, we asked for the IT and AI knowledge of the participants. Out of all participants, 156 (68.7%) stated that they would rate their IT knowledge as high or very high. Only 48 participants (21.5%) stated that they would rate their AI knowledge as high or very high. Manipulation and attention checks were performed to ensure participants were able to relate to the shown medical scenario. The survey was conducted in February 2023.

4.1 Manipulations

All participants were presented with the same medical scenarios and were asked to solve the same task, i.e., deciding on which diagnosis likely persists for the given patient in cooperation with the AI system. The control group was asked to diagnose the patients with an AI system which only presented the prediction of the system, with no further information. The treatment group with the inoculation scenario was presented with an inculcation message which warned them about possible AI mistakes. The formulation chosen for the message was based on prior literature but adapted to our context [6]. The explicit formulation chosen was: "The algorithm is still learning and produces errors. Consider that the wrong assessment of medical information by the AI system can have severe consequences for the patient." For the explanation scenario, the participants were shown an explanation for the given AI advice. Here, we based the presented structure on prior literature [9] and made sure that it was in line with other similar experimental set-ups [23]. The fourth group received the inoculation message as well as the explanations. These four groups (1) control, (2) inoculation, (3) explanation, (4) inoculation and explanation) represent our 2×2 between-subjects design. Examples of the described treatment groups can be seen in Fig. 1.

4.2 Procedure

We set up the participants in a medical scenario in which they were supposed to solve three medical tasks in collaboration with the AI system. Even though the AI system used was only a mock-up version that presented the participants with the screenshots of the final decision, the functioning still closely aligns with those of a fully-implemented medical AI system [24]. For each of the cases, a different hypothetical patient with respective symptoms was presented. After being shown the AI advice (either control, inoculation, or explanation), the expert was asked to indicate whether they agree or disagree with the diagnosis. The procedure consisted of four main steps (see Fig. 2):

(1) The experiment started with a short introduction to the participants that included information about the experimental procedure and instructions for the task. The participants were asked to put themselves into a situation where they adopt an AI system as a primary care doctor which analyzes the medical documents of the patients and supports them in their diagnosing process. The specific formulation was following: "Please imagine that you are a primary care doctor which looks into the medical cases of your patients to decide on what disease persists, based on present symptoms. In this context, you are able to use a new Artificial Intelligence (AI) based system, called AuMEDa, that supports you in deciding what disease persists for the given patient based on the analysis of the symptoms.". We told the participants that the entire study consisted of six

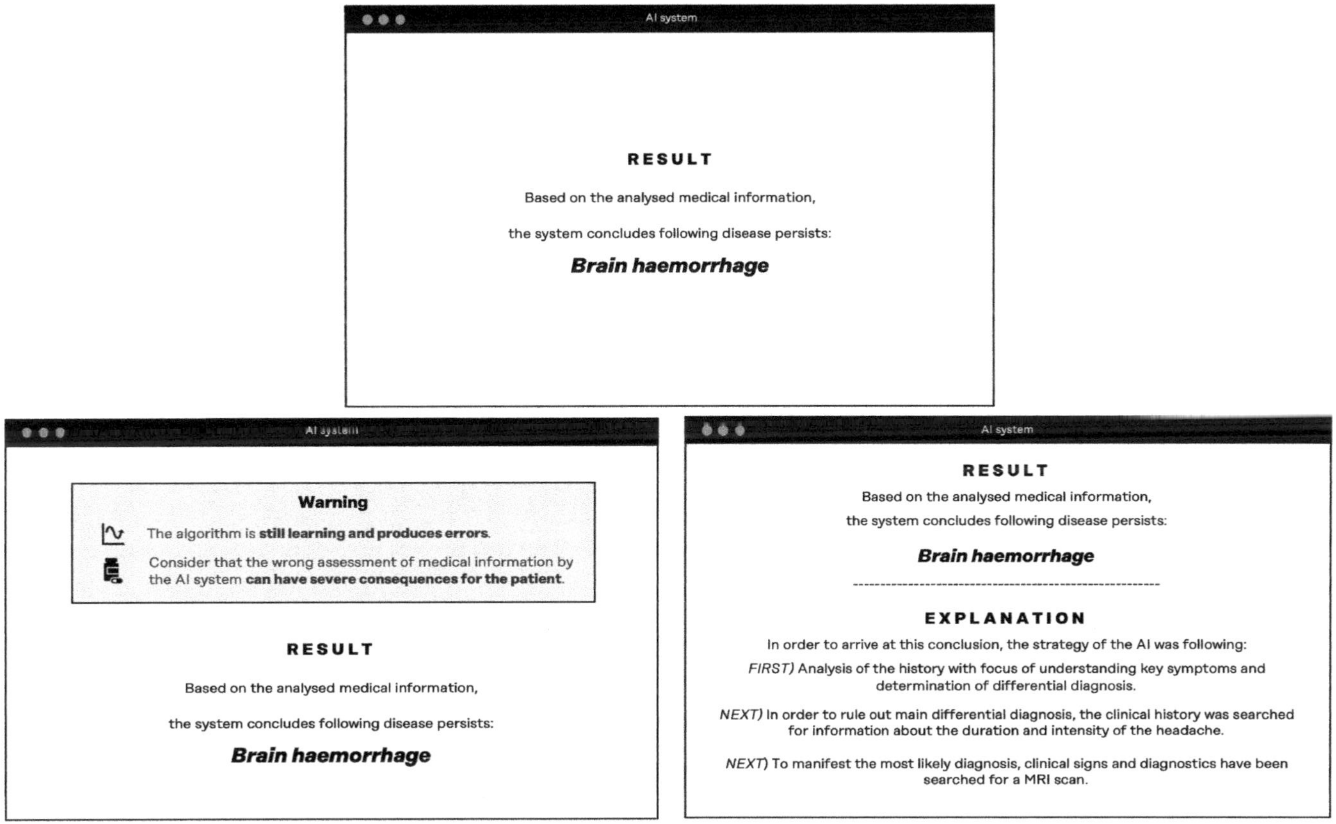

Fig. 1 Control scenario (top), inoculation scenario (bottom left) and explanation scenario (bottom right)

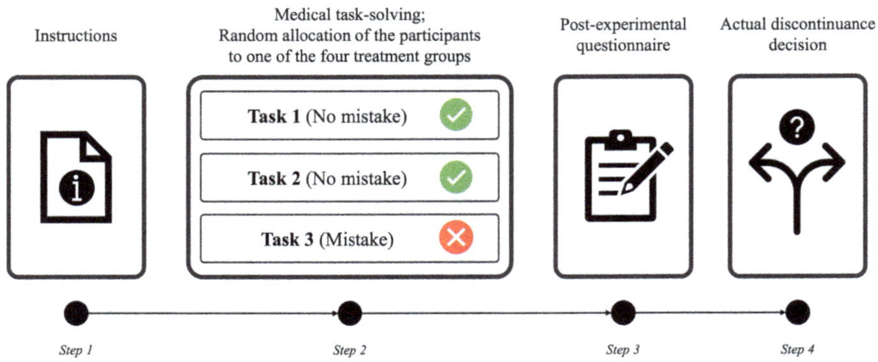

Fig. 2 Experimental procedure

medical tasks and after half of the tasks, they would be asked to complete a questionnaire. After the questionnaire, they would decide whether to continue with or without the AI system for the second half of the experiment. In actuality, the experiment ended after the first three tasks and the questionnaire, but we used this dissimulative design based on prior literature [6] as we wanted to capture the medical experts' actual discontinuance decisions rather than only statements of intent.

(2) Next, the participants were randomly allocated to one of the four treatment groups. The participants were asked to diagnose the following three medical cases with the help of an AI system: 1) A 20-year-old female with *appendicitis*, 2) A 67-year-old male with a *myocardial infarction*, and 3) A 34-year-old female with a *severe migraine*. For each of the cases, the medical experts were presented with realistic symptoms based on the workshop we conducted with the doctors. Crucially, while the first two cases were assessed correctly by the AI system, it made a mistake in the third task. While the symptoms indicated a severe migraine for the 34-year-old female patient, the system gave the (wrong) diagnosis of *brain hemorrhage* as it incorrectly interpreted the MRI results.

(3) After the completion of the third task, participants answered the post-experimental questionnaire about their experience with the AI system and other questions, capturing our control variables. We also measured latent constructs to gain a deeper understanding of how the medical experts perceived the treatment.

(4) Finally, participants could decide whether they would like to continue the second part of the experiment with the AI system or without it. This decision was used as the dependent variable.

After capturing the participants' discontinuance decision, we debriefed them and thanked them for their participation.

4.3 Operationalization

We measured our dependent variable (actual discontinuance), as a binary coded variable by asking the medical experts to choose between the two options: "I would like to continue using the AI system" or "I would like to discontinue using the AI system". Since our dependent variable is binary coded, we conducted a logistic (logit) regression, a probabilistic discriminative classifier, to understand the impact of our treatments on the dependent variable, an approach that is in line with related research [6, 25].

Further, we made sure that the two right and one wrong (i.e., the AI mistake) diagnoses by the system were perceived as such. For this, we asked the participants to indicate whether they would agree or disagree with the provided AI prediction and specify what they believed was the correct diagnosis if they disagreed. For our first task, in which the AI system provided the correct diagnosis, on average over all treatments, 97.9% of all participants (223 participants) agreed with the prediction. For task two, in which the AI system also provided the correct diagnosis, on average over all treatments, 95.2% of all participants (216 participants) agreed with the prediction. For the third task, for which we deliberately planned an AI mistake, on average over all treatments, 86.0% of all participants (195 participants) disagreed with the given prediction, of which a majority indicated that they would rather conclude that a migraine persists (which was the correct assessment). This indicates that the last task was sufficiently perceived as an AI mistake of the system, as planned for in our manipulation.

The respective numbers, detailed for the given treatment group, can be seen in Table 1. To sum up, the data shows that the predictions in the first two tasks were sufficiently perceived as the correct diagnoses whereas the prediction in the third was perceived as an AI mistake.

In addition, we measured latent constructs such as perceived enjoyment [26], perceived transparency [27], and perceived usefulness [28] all on a 7-point-Likert scale ranging from strongly disagree to strongly agree. We chose these constructs to understand the overall interaction between the expert and AI system in more detail, as prior research has shown that they can play a relevant factor in the interaction [23, 29, 30]. We establish internal consistency and reliability by examining Cronbach's

Table 1 Perception of the correct diagnoses and AI mistake

	Task 1 (Correct diagnosis)		Task 2 (Correct diagnosis)		Task 3 (Incorrect diagnosis)	
	Agree	Disagree	Agree	Disagree	Agree	Disagree
Control	52	1	49	4	6	47
Inoculation	53	3	51	5	7	49
Explanation	58	1	58	1	9	50
Inoculation & Explanation	59	0	58	1	10	49

alpha and composite reliability. Both of these are fulfilled if the threshold of 0.7 is met [31, 32], which is the case for all our scales. Further, the results indicate that all discriminant validity requirements were met, as each scale's average variance extracted exceeded the multiple squared correlations [33].

5 Data Analysis and Results

First, we present some descriptive analysis of the data by highlighting the rate of discontinuance in percentage (see Table 2). For our control scenario (no inoculation and no explanation), after the AI made a mistake, 15 out of 53 medical experts decided to discontinue the use of the AI system, which is a discontinuance rate of roughly 28.3%. For our inoculation scenario, 7 out of 56 medical experts decided to discontinue the use of the AI system, amounting to a discontinuance rate of only 12.5%. For the explanation scenario, 7 out of 59 medical experts decided to discontinue the system, which is a discontinuance rate of 11.9%. Lastly, for the group that received the inoculation message and the explanation, 6 out of 59 experts decided to discontinue their system use, amounting to a discontinuance rate of 10.2%.

The discontinuance rates show that, generally, most people would like to continue using the AI system despite the mistakes it makes. Nevertheless, we also see that the discontinuance rates are lower for the inoculation and explanation treatment group, showing indications toward the hypothesized positive effect of inoculation messages and explanations on the user's information processing and subsequent decision to discontinue usage.

To test the hypotheses, we conducted a logit regression analysis on our binary-coded dependent variable *actual discontinuance* (see Table 3). The results demonstrate that providing an inoculation message negatively impacted the dependent variable (actual discontinuance) ($\beta = -1.0758$, $p = .0332$), i.e., proving lower levels of discontinuance. Hence, **hypothesis 1 is supported**. Additionally, the results demonstrate that the AI explanation also negatively impacted the dependent variable ($\beta = -1.0164$, $p = .0447$). Therefore, we find **support for hypothesis 2** as well.

As mentioned above, we measured perceived levels of enjoyment, transparency, and usefulness to gain a better understanding of how the overall interaction with the

Table 2 Discontinuance rate of the treatment groups

	n	Decision to continue (with the AI system)	Decision to discontinue (with the AI system)	Discontinuance rate
Control	53	38	15	28.3%
Inoculation	56	49	7	12.5%
Explanation	59	52	7	11.9%
Inoculation & Explanation	59	53	6	10.2%

Table 3 Results of logistic regression on the dependent variable actual discontinuance in relation to control group

	β	Std. error	z value	*p*-value
Intercept	−0.9295	0.3049	−3.048	0.0023 **
Inoculation	−1.0758	0.5050	−2.130	0.0332 *
Explanation	−1.0164	0.5062	−2.008	0.0447 *

Note n = 227, $R^2 = 0.202$ (Cox & Snell), $*p < .05$; $**p < .01$

AI system was perceived by the medical experts. Here, we conducted ANOVAs to investigate the effect of the treatment groups on the construct's enjoyment, transparency, and usefulness. We find, that for a *p*-level < .05, medical experts receiving the inoculation messages reported significantly higher levels of transparency ($\beta = .134, p = .024$) and enjoyment ($\beta = .151, p = .011$). For the same p-level, the medical experts receiving an explanation reported significantly higher levels of transparency ($\beta = .407, p = < .001$) and usefulness ($\beta = .199, p = < .001$), but not enjoyment.

Further, we tested our dependent variable for our controlled variables and found that all control variables (age, gender, medical expertise, IT knowledge, and AI knowledge) do not have a significant effect on our dependent variable.

In summary, the conducted logistic regression show support for both our hypotheses, indicating that inoculation messages and AI explanations can lower the tendency of medical experts to discontinue their use of an AI system after it makes a mistake. The conducted analysis of the latent constructs reveals, among other things, that despite the positive effect of AI explanation on discontinuance, it is not perceived as enjoyable as the inoculation treatment.

6 Discussion

Since the existing literature does not address the effect of AI explanations on users' behavior in terms of discontinuance after an AI mistake, our study addresses this gap by showing that explanations can act as a powerful tool to significantly reduce a user's tendency to stop using an AI system. Our experiment shows that AI explanations, like inoculation messages, can influence medical experts processing process by allowing them to compare the AI system's process of arriving at a diagnosis with their own. Giving them this option (which would not be possible with only an AI prediction) allows users to be more forgiving when an AI mistake occurs.

Our analysis of latent constructs reveals that the inoculation group experiences higher levels of enjoyment compared to the explanation group. This could be attributed to the greater cognitive effort needed to fully understand the provided explanations. This suggests that the implementation of explanations in AI systems must be approached with caution, considering both potential positive and negative impacts on users. In the following, we discuss the implications of these findings for the literature and practice and point out future research opportunities.

6.1 Contributions to Literature and Practice

Our study contributes to both to literature and practice in several ways. In terms of literature, our study contributes to the growing literature on the influence of AI explanations on users' cognitive information processing. As shown in the research background, prior literature established that explanations can have a unique impact on users by influencing which and how information are perceived in a decision-making process [10, 11, 34]. We contribute to this literature by indicating that such influence on the cognitive processes of users can be used to trigger a desirable behavioral outcome. Prior research shows that for many domains a state of human-AI collaboration is preferable [35], implying that we would not want the user to stop the use of the AI system after a mistake. In this context, our experiment indicates that providing explanations alters the cognitive process of medical experts and leads them to be more forgiving towards the AI system. This leads to the desired outcome that they are less likely to discontinue the AI system use following a mistake. Thus, we strengthen the literature on the influence of explanations on cognitive processes by showing how such influence lowers the discontinuance rates of AI systems.

In terms of practice, our study shows medical managers that explanations can be used as a strategic tool against the discontinuance of the use of AI. As the overall diffusion of AI promises immense potential for the medical and healthcare sector, there is growing pressure for medical managers to ensure that their organizations invest in and adopt AI systems. Among other factors, this will ensure that their organization does not miss a major technological development and prepare their organization for the future. This trend is proven by the ever-growing sums that are being invested in the global medical AI market [36]. However, while AI for medical applications gets more and more important, medical managers struggle with the question of how to positively affect the adoption of such systems by the end-users, i.e., medical experts. Ultimately, the success of deployed medical AI systems depends on whether the users use and continue using them. Here, our study shows that explanations, as a system functionality, can be used strategically against the discontinuance of AI systems after an AI mistake. As discussed, AI mistakes, due to the very probabilistic nature of AI systems, cannot be completely ruled out. Hence, our study shows that explanations can be used as a countermeasure against a problem present today, which will also stay relevant in the future. This potential of explanations promises to be a great advantage for medical managers and organizations that heavily invest in AI systems and consequently hope to reap the benefits of such financial investment.

6.2 *Limitations and Opportunities for Future Research*

Despite the illustrated contributions, we note two important areas in which future research could strengthen and extend the results of our study. First, we must note the importance of our decision on what type of mistake to build into the experiment. AI systems are complex systems based on many internal parameters so there are various types of mistakes that such systems can make. Here, we can expect that different forms of mistakes can trigger different types of reactions from the users. Second, we recognize that for better medical generalizability, the test of more diverse medical cases is needed. We considered this aspect in the joint workshop with the doctors and proactively designed cases that are not only limited to one medical specialty (appendicitis, myocardial infarction, and migraine are problems associated with different parts of the body), why we believe that our findings are not only bounded to one medical specialty. However, we recognize that different medical cases that also vary in their complexity and scope would help strengthen our results and make the presented findings more generalizable.

7 Conclusion

In conclusion, our work provides valuable insights into how AI explanations lower the likelihood of discontinuance of use after an AI mistake in the medical field. By conducting a between-subject online experiment (n = 227) with medical experts we show that explanations, which allow the medical experts to compare their own decision with that of the system, make them more forgiving by significantly alleviating users' discontinuance decision. While other forms of messages, such as inoculation messages, must be designed on purpose, there is a strong regulatory push to implement explanations in AI systems for sensitive applications, such as the medical field. As organizations continue to adopt AI-based systems, they will have to implement more explainability measures due to regulatory pressure. In this context, our study highlights an advantage of explanations, previously unknown. Our study sheds light on the important effect of explanations in the event of an AI mistake, which will continue to be a challenge for the adoption of such a system as they will likely never reach a state of "infallibility". Hence, we contribute to the literature by showcasing a further example of how explanations influence the cognitive processes of users, by demonstrating the effect on discontinuance behavior. Additionally, we contribute to practice by offering a strategic tool for organizations as a countermeasure against the discontinuance of AI systems, in which medical organizations invest heavily.

Acknowledgements This research was supported by the AuMEDa project, which is a joint research project between the University Medical Center Goettingen (UMG) and the University of Goettingen, Chair of Information Management.

References

1. Mehta, N., & Pandit, A. (2018). Concurrence of big data analytics and healthcare: A systematic review. *International Journal of Medical Informatics, 114*, 57–65. https://doi.org/10.1016/j.ijmedinf.2018.03.013
2. Roski, J., Bo-Linn, G. W., & Andrews, T. A. (2014). Creating value in health care through big data: Opportunities and policy implications. *Health Affairs, 33*, 1115–1122. https://doi.org/10.1377/hlthaff.2014.0147
3. Ali, O., Abdelbaki, W., Shrestha, A., Elbasi, E., Alryalat, M. A. A., & Dwivedi, Y. K. (2023). A systematic literature review of artificial intelligence in the healthcare sector: Benefits, challenges, methodologies, and functionalities. *Journal of Innovation & Knowledge, 8*, Article 100333. https://doi.org/10.1016/j.jik.2023.100333
4. Holzinger, A., Langs, G., Denk, H., Zatloukal, K., & Müller, H. (2019). Causability and explainability of artificial intelligence in medicine. *Wiley Interdisciplinary Reviews: Data Mining and Knowledge Discovery, 9*, 1–13. https://doi.org/10.1002/widm.1312
5. Adam, M., Wessel, M., & Benlian, A. (2021). AI-based chatbots in customer service and their effects on user compliance. *Electron Markets, 31*, 427–445. https://doi.org/10.1007/s12525-020-00414-7
6. Weiler, S., Matt, C., & Hess, T. (2022). Immunizing with information – Inoculation messages against conversational agents' response failures. *Electronic Markets, 32*, 239–258. https://doi.org/10.1007/s12525-021-00509-9
7. McGuire, W. J. (1964). Some Contemporary Approaches. In *Advances in Experimental Social Psychology* (pp. 191–229). Elsevier.
8. Commission, E. (2021). Artificial Intelligence Act COM (2021) 206 final. *Brussels, 0106*, 1–108.
9. Ribera, M. & Lapedriza, A. (2019). *Can we do better explanations? A proposal of user-centered explainable AI*. CEUR Workshop Proceedings 2327.
10. Bauer, K., von Zahn, M., & Hinz, O. (2023). Expl(AI)ned: The Impact of Explainable Artificial Intelligence on Users' Information Processing. *Information Systems Research, 34*, 1582–1602. https://doi.org/10.1287/isre.2023.1199
11. Jussupow, E., Spohrer, K., Heinzl, A., & Gawlitza, J. (2021). Augmenting medical diagnosis decisions? An investigation into physicians' decision-making process with artificial intelligence. *Information Systems Research, 32*, 713–735. https://doi.org/10.1287/ISRE.2020.0980
12. Limayem, H. C. (2007). How Habit Limits the Predictive Power of Intention: The Case of Information Systems Continuance. *MIS Quarterly, 31*, 705–737. https://doi.org/10.2307/25148817
13. Maillet, É., Mathieu, L., & Sicotte, C. (2015). Modeling factors explaining the acceptance, actual use and satisfaction of nurses using an Electronic Patient Record in acute care settings: An extension of the UTAUT. *International Journal of Medical Informatics, 84*, 36–47. https://doi.org/10.1016/j.ijmedinf.2014.09.004
14. Straub, D., Limayem, M., & Karahanna-Evaristo, E. (1995). Measuring System Usage: Implications for IS Theory Testing. *Management Science, 41*, 1328–1342. https://doi.org/10.1287/mnsc.41.8.1328
15. Turner, M., Kitchenham, B., Brereton, P., Charters, S., & Budgen, D. (2010). Does the technology acceptance model predict actual use? A systematic literature review. *Information and Software Technology, 52*, 463–479. https://doi.org/10.1016/j.infsof.2009.11.005
16. Meske, C., Bunde, E., Schneider, J., & Gersch, M. (2020). Explainable Artificial Intelligence: Objectives, Stakeholders, and Future Research Opportunities. *Information Systems Management, 39*, 53–63. https://doi.org/10.1080/10580530.2020.1849465
17. Dietvorst, B. J., Simmons, J. P., & Massey, C. (2015). Algorithm Aversion: People Erroneously Avoid Algorithms After Seeing Them Err. *Journal of Experimental Psychology: General, 144*, 114–126. https://doi.org/10.1037/xge0000033

18. Jones-Jang, S. M., & Park, Y. J. (2022). How do people react to AI failure? Automation bias, algorithmic aversion, and perceived controllability. *Journal of Computer-Mediated Communication*. https://doi.org/10.1093/jcmc/zmac029
19. Reich, T., Kaju, A., & Maglio, S. J. (2023). How to overcome algorithm aversion: Learning from mistakes. *Journal of Consumer Psychology, 33*, 285–302. https://doi.org/10.1002/jcpy.1313
20. Compton, J. (2013). Inoculation theory. *The Sage handbook of persuasion: Developments in theory and practice* (pp. 220–236). SAGE Publications.
21. Mahmood, A., Fung, J. W., Won, I., & Huang, C. M. (2022). Owning Mistakes Sincerely: Strategies for Mitigating AI Errors. *CHI Conference on Human Factors in Computing Systems*. https://doi.org/10.1145/3491102.3517565
22. Spreng, R. A., Harrell, G. D., & Mackoy, R. D. (1995). Service recovery: Impact on satisfaction and intentions. *Journal of Services Marketing, 9*, 15–23. https://doi.org/10.1108/08876049510079853
23. Aslan, A., Greve, M., Braun, M., & Kolbe, L. M. (2022). Doctors ' Dilemma—Understanding the Perspective of Medical Experts on AI Explanations. In *International Conference on Information Systems 2022 0–17*.
24. Panigutti, C., Perotti, A., Pedreschi, D. (2020). Doctor XAI: an ontology-based approach to black-box sequential data classification explanations. In *Proceedings of the 2020 Conference on Fairness, Accountability, and Transparency* (pp. 629–639). https://doi.org/10.1145/3351095.3372855
25. Murphy, K. P. (2012). *Machine learning: A probabilistic perspective*. The MIT Press.
26. Koufaris, M. (2002). Applying the technology acceptance model and flow theory to online consumer behavior. *Information Systems Research, 13*, 205–223. https://doi.org/10.1287/isre.13.2.205.83
27. Schnackenberg, A. K., Tomlinson, E., & Coen, C. (2021). *The dimensional structure of transparency: A construct validation of transparency as disclosure, clarity, and accuracy in organizations*.
28. McKinney, V., Yoon, K., & Zahedi, F. (2002). The measurement of Web-customer satisfaction: An expectation and disconfirmation approach. *Information Systems Research, 13*, 296–315. https://doi.org/10.1287/isre.13 3.296.76
29. Araujo, T., Helberger, N., Kruikemeier, S , & De Vreese, C. H. (2020). In AI we trust? Perceptions about automated decision-making by artificial intelligence. *AI & SOCIETY, 35*, 611–623. https://doi.org/10.1007/s00146-019-00931-w
30. Bao, Y., Cheng, X., De Vreede, T., & De Vreede, G.-J. (2021). Investigating the relationship between AI and trust in human-AI collaboration. *Hawaii International Conference on System Sciences, 2021*, 607–616.
31. Ko, K. K. (2005). Antecedents of Knowledge Transfer from Consultants to Clients in Enterprise System Implementations. *MIS Quarterly, 29*, 59. https://doi.org/10.2307/25148668
32. Nunnally, J. C., & Bernstein, I. H. (1994). The Assessment of Reliability. *Psychometric Theory* (pp. 248–292). McGraw-Hill.
33. Fornell, C., & Larcker, D. F. (1981). Evaluating Structural Equation Models with Unobservable Variables and Measurement Error. *Journal of Marketing Research, 18*, 39–50. https://doi.org/10.2307/3151312
34. Ebermann, C., Selisky, M., & Weibelzahl, S. (2022). Explainable AI: The Effect of Contradictory Decisions and Explanations on Users' Acceptance of AI Systems. *International Journal of Human-Computer Interaction*. https://doi.org/10.1080/10447318.2022.2126812
35. van den Broek, E., Sergeeva, A , & Huysman, M. (2021). When the machine meets the expert: An ethnography of developing ai for hiring. *MIS Quarterly, 45*, 1557–1580. https://doi.org/10.25300/MISQ/2021/16559
36. ReportLinker. (2021). *Artificial Intelligence in Healthcare Market by Offering, Technology, Application, End User and Geography - Global Forecast to 2027*.

Navigating AI Adoption: A Methodology for German SMEs

Research in Progress

Elias Werner and Kian Schmalenbach

Abstract Despite its growing potential for value creation, German small and medium-sized enterprises (SMEs) face significant challenges in identifying strategies for adopting artificial intelligence (AI) in their operations. To address this important issue in a comprehensive practical guide, we follow a design science approach to develop a novel, tailored methodology for improving AI integration. Consisting of two phases—success factor analysis and roadmap identification—our methodology aims to equip SMEs with knowledge for AI integration based on the TOE (Technology, Organization, Environment) framework. While we demonstrate the application of our methodology within a single case study and present a brief evaluation to assess its effectiveness, our research in progress leaves the systematic identification of areas to refine our methodology to future research. Nevertheless, our findings contribute to research and practice by providing an applicable, theory-based methodology specifically designed to guide German SMEs in identifying actionable steps toward AI adoption.

1 Introduction

As the backbone of German economy, German small and medium-sized enterprises (SMEs) have proven to be irreplaceable for the country's economic strength over the past decades and continue to be a key driver of employment [5, 22]. Known as "hidden champions," German SMEs contribute to ground-breaking innovations and are a decisive factor for world-market leaders in niche indus- tries [27]. According to

Supplementary Information The online version contains supplementary material available at https://doi.org/10.1007/978-3-032-08480-4_6.

E. Werner (✉) · K. Schmalenbach
Institute of Information Systems, FAU Erlangen-Nürnberg, Nuremberg, Germany
e-mail: elias.werner@fau.de

K. Schmalenbach
e-mail: kian.schmalenbach@fau.de

C. M. Flath et al. (eds.), *Artificial Intelligence, Data, and Decision-Making*, Lecture Notes in Information Systems and Organisation 82,
https://doi.org/10.1007/978-3-032-08480-4_6

the European [12], the term "German SMEs" comprises companies with fewer than 250 employees and limited financial metrics. In this work, we will also include larger companies if they possess the qualitative characteristic of being owner- or family-managed (in line with, e.g., [5]). From a qualitative perspective, German SMEs can be further characterized by resource scarcity and a distinct Mittelstand mindset, which emphasizes long-term values and sustainability over rapid technological adoption, setting them apart from larger competitors [7, 23, 30].

The rapid advancement of information technology and artificial intelligence (AI) is reshaping industries, driving companies to adapt to new business environments and leverage AI for new opportunities. Over the last years, the rapid growth of networks and enhanced data processings speeds, coupled with advancements in hardware, are propelling AI to a level of commercial viability (e.g., [18]). In general terms, AI can be regarded as a technology that enables organizations "to interpret external data correctly, to learn from such data, and to use those learnings to achieve specific goals and tasks through flexible adaptation" ([17], p. 17). In certain areas, it is already possible today to achieve results that are on a par with those of humans, without adhering to predefined rules or fixed action sequences [11]. This transformation is accelerated by significant investments from leading tech companies, highlighting AI's commercial viability and its role as a critical factor in maintaining competitive advantage [1].

In light of the immense potential that the use of AI holds, the German SME sector is facing the challenge of how to approach this technology. Currently, the opinion of German SMEs on this technology is mostly reserved [10, 20, 21]. However, a majority of these companies [10] and an overwhelming majority of experts from the German SME sector [20, 21] consider engagement at a strategic level with the resource AI as necessary. This necessity is also demonstrated by the fact that underestimating the strategic significance of AI could allow other companies to gain competitive advantages through AI that may be difficult or impossible to recover from later on. The German SME sector being left behind would then have both economically and politically enormous consequences, given its innovation and employment strength. Against this backdrop, a critical examination of the organizational implementation of AI technology seems essential for German SMEs.

This paper employs a design science research (DSR) approach [15] to develop a methodology for German SMEs to approach AI strategically. Currently, there is a lack of guidelines for German SMEs that are grounded in theory, pragmatic, and easy to use. These guidelines would enable German SMEs to discuss AI adoption from a strategic point of view. Consequently, we posit that scientific works designed to assist German SMEs in preparing for the future use of AI technology and outlining potential steps to take represent a significant research gap. To address this research gap, we first describe design objectives and then the development of our artifact, namely the methodology. Subsequently, we demonstrate the efficacy of the methodology in a real- world context through the evaluation of empirical qualitative data collected in a single case study. Our research outcome is a two-step methodology that directly addresses the aforementioned research gap. As research in progress, our objective is to establish a robust foundation for future research endeavors.

In the remainder of this paper, we first motivate our research question through a brief review of pertinent literature. Subsequently, we present the developed artifact and its various components, followed by a preliminary evaluation of the artifact within a single case study from a German SME. Finally, we conclude with a discussion of the findings in the broader research context.

2 Research Background and Related Work

The study of IT innovation adoption, especially at the organizational level, is crucial in IS research, highlighting the importance of understanding the mechanisms behind it. In general, research that discusses the status quo of AI adoption in the German SME sector is rather scarce. A recent study reveals that the actual integration of AI into these organizations remains rather low [20], despite numerous advantages such as process automation, efficient data utilization, or process acceleration [10]. Literature shows that smaller companies especially have difficulty in analyzing and structuring large data sets [19]. The scientific exploration into AI adoption has increasingly identified success factors, employing frameworks like TOE for better understanding (e.g., [2, 25, 28]), alongside practical strategies to guide organizations in AI integration (e.g., [6, 14]). However, existing work often lacks concrete steps for starting AI adoption, prompting a need for methodologies that offer direct applicability, especially for German SMEs. This paper aims to address these gaps by proposing a practical, two-phase methodology tailored to German SMEs. We provide a robust framework to give a first strategic orientation towards AI, primarily for companies starting their AI adoption journey.

3 Research Methodology

The study integrates DSR within the Information Systems (IS) field to present an artifact designed to address identified organizational problems [15]. Utilizing the [24] model, enhanced by insights from [16], the research follows a systematic approach to designing an artifact, marking a novel contribution at the intersection of AI adoption and DSR (see Fig. 1).

Our research follows [24] five-phase process model, augmented by [16] cycles of relevance and rigor to ensure real-world applicability and scientific validity. This dual emphasis guarantees the practical applicability and scholarly value of our findings. In particular, we chose a DSR-based approach for three main reasons. First, as a problem-solving paradigm, research efforts within DSR are primarily focused on generating practical (or prescriptive) knowledge [15]. Second, following the DSR approach allows us to gradually arrive at a satisfactory solution without knowing exactly what the developed methodology would look like at the beginning. By employing this iterative approach, an early version of the artifact can be introduced,

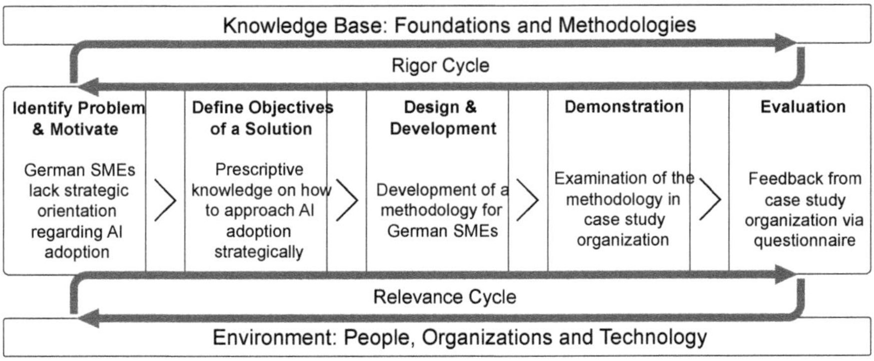

Fig. 1 DSR framework (adapted from [24] and [16])

thereby obtaining important feedback for further design cycles. Third, we view the identification of relevance and rigor cycles as crucial for directing the development process of our methodology. In this vein, it is important to note that our methodology aims not to increase AI adoption per se but to enhance awareness and strategic planning for AI integration within these SMEs. To achieve scientific standards in the IS field, we adhered to the seven design principles suggested by [15] to ensure the rigorous execution of our design, development, and evaluation processes.

4 Results

In alignment with the phases depicted in Fig. 1, this section presents our methodology for assisting German SMEs in navigating their distinctive AI adoption journey.

4.1 Problem Identification and Design Objectives

Given the current situation of German SMEs, we define our main problem as companies within this sector lacking strategic orientation regarding AI adoption. Thus, following the DSR paradigm, the artifact we create should align with clear objectives that seek to enhance the initially posed problematic situation. We therefore intend to design a methodology that is grounded in theory and serves as a tool for practitioners, offering a comprehensive guide to aid decision-makers in German SMEs. It should be flexible to meet the diverse needs of German SMEs and adapt to individual contexts, avoiding a one-size-fits-all approach. Designed for this specific sector, it takes into account resource constraints and supports incremental investments. Furthermore, the developed methodology must significantly augment strategic knowledge in AI adoption, which is the central focus of this research project. In order to assess this, a thorough evaluation of the methodology in a real-world context must be conducted in order to ensure that users from practice also perceive the methodology in this way.

4.2 Design and Development

Our developed methodology comprises two steps, which are conducted consecutively, each in a workshop-like format. Appropriate concepts from the knowledge base were chosen with care to ensure a robust and rigorous methodology. The two phases of the methodology were developed sequentially within the DSR project, with each phase building on the previous one. An overview of our developed methodology is provided in Fig. 2.

The first step is grounded in Grant's resource-based strategy (1999), suggesting an analysis of one's own resources and capabilities to lay a foundation for further strategic decisions. Therefore, we introduce success factor analysis to cultivate a fundamental awareness of key factors influencing AI adoption. For a conceptual basis of relevant success factors, we draw on [25] extended TOE framework, specifically geared towards the adoption of AI. The core focus of this phase is to map the company onto the success factors of AI adoption, laying the foundation for the determination of the company's specific AI maturity level. In our methodology, we rely on the AI maturity model presented by [29], which is specifically tailored for SMEs. We provide an extensive description of these factors and of the different AI maturity levels in our electronic appendix, where all supplementary materials can be found.[1] The outcome of the first phase is a comprehensive assessment of key success factors for AI adoption, along with the assignment of a specific AI maturity level. We view this phase as a solid foundation for further strategic considerations.

In seeking options for how to proceed after the initial phase, we drew inspiration from Alsheibani et al.'s [3] and Radhakrishnan et al.'s [26] approach, which integrates the notion of learning from other successful AI adoption journeys. Therefore, we conducted a literature review to identify past research that offers practitioners actionable guidance on AI adoption. We introduce the construct of an area to attack (ATA) to define critical domains for enhancing the adoption of AI. This construct acknowledges that effective AI adoption requires a multifaceted approach. A description of ATAs can be found in the supplementary material. The aim of this second phase is to derive concrete activities from the ATAs that are suitable for the current situation of the company. This enables the identification of an individual roadmap aligned with the company's plans for the adoption of AI. The strength of this phase lies in the fact that the identified ATAs have shown to be the focus of numerous discussions in previous research. The outcome of the second phase is a prioritized list of activities that could be implemented in the company to advance the adoption of AI. In doing so, we offer German SMEs a structured framework to provide initial strategic guidance on AI.

---

[1] See https://github.com/publicationWI2024

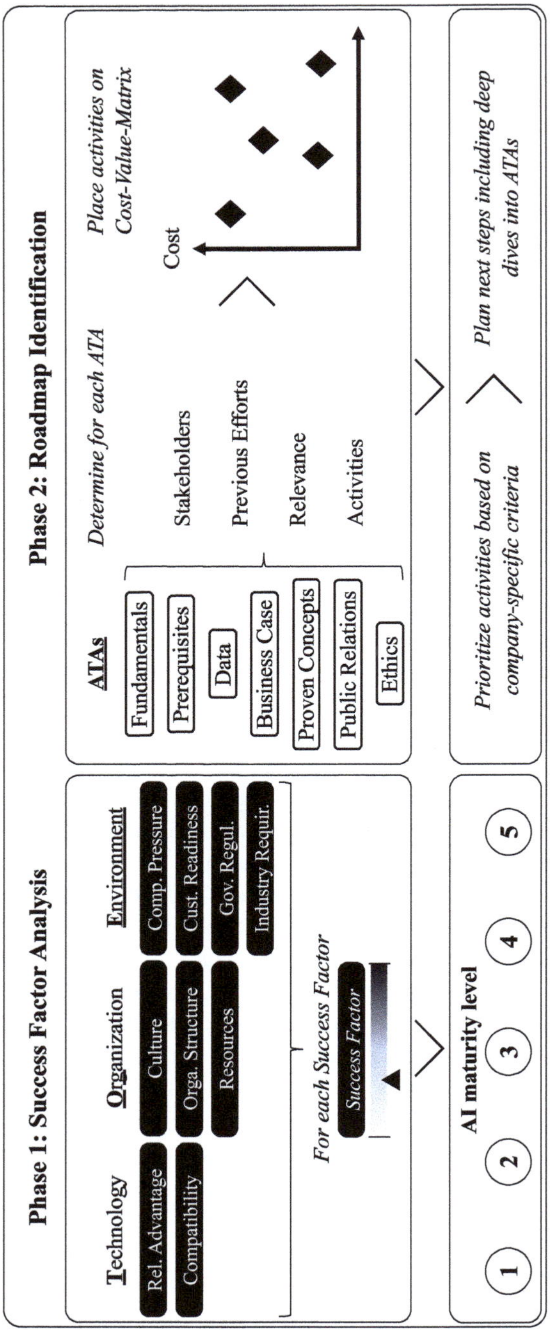

Fig. 2 Two phases of the developed methodology

4.3 *Demonstration and Evaluation*

Concluding the first design cycle, we conducted a preliminary evaluation based on a single case study in a German manufacturing SME. Two workshops were conducted to run through both phases of our methodology. A questionnaire (see supplementary materials) was used to evaluate the efficacy of our methodology at the end of both workshops. For the evaluation, we rely on two IS concepts, perceived usefulness and perceived ease of use [9], to compare the methodology with the original design objectives. While limited in terms of external validity, our preliminary results already show that the methodology can be a suitable tool for providing strategic guidance on the introduction of AI. The workshop participants rated the developed methodology as clear and easy to use. Furthermore, they indicated that the methodology enabled them to identify initial concrete actions that facilitate AI adoption within their company.

5 Discussion and Outlook

AI holds significant potential for use in the business context, yet many companies, in particular German SMEs, face obstacles when implementing this technology. In this DSR paper, we present a practical two-phase methodology tailored for German SMEs, allowing them to generate strategic knowledge of AI adoption for their company-specific situation. In developing our methodology, we incrementally approached a solution and relied on the existing knowledge base of previous research to ensure a rigorous and scientifically valid contribution. Following the DSR procedure model outlined by [24], we identified a relevant problem from practice, defined objectives for a solution and developed a two-phase methodology. Later, we proceeded to the demonstration phase, where we tested our methodology in a German SME. In doing so, we laid the groundwork for a more detailed demonstration and an in-depth evaluation, which goes beyond the scope of this research in progress paper.

With our work, we have made a substantial contribution at the intersection of research, entrepreneurial practice, and AI adoption. Our research outcome serves as a tool for practitioners, providing a comprehensive guide to help decision makers in German SMEs create an individual roadmap for responsible AI adoption. In addition, our research findings re-emphasize the relevance of the TOE model, a well-established framework for studying technology adoption in IS. Our first phase confirms the suitability of the TOE model for AI adoption, especially in the context of German SMEs.

However, in order to demonstrate the efficacy of our methodology, we limited ourselves to a single case study, suggesting a potential improvement in terms of generalizability. Therefore, subsequent research activities should apply our methodology across various German SMEs to derive generalizable findings regarding its operation. Subsequently, the observed results from the application of the methodology in the case study setting should be compared with the initially formulated objectives of the artifact in Sect. 3.1 for a detailed evaluation of our artifact. Further research should also examine whether the case study should be expanded to include other evaluation methods to provide a more precise assessment of our artifact. This may reveal shortcomings for subsequent design iterations of our methodology.

References

1. Alsheibani, S. A., Cheung, Y., Messom, C., & Alhosni, M. (2020a). Winning AI strategy: six steps to create value from artificial intelligence. In *AMCIS 2020 Proceedings.*
2. Alsheibani, S. A., Messom, C., Cheung, Y., & Alhosni, M. (2020b). Artificial Intelligence beyond the hype: exploring the organization adoption factors. In *ACIS 2020 Proceedings.* https://aisel.aisnet.org/acis2020/33
3. Alsheibani, S. A., Messom, C., Cheung, Y., & Alhosni, M. (2020c). Reimagining the strategic management of artificial intelligence: Five recommendations for business leaders. In *AMCIS 2020 Proceedings.* https://aisel.aisnet.org/amcis2020/is_leadership/is_leadership/4
4. Amabile, T. M. (1988). A model of creativity and innovation in organizations. *Research in Organizational Behavior, 10*, 123–167.
5. BVMW. (2022). Der Mittelstand ist Garant für Stabilität und Fortschritt. https://www.bvmw.de/de/der-verband/über-uns/zahlen-fakten. Retrieved 5 Jul 2023
6. Beiner, S., Kandler, M., Richer, D., May, M. C., Kinkel, S., & Lanza, G. (2023). Artificial Intelligence implementation strategy for industrial companies using the AI tool box - a morphology for selecting relevant ai use cases. In *Proceedings of the 9th Changeable, Agile, Reconfigurable and Virtual Production Conference (CARV2023) and the 11th World Mass Customization & Personalization Conference (MCPC2023), Bologna, Italy, June 2023.* https://doi.org/10.1007/978-3-031-34821-1_83
7. Cassells, S., & Lewis, K. (2011). SMEs and environmental responsibility: Do actions reflect attitudes? *Corporate Social Responsibility and Environmental Management, 18*(3), 186–199. https://doi.org/10.1002/csr.269
8. Damanpour, F., & Wischnevsky, J. D. (2006). Research on innovation in organizations: Distinguishing innovation-generating from innovation-adopting organizations. *Journal of Engineering and Technology Management, 23*(4), 269–291. https://doi.org/10.1016/j.jengtecman.2006.08.002
9. Davis, F. D. (1989). Perceived usefulness perceived ease of use and user acceptance of information technology. *MIS Quarterly, 13*(3), 319–340. https://doi.org/10.2307/249008
10. Deloitte Private. (2021). Künstliche Intelligenz im Mittelstand. https://www2.deloitte.com/content/dam/Deloitte/de/Documents/Mittelstand/Erfolgsfaktorenstudie_Künstliche%20Intelligenz%20im%20Mittelstand.pdf. Retrieved 4 May 2023.
11. Demlehner, Q., & Laumer, S. (2020). Shall we use it or not? Explaining the adoption of artificial intelligence for car manufacturing purposes. In *ECIS 2020 Proceedings.* https://aisel.aisnet.org/ecis2020_rp/177
12. European Commission. (2022). SME definition. https://single-market-economy.ec.europa.eu/smes/sme-definition_en. Retrieved 6 Jul 2023.
13. Grant, R. M. (1999). The resource-based theory of competitive advantage: Implications for strategy formulation. *California Management Review, 33*(3), 114–135. https://doi.org/10.1016/B978-0-7506-7088-3.50004-8
14. Gudigantala, N., Madhavaram, S., & Bicen, P. (2023). An AI decision-making framework for business value maximization. *AI Magazine, 44*, 67–84. https://doi.org/10.1002/aaai.12076

15. Hevner, A. R., March, S. T., Park, J., & Ram, S. (2004). Design science in information systems research. *MIS Quarterly, 28*(1), 75–105. https://doi.org/10.2307/25148625
16. Hevner, A. R. (2007). A three cycle view of Design Science Research. *Scandinavian Journal of Information Systems, 19*(2), 87–92. https://aisel.aisnet.org/sjis/vol19/iss2/4
17. Kaplan, A., & Haenlein, M. (2019). Siri, Siri, in my hand: Who´s the fairest in the land? On the interpretations, illustrations, and implications of artificial intelligence. *Business Horizons, 62*(1), 15–25. https://doi.org/10.1016/j.bushor.2018.08.004
18. Kim, J.-S., & Seo, D. (2023). Foresight and strategic decision-making framework from artificial intelligence technology development to utilization activities in small-and-medium-sized enterprises. *Foresight*. https://doi.org/10.1108/fs-06-2022-0069
19. Kinkel, S., Baumgartner, M. & Cherubini, E. (2022). Prerequisites for the adoption of AI technologies in manufacturing – Evidence from a worldwide sample of manufacturing companies. *Technovation, 110*, 102375. https://doi.org/10.1016/j.technovation.2021.102375
20. Lundborg, M., & Gull, I. (2021). Künstliche Intelligenz im Mittelstand: so wird KI für kleine und mittlere Unternehmen zum Game Changer. https://www.mittelstand-digital.de/MD/Redaktion/DE/Publikationen/ki-Studie-2021.pdf?__blob=publicationFile&v=1. Retrieved 2 May 2023.
21. Lundborg, M., & Märkel, C. (2019). Künstliche Intelligenz im Mittelstand: Relevanz, Anwendungen, Transfer. https://www.mittelstand-digital.de/MD/Redaktion/DE/Publikationen/kuenstliche-intelligenz-im-mittelstand.pdf?__blob=publicationFile&v=5. Retrieved 2 May 2023.
22. Muzyka, D., Breuninger, H., & Rossell, G. (1997). The secret of new growth in old German "Mittelstand" companies. *European Management Journal, 15*(2), 147–157. https://doi.org/10.1016/s0263-2373(96)00084-9
23. Pahnke, A., Welter, F., & Audretsch, D. B. (2023). In the eye of the beholder? Differentiating between SMEs and Mittelstand. *Small Business Economics, 60*(2), 729–743. https://doi.org/10.1007/s11187-022-00612-x
24. Peffers, K., Tuunanen, T., Rothenberger, M. A., & Chatterjee, S. (2007). A design science research methodology for information systems research. *Journal of Management Information Systems, 24*(3), 45–77. https://doi.org/10.2753/mis0742-1222240302
25. Pumplun, L., Tauchert, C., & Heidt, M. (2019). A new organizational chassis for artificial intelligence - exploring organizational readiness factors. In *ECIS 2019 Proceedings*.
26. Radhakrishnan, J., Gupta, S., & Prashar, S. (2022). Understanding organizations' artificial intelligence journey: a qualitative approach. *Pacific Asia Journal of the Association for Information Systems, 14*(6), 43–77. https://doi.org/10.17705/1pais.14602
27. Schenkenhofer, J. (2022). Hidden champions: A review of the literature & future research avenues. *Management Review Quarterly, 72*, 417–482.
28. Schmiegelow, F., & Melo, F. C. L. (2023). A market research on challenges influencing artificial intelligence adoption. *Versl Tecr Prakt, 24*(1), 250–257.
29. Schuster, T., Waidelich, L., Camarinha-Matos, L. M., Ortiz, A., Boucher, X. & Osório, A. L. (2022). *Collaborative Networks in Digitalization and Society 5.0 23rd IFIP WG 5.5 Working Conference on Virtual Enterprises, PRO-VE 2022, Lisbon, Portugal September 19–21, 2022, Proceedings Maturity of Artificial Intelligence in SMEs: Privacy and Ethics Dimensions* (pp. 274–286). Springer International Publishing.
30. Thong, J. Y. L., Yap, C. S., & Raman, K. S. (1997). Environments for information systems implementation in small businesses. *Journal of Organizational Computing and Electronic Commerce, 7*(4), 253–278.
31. Tornatzky, L. G., & Fleischer, M. (1990). *The processes of technological innovation*. Lexington Books.
32. Zaltman, G., Duncan, R., & Holbeck, J. (1973). *Innovations and organizations*. Wiley.

Optimizing Household Energy Use: An Activity-Based Recommendation System for Reducing CO_2 Emissions

Alona Zharova, Laura Löschmann, and Stefan Lessmann

Abstract The energy consumption of households accounts for approximately 30% of the total global energy consumption, leading to a significant portion of CO2 emis-sions from energy production. Enhancing energy efficiency by managing demand, such as through load shifting, presents a viable strategy for reducing CO2 emissions. This study introduces an innovative activity-based multi-agent recommendation system aimed at reducing CO2 emissions in households. By shifting household activities rather than individual appliance usage, we propose a more intuitive approach to energy efficiency grounded in the social practices of domestic life. Using real-world data, the system provides personalized, ac-tionable recommendations. Our contributions encompass the development of an Activity Agent, the introduction of a performance measure, and a practical im-plementation strategy requiring minimal user input. Our approach not only en-courages sustainable behavior among households but also contributes to the IS field by demonstrating how AI can play a pivotal role in addressing climate change challenges.

1 Introduction

As we face the intensifying challenges due to the climate change, artificial intelligence (AI) is increasingly emerging as a driver of sustainable solutions. This study leverages AI-based systems to address the significant carbon footprint of residential buildings. The energy consumption of private households amounts to approximately 30% of the total global energy consumption [3], causing a large share of the CO2 emissions through energy production. Increasing the efficiency of energy consumption through managing the demand, for instance, through load shifting, is a feasible way to reduce CO2 emissions.

For the practical implementation of load shifting, private households require data-driven decision support. Recommendation systems provide a framework by

A. Zharova (✉) · L. Löschmann · S. Lessmann
Chair of Information Systems, Humboldt-Universität zu Berlin, Berlin, Germany
e-mail: alona.zharova@hu-berlin.de

C. M. Flath et al. (eds.), *Artificial Intelligence, Data, and Decision-Making*, Lecture Notes in Information Systems and Organisation 82,
https://doi.org/10.1007/978-3-032-08480-4_7

suggesting energy-efficient actions. Existing literature on recommender systems for load shifting in residential houses mainly focuses on rescheduling the device usage [11, 20]. However, recommending residents when to use appliances does not resonate with the way people spend their time at home. The domestic use of energy is a result of deeply embedded social practices [19], which can be depicted as activities (i.e., cooking, laundering). Dwellers can more easily understand and follow the recommendations on shifting their activities instead of devices [39], thus, fostering the acceptance and usage of the system over a longer period. For instance, an activity-based recommendation might suggest "do your laundry at 7 AM", rather than a device-based suggestion to "turn on the washing machine at 7 AM". This approach aligns with how people plan their daily activities, making the recommendations more intuitive and actionable for residents.

Only a few works explore activity-aware systems and recommend the shifting of domestic activities corresponding to energy-consuming devices [29, 43]. However, these works rely on various sensor data with activity labels. The high amount of sensors increases the implementation effort and costs in real-life applications. Moreover, the requirement of tracking residents' activities for a sufficient amount of time burdens users and is, thus, not feasible for real-life applications.

This research focuses on user-centered energy-efficiency improvements in residential households. In particular, we propose a new activity-based framework for a multi-agent recommendation system to encourage behavioral changes. We summarize our key contributions as follows.

First, we design and implement an Activity Agent that applies a vector space model to calculate the activity probabilities for every hour in contrast to other works that utilize daily device-usage probabilities [16, 35]. This facilitates recommending the activity-shifting schedule that is based on social practices from the users' domestic life. Therefore, recommendations can be easier integrated into daily life, fostering the acceptance of the system in a long-term perspective [18, 46].

Second, we suggest a measure to evaluate the performance of the Activity Agent. In particular, an EQUAL score indicates how many hourly sets of activities out of 24 hourly sets the Activity Agent can correctly predict on average.

Finally, in terms of practical deployment, our system needs minimal user input, and appliance-level energy consumption data (i.e., from low-cost smart plugs) and does not require activity labels or other sensors. Moreover, the system solves the cold start problem in two to six months for most studied households. We provide the user with the utility option to focus on saving CO2 emissions or energy costs, or both. The user can also adjust the utility preferences when the system is already in use.

2 Literature Review

The paper draws on previous research on recommendation systems and activity recognition to develop an activity-based multi-agent recommendation system. First, we outline the research on existing recommendation systems for energy efficiency.

Second, we describe the state-of-the-art in multi-agent systems. Next, we explain the pivotal role of activity-based approaches and summarize the literature across three dimensions. Finally, we review the few existing works on activity-aware recommendation systems.

2.1 Recommendation Systems

Demand response programs strive to align the consumption of energy with the available supply. Better alignment of demand and supply raises the efficiency of energy utilization [28, 47]. Recommendation systems can motivate energy consumers to adapt their use of energy [5]. Provided consumers have information on when energy prices are low or other incentives are attainable (e.g., lower emissions), they may obtain notable advantages from participation in demand response programs [6].

Numerous studies focus on algorithms for recommendations and different forms of recommendation systems [22]. Prior research on energy efficiency in buildings has has explored content-based [21, 27]), goal-based context-aware [37, 38], collaborative filtering-based [14, 26], fuzzy logic-based [20], user behavior-based [17], genetic-based [49], micro-moments-oriented [45], and multi-agent systems [16, 33]. The latter architecture offers additional flexibility. A multi-agent system comprises a collection of several intelligent agents that communicate and coordinate their actions to pursue the overall goal of the recommendation system [12]. For example, [11] introduce a smart home device scheduling system that aims to minimize energy use in peak hours. Each agent of their multi-agent system controls a set of appliances and sensors in a smart home. [16] implement a multi-agent recommendation system using energy consumption data from smart plugs. Their system incentivizes users with monetary rewards to distribute energy consumption along different hours of the day. A utility-based context-aware multi-agent recommendation system by [35] generates device-usage schedules for a 24-h time window based on appliance-level energy consumption data as well as device-specific load profiles. To facilitate energy cost savings, the system takes account of the day-ahead energy prices and users' availability.

A limitation of previous work is that recommendations on shifting the device usage times may not align with individuals' daily routines at home. Domestic energy consumption is influenced by ingrained social practices, represented by various activities such as cooking, laundry, and cleaning [19]. Residents find it more intuitive to follow recommendations related to shifting activities rather than device usage [39].

2.2 Activity-Based Systems

Activity-based systems can be categorized into data-driven and knowledge-driven approaches. Data-driven methods use sensor data to build, infer, and calibrate an activity recognition model [36]. However, due to the complex nature of activities, mapping sensor events to activity labels poses a challenge. Previous research employs supervised learning algorithms like Decision Trees [23], Random Forest [2], Hidden Markov Models [4], Naïve Bayes Classifier [29], probabilistic models [24], and sequential models [8] to recognize activities through inductive reasoning. These techniques require substantial amounts of training data. Acquiring a labelled and diverse activity-based training dataset is time-consuming and often done manually by the residents. Residents may also perceive sensors as intrusive and refrain from sharing their data due to privacy issues [32]. To overcome these limitations, a few studies examine unsupervised learning [44]. However, their models lack performance and generalizability, often being tailored to the trained subject in particular environment [42].

The knowledge-driven approach to activity recognition uses contextual relationships within ontologies and deductive reasoning to identify new instances. Ontologies provide a structured and machine-understandable representation of knowledge, supporting the deductive reasoning process [42]. However, ontologies may be overly generic and static, contrasting with the dynamic nature of context data sources that are unknown in advance [36].

Hybrid activity recognition approaches, which combine data- and knowledge-driven techniques, promise to overcome these limitations. Ontological reasoning enables the detection of complex activities, while data-driven reasoning facilitates the discovery of simpler ones [39] use appliance-level energy consumption data alongside an ontology of activities to predict activities. They gather data through semi-structured household interviews to create the ontology and map appliances to corresponding activities [1] use data from power meters, motion, and light sensors to detect actions defined as specific environmental changes. Using a description logic language and unsupervised learning, they match identified actions with relevant activities. However, both works require substantial effort to initialize the system, such as constructing the knowledge base.

Activity-aware recommendation systems for efficient energy management can adapt to the residents' social behavior [34], which is crucial for long-term system use. Only a few works explore such systems and recommend shifting of domestic activities corresponding to energy-consuming devices [43] introduce an activity-aware energy-efficient automation system that predicts the type and timing of activities within the next ten minutes. The system aims to deactivate appliances not required for the current activity. Similarly, [30] propose a system for reducing energy consumption, relying on activity recognition and prediction algorithms that require sensor data with labelled activities. Yet, both approaches rely on multiple sensors with activity labels, increasing implementation effort and costs in real-world scenarios. Additionally, the need to track residents' activities for a sufficient duration imposes a burden on users and may be impractical in real-world settings.

3 Methods

In this study, we introduce a framework for an activity-based recommendation system. This recommendation system leverages the multi-agent architecture proposed by [35]. Our system includes seven agents: Price Agent, CO2 Emissions Agent, Preprocessing Agent, Availability Agent, Usage Agent, Activity Agent, and Recommendation Agent (see Fig. 1). The **Price Agent** collects the predicted electricity prices for the next 24 h from an external API. After the data preparation, it outputs a vector of electricity price signals for every hour of the 24-h recommendation horizon, in the form $p_{24h} = (p_1, \ldots, p_{24})_{24h}$. The **CO2 Emissions Agent** requests the hourly data indicating the predicted amount of CO2 emissions that will be generated during the power production within the next 24 h. It outputs a vector of CO2 emission predictions for every hour of the 24-h recommendation horizon, in the form $c_{24h} = (c_1, \ldots, c_{24})_{24h}$.

The **Preprocessing Agent** takes the appliance-level energy consumption data as input and performs several preprocessing steps on the data. Firstly, it groups the consumption data per appliance on an hourly level. Secondly, time features like the month, the day of the week, and the hour of the day are added to the dataset. The Preprocessing Agent outputs a large dataset comprising the preprocessed hourly consumption data as well as features the following agents can choose from.

The **Availability Agent** takes all time features as well as the time lag features referring to the availability as input with the goal to output probabilities indicating the user's availability for every hour of the 24-h recommendation horizon, in the form $(\pi_1^{AV}, \ldots, \pi_{24}^{AV})$. As a benchmark, we use a logistic regression (LR) model. Additionally, we apply random forest (RF) and feed-forward neural network (NN) models.

The **Usage Agent** calculates usage probabilities for the devices used for carrying out shiftable activities for every hour during the recommendation horizon, in the form $(\pi_1^{DEVi}, \ldots, \pi_{24}^{DEVi})$. The agent receives the time features as well as the time lag features referring to the usage of the individual appliances as input. Similarly to the Availability Agent, we apply LR, RF, and NN models for the prediction task. Since the Availability and the Usage Agents perform a binary classification task with supervised learning, we measure their performance using an Area Under the ROC-Curve (AUC) score.

The **Activity Agent** receives the usage probabilities and activity-device mappings as an input and outputs activity probabilities for every shiftable activity within the 24-h recommendation horizon, in the form of $(\pi_1^{ACTi}, \ldots, \pi_{24}^{ACTi})$. The activity-device mapping is a vector representation of the association of the devices with corresponding activities characterizing domestic life. For example, washing machine and tumble dryer are associated with laundering, whereas stove and kettle are associated with cooking. The system creates the activity-device mappings from the user input during the installation of the system. In particular, the user has to specify which household devices correspond to which activities. This further ensures that there are no activities associated with the same set of devices. With this mapping, the Activity

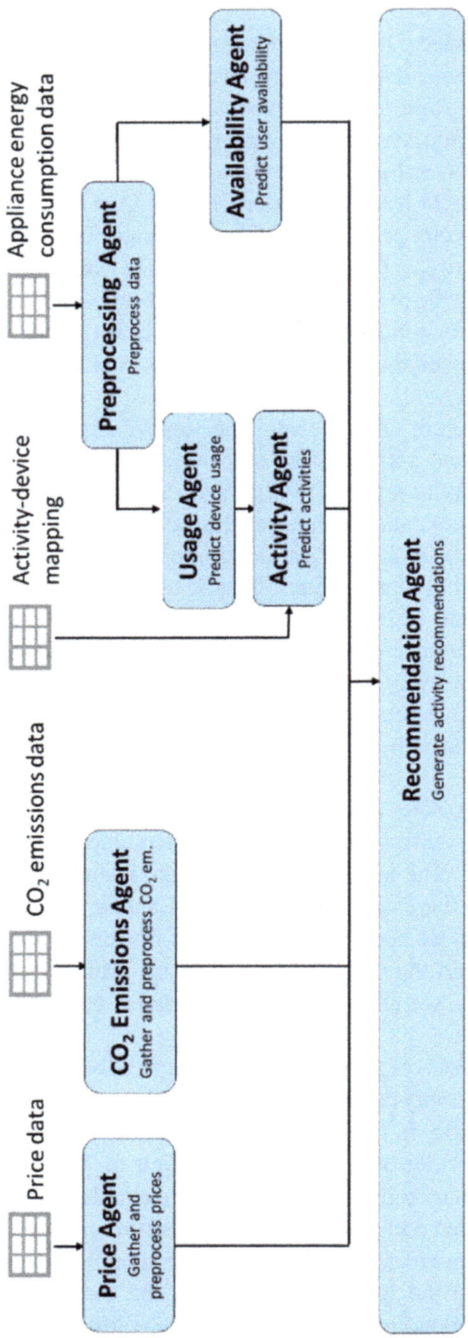

Fig. 1 Architecture of the activity-based multi-agent recommendation system

Agent receives a vector representation for every activity A^i in the form of $A^i = (R_{d1}, R_{d2}, \ldots, R_{dn})$ with R_{dn} specifying the relation R in numerical form between device d_n and A^i as input for the vector space model.

The Activity Agent applies a vector space model to calculate the cosine similarity for the activity vectors. In detail, the vector space model has two input vectors each of the length equal to the number of devices n_d considered by the recommendation system. Hence, the vector space has n_d dimensions, one for each appliance ranging from 0, no device usage, to 1, definite device usage. The first vector in the vector space is the vector representing the device usage probabilities per hour (vector A). The second vector is the activity-device mapping vector for an individual activity (vector B). To determine the similarity of these two vectors, we use the cosine similarity, as follows:

$$similarity = \begin{cases} 0, & if\ \|A\| = 0\, or \|B\| = 0 \\ \cos(\vartheta) = \dfrac{A * B}{\|A\| * \|B\|} = \dfrac{\sum_{i=1}^{n} A_i * B_i}{\sqrt{\sum_{i=1}^{n} A_i^2} * \sqrt{\sum_{i=1}^{n} B_i^2}} & Otherwise \end{cases} \quad (1)$$

where A and B are the two vectors whose similarity is calculated, n is the number of vector components and i is the iterator. The Activity Agent takes vector A of a specific hour and compares it with vector B of each activity of the same specific hour. The result is one cosine similarity measurement for each activity of the private household per hour. The higher the cosine similarity measurement, the closer are the compared vectors due to a similar orientation specifying that the probably used devices indicated by vector A are similar to the devices that are used to carry out a certain activity indicated by vector B. This procedure also enables the detection of concurrent activities. The cosine similarity of each activity vector is calculated and even though vector A states a high usage probability of identifying devices of different activities, both will be considered with a respective similarity measurement since the vector orientation will be closer to a vector indicating the usage of the identifying devices than to a vector not specifying such usage. To provide the activity probabilities for every shiftable activity the computed cosine similarity calculations are transformed into probabilities by dividing each measurement by the sum of all measurements of that hour.

The activity-based recommendation system is designed to provide personalized recommendations by using device-usage data to analyze the context, specifically the device-usage patterns. Therefore, the recommendation system can provide recommendations only for activities that have associated devices with energy consumption data used as input [48] shows that out of nearly 40 daily household activities, only ten are directly related to device energy consumption.

Following our middle-term aim of practical deployment of the system with minimal user input, we develop an EQUAL score to evaluate the Activity Agent's performance. In simple words, the EQUAL score indicates how many hourly sets of activities out of 24 hourly sets the Activity Agent can correctly predict on average. More detailed, the predictions of the Activity Agent are based on the device usage probabilities. If a device's usage is likely in a certain hour, the associated activity is also likely to be carried out. Taking this principle, every hour a set of devices S^i_{dev} that are predicted with a probability higher than a certain usage threshold can be translated into a set of activities S^i_{act} containing all associated activities. As a result, S^i_{act} can be used as a target variable to compare the predictions of the Activity Agent with.

The output of the Activity Agent is the activity probabilities for every possible activity per hour. An hourly set of the predicted activities $S^i_{\widehat{act}}$ can be compiled by taking all activities higher than a certain activity threshold. To measure the performance of the Activity Agent both sets need to be compared and checked for equality, meaning both contain the same activities, as follows

$$ID_{act} = \{dev|P(dev) = 1\}, \tag{2}$$

where ID_{act} is the set of identifying devices for each possible activity of the private household. The values for $P(dev)$ are provided by the activity-device mapping vector, where 1 represents an identifying relation between the activity and the device.

$$S^i_{dev} = \left\{dev|\pi^{dev} > use_{th}\right\}, \tag{3}$$

where S^i_{dev} describes the set of devices, whose device usage probability of hour i is greater than the usage threshold use_{th}.

$$S^i_{act} = \left\{S_{act}|dev \in S^i_{dev} \wedge \widehat{dev} \in ID_{act}\right\}, \tag{4}$$

where S^i_{act} is the set of activities that have an identifying activity-device relationship with the devices of S^i_{dev}.

$$S^i_{\widehat{act}} = \left\{\widehat{act}|\pi^{\widehat{act}} > act_{th}\right\}, \tag{5}$$

where $S^i_{\widehat{act}}$ describes the set of activities that are predicted by the Activity Agent with a probability greater than the activity threshold act_{th}.

$$EQUAL_{act} = \sum_{i=1}^{n}\left(S^i_{act} = S^i_{\widehat{act}}\right)/n \tag{6}$$

where $EQUAL_{act}$ is the ratio of the sum of equal activity sets per hour i over n, with n being the total number of hourly activity sets in the recommendation horizon, in this case, 24. For example, if the Activity Agent can accurately make predictions for 12 h out of 24 h on average, then the EQUAL score is 0.5.

The **Recommendation Agent** receives the output of the Price Agent, the CO2 Emissions Agent, the Availability Agent, and the Activity Agent and calculates an activity schedule for the next 24 h. It also takes an availability threshold (i.e., the minimum predicted probability that the user will be available), an activity threshold (i.e., the minimum predicted probability that an activity will be carried out), a CO2 emissions ratio (i.e., to which extent the Recommendation Agent has to consider CO2 emissions over energy prices), a Boolean variable *aval-off* (i.e., indicating whether the system should consider the user availability hours or not), and an average energy consumption per device.

4 Experimental Design

To analyze and evaluate the proposed recommendation system, we use the REFIT Electrical Load Measurements dataset [31] that contains appliance-level electrical consumption data in Watts, timestamped, and sampled at eight-second intervals. The energy consumption data was collected from October 2013 to June 2015 in 20 households, for nine different devices each, in Loughborough, United Kingdom. To validate the findings, we do the performance evaluation using data from households 1 to 5. Additionally, we use the carbon intensity data provided by the National Grid Electricity System Operator (ESO, 2022). ESO provide data on the national and regional carbon intensity of the electricity system in Great Britain. Further, we use day-ahead industry energy prices for the United Kingdom (entsoe, 2022). These prices are not the actual consumption prices paid by the households, but they are a realistic proxy in the case of variable prices on the household level since higher industry prices are a result of higher market demand which also results in higher energy prices for households with variable tariffs.

During the launch of the system, users have to provide four inputs: for which activities users would like to receive shifting recommendations, which devices correspond to these activities, whether users would like to focus on saving CO2 emissions or costs or both, and at which time they would like to get daily recommendations.

For our empirical study, we manually associate the devices with the corresponding activities for every household to prepare the activity-device mappings [25] show that green defaults maximize energy savings. Therefore, we initialize the system with hyperparameter values (i.e., the availability threshold, the activity threshold, and the aval-off value) that lead to the highest possible savings. For optimal initialization, we analyze changes in the distribution of the recommended activity launching hours and in the performance measures due to hyperparameters changes. We also perform a grid search for the highest total savings on the household level to confirm suitable parameters have been identified. Only hours with the probability of user availability and activity higher than a threshold are considered for a recommendation. The recommendation system further requires the value of the emissions ratio from the user as an input (i.e., 1.0 in case of focusing on emission savings, 0.0 for cost saving, or 0.5 for both equally).

The Availability Agent takes five features as input: month, day, and hour of appliance use, the resident's availability one hour and one week ago based on the use of appliances that ensure the resident is at home. The Usage Agent takes the time features (month, day, and hour) and time lag one-hot-encoded features (one hour and one week ago) indicating the usage of each household appliance. We train the LR, RF, and NN models on the first four weeks of data for each household before they make their first prediction to address the cold start problem. We calculate the AUC using the fifth week as a test set. The models are tuned every four months using the new energy consumption data and cutting off the oldest two months of data to focus on the current energy consumption behavior. The NN model outperforms and, therefore, is used further. The codes for the recommendation system are provided in GitHub (GitHub, n.d.).

5 Empirical Results

The total performance of the recommendation system depends on the performance of its single agents. Therefore, we first measure the performance of the individual agents. Next, we quantify the challenge of the cold start problem by evaluating the agents' performance over time. Last, we analyze the potential CO2 emissions and cost savings of the overall recommendation system.

5.1 Performance of Individual Agents

To evaluate the performance of the individual agents, we calculate the AUC scores for the Availability Agent and the Usage Agent, along with the EQUAL score for the Activity Agent across households 1 to 5. There is only little variation of the Availability Agent's and the Usage Agent's performance being overall on a high level of AUC scores. We observe a higher variance in the AUC scores of the Availability Agent for household 1 compared to household 3, and variations in the Usage Agent's performance between household 1 and households 2 to 5 (see Table 1). Yet, a visual inspection of the energy consumption data of the households do not reveal a specific pattern. However, the prediction performance could be influenced by variations in device usage throughout the day and over time. Moreover, fluctuations in user availability, particularly during weekend trips or longer vacations, may further impact prediction accuracy.

The performance of the Activity Agent depends on the performance of the Usage Agent, which explains high scores observed for households 3, 4, and 5 compared to household 1. While household 2 exhibits strong Usage Agent performance, this is not fully reflected in the Activity Agent's score. One possible explanation is

Table 1 Performance evaluation of the individual agents for the households (HH) 1 to 5. The neural network model used for the predictions of the availability and the usage agents

	AUC	AUC								EQUAL
HH	Availability	Usage Dev1	Dev2	Dev3	Dev4	Dev5	Dev6	Dev7	Dev8	Activity
1	0.87	0.74	0.82	0.78	0.86	1.00	–	–	–	0.46
2	0.84	0.92	0.94	0.98	0.93	0.89	0.99	0.98	–	0.57
3	0.78	0.96	0.95	0.89	0.95	0.80	0.88	1.00	–	0.69
4	0.84	0.82	0.98	0.95	0.95	0.99	1.00	–	–	0.64
5	0.87	0.95	0.91	0.88	0.90	0.95	0.96	0.99	0.89	0.79

the reliance of the EQUAL score calculation on thresholds. These thresholds are necessary for filtering activities based on probabilities of device use and activity occurrence, ensuring the score's accuracy. Optimization of the thresholds for the highest EQUAL score could be considered but would require considerable time and resources. Therefore, the EQUAL score serves as an approximation for the quantification of an unsupervised learning problem. For instance, a EQUAL score of 0.79 for household 5 implies that the Activity Agent accurately predicts around 19 out of 24 hourly activity sets on average.

5.2 *Cold Start Problem Evaluation*

Every recommendation system is challenged by the cold start problem. Systems require training data to generate good recommendations. However, during the initial stages of system launch, this data may be unavailable. Hence, the recommendation system might not be able to provide proper recommendations. The problem could be overcome by requesting more user input initially. However, this would conflict with the goal of minimal user input. To measure the impact of the cold start problem on the recommender system, we evaluate the Availability, Usage, and Activity Agents using varying lengths of training data. We also analyze how their performance evolves with increasing dataset sizes. Additionally, we ensure comparability by evaluating the performance of all models using the same test data. The cold start problem of the recommendations system is solved when all individual agents of the system solve it.

Table 2 shows the solution to the cold start problem. The Availability Agent reaches acceptable performance relatively quickly, overcoming the cold start problem in approximately 2.5 months, a trend consistent across households. In contrast, the cold start scores of the Usage Agent vary across different devices and households. While for some devices the cold start problem can instantly be solved after 28 days, others require 2 to 6 months, or even up to a year, as seen in Dev1 of household 1. This variability may stem from infrequent use of devices or erratic use, which is not following a daily pattern. Discarding old usage data at every new tuning step

Table 2 Cold start scores in days for households 1 to 5

	Availability	Usage								Activity	System
HH		Dev1	Dev2	Dev3	Dev4	Dev5	Dev6	Dev7	Dev8		
1	81	365	74	80	103	28	–	–	–	51	365
2	72	28	41	30	28	67	28	28	–	35	71
3	73	99	33	29	28	28	120	29	–	37	120
4	72	186	75	84	78	32	29	–	–	32	186
5	78	28	28	98	28	28	28	28	28	30	98

makes the model focus on the current device use and learn new habits and unlearn old ones. The cold start problem for the Activity Agent is typically solved within approximately one month, consistently observed across households.

The recommendation system solves the cold start problem when all agents overcome it. For instance, in household 5, all three agents solve the cold start problem in 98 days at the earliest. Consequently, the cold start problem for the entire system is solved in 98 days. As a result, the recommendation system solves the cold start problem in two to six months for most households.

5.3 Performance of the Recommendation System

The primary objective of the system is to empower users to reduce CO2 emissions and/or energy costs. Therefore, we evaluate the performance of the recommendation system by quantifying how much a user could save when using the system for one year. For this purpose, the system generates acceptable recommendations (i.e., when the predicted probability of user availability and specific activities are higher than a threshold). Next, we compute the CO2 emissions and energy costs for executing the activities with and without following the recommendations. The potential CO2 emissions savings are calculated by using the day-ahead CO2 emission predictions provided by the CO2 Emissions Agent. The possible energy cost savings are computed by using the day-ahead energy prices provided by the Price Agent. Both inputs are based on the true energy consumption data of the appliances used for the predicted activities.

Total emissions and cost savings vary across households due to the factors such as the number of activities, devices used, and individual agent performance. The recommendation system for household 1, for example, considers only 4 activities using 5 devices in total (see Table 3). Moreover, the performance of individual agents in household 1 consistently lags behind that of agents in other households. Another factor contributing to the variance in total savings is the behavior of the user. In cases where users already demonstrate energy efficiency in carrying out domestic activities without reliance on a recommendation system, potential savings naturally diminish. This could explain the relatively lower total savings observed in household 4.

Table 3 Performance evaluation results for households 1 to 5 with an emissions ratio of 0.0 compared to an emissions ratio of 1.0 and constant availability and activity thresholds of 0.15

			emissions ratio = 0.0				emissions ratio = 1.0			
			emissions sav		price sav		emissions sav		price sav	
HH	#rec	#rec /day	total	relative	total	relative	total	relative	total	relative
1	1,837	5	123.37	0.07	79.84	0.22	261.32	0.14	21.65	0.06
2	3,231	9	188.35	0.07	109.54	0.20	345.72	0.13	40.45	0.07
3	3,084	8	184.85	0.06	119.63	0.20	355.63	0.12	32.66	0.06
4	2,216	6	30.43	0.03	27.76	0.13	80.15	0.07	-0.38	0.00
5	3,893	11	219.30	0.07	136.46	0.25	350.97	0.13	74.77	0.14

The empirical findings presented in Table 3 highlight that while focusing on CO2 emissions (emissions ratio = 1.0), the system provides an average of 12% reduction in CO2 emission and 7% reduction in electricity costs. When prioritizing energy costs (emissions ratio = 0.0), households can achieve an average of 6% emissions and 20% electricity costs reductions, provided they accept the recommendations.

6 Discussion

The proposed recommendation system exhibits similarities with previous approaches. We utilize simple hardware, adopt the flexible architecture of a multi-agent system, and use similar logic to generate recommendations. However, our system improves and extends previous systems and findings in several aspects.

Firstly, [35] focus on shifting the use of flexible devices (i.e., dishwasher), [16] cover all shiftable devices but limit the number of recommendations per device to avoid overloading the user with too many recommendations. Recommending the rescheduling of activities reduces the number of recommendations per se, as activities represent a specific number of devices used to carry out the activity.

Secondly, the recommendation systems by [35] and [16] generate at most one recommendation per device and day. In contrast, our recommendation system provides one recommendation for every time the probability for an activity occurring exceeds the activity threshold within the recommended time horizon. This approach is more realistic since domestic activities such as cooking or laundering can occur multiple times a day.

Thirdly, the proposed system extends the predicted time horizon compared to [43] (10 min) and [29] (9 h) to a period of 24 h. Additionally, while [29] consider one appliance per activity, the proposed system also supports using several devices for an activity, which is more realistic.

Fourthly, while the recommendation systems of [35] and [16] aim at saving energy costs with load shifting, the proposed system enhances the utility dimension by offering the option to focus on saving CO2 emissions or electricity costs, or both. This feature enables the system to reach a wider target audience. In addition, users can switch the focus of the system while using it.

Finally, our medium-term goal is to integrate the recommendation system with an existing smart home platform used in German private households, to perform an experimental study, and study the rebound effects. For deployment, the system requires a low-cost credit-card-sized computer Raspberry Pi and smart plugs, making it an inexpensive solution. The recommendation system works with energy consumption data and does not require additional sensorial data or activity labels. This reduces the implementation effort and costs, ensures minimal user input, and leaves users in control of their highly sensitive data.

7 Conclusions

This paper introduces a novel activity-based framework for a multi-agent recommendation system that aims at human-centered energy-efficiency improvements in residential houses to tackle climate change. We offer both a theoretical framework and practical implementation, accompanied by a proposed performance evaluation method. Empirical results show the system's potential to reduce CO2 emissions and energy costs by shifting domestic activities. Our system targets a segment of the population that is open to receiving data-driven decision support and has a higher acceptance of AI technology. Implementing the proposed system raises awareness that residents can influence CO2 emissions from energy production and energy costs through their daily energy consumption behavior. Our system can be used within a smartphone application or existing smart home systems, making it a feasible tool for climate change mitigation in low-, middle-, and high-income countries alike.

References

1. Ahmadi-Karvigh, S., Ghahramani, A., Becerik-Gerber, B., & Soibelman, L. (2018). Real-Time Activity Recognition for Energy Efficiency in Buildings. *Applied Energy, 211*, 146–160.
2. Alhamoud, A., Xu, P., Englert, F., Reinhardt, A., Scholl, P., Boehnstedt, D., & Steinmetz, R. (2015). Extracting Human Behavior Patterns from Appliance-Level Power Consumption Data. In *European Conference on Wireless Sensor Networks* (pp. 52–67). Springer.
3. Allouhi, A., El Fouih, Y., Kousksou, T., Jamil, A., Zeraouli, Y., & Mourad, Y. (2015). Energy Consumption and Efficiency in Buildings: Current Status and Future Trends. *Journal of Cleaner production, 109*, 118–130.
4. Asghari, P., Soleimani, E., & Nazerfard, E. (2020). Online Human Activity Recognition Employing Hierarchical Hidden Markov Models. *Journal of Ambient Intelligence and Humanized Computing, 11*(3), 1141–1152.
5. Bichler, M., Gupta, A., & Ketter, W. (2010). Research Commentary—Designing Smart Markets. *Information Systems Research, 21*(4), 688–699.

6. Bichler, M., Knörr, J., & Maldonado, F. (2023). Pricing in Nonconvex Markets: How to Price Electricity in the Presence of Demand Response. *Information Systems Research., 34*(2), 652–675.
7. Destatis, Statistisches Bundesamt. Entwicklung der Privathaushalte bis 2040. https://www.destatis.de/DE/Themen/Gesellschaft-Umwelt/Bevoelkerung/Haushalte-Familien/Publikationen/Downloads-Haushalte/entwicklung-privathaushalte-5124001209004.pdf?__blob=publicationFile. Accessed: 14.03.2024.
8. Du, Y., Lim, Y., & Tan, Y. (2019). A Novel Human Activity Recognition and Prediction in Smart Home Based on Interaction. *Sensors, 19*(20), 4474.
9. Entsoe. (n.d.). Transparency Platform. Day-Ahead Prices [online database]. https://transparency.entsoe.eu/transmission-domain/r2/dayAheadPrices/show. Accessed: 14.03.2024.
10. ESO National Grid. (n.d.). Carbon Intensity Api [online database]. https://www.carbonintensity.org.uk/. Accessed: 14.03.2024.
11. Fioretto, F., Yeoh, W., & Pontelli, E. (2017). A Multiagent System Approach to Scheduling Devices in Smart Homes. In *Workshops at the Thirty-First AAAI Conference on Artificial Intelligence* (pp. 240–246) AAAI.
12. Gelvez García, N. Y., Ballén Duarte, A. D., & Espitia Cuchango, H. E. (2019). Multi-Agent System Used for Recommendation of Historical and Cultural Memories. *Tecciencia, 14*(26), 43–52.
13. GitHub. (n.d.). Public Repository "Activity-Based Recommendations for Demand Response in Smart Sustainable Buildings". https://github.com/AlonaZharova/Activity-based_recommendations. Accessed: 28.06.2024.
14. Hasegawa T., & Hayashi, T. (2013). Collaborative filtering based spot recommendation seamlessly available in home and away areas. In *Proceedings IEEE/ACIS 12th International Conference on Computer and Information Science (ICIS)* (pp. 547–548).
15. Icha, P., Lauf, T., & Kuhs, G. (2022). Entwicklung der spezifischen Kohlendioxid—Emissionen des deutschen Strommix in den Jahren 1990–2020. *Umweltbundesamt. Climate Change*, 15.
16. Jiménez-Bravo, D. M., Pérez-Marcos, J., De la Iglesia, D. H., Villarrubia González, G., & De Paz, J. F. (2019). Multi-Agent Recommendation System for Electrical Energy Optimization and Cost saving in Smart Homes. *Energies, 12*(7), 1317.
17. Kar, P., Shareef, A., Kumar, A., Harn, K. T., Kalluri, B., & Kumar Panda, S. (2019). Revicee: A Recommendation Based Approach for Personalized Control, Visual Comfort & Energy Efficiency in Buildings. *Building and Environment, 152*, 135–144.
18. Karahanna, E., Agarwal, R., & Angst, C. M. (2006). Reconceptualizing Compatibility Beliefs in Technology Acceptance Research. *MIS Quarterly, 30*(4), 781–804.
19. Katzeff, C., & Wangel, J. (2015). Social Practices, Households, and Design in the Smart Grid, In *ICT Innovations for Sustainability* (pp. 351–35). Springer.
20. Khalid, R., Javaid, N., Hassan Rahim, M., Aslam, S., & Sher, A. (2019). Fuzzy Energy Management Controller and Scheduler for Smart Homes. *Sustainable Computing: Informatics and Systems, 21*, 103–118.
21. Kottage, G. N., Keshawa Jayathilake, D., Chankuma, K. C., Upeksha Ganegoda, G., & Sandanayake, T. (2018), Preference Based Recommendation System for Apparel E-Commerce Sites. In *IEEE/ACIS 17th International Conference on Computer and Information Science (ICIS).*
22. Lee, D., Gopal, A., & Park, S.-H. (2020). Different but Equal? A Field Experiment on the Impact of Recommendation Systems on Mobile and Personal Computer Channels in Retail. *Information Systems Research, 31*(3), 892–912.
23. Lima, W. S., Souto, E., Rocha, T., Pazzi, R., & Pramudianto, F. (2015). User Activity Recognition for Energy Saving in Smart Home Environment. In *Proceedings 2015 IEEE Symposium on Computers and Communication (ISCC)*. IEEE.
24. Liu, L., Wang, S., Su, G., Huang, Z.-G., & Liu, M. (2017). Towards Complex Activity Recognition Using a Bayesian Network-Based Probabilistic Generative Framework. *Pattern Recognition, 68*, 295–309.

25. Loock, C.-M., Staake, T., & Thiesse, F. (2013). Motivating Energy-Efficient Behavior with Green IS: An Investigation of Goal Setting and the Role of Defaults. *MIS Quarterly, 37*(4), 1313–1332.
26. Luo, F., Ranzi, G., Kong, W., Liang, G., & Yang Dong, Z. (2021). Personalized Residential Energy Usage Recommendation System Based on Load Monitoring and Collaborative Filtering. *Proceedings IEEE Transactions on Industrial Informatics, 17*(2), 1253–1262.
27. Luo, F., Ranzi, G., Kong, W., Yang Dong, Z., Wang, S., & Zhao, J. (2017). Non–Intrusive Energy Saving Appliance Recommender System for Smart Grid Residential Users. *IET Generation, Transmission & Distribution, 11*(7), 1786–1793.
28. Malhotra, A., Melville, N. P., & Watson, R. T. (2013). Spurring Impactful Research on Information Systems for Environmental Sustainability. *MIS Quarterly, 37*(4), 1265–1274.
29. Marcello, F., & Pilloni, V. (2020). Smart Building Energy and Comfort Management Based on Sensor Activity Recognition and Prediction. *Sensors, 1*, Article s2.
30. Marcello, F., Pilloni, V., & Giusto, D. (2019). Sensor-Based early Activity Recognition Inside Buildings to Support Energy and Comfort Management Systems. *Energies, 12*(13), 2631.
31. Murray, D., Stankovic, L., & Stankovic, V. (2017). An electrical Load Measurements Dataset of United Kingdom Households from a Two-Year Longitudinal Study. *Scientific data, 4*(1), 1–12.
32. Nitti, M., Stelea, G. A., Popescu, V., & Fadda, M. (2019). When Social Networks Meet D2D Communications: A Survey. *Sensors, 19*(2), 396.
33. Pinto, T., Faia, R., Navarro-Caceres, G., Santos, M., Corchado, H. M., & Vale, Z. (2019). Multiagent-Based Cbr Recommender System for Intelligent Energy Management in Buildings. *IEEE Systems Journal, 13*(1), 1084–1095.
34. Reinecke, K., & Bernstein, A. (2013). Knowing What a User Likes: A Design Science Approach to Interfaces that Automatically Adapt to Culture. *MIS Quarterly, 37*(2), 427–453.
35. Riabchuk, V., Hagel, L., Germaine, F., & Zharova, A. (2022). Utility-Based Context-Aware Multi-Agent Recommendation System for Energy Efficiency in Residential Buildings. arXiv: 2205.02704, 2022.
36. Rodríguez, D., Cuéllar, M. P., Lilius, J., & Calvo-Flores, M. D. (2014). A Survey on Ontologies for Human Behavior Recognition. *ACM Computing Surveys, 46*(4), 1–33.
37. Sardianos, C., Varlamis, I., Chronis, C., Dimitrakopoulos, G., Alsalemi, A., Himeur, Y., Bensaali, F., & Amira, A. (2021). The Emergence of Explainability of Intelligent Systems: Delivering Explain a bleand Personalized Recommendations for Energy Efficiency. *International Journal of Intelligent Systems, 36*(2), 656–680.
38. Sardianos, C., Varlamis, I., Dimitrakopoulos, G., Anagnostopoulos, D., Alsalemi, A., Bensaali, F., Himeur, Y., & Amira, A. (2020). Rehab-c: Recommendations for Energy Habits Change. *Future Generation Computer Systems, 112*, 394–407.
39. Stankovic, L., Stankovic, V., Liao, J., & Wilson, C. (2016). Measuring the Energy Intensity of Domestic Activities from Smart Meter Data. *Applied Energy, 183*, 1565–1580.
40. Statista. Research department. (2022). Jährlicher Stromverbrauch eines privaten Haushaltes in Deutschland in den Jahren 1991 bis 2021 (in Kilowattstunden). [Infographic], 2022. https://de.statista.com/statistik/daten/studie/245790/umfrage/stromverbrauch-eines-privathaushalts-in-deutschland/. Accessed: 14.03.2024.
41. Statista. Research department. (2021), Prognose zur Anzahl der Smart Home Haushalte nach Segmenten in Deutschland f¨ur die Jahre 2017 bis 2025 (in Millionen). [Infographic]. https://de.statista.com/prognosen/801573/anzahl-der-smart-home-haushalte-nach-segmenten-in-deutschland. Accessed: 14.03.2024.
42. Sukor, A., Syafiq, A., Ammar, Z., Norasmadi, A. R., Latifah, K., Rossi, S., & Hiromitsu, N. (2019). A Hybrid Approach of Knowledge-Driven and Data-Driven Reasoning for Activity Recognition in Smart Homes. *Journal of Intelligent & Fuzzy Systems., 36*(5), 1–12.
43. Thomas, B. L., & Cook, D. J. (2016). Activity-Aware Energy-Efficient Automation of Smart BUILDINGS. *Energies, 9*(8), 624.
44. Trabelsi, D., Samer, M., Faicel, C., Latifa, O., & Yacine, A. (2013). An Unsupervised Approach for Automatic Activity Recognition Based on Hidden Markov Model Regression. *IEEE Transactions on automation science and engineering, 10*(3), 829–835.

45. Varlamis, I., Sardianos, C., Chronis, C., Dimitrakopoulos, G., Himeur, Y., Alsalemi, A., Bensaali, F., & Amira, A. (2022). Smart Fusion of Sensor Data and Human Feedback for Personalized Energy-Saving Recommendations. *Applied Energy, 305*, Article 117775.
46. Venkatesh, V., Morris, M. G., Davis, G. B., & Davis, F. D. (2003). User 'Acceptance of Information Technology: Toward a Unified View.' *MIS Quarterly, 27*(3), 425–478.
47. Watson, R. T., Boudreau, M.-C., & Chen, A. J. (2010). Information Systems and Environmentally Sustainable Development: Energy Informatics and New Directions for the IS Community. *MIS Quarterly, 34*(1), 23–38.
48. Yilmaz, S., Rinaldi, A. & Patel, M. (2020). 'DSM Interactions: What is the Impact of Appliance Energy efficiency measures on the demand response (peak load management)? *Energy Policy,139.*
49. Yuce, B., Rezgui, Y., & Mourshed, M. M. (2016). Ann–ga Smart Appliance Scheduling for Optimised Energy Management in the Domestic Sector. *Energy and Buildings, 111*(2), 311–325.

Reproducible AutoML: An Assessment of Research Reproducibility of No-Code AutoML Tools

Sabrina Pletzl, Armin Haberl, Tony Ross-Hellauer, and Stefan Thalmann

Abstract Technical advances in machine learning (ML) and artificial intelligence (AI) are shaping the transformation in organisations, society and research. Yet, adoption lags behind as implementation is costly and requires experts which are scarce on the market. Automated ML (autoML) promises to overcome these barriers and help to democratize ML by empowering domain specialists to develop ML models in an easy and cheap way. However, the usage of autoML by non-experts in science raises concerns regarding reproducibility, undermining research credibility. This paper examines the extent to which users without in-depth ML knowledge are supported by no-code autoML tools in ensuring research reproducibility. The results of this study uncover human-related and tool-related opportunities and challenges. Addressing these requires a multifaceted design-oriented approach that incorporates open science principles. In this way, the full potential of no-code autoML tools can be realized while ensuring reproducibility and ultimately the credibility of research.

1 Introduction

Over the past decade, machine learning (ML) methods and artificial intelligence (AI) have seen a surge in adoption in both research and business applications [20]. However, this required substantial technical skills and thus created a bottleneck for AI adoption in industry and science. This changes with the introduction of automated

S. Pletzl
Computational Social Systems, Graz University of Technology, Graz, Austria
e-mail: sabrina.pletzl@student.tugraz.at

A. Haberl · S. Thalmann (✉)
Business Analytics and Data Science Center, University of Graz, Graz, Austria
e-mail: stefan.thalmann@uni-graz.at

A. Haberl
e-mail: armin.haberl@uni-graz.at

T. Ross-Hellauer
Institute of Interactive Systems and Data Science, Graz University of Technology, Graz, Austria
e-mail: ross-hellauer@tugraz.at

C. M. Flath et al. (eds.), *Artificial Intelligence, Data, and Decision-Making*, Lecture Notes in Information Systems and Organisation 82,
https://doi.org/10.1007/978-3-032-08480-4_8

ML (autoML) tools [41]. In particular, no-code applications enable domain experts without extensive ML expertise to efficiently create performant ML models [29, 33, 43]. The tools offer varying levels of automation ranging from the automation of single components of the ML pipeline to almost full automation [2, 21]. This simplified access to ML is often referred to as the *democratization* of ML [43].

Despite the promising application scenarios of autoML, there are rising concerns about the lack of transparency provided by these tools [32]. Many autoML tools are designed as black-boxes that do not give the user full insight into the actions performed and parameters set [43]. This missing transparency significantly impairs the reproducibility potential of research utilizing autoML. These doubts are substantiated by the study of [16] that showed significant shortcomings in the reproducibility of autoML experiments, with many autoML tools failing to fulfil the reproducibility functions recommended by the authors. There are no studies on the requirements of different user groups of autoML tools to ensure research reproducibility, representing a substantial evidence gap. However, the study of Crisan and Fiore-Gartland [2] indicates that the degree of automation and user guidance provided by the tool must be adapted to the ML skills of the different user groups. Some authors also claim that autoML tools have the potential to improve the reproducibility and credibility of AI research by standardizing and automating data science practices [30, 41].

These contradictory findings of previous studies call for further investigation of the reproducibility challenges and opportunities associated with the use of autoML in research applications. Therefore, this research paper aims to answer the following research question:

Do no-code autoML tools provide sufficient support in ensuring research reproducibility for users without in-depth ML knowledge?

Considering that no-code autoML tools increasingly attract the user group of individuals without ML knowledge, this paper aims to close the research gap on the needs of this specific user group regarding the reproducibility of their results. Therefore, a reproducibility experiment is conducted and its findings are used to identify tool-related and human-related implications and to counteract the reproducibility crisis in autoML-driven research. This paper is structured as follows: Sect. 2 covers the theoretical background of autoML and research reproducibility, followed by an explanation of the empirical method and procedure in Sect. 3. The results of the study are presented in Sect. 4 and concluded in Sect. 5.

2 Theoretical Background

No-code autoML tools simplify the creation and deployment of ML models so that even individuals with limited knowledge of data science can use them [43]. This is done by hiding the complexity associated with traditional ML, such as the need to understand algorithms and programming languages [42]. The tools are accessible via a graphical user interface (GUI) that allows the user to navigate through the individual steps of the ML pipeline and set parameters as needed [4]. Crisan and Fiore-Gartland [2] emphasize that there are currently no autoML tools that work entirely without human interaction. In their study the authors used the levels of automation proposed by [24, 26] and revealed that particularly in the step of data preparation, model interpretation and governance considerable human involvement is required. Francia et al. [9] argue that autoML tools should prioritize simplicity and reproducibility over extensive human involvement, but should actively require human oversight where it is necessary. Accordingly, users need some basic knowledge about AI and ML as well as a suitable representation and tool guidance to use AI in an responsible way.

One of the first autoML tools on the market was Auto-WEKA in 2013 [36]. It is an open-source tool suitable for non-experts, providing a simple GUI for combined algorithm selection and hyperparameter optimization (CASH) problems [40]. Since then, the uptake of autoML has experienced continuous growth [1, 37]. Domain specialists of various fields have been leveraging autoML tools to streamline the development of ML models [30]. According to a study from [38], the adoption is highest for research, followed by tech companies. This might result from the fact that particularly big technology companies, which produce large amounts of data, benefit from automating data science and analytics work [2]. AutoML is not widely used among non-tech companies and governmental organizations, most likely because they are less tech-savvy and are concerned about their sensitive data [38]. Yet, the high effort put into the development of autoML led to reasonable technical advancements. Promising findings on the performance and robustness of autoML results increased confidence in the applications [4, 18]. However, in addition to the above-mentioned problem of transparency, lacking usability [24] and control [2], the issue of reproducibility of results from autoML-driven research represents a fundamental challenge in this area [16].

As for science in general, the topic of reproducibility has long been an unsolved issue in ML research [11]. There are different barriers associated with ML reproducibility. Semmelrock et al. [31] categorizes them into computational problems, missing data and code, methodological errors and structural problems. Computational problems cover the lack of fixed random seeds and the use of different hardware environments. Methodological errors are often attributed to data leakage, a common problem among non-experts [10]. Structural problems comprise privacy and competition concerns [13]. The documentation enabling reproducibility requires a lot of time and effort, and offers no direct incentives [3, 13]. Peng [27] emphasizes the lack of a 'culture of reproducibility' as the core problem. If there was a community that facilitates and requires the fulfillment of reproducibility measures, applications would be developed and research prepared accordingly.

In general, it is task of AI researchers to ensure proper documentation and thus enable the reproducibility of their results [3, 19]. Yet, particularly in the use of no-code autoML tools that usually have a high automation component in combination with a black-box-like tool design, researchers are highly dependent on proper documentation by the tool. Accordingly, the more documentation, the higher the transparency and the better the potential to reproduce the research [14]. While there are many and at times competing interpretations of the term 'reproducibility' [28], there is a general consensus that the overarching goal is the ability to re-perform the original research and obtain the same or highly identical results that serve as a minimum level of validation for a scientific claim [15, 27]. This is a particular challenge for autoML research due to the automation of several steps along the ML pipeline and the associated lack of transparency [4]. The black-box character of autoML tools makes it particularly difficult for the user to understand and document model training, feature selection and hyperparameter optimization [2, 43]. Thus, it is not clear if and how researchers can document their research conducted with the help of autoML in such a way, that it can be reproduced by other researchers acting as reviewers for example. This study aims at targeting this research gap using an experimental approach.

3 Method and Procedure

Experimental research was carried out as part of this study, which is summarized in Table 1. First, a think-aloud study explored the opportunities and challenges the tools create for the producers in ensuring reproducibility of their results. Second, a reproducibility experiment was conducted to determine whether the documentation provided by the tool and the producers is sufficient for the reproducers with a similar skill set. The aim is to determine design implications for the future design of autoML tools used in research.

In both phases, version 3.44.0.2 of H2O Flow, the no-code web GUI of the autoML tool H2O.ai, was used. H2O.ai is widely applied in science which is made apparent by the number of references to the paper [23]. H2O Flow provides a simple interface for data preparation, feature engineering and ML tasks that does not require any programming knowledge. It can therefore be considered as no-code tool and is well suited for users with limited ML skills.

In total, 11 participants were recruited for voluntary participation in this study, none of whom had any experience in the field of ML. For the purpose of generalization, the participants were divided into two groups, with each group having domain-specific knowledge in a different area. Six individuals had expertise in business administration and five in journalism or content marketing (i.e., domain expertise related to the datasets used in the subsequent tasks). The division into exactly two areas was made to allow a qualitative comparison of the results obtained by participants in the same area. This allows potential participant-related biases to become more apparent. The aim to select two rather contrasting domains (marketing/journalism = creative/emotional domain vs. business = objective/fact-based domain) was to recognize potential domain-related differences in the challenges posed. In the recruitment process, attention was paid to a balanced ratio between the genders of the participants. To avoid challenges with the tool and basic tool discussions, all participants received the same training video about the basics of ML (in particular regression tasks), autoML and the tool to be used in the experiments, as

Table 1 Overview of research procedure

Phase	Phase 1	Phase 2
Method	**Think-aloud-study**	**Reproducibility experiment**
Perspective	Producer	Reproducer
Participants	2 Domain experts	9 Domain experts
Data	Domain 1: prediction of the number of bike sharing rentals (9 numeric and 4 symbolic features) [6] Domain 2: predication of number of article shares in social networks (60 numeric and 1 symbolic feature) [7]	
Output	Challenges and opportunities for research reproducibility; perceived importance of AutoML tool support	

Table 2 Overview of the participant profiles

Domain	Domain 1	Domain 2
Number of participants	6 (P1, P3-P7)	5 (P2, P8-P11)
Gender	3 female/3 male	3 female/2 male
Education	Business administration	Journalism/Content marketing
ML knowledge	No prior experience in the field of ML	
Age bracket	25-35 years old	

well as research reproducibility and the framework of [16]. This should ensure that everyone had the same level of understanding about the topics and knowledge about the usage of the autoML tool (Table 2).

The participants of domain 1 worked with data about bike sharing demand [6] and those of domain 2 with data about online news popularity [7]. The data was retrieved from OpenML on the basis of four criteria: First, it should come from two different domains that entail easy recruiting of potential study participants. Second, the data should be suitable for a general ML task. This focus can be attributed to the fact that autoML tools are most mature in this area and therefore provide a stable research environment [8]. Third, there should be a sufficient number of data instances (at least 10,000 rows) so that robust models can be built [5]. Fourth, a license for the use of the data should be provided. Prior to both the think-aloud study and the reproducibility experiment, a "knowledge-check" was conducted with participants answering five single-choice questions about the provided training contents to assess their understanding of ML and reproducibility. For each correct answer they received one point. The level of knowledge was included as a control variable in the analysis.

3.1 Think-Aloud Study

From each of the two domains, the participant with the best fitting domain skill set has been designated as the producer. The selection was based on the education and profession in the exact domains. The participants were required to implement an autoML run on the tool while ensuring research reproducibility according to the 22 variables of the framework by [16]. Details about the data sets were not known until the experiment started. Hence, the participants had to examine the data and establish a hypothesis before starting the ML process. The only restrictions imposed on the execution of the autoML run included the implementation of exactly five regression models and the exclusion of the Stacked Ensembles and XGBoost algorithms to save computing time and thus execution time during the experiments. All other parameters should be set using the personal domain knowledge. Both participants worked from the same computer with equal hardware and software settings. As the task was conducted as part of a think-aloud study, participants were asked to verbalize all thoughts during the process and justify their actions. This research method was applied because it is widely used in usability tests and provides a large amount of accurate information due to the possibility of direct confrontation with the user [25]. After conducting the autoML run and producing five models, the two participants had to select one regression model to make their research claims and document the research according to the reproducibility framework. Before closing the experiment, the participants were asked to rate the accessibility, usability and perceived helpfulness of each reproducibility variables on a Likert scale from one (best grade) to five (worst grade). The intention of this additional quantitative method was to challenge the qualitative findings by asking for a direct assessment of the individual reproducibility functions. The Likert scale represents a simple and effective tool for this purpose since it allows to perform arithmetic calculations on top of the user ratings [35]. Once all tasks were completed, the documentation flow of the regression model was downloaded and saved on the computer's local drive. The think-aloud study was recorded on video and audio via OBS studio. The recordings were transcribed using aTrain [17] and analyzed in two steps using a qualitative content analysis according to [22]. First, a deductive approach was followed to encode challenges, opportunities and perceptions about the reproducibility functions. Thereafter, an inductive approach was used to determine the subcategories of the pre-defined categories. In addition, the average rating of each reproducibility variable was calculated. Given the small number of instances (n=2), the quantitative result makes no claim to robustness and is only intended to support the qualitative analysis.

3.2 Reproducibility Experiment

Following the implementation of the producers, the remaining nine participants had the task of reproducing the documentation flows that emerged from the think-aloud study. The reproducibility experiment was carried out in a computer lab where all participants used computers with the same hardware and software settings, which differed from those of the producers in terms of working memory (8GB versus 16GB) and operating system (Windows 10 Enterprise versus Windows 11 Home). The participants were randomly assigned to a computer by drawing a card with the number of the workstation. For the reproduction attempt the documentation of the producer was imported into the autoML tool. The participants had to add a new model to the loaded notebook and build it according to the available information. Once they had run their model, they were asked to compare the results with those of the producer. The reproducibility attempt was considered successful, if their created model applied the same feature importance as that of the producers. There are two reasons behind this research design. First, the task was to determine, which features have the biggest impact on the bike sharing demand (Domain 1) or on the distribution of news articles (Domain 2). This is why the participants of the think-aloud study as well as of the reproduction experiment aimed to determine the feature importance of the produced model. Second, because the experiment involved participants with little to no ML knowledge and the focus of the study was on examining the reproducibility of the results generated using autoML tools rather than the results themselves, the feature importance of the model was chosen as the criterion for successful reproduction to reduce complexity for the study participants. On the basis of feature importance, it was investigated whether the participants would derive the same result for the given problem, which was considered sufficient for the purpose of this study. Similar as for the think-aloud study, this phase of the research procedure was also supported by additional quantitative data. However, this time the participants had to rate the accessibility, the scope of the provided description, the interpretability and the perceived helpfulness of each reproducibility variable, again, on a Likert scale from one (best grade) to five (worst grade). As low transparency, explainability and usability are common issues related to autoML tools, the evaluation categories aimed at capturing whether participants experienced challenges in (1) finding the function, (2) having a proper description, (3) interpreting the function, or (4) finding the function useful for the purpose of reproduction. Once all tasks were completed, the documentation flow of the reproduced regression model was downloaded and saved on the computer's local drive. The qualitative analysis of the reproducibility experiment comprised the observation of the video recording which was carried out via OBS studio. The goal of the observation was to determine the reasons for the (un)successful reproduction of research results. The observation represents a valuable method for the discrete collection of data [34]. Hence, the individual strategies and struggles encountered along the process of reproduction could be investigated.

4 Results

Overall, the investigation of the no-code autoML tool revealed high potential in supporting the reproducibility of research. However, the lack of ML knowledge of our participants hindered an effective utilization of the tool for both user groups: The producers on making informed decisions about configurations, and the reproducers in the interpretation of the set parameters. The results are divided into three sub-areas, namely (1) opportunities and challenges that the producers faced in ensuring the reproducibility of their experiments, (2) challenges that the reproducers experienced in their reproduction attempts, and (3) differences in the perceived importance of the reproducibility functions between the two user groups.

4.1 Opportunities and Challenges for Producers

In ensuring the reproducibility of their own research, the participants of the think-aloud study encountered opportunities and challenges that were related to personal skills (human-related) and tool functionalities (tool-related), summarized in Table 3.

Table 3 Opportunities and challenges in ensuring research reproducibility

	Opportunities	Challenges
Human-related	Easy manual documentation of design decisions	Lack of ML knowledge and reproducibility awareness
Tool-related	Simple user guidance through workflow and automatic documentation of parameters and configurations	Poor usability, explainability and trust in results

Concerning human-related opportunities and challenges, the participants had no difficulties in providing their own textual documentation in markdown cells. The functionality was clear and concise, and simple to implement. As one participant specified *"That was actually easy, because I knew what I was doing." [P2]*. Yet, this does not refer to setting ML parameters other than the selection of the features. Although the tool offered many opportunities to incorporate personal design decisions into the ML process, participants did not feel able to make informed decisions about individual settings. Both participants expressed their insecurity multiple times: *"I have no idea. I don't have a subjective opinion on that either, because I don't know what it [parameter] will do." [P1]* and *"Yes, I mean, you have to know your way around so that you understand what it [parameter description] says." [P2]*. Both quotes indicate a lack of knowledge in the field of ML which can be expected from non-AI experts as a typical user group for no-code autoML. This result shows that developers should pay more attention to the implementation of help functions, chats and the provision of documentation. Training videos and exercises could also be provided to make it easier for users to use the tool. The missing knowledge also contributed to their unawareness of necessary measures for reproducibility. One participant emphasized that the reproducibility variables required deeper understanding of ML in general to get the intent behind them—*"The difficulty with the task of making it reproducible, was essentially, that I don't know my way around." [P2]*. The lack of knowledge about ML led to the strategy of limiting the design decisions to the required fields and letting the tool decide on other fields. In this regard, the clear outline of mandatory fields and the streamlined guidance through the workflow represent a reasonable tool-related opportunity for autoML developers minimizing application errors as one participant stated: *"If it's not mandatory to select something, then it [auto settings] will be fine. [...] I'll trust it [tool] on that one [auto setting]." [P1]*. Thus, the lack of knowledge is compensated by trust in the automatic capabilities, suggestions and documentation of the tool. Developers may increase the users' confidence in own decisions by providing more explanations about how the ML model could be influenced by the respective parameters. However, poor usability and explainability represented fundamental tool-related challenges for the participants. They complained about time-consuming navigation, little overview of the workflow and the results. One participant stated *"I had to spend a lot of time to understand the whole use of the tool. And there was a lot of going back and forth,*

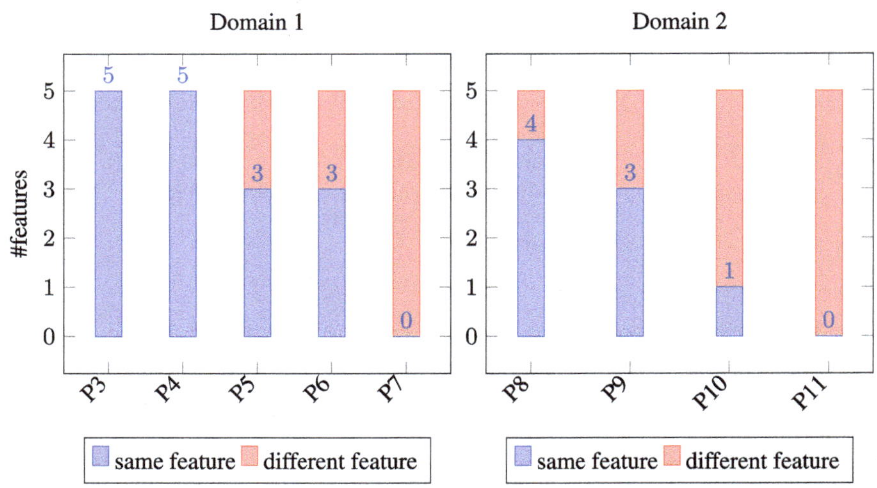

Fig. 1 Reproduction success per participant of the two domains

scrolling up and down, checking and unchecking." [P2]. According to them, additional visualizations would have been helpful. They also criticized the fact that the descriptions given when configuring the model contained a lot of technical terms and were not adapted to their technical knowledge. Difficulties were *"Too many outputs, too little explanations." [P2]* and *"I was provided with information, so far I would say. Because the descriptions were standing next to it [parameter selection], they were indeed immediately recognizable. [...] But they [descriptions] didn't help me." [P2]*. Descriptions of the outputs were completely lacking. This finding implies a fundamental need to provide personalized and especially domain-specific descriptions and explanations. All in all, the participants expressed little confidence in their results - *"[...] whether it's [own results] technically meaningful, I don't dare to judge it." [P1]* (Fig. 1).

4.2 Challenges for Reproducers

Out of the nine participants only two managed to create a model with the same feature importance ranking as the producers. The features are an indicator for the nature of the model. Different features indicate a different model, even if they could lead to the same interpretation of the results. Based on the screen recordings and qualitative feedback, the challenges lay in the lack of interpretability and information overflow. The participants reported *"I think I found the results, but I can't interpret them." [P10]*, *"Graphics are easy to understand and find, but what I see is not explained." [P3]*, and *"I see general ML knowledge as absolutely essential." [P7]*. Many of participants followed the strategy of matching the parameters with those of

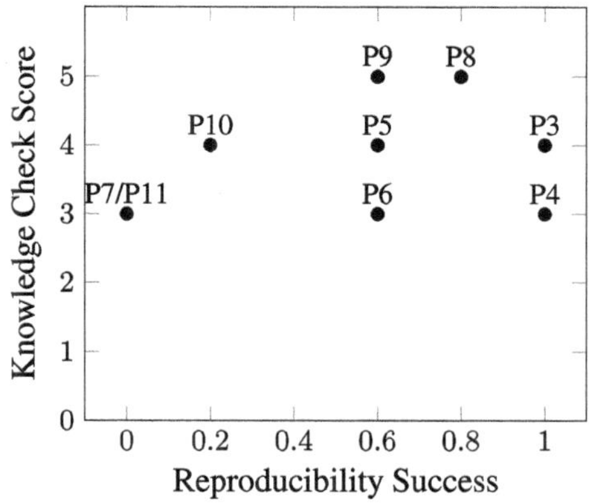

Fig. 2 Relation between reproducibility success (% of correct feature reproduction) and knowledge check score (score max: 5 points)

the original experiment, sometimes without even properly understanding what they meant. One participant explained *"I was checking the specifications, but I didn't really understand it." [P5]*. The large amount of information led to some of the established parameters not being taken into account, which produced different results to those of the producers. When comparing the results of the knowledge check with the reproduction success of the individual participants, no clear picture emerges. Both participants who received full points (5/5) in the knowledge check failed to reproduce the experiment. The participants who succeeded in reproducing the model achieved average scores (3/5 and 4/5) in the knowledge check. Figure 2 depicts the relation between the percentage of correct feature reproduction and the knowledge check score.

4.3 Differences in Perceived Importance of Functions

As Table 4 outlines, the producers considered almost all variables of the reproducibility framework to be very important. Exceptions represented the variables hardware, workflow execution, code metadata, justification and software of the factor *experiment*, which were rated as neutral to not very important. In contrast, the participants in the reproducibility experiment placed particular emphasis on five variables, namely data repository, results, code repository, problem description and setup. Significantly different perceptions on the variable importance have been observed for the variables workflow execution, licensing and citation, outline, analysis and prediction. For each of those variables, the producers assigned a higher value than the reproducers, with the exception of workflow execution. According to the reproducers, the structured, chronologically ordered steps along the workflow were helpful for a better understanding of the performed actions. However, there is still room for improvement -*"Comprehensible but tedious to scroll through." [P8]*.

Table 4 Comparison of mean grades per reproducibility function of think-aloud study (n=2) and reproducibility experiment (n=9)

Reproducibility function	Mean grade of producers	Mean grade of reproducers
Results	1	1
Analysis	1	3.3
Justification	3	3.8
Workflow	2	2.4
Workflow execution	3.5	2.2
Hardware	4	4.9
Software	3	2.2
Citation export	2.5	3.8
Code repository	1	1.4
Code meta data	3.5	3.3
Code license	2	3.4
Code citable	1.5	3.9
Hypothesis	1	2.1
Prediction	1	3.4
Setup	1	1.9
Problem description	1	1.9
Outline	1	4.1
Pseudo code	1	4.1
Data repository	1	1
Data meta data	1.5	2.1
Data license	1.5	3.4
Data citable	1.5	3.9

5 Discussion and Outlook

There are already a number of commercial and free to use autoML tools that are targeting domain experts with little to no experience in data science. As part of this paper, H2O Flow was used by non-specialists to investigate reproducibility of a regression task.

Our findings are threefold: (1) We showed that current autoML tools offer several features to document the model building process, but their usage is not intuitive. In literature, the assumption of the low transparency of the autoML workflow leading to incomplete documentation is frequently stated [2, 4, 39, 43]. Instead, it became apparent that the tool might indeed be an enabler of reproducibility in this regard since the parameters and configurations were automatically documented. However, as the participants were overwhelmed with the high complexity of ML configuration options, we conclude that simplicity must take precedence over human involvement, as stated in the literature. Additionally further efforts must be placed in the development of built-in reproducibility functions, particularly those that support the citation, licensing and sharing of code and data.

(2) We showed that even with much effort and awareness to ensure reproducibility, the reproduction of outcomes could not be consistently ensured. Only two out of nine participants were able to reproduce the regression model. This finding is in line with the study outcomes of [2, 38] who revealed that domain experts have major difficulties in adopting autoML due to a lack of technical knowledge. In this study, the feature importance applied by the produced ML model was used as an indicator for research reproducibility. Literature shows that models with different features can lead to the same predictions or interpretations [14]. However, the scope of this study lies in the minimum requirement for reproducibility, which aims to re-perform the original research and obtain the same or almost identical results. Since we did not test for another level of reproducibility, this remains an interesting topic for future research.

(3) We showed that ML knowledge and education is also needed to know how best to document autoML research. Apparently, the democratization of ML has so far been more of a theoretical concept and there are still some problems with its practical implementation. For the non-expert user group, it is not enough to simply provide access to autoML tools. As outlined in Sect. 4, there are human-related and tool-related challenges to tackle. Human-related factors include the provision of fundamental user training and spread of awareness about the importance and considerations of research reproducibility. To compensate the knowledge gap, tool-related measures such as enhanced user-guidance and explainability of tool functions, ML methods and results must be implemented. As suggested by Crisan and Fiore-Gartland [2] the degree of support must be adapted to the level of user know-how. Further, guidelines for how to document autoML research are needed, particularly for the user group without ML knowledge. Thus, we call for (domain-specific) policies and guidelines from editors and conference chairs as already suggested by [12, 15, 27].

This exploratory study does not come without limitations. The results of the study are based on a small sample. Therefore, the reader must be aware that it provides first insights and that the findings cannot be generalized. The quantitative part of the study merely serves to draw a broader picture of the topic and must be validated in a further study with a larger sample. Finally, we answered our research question *Do no-code autoML tools provide sufficient support in ensuring research reproducibility for users without in-depth ML knowledge?* in a nuanced way. Whereas the quantitative measures of our experiment showed that this is not the case now, the qualitative research offered a more nuanced and user-centric perspective. Based on the results of this study it becomes evident that a multifaceted approach is required to achieve an effective utilization of no-code autoML tools and reproducible research through individuals without in-depth ML knowledge. By focusing on design-oriented research and development and adhering to open science principles, such as reproducibility, transparency and collaboration, autoML tools can be developed that meet the needs and challenges of the respective user group and, ultimately, counteract the credibility crisis.

References

1. Chauhan, K., Jani, S., Thakkar, D., Dave, R., Bhatia, J., Tanwar, S. & Obaidat, M. S. (2020). Automated machine learning: The new wave of machine learning. In *2020 2nd International Conference on Innovative Mechanisms for Industry Applications (ICIMIA), IEEE* (pp. 205–212).
2. Crisan, A., & Fiore-Gartland, B. (2021). Fits and starts: Enterprise use of autoML and the role of humans in the loop. In *Proceedings of the 2021 CHI Conference on Human Factors in Computing Systems* (pp. 1–15).
3. Donoho, D. L., Maleki, A., Rahman, I. U., Shahram, M., & Stodden, V. (2008). Reproducible research in computational harmonic analysis. *Computing in Science & Engineering, 11*(1), 8–18.
4. Drozdal, J., Weisz, J., Wang, D., Dass, G., Yao, B., Zhao, C., Muller, M., Ju, L., & Su, H. (2020). Trust in autoML: Exploring information needs for establishing trust in automated machine learning systems. In *Proceedings of the 25th International Conference on Intelligent User Interfaces* (pp. 297–307).
5. Elshawi, R., Maher, M., & Sakr, S. (2019). Automated machine learning: State-of-the-art and open challenges. arXiv:1906.02287.
6. Fanaee-T, H., & Gama, J. (2014). Event labeling combining ensemble detectors and background knowledge. *Progress in Artificial Intelligence, 2*, 113–127.
7. Fernandes, K., Vinagre, P., & Cortez, P. (2015). A proactive intelligent decision support system for predicting the popularity of online news. In *Progress in Artificial Intelligence: 17th Portuguese Conference on Artificial Intelligence, EPIA 2015, Coimbra, Portugal, September 8–11, 2015. Proceedings 17* (pp. 535–546). Springer.
8. Ferreira, L., Pilastri, A., Martins, C. M., Pires, P. M., & Cortez, P. (2021). A comparison of autoML tools for machine learning, deep learning and XGBoost. In *2021 International Joint Conference on Neural Networks (IJCNN), IEEE* (pp. 1–8).
9. Francia, M., Giovanelli, J., & Pisano, G. (2023). Hamlet: A framework for human-centered autoML via structured argumentation. *Future Generation Computer Systems, 142*, 182–194.
10. Gibney, E. (2022). Is AI fuelling a reproducibility crisis in science. *Nature, 608*(7922), 250–251.
11. Goodman, S. N., Fanelli, D. & Ioannidis, J. P. (2016). What does research reproducibility mean? *Science Translational Medicine,* **8**(341), 341ps12–341ps12.
12. Gundersen, O. E. (2019). Standing on the feet of giants-reproducibility in AI. *Ai Magazine, 40*(4), 9–23.
13. Gundersen, O. E. (2020). The reproducibility crisis is real. *AI Magazine, 41*(3), 103–106.
14. Gundersen, O. E. (2021). The fundamental principles of reproducibility. *Philosophical Transactions of the Royal Society A, 379*(2197), 20200210.
15. Gundersen, O. E., Gil, Y., & Aha, D. W. (2018). On reproducible AI: Towards reproducible research, open science, and digital scholarship in AI publications. *AI Magazine, 39*(3), 56–68.
16. Gundersen, O. E., Shamsaliei, S., & Isdahl, R. J. (2022). Do machine learning platforms provide out-of-the-box reproducibility? *Future Generation Computer Systems, 126*, 34–47.
17. Haberl, A., Fleiß, J., Kowald, D., & Thalmann, S. (2024). Take the atrain. Introducing an interface for the accessible transcription of interviews. *Journal of Behavioral and Experimental Finance,* **41**, 100891. https://www.sciencedirect.com/science/article/pii/S2214635024000066
18. Hanussek, M., Blohm, M., & Kintz, M. (2020). Can AutoML outperform humans? An evaluation on popular OpenML datasets using AutoML benchmark. In *2020 2nd International Conference on Artificial Intelligence, Robotics and Control* (pp. 29–32).
19. Heil, B. J., Hoffman, M. M., Markowetz, F., Lee, S.-I., Greene, C. S., & Hicks, S. C. (2021). Reproducibility standards for machine learning in the life sciences. *Nature Methods, 18*(10), 1132–1135.
20. Hutter, F., Kotthoff, L., & Vanschoren, J. (2019) , *Automated machine learning: Methods, systems, challenges*. Springer Nature.

21. Karmaker, S. K., Hassan, M. M., Smith, M. J., Xu, L., Zhai, C., & Veeramachaneni, K. (2022). AutoML to date and beyond Challenges and opportunities. *ACM Computing Surveys, 54*(8), 1–36.
22. Kuckartz, U., & Rädiker, S. (2023). *Qualitative content analysis: Methods, practice and software*. Sage.
23. LeDell, E., & Poirier, S. (2020). H2o autoML: Scalable automatic machine learning. In *Proceedings of the AutoML Workshop at ICML*.
24. Lee, D. J.-L., & Macke, S. (2020). A human-in-the-loop perspective on autoML: Milestones and the road ahead. *IEEE Data Engineering Bulletin*.
25. McDonald, S., Cockton, G., & Irons, A. (2020). The impact of thinking-aloud on usability inspection. *Proceedings of the ACM on Human-Computer Interaction, 4*(EICS), 1–22.
26. Parasuraman, R., Sheridan, T. B., & Wickens, C. D. (2000). A model for types and levels of human interaction with automation. *IEEE Transactions on Systems, Man, and Cybernetics-Part A: Systems and Humans, 30*(3), 286–297.
27. Peng, R. D. (2011). Reproducible research in computational science. *Science, 334*(6060), 1226–1227.
28. Plesser, H. E. (2018). Reproducibility vs. replicability: A brief history of a confused terminology. *Frontiers in Neuroinformatics, 11*, 76.
29. Polzer, A. K., & Thalmann, S. (2022). The impact of autoML on the AI development process. In *Proceedings of the 2022 Pre-ICIS SIGDSA Symposium*.
30. Scriven, A., Kedziora, D. J., Musial, K. & Gabrys, B. (2022). The technological emergence of autoML: A survey of performant software and applications in the context of industry. arXiv:2211.04148 .
31. Semmelrock, H., Kopeinik, S., Theiler, D., Ross-Hellauer, T., & Kowald, D. (2023). Reproducibility in machine learning-driven research. arXiv:2307.10320
32. Sun, Y., Song, Q., Gui, X., Ma, F., & Wang, T. (2023). AutoML in the wild: Obstacles, workarounds, and expectations. In A. Schmidt, K. Väänänen, T. Goyal, P. O. Kristensson, A. Peters, S. Mueller, J. R. Williamson & M. L. Wilson (Eds.), *Proceedings of the 2023 CHI Conference on Human Factors in Computing Systems* (pp. 1–15). ACM.
33. Sundberg, L., & Holmström, J. (2023). Democratizing artificial intelligence: How no-code AI can leverage machine learning operations. *Business Horizons, 66*(6), 777–788.
34. Tang, J. C., Liu, S. B., Muller, M., Lin, J., & Drews, C. (2006). Unobtrusive but invasive: Using screen recording to collect field data on computer-mediated interaction. In *Proceedings of the 2006 20th Anniversary Conference on Computer Supported Cooperative Work* (pp. 479–482).
35. Tanujaya, B., Prahmana, R. C. I., & Mumu, J. (2022). Likert scale in social sciences research: Problems and difficulties.
36. Thornton, C., Hutter, F., Hoos, H. H., & Leyton-Brown, K. (2013). Auto-weka. In R. Ghani, T. E. Senator, P. Bradley, R. Parekh, J. He, R. L. Grossman, R. Uthurusamy, I. S. Dhillon & Y. Koren (Eds.), *Proceedings of the 19th ACM SIGKDD International Conference on Knowledge Discovery and Data Mining* (pp. 847–855). ACM.
37. Truong, A., Walters, A., Goodsitt, J., Hines, K., Bruss, C. B., & Farivar, R. (2019). Towards automated machine learning: Evaluation and comparison of autoML approaches and tools. In *2019 IEEE 31st International Conference on Tools with Artificial Intelligence (ICTAI)* (pp. 1471–1479). IEEE.
38. Van der Blom, K., Serban, A., Hoos, H., & Visser, J. (2021). AutoML adoption in ml software. In *8th ICML Workshop on Automated Machine Learning (AutoML)*.
39. Wang, Q., Ming, Y., Jin, Z., Shen, Q., Liu, D., Smith, M. J., Veeramachaneni, K., & Qu, H. (2019). Atmseer: Increasing transparency and controllability in automated machine learning. In *Proceedings of the 2019 CHI Conference on Human Factors in Computing Systems* (pp. 1–12).
40. Waring, J., Lindvall, C., & Umeton, R. (2020). Automated machine learning: Review of the state-of-the-art and opportunities for healthcare. *Artificial Intelligence in Medicine, 104*, Article 101822.
41. Xin, D., Wu, E. Y., Lee, D. J.-L., Salehi, N., & Parameswaran, A. (2021). Whither autoML? Understanding the role of automation in machine learning workflows. In Y. Kitamura,

A. Quigley, K. Isbister, T. Igarashi, P. Bjørn & S. Drucker (Eds.), *Proceedings of the 2021 CHI Conference on Human Factors in Computing Systems* (pp. 1–16). ACM.

42. Yao, Q., Wang, M., Chen, Y., Dai, W., Li, Y.-F., Tu, W.-W., Yang, Q., & Yu, Y. (2018). Taking human out of learning applications: A survey on automated machine learning. arXiv:1810.13306
43. Zöller, M.-A., & Huber, M. F. (2021). Benchmark and survey of automated machine learning frameworks. *Journal of Artificial Intelligence Research, 70*, 409–472.

Stereotypical Bias Peaks in First Responses of DALL-E3

Stefan Arnold

Abstract This study investigates the presence of stereotype bias in the first images produced by repeatedly prompting text-to-image systems, particularly DALL-E3. The motivation for this study lies in the concern that the primacy effect could amplify stereotypical biases in users' perceptions. Through a questionnaire survey, participants were asked to rank images based on perceived stereotypical content. Results indicate a pronounced bias in the first images generated, with statistical analysis confirming a significant association between the order of image presentation and the perception of stereotypical bias.

1 Introduction

In the field of artificial intelligence, text-to-image synthesis emerged as a groundbreaking technology that enables the conversion of textual descriptions into detailed images. This area witnessed the advent of advanced systems such as DALL-E [15, 16] and IMAGEN [17], showcasing remarkable capabilities in generating photorealistic images from textual prompts.

However, these systems grapple with challenges related to bias and stereotyping. Naik and Nushi [14] identified the issue of over-representation of white individuals in images generated, raising significant concerns about fairness. [5] uncovered disparities in gendered occupations, noting a propensity towards generating males for certain professions. This pattern of gender and racial bias is corroborated by several studies [2, 6, 23] and is linked to training images embedded with social stereotypes [18].

Building upon the existing knowledge on stereotypical biases in text-to-image synthesis systems, this study aims to delve deeper into the dynamics of bias emergence across a sequence of generated images. Understanding the dynamics of bias in generated images is crucial given the influence of the primacy effect [13] on per-

S. Arnold (✉)
FAU Erlangen-Nürnberg, Nürnberg, Germany
e-mail: stefan.st.arnold@fau.de

C. M. Flath et al. (eds.), *Artificial Intelligence, Data, and Decision-Making*, Lecture Notes in Information Systems and Organisation 82,
https://doi.org/10.1007/978-3-032-08480-4_9

ception and memory. Studies in social cognition highlight that initial impressions disproportionately influence subsequent judgments [22].

By investigating the bias distribution across the order of generation, this study seeks to expand the current understanding of stereotypical bias and offer valuable insights into the tendency to display stereotypical images at a user's initial prompt. Specifically, we test the hypothesis that the initial images produced by `DALL-E3` in response to a textual prompt tend to manifest more stereotypical bias compared to subsequent images generated from the same prompt. Since biases in initial images can have a cascading effect, potentially influencing individual perceptions and reinforcing stereotypes in society, we expect this study to uncover critical patterns in bias emergence and help to identify strategies for altering the generative process to mitigate undesirable content.

2 Related Work

2.1 Stereotypical Bias

Recent research delved into the examination of stereotypical biases in image synthesis, particularly in contexts where models are prompted to generate images of persons with specific demographic traits, such as gender [2, 23], profession [5, 23] or racial identity [14].

[2] noticed that a broad range of ordinary prompts mentioning traits, descriptors, occupations, or objects are prone to amplifying demographic stereotypes. Their analysis demonstrates that these systems frequently generate images that reinforce biases on gender, race, and other demographic markers. Naik and Nushi [14] identified that white persons are overrepresented in the visual outputs. Cho et al. [5] discovered disparities in the level and direction of biases related to occupation. Despite seemingly non-stereotypical generations for single persons, [23] unveiled gendered occupational and power associations by portraying men as managers and women as assistants in paired generations. Fraser et al. [6] explored how text-to-image systems resort to stereotypes in response to vague descriptions, suggesting that these systems rely on prevalent stereotypes to interpret missing information when descriptions lack specificity. Seshadri et al. [18] attributed this bias amplification to a distribution shift in the gender indicators in the captions of the training images.

While prior studies highlighted the presence of bias within text-to-image systems, our investigation examines the temporal dimension of (perceived) bias in visual content stemming from repeated and identical prompts. Specifically, we test whether the first image produced by `DALL-E3` displays more pronounced bias compared to subsequent images. This unique angle offers insights into the dynamics of bias emergence in systems for text-to-image generation.

(a) 1st (b) 2nd (c) 3rd (d) 4th

Fig. 1 Images for prompt 'A German man enjoying his free time.' in sequential order

2.2 *Primacy Effect*

Our emphasis on the timing of bias in the generation of visual content is motivated by psychological insights related to the order of information presentation and its impact on human perception and memory. This is encapsulated in the concept of the primacy effect [13]. The primacy effect claims that information presented early disproportionately influences the formation of first impressions [22]. It is notoriously resistant to change due to the way information is processed and remembered, and can explain why first impressions are considered so memorable.

The mechanisms behind the primacy effect are multifaceted. Humans may interpret subsequent information so that it aligns with their prior knowledge and biases, either due to a desire for consistency or because they use early information as an anchor [8, 20]. Humans may also believe that the most critical information is presented first [7] or simply due to diminishing attention over time [21].

The primacy effect profoundly impacts various cognitive processes as supported by empirical evidence across various domains. Jones et al. [9] demonstrated that the sequence of information presentation significantly influences the attribution of intellectual abilities, while [11] found that the order in which information is presented affects the activation of stereotypes. Benassi [1] revealed that the order of presentation also impacts perceptions of attractiveness, with individuals being more likely to attribute positive qualities to those presented earlier. These findings underscore the importance of the primacy effect in understanding how impressions and judgments on attractiveness, intellectual ability, and stereotypes are formed.

3 Methodology and Findings

Our hypothesis was tested through a questionnaire survey. Drawing inspiration from prior tests on stereotypical association [3, 4], we curated a set of textual prompts covering a range of topics and concepts that evoke varied visual content covering stereotypical representations about *gender*, *race*, and *cultures*.

Table 1 Count statistics of the image in a sequence of prompts that respondents perceived to display the most stereotypical content. Since this study investigates the primacy effect, we only count whether the first image or any subsequent images was perceived stereotypical

	Example 1	Example 2	Example 3	Example 4	$\sum$
First	93	77	24	82	276
Subsequent	7	23	76	18	124

Using DALLE-E3, we generated four images in sequence in response to each prompt. We than launched a questionnaire survey. The questionnaire survey was administered using *SurveyMonkey*. To ensure a diverse and unbiased sample, participants were recruited through online platforms. For each prompt, participants were asked to select the image that they considered to have the highest degree of stereotypical content. Figure 1 shows an example selection for a sequence of images generated from a prompt. To mitigate order effects and minimize bias in participant responses, we randomized the order of the generated images for each prompt, thereby ensuring that participants encountered different sequences of images per prompt during evaluation. This methodology allowed for efficient data collection while ensuring participant anonymity and convenience.

To determine the frequency with which the first image generated by DALL-E3 was identified as the most stereotypical compared to all subsequent prompts, we counted the responses from 100 participants. Table 1 presents the count frequencies for the perceived extent of stereotypical content, grouped by its position in a sequence of repeated prompts. Upon analyzing the responses of participants, we find that the likelihood of the first image being perceived as containing more stereotypical content, relative to any of the three subsequent images, is approximately 2.23 to 1. This ratio suggests that a significant majority of respondents perceive the first image as embodying more stereotypical content. To evaluate the statistical significance of this observation, we applied the χ^2 test for contingency tables. The test yielded a statistic of 132.49, with an associated $p < 0.05$ and 3 degrees of freedom, indicating a highly significant association between the order of generated pictures and participants' perceptions of stereotypical content.

When asked whether the participants approve stereotypical portrayals, a majority of the participants reject them. However, when asked whether the stereotypical content influences their decision to continue using DALLE-E3, most participants deny such an influence on their continuation. This discrepancy suggests an intention-behavior gap [19]. Understanding this gap could provide insights into user tolerance of biased content despite recognizing their negative implications and could inform strategies to enhance user awareness and promote ethical use.

4 Discussion and Conclusion

This study embarked on an investigation whether the first image generated by text-to-image synthesis systems like DALL-E3 contain more bias, a concern given the primacy effect's influence on shaping stereotypes such as cultural narratives [10]. Findings confirm that the first images are perceived as more stereotypically biased. Recognizing these issues holds implications for the development and deployment of text-to-image systems and underscores the need for awareness of how these systems perpetuate stereotypes and how this effects on human behavior [12].

Limitations. This study is constrained by several limitations. The types and degrees of biases observed in DALL-E3 may vary with different textual prompts, suggesting a need to examine the reproducibility of these findings across various prompts, models, domains, and cultural contexts. Moreover, future research should explore whether bias in the generated images incentivizes users to issue more prompts than usual. This behavior could arise as users attempt to obtain less biased images, offering further insights into user interaction patterns and the broader implications of bias on user engagement.

References

1. Benassi, M. A. (1982). Effects of order of presentation, primacy, and physical attractiveness on attributions of ability. *Journal of Personality and Social Psychology, 43*(1), 48.
2. Bianchi, F., Kalluri, P., Durmus, E., Ladhak, F., Cheng, M., Nozza, D., Hashimoto, T., Jurafsky, D., Zou, J., & Caliskan, A. (2023). Easily accessible text-to-image generation amplifies demographic stereotypes at large scale. In *Proceedings of the 2023 ACM conference on fairness, accountability, and transparency* (pp. 1493–1504).
3. Bolukbasi, T., Chang, K. W., Zou, J. Y., Saligrama, V., & Kalai, A. T. (2016). Man is to computer programmer as woman is to homemaker? debiasing word embeddings. In *Advances in neural information processing systems* (Vol. 29).
4. Caliskan, A., Bryson, J. J., & Narayanan, A. (2017). Semantics derived automatically from language corpora contain human-like biases. *Science, 356*(6334), 183–186.
5. Cho, J., Zala, A., & Bansal, M. (2023). Dall-eval: Probing the reasoning skills and social biases of text-to-image generation models. In *Proceedings of the IEEE/CVF international conference on computer vision* (pp. 3043–3054).
6. Fraser, K. C., Kiritchenko, S., & Nejadgholi, I. (2023). A friendly face: Do text-to-image systems rely on stereotypes when the input is under-specified? arXiv preprint arXiv:2302.07159
7. Hendrick, C., & Costantini, A. F. (1970). Effects of varying trait inconsistency and response requirements on the primacy effect in impression formation. *Journal of Personality and Social Psychology, 15*(2), 158.
8. Hogarth, R. M., & Einhorn, H. J. (1992). Order effects in belief updating: The belief-adjustment model. *Cognitive Psychology, 24*(1), 1–55.
9. Jones, E. E., Rock, L., Shaver, K. G., Goethals, G. R., & Ward, L. M. (1968). Pattern of performance and ability attribution: An unexpected primacy effect. *Journal of Personality and Social Psychology, 10*(4), 317.
10. Kashima, Y. (2000). Maintaining cultural stereotypes in the serial reproduction of narratives. *Personality and Social Psychology Bulletin, 26*(5), 594–604.

11. London, M., & Hakel, M. D. (1974). Effects of applicant stereotypes, order, and information on interview impressions.
12. Mogaji, E., Viglia, G., Srivastava, P., & Dwivedi, Y. K. (2024). Is it the end of the technology acceptance model in the era of generative artificial intelligence? *International Journal of Contemporary Hospitality Management*.
13. Murdock, J., & Bennet, B. (1962). The serial position effect of free recall. *Journal of Experimental Psychology, 64*(5), 482.
14. Naik, R., & Nushi, B. (2023). Social biases through the text-to-image generation lens. arXiv preprint arXiv:2304.06034
15. Ramesh, A., Dhariwal, P., Nichol, A., Chu, C., & Chen, M. (2022). Hierarchical text-conditional image generation with clip latents. arXiv preprint arXiv:2204.06125 **1**(2), 3 (2022)
16. Ramesh, A., Pavlov, M., Goh, G., Gray, S., Voss, C., Radford, A., Chen, M., & Sutskever, I. (2021). Zero-shot text-to-image generation. In *International conference on machine learning* (pp. 8821–8831). PMLR.
17. Saharia, C., Chan, W., Saxena, S., Li, L., Whang, J., Denton, E. L., Ghasemipour, K., Gontijo Lopes, R., Karagol Ayan, B., Salimans, T., et al. (2022). Photorealistic text-to-image diffusion models with deep language understanding. *Advances in Neural Information Processing Systems, 35*, 36479–36494.
18. Seshadri, P., Singh, S., & Elazar, Y. (2023). The bias amplification paradox in text-to-image generation. arXiv preprint arXiv:2308.00755
19. Sheeran, P., & Webb, T. L. (2016). The intention-behavior gap. *Social and Personality Psychology Compass, 10*(9), 503–518.
20. Steiner, D. D., & Rain, J. S. (1989). Immediate and delayed primacy and recency effects in performance evaluation. *Journal of Applied Psychology, 74*(1), 136.
21. Stewart, R. H. (1965). Effect of continuous responding on the order effect in personality impression formation. *Journal of Personality and Social Psychology, 1*(2), 161.
22. Tetlock, P. (1983). Accountability and the perseverance of first impressions. *Social Psychology Quarterly*, 285–292.
23. Wan, Y., & Chang, K. W. (2024). The male ceo and the female assistant: Probing gender biases in text-to-image models through paired stereotype test. arXiv preprint arXiv:2402.11089

The Impact of the EU AI Act's Transparency Requirements on AI Innovation

Luca Holst, Valentin Mayer, Luis Lämmermann, Nils Urbach, and Domenik Wendt

Abstract The increasing capabilities of Artificial Intelligence (AI) raise concerns about the risks associated with the technology. The European Union, therefore, proposed the Artificial Intelligence Act aiming to mitigate the risks of AI by fostering their safety and transparency. However, there is controversial debate about its impact on AI innovation. While the AI Act aims to provide legal certainty guiding innovation, the criticism refers to exaggerated bureaucratic burden such as transparency requirements impeding innovation. Based on a multivocal literature review, we examine the impact of the AI Act's transparency requirements on patenting as a means for AI innovation. Our results indicate that the transparency requirements do not necessarily hinder the patentability of AI innovations. Instead, existing concerns primarily rely on uncertainties within key terms of the AI Act. Accordingly, we propose an improvement suggestion focusing on resolving existing uncertainties.

L. Holst · V. Mayer (✉)
University of Bayreuth, Bayreuth, Germany
e-mail: valentin.mayer@fim-rc.de

L. Holst
e-mail: luca.holst@uni-bayreuth.de

V. Mayer · L. Lämmermann · N. Urbach
Branch Business & Information Systems, Engineering of the Fraunhofer FIT, Bayreuth, Germany

FIM Research Center, Bayreuth, Germany

L. Lämmermann
e-mail: luis.laemmermann@fit.fraunhofer.de

N. Urbach
e-mail: nils.urbach@fb3.fra-uas.de

L. Lämmermann · N. Urbach · D. Wendt
Frankfurt University of Applied Science, Frankfurt, Germany
e-mail: wendt@fb3.fra-uas.de

C. M. Flath et al. (eds.), *Artificial Intelligence, Data, and Decision-Making*, Lecture Notes in Information Systems and Organisation 82,
https://doi.org/10.1007/978-3-032-08480-4_10

1 Introduction

The rapidly advancing AI capabilities and associated risks have fueled the need for regulation and governance of AI systems. As a consequence, the European Union introduced the AI Act inducing pivotal change in the regulatory landscape which significantly influence the AI innovation capabilities of firms. The goal of the AI Act is "to improve the functioning of the internal market and promote the uptake of human-centric and trustworthy [AI], while ensuring a high level of protection of health, safety [and] fundamental rights [...] against the harmful effects of [AI systems] in the Union, and to support innovation" (Art. 1 (1) AI Act as adopted on March 13, 2024). Although experts welcomed the AI Act recognizing it as a significant milestone in regulating AI (Cozzi et al., 2023), the potential benefits of the AI Act for the EU as a "global leader in developing secure, trustworthy, and ethical AI" (European Council, 2020, p. 6) are uncertain. While previous research recognizes the transparency as one of the main rationales behind the AI Act (Li, 2023; Panigutti et al., 2023), its impact on the innovation remains unclear. For instance, transparency requirements of the AI Act impede innovation could potentially restrict the firms' ability to protect AI innovation as intellectual property. Thus, we ask: What is the impact of the AI Act's transparency requirements on patenting as a tool for commercializing AI innovations?

To answer our research question, we conduct a multivocal literature review examining the impact of the AI Act's transparency requirements on patenting as a means for AI innovation. We rely on both academic and non-academic literature, as the AI Act has just been passed and academic literature rigorously evaluating the effects of the AI Act on innovations is scarce. Thus, a multivocal literature review is suitable, capturing up to date business perspectives (DIHK, 2023), approaches to patent law (Lankinen, 2019) and transparency within AI (Hacker & Passoth, 2022).

Our results indicate that the transparency requirements may affect innovation, yet, they are unlikely to have a significant impact on innovative ability if the legislator clarifies specific requirements and legal definitions of terms used in the AI Act. Our paper addresses the research gap on the link between transparency requirements and innovation, potentially shedding light on improvements to AI regulations to ensure benefitting companies. We conclude that the transparency mandates of the AI Act do not hinder patentability of AI inventions. However, the number of patents may still reduce because of the uncertain level of transparency required under the AI Act resulting from undefined key terms. Finally, we give an improvement suggestion to the legislators on how to clear up this uncertainty to prevent any negative impact caused by the AI Act on the innovative ability of companies. We consider our results, which are grounded in the current body of literature, as a valuable starting point that requires further empirical data from business field studies and expert opinions.

2 Background

2.1 Possibilities of Economic Usability and Requirements for the Patentability of Technical Inventions

Economic usability means the adequate form of monetization or sale of objects or intellectual property (IP), to generate financial proceeds (white ip, 2021). One possibility of monetization of AI innovation is technological leadership, meaning that the innovation is sufficiently advanced so that other companies do not have the means to copy it. Secondly, companies can keep the functioning of their AI innovations a trade secret. As there is few public information available on the number of AI innovations protected through technological leadership and AI trade secrets, these options are unsuitable to be analyzed by our research. A further look is taken at legal instruments allowing protection to the use of AI innovation. For simplicity, the legal situation in most member states of the EU will be the scale for the following remarks which is possible as IP law is largely harmonized. Copyrights are initially owned by the creator of a work (Ginsburg, 2017) and can be licensed. While trademark rights and rights of distinguishing marks protect the identification of products as belonging to a company (DPMA a, 2024), registered design focuses on a product's appearance (DPMA b, 2021). Therefore, these options are not suitable as measures for economic usability of AI. Patents and (the unharmonized!) utility models have the same requirements (European Commission, o. D.) and offer their owners the same saleable and licensable rights (DPMA c, 2020). The process of granting a utility model, however, is faster in return its protection expires faster (DPMA d, 2021). The requirements of utility models are not examined in the registration procedure (European Commission, o. D.), which increases the risk of them being challenged or cancelled. Patents on the other side are more commonly registered than utility models (DPMA e, 2023; DPMA f, 2023).

Overall, patents represent a good measure of economic usability to be considered in context of the AI Act as patent law is harmonized across the EU, refers to the product itself and is commonly used for economic usability. In contrast to copyright, it protects the functionality or the idea, procedure, or method of operation itself and not just format and expression of the idea (Art. 9 (2) TRIPS, 1994) which plays a secondary role regarding AI inventions. Moreover, the number of granted patents is established as an indicator of innovation within academic literature (Bahoo et al., 2023; Igna & Venturini, 2023; Van Roy et al., 2020).

The requirements for registering a patent are novelty, inventive step, industrial applicability of the innovation and technical character. According to Art. 54 EPC, novelty is given if the invention "does not form part of the state of the art" with the latter being "everything made available to the public by means of a written or oral description, by use, or in any other way". The invention involves an inventive step if it is not obvious to a skilled practitioner in the relevant field of technology with average knowledge and ability (European Patent Office (EPO), 2024). As indication for industrial applicability (Art. 57 EPC), it could have a "sound and concrete technical basis [so] that the skilled person can recognize that [the invention's] contribution to the art could lead to practical exploitation in industry" (EPO a, 2006). Lastly a technical character of the invention is required (EPO b, 2006).

2.2 The AI Act and Its Transparency Requirements

AI systems are assigned to a risk category according to the risk their use poses especially to fundamental rights and Union values (Explanatory Memorandum in Proposal for AI Act, COM/2021/206 final, 2021). The risk categories are minimal or no risk, limited risk, high risk and unacceptable risk. Depending on the risk category of an AI system, it must meet certain requirements, except for AI systems posing an unacceptable risk which will be completely banned. Limited risk AI systems interacting with natural persons and general-purpose AI (GPAI) systems must only meet certain transparency obligations as set out in Art. 52 respectively Art. 52c AI Act. AI systems with minimal risk do not have to follow any obligations.

If we take a closer look at a possible definition of transparency to consider which provisions of the AI Act should be grouped under this term, we find that transparency is interpreted differently depending on the subject under consideration. Within transparency in the context of regulatory frameworks, a differentiation is made between enabling, technical, and protective transparency (Hacker & Passoth, 2022). Enabling transparency distinguishes between rights-enabling, review-enabling, and decision-enabling transparency (Hacker & Passoth, 2022). The ability of individuals to exercise their rights against the AI system falls under rights-enabling transparency, while the ability to make informed decisions is subsumed under decision-enabling transparency (Hacker & Passoth, 2022). Review-enabling transparency enables to initiate legal reviews of the AI system (Hacker & Passoth, 2022). Technical transparency means informed decision making on the side of technical operators of the system who might improve the functioning of the AI application (Hacker & Passoth, 2022). Lastly, protective transparency describes the opportunity to reduce significant risks being posed from AI systems (Hacker & Passoth, 2022).

Next, we discuss which transparency requirements result from the AI Act (as adopted on March 13, 2024) considering these transparency definitions. The main transparency requirements can be found in Art. 13 AI Act. According to that, high-risk AI systems, including open-source AI systems, "shall be designed and developed in such a way to ensure that their operation is sufficiently transparent to enable deployers to interpret the system's output and use it appropriately". They "shall be accompanied by instructions for use [...] that include concise, complete, correct and clear information that is relevant, accessible and comprehensible to deployers", including i.e. characteristics, capabilities, and limitations of performance of the AI system. These requirements contribute to the aim of understandable AI systems, and output being interpretable. The information to be provided will enable providers to assess for themselves the risks of AI decision-making, in particular the risk of biased algorithms and possible gaps in data protection. It also facilitates surveillance by supervisory organizations or other third parties.

According to Art. 50 AI Act, AI systems must be designed and developed in such a way that natural persons are informed interacting with an AI system and, where appropriate, are provided with further information. Natural persons shall also be informed, and their consent be obtained if they are exposed to an emotion recognition system or biometric categorization system and deep fakes must be disclosed as such.

Disclosing certain information to register a high-risk AI system in a public EU database according to Art. 49, 71 AI Act is a decision- and review-enabling transparency measure. The additional disclosure of contact details of the provider may be important as it gives a user the option to exercise rights against him regarding the infringement of his personal rights. Lastly, affected parties have the right to explanation of individual decision-making taken by the deployer regarding the role of the AI system in the decision-making procedure, main parameters of the decision and related input data under some conditions (Art. 68c). In summary, the AI Act contains rules fulfilling all definitions of transparency. However, as the AI Act only uses the term "transparency" within 13 and 50 AI Act, the focus will be on these articles.

3 Research Method

Although an academic literature review that solely includes peer-reviewed papers is the optimum to ensure the quality of the research under consideration, it would be insufficient and not expedient to gain a comprehensive insight because of the small number of papers on such an emerging topic being published yet. Therefore, we believe that a multivocal literature review is an appropriate method to obtain a broader range of assessments of the research question. That means that apart from academic literature, we consider "grey literature", meaning literature which is produced at all levels of government, academia, business, industry in print and electronic form, but is not controlled by commercial publishers (Farace & Schöpfel, 2010). To identify relevant academic literature, we first defined a suitable search string. To this end, we included the three major components of the research question, being "AI" "Act" and "transparency" or "patent". To avoid the possibility of exclusion of relevant literature, we added synonyms or generic terms, leading to the final search string:

(Act OR Legislation OR Law OR Regulation) AND (Transparency OR Innovation OR Patent OR "Intellectual Property" OR IP) AND (AI OR "Artificial Intelligence" OR "Machine Learning").

We applied this search string to two reputable databases for academic literature, Web of Science and Beck-online, to cover both general scientific and legal literature. As Beck-online is a German database, we translated the search string. Considering all papers and essays on the databases published before January 1, 2024, we identified 855 academic papers. Then, we set criteria to exclude items that (1) were published before January 1, 2017, and (2) were not available in English or German. Content-related, we excluded papers that discussed AI-generated innovations instead of the innovations being AI systems, and papers that set a non-European or too specific focus like AI innovations in healthcare etc. We applied these criteria in title, abstract, and full-text screening leading to 17 papers being left. Through backward and forward search, in which we used the reference list of found papers or citations to them to identify additional items, we did not add any papers to the final set as the cited literature usually was too specific to answer another question but this papers' question.

For identifying grey literature, using the search string in search engines would have led to a variety of results lacking qualitative discussions as blog entries, newspaper articles and so on often only represent the views of a single person without underlying in-depth analysis of the topic. This is a risk to be considered regarding grey literature as it does not follow a peer-reviewed publishing process. Therefore, and despite the risk of a too narrow research, we focused the grey literature research specifically on the most important players with expertise in the legal and / or AI sector including business consulting companies like McKinsey & Company, major law firms like Taylor Wessing and industry associations like the Chamber of Commerce and Industry. To this end, we filtered their websites through a website-intern search function for results referring to the "AI Act". We only included position papers, expert statements etc. in the research. We excluded literature that is not available in full or in English, search results that did not contribute to the state of knowledge, and results that did not include well-founded critical appraisal as the result of an investigation. Additionally, we used material from the website of the EPO regarding "Artificial Intelligence" as the aspect of patentability of AI was not made a main topic in the found literature but is essential to properly answer the research question. As found literature did mostly not cite other sources, we found only one paper in the backward and forward search.

Following Gramlich et al. (2023), to ensure a qualitative selection of literature, we evaluated our literature sample according to certain criteria categories: authority of the producer, objectivity of the source, methodology, date, related sources, novelty, and impact. If we rated the item as negative in most of the categories, meaning in at least four of the named categories, we excluded it from further consideration. Ultimately, we obtained 12 grey literature sources for the final set. Thereby, we finally maintained a set of 29 literature sources for a multivocal analysis.

4 Results

We categorized the grey and academic literature sources as follows: First, we analyzed the focus of the item analyzed and second, we determined whether the item provided an improvement concept (see Table 1).

Items published before the AI Act's proposal gave us important implications to evaluate improvement concepts although they could not refer to the Act itself.

Table 1 Focus of the items and existence of concepts

Focus of the items	
AI Act's transparency requirements (17)	Bell et al. (2023), Bomhard and Merkle (2021), Buiten (2019), Ebers et al. (2021), Gacutan and Selvadurai (2020), German AI Association (2023), Hacker and Berz (2023), Hacker and Passoth (2022), Hupont et al. (2023), Nannini et al. (2023), Nastasa et al. (2023), Panigutti et al. (2023), PwC (2023), Raposo (2022), Reed (2018), VDA (2023), Wojtczak & Księżak (2021)
Connection between AI Act requirements without a focus on transparency or innovative ability (6)	Applied AI Initiative (2022), Block et al. (2023), Bomhard and Merkle (2021), DIHK (2023), Meyer (2018), Mylly (2023), Verdi (2022)
Connection between transparency requirements and innovative ability or trade secrets (7)	Bitkom (2023), Buiten (2019), DIHK (2023), DIHK (2021), Nastasa et al. (2023), Raposo (2022), Wojtczak & Księżak (2021)
Patentability of AI (5)	Bailas and Thums (2018), EPO (2023), EPO (2009), Lankinen (2019), Méniere and Pihlajamaa (2019)
Existence of concept	
Items including improvement concepts (6)	Bell et al. (2023), Buiten (2019), Gacutan and Selvadurai (2020), German AI Association (2023), Hacker and Berz (2023), Reed (2018)
Items not including improvement concepts (17)	appliedAI Initiative (2023), Bitkom (2023), Bomhard and Merkle (2021), DIHK (2023), DIHK (2021), Ebers et al. (2021), Hacker and Passoth (2022), Meyer (2018), Mylly (2023), Nannini et al. (2023), Nastasa et al. (2023), Panigutti et al. (2023), PwC (2023), Raposo (2022), VDA (2023), Verdi (2022), Wojtczak & Księżak (2021)

4.1 Patentability of AI

While three of the four prerequisites of patentability (novelty, inventive step, and industrial applicability) do not show any special features in the patentability of AI systems, the technical character of AI inventions is discussed more strongly. Inventions involving computer programs that solely implement mathematical methods are not patentable according to Art. 52 (2) and (3) EPC. The mathematical method or algorithm of the AI needs to be used in a technical process carried out on a physical entity by technical means resulting in a change of the physical entity to be patentable (Lankinen, 2019). Besides technical character, the invention must describe a not purely abstract or intellectual concept and be implemented by using a computer, computer network or other programmable apparatus with technical effect (Bailas &

Thums, 2018). Thereto, the invention has to be described "sufficiently clear[ly] and complete[ly] to be carried out by persons skilled in the art" (EPO, 2024, p. 401). It was mentioned that in the drafting of claims, "black boxes" shall be avoided (Bailas & Thums, 2018). Additionally, the EPO approved that, when AI relies on mathematical methods, they must be disclosed in sufficient detail so that the invention can be reproduced (European Patent Office, 2023). Disclosing the source code is not per se necessary (EPO, 2009) although algorithm and training data are often needed to reproduce the AI invention in practice (Méniere & Pihlajamaa, 2019). However, unveiling the mathematical methods and algorithms might not be clear enough to fulfil the patent requirements because of the lack of understanding of machine learning and possibilities to track the steps of the AI system in its output generation. Lankinen proposes that the definition of input and output of an AI system might be sufficient for a skilled practitioner in the relevant field of technology—here being AI—to understand the innovation's extent of protection and crucial features but questions whether the process leading to the output must be explained as well (2019).

In summary, the patentability of AI does not overly differ from the patentability of other products. The issue would lie on the obligation to disclose further information about the AI system in the patent application to properly explain the functioning of the system to the person skilled in the art. This is significant for "black box" AI systems in which even the developer of the system may not understand the decision-making process. Apart from that, the requirements for the patentability of AI systems were not evaluated as innovation-inhibiting indicated by the tripling of the number of AI inventions registered by the EPO between 2010 and 2017 (Méniere & Pihlajamaa, 2019).

4.2 AI Act Transparency Requirements and Innovative Ability

After we determined the specialties in the patentability of AI systems, we evaluated the influence of transparency requirements in this regard. First, we analyzed what kind of challenges to the transparency requirements are addressed in the literature.

A non-scientific survey conducted by the appliedAI initiative (2022) found that at least a third of the startups would classify themselves as high-risk AI systems whereas the assumption of the EU Commission was at most 15%. This is important as the transparency obligations of Art. 13 would under this assumption be applicable for way more startups than estimated. The survey found that more than 50% of the startups see the obligation to transparency and provision of information to users at least as "somewhat difficult". This concern is shared especially regarding missing technical abilities of AI systems to justify their decisions comprehensibly (Bomhard & Merkle, 2021; Buiten, 2019; PwC, 2023; Raposo, 2022. Existing explainability methods are often not practical as they are imprecise, vulnerable for attacks, inconsistent and many AI designers are unaware of these methods (Nannini et al., 2023; Panigutti et al., 2023). In addition, a relatively complex AI system might even be harder to explain in a way that is understood by individuals (Gacutan & Selvadurai, 2020; PwC, 2023). Raposo (2022), however, counters this by stating that not a precise understanding of the AI System but rather the main limitations of the system and its shortcomings are subject to transparency requirements of the AI Act. Panigutti et al. (2023) suggest that the transparency requirements of the AI Act can be met by describing the action, including the intended use, and by explaining how the system can be used, with detailed instructions for use and outputs, and by creating an ideally simple and consistent human-AI interface design alongside human oversight measures. This course could signal when the AI system is uncertain or unable to provide an answer, the system could provide a range of outputs rather than a single word answer or encourage user evaluation before generating an output (Panigutti et al., 2023). Moreover, Bomhard and Merkle comment that notices to be given to users according to Art. 52 AI Act-E (new Art. 50 AI Act) must be discreet and sufficiently transparent at the same time (2021), in any case, risk adequate (VDA, 2023). The VDA criticizes in this matter the vague wording "obvious from the circumstances and the context of use" in Art. 52 (1) AI Act-E (now Art. 50 AI Act) (2023).

Although the risk-based approach in transparency is appreciated (Buiten, 2019; DIHK, 2021; Ebers et al., 2021), a discussion about the inclusion of stricter transparency requirements particularly for GPAI systems has come up. The European Digital SME Alliance (2022) encouraged stricter rules on AI systems for the benefit of smaller players, while the German AI Association (2023) noted that transparency requirements were unproportionate to the level of risk and specific use cases. This is supported by the assumption that GPAI systems could be particularly challenged by the obligation of transparency, as they tend to be extremely complex due to their development through the accumulation of multiple AI systems (Nannini et al., 2023). In addition, Bitkom noted that transparency obligations would go far beyond the purpose of product safety and market regulation (2023).

A key point of criticism is that the way in which transparency and interpretability are to be implemented remains unclear, making it impossible to define them and thus to ensure legal certainty. (Bell et al., 2023; Ebers et al., 2021; Gacutan & Selvadurai, 2020; Nannini et al., 2023; Nastasa et al., 2023). The term of "sufficient transparency" in Art. 13 AI Act adds to the uncertainty but gives the provider leeway in the interpretation (Nannini et al., 2023). However, some state-of-the-art AI and dataset transparency approaches have been found to be "highly suitable to provide concise and accessible technical information for users of high-risk AI systems" (Hupont et al., 2023, p. 26), which implies that an overall standard for Art. 13 might become subject to a standard already being used currently. Only little extensions must be made to guarantee that users understand and use high-risk AI systems properly (Hupont et al., 2023). However, it is questionable whether the information to be disclosed is useful at all as the information provided would rarely be understandable for users without AI development or practice (Hacker & Passoth, 2022). It remains problematic that providers can generally self-certify that they meet the transparency requirements, which makes enforcement of this provision difficult, and leaves open the possibility of ethical whitewashing. (Hacker & Passoth, 2022; Nannini et al., 2023). Nevertheless, the AI Act's transparency obligations around use, documentation and data quality are assessed as an overall successful part of the AI Act (Hacker & Berz, 2023; Reed, 2018).

Two-thirds of startups surveyed by the appliedAI initiative (2022) expect the AI Act to have a negative impact on AI innovation in their own startups, and almost 80% of venture capitalists see a decline in the competitiveness of EU-based AI startups. These findings should, however, be treated with caution as they solely result from named non-scientific study. According to the European Digital SME Association (2022), the requirements of the AI Act will overburden small and medium-sized enterprises (SMEs) with high compliance costs. This is of specific importance as SMEs are on top of innovation in the EU (DIHK, 2023). It also notes that unclear and unspecific rules that do not provide the necessary legal certainty in the use of AI systems could risk hampering innovation. (Bomhard & Merkle, 2021; DIHK, 2023; Verdi, 2022).

It is mentioned that the transparency obligations of the AI Act carry the risk of disclosing trade secrets and proprietary information (Bitkom, 2023; DIHK, 2021; Nastasa et al., 2023; VDA, 2023; Wojtczak & Księżak, 2021). Specifically, the underlying algorithms of an AI system are complex, difficult to develop and create the unique selling point of a business model, and therefore must not be disclosed (DIHK, 2021). In this regard, Mylly (2023) clarified that the requirements under the AI Act rarely contain information categorized as trade secrets, especially a disclosure to legislative instruments does not qualify as the disclosure of a trade secret. Additionally, it must be noted that the information to be disclosed is usually excluded from trade secret protection (Mylly, 2023) or loses its status as a trade secret with its availability for public. Nevertheless, public availability of information comes with the liberty of use by the public without infringing IP rights (Mylly, 2023), which might not lie in the interest of AI inventors (PwC, 2023). In general, there are fears that disproportional obligations will create a competitive risk and inhibit for startups and investors (Bitkom, 2023; Buiten, 2019). However, the DIHK (2023) points out that the reliability and transparency of foundation models will play a crucial role for the successful use of an AI system in the market, especially regarding a value chain between deployers and users. Nastasa et al. (2023) see the transparency requirements as crucial to build citizen trust.

4.3 Improvement Concepts for the Transparency Requirements of the AI Act

The appliedAI initiative (2022) proposes reducing high-risk cases of AI systems so that no more than 15% of such systems are affected. It emphasizes the importance of considering the needs of AI startups. Similarly, Bell et al. (2023) suggest a stakeholder-first approach, which involves establishing stakeholders, goals, and purposes for transparency requirements that meet the needs of the system's users. This should be done under a transparency method chosen by a technologist. In relation to the issue of transparency in black box AI systems, Buiten (2019) proposed an approach suggesting that disclosing potential flaws and risks of the AI system in a way that is both understandable and technically feasible could be sufficient to support the informed decision-making by users. This approach prioritizes problem-solving and risk management in technology by identifying biases through learning from existing data and testing. This is considered a feasible method for achieving transparency in algorithms, while also considering the associated costs and benefits for the specific requirements. The focus is on transparency of the technology rather than subjective evaluations (Buiten, 2019). The German AI Association (2023) proposes an approach for regulating foundation models, in the latest draft GPAI systems. According to this approach, developers of foundation models are only required to make documentation available to authorities upon request, as a transparency requirement. Commercial providers that use foundation models must inform end users understandably about "[...] the model's power and limitations [...]" (German AI Association, 2023, p. 11) instead of requiring higher levels of traceability and explainability. Finally, it is proposed that Art. 52 of the AI Act should include an obligation to label works generated by AI systems using cryptography or watermarks. This will enable third parties to verify whether a post is a generated work (Hacker & Berz, 2023). In summary, while transparency requirements are seen as a positive step, there is strong debate about the specifics of their implementation. A uniform suggestion for improvement is barely discernible.

5 Discussion

Overall, it appears that transparency requirements have little impact on the patentability of AI. The AI Act's criticism did not mention patentability, suggesting its limited significance in this regard. The disclosure of how AI systems function could result in a quicker advancement in the state of the art, as required by Art. 54 EPC. This could make it more challenging to obtain a patent for AI systems that only show minor progress compared to similar-functioning AI systems. However, if the AI system serves a different purpose that is reflected in technical terms, novelty could still be fulfilled. Since transparency mandates do not affect the economic usability or technical character of the invention, they only play a limited role in the patent application of AI systems.

It is uncertain whether transparency obligations have a negative impact on innovative ability. One concern raised is the level of transparency required for certain AI systems under Art. 13 AI Act. The complexity of GPAI systems has raised concerns about the transparency of their operations. The issue, however, is not an explainable design of an AI system but the uncertainty of the terms the AI Act used. For example, the terms "transparency" and "interpretability" are not defined. The assumption that definitions are the crucial issue is supported by the statement of several interest groups that unclear regulations could hinder innovation (Bomhard & Merkle, 2021; DIHK, 2023; Verdi, 2022). Inventors could under this assumption be deterred by the uncertainty and refrain from inventing AI systems, leading to a decline in patenting. There is also a widespread concern that transparency obligations may inhibit innovation, particularly in the startup sector (appliedAI initiative, 2022; DIHK, 2023; Verdi, 2022). It is unclear whether all AI Act regulations can be evaluated solely based on transparency regulations. When concerns were raised about overregulation, they were often overlooked and instead portrayed as just one piece of a larger bureaucratic burden. Next, even though the fear of disclosing trade secrets through the requirement of Art. 13 AI Act was dispelled by Mylly (2023), inventors fear that their business model could be revealed under the amount of information to be publicly disclosed. This statement appears to be unfounded. To obtain a patent, an invention must be described in sufficient detail to enable a person skilled in the relevant field to carry it out. This requirement is equivalent to a certain level of transparency, which is not affected by the transparency obligations of the AI Act. This can be countered by the fact that the disclosure in patent application is only made to authorities and not users. Nevertheless, as stated by the DIHK (2023), transparency obligations are crucial for the successful use of an AI system on the market and therefore increase innovative ability.

However, it is uncertain whether addressing the issues is adequate. As two third of startup owners anticipate a negative impact from the AI Act and AI innovation on their own startups, providers are already biased towards the development of AI systems. Therefore, we recommend policymakers to clarify the practical implications of the AI Act obligations, including transparency requirements, to eliminate this bias.

Improvement proposals in the literature aim to balance user information, limit risks from AI systems, and consider the interests of system deployers. This forms the basis for the following improvement suggestion. Firstly, the AI Act should legally define the term 'interpretability' to allow for the development of black box AI systems on the EU market without violating transparency requirements. Secondly, it is encouraged to implement the approach of Hacker and Berz (2023) to label works created by generative AI through cryptography or watermarks as a transparency requirement. This will strengthen public trust in AI systems.

Further consideration of European competitiveness and stakeholder needs is necessary. The burden of compliance costs on SMEs should be compensated to encourage informed decisions. Transparency requirements regarding SMEs should not be reduced as users cannot differentiate between the types of companies behind AI systems. Reducing high-risk cases is also not expedient. Restricting the application of AI systems could result in significant loss of trust and potentially undermine the EU's unique selling proposition of providing trustworthy AI systems to support businesses. Standardized templates could be provided as a guide for fulfilling transparency obligations and understanding the transparency requirements. The named improvement suggestions aim to clarify uncertainties and dispel bias towards an overburden of compliance requirements for deployers of AI systems. This should encourage innovation in the AI sector, leading to an increase in patents and innovation in the EU.

The research on the AI Act is expected to expand radically as the AI Act was just passed in March 2024, which is why this paper is based on just a minute part of criticism of the AI Act. Additionally, research was conducted using two databases covering legal and general scientific literature, including a backward and forward search, as well as carefully selected position papers and statements by 'big players' in the legal, AI, and economic sectors. The text could benefit from the inclusion of sociological aspects to better understand the effects of transparency on user behavior. The research was mainly limited to a search string, which posed a risk of missing relevant items, despite the inclusion of synonyms to avoid excluding too many papers. Most gray literature items are views by interest groups representing potential providers of AI systems. They could possibly describe the situation one-sidedly focusing on burdens for providers without acknowledging benefits for deployers. Lastly, it must be noted that the base of this paper relies on an interplay of predictions and does not display empirical research.

Based on our results that are grounded on the current state of literature on the transparency requirements of the AI Act, future research could focus on empirical findings. Future research should examine options to support SMEs in coping with the compliance requirements under the AI Act to further support innovation. Furthermore, it is important to explore options for meeting the transparency requirements outlined in the AI Act when deploying a black box AI system. This investigation may result in the development of a standardized template that the European Parliament can propose to guide deployers of AI systems.

This paper contributes to academic research on transparency requirements of the AI Act and provides legal insight into the practical reality of deploying AI systems. It aims to clarify the uncertainty surrounding transparency obligations and address current concerns. Although no severe obstacles were found that could decrease the EU's innovative ability through transparency requirements, this paper appeals to European legislators to address the gaps found within these requirements, particularly the lack of legal definitions, and to provide a concept for how they can be fulfilled to achieve legal certainty.

6 Conclusion

This paper examines the transparency requirements proposed in the AI Act in relation to the patentability of AI within the EU. While some expressed concerns that these requirements may hinder innovation, most of the criticism has been directed towards the rules for high-risk and GPAI systems, and specifically towards the possible interpretations of terms in the AI Act that are not yet legally defined. The need for transparency in patent applications does not necessarily preclude the patentability of black box AI systems. We assume that the same applies to transparency regulations under the AI Act, but legal definitions of key terms related to transparency within the AI Act are still needed. Improvement suggestions in the literature were only partially helpful in maintaining a balance between protecting the rights of users of AI systems and complying with the associated costs of deployment. This often depends on the respective interest group represented in position papers. Our research identified weaknesses in regulations from an economic perspective opening the door for further improvement.

For citations of references, we prefer the use of square brackets and consecutive numbers. Citations using labels or the author/year convention are also acceptable. The following bibliography provides a sample reference list with entries for journal articles [1], an LNCS chapter [2], a book [3], proceedings without editors [4], as well as a URL [5].

References

appliedAI initiative. (2022, December 12). *AI-act Impact Survey, Pan-European Survey of AI Startups and Vcs About The Impact of The AI Act, Appliedai Initiative.* https://www.appliedai.de/assets/files/AI-Act-Impact-Survey_Slides_Dec12.2022.pdf. (accessed: March 14, 2024).

Bahoo, S., Cucculelli, M., & Qamar, D. (2023). Artificial Intelligence and Corporate Innovation: A Review and Research Agenda. *Technological Forecasting and Social Change, 188*, S. 122264. https://doi.org/10.1016/j.techfore.2022.122264.

Bailas, A., & Thums, D. (2018, June 5). *Patentability of AI Related Inventions – The EPO Perspective.* https://www.grur.org/uploads/tx_meeting/05_EPO_GRUR_BRU_30_05_final_v4.pptx (accessed: March 14, 2024).

Bell, A., Nov, O., & Stoyanovich, J. (2023). Think About The Stakeholders First! Toward An Algorithmic Transparency Playbook for Regulatory Compliance. *Data & Policy, 5.* https://doi.org/10.1017/dap.2023.8.

Bitkom. (2023, November). Bitkom *Position on the AI Act Trilogue Negotiations on requirements referring to copyright, Bitkom.* https://www.bitkom.org/sites/main/files/2023-11/bitkom-position-paper-ai-act-trilogue-requirements-copyright112023.pdf (accessed: March 14, 2024).

Block, M., Jung, C., & Wendt, D. (2023). Requirements for legal tech AI systems—Reflections on the negotiated AI act with regard to legal technology using AI. *Computer Law Review International, 24*(4).

Bomhard, D., & Merkle, M. (2021). Regulation of Artificial Intelligence—The EU Commision's Proposal of an AI Act. *EuCML*, (6), 257–262. https://beck-online.beck.de/Dokument?vpath=bibdata%2Fzeits%2Feucml%2F2021%2Fcont%2Feucml.2021.257.1.htm&pos=1&hlwords=on (accessed: March 14, 2024).

Buiten, M. C. (2019). Towards Intelligent Regulation of Artificial Intelligence. *European Journal of Risk Regulation, 10*(1), 41–59. https://doi.org/10.1017/err.2019.8

Cozzi, F., Mechelli, S., Maisnier-Boché, L., Moruzzi, M., & Arzuaga, P. (2023, July 31). *The EU Artificial Intelligence Act: What's the impact? MWE*, https://www.mwe.com/insights/the-eu-artificial-intelligence-act-whats-the-impact/ (accessed: March 14, 2024).

DIHK. (2021, August 5). Zu dem Vorschlag der EU-Kommission für ein Europäisches Gesetz über Künstliche Intelligenz (in German), DIHK. https://www.dihk.de/resource/blob/56630/41978574822e9ed4283e8d67f48a73a8/dihk-stellungnahme-ki-gesetz-data.pdf (accessed: March 14, 2024).

DIHK. (2023, November 15). DIHK-Impulspapier zum AI Act (in German), DIHK. https://www.dihk.de/resource/blob/108286/ced2065567fb479044a9c34084cd0acb/dihk-impulspapier-ai-act-und-weitere-data.pdf (accessed: March 14, 2024).

DPMA a | Trade Mark Protection. (2024, March 21). *German Patent and Trade Mark Office.* https://www.dpma.de/english/trade_marks/trade_mark_protection/index.html (accessed: March 14, 2024).

DPMA b | Design protection. (2021, March 21). *German Patent and Trade Mark Office*. https://www.dpma.de/english/designs/design_protection/index.html (accessed: March 14, 2024).
DPMA c | Utility Models. (2020, October 20). *German Patent and Trade Mark Office*. https://www.dpma.de/english/utility_models/index.html (accessed: March 14, 2024).
DPMA d | FAQ. (2021, July 21). *German Patent and Trade Mark Office*. https://www.dpma.de/english/utility_models/faq/index.html (accessed: March 14, 2024).
DPMA e | Patents. (2023, June 22). *German Patent and Trade Mark Office*. https://www.dpma.de/english/our_office/publications/statistics/patents/index.html (accessed: March 14, 2024).
DPMA f | Utility Models. (2023, June 22). *German Patent and Trade Mark Office*. https://www.dpma.de/english/our_office/publications/statistics/utility_models/index.html (accessed: March 14, 2024).
Ebers, M., Hoch, V. R. S., Rosenkranz, F., Ruschemeier, H., & Steinrötter, B. (2021). Der Entwurf für eine EU-KI-Verordnung: Richtige Richtung mit Optimie-rungsbedarf (in German). *RDi*, (11), 528–537, https://beck-online.beck.de/Dokument?vpath=bibdata%2Fzeits%2Frdi%2F2021%2Fcont%2Frdi.2021.528.1.htm&pos=3&hlwords=on (accessed: March 14, 2024).
European Commission. (o.D.). *Utility models*. https://single-market-economy.ec.europa.eu/industry/strategy/intellectual-property/patent-protection-eu/utility-models_en (accessed: March 14, 2024).
European Council. (2020, October 2). *Special Meeting of the European Council (1 and 2 October 2020) - Conclusions, EUCO 13/20*, https://www.consilium.europa.eu/media/45910/021020-euco-final-conclusions.pdf (accessed: March 14, 2024).
European Patent Office. (2023). *Convergence of Practice*, http://documents.epo.org/projects/babylon/eponet.nsf/0/797E6BDF8942E8D1C125898F002CC1DC/$File/common_practice_cii_ai_for_convergence_website_en.pdf
European Patent Office a. (2006). ECLI: EP: BA: 2006: T089805.20060707, https://www.epo.org/en/boards-of-appeal/decisions/t050898eu1 (accessed: March 14, 2024).
European Patent Office b. (2006). ECLI: EP: BA: 2006: T061902.20060322, https://www.epo.org/en/boards-of-appeal/decisions/t020619ex1 (accessed: March 14, 2024).
European Patent Office. (2009). *Patents for software? European law and practice*. https://ciencias.ulisboa.pt/sites/default/files/fcul/inovacao/PI-Pack-INPI-E-Patents-for-Software-EPO.pdf. (accessed: March 14, 2024).
European Patent Office. (2024, March). *Guidelines for Examination in the European Patent Office*, https://link.epo.org/web/legal/guidelines-epc/en-epc-guidelines-2024-hyperlinked.pdf (accessed: March 14, 2024).
Farace, D. J., & Schöpfel, J. (2010). *Grey Literature in Library and Information Studies*. De Gruyter Saur.
Gacutan, J., & Selvadurai, N. (2020). A Statutory Right To Explanation For Decisions Generated Using Artificial Intelligence. *International Journal of Law and Information Technology, 28*(3), 193–216. https://doi.org/10.1093/ijlit/eaaa016
German AI Association. (2023, July 4). The EU AI Act: Towards the finish line: Key issues and proposals for the trilogue negotiations. *KI-Bundesverband*. https://ki-verband.de/wp-content/uploads/2023/07/Position-Paper_AI-Act-Trilogue_GermanAIAssociation.pdf (accessed: March 14, 2024).
Ginsburg, J. (2017). Copyright. In *The Oxford Handbook of Intellectual Property*, (pp. 487–516).
Gramlich, V., Guggenberger, T., Principato, M., Schellinger, B., & Urbach, N. (2023). A Multivocal Literature Review of Decentralized Finance: Current Knowledge and Future Research Avenues. *Electron Markets, 33*(1). https://doi.org/10.1007/s12525-023-00637-4.
Hacker, P., & Berz, A. (2023). Der AI Act der Europäischen Union—Überblick, Kritik und Ausblick (in German). *ZRP*, (8), 226–229. https://beck-online.beck.de/Dokument?vpath=bibdata%2Fzeits%2Fzrp%2F2023%2Fcont%2Fzrp.2023.226.1.htm&pos=1&hlwords=on (accessed: March 14, 2024).
Hacker, P., & Passoth, J. (2022). Varieties of AI Explanations Under the Law. From the GDPR to the AI Act, and Beyond. In A. Holzinger, R. Goebel, R. Fong, T. Moon, K.-R. Müller & W.

Samek (Hg.):*xxAI—Beyond Explainable AI*, Bd. 13200 (pp. 343–373). Springer International Publishing (Lecture Notes in Computer Science).

Hupont, I., Micheli, M., Delipetrev, B., Gómez, E., & Garrido, J. S. (2023). Documenting High-Risk AI: A European Regulatory Perspective. *Computer, 56*(5), 18–27. https://doi.org/10.1109/MC.2023.3235712

Igna, I., & Venturini, F. (2023). The determinants of AI innovation across European firms. *Research Policy, 52*(2), S. 104661. https://doi.org/10.1016/j.respol.2022.104661.

Lankinen, A. (2019*). Patentability of Artificial Intelligence in Europe: Is Artificial Intelligence Patentable According to the European Patent Convention and is the Current Legal Framework for Patents Suitable for Patenting Artificial Intelligence*? Final Thesis for the Law Program, Örebro Universitet, https://www.diva-portal.org/smash/get/diva2:1426056/FULLTEXT01.pdf (accessed March 14, 2024).

Li, Z. (2023). Why the European AI Act Transparency Obligation is Insufficient. *Nature Machine Intelligence, 5*(6), 559–560. https://doi.org/10.1038/s42256-023-00672-y.

Ménière, Y., & Pihlajamaa, H. (2019). Künstliche Intelligenz in der Praxis des EPA (in German). *GRUR*, (4), 332–336. https://beck-online.beck.de/Dokument?vpath=bibdata%2Fzeits%2Fgrur%2F2019%2Fcont%2Fgrur.2019.332.1.htm&pos=10&hlwords=on (accessed: March 14, 2024).

Meyer, S. (2018). Künstliche Intelligenz und die Rolle des Rechts für Innovation (in German). *ZRP*, (8), 233–238, https://beck-online.beck.de/Dokument?vpath=bibdata%2Fzeits%2Fzrp%2F2018%2Fcont%2Fzrp.2018.233.1.htm&pos=15&hlwords=on (accessed: March 14, 2024).

Mylly, U. M. (2023). Transparent AI? Navigating Between Rules on Trade Secrets and Access to Information. *IIC, 54*(7), 1013–1043. https://doi.org/10.1007/s40319-023-01328-5.

Nannini, L., Balayn, A., & Smith, A. L. (2023). Explainability in AI Policies: A Critical Review of Communications, Reports, Regulations, and Standards in the EU, US, and UK. In 2023 ACM Conference on Fairness, Accountability, and Transparency, FAccT'23: The 2023 ACM Conference on Fairness, Accountability, and Transparency (pp. 1198–1212). ACM.

Nastasa, A., Maer M., Monica M., & Mocanu, C. (2023). Artificial Intelligence: Friend or Foe? Experts' Concerns on European AI Act. *ECECSR, 57*(3), 5–22. https://doi.org/10.24818/18423264/57.3.23.01.

Panigutti, C., Hamon, R., Hupont, I., Fernandez Llorca, D., Fano Yela, D., & Junklewitz, H. et al. (2023). The Role of Explainable AI in the Context of the AI Act. In 2023 ACM Conference on Fairness, Accountability, and Transparency, FAccT'23: The 2023 ACM Conference on Fairness, Accountability, and Transparency, pp. 1139–1150. ACM.

PricewaterhouseCoopers. (2023, November). Trustworthy AI: European regulation and its implementation. *PWC*. https://www.pwc.de/en/risk-regulatory/responsible-ai/european-ai-regulation-and-its-implementation.html (accessed: March 14, 2024).

Raposo, V. L. (2022). Ex machina: Preliminary Critical Assessment of the European Draft Act on artificial intelligence. *International Journal of Law and Information Technology, 30*(1), 88–109. https://doi.org/10.1093/ijlit/eaac007

Reed, C. (2018). How Should We Regulate Artificial Intelligence? In Philosophical trans-actions. *Series A, Mathematical, physical, and engineering sciences*, 376 (2128), https://doi.org/10.1098/rsta.2017.0360.

Van Roy, V., Vertesy, D., & Damioli, G. (2020). AI and Robotics Innovation. In F. Klaus, *Zimmermann: Handbook of Labor, Human Resources and Population Economics*, (pp. 1–3). Springer International Publishing; Imprint: Springer.

Verband der Automobilindustrie. (2023, July 18). Position Artificial Intelligence Act. *VDA*, https://www.vda.de/dam/jcr:298c439d-31ec-45ab-95de-6b1089b6fb4c/Positionspapier_KI-Verordnung.pdf (accessed: March 14, 2024).

Verdi, G. (2022, October 5). General-Purpose AI fit for European small-scale innovators. *European Digital SME Alliance*, https://www.digitalsme.eu/general-purpose-ai-fit-.for-european-small-scale-innovators/?utm_source=substack&utm_medium=email (accessed: March 14, 2024).

white ip, Patent & Legal, Business Solutions, Tax. (2021, August 9). Business strategy: Exploitation of intellectual property. *white ip group*, https://www.white-ip.com/en/business-solutions/business-strategy/exploitation-of-intellectual-property/ (accessed: March 14, 2024).

Wojtczak, S., & Księżak, P. (2021). Causation in Civil Law and the Problems of Transparency in AI. *ERPL, 29*(4), 561–582. https://doi.org/10.54648/erpl2021030.

Understanding the Challenges of AI Implementation: Insights from an Empirical Study of Manufacturing Companies

Leon Oldemeyer, Andreas Jede, and Frank Teuteberg

Abstract The increasing importance of artificial intelligence on manufacturing competitiveness is a prevalent topic in contemporary studies. Thereby, the potential of AI extends across companies of all sizes. However, small and medium-sized enterprises in particular see major challenges in AI implementation. As a result, our study determined the variations in the perceived barriers to AI realization among different company sizes and the obstacles that notably impede the willingness to implement AI. To achieve this, a factor analysis and structural equation modeling were carried out. Our findings highlight that the different challenges for AI implementation can be divided into four groups economic, technological, social, and political. Thereby the perception of economic challenges varies the most among distinct enterprise sizes, whereas the social challenges correlate extremely weakly. Regarding the willingness to implement AI, political challenges show the strongest negative correlation, while technological challenges, contrary to prior assumptions, lack significant influence.

1 Introduction

The growing prevalence of artificial intelligence (AI) has a substantial impact on manufacturing companies in particular [1]. Considerable potential, for example in the optimization of production processes [2], provides these enterprises with the opportunity to improve their economic situation. On the other hand, however, there is also a risk of losing competitiveness if the new technology is not implemented [3]. Despite the importance of AI, studies indicated that the vast majority of manufacturing companies have not yet implement AI applications [4]. In the case of European small and medium-sized enterprises (SMEs), the adoption rate is only around 10%

L. Oldemeyer (✉) · A. Jede
Osnabrück University of Applied Sciences, Osnabrück, Germany
e-mail: leon.oldemeyer@hs-osnabrueck.de

F. Teuteberg
University of Osnabrück, Osnabrück, Germany

C. M. Flath et al. (eds.), *Artificial Intelligence, Data, and Decision-Making*, Lecture Notes in Information Systems and Organisation 82,
https://doi.org/10.1007/978-3-032-08480-4_11

[5, 6]. The barriers to AI implementation are defined as the main reason for this state of affairs [7]. Various case studies and surveys showed a wide range of different challenges that businesses are confronted with [8]. However, these vary substantially depending on the size of the company [9]. On one hand, SMEs frequently contend with limited financial resources, making the risk of failure a more significant factor [10]. On the other hand, their initial conditions often differ substantially. For instance, smaller companies are more likely to struggle with issues related to data availability and data quality [11]. The demands for a potential AI solution also vary greatly according to business size in terms of the required complexity [12].

However, empirical studies of the challenges of AI implementation in the manufacturing sector are still limited compared to other sectors. Moreover, we conducted a factor analysis to facilitate an open and alternative approach to categorizing the identified challenges from the literature review. This differs from previous classifications that have often been based on established models such as the Organization-Environment framework (TOE) [4, 13]. In addition, country-specific characteristics such as the degree of industrialization, the education level of the population, or legal regulations are considered because they can also influence the challenges and willingness to implement new technologies in companies [14, 15]. As Kinkel et al. [13] have already compared the perceived challenges of AI implementation in different countries, we will focus on manufacturing companies located exclusively in the industrialized nation of Germany. Germany is well-known for its broad "German Mittelstand" [16], which encompasses many companies of all sizes. This leads to our first research question:

- RQ1: How does the size of German manufacturing companies influence the perceived challenges of an AI implementation?

Although many researchers perceived similar obstacles to AI implementation in their studies, there are substantial discrepancies between the assessment of the influence of the different challenges on the willingness to realize an AI project. While some studies emphasized the role of knowledge as the most substantial entry barrier [17, 18], others highlighted the costs associated with implementation as the primary obstacle [19]. Moreover, other factors such as acceptance [20], or data [21] were also deemed critical for AI implementation by some researchers. Therefore, there is no consensus on the influential factors concerning AI realization. This aligns with the research gap identified by Kinkel et al. [13], in investigating various challenges related to the effect of readiness to introduce AI. As such, we deploy the second research question:

- RQ2: How do the various perceived challenges of AI implementation influence the willingness of German manufacturing companies to implement AI solutions?

Our study contributes to theory and practice in different ways. First, we did a data-based grouping of the various challenges for a structured overview. We anticipate that this approach will contribute added value in terms of new focal points and new perspectives on the topic of implementation barriers and their correlation with the willingness to realize. Furthermore, we were also able to identify the areas where the challenges exhibit the greatest variance across the enterprise sizes. In these, greater differentiation should be made between the sizes, both in political considerations and in the context of further research. Besides, we were able to empirically investigate the influence of the various challenge groups on the willingness to implement AI in order to identify the greatest lever for increasing the spread of AI in manufacturing companies.

2 Hypothesis Development and Research Model

The development of the following hypotheses and the research model are based on the findings of our literature review and a subsequent factor analysis, which are described in detail in Sect. 3.

One of the primary challenges of AI implementation relates to the costs and their associated budget. Nonetheless, variations among different enterprise sizes have been emphasized. For instance, Barton et al. [10] pointed out that financial resources represent the most substantial distinction between SMEs and larger enterprises regarding AI implementation. Similarly, studies by Szedlak et al. [22] and Ulrich und Frank [18] highlighted that costs and the financial risk of failure are considerably higher for smaller companies. The availability of AI solutions on the market is also perceived differently among various business sizes. While this is frequently discussed in the context of SMEs [12, 23], larger firms tend to pay less attention to this concern. In summary, we derive our first hypothesis, H1: As the **size of the company** increases, the perceived **economic** challenges of AI implementation decrease.

Even though data availability and quality are widely acknowledged as barriers in AI implementation for both smaller and larger companies, it is apparent that smaller enterprises are more affected by these challenges. Mittal et al. [24] also recognized this observation in their study, attributing this to lower maturity levels in smaller firms. Jain et al. [12] additionally noticed technical barriers in SMEs primarily due to the lack of an IT infrastructure. This context leads to the formulation of our second hypothesis, H2: As the **size of the company** increases, the perceived **technological** challenges of AI implementation decrease.

Knowledge is a major barrier to the utilization of AI, especially for companies with lower revenues and a smaller workforce. In a survey of experts conducted by Hansen und Bøgh [25], none of the respondents from SMEs concurred with the statement that their firms possessed sufficient knowledge and expertise in AI. This challenge exerts a more pronounced impact on smaller companies compared to their larger counterparts. Furthermore, research on management also revealed a correlation between the size of enterprises and the perceived barriers to the introduction of AI. Consequently, a greater number of SMEs did not identify a potential application area for AI within their company [25, 27]. In addition the review of Lu et al. [28] showed that SMEs face other ethnic challenges than lager enterprises as these companies have often no expertise in this area and are more dependent on external data exchange. These findings from various perspectives on the social challenges emerge our third hypothesis, H3: As the **size of the company** increases, the perceived **social** challenges of AI implementation decrease.

Research conducted has also found disparities between companies of different sizes concerning the political challenges, chiefly about regulations and the lack of government support. SMEs, facing limited resources and a deficit in expertise, encounter greater challenges when it comes to understanding and complying with legal requirements [7, 12]. In this regard, but also advice on how to get started, small companies often find themselves lacking the required support [25]. Consequently, our fourth hypothesis, H4, is: As the **size of the company** increases, the perceived **political** challenges of AI implementation decrease.

Furthermore, prior research has delved into the connection between perceived challenges and the willingness to realize an AI solution. In consideration of the economic barriers, such as the quandary of the monetary valuation (cost–benefit-effect) of a prospective AI application [29], or the lack of a budget [30], many studies often presented these as frequent obstacles to a company's willingness to implement an AI solution. In addition, the often unpredictable durations and the uncertainty regarding a successful introduction of the project, as they often follow a trial-and-error approach, diminish the readiness to initiate such solutions [31]. Hypothesis H5 is thus formulated as follows: As the perceived **economic** challenges increases, the **willingness** of AI implementation decreases.

Especially with regard to AI, data is a particularly critical factor and often represents a major challenge in the realization process. Some researchers even have identified data as the most substantial problem in this context [21]. This encompasses concerns related to data availability, data quality, and data flow [19]. Neglecting these aspects during the implementation process carries a considerable risk of failure. Given that decision-makers are also aware of this, the quality and availability of data are substantial factors in the willingness to AI implementation. Also, in the case where an enterprise lacks an adequate IT infrastructure, decision-makers are frequently hesitant to embark on potential AI projects. This is often even the reason why the subject is not explored in greater depth [17]. This leads to the formulation of the sixth hypothesis, H6: As the perceived **technological** challenges increases, the **willingness** of AI implementation decreases.

Although, as already shown, the lack of knowledge among SMEs is perceived as a greater obstacle to the adoption of AI compared to larger companies, research has indicated that this barrier has an adverse effect on the readiness to implement AI for companies of all sizes [32]. Apart from knowledge, management, and decision-makers also have a significant influence on realization. In this context, Iftikhar und Nordbjerg [27] pointed out that, management is the biggest hurdle to realize an AI project in a business. Other researchers instead presented acceptance and trust in AI solutions as the biggest determinant of the willingness to implement AI [20]. However, the ethnical aspects of an AI implementation are also a frequently identified challenge that influences the readiness [33, 34]. Consequently, we propose the following hypothesis, H7: As the perceived **social** challenges increases, the **willingness** of AI implementation decreases.

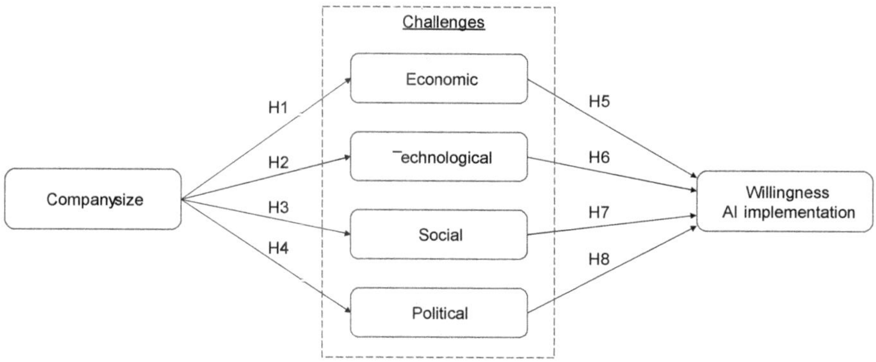

Fig. 1 Research model

Analogous to the barrier of knowledge, regulatory requirements are often perceived as a more significant challenge by SMEs. Yet they also negatively influence the willingness of larger businesses to implement AI, as noted by Prem [31]. Furthermore, there is a shared criticism among companies of all sizes regarding the lack of research in this area. Smaller firms are particularly impacted by the scarcity of use cases that are specifically designed to cater to their initial situation and their needs [26]. Conversely, larger companies are more affected by the frameworks. Government incentives are deemed necessary to mitigate financial risk, as pointed out by Davila Delgado et al. [35]. Consequently, this current lack has a major impact on the companies' willingness to implement AI. This remark extends also to advisory offers. The dearth of free or low-cost government alternatives further dampens companies' readiness to embark on AI realization [28]. This results in the final hypothesis, H8: As the perceived **political** challenges increases, the **willingness** of AI implementation decreases.

A summary of the included challenges of the four groups can be taken from the factor analysis in the following section. From the conducted hypotheses we designed our model in the next step, which is depicted in Fig. 1. For each group of challenges, we created a formative construct. The individual items, representing the identified barriers, constitute the basis of these constructs.

3 Research Method

According to Gable [36], our method can be divided into four steps: 1. development of the research model, 2. development of the items, 3. data collection, and 4. data analysis.

Development of the research model. First, we conducted a literature review to identify the perceived challenges in companies regarding the introduction of AI. We searched the scientific databases Scopus, Web of Science, EBSCO, and ProQuest using the search string ("AI" AND "Challenges" AND "Manufacturing") for journal papers and proceeding articles written in English and published from 2010 onwards. From the selected articles, we derived the major barriers and categorized them into groups using an exploratory factor analysis, followed by Hayton et al. [37]. A screeplot analysis indicated that a four-factor solution would be most appropriate for the collected data. Following the thematic assignment of challenges by the factor analysis, the identified groups could be named into economic, technological, social, and political. The results can be accessed at: https://bit.ly/436Z4z8. For a better overview, coefficients below 0.2 were suppressed. Subsequently, we developed eight hypotheses to explore the interconnection between these groups to enterprise size and willingness for AI implementation, as outlined in section two. Thereby the size of the enterprises is determined based on turnover and the number of employees.

Development of the items. During this step, we selected relevant measurement items for each construct, based on their incidence and importance. These can be called up at https://bit.ly/3TrgYJB. All of these are measured on a five-point Likert scale. The data collection for the structural equation model was conducted through an online survey. To enhance comprehensibility and improve the questionnaire's quality, two preliminary tests were executed. The feedback received regarding the wording, item assessment, and overall clarity was considered in the revised versions of the questionnaire.

Data collection. As our research focuses on the perceived challenges and their connection to the willingness to implement AI, we specially targeted potential decision-makers for AI implementation when distributing the questionnaire. These are on the one hand the owners or the management in smaller companies and on the other hand the heads of IT departments in larger enterprises. The addresses were identified from both the company's website and the networking platform (xing.com). The selection of recipients can be characterized as random sampling, where individuals were chosen at random from the total population, following Nassiuma [38].

The survey was conducted until the beginning of October 2023 and was limited to enterprises in Germany. A total of 168 responses were obtained. We meticulously reviewed these answers for completeness and trustworthiness, employing control questions as a means of verification. Consequently, 110 questionnaires were deemed suitable for inclusion in the statistical analysis. By doing so, we adhered to the common practice of PLS analysis, which suggests that the sample size should be at least ten times the largest number of variables measured for a dependent variable [39]. In the chosen data sets, 63 participants identified their roles as the head of the IT department, while only 47 categorized themselves as owner or personnel of the top management. Notably, over 75% of the responders were male. When classifying the companies into industrial and handicraft enterprises, the distribution was approximately 62.7% to 37.3%. The sizes of the participating companies were fairly evenly distributed (available at: https://bit.ly/3VxNTfm), with the lowest willingness to take part among micro companies. Additionally, we checked for nonresponse or common method bias. As no significant abnormalities were found, the mentioned biases can be considered inconsequential in this study.

Data analysis. During phase four, data analysis was carried out using structural equation modeling (SEM). We employed the approach of component-based least squares (PLS) due to its advantages in handling complex structures, smaller sample sizes, and avoiding biases [40]. For the execution, we used the software SmartPLS4 (www.smartpls.com). The subsequent procedure can be divided into two steps: one for assessing the measurement model and the other for assessing the structural model, as outlined by Hair et al. [41]

Measurement model assessment. In our study, we utilized formative as well as reflective measurements. The evaluation of the formative constructs involved investing the multicollinearity and examining the outer loadings along with their weights and significances. Multicollinearity was assessed using the variance inflation factors (VIF). During our testing, the VIF values consistently ranged from 1.100 to 1.712, therefore remaining below 5, indicating the absence of multicollinearity in this study [41]. In addition, we conducted significance tests on the outer loadings. Items that satisfied both conditions 'significance' and 'a loading greater than 0.5' remained in our construct [42]. As a result, we eliminated six items.

Given that the assessment differs between formative and reflective constructs, we scrutinized the following aspects for the reflective measurement: Indicator reliability, internal consistency reliability, convergent validity, and discriminant validity. All loadings of the items within the reflective measurement are significant and have a value greater than 0.85, surpassing the required level of 0.707 [43]. Hence, the indicator reliability is given in this study. Moving forward, we assessed the internal consistency reliability using both Cronbach's alpha (CA) and composite reliability (CM). The CA value yields a result of 0.721, while the CM value is 0.876. Consequently, both tests report a satisfactory reliability of over 0.7 [44]. For the convergent validity, the average extracted variance (AVE) must exceed the accepted minimum threshold of 0.5 [41]. In our study, this condition is met, as the AVE value is 0.780. In the subsequent step, we assessed discriminant validity. Both the criteria according to Fornell und Larcker [45] and the heterotrait-monotrait ratio (HTMT) are met. As per Henseler et al. [46] recommendation, the critical value of 0.85 for HTMT was not passed, with a correlation of 0.564. This implies that both reliability and validity are given for the model. The detailed results can be accessed at: https://bit.ly/4abYEtC.

Structural model assessment. In the structural model we determined the significance of the paths and loadings through bootstrapping. This technique involved generating 5,000 resamples to calculate standard errors and t-values [42]. Figure 2 shows all R2, path coefficients, p-values, and t-values.

The constructed model elucidates 38.7% of the variance (R2) in the willingness to introduce an AI solution, considering various challenges. In contrast, 32.6% of the variance is accounted for by perceived economic barriers, 21.0% by technological obstacles, and 17.3% by the variance of the political challenges. According to Chin [43], R2 values should exceed the threshold of 0.19, while other researchers already defined the minimum acceptable level at 0.1 [47]. Accordingly, only the variance of the social challenges with an R2 value of 0.054 does not meet this requirement.

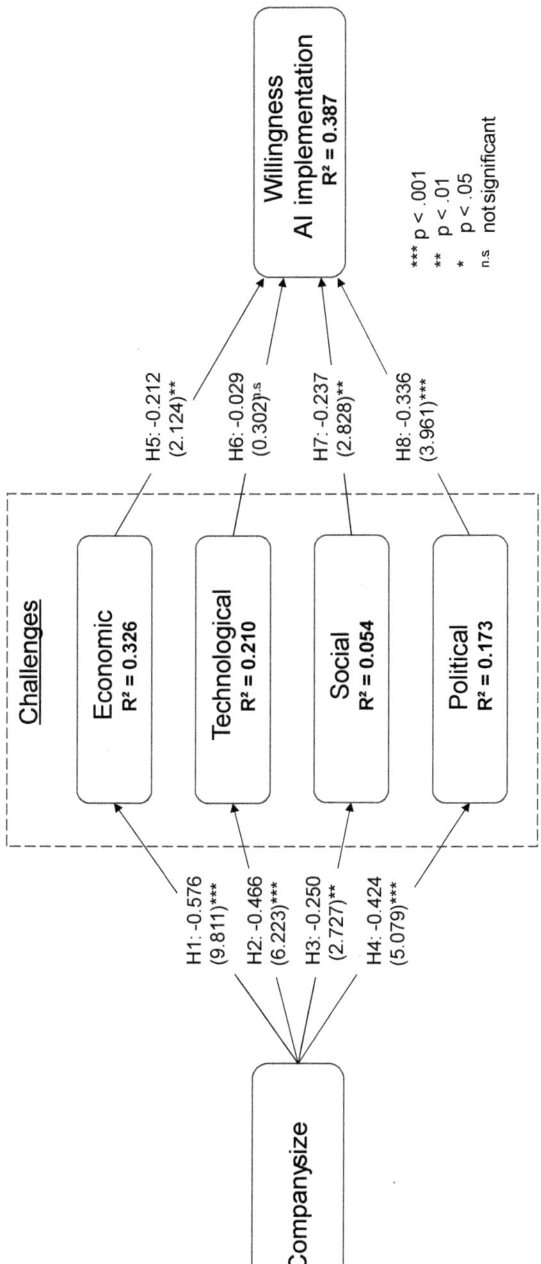

Fig. 2 Evaluation of the research model

Table 1 Evaluation of the test criteria of the structural model

Hypothesis	Path coefficient	t-value	*p*-value	Effect strength f2	Decision
H1	−0.576	9.811	0.000	0.497	Supported
H2	−0.466	6.223	0.000	0.277	Supported
H3	−0.250	2.727	0.006	0.067	Supported
H4	−0.424	5.079	0.000	0.220	Supported
H5	−0.212	2.124	0.034	0.043	Supported
H6	−0.029	0.302	0.763	0.001	Rejected
H7	−0.237	2.828	0.005	0.070	Supported
H8	−0.336	3.961	0.000	0.133	Supported

Moreover, it is essential to consider, on the one hand, the critical p-values ($*p <$ 0.05), and on the other hand, the path coefficients, which are anticipated to surpass the critical value of 0.2 Chin [43]. The only path failing to satisfy these criteria is the relationship between technological barriers to the willingness to AI implementation, therefore H6 is rejected. The remaining significant path coefficients vary between −0.212 and −0.576 and the t-values between 2.124 and 9.811. Thereby the relationship between company size and the perceived economic barriers exhibits the strongest correlation (−0.576, t-value: 9.811). Furthermore, the paths from size to technological challenges (−0.466, t-value: 6.223) and to political challenges (−0.424, t-value: 5.079) also display significant and substantial influences. However, the path from enterprise size to the social obstacles is significant, the coefficient is notably less pronounced (−0.250, t-value: 2.727), in addition to the previously mentioned low R2 of this variable.

When analyzing the path from challenges to willingness, it is evident that all these coefficients display a less meaningful significance when compared to the relationships with the company's size. However, except for the technological barriers, all these paths meet the critical value threshold. The path from political challenges to willingness (−0.366, t-value: 3.961) has the greatest correlation, while the paths from economic (−0.212, t-value: 2.124) and social (−0.237, t-value: 2.828) to willingness are close to each other. Table 1 provides a summary of the results and the subsequent determination of supported and rejected hypotheses.

4 Discussion and Implications

Our study found evidence regarding our two research questions of whether company size has a significant influence on the perceived challenges during an AI implementation (RQ1), and which barriers have a particularly substantial impact on the willingness to implement AI in companies (RQ2).

Grouping challenges. The open and alternative approach to grouping the various challenges using a factor analysis enabled us to structure the various challenges into the four categories of economic, technological, social, and political, based on the data. This classification can be used as a starting point for future analyses and discussions of AI challenges to present them in a summarized and clear manner.

5 Relation of Company Size and Challenges of AI Implementation

Concerning our first research question, the analysis reveals a significant correlation, especially in economic and technological challenges, as well as the political challenges. Compared to previous research [6, 21, 27], our findings not only show the variations in the perceived challenges of AI implementation across different company sizes but also afford the possibility to quantify the extent of this influence.

Economic challenges. Our findings indicate that the company size exerts the most significant influence on the economic challenges when compared with the other three categories (technological, social, and political challenges). This category predominantly encompasses the costs, profitability, and solutions on the market associated with an AI implementation. We see various reasons for the different perceptions of the economic barriers. On the one hand, along with the results of Lu et al. [28], we consider the often limited financial capacity of smaller companies and the associated effects of a potential failure of the project as one of the main reasons. On the other hand, however, we see the calculation or estimation of the cost–benefit ratio as another important factor, which differs between smaller and larger enterprises. Bunte et al. [48] showed in a survey that only 5% of SMEs that implement AI were also able to determine the economic benefit. The limited expertise in calculating the return on investment (ROI) often compels smaller firms to rely on intuition rather than concrete financial metrics. Therefore, we recommend raising awareness among SMEs about the possibilities of simple and cost-effective AI applications. In addition to free software such as ChatGPT (openai.com), Kim et al. [49] presented that partially individual AI solutions are already possible for less than $500. This stands in contrast to the findings of our survey, in which SMEs, on average, indicated that the expected implementation cost of at least 43,236€ (median: 27,500€) for a basic AI application. It is reasonable to assume that many SMEs may be overestimating the cost barrier on these assumptions, leading them to overlook the potential benefits of adopting AI in their businesses.

Social challenges. A further noticeable aspect of our analysis is the relationship between the size of a company and the perceived social barriers. Contrary to previous publications that mainly associate social challenges in the context of an AI implementation, such as knowledge gaps, management issues, and ethical concerns, with smaller companies [17, 49], our model shows only a very weak correlation with an exceptionally weak coefficient of determination. One explanation is the diverse interpretation of these barriers. For instance, smaller firms may be more inclined to refer to general AI-related knowledge gaps (e.g., understanding of the technology, use cases, and implementation processes). In contrast, larger companies might perceive knowledge as a challenge in more specific and detailed areas such as the selection of the right AI method or algorithm. This highlights the necessity for precise definitions and underscores the importance of recognizing that different aspects can be addressed even when mentoring the same challenge. The result further implies that certain social challenges, such as employee acceptance, remain consistent across different company sizes. This aligns with prior research findings that have identified acceptance as a common barrier to AI realization, both in SMEs and large businesses [10].

Technological and political challenges. Furthermore, our study shows similarly strong correlations between the technological and the political challenges with regard to the different company sizes (H2, H4). This is unexpected, as existing research on AI implementation mainly only differentiated between company sizes in terms of the technological starting conditions and challenges, such the different data availability, data quality, and the existing IT infrastructure [7, 10]. Conversely, the political challenges are typically portrayed in an undifferentiated manner in previous publications [50]. This stands in contrast to our findings, which indicate that the perception of political challenges varies between the company sizes to a similar degree as technological challenges. Consequently, we contend the political challenges must be more strongly distinguished according to the diverse business sizes. So, governments should leverage these insights to tailor their support and proposal more effectively. A potential approach could be to trailer access to these resources to the needs of the respective size of firms and to make them only available to a specific target group, akin to other supportive initiatives. Furthermore, we propose a greater distinction in the realm of research between the different company sizes or at least, a more detailed exposition of the group under consideration in the study. This is predicated on the understanding that frameworks and use cases, developed based on large businesses, can only be transferred to other sizes of enterprises to a limited extent due to the varying initial conditions.

Smaller companies perceive more challenges. The negative correlation that can be observed between the size of the company and the economic, technological, social, and political challenges, confirm the assumption that smaller businesses perceive more barriers to AI implementation, making them more cautious and slower to initiate the new technology. These findings align with earlier studies on the relationship between enterprise size and the realization of other new technologies [24]. Our study has now also empirically confirmed this correlation for AI technology. We, therefore, recommend differentiating more strongly between the various company sizes when considering aspects of an AI implementation.

6 Relation of Challenges and Willingness to Implement AI

Political challenges. This finding is also related to the second research question (RQ2), which examined the effects of perceived challenges on the willingness to implement AI, regardless of the size. Our structural equation model elucidates that the connection between obstacles arising from the political challenges and the willingness to implement AI exhibits the most substantial correlation. In comparison to previous studies, our findings not only identify a connection but also indicate that it surpasses the economic, technological, and social challenges of an AI implementation. Following Huang et al. [51] and Lu et al. [28], the existing deficiency in regulations and statutory frameworks regarding AI is an important factor in shaping this assessment. The establishment of comprehensive regulatory and ethical directives, along with well-defined constraints for AI, ideally coordinated globally, is essential. However, our findings extend beyond this, highlighting that apart from the missing regulation, the lack of financial support or advisory services within the political challenges also exerts another important influence on the willingness to implement. We therefore encourage more governmental support elements in this field. Despite the previous fact that these requirements pose a notably greater obstacle for SMEs, it is important to acknowledge that these aspects nevertheless have an impact on the willingness to implement AI across all company sizes.

Technological challenges. Equally important is the rejection of hypothesis six. Even though the recurrent emphasis on different technological obstacles in previous research [10, 17], our model contrasts this by revealing that the technological barriers do not exert a significant influence on the willingness to realize. We attribute this to two reasons. Firstly, our survey exclusively targets German enterprises, distinguishing it from the other studies. By specifically examining companies within an industrial location, they tend to be more advanced technologically on average. For example, more enterprises have modern machines that automatically collect large amounts of data. This contributes to the observation that technological challenges in Germany are less decisive regarding the willingness to implement AI.

Triad of economic, social, and political challenges. Moreover, our findings indicate that the willingness to implement AI is significantly influenced by a triad of economic, social, and political barriers. Consequently, we propose a holistic approach to addressing the perceived challenges faced by companies. Both from a political and scientific standpoint, therefore, it is insufficient to put the focus solely on one of these dimensions.

7 Limitations and Conclusions

There are some limitations to our research. First, our research refers to AI in general, although the different characteristics and subfields of AI can lead to different results. But the general approach enabled us to achieve greater acceptance in our survey of smaller companies or companies that had previously only dealt with AI in a rudimentary way than if AI had been specified in greater detail. Further research should therefore refine our analysis with regard to individual subfields of AI and identify the challenges that differ significantly from our general approach. The factor analysis consolidates various challenges into a single group. The classification of the groups in economic, technological, social, and political represents a method-specific limitation due to different possibilities for naming the clusters and interpreting the chosen terms.

Our study contributes to a better understanding of the challenges associated with AI implementation in manufacturing companies and its impact on willingness to implement AI. Thereby, we differentiate between the enterprise sizes to investigate how this factor influences the perception of the barriers. This research was conducted using data collected from an online survey of German manufacturing companies, which was subsequently analyzed through a factor analysis and a structural equation model.

The findings regarding the first research question could empirically prove that the influence of company size on the perceived economic challenges is greatest in comparison to the technological, social, and political challenges. This can be attributed primarily to variations in the perception of financial risks and the complexity involved in assessing the cost–benefit impact. The very weak correlation with an extremely weak coefficient of determination between company size and the perceived social challenges is also noteworthy. Despite the very different starting conditions in the various company sizes with regard to social challenges, such as existing knowledge, there are no substantial differences in the assessment of these obstacles across different company sizes. We attribute this to different interpretations of the evaluation of the challenges and therefore call for awareness to be raised in studies and politics.

According to our second research question, our findings reveal that the political challenges have the most substantial correlation to the willingness to implement AI and therefore have a greater influence than the economic, technological, and social challenges. We attribute this to the absence of comprehensive regulations but also to the inadequate government support services, including subsidies and independent advisory services. Additionally noteworthy is the rejection of hypothesis six and, consequently, the absence of a significant correlation in terms of perceived technological barriers, such as data, concerning the willingness to implement AI. There is a risk that companies may perceive technological obstacles as part of the normal implementation process rather than as hurdles that need to be addressed before AI implementation.

References

1. Teerasoponpong, S., & Sopadang, A. (2021). A Simulation-optimization Approach for Adaptive Manufacturing Capacity Planning in Small and Medium-Sized Enterprises. *Expert Systems with Applications, 168*, Article 114451.
2. Cheng, E-S., Yang, J-Y., & Lee, J-D. (2021). AIoT Module Development for Automated Production. In *International Conference on Consumer Electronics Taiwan* (pp. 1–2). IEEE.
3. Dwivedi, Y. K., Rana, N. P., Jeyaraj, A., Clement, M., & Williams, M. D. (2019). Re-Examining the Unified Theory of Acceptance and Use of Technology (UTAUT): Towards a Revised Theoretical Model. *Information Systems Frontiers, 21*(3), 719–734.
4. Maslej, N., Fattorini, L., Brynjolfsson, E., Etchemendy, J., Ligett, K., Lyons, T., Manyika, J., Ngo, H., Niebles, J. C., Parli, V., Shoham, Y., Wald, R., Clark, J., & Perrault, R. (2023). *Artificial Intelligence Index Report 2023*. Stanford University.
5. Willenbacher, M., Scholten, J., & Wohlgemuth, V. (2021). Machine Learning for Optimization of Energy and Plastic Consumption in the Production of Thermoplastic Parts in SME. *Sustainability, 13*(12), 6800.
6. Szedlak, C., Leyendecker, B., Reinemann, H., Kschischo, M., & Pötters, P. (2021). Risks and Benefits of Artificial Intelligence in Small-and-Medium Sized Enterprises. In *Proceedings of the International Conference on Industrial Engineering and Operations Management* (pp. 195–205) IEOM.
7. Bettoni, A., Matteri, D., Montini, E., Gladysz, B., & Carpanzano, E. (2021). An AI Adoption Model for SMEs: A Conceptual Framework. *IFAC-PapersOnLin, 54*(1), 702–708.
8. Oldemeyer, L., Jede, A., & Teuteberg, F. (2024). Investigation of Artificial Intelligence in SMEs: A Systematic Review of the State of the Art and the Main Implementation Challenges. *Management Review Quarterly*, 1–43.
9. Heizmann, M., Braun, A., Glitzner, M., Günther, M., Hasna, G., Klüver, C., Krooß, J., Marquardt, E., Overdick, M., & Ulrich, M. (2022). Implementing Machine Learning: Chances and Challenges. *At-Automatisierungstechnik, 70*(1), 90–101.
10. Barton, M., Budjac, R., Tanuska, P., Gaspar, G., & Schreiber, P. (2022). Identification Overview of Industry 4.0 Essential Attributes and Resource-Limited Embedded Artificial-Intelligence-of-Things Devices for Small and Medium-Sized Enterprises. *Applied Sciences, 12*(11), 5672.
11. Chen, Y.-C., Ting, K.-C., Chen, Y.-M., Yang, D.-L., & Chen, H.-M. (2019). Ying JJ-C: A Low-Cost Add-On Sensor and Algorithm to Help Small- and Medium-Sized Enterprises Monitor Machinery and Schedule Processes. *Applied Sciences, 9*(8), 1549.
12. Jain, V., Tewary, T., & Gopalakrishnan, B. N. (2021). Unlocking Technology Adoption for a Robust Food Supply Chain: Evidence from Indian Food Processing Sector. *HSE Economic Journal, 25*(1), 147–164.
13. Kinkel, S., Baumgartner, M., & Cherubini, E. (2022). Prerequisites for the Adoption of AI Technologies in Manufacturing—Evidence from a Worldwide Sample of Manufacturing Companies. *Technovation, 110*, Article 102375.
14. Tornatzky, L., Fleischer, M., & Chakrabarti, A. (1990). *The Processes of Technological Innovation*. Lexington.
15. Vagnani, G., Gatti, C., & Proietti, L. (2019). A Conceptual Framework of the Adoption of Innovations in Organizations: A Meta-Analytical Review of the Literature. *Journal of Management and Governance, 23*(4), 1023–1062.
16. Pahnke, A., & Welter, F. (2019). The German Mittelstand: Antithesis to Silicon Valley entrepreneurship? *Small Business Economics, 52*(2), 345–358.
17. Kumar, A., & Kalse, A. (2021). Usage and Adoption of Artificial Intelligence in SMEs. *Materials Today: Proceedings*.
18. Ulrich, P., & Frank, V. (2021). Relevance and Adoption of AI Technologies in German SMEs—Results Survey-Based Research. *Procedia Computer Science, 192*, 2152–2159.
19. Kim, M., Lee, J., Lee, C., & Jeong, J. (2022). Framework of 2D KDE and LSTM-Based Forecasting for Cost-Effective Inventory Management in Smart Manufacturing. *Applied Sciences, 12*(5), 2380.

20. Garrel, J., & Jahn, C. (2022). Design Framework for the Implementation of AI-Based (service) Business Models for Small and Medium-Sized Manufacturing Enterprises. *Journal of the Knowledge Economy, 14*(3), 3551–3569.
21. Bauer, M., Dinther, C., & Kiefer, D. (2020). Machine Learning in SME: An Empirical Study on Enablers and Success Factors In *26th Americas Conference on Information Systems* pp. 1–10. Online.
22. Szedlak, C., Poetters, P., & Leyendecker, B. (2020). Application of Artificial Intelligence in Small and Medium-Sized Enterprises. In *Proceedings of the 5th NA International Conference on Industrial Engineering and Operations Management* (pp. 1574–1582). IOEM, Online.
23. Brezani, S., Hrasko, R., & Vojtas, P. (2022). Smart Extensions to Regular Cameras in the Industrial Environment. *Procedia Computer Science, 200*, 298–307.
24. Mittal, S., Khan, M. A., Romero, D., & Wuest, T. (2018). A Critical Review of Smart Manufacturing & Industry 4.0 Maturity Models: Implications for Small and Medium-sized Enterprises (SMEs). *Journal of Manufacturing Systems, 49*, 194–214.
25. Hansen, E. B., & Bøgh, S. (2021). Artificial Intelligence and Internet of Things in Small and Medium-Sized Enterprises: A Survey. *Journal of Manufacturing Systems, 58*, 362–372.
26. Husson, D., Holland, A., Fathi, M., & Arteaga Sanchez, R. (2021). *Analysis and Illustration of the Practical Impact of Artificial Intelligence and Intelligent Personal Assistants on Business Processes in Small- and Medium-Sized Service Enterprises.* In International Conference on Systems, Man, and Cybernetics (pp. 3303–3310). IEEE, Online.
27. Iftikhar, N., & Nordbjerg, F. E. (2021). Adopting Artificial Intelligence in Danish SMEs: Barriers to Become a Data Driven Company, Its Solutions and Benefits. In *2nd International Conference on Innovative Intelligent Industrial Production and Logistics* (pp. 131–136). IN4PL, Online.
28. Lu, X., Wijayaratna, K., Huang, Y., & Qiu, A. (2022). AI-Enabled Opportunities and Transformation Challenges for SMEs in the Post-Pandemic Era: A Review and Research Agenda. *Frontiers in Public Health, 10*, Article 885067.
29. Kaymakci, C., Wenninger, S., Pelger, P., & Sauer, A. (2022). A Systematic Selection Process of Machine Learning Cloud Services for Manufacturing SMEs. *Computers, 11*(1), 14.
30. Sharma, P., Shah, J., & Patel, R. (2022). Artificial Intelligence Framework for MSME Sectors with Focus on Design and Manufacturing Industries. *Materials Today: Proceedings, 62*, 6962–6966.
31. Prem, E. (2019). Artificial Intelligence for Innovation in Austria. *Technology Innovation Management Review, 9*(12).
32. Bencsik, A. (2020). Challenges of Management in the Digital Economy. *International Journal of Technology, 11*(6), 1275–1285.
33. Chalmers, D., MacKenzie, N. G., & Carter, S. (2021). Artificial Intelligence and Entrepreneurship: Implications for Venture Creation in the Fourth Industrial Revolution. *Entrepreneurship Theory and Practice, 45*(5), 1028–1053.
34. Zang, H., Li, S., Dong, X., Ma, D., & Dang, B. (2024). Evaluating the Social Impact of AI in Manufacturing: A Methodological Framework for Ethical Production. *Academic Journal of Sociology & Management, 2*(1), 21–25.
35. Davila Delgado, J. M., Oyedele, L., Beach, T., & Demian, P. (2020). Augmented and Virtual Reality in Construction: Drivers and Limitations for Industry Adoption. *Journal of Construction Engineering and Management, 146*(7), 04020079.
36. Gable, G. G. (1994). Integrating Case Study and Survey Research Methods: An Example in Information Systems. *European Journal of Information Systems, 3*(2), 112–126.
37. Hayton, J. C., Allen, D. G., & Scarpello, V (2004). Factor Retention Decisions in Exploratory Factor Analysis: A Tutorial on Parallel Analysis. *Organizational Research Methods, 7*(2), 191–205.
38. Nassiuma, D. (2001). *Survey Sampling: Theory and Methods*. University of Nairobi.
39. Chin, W. (1998). Commentary: Issues and Opinion on Structural Equation Modeling. *MIS quarterly, 22*(1), 7–16.

40. Sarstedt, M., Hair, J. F., Ringle, C. M., Thiele, K. O., & Gudergan, S. P. (2016). Estimation Issues with PLS and CBSEM: Where the Bias Lies! *Journal of Business Research, 69*(10), 3998–4010.
41. Hair, J. F., Ringle, C. M., & Sarstedt, M. (2011). PLS-SEM: Indeed a Silver Bullet. *Journal of Marketing Theory and Practice, 19*(2), 139–152.
42. Hair, J., Hollingsworth, C. L., Randolph, A. B., & Chong, A. Y. L. (2017). An Updated and Expanded Assessment of PLS-SEM in Information Systems Research. *Industrial Management & Data Systems, 117*(3), 442–458.
43. Chin, W. (1998). The Partial Least Squares Approach to Structural Equation Modeling. *Modern Methods for Business Research, 295*(2), 295–336.
44. Nunnally, B. (1994). *Psychometric Theory New York*. McGraw-Hill.
45. Fornell, C., & Larcker, D. F. (1981). Evaluating Structural Equation Models with Unobservable Variables and Measurement Error. *Journal of Marketing Research, 18*(1), 39–50.
46. Henseler, J., Hubona, G., & Ray, P. A. (2016). Using PLS Path Modeling in New Technology Research: Updated Guidelines. *Industrial Management & Data Systems, 116*(1), 2–20.
47. Falk, R., & Miller, N. (1992). *A Primer for Soft Modeling*. The University of Akron.
48. Bunte, A., Richter, F., & Diovisalvi, R. (2021). Why It is Hard to Find AI in SMEs: A Survey from the Practice and How to Promote It. In *Proceedings of the 13th International Conference on Agents and Artificial Intelligence* (pp. 614–620). ICAART, Online.
49. Kim, H., Jung, W.-K., Choi, I.-G., & Ahn, S.-H. (2019). A Low-Cost Vision-Based Monitoring of Computer Numerical Control (CNC) Machine Tools for Small and Medium-Sized Enterprises (SMEs). *Sensors, 19*(20), 4506.
50. Sharma, M., Luthra, S., Joshi, S., & Kumar, A. (2022). Implementing Challenges of Artificial Intelligence: Evidence from Public Manufacturing Sector of an Emerging Economy. *Government Information Quarterly, 39*(4), Article 101624.
51. Huang, X., Yusoff, Z, M., Nor, Nor, M. Z. B. M., & Labanieh, M, F. (2024). The Legal Challenges and Regulatory Responses to Artificial Intelligence (AI) in China. In *12th UUM International Legal Conference* (pp. 335–347). UUMILC.

Unlocking AI-Based Knowledge Management Potential for SMEs: Exploring Semantic Search Adoption

Timo Grüneke, Tobias Guggenberger, Jakob Nusser, Anna Maria Oberländer, Jan Stramm, and Alexander Varrentrapp

Abstract Small and medium-sized enterprises (SME) thrive on knowledge-intensive operations, making effective knowledge management critical to their success. Contemporary developments, such as semantic search applications (SSA) leveraging artificial intelligence (AI), promise significant benefits for knowledge management. However, the adoption of such AI-based applications in the context of SME remains still notably limited. Building upon the groundwork laid by previous research on the socio-technical dimensions of AI adoption, we thus investigate the adoption of SSA in a multiple case study within the German manufacturing sector. Hence, contextualizing the adoption of SSA in SMEs using a grounded theoretical

T. Grüneke (✉) · T. Guggenberger · J. Nusser · A. M. Oberländer · J. Stramm · A. Varrentrapp
University of Bayreuth, Bayreuth, Germany
e-mail: timo.grueneke@uni-bayreuth.de; timo.grueneke@fim-rc.de; timo.grueneke@fit.fraunhofer.de

T. Guggenberger
e-mail: tobias.guggenberger@uni-bayreuth.de; tobias.guggenberger@fim-rc.de; tobias.guggenberger@fit.fraunhofer.de

J. Nusser
e-mail: jakob.nusser@uni-bayreuth.de

A. M. Oberländer
e-mail: anna.oberlaender@uni-bayreuth.de; anna.maria.oberlaender@fit.fraunhofer.de; anna.oberlaender@fim-rc.de

J. Stramm
e-mail: jan.stramm@uni-bayreuth.de; jan.stramm@fim-rc.de; jan.stramm@fb3.fra-uas.de; jan.stramm@fit.fraunhofer.de

A. Varrentrapp
e-mail: alexander.e.a.varrentrapp@uni-bayreuth.de

T. Grüneke · T. Guggenberger · A. M. Oberländer · J. Stramm
FIM Research Center, Bayreuth, Germany

Branch Business & Information Systems Engineering of the Fraunhofer FIT, Bayreuth, Germany

J. Stramm
Frankfurt University of Applied Sciences, Frankfurt, Germany

C. M. Flath et al. (eds.), *Artificial Intelligence, Data, and Decision-Making*, Lecture Notes in Information Systems and Organisation 82,
https://doi.org/10.1007/978-3-032-08480-4_12

framework. Our findings highlight the intricate interplay of organizational readiness, external support, and user satisfaction in facilitating SSA adoption. We believe our framework holds significant potential to guide the adoption of SSA and thus offers valuable insights for navigating the complexities of harnessing the potential of AI-based applications for effective knowledge management in SMEs.

1 Introduction

In the digital era, the rapidly expanding volume of information makes it increasingly difficult for organizations and humans alike to manage and make sense of information effectively. However, the ability to quickly navigate knowledge is crucial for organizational success as the productivity of corporations is predominantly contingent upon their intellectual capabilities rather than tangible assets [47]. This enforced the evolution of information technology to effectively capture, store, and disseminate knowledge across the organization. Integrating Artificial Intelligence (AI) marks a pivotal shift, offering unprecedented opportunities to provide intelligent ways for capturing, retrieving, and transmitting data and information [22]. Emerging AI-based technologies offer novel knowledge management solutions within the framework of digital transformation. This is particularly pertinent due to the rising complexity and volume of data [7]. Within this framework, semantic search applications (SSA) are regarded as a unique form of AI-based knowledge management. They supersede traditional lexical search methods by employing intelligent search systems based on semantic text analysis, representing a promising technological advancement in knowledge management practices [21, 46].

Particularly in the digital realm, knowledge management emerges as a critical area for small and medium-sized enterprises (SMEs) as it facilitates the capture, dissemination, and effective use of knowledge, which is crucial for sustaining innovation and competitive advantage in rapidly changing markets [11]. Especially as SMEs, which constitute the backbone of the economy, particularly in Germany, are renowned for their specialized niche expertise and global market dominance, often being recognized as hidden champions. SMEs, thrive on technologically innovative manufacturing practices, significantly contributing to an advanced technological innovation landscape [49]. Nevertheless, in SMEs, where competitive advantage is rooted in specialized and knowledge-intensive processes and products, notable shortcomings emerge concerning knowledge management, particularly within the digital realm [16, 17]. Despite the promising technological advancement of AI-based knowledge management, such solutions see little practical application in the context of SMEs [39].

Regardless of SMEs' leading role in production-related technology innovation, they show only limited structured work processes, inadequate data infrastructures (resulting in data fragmentation across various databases and formats), and dependence on external Information Systems (IS) expertise [25, 53, 54]. Thus, the technological capabilities of AI-based knowledge management implementation are often hampered by SME-specific technological barriers and capacity constraints. This technological aspect is magnified in recent developments where large corporations devote billions to technical AI development and adoption annually [41] whereas SMEs struggle to catch up with implementing and using AI, having limited internal resources, capacities, and knowledge in that domain [52].

In addition to the technological aspects, research found the adoption of AI to be two-sided: besides the technical component there is a social component as AI adoption includes culture and workforce [38]. Concerning AI-based knowledge management, it is, therefore, essential to recognize that AI is not a static or closed digital technology in the traditional sense. Instead, it represents a dynamic and ongoing boundary shift across all levels, extending beyond conventional digital technologies [7]. The dynamic characteristic of AI, thus, requires a reevaluation of adoption strategies [7]. To fully exploit and convert the existing potential into value, socio-technical aspects regarding the willingness and motivation of individuals and organizations to utilize the technology must, therefore, be considered, extending beyond purely technical aspects. To give guidance for AI-based knowledge management adoption in SMEs, our research question is as follows:

How is the adoption of semantic search applications, as a form of AI-based knowledge management in SMEs, affected by socio-technical dimensions?

To answer our research question, we developed a grounded theoretical framework for SSA adoption in SMEs. Since the results of empirical studies in the IS literature cannot be easily generalized to SMEs [18], we conducted a multiple case study including three SMEs located in the German manufacturing business-to-business (B2B) sector following Eisenhardt's [19] case study approach. In addition, we investigated stakeholder needs in its natural setting in SSA adoption to unleash the potential of AI-based knowledge management for SMEs. We focused on a specific AI technology: Natural Language Processing (NLP) [37].

The paper is structured as follows: We first provide an overview of knowledge management in SMEs and AI adoption. Then, we describe our multiple case study design, the data collection, and the data analysis. Subsequently, we present and interpret our main findings by developing a grounded theoretical framework for SSA adoption in SMEs. We close with the discussion and conclusion of our key findings, limitations, and possible directions for future research in the field of SSA adoption.

2 Theoretical Background

2.1 *Knowledge Management in Small and Medium-Sized Enterprises*

As SMEs face significant challenges in managing knowledge, SSAs are becoming increasingly important as part of the digital transformation of SMEs [7, 13, 25, 54]. The already existing complexity of the environment SMEs are embedded in is rising due to digitalization and requires careful and strategic management of knowledge [39]. Especially in SMEs, searching with conventional knowledge management tools, e.g., intranet, can be frustrating due to insufficient user training, implementation obstacles, and data-related issues [8, 55]. In comparison to conventional knowledge management systems, AI-based knowledge management systems not only handle the complexity but also unlock new potential for the company [39]. Knowledge management is characterized as a prerequisite of productivity in SMEs and includes the implementation, perception, and transfer of knowledge [16, 17, 47]. The soaring success of AI changes the implementation, perception, and transfer of knowledge significantly by providing new AI technologies, such as NLP [39]. NLP is a convergence of computer science, AI, and linguistics involving a range of methods and tasks designed to empower computers to understand, interpret, and generate human language [30, 37]. Herein, SSAs are a subfield within the broader field of NLP [13, 30, 37]. Compared to lexical search, SSAs provide a more advanced and intelligent information retrieval method, giving users more precise, pertinent, and customized search results [5]. SSAs involve information extraction by entering a search query and receiving a response with the information that most closely matches the search query [13]. Thus, users can understand the context of a search query and the relevance of search results increases [13, 27]. To unlock the potential of new and promising knowledge management tools in the context of SSAs, the successful adoption of AI becomes increasingly important for SMEs.

3 AI Adoption

AI adoption is a preliminary stage for AI implementation [23]. Based on the adoption of innovation and technology, AI adoption can be defined as the preparedness related to integrating new AI innovations [3]. The process of AI adoption reflects the sequence of initiation, adoption decision, and implementation [35]. Initiation is characterized by the awareness, consideration, and intention to implement AI in the company to identify AI innovations [14, 35, 48]. SMEs in particular find it difficult to implement AI technologies due to a lack of AI expertise [58]. The adoption decision includes evaluating innovation ideas and allocating resources [14, 35]. Because of the SME-specific relevance of social factors [35, 38], the adoption decision is a crucial step in the adoption process for SMEs. Implementation involves adapting and integrating the innovation within the organization until it becomes routine for its users [14, 35]. In SMEs, the strong dependence on external IT service providers hinders successful AI implementation [54]. External IT support by IT service providers is a central factor for AI adoption in SMEs as SMEs depend on external support due to the sophistication of IS and the scarcity of IS staff [10, 33]. Employee training is one factor through which external support (technology supplier) influences the adaptation of technological change in SMEs [10, 45].

Besides technical drivers, Jöhnk et al. [35] highlight the various challenges emerging from non-technical drivers. Within the context of socio-technical literature, assimilating AI into organizational frameworks demands a holistic approach that also considers organizational readiness [35]. Organizational readiness emerges as a central factor influencing the adoption process of AI within SMEs [4, 10, 35] and can be defined as the organization's ability to execute digital transformation including AI-based technologies [3]. To ensure a successful AI adoption the assessment of the organizational readiness identifies potential gaps within the adoption process [2, 35]. Organizational readiness assessment includes the four steps of identification, prioritization, assessment, and adaption of organizational necessities and factors [35]. In sum, external support and organizational readiness are the crucial socio-technical factors for AI adoption.

4 Method

To examine how SMEs adopt AI, we conducted a qualitative case study research following Eisenhardt's [19] method for building theories from multiple cases. We firmly believe that qualitative research methodologies, as emphasized by Vogelsang et al. [57] and Guggenberger et al. [29], offer invaluable insights into the realm of SSA adoption research.

Aligned with Eisenhardt's [19] methodology, the cornerstone of our research lies in the specific use case scenarios observed within the participating companies and partners (see Table 1). Over a comprehensive two-year period, a consortium comprising three application partners (ID 1–3), two development partners, and two research partners (ID 4) investigated the intricacies of SSA adoption within SME environments. Each of the three application partners (ID 1–3) falls under the SME category, a demographic that constitutes a substantial portion of Germany's economic landscape. The companies operate in diverse sectors including agriculture, mechanical engineering, metal processing, and the manufacturing of technical glass and ceramic beads. Their engagement with SSAs stems from a collective effort as part of a public initiative (KIWise) funded by the Federal Ministry of Education and Research. This collaborative endeavor sought to explore the practical implementation of SSAs as a knowledge access tool within SMEs, with a particular focus on enhancing knowledge accessibility for employees through AI-based tools.

Table 1 Overview of cases with use case characteristics and interviews

ID	Case description and organization	Use case characteristics	Interviewee background and No. of interviewees (#)
1	Agricultural and mechanical engineering: Implementation of a SSA in service and sales of livestock farming technology for agriculture	Technical training Sales enquiries Service enquiries	Service technician (3)
2	Metal processing: Implementation of a SSA to increase efficiency and effectiveness in production processes	Improved work preparation Reduction of idle times Quick knowledge access	Assistance to the board (1) Machine operator (3)
3	Technical glass and ceramic beads manufacturing: Implementation of a SSA in the sales department and research and development	Complaints management Procurement process Find visit and fair reports	IT (1) R&D (2) Sales (3)
4	Development and research partner: Support in the derivation of use cases for a SSA and support in the derivation of functional and non-functional requirements	Technical support Identification of potential areas of application	Developer (1) Researcher (2)

Our research methodology encompassed both primary and secondary data collection to identify potential barriers hindering the effective utilization of SSAs. Primary data was gathered through in-depth semi-structured interviews conducted with representatives from the three SMEs in the manufacturing sector, as well as the company responsible for developing the SSA. These interviews, each spanning approximately 45 min, provided rich insights into stakeholder experiences, facilitated by follow-up questions to delve deeper into the phenomenon under study. An overview of the interview questions can be found here: https://doi.org/https://doi.org/10.5281/zenodo.12581478. Additionally, secondary data analysis involved scrutinizing unsolicited and official project documents to uncover potential barriers that may not have surfaced during primary data collection [20, 51].

The collected data underwent meticulous analysis using the coding approach outlined by Gioia et al. [26], supported by MAXQDA. MAXQDA is a comprehensive tool that enhances the rigor of qualitative data analysis through efficient coding, annotation, retrieval, organization, and visualization of qualitative data, as well as offering features for mixed methods research from sources such as interviews, surveys, and focus groups. A total of 16 interviews were conducted across various functional roles within the participating companies supplemented by the analysis of

50 documents comprising presentations, manuals, protocols, and textual documents in various formats (pdf, excel, word). To ensure the reliability of our analysis, we conducted a second round of coding two months later, adhering to Mayring's [42] framework. Our iterative coding process, conducted by established guidelines [50], resulted in the identification of 357 labeled statements and text passages (256 from interviews, 101 from documents).

Additionally, we organized workshops involving multiple researchers within the IS discipline to validate our findings and facilitate an iterative process for theory development. Throughout this journey, we maintained a transparent and collaborative approach, providing feedback documents to the observed SMEs based on the insights gleaned from our interviews and document analysis.

5 Results

5.1 Main Findings

The SSA adoption for AI-based knowledge management is intricately influenced by various socio-technical dimensions in SMEs. Our investigation has unveiled three primary dimensions driving this influence: organizational readiness, external support, and user satisfaction. Through a careful coding process, we initially identified 30 first-order concepts, which were then refined into eight second-order themes and eventually synthesized into three aggregate dimensions [26]. As we progressed with our analysis, we continuously refined our coding framework to ensure its alignment with the rich content we encountered [42]. While repeating the theory building, we rearranged them into 18 first-order concepts, eight second-order themes, and three dimensions (see Table 2). In addition, Tables 3, 4, And 5 list sample quotes from the interviews for each of the 18 first-order concepts.

Organizational readiness: We understand organizational readiness as the extent to which SMEs navigate the interplay between use case context, technology readiness, and data privacy and data security. Building upon our observations use case context encompasses the boundary conditions for defining and focusing on specific, practical scenarios in which the SSA is applied to solve real-world problems depending on the company size and industry sector. Regarding company size, we observed that smaller organizations struggle with identifying appropriate use cases for the SSA because of their limited data resources. In contrast, larger organizations have access to more extensive datasets, enabling them to explore a wider array of applications and leverage more advanced SSA capabilities. Additionally, the unique needs and regulatory challenges of different industry sectors give distinct contexts for how SSAs are selected and implemented. We observed that technology readiness refers to the degree to which an organization (IT-infrastructure) or individual (IT-Qualifications) is prepared and equipped to effectively utilize a specific technology.

Table 2 Data structure. Own representation based on Gioia et al. [26]

1st order concepts	2nd order themes (# of codes)	Dimensions (# of codes)
Company size	Use case context (58)	Organizational readiness (130)
Industry sector		
IT-Infrastructure	Technology readiness (44)	
IT-Qualifications		
Expansion of the database	Data privacy and data security (28)	
Data storage location (online/offline)		
Access management to the database		
User-friendly interface	Onboarding (68)	External support (179)
Helpful introductions		
Reliability of search results	Technical capabilities (111)	
Technical improvements		
Explanations of search results	Interpretability of decision-making (26)	User satisfaction (48)
Restart duration		
Perceived Usefulness	User expectations (22)	
Trustworthiness		
Economy of time		
Accuracy of search results		
Compatibility with daily routine		

Regarding IT-infrastructure, we observed that data management and data preprocessing is a big issue in SMEs. In addition, we noticed that the IT-qualifications are medium-qualified in SMEs as users show only little interest in in-depth technological understanding. A reinforcing factor for insufficient IT-qualifications in SMEs is the inadequate IT infrastructure compared to large companies. As data privacy focuses on handling personal information and data security protects data from unauthorized access, in SMEs both are essential components of effective information management concerning the expansion of the data storage location, database, and access management to the database. The users want to know where data is processed, and they prefer local data storage. Local data storage significantly increases the sense of security as users feel more comfortable with it because the data remains within the company. When expanding the database, carefully managing access management is crucial as users were concerned that plenty of people have access to their data like e-mails.

External support: Our findings suggest that external support relates to how effectively SMEs manage the interaction between onboarding and technical capabilities. Onboarding is the process through which the users in our study were introduced to

Table 3 Example quotes from the interviews for organizational readiness

Example Quotes	1st order concepts	2nd order themes
"So, my impression is that, of course, a lot more energy in SMEs had to be invested in finding the use case at the start because the data material is simply not as large as in large companies."	Company size	Use case context
"I would have expected to get more results. But as I said, that was probably mainly because of the tables [specific to the manufacturing industry]."	Industry sector	
"In general, you have to say that data management and data preprocessing is always a big issue and that was also a big issue here. It's simply not easy for many people."	IT-Infrastructure	Technology readiness
"Interested [in AI], but not in depth. You just get to see what is already working in, let us say, the popular media. You try the whole thing out for yourself."	IT-Qualifications	
"What do I upload to this whole thing, where does it all end up and who guarantees that it stays right there and that only I have access to it? Of course, that is one story, always the question, so as local as possible."	Expansion of the database	Data privacy and data security
"As long as it is limited to the server here, not really at all, because then I look for it and I know where […]"	Data storage location (online/offline)	
"We once discussed whether the whole thing could be extended to include emails or other points. Then the question is again, who can find what?"	Access management to the database	

Table 4 Example quotes from the interviews for external support

Example Quotes	1st order concepts	2nd order themes
"The user interface and the general operation, as far as we have used it, is relatively intuitive and not that difficult to understand, at least for me."	User-friendly interface	On-boarding
"We had a very short briefing. It's relatively self-explanatory."	Helpful introductions	
"Partly, partly. So. Better than when I started using it. In any case."	Reliability of search results	Technical capabilities
"The only negative thing about the application is that it cannot display images or graphics."	Technical Improvements	

the SSA. User-friendly interfaces and informative introductions were identified as key elements of effective onboarding, facilitating seamless user experiences. The user interface of the SSA was very intuitive and easy to understand for the users and the introduction to the SSA was helpful as it was self-explanatory. While some

Table 5 Example quotes from the interviews for user satisfaction

Example Quotes	1st order concepts	2nd order themes
"I would like to see a little oops, we could not find that or something like that, for example. Or please ask the question differently."	Explanation of search results	Inter-pretability of decision-making
"When I need the application, I start it and then I have to wait two minutes. I don't know why, but it's extremely annoying. Even though you know it."	Restart duration	
"But it is less relevant for day-to-day production."	Perceived Usefulness	User expectations
"So how much can you trust a solution like that? Because you always have a machine with you. Very quickly, you have a machine breakdown."	Trustworthiness	
"Well, it actually has to be quick. I need more time to assess it than if I search in the table of contents myself."	Economy of time	
"Sometimes I had the feeling that I could search for the same thing three times and get different results three times, so that was extreme, for example."	Accuracy of search results	
"It can help us with the simple things, but it's not much use with the difficult things like technical documents we use in our daily routine."	Compatibility with daily routine	

users expressed a desire for further education, the majority found the initial technical introduction provided by developers sufficient. We noticed that technical capabilities refer to the techniques, methodologies, and tasks of the SSA ensuring reliable search results and potential for technical improvements. Throughout the project's duration, the reliability of search results provided by the SSA experienced enhancements. Suggestions for improvement include tables and graphics to increase the reliability of search results.

User satisfaction: The user satisfaction in our study encompasses the interplay between the interpretability of decision-making and user expectations. We see the interpretability of decision-making as the degree to which the users can understand, explain, and validate the rationale, process, and outcomes of decisions made within the SSA. The explanation of search results and the restart duration of the SSA are pivotal for the extent of interpretability of decision-making. Users desire to receive a notification if the SSA fails to find a satisfactory result or if the user needs to refine the query. The user expectations in our study refer to the anticipated standards, requirements, or desires that users have regarding the performance, features, and quality of the SSA. The extent of user expectations exists of the perceived usefulness, trustworthiness, economy of time, accuracy of search results, and compatibility with daily routine. We view perceived usefulness as how the users assess if the SSA will enhance their performance or well-being in achieving specific tasks and goals. The usefulness of the SSA is limited in everyday working life. Trustworthiness refers to the reliability of the SSA. Users were afraid of consequences when someone relied solely on the search results without scrutinizing them. In our understanding, economy of time is the efficient and effective use of time to achieve the users' desired objectives or goals. Dissatisfaction was particularly noted with the duration of SSA restarts, with users expressing frustration over extended wait times. The SSA's accuracy of search results is the perceived degree of correctness of the information retrieved by the SSA in response to a user query. Users were confused about the varying quality of search results. We see the compatibility with daily routine as the degree to which the SSA fits into the users' routine in their working lives. Users prefer the SSA for simple tasks, but they are not convinced of its compatibility with daily routine when it comes to more complex tasks.

In conclusion, our study highlights the multifaceted nature of SSA adoption in SMEs, underscoring the critical role played by socio-technical dimensions in shaping organizational readiness, external support, and user satisfaction. To enhance the utility of SSAs in the manufacturing SME context, our findings underscore the importance of addressing specific areas for improvement. These include optimizing the analysis of tables and graphics, automating the display of exact text positions in search results, and addressing issues related to SSA restart times to mitigate user dissatisfaction.

6 Grounded Theoretical Framework

Our investigation into the adoption of the SSA in SMEs has culminated in the development of a grounded theoretical framework, as illustrated in Fig. 1. The framework serves as a comprehensive outline for understanding the interplay of the observed socio-technical dimensions influencing the adoption of SSA solutions in SMEs. The initial element of our grounded theoretical framework is the reciprocal relationship between organizational readiness and external support [1a.]. Within the realm of organizational readiness, our framework includes three key determinants: use case context, technology readiness, data privacy, and data security. In contrast, external support is characterized through the onboarding processes of both deployers and users, as well as the technical capabilities of the SSA. Our findings show that organizational readiness within SMEs is linked to the extent of external support it receives as organizational readiness can impact the utilization and effectiveness of external support. SMEs that are well-prepared and committed to the SSA are more likely to leverage external support effectively to achieve a successful adoption process. External support in turn shapes the organizational readiness to embrace SSAs effectively by providing technical capabilities and onboarding. On top of that, our framework delineates the separate influence of organizational readiness [1b.] and external support on user satisfaction [1c.] independently from their reciprocal relationship [1a.]. Organizational readiness sets the stage for a successful SSA adoption influencing user satisfaction directly by providing a fitting use case context, considering

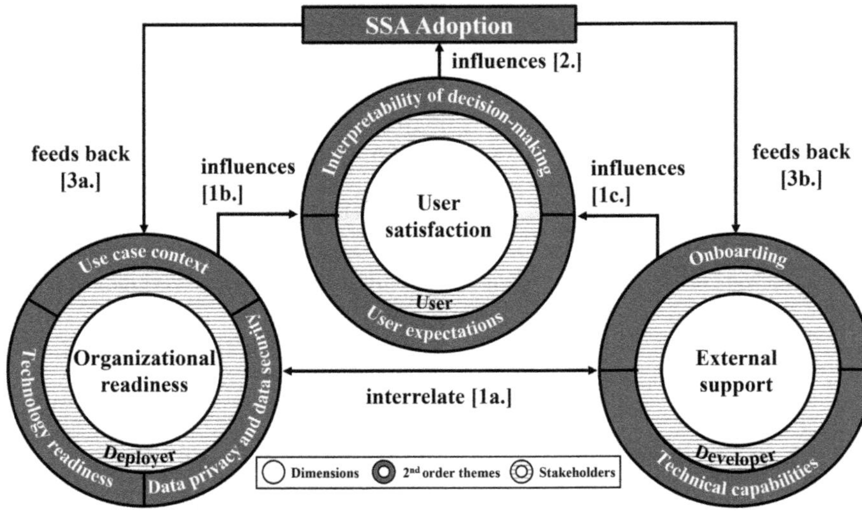

Fig. 1 Grounded theoretical framework for SSA adoption in SMEs

data privacy and data security, and being technologically ready. Similarly, our framework suggests that the quality and extent of support provided by developers significantly contribute to user satisfaction levels within SMEs. Our framework conceptualizes the influence of user satisfaction on SSA adoption [2.] based on how well the SSA aligns with user expectations and enables users to understand the decision-making process of the SSA. SSA adoption triggers a feedback process that leads to advanced organizational readiness [3a.] and external support [3b.]. By requiring adjustments to organizational infrastructure and procedures, the adoption of the SSA influences organizational readiness. SSA adoption also influences the requirement for external support to successfully guide the adoption process. To guarantee the effective adoption and integration of the SSA into their operations, SMEs need to evaluate their organizational readiness and ascertain the extent of external support needed. By employing this grounded theoretical framework, we aim to provide a holistic understanding of the complex dynamics underlying the adoption of SSAs in SMEs.

7 Discussion

Based on our socio-technical understanding of AI adoption [35], we conceptualized the adoption of SSAs. Thereby, our research findings offer a novel perspective unveiling the central role of user satisfaction in fostering the successful adoption of AI-based knowledge management within SMEs.

Our findings resonate with the established discourse within IS literature, underscoring the interplay between organizational readiness and external support [15, 35, 36, 40]. However, existing IS research has highlighted a direct correlation between organizational readiness and external support with the adoption of AI-based technologies [10, 35]. In contrast, our grounded theoretical framework suggests for SSAs, that organizational readiness and external support determine the adoption specifically indirectly through influencing user satisfaction. Hereby, we underscore the importance of focusing on end-user experiences and satisfaction as core elements for the adoption process of AI technology in SMEs.

In alignment with the findings of Jo and Bang [34], our study has unveiled AI adoption drivers. Thus, applying as well as extending the body of knowledge about such drivers from the context of generative (e.g., ChatGPT) towards extractive AI (in the form of SSA). In this context, our research reveals that external support significantly drives user satisfaction during the adoption of an AI tool designed for knowledge extraction. Smooth onboarding processes and strong technical functionalities emerged as pivotal specific adoption drivers. Echoing Acton and Golden [1], who explored the effect of IT training on user satisfaction, our research further underscores the vital importance of well-executed onboarding in enhancing user satisfaction. The effectiveness of the onboarding is, thus, paramount for SSA adoption, as it reduces the users' cognitive load upon technology contact and fosters the core intent to retrieve knowledge effectively supported by AI.

For organizations it is deemed crucial to mobilize and deploy IT-based resources for the rapid development and implementation of new technologies [9], thereby enhancing their ability to respond promptly to internal or external changes [11]. However, Nevo et al. [43] highlight the importance of external technical support, which is in line with our observations. In our context, the external support provided by developers reduced the prohibitive effect of making upfront investments associated with developing, deploying, and maintaining sophisticated AI systems. Furthermore, in-house specialized knowledge is superfluous, as the technological expertise to effectively deploy and maintain AI-based systems can be leveraged while maintaining focus on the primary core business.

Supporting current research, we emphasize the vital importance of the use case context in connection with organizational readiness [56]. Our insights, therein, echo the perspectives expressed by Burton-Jones and Grange [12] and Orlikowski [44], emphasizing the foundational role of understanding the specific use case context for driving effective technological utilization. The meticulous and especially purposeful selection of AI use cases is of utmost importance [31], particularly within the SMEs investigated in our research. We found that comprehending the context, pinpointing domain-specific issues, and aligning AI solutions with the scale of the companies' use cases play a pivotal role in configuring and ultimately adopting SSA. Moreover, our research underscores the critical importance of data privacy and data security considerations in fostering organizational readiness, especially within the initial stages of SSA adoption within SMEs [24, 28]. Our findings highlight the significant impact of these considerations, which we observed to result in increased user satisfaction, particularly arising from factors such as the location of data storage, expansion of the database, and access management [6, 59].

Throughout phases of creation, delivery, and utilization of SSA adoption in SMEs, users, developers, and deployers emerged as the relevant stakeholders from our study. The relationship between them is defined by a feedback loop in which decisions about the development and deployment of the SSA are influenced by the user's satisfaction based on how the SSA matches the user's expectations and allows the user to interpret the SSA's decision-making. Recognizing the importance of involving all relevant stakeholders, we advocate for a collaborative approach to prevent costly errors and maximize the benefits of AI-based initiatives within the SME environment [32].

In essence, our study advances our understanding of the complex dynamics underlying SSA adoption in SMEs, offering valuable insights into the interplay between organizational readiness, external support, and user satisfaction. Through our nuanced exploration, we aim to pave the way for informed decision-making and effective implementation strategies in leveraging SSAs within SME.

8 Conclusion

Given the pivotal role SMEs play in the German economic landscape, embarking on a successful digital transformation journey becomes imperative. In our endeavor to catalyze the adoption of the SSA within SMEs, we crafted a grounded theoretical framework. This framework includes a dynamic interplay between organizational readiness and external support, resulting in increased user satisfaction, a cornerstone for driving the SSA adoption. Our framework gives guidance to practitioners by offering an overview of the diverse stakeholders crucial for the seamless adoption of SSAs within SMEs. It delineates their interactions, empowering practitioners with invaluable insights into the needs and nuances of each stakeholder group. Armed with this comprehensive understanding, practitioners can navigate the SSA's implementation journey with confidence, ensuring a successful outcome. However, it is important to acknowledge the limitations of our study. Our observations were confined to the developer of the SSA, along with the user and deployer of three SMEs within the sector of German manufacturing. As such, our insights are bounded by the scope, industry sector, company size, and stakeholder composition of the observed entities. Future research should aim to broaden the scope of analysis, encompassing a diverse array of stakeholders and exploring SSA adoption dynamics across various industries.

Acknowledgements We gratefully acknowledge the "Federal Ministry of Education and Research" and its "Project Management Agency Karlsruhe" for their support of the "Innovative Arbeitswelten im Mittelstand - 2021 bis 2022" within the project "KIWise - Einsatz- und Akzeptanzanalyse von KI-basierten Wissenszugängen in KMU am Beispiel einer semantischen Suche" that made this paper possible (Funding number: 02L21B030, 02L21B031).

References

1. Acton, T., & Golden, W. (2003). Training the Knowledge Worker: A Descriptive Study of Training Practices in Irish Software Companies. *Journal of European Industrial Training, 27*, 137–146.
2. Alshawi, M. (2007). *Rethinking IT in construction and engineering*. Routledge.
3. Alsheibani, S., Cheung, Y. & Messom, C. (2018). Artificial intelligence adoption: AI-readiness at firmlevel. In *PACIS 2018 Proceedings*. Yokohama.
4. Alsheibani, S. A., Cheung, Y. & Messom, C. (2019). Factors inhibiting the adoption of artificial intelligence at organizational-level: A preliminary investigation. In *AMCIS 2019 Proceedings*. Cancún.
5. Bast, H., Buchhold, B., & Haussmann, E. (2016). Semantic Search on Text and Knowledge Bases. *Foundations and Trends in Information Retrieval, 10*(2–3), 119–271.
6. Bélanger, F., & Crossler, R. E. (2011). Privacy in the Digital Age: A Review of Information Privacy Research in Information Systems *MIS Quarterly, 35*(4), 1017–1041.
7. Berente, N., Gu, B., Recker, J. & Santhanam, R. (2021) Special Issue Editor's Comments: Managing Artificial Intelligence. *MIS Quarterly, 45*(3), 1433–1450.
8. Bergamaschi, S., Martoglia, R., & Sorrentino, S. (2015). Exploiting semantics for filtering and searching knowledge in a software development context. *Knowledge and Information Systems, 45*, 295–318.
9. Bharadwaj, A. S. (2000). A Resource-Based Perspective on Information Technology Capability and Firm Performance: An Empirical Investigation. *MIS Quarterly, 24*(1), 169–196.
10. Bruque, S., & Moyano, J. (2007). Organisational Determinants of Information Technology Adoption and Implementation in SMEs: The Case of Family and Cooperative Firms. *Technovation, 27*, 241–253.
11. Buck, C., Grüneke, T. & Stelzl, K. (2021). Structuring the Jungle of Capabilities Fostering Digital Innovation. In Ahlemann, F., Schütte, R. & Stieglitz, S. (eds) Innovation Through Information Systems. WI 2021. Lecture Notes in Information Systems and Organisation (Vol. 48). Springer.
12. Burton-Jones, A., & Grange, C. (2012). From Use to Effective Use: A Representation Theory Perspective. *Information Systems Research, 24*(3), 632–658.
13. Cambria, E., & White, B. (2014). Jumping NLP curves: A review of natural language processing research. *IEEE Computational Intelligence Magazine, 9*(2), 48–57.
14. Damanpour, F., & Schneider, M. (2006). Phases of the adoption of innovation in organizations: Effects of environment, organization and top managers. *British Journal of Management, 17*, 215–236.
15. DeLone, W. H., & McLean, E. R. (1992). Information Systems Success: The Quest for the Dependent Variable. *Information Systems Research, 3*(1), 60–95.
16. Despres, C., & Chauvel, D. (1999). Knowledge management(s). *Journal of Knowledge Management, 3*(2), 110–120.
17. Durst, S., Edvardsson, I. R., & Foli, S. (2023). Knowledge management in SMEs: A follow-up literature review. *Journal of Knowledge Management, 27*(11), 25–58.
18. Dutot, V., Bergeron, F., & Raymond, L. (2014). Information management for the internationalization of SMEs: An exploratory study based on a strategic alignment perspective. *International Journal of Information Management, 34*(5), 672–681.
19. Eisenhardt, K. M. (1989). Building theories from case study research. *Academy of Management Review, 14*, 532–550.
20. Flick, U. (2018). *The SAGE handbook of qualitative data collection*. SAGE Reference.
21. Formica, A., Missikoff, M., Pourabbas, E., & Taglino, F. (2013). Semantic search for matching user requests with profiled enterprises. *Computers in Industry, 64*(3), 191–202.
22. Fowler, A. (2000). The role of AI-based technology in support of the knowledge management value activity cycle. *Journal of Strategic Information Systems, 9*(2–3), 107–128.

23. Frambach, R. T., & Schillewaert, N. (2002). Organizational innovation adoption: A multi-level framework of determinants and opportunities for future research. *Journal of Business Research, 55*, 163–176.
24. Fu, Z., Huang, F., Ren, K., Wang, C., & Weng, J. (2017). Privacy-Preserving Smart Semantic Search Based on Conceptual Graphs Over Encrypted Outsourced Data. *IEEE Transactions on Information Forensics and Security, 12*(8), 1874–1884.
25. Garbellano, S., & Da Veiga, Md. R. (2019). Dynamic capabilities in Italian leading SMEs adopting industry 4.0. *Measuring Business Excellence, 23*(4), 472–483.
26. Gioia, D. A., Corley, K. G., & Hamilton, A. L. (2013). Seeking Qualitative Rigor in Inductive Research: Notes on the Gioia Methodology. *Organizational Research Methods, 16*(1), 15–31.
27. Grant, G. H., & Conlon, S. J. (2006). EDGAR extraction system: An automated approach to analyze employee stock option disclosures. *Journal of Information Systems, 20*(2), 119–142.
28. Guan, Z., Li, Y., Liu, X., Wu, J., Wu, L., Xu, R., & Zhang, J. (2020). Cross-lingual multi-keyword rank search with semantic extension over encrypted data. *Information Sciences, 514*, 523–540.
29. Guggenberger, T., Neubauer, L., Stramm, J., Völter, F. & Zwede, T. (2023). Accept Me as I Am or See Me Go: A Qualitative Analysis of User Acceptance of Self-Sovereign Identity Applications. In *Proceedings of the 56th Hawaii International Conference on System Sciences (HICSS)* (pp. 6560–6569). Honolulu, HI.
30. Hirschberg, J., & Manning, C. (2015). Advances in natural language processing. *Science, 349*(6245), 261–266.
31. Hofmann, P., Jöhnk, J., Protschky, D. & Urbach, N. (2020). Developing Purposeful AI Use Cases—A Structured Method and Its Application in Project Management. In *WI2020 Zentrale Tracks, GITO Verlag: Berlin, Germany* (pp. 33–49).
32. Humpert, L., Albers, A., Anacker, H., Dumitrescu, R., Horstmeyer, S., & Wäschle, M. (2023). Stakeholder-oriented Elaboration of Artificial Intelligence use cases using the example of Special-Purpose engineering. *Procedia CIRP, 119*, 693–698.
33. Igbaria, M., Cavaye, A., Cragg, P., & Zinatelli, N. (1997). Personal computing acceptance factors in small firms: A structural equation model. *MIS Quarterly, 21*(3), 279–305.
34. Jo, H., & Bang, Y. (2023). Analyzing ChatGPT adoption drivers with the TOEK framework. *Scientific Reports, 13*, 22606.
35. Jöhnk, J., Weißert, M., & Wyrtki, K. (2021). Ready or Not, AI Comes–An Interview Study of Organizational AI Readiness Factors. *Business & Information Systems Engineering, 63*(1), 5–20.
36. Lee, J.-C., & Chen, C.-Y. (2019). Exploring the determinants of software process improvement success: A dynamic capability view. *Information Development, 35*(1), 6–20.
37. Li, Y., & a Thomas, M. & Liu, D. (2020). From semantics to pragmatics: where IS can lead in Natural Language Processing (NLP) research. *European Journal of Information Systems, 30*(5), 569–590.
38. Madan, R., & Ashok, M. (2023). AI adoption and diffusion in public administration: A systematic literature review and future research agenda. *Government Information Quarterly, 40*(1), Article 101774.
39. Majumder, S. & Dey, N. (2022). AI-empowered Knowledge Management. In J. Kacprzyk (Ed.), *Studies in Big Data* (pp. 1–114). Springer Nature.
40. Markus, M. L., & Robey, D. (1988). Information Technology and Organizational Change: Causal Structure in Theory and Research. *Management Science, 34*(5), 583–598.
41. Marr, B. (2019). *Artificial intelligence in practice: How 50 Successful Companies Used AI and Machine Learning to Solve Problems*. John Wiley & Sons.
42. Mayring, P. (2010). Qualitative Inhaltsanalyse. In Mey, G., Mruck, K. (Eds.) *Handbuch Qualitative Forschung in der Psychologie*. VS Verlag für Sozialwissenschaften.
43. Nevo, S., Cook, W. D., & Wade, M. R. (2007). An examination of the trade-off between internal and external IT capabilities. *Journal of Strategic Information Systems, 16*(1), 5–23.
44. Orlikowski, W. J. (2000). Using Technology and Constituting Structures: A Practice Lens for Studying Technology in Organizations. *Organization Science, 11*(4), 404–428.

45. Premkumar, G. (2003). A Meta-Analysis of Research on Information Technology Implementation in Small Business. *Journal of Organizational Computing and Electronic Commerce, 13*(2), 91–121.
46. Pustejovsky, J., & Boguraev, B. (1993). Lexical knowledge representation and natural language processing. *Artificial Intelligence, 63*, 193–223.
47. Quinn, J., Anderson, P., & Finkelstein, S. (2005). Leveraging intellect. *Academy of Management Executive, 19*(4), 1.
48. Rogers, E. M. (2003). *Diffusion of innovations* (5th ed.). Free Press.
49. Rovira Nordman, E., & Tolstoy, D. (2011). Technology Innovation in Internationalising SMEs. *Industry and Innovation, 18*, 669–684.
50. Saldaña, J. (2013). *The Coding Manual for Qualitative Researchers* (2nd ed.). Sage.
51. Scott, J. (1990). *A Matter of Record: Documentary Sources in Social Research.* Cambridge, UK: Polity Press.
52. Statistisches Bundesamt. (2023). Kleine und mittlere Unternehmen. https://www.destatis.de/DE/Themen/Branchen-Unternehmen/Unternehmen/Kleine-Unternehmen-Mittlere-Unternehmen/_inhalt.html. Accessed February 14, 2024.
53. Teece, D. J. (2018). Business Models and Dynamic Capabilities. *Long Range Planning, 51*, 40–49.
54. Thong, J. Y. L., Raman, K. S., & Yap, C.-S. (1996). Top Management Support, External Expertise and Information Systems Implementation in Small Businesses. *Information Systems Research, 7*(2), 248–267.
55. Ulrich, P., & Frank, V. (2021). Relevance and adoption of AI technologies in German SMEs - results from survey-based research. *Procedia Computer Science, 192*, 2152–2159.
56. Venkatesh, V., Davis, F. D., Davis, G. B., & Morris, M. G. (2003). User Acceptance of Information Technology: Toward a Unified View. *MIS Quarterly, 27*(3), 425–478.
57. Vogelsang, K., Hoppe, U. & Steinhüser, M. (2013). A Qualitative Approach to Examine Technology Acceptance. In *International Conference on Information Systems (ICIS 2013): Reshaping Society Through Information Systems Design.*
58. Wei, R., & Pardo, C. (2022). Artificial intelligence and SMEs: How can B2B SMEs leverage AI platforms to integrate AI technologies? *Industrial Marketing Management, 107*, 466–483.
59. Yang, P., Ren, J., & Xiong, N. (2020). Data Security and Privacy Protection for Cloud Storage: A Survey. *IEEE Access., 8*, 131723–131740.

Part II
IT Strategy, Governance & Management

Bridging Fields of Practice: How Boundary Objects Enable Collaboration in Data Science Initiatives

Nils Rahlmeier and Konstantin Hopf

Abstract Data-intensive technologies draw high investments. Yet, data science projects are reported to suffer from poor collaboration, unrealistic expectations, and difficulties in realizing practical solutions between business and data science units. Moving beyond the currently prevalent approach to study data science practices, our study emphasizes the use of boundary objects between data science and collaborating fields. We interviewed collaborators from diverse fields in six organizational data science initiatives. Our inductive analysis of this rich data source uncovered six distinct mechanisms and six archetypes of boundary objects in data science projects. While archetypes that we label Alignment, Temporary, Collaboration, and Outcome are procedural and appear in selective stages of the data value creation process, the archetypes Infrastructure and Upskilling support projects along the value creation process. The archetypes and their mechanisms inform the management of data science initiatives, help to advance boundary object theory, and provide instruments to study data science initiatives.

1 Introduction

Companies have been investing heavily in data-intensive technologies (e.g., big data, business analytics, artificial intelligence) in recent years, hoping to add value by making more effective, objective, and neutral decisions [6, 24, 37] or increasing their efficiency [21]. Yet, many organizations struggle to carry out the data science

N. Rahlmeier · K. Hopf
Information Systems and Energy Effieicnt Systems, University of Bamberg, Bamberg, Germany
e-mail: nils.rahlmeier@e-vc.org

N. Rahlmeier
e.Venture Consulting, Berlin, Germany

K. Hopf (✉)
Information Systems and Business Analytics, Chemnitz University of Technology, Chemnitz, Germany
e-mail: konstantin.hopf@wiwi.tu-chemnitz.de

C. M. Flath et al. (eds.), *Artificial Intelligence, Data, and Decision-Making*, Lecture Notes in Information Systems and Organisation 82,
https://doi.org/10.1007/978-3-032-08480-4_13

initiatives that are necessary to adopt and leverage these technologies (Joshi et al., [19, 30]. Many such projects are reported to be ad-hoc initiatives that never leave the pilot phase [11]. Literature cites several reasons why data science initiatives fall short of delivering business value. For example, poor collaboration between business and data science units, unrealistic expectations about the technology, and the long way from "doing data science" to implementing operational solutions [14, 19]. Many challenges can be directed to a mismanagement of the interfaces between data science and other multidisciplinary collaborators [16].

The field of data science has evolved over the past decade [7, 8]. It is characterized by interdisciplinary knowledge work [30] and follows a non-linear explorative path involving cross-disciplinary expertise from multiple actors from different fields of practice [2, 25, 27]. Several studies demonstrate that data science projects are qualitatively different from other IT or non-IT projects, mainly because they use data as their material. Data is a constantly changing resource, which leads to constantly changing and unstable outputs of data science projects [17, 25]. The tools used also differ, as many data science projects rely on learning algorithms that automatically extract patterns from large amounts of data [10]. This often leads to "black boxes" in which many outputs and data representations are difficult to understand and interpret [1]. In conventional software, by contrast, all instructions must be explicitly programmed.

At the center of this complex work environment is the *data scientist*, who appears to be the most important link between the different fields of practice [29]. Originally described as barely existent experts, the "hybrid of data hacker, analyst, communicator, and trusted adviser. The combination is extremely powerful—and rare" [7, p. 73], these individuals are key players in creating value from data [29] by integrating different parts of organizations.

Information systems (IS) research has made efforts to understand the practices that data scientists employ while they interact with technology (e.g., [15]), domain experts (e.g., [5, 33]), and managers [16] separately. Yet, our knowledge of how data scientists work together with the variety of other actors in organizations is limited. This lack of clarity makes it difficult to establish appropriate working conditions for effective data science work and to manage collaboration in data science initiatives.

Our study addresses this knowledge gap by exploring the underlying dynamics of collaboration in data science projects. We selected *boundary objects* [4, 32]) as the unit of analysis, which are objects "intersecting social worlds ... *and* satisfy the informational requirements of each of them" [32, p. 393]. These objects are exchanged between data scientists and other actors from diverse fields of practice. Effective boundary objects in place decrease the need for coordination and allow shifting concerns between local and global focus [18]. They establish focal points that foster collaboration and bridge the gap between various knowledge domains. Boundary objects are an established theoretical frame in an organization and IS research when it comes to understanding and improving the collaboration of different stakeholders. Thus, this paper explores the question: *How do data scientists collaborate with other fields of practice (e.g., management, frontline employees, and IT) through the use of boundary objects?*

Our research uncovers six mechanisms and archetypes of boundary objects, and we explain their functions within data science projects and organizations. We position the identified boundary objects within the value creation process and emphasize the significance of approaching and developing a specific subset of them strategically. Furthermore, our research highlights the data scientist's pivotal role in bridging different fields of practice through the use of boundary objects while also serving as an educator within the organization. Before we give a detailed account of our study and its result, we introduce the phenomenon of data science and the theory of boundary objects.

2 Theoretical Background

2.1 Management of Data Science Initiatives

The scholarly discourse on the management and strategy related to data-intense technologies began a decade ago with the realization that "big data" exists in corporate IT systems (e.g., [6]). Literature acknowledges that a complex process is necessary to create value from data [28, 34] and that advanced analytics (using statistics and machine learning) is necessary to lift any potential from data. So far, IS literature has examined issues related to technology design (e.g., [20]), the interaction of individuals with the technology [5, 15], or how data-intensive technologies might change the work of individuals [36].

Increasing interest is paid to the work of data scientists, who are the actors in organizations that develop data-intensive applications [25]. Yet, empirical studies come to partly conflicting results: On the one hand, studies put data scientists into a strong position by demonstrating that they deliberately include and exclude domain experts or ML models to develop AI applications (van den [5] or that are the key resource orchestrators in corporate AI initiatives [29]. On the other hand, Stice-Lusvardi et al. [33] find that data scientists compromise their "good" practices in order to get their work accepted by others. Other studies show that the identity of data scientists is subject to constant change because of the emergence of their occupation [2, 35].

To create effective work environments and successfully manage data science initiatives, a more advanced understanding of the data science work boundaries with other fields of practice is necessary. To operationalize this investigation, we leverage boundary objects as the unit of analysis.

2.2 *Boundary Objects*

When heterogeneous actors from different social worlds collaborate, a central tension appears between divergent viewpoints and the need for generalizable findings. Star and Griesemer [32] found that individuals use boundary objects to manage this tension to achieve a common goal or interest. These objects must be "plastic enough to adapt to local needs and the constraints of the several parties employing them, yet robust enough to maintain a common identity across sites" [32, p. 393]. They identified four types of boundary objects in their study,[1] and over time, several additional types and classifications of boundary objects from different fields were contributed [22, 31].

Boundary objects are artifacts that convey status information, discussions, and agreements (e.g., [9]) across the boundaries of organizations and stakeholder groups. Levina and Vaast [22] identify the active use of an object by project participants from different fields of practice as a criterion that separates boundary objects from other types of objects. This is reflected in the concept of "designated boundary objects" versus "boundary objects-in-use" [22]. The latter class describes objects that emerge locally and create usefulness in a joint field. Marabelli et al. [23] expanded the theory by examining temporal aspects of boundary objects. Although boundary objects have been analyzed in the context of information systems [23] and agile software development projects (e..g., [3, 38]), their role in data science project environments has yet to be explored.

3 Method

We conducted an exploratory study of six cross-functional data science projects. At the core of our study are data scientists and their work relations to one or two collaborators from different fields of practice, which we refer to as a case. In total, we conducted 14 semi-structured interviews between Jan and Feb 2023 (average duration: 52 min, with a standard deviation of 8 min, in total 12 h).

Study Design—A comprehensive understanding of boundary objects requires soliciting the perspectives of representatives from different social worlds. Consequently, we sought to represent *at least two perspectives on the same project from different fields of practice* to avoid bias that could arise by only interviewing data scientists. Hence, our study centers around one data scientist and at least one collaborator (see Table 1).

---

[1] Without the intention of being exhausting, Star and Griesemer [32] describe four boundary object types: *Repositories* (ordered pile of data or shared resource collections used by multiple stakeholders), *Ideal types* (conceptual models that capture essential features), *Coincident boundaries* (points where different perspectives overlap and require coordination), and *Standardized forms* (agreed-upon formats that facilitate communication and collaboration).

Table 1 Case overview and interview participants

#	Participants (Interview duration in minutes)	Industry	Size	Project goal	Location of data science
1	Product Owner (IP12, 51); Sen. Data Analyst (IP 13, 50); Data Science Lead (IP14, 56)	E-Commerce	> 2500	Classify and recommend relevant influencer videos that feature products for users of an e-commerce app	Internal
2	Product Owner (IP3, 51); Data Scientist (IP4, 52); Data Scientist (IP5, 51)	E-Commerce	500–2500	Predicting trustworthiness of customers to offer additional payment methods; Advanced forecasting for employee capacities and product quantities	Internal
3	Lead Data Scientist (IP1, 63); Software Developer (IP2, 39)	Optical technologies	>2500	Automated forwarding of online submitted contact forms based on document understanding to internal recipients	Internal
4	Project Manager (IP7, 47); Data Scientist (IP6, 44)	Analytics Consulting	500–2500	Digitization and document understanding of analog forms for a retail bank	External
5	Manager (IP10, 43); Data Scientist (IP11, 61)	Analytics Consulting	>2500	Advanced time-series models for revenue forecasts with automated retraining	External
6	Managing director (IP8, 65); Data Scientist/ Software Engineer (IP9, 47)	Optical Engineering	<25	Predictive adjustment of production parameters on the basis of sensor data in order to increase quality of output	External

Sampling Strategy—We tried to achieve a broad coverage of boundary objects by using a maximum variation sampling [26, p. 243] and involved different organizational contexts and participants at various levels. Although all employers of the interview partners had locations in Germany, almost all of them have an international presence, which resulted in half of the interviews being conducted in German and the other half in English. We contacted 161 individuals via personal contact or searching for data scientists' profiles on LinkedIn, and received a response from 75 of them. Given that all potential interviewees had to find colleagues they have worked with in a cross-functional team, we could schedule 18 interviews. Four of them (where we had only a data scientist but no collaborator) served as pilot tests to refine our interview guide and identify potential issues. These four pilot interviews were excluded from the analysis sample. Prior to the interview, we had a phone call with the data scientist to determine if the person had been involved in a data science project (currently or in the past) and if other colleagues were available to be interviewed as part of the study. After conducting around ten interviews and covering four cases, recurring themes began to emerge, and the acquisition of new information during the latter interviews declined.

Structure and Contents of the Interviews—The interviews were structured around using and managing boundary objects in one data science project of the company. The interview guide remained relatively stable over time and had three sections: First, we asked contextual questions regarding the person, their organization, and the focal project. Second, we clarified project-related boundaries and objects. Third, we delved into the use and management of boundary objects to conduct an in-depth discussion of selected objects. To facilitate this discussion, the objects and project participants were listed on a shared screen, and we discussed the use, creation, and management of these objects in relation to the project participants. Third, we asked about the roles and boundary activities that the interview partners performed in the team.

Data Analysis—Both audio and screen sharing were recorded and transcribed verbatim, leading us to 205 pages of original text. We analyzed all data (including the notes and tables created and used within the interview) using the software MAXQDA. We used a multi-stage coding process, starting with initial open coding and establishing a focus for subsequent rounds by comparing it to the literature. We then did five (partly iterative) rounds of open, axial, and selective coding, addressing disagreements between researchers and constant comparison to ensure our theory was grounded in data:

Codig step 1: Initial screening and open coding—We started with open coding to give "extraordinary voice" to our informants while also aligning ourselves closely with their unique terminologies [12]. We came to a high number of 1192 open codes that covered diverse topics, e.g., agile working, collaborative tools, and culture.

Coding step 2: Focused and axial coding to identify boundary object instances—In our next iteration, we included our theoretical focus on boundary objects and first grouped all codes related to what indicates a boundary object. Our coding process encountered difficulties in classifying boundary objects, and we began with a large set of over 80 objects—a challenge that other studies also had to cope with [31]. We started with a subsequent axial coding using researcher-centric notions [12] to develop categories representing boundary objects or the functions of boundary objects in data science. To enhance validity and reliability, we established clear criteria of inclusion—objects that are positioned and used over the boundaries of different social worlds [32],neither used solely as pure input or output and objects that are in use [22]—and exclusion—objects that are only created and used by one person, are used on a small scale [31], objects not plastic enough [32] and objects that are collaborative tools. With these criteria, we reduced the inventory to 54 instances of boundary objects.

Coding step 3: Finding mechanisms of boundary objects—In addition to the codes that helped us to find instances of boundary objects, we analyzed the remaining codes to understand the functions of boundary objects. That is, how boundary objects help individuals to coordinate and communicate across diverse fields of practice. We grouped the functions into mechanisms of boundary objects. Thereby, we tried to eliminate deviations in the formed dimensions and achieve theoretical saturation [13]. In the end, we identified six mechanisms of how boundary objects facilitate collaboration between different fields of practice in data science.

Coding step 4: Conceptualization of boundary objects—In our next analysis step, we aimed to aggregate the boundary object instances into a low number of archetypes of boundary objects. To do so, we engaged in an iterative selective coding process to group together boundary objects that serve the same mechanism (as identified previously).

Coding step 5: Value creation mapping—In our last analysis step, we mapped the discovered boundary object (archetypes) onto the data value creation process [28, 34]. This approach allowed us to take an all-encompassing perspective beyond a mere operational view to encompass a strategic and organizational perspective. We assigned the archetypes by reviewing the literature on the various phases of value creation and the challenges at the transitions (see Fig. 1).

4 Findings

The data science projects in our sample spanned across several fields of practice with different understandings of data science work. Yet, 13 out of 14 interviewees indicated a joint field could be established, also through the use of boundary objects. Before we describe archetypes of those, we describe mechanisms that boundary objects fulfilled.

4.1 Mechanism of Boundary Objects in Data Science

In our third analysis step, we inductively derived the boundary object mechanisms reported by informants from the data and coded them as aggregate dimensions:

1. *Understand & Define the Problem (UDP)*, identify and understand the client's business needs, and agree on and specify requirements.
2. *Coordination & Management (CM)*, reviewing and coordinating tasks and capacities, maintaining central project information for documentation and orientation, and summarizing and communicating project status.
3. *Create Common ground (CCG)*, actively train collaborators, and improve intra-team relationships.

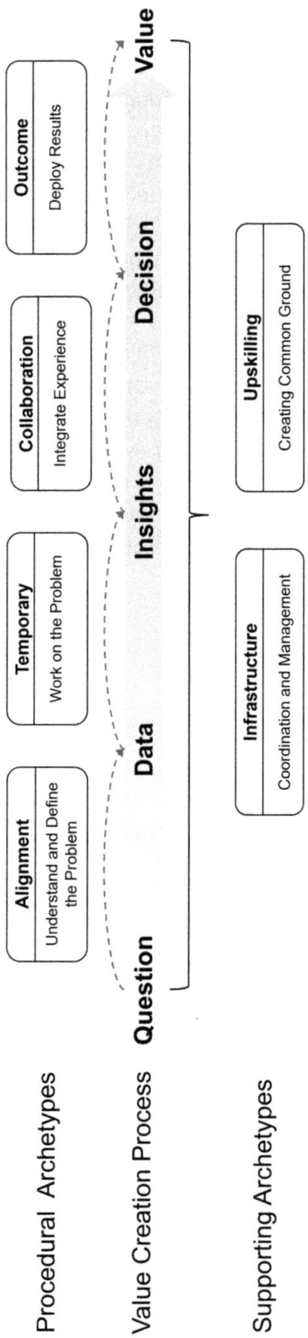

Fig. 1 Overview Procedural and Supporting archetypes

4. *Solve problems (SP)*, establish a framework for collaborative work, regular reviews and challenges of work in progress, and discuss the current solution approach.
5. *Integrate Experience (IE)*, collaboratively integrating customer understanding, discussing and negotiating project-wide solution approach, and involving expert communities in the exchange.
6. *Share Results (SR)*, delivering actionable insights to the client, enriching their knowledge, and making results understandable for their decision-making.

4.2 Archetypes of Boundary Objects

Each archetype that we found describes a set of boundary object instances that effectively fulfill the same core function. The identified archetypes are shown in **Fehler! Verweisquelle konnte nicht gefunden werden.** and we describe each of them briefly in the next section. To better represent the complexity of the objects in each archetype, we visually represent a frequency distribution of their functions (according to the six mechanisms mentioned above). For these figures, we determine the relative frequency of codes regarding mechanisms in each archetype after the third coding step. That means we counted the number of times each mechanism was mentioned for each archetype and divided this by the total number of mechanism codes per archetype. We show these numbers in a radar chart in Table 2 using the abbreviated mechanisms.

4.3 Boundary Objects Along the Data Value Creation Process

The archetypes stretch throughout the entire trajectory of data science projects. While the Alignment (I) and the Upskilling (II) archetypes particularly supported the pre-development phase of projects, the Temporary (III) and Infrastructural (VI) archetypes were mainly present in the development phase of projects, the Collaboration (IV) and Outcome (V) archetypes in the refinement and deployment phase of projects. We use the data value creation process [28, 34] to locate the main use of this archetype along the process model, as we illustrate in Fig. 1.

The *Alignment Archetype (I)* consists of boundary objects that help reach a consensus on defining a problem across diverse fields of practice (e.g., requirements document, problem statement). The archetype supports and engages the articulation of each field of practice's unique view, goals, and priorities, and makes their perspective visible to the whole team. The archetype helps to overcome the *"huge communication gap between the business and the data scientist. With incomplete understanding … you start working … and when you present results, you will get the feedback: 'But that's not what we were interested in.'" (Data scientist, IP3)* The

Table 2 Boundary object archetypes

Type and Description	Examples	Functions (Categories)	Impact
I. Alignment: Support and represent the process of finding and formulating the consensus on the problem definition from different social worlds	Requirement Catalogue, Service Agreement, Problem Statement	(1) Identifying and understanding the business needs of the client (2) Agree on & specify requirements	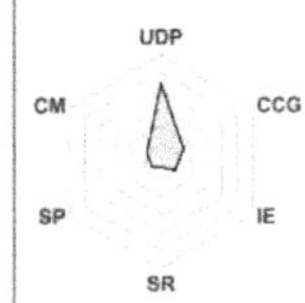
II. Upskilling: Boundary objects whose content is purposefully designed and used to convey one's own social world to another	Upskilling Documents/ Slides, Explanation/ Interpretation aids	(1) Actively train the client (2) Improve team-client relationship	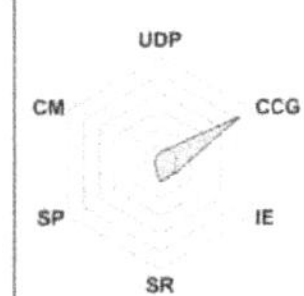
III. Temporary: Temporary outcomes, used as a facilitator for multiple people to work together on complex problems	Mock-Ups, Sketches, Working Documents	(1) Framework for collaborative work (2) Review and challenge work in progress (3) Discuss current solution approach	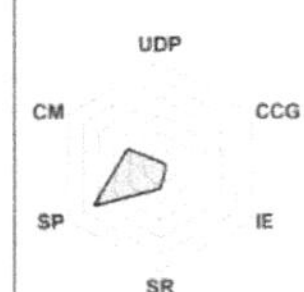
IV. Collaboration: Content encourages different social worlds to discuss their views with the aim to integrate and enrich knowledge from other social worlds	Dashboards/ Metrics Ideation Catalogue, User Stories, Project Goals, Review Presentation	(1) Incorporating customer's business understanding (2) Project-wide discussion and negotiation of solution approach (3) Exchange and involvement of expert communities	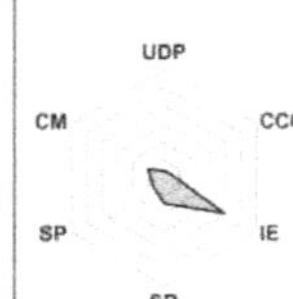

(continued)

Table 2 (continued)

Type and Description	Examples	Functions (Categories)	Impact
V. Outcome: Pool the output of other objects and grow over the course of the project from a preview to the finished project deliverable	Application, final analysis presentation, Use Case Documentation, Data as a result	(1) Presenting results for customer's decision-making (2) Handover results and enrich knowledge (3) Making insights understandable for the client	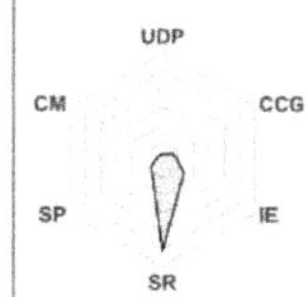
VI. Infrastructure: Content represents a comprehensive overview as orientation across all social worlds nevertheless, each social world can adapt the content to their own	Roadmap, Backlog, Tickets, Project Charter	(1) Review and coordination of tasks and capacities (2) Central project information for documenta orientation (3) Summarize and communicate project status	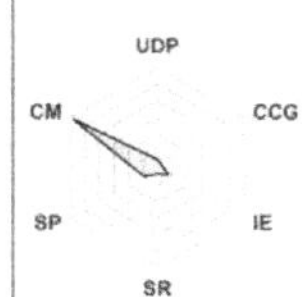

boundary object instances of the Alignment type are created by the client or collaboratively at the start of a project. After fast-paced development, these objects serve as orientation throughout the whole project. They are not actively terminated, rather no longer used as the project progresses, but may be transformed into other boundary objects.

The *Upskilling Archetype (II)* is used to communicate one's social world to others. These boundary objects come in the form of introductory slides, interpretation aids, etc. They actively train collaborators to build a common understanding and to improve team-client relationships to foster communication, collaboration, expectations, and trust between the data science team and the client. A senior data scientist and manager described the effect of actively upskilling the client: *"We need their [business side] help regarding internal drivers to create a feeling for what is important, to enable them to work with us, but also to make the collaboration more productive." (IP10)* Upskilling the client is about enabling the team to work more productively on the project while preparing them for long-term use of the project outcome. The boundary objects also increase the acceptance of the project and motivation of all participants by generating transparency. By actively training and involving the client, the boundary objects can foster shared ownership of the project and promote a sense of partnership. Upskilling boundary objects are created by experts independent of specific projects and are continuously developed based on years of professional experience.

The *Temporary Archetype (III)* facilitates collaboration on complex problems among multiple people. Examples are mock-ups and sketches that help to "*break down problem complexity. When you ... have to get a feel for [a problem]. ... Sometimes, it is also a matter of simply discussing what the best way to program something or to explain something quickly is, there is a visualization option." (Data scientist, IP11)* These boundary object instances are focused on improving the quality and effectiveness of teamwork within a complex problem-solving environment. By encouraging critical thinking, open communication, and constructive feedback using these boundary objects, teams can work together to develop more sophisticated and effective solutions. Temporary problem-solving objects are created spontaneously and unplanned during the project's progress, are updated continuously while in use. They are used only for a short time after their creation and, if deemed unhelpful, are terminated immediately. If they served their purpose, they may be transferred to other boundary objects.

The *Infrastructure Archetype (IV)* refers to critical components of effective project management (e.g., project roadmaps, product backlog). *"We use them to send to higher management, to newcomers, to people who are interested in the project, show them where we are, what we've done, what it looks like." (Product Owner, IP13)* They enable team-internal and project-wide evaluation of progress, coordinating tasks, and capacities. They provide orientation, communicate project status, documentation, and ensure access to necessary resources. They can also be used as an abstract high-level snapshot of the whole data science initiative to inform new team members or further uninvolved fields of practice. The Infrastructure boundary objects are either pre-existing templates in the departments adopted by the data science team or created anew by them. These objects become more specific and granular during the project, forming sub-types tailored to more specific use cases. They are continuously used and extended throughout the project and are not actively terminated but may no longer be used or transferred to another object when their purpose is fulfilled.

The *Collaboration Archetype (V)* facilitates discussion and the integration of knowledge from different social worlds (e.g., dashboards, user stories). *"We present something, and the [business side] will give their opinion ..., further suggestions ..., maybe 'you can also add this parameter', or 'from our experience, we have seen that this is something which might improve the detection rate'." (Data scientist, IP3)* These boundary objects facilitate project-wide discussion and negotiation of the solution approach by engaging team members to leverage their diverse expertise and identify potential issues. Collaboration archetypes are created within the project process by the data science team or collaboratively with the client for specific use cases. The content of these objects undergoes continuous development during the project through evaluation, reflection, consolidation, adaptation, and refinement while the format remains consistent. They are used continuously at specific points in the project and serve as a basis for initiating further steps. Once their purpose has been fulfilled and their content transferred to another object, they are dropped.

The *Outcome Archetype (VI)* merges and combines boundary objects that were created earlier and evolves from a preview to the final deliverable (e.g., application, final analysis). They are linked by their focus on effectively communicating knowledge to the client. Presenting results for customer decision-making involves clear and concise communication to enable informed decision-making. A data scientist explained *"At the end of the day it is about investments. For us, it was our final deliverable. And for the customer it is just the next means for the subsequent communication meetings." (Data scientist, IP9)* Handing over results and enriching knowledge involves the transfer of information in an understandable way. Prioritizing clear communication and ongoing support enables customers to make informed decisions and fully utilize the insights gained, leading to better outcomes. The Outcome boundary objects are continuously developed across the project, refined, streamlined, and finalized by the data science team. Upon completion, the object is handed over and responsibility is transferred to the appropriate individuals or teams.

4.4 Procedural and Supporting Archetypes

We observed that certain aspects of data science extend beyond operational activities during a project's life cycle and are better viewed with a strategic perspective on value creation for the organization. Thus, we mapped the primary use of the six archetypes to phases in the data value creation process [28, 34], as we show in Fig. 1. As a result, we found four archetypes whose primary functions support the transition in the value creation (we describe those as *procedural archetypes*). The two remaining archetypes (Infrastructure and Upskilling) act *supportively* and throughout the entire process.

Supporting archetypes are just as essential for the overall project outcome as the other archetypes, yet, they have an "indirect" impact on the transitions in the value creation in data science. These archetypes are employed to enhance the performance of other archetypes or to mitigate their weaknesses. The use of Infrastructure and Upskilling boundary objects often appeared in combination with boundary objects of the other archetypes. Surprisingly, we found that boundary objects with the main function of educating collaborators from other fields of practice come along with all other boundary object archetypes. With regard to the scoping phase of a project (where mainly Alignment boundary objects are used), a senior data scientist described the importance of using Upskilling boundary objects to create common ground: *"You cannot really get everyone on board without [upskilling]. That is essential for the project to succeed. … If people do not understand it, they will not use it."* (IP10) Furthermore, upskilling has positive side effects, as it enables the business side to imagine data science applications: *"Initially, the data science team had to approach the business department. Now the business department is actively approaching the data science team for assistance in obtaining and understanding data to gain insights."* (IP5).

5 Discussion

Our investigation is—to the best of our knowledge—the first study that unfolds the nature and use of boundary objects in the field of data science. It is therefore a contribution to the current discourse on the effective organization of data science work [25]. We found six *mechanisms* and six *archetypes* of boundary objects that are different from earlier boundary object archetypes that were suggested for other fields (e.g., [3, 32]).

Knowledge of the functions and use of domain-specific boundary objects helps researchers to further study the domain and practitioners to effectively design and use these boundary objects. While previous studies on data science initiatives focused on the relation and interactions between data scientists and experts [5, 33] or the interaction of data scientists with intelligent technologies (e.g., [15]), the boundary objects we identified allows to better manage and study of the interaction of data scientists with other fields of practice on a more granular level. Thus, *the identified boundary objects are instruments that future studies can use as sensitizing devices.*

In addition, we made two observations that inform the theory of boundary objects. First, one property of boundary objects is that they work as "a 'lowest common denominator' which satisfies the minimal demands of each world by capturing properties that fall within the minimum acceptable range of all concerned worlds" [32, p. 404]. Thereby, the objects can bridge boundaries and manage conflicting views. In our study, however, data scientists struggled to create objects that serve as the lowest common denominators when making insights understandable to collaborators with low data skills. Instead of "dumping down" the complexity to match the lowest denominator, data scientists started to train their collaborators, for example, using Upskilling boundary objects. Hence, in their effort to collaborate with other social worlds, data scientists have to identify and raise the lowest denominator and evaluate how they *can keep a certain required level of the complexity of their own work environment* across multiple social worlds. This is important for data science because many models are very complex or black boxes, making it essential for data scientists to explain limitations and potential risks associated with their use.

Second, our study found that some boundary objects fulfilled functions that were, at first sight, not reflected in their primary function. Temporary objects such as mock-ups and sketches are primarily utilized as frameworks for collaborative work on complex problems and for challenging current working results. However, beyond their primary functions, these objects also serve to provide orientation in project planning. They spark extensive project-wide reviews and coordination of tasks and capacities, which are integral aspects of the primary functions of infrastructural archetypes. These secondary functions and contributions of temporary boundary objects are sustained and transferred through their use in renewing and iterating infrastructural objects. Thus, it is crucial to perceive boundary object archetypes not only as discrete entities but also in relation to each other and how they interact within their social contexts.

6 Conclusion and Future Research

Our study demonstrates that a focus on boundary objects helps to better understand the current (sometimes unsatisfactory) outcomes of data science initiatives. This is because collaboration can be broken down and explored to the expectations as well as value propositions of individual detailed activities for interdisciplinary collaboration.

Implications for practice—The six mechanisms and six archetypes of boundary objects for data science projects are helpful in practice in three ways. First, the mechanisms and archetypes help to classify artifacts in data science projects as boundary objects. Practitioners can thereby better understand the functions of the different artifacts. Our findings can also be used to identify potential missing boundary object types that practitioners have not deployed. Second, data scientists can improve the design of boundary objects using the identified mechanisms to leverage them to enhance collaboration across different stages of data science initiatives, e.g., by formulating requirements for collaboration documents. Third, activities such as actively training non-data scientist staff and building working relationships with various other departments should be recognized by management and included in the scope of data scientist activities.

Limitations and future research—Future research should extend our study to enhance the empirical basis of our findings. Our data analysis indicated a point of theoretical saturation already in the 14 interviews with informants from six organizations. For a more thorough understanding of boundary work in data science, our research approach should be continued We cannot exclude a bias in the selection of our cases and informants, as all companies were located in Germany. It was very hard to find cases where the data scientist was confident or willing to approach other colleagues to join the study. Consequently, we may have sampled participants where a healthy work environment (or a more open organizational culture) was already established, and the relationships may have been stronger than in the average organizational setting. Further analysis should also focus on the temporal dynamics of boundary objects, which will help to identify success factors to design and realize boundary objects for the effective management of data science projects.

References

1. Anthony, C. (2021). When knowledge work and analytical technologies collide: The practices and consequences of black boxing algorithmic technologies. *Administrative Science Quarterly*, *66*(4), 1173–1212. Available at: https://doi.org/10.1177/00018392211016755

2. Avnoon, N. (2021). Data scientists' identity work: omnivorous symbolic boundaries in skills acquisition. *Work, Employment and Society*, *35*(2), 332–349. Available at: https://doi.org/10.1177/0950017020977306
3. Ben Chouikha, M., & Dakhli, S. B. D. (2015). Knowledge sharing in computerization projects: An approach based on boundary objects. *MCIS 2015 Proceedings* [Preprint].
4. Bowker, G. C., & Star, S. L. (1999). *Sorting things out: Classification and its consequences*. MIT Press (Inside technology).
5. van den Broek, E., Sergeeva, A., & Huysman, M. (2021). When the machine meets the expert: An ethnography of developing AI for hiring. *MIS Quarterly*, *45*(3), 1557–1580. Available at: https://doi.org/10.25300/MISQ/2021/16559
6. Chen, H., Chiang, R., & Storey, V. (2012). Business intelligence and analytics: From big data to big impact. *MIS Quarterly, 36*(4), 1165–1188.
7. Davenport, T. H., & Patil, D. J. (2012). Data scientist: The sexiest job of the 21st century. *Harvard Business Review* [Preprint]. Available at: https://hbr.org/2012/10/data-scientist-the-sexiest-job-of-the-21st-century (Retrieved 4 February 2018)
8. Davenport, T. H., & Patil, D. J. (2022). Is data scientist still the sexiest job of the 21st century?. *Harvard Business Review*, 15 July. Available at: https://hbr.org/2022/07/is-data-scientist-still-the-sexiest-job-of-the-21st-century (Retrieved 17 May 2024).
9. Doolin, B., & McLeod, L. (2012). Sociomateriality and boundary objects in information systems development. *European Journal of Information Systems*, *21*(5), 570–586. Available at: https://doi.org/10.1057/ejis.2012.20
10. Faraj, S., Pachidi, S., & Sayegh, K. (2018). Working and organizing in the age of the learning algorithm. *Information and Organization*, *28*(1), 62–70. Available at: https://doi.org/10.1016/j.infoandorg.2018.02.005
11. Fountaine, T., McCarthy, B., & Saleh, T. (2019). Building the AI-powered organization. *Harvard Business Review*, 1 July. Available at: https://hbr.org/2019/07/building-the-ai-powered-organization (Retrieved 19 February 2020).
12. Gioia, D.A., Corley, K.G., Hamilton, A.L. (2013). Seeking qualitative rigor in inductive research: Notes on the Gioia methodology. *Organizational Research Methods*, 16(1), pp. 15–31. Available at: https://doi.org/10.1177/1094428112452151
13. Glaser, B., & Strauss, A. (1967). *The discovery of grounded theory: Strategies for qualitative research*. Aldine Transaction.
14. Glushko, R. J. (2023). Seven ways to make a data science project fail. *Data and Information Management*, *7*(1), 100029. Available at: https://doi.org/10.1016/j.dim.2023.100029
15. Grønsund, T., & Aanestad, M. (2020). Augmenting the algorithm: Emerging human-in-the-loop work configurations. *The Journal of Strategic Information Systems*, *29*(2), 101614. Available at: https://doi.org/10.1016/j.jsis.2020.101614
16. Hopf, K., et al. (2023). Organizational implementation of AI: Craft and mechanical work. *California Management Review*, *66*(1). *Available at*. https://doi.org/10.1177/00081256231197445
17. Hopf, K. et al. (2024). Crafting ever-changing data products: Towards a human-centered process model of data work. In *ECIS 2024 proceedings. 32. European conference on information systems*. AIS electronic library. Available at: https://aisel.aisnet.org/ecis2024/track01_peoplefirst/track01_peoplefirst/3
18. Huvila, I. et al. (2017). Boundary objects in information science. *Journal of the Association for Information Science and Technology*, *68*(8), 1807–1822. Available at: https://doi.org/10.1002/asi.23817
19. Joshi, M. P. et al. (2021). Why so many data science projects fail to deliver. *MIT Sloan Management Review*, 2 March. Available at: https://sloanreview.mit.edu/article/why-so-many-data-science-projects-fail-to-deliver/ (Retrieved 28 July 2021).
20. Kane, G. C. et al. (2021). Avoiding an oppressive future of machine learning: A design theory for emancipatory assistants. *MIS Quarterly*, *45*(1), 371–396. Available at: https://doi.org/10.25300/MISQ/2021/1578

21. Krakowski, S., Luger, J., & Raisch, S. (2022). Artificial intelligence and the changing sources of competitive advantage. *Strategic Management Journal* [Preprint]. *Available at.* https://doi.org/10.1002/smj.3387
22. Levina, & Vaast. (2005). The emergence of boundary spanning competence in practice: Implications for implementation and use of information systems. *MIS Quarterly*, *29*(2), 335. Available at: https://doi.org/10.2307/25148682
23. Marabelli, M., Newell, S., & Vaast, E. (2017). Boundary objects survival over time: insights from the field of healthcare coordination. In *Academy of Management Proceedings.*
24. Müller, O., Fay, M., & Brocke, J. vom. (2018). The effect of big data and analytics on firm performance: An econometric analysis considering industry characteristics. *Journal of Management Information Systems*, *35*(2), 488–509. Available at: https://doi.org/10.1080/07421222.2018.1451955.
25. Parmiggiani, E., Østerlie, T., & Almklov, P. G. (2022). In the backrooms of data science. *Journal of the Association for Information Systems*, *23*(1), 139–164. Available at: https://doi.org/10.17705/1jais.00718
26. Patton, M. Q. (2002). *Qualitative research and evaluation methods* (3rd ed.). Sage Publications.
27. Pawlowski, S. D., & Robey, D. (2004). Bridging user organizations: Knowledge brokering and the work of information technology professionals. *MIS Quarterly, 28*(4), 645–672.
28. Sharma, R., Mithas, S., & Kankanhalli, A. (2014). Transforming decision-making processes: a research agenda for understanding the impact of business analytics on organisations. *European Journal of Information Systems*, *23*(4), 433–441. Available at: https://doi.org/10.1057/ejis.2014.17
29. Shollo, A. et al. (2022). Shifting ML value creation mechanisms: A process model of ML value creation. *The Journal of Strategic Information Systems*, *31*(3), 101734. Available at: https://doi.org/10.1016/j.jsis.2022.101734
30. Someh, I. et al. (2023). Configuring relationships between analytics and business domain groups for knowledge integration. *Journal of the Association for Information Systems*, *24*(2), 592–618. Available at: https://doi.org/10.17705/1jais.00782
31. Star, S. L. (2010). This is not a boundary object: reflections on the origin of a concept. *Science, Technology, & Human Values*, *35*(5), 601–617. Available at: https://doi.org/10.1177/0162243910377624
32. Star, S.L. and Griesemer, J. R. (1989). Institutional ecology, 'translations' and boundary objects: Amateurs and professionals in Berkeley's Museum of Vertebrate Zoology, 1907–39. *Social Studies of Science*, *19*(3), 387–420. Available at: https://doi.org/10.1177/030631289019003001
33. Stice-Lusvardi, R., Hinds, P. J., & Valentine, M. (2023). Legitimating illegitimate practices: how data analysts compromised their standards to promote quantification. *Organization Science* [Preprint]. *Available at.* https://doi.org/10.1287/orsc.2022.1655
34. Thiess, T., & Müller, O. (2018). Towards design principles for data-driven decision making – an action design research project in the maritime industry. In *ECIS 2018 proceedings. 26. European conference on information systems.* AIS electronic library.
35. Vaast, E., & Pinsonneault, A. (2021). When digital technologies enable and threaten occupational identity: The delicate balancing act of data scientists. *MIS Quarterly*, *45*(3), 1087–1112. Available at: https://doi.org/10.25300/MISQ/2021/16024
36. Waardenburg, L., Huysman, M. & Sergeeva, A. V. (2022). In the land of the blind, the one-eyed man is king: knowledge brokerage in the age of learning algorithms. *Organization Science*, *33*(1), 59–82. Available at: https://doi.org/10.1287/orsc.2021.1544
37. Wu, L., Hitt, L., & Lou, B. (2019). Data analytics, innovation, and firm productivity. *Management Science*, *66*(5), 2017–2039. Available at: https://doi.org/10.1287/mnsc.2018.3281
38. Zaitsev, A., Tan, B., & Gal, U. (2016). Collaboration Amidst volatility: the Evolving Nature of boundary Objects in Agile Software Development. In *ECIS 2016 proceedings.*

Governance Requirements for Decentralized Blockchain-Based Supply Chain Consortia

Maximilian Greiner, Christian Zeiß, Nicolas Neis, Karl Seidenfad, Ulrike Lechner, and Axel Winkelmann

Abstract As global logistics becomes increasingly complex, supply chain automation has become a key aspect in improving operational efficiency and transparency. Blockchain technology presents itself as a viable option, providing the potential for transformative advancements in supply chain management without a central authority through decentralization, transparency, and immutability. This study emphasizes the importance of effective governance for blockchain-based supply chain consortia, aiming to identify governance requirements (GR) for a decentralized supply chain environment. In this article, we use a mixed-method approach, including a structured literature review, expert interviews (n=13), and a two-sided evaluation strategy involving a focus group (n=5) and a survey (n=199) to derive 24 GR from the provider and user perspectives. These GRs lay the foundation for developing governance strategies within decentralized blockchain consortia in supply chains, addressing aspects such as roles, rules, incentives, structures, and decision-making processes, offering valuable insights to researchers and practitioners.

M. Greiner (✉) · K. Seidenfad · U. Lechner
University of the Bundeswehr Munich, 85578 Neubiberg, Germany
e-mail: maximilian.greiner@unibw.de

K. Seidenfad
e-mail: karl.seidenfad@unibw.de

U. Lechner
e-mail: ulrike.lechner@unibw.de

C. Zeiß · N. Neis · A. Winkelmann
University of Würzburg, 97070 Würzburg, Germany
e-mail: christian.zeiss@uni-wuerzburg.de

N. Neis
e-mail: nicolas.neis@uni-wuerzburg.de

A. Winkelmann
e-mail: axel.winkelmann@uni-wuerzburg.de

C. M. Flath et al. (eds.), *Artificial Intelligence, Data, and Decision-Making*, Lecture Notes in Information Systems and Organisation 82,
https://doi.org/10.1007/978-3-032-08480-4_14

1 Introduction

Supply chain automation has emerged as a critical aspect in improving efficiency and transparency in the global logistics landscape [11, 38]. In this context, blockchain technology arises as a particularly promising innovation that offers the potential to further revolutionize supply chain management (SCM) through its inherent properties of decentralization, transparency, and immutability [37, 43]. Thus, new collaborations, also known as consortia, have formed that use the capabilities of blockchain to reinvent industries [14, 66]. Blockchain technology steps toward technological maturity through the introduction of design patterns [18, 25], taxonomies [58], feasibility studies [13, 46, 47], and a growing number of projects in practice, e.g., SCM applications such as IBM's TradeLens [20], and BMW's PartChain [36].

When implementing blockchain applications, governance is cited as one of the most critical challenges [24]. Especially in the supply chain environment, governance is necessary to address key challenges such as ensuring consensus on system changes, maintaining immutability and decentralization, fostering reliable data entry and standards for interoperability, and coordinating stakeholder decisions to prevent fragmentation and system degradation [66]. In this article, we follow the idea of a scenario with a higher degree of decentralization from a technological and organizational perspective without a central service provider or authority [15]. This structure assumes self-management and self-governance of the technology and participating actors, meaning that each stakeholder is individually responsible for managing and governing the technology, ensuring that their actions and decisions align with the overall objectives and protocols of the blockchain system. However, research and practice highlight the importance of addressing organizational governance issues, such as decision making, accountability, structures, and incentives, within decentralized supply chain consortia using a private permissioned blockchain [3, 31, 66]. As our idea assumes self-governance and self-management of technology and the participating stakeholders, collective requirements must be created for the design of governance structures. Our focus is on a specific environment, the coffee supply chain, which is characterized by diverse stakeholders with varying technological capabilities and interests. We emphasize the highly relevant topic of governance in blockchain-based supply chain consortia and aim to establish the foundation for a successful decentralized governance strategy by identifying governance requirements (GR) from both user and provider perspectives, thereby standardizing a governance structure through the consortium. This approach leads to the following research question:

> *What governance requirements do users and providers expect from the governance of blockchain-based consortia?*

To answer this research question, we follow a participatory design (PD) process using a mixed-method approach (expert interviews, focus group, and survey) to develop and evaluate our GRs (user and provider) that provide governance needs for blockchain-based applications in a decentralized supply chain environment.

2 Theoretical Background

2.1 Blockchain in a Nutshell

Blockchain refers to the decentralized peer-to-peer management of tamper-proof data through an append-only list known as the ledger. All nodes in a blockchain network maintain a replica of the ledger, and new ledger entries are added using a consensus protocol. The National Institute of Standards and Technology presents a comprehensive definition of distributed ledger technologies, with a particular focus on blockchain [59]. Blockchain technologies can be differentiated by their right to participate in the consensus process or by their level of network exposure [7]. The network structure of blockchains can be customized to fit various scenarios [9]. Public, private, and consortium (hybrid) blockchains are decentralized networks that have different characteristics, uses, and benefits [48]. A public blockchain is accessible to all network users and is implemented through a peer-to-peer network with freely given writing and reading rights. A private blockchain provides a closed network that limits participation to a selected group and assigns predefined roles to participants. These roles determine permissions to write and read on the blockchain. Consortium blockchains are a hybrid of previous forms, allowing a group of pre-approved participants and assigned read and write permissions based on the number of participants to work together while maintaining some level of decentralization [27]. Realizing the business potential of blockchain (e.g., in accounting [26], business process management [32] and monitoring [55]) is crucially dependent on advanced design and engineering methods. However, advanced methods are lacking to design governance mechanisms within the entire organizational context.

2.2 Blockchain Governance

The governance of blockchain applications depends on the technological (e.g., hosting the blockchain nodes, smart contract development) and organizational (e.g., onboarding, risk management) configuration (whether centralized, decentralized, or mixed) of the consortium [15, 23, 54, 66]. Blockchain technology distinguishes between on-chain (encoding of rules, protocols, and decision-making processes directly in the chain code) and off-chain (non-technical regulations and decision-making procedures that influence the development and operation of the system) governance [44]. Blockchain governance has been investigated through the lens of several theories, such as IT governance [3], platform governance [41], collaborative economy [10], or stakeholder theory [4]. Recent studies have identified various components of blockchain governance, depending on whether the analysis was conducted through a theoretical framework or used an atheoretical descriptive research methodology. For example, Beck et al. [3] discuss the dimensions (decision rights, responsibilities, and incentives) of IT governance defined by Weill [57] along the blockchain economy and propose key issues in the form of a research agenda.

Other researchers, such as Li et al.[31] , Pelt et al. [40], Katina et al. [21] or Laatikainen et al. [23] focus on defining blockchain governance. Pelt et al. [40] define blockchain governance using six dimensions: formation and context, roles, incentives, membership, communication, and decision-making, in three layers: off-chain community, off-chain development, and on-chain protocol. Additionally, Additionally, Laatikainen et al. [23] suggest that blockchain governance includes technical and social decision-making at various levels (individual, organization, national) related to actors, roles, rights, incentives, responsibilities, and rules throughout the blockchain life cycle. Katina et al. [21] emphasize three essential aspects of blockchain governance: direction, oversight, and accountability, which ensure control, communication, and integration of the system and its entities.

Furthermore, research on blockchain governance also focuses on frameworks and mechanisms. Hofman et al. [17] have developed a governance analysis framework specifically designed to understand how blockchain solutions are integrated within a larger global context, analyzing the interconnections and influence of blockchain technology in relation to the broader world. In addition, Rikken et al. [45] classifies blockchain governance based on a framework consisting of different layers (infrastructure, application, company, and institution/country) and stages (design, operate, evolve/crisis). From a contractual and relational governance perspective, Lumineau et al. [33] present an analysis focusing on the role of governance mechanisms and discuss how blockchain governance interacts with traditional governance structures both in substitutive and complementary ways.

2.3 *Governance in Blockchain-Based Consortia*

While the latter blockchain governance approaches focus on public blockchain networks, where participation is open to all and actors are largely unknown, few researchers advance the study of private and consortial environments, respectively, where participants are known and roles are clearly assignable, such as in our scenario idea.

For success in a blockchain consortium, early alignment in relational and technological integration is crucial. Unlike typical IT projects, a blockchain consortium requires early negotiation of collaboration rules among users, embedding these rules within the immutable ledger [14]. Yue et al. [60] propose a framework comprising six governance attributes and 13 subattributes, including decision-making processes, accountability and verifiability, privacy and security, trust, incentives, and effectiveness. Evidence on the importance of governance for the success of a consortium is provided by Ziolkowski et al. [66], which presents the setup of a blockchain-based car dossier consortium managing car data and seeks to improve collaboration between players in terms of management, governance and value creation. In addition to the organizational steps of consortium establishment, they also describe tensions in terms of consortium, business value, and governance [62]. In a multi-case study,

Viguerie et al. [54] explore the dynamics of participant and platform openness by theorizing formative archetypes (chief, clan, custodian and consortium) in enterprise blockchains.

These approaches highlight key success factors in a blockchain consortium, emphasizing early alignment in relational and technological integration, and negotiating collaboration rules within the immutable ledger. Governance is crucial, as illustrated by a blockchain-based car dossier consortium and the exploration of participant and platform openness in enterprise blockchains.

3 Research Design

Overview: Our research aims to investigate GRs in decentralized blockchain-based supply chain consortia. Our research approach follows an iterative DSR framework of Hevner et al. [16] guided by a participatory design (PD) process (see Fig. 1). PD is a method that emphasizes the involvement of stakeholders and iterative development in the creation of technological solutions [50]. We use the PD concept to involve the provider and the user in our solution design. The problem space is provided by our idea of a decentralized (technological and organizational) blockchain-based supply chain consortium, where self-management and self-governance of the technology and the participating stakeholders prevail. We define the goals of our GRs artifact by building a knowledge base that mixes expertise from literature theory and practical expert interviews. Additionally, we design and develop our requirements considering the provider and the users (coffee supply chain stakeholder) as we perform workshops as part of our PD [50]. We evaluate our GRs with a mixed-method approach [6].

Literature Review: To derive the GRs, we conducted a literature review following the comprehensive approach proposed by vom Brocke et al. [5]. We carried out a topic-based database search in seven IS-related databases according to Webster and Watson [56]. The research team searched *Web of Science, ACM Digital Library, EBSCOhost Business Source Premier, Science Direct, Emerald Insight, IEEE Xplore, and AIS eLibrary* to identify 10248 potential contributions. Based on our focus on intercompany blockchain consortia, we defined a generic query string: *(consortium AND blockchain governance AND (collaboration OR intermediary OR provider OR trust))*. After screening the titles, abstracts, and full texts, we identified a final set of 32 relevant contributions that we used to derive the first requirements. We present an overview of the literature review process and the inclusion and exclusion criteria used in Fig. 2.

Interview Study: Furthermore, we conducted semi-structured expert interviews (n=13) with blockchain as well as supply chain experts and stakeholders in the coffee supply chain (coffee farmer, processor, importer, roaster and distributor). Blockchain and supply chain experts represent the provider's perspective in our research, and coffee supply chain stakeholders are used to adopt the user's perspective. The requirements that the interviewees mentioned regarding the governance of the system serve as the foundation for our coding procedure for the transcribed interviews [51]. The

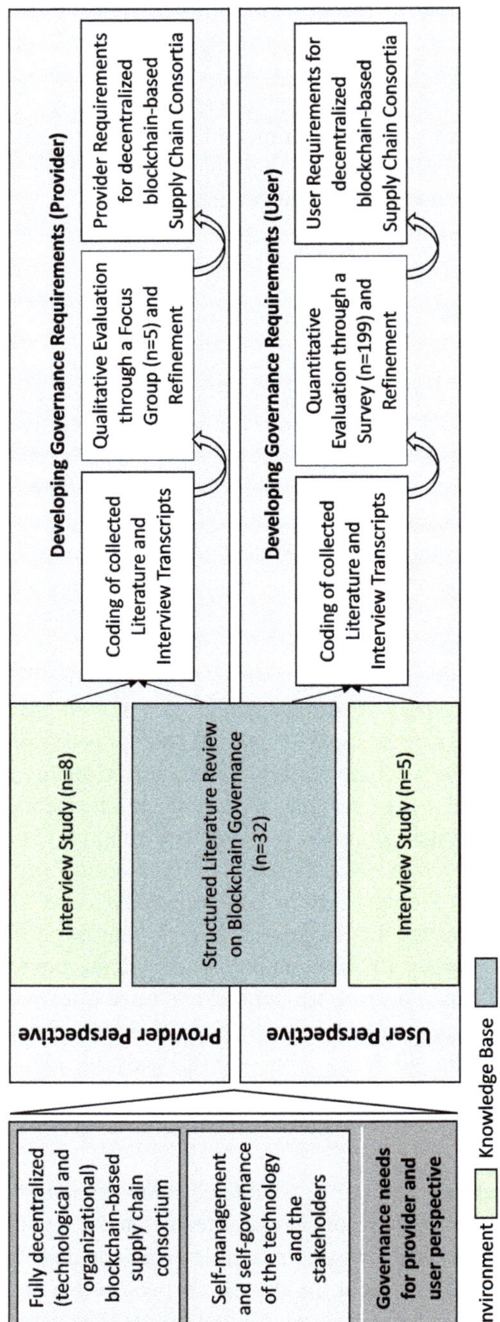

Fig. 1 Research design

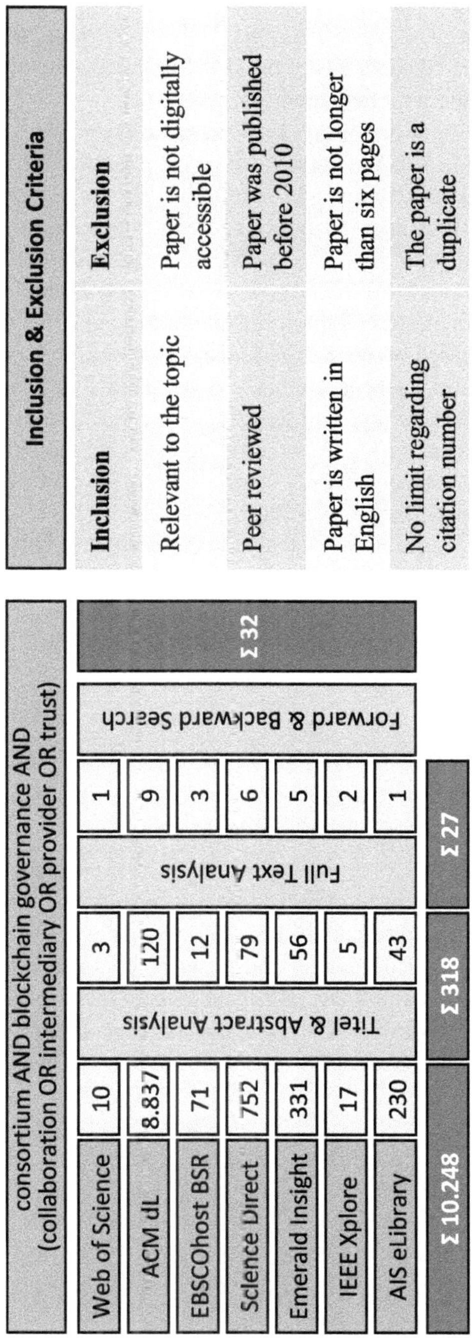

Fig. 2 Overview of literature review procedure

open coding activities lead to approximately n=50 open codes, which were then analyzed by Axial Coding to identify the relationships between the codes and derive a final set of 6 categories: *Decision making, Accountabilities, Incentives, Security, Technology, Verifiability*. The results of the structured literature review then complemented the results of the interview analysis.

Evaluation: Our validation follows the Framework for Evaluation in Design Science Research (FEDS) [53]. We deploy a mixed-methods approach by Bryman et al. [6] as we combine quantitative and qualitative research by conducting a quantitative survey (n=199) for users to demonstrate their agreement with our GRs and a focus group [49, 64] with providers (n=5). A story-based online study was conducted on the Prolific platform to classify GRs [52, 63]. Participants who work in supply chain management and collaboration completed our survey questionnaire. We selected participants based on their experience and workplace, as they are potential user best placed to assess user requirements (UR). They rated their agreement with our GRs, including the keyword and descriptions, on a 7-point Likert scale ranging from 1 (strongly disagree) to 7 (strongly agree). Our focus group consisted of five blockchain governance and supply chain experts. We explain our decentralized blockchain-based supply chain consortium and demonstrate our GRs for governance on the provider side. In addition, we discuss the requirements. Our experts mentioned the practical relevance of our provider requirements (PR) and the need for prioritization when operating the requirements. In the following, we present the final draft of URs and PRs including our evaluation findings.

4 Governance Requirements—User and Provider Perspective

The decentralized application of blockchain without a central service provider or authority forces the actors in the blockchain consortium to consider the tasks for both sides, the user perspective, and the provider perspective. This chapter comprises the resulting GR catalogs from a user and provider perspective. In addition to the descriptions supported by the analysis of our expert interviews (EI1-13) and the results of our literature review, expression measures that show whether they are part of technical or organizational areas of responsibility are outlined.

4.1 User Requirements

From the user's point of view, there are distinct GRs related to system utilization within our consortium (see Fig. 3). Our first GR (**UR1**) covers the accessibility and user-friendliness of the blockchain system. Due to the heterogeneity of the levels of computer literacy of the participants, it is necessary to design user interfaces and

ID	Requirement	Description	Expression Measure
UR1	**Accessibility & user friendliness**	Focus on user-friendliness due to the varying computer literacy levels of participants from different countries. The system, including user interfaces and network operations, should be simple and accessible regardless of technical skills or capabilities.	Technical
UR2	**Education and awareness**	Counteracting skepticism and ignorance by raising awareness towards blockchain and the associated risks within the operation.	Organizational
UR3	**Type and scope of data collection**	Ensure that only data relevant to the participants can be stored on the network to keep the data model lean as information is collected across the entire supply chain. This will have a decisive impact on decision-making processes of stakeholders.	Organizational
UR4	**Stakeholder communication**	Establishment of a secure (live) communication platform whether on-chain or off-chain in addition to the data available from the blockchain to support exchange among participants and strengthen relationships.	Organizational/ technical
UR5	**Data privacy mechanisms**	Introduction of mechanisms that enable certain data with high sensitivity to be additionally encrypted or concealed from unauthorized participants.	Technical
UR6	**Criteria for participation**	Definition of a catalog that defines criteria for on-boarding (e.g., required certificates) and off-boarding (e.g., sanctions).	Organizational
UR7	**Data integrity mechanisms**	Implementation of mechanisms for data verification (e.g., an external auditor) before storing on the blockchain network to enhance IT security. Furthermore, an option for correcting wrong-entered data needs to be considered.	Technical
UR8	**Co-development procedures**	Requirement of a co-determination right of participants for the establishment, operation, and further development of the blockchain consortium concerning functions, purpose, and strategic alignment.	Organizational
UR9	**Cost effectiveness**	Implementation of measures to justify the costs incurred by users with regard to human resources and Unique Selling Point (USP) of the product.	Organizational
UR10	**Added value creation**	Identification of added values (e.g., financing opportunities in production countries) besides the actual business purpose of the track and trace system, to maximize the consortium potential.	Organizational
UR11	**Consortium scalability**	Determination of the scalability of the consortium with regard to a critical number of participants.	Technical
UR12	**Incentive allocation**	Users require incentives that are compelling enough to ensure that the system is used carefully and consistently. Each actor has to identify benefits for participation.	Organizational
UR13	**IT/Business Alignment**	Each stakeholder has to ensure the adaption of its business model to the shared use of the technology within the consortium individually.	Organizational

Fig. 3 Requirements catalog from an user perspective

network operations in a simple and accessible way regardless of technical skills or capabilities [3]. Here, all experts agreed that the complexity must be reduced for a successful use. Furthermore, the high complexity of the technology and the inter-organizational environment without a central service provider forces organizations to raise awareness and train their employees (**UR2**) with regard to the risks involved in dealing with blockchain [29]. The immutability and persistence of the data and cross-company use require a clear definition of the scope and type of data collection (**UR3**). The substantial volume of data collected throughout the supply chain necessitates the development of streamlined data models for effective utilization and decision making.

UR4 covers stakeholder communication, which is a critical component for the success of the consortium. More than half of the experts interviewed indicated that exchange between participants is essential for the success of the consortium. In addition to proven communication platforms, the blockchain within Hyperledger Fabric offers a "channel" option that can be connected on-chain to the network [1]. Participants may be included or excluded from this process as necessitated by the requirements. In addition to data that are accessible to all participating stakeholders, individual companies can also choose to share sensitive or business-critical data via the blockchain (**UR5**). For this purpose, users require mechanisms that further encrypt these data or keep them hidden from unauthorized participants [30, 31].

Furthermore, **UR6** outlines the need for a participation strategy. It is imperative to establish precise guidelines and criteria, depending on the objectives of the consortium, delineating the characteristics required for potential participants. Concurrently, it is essential to define sanctions for any violation of established rules [19, 39, 42]. To enhance IT security and data integrity, mechanisms are required to verify data before they are recorded on the network (**UR7**) [17, 21]. *"It is crucial to ensure that the entered data is correct from the beginning. For example, incorrect data input into the blockchain without knowing can be problematic since the blockchain is a permanent system"* (EI3). Additionally, corrective measures that are acceptable to participating stakeholders should be defined. Co-development procedures (**UR8**) within blockchain consortia can strengthen collaboration between players in the ecosystem, potentially improving value creation [62].

Collaboration in the consortium is based on transparency in handling costs and benefits for individual stakeholders and users [29]. Cost effectiveness (**UR9**) must be attractive, especially for users. In particular, stakeholders in the coffee supply chain noted that participation depends on how costs can be covered. (**UR10**) discusses the need to create added value through collaboration in the consortium in addition to the existing business by establishing new business models [62]. To ensure a large user base, the technical, infrastructural, and conceptual components of the consortium must be scalable (**UR11**) [60]. During the discussions with the interview partners, it was noted several times that the scalability of the entire consortium is currently difficult to determine due to the technological maturity.

To achieve consensus, it is crucial to allocate incentives (**UR12**) and manage them effectively in the blockchain economy [3, 30, 60, 65]. *"I think more motivation means that people will be more willing to engage and contribute resources to the consortium"* (EI5). When entering a blockchain-based consortium, the processes and structures of each participant must be adapted to the underlying technology and the consortium (**UR13**). Continuous evolution must also be taken into account.

4.2 User Evaluation

The evaluation achieves an average agreement of 83,5% for our GRs (see Fig. 4). The user side shows the highest confirmation score for the requirements of data privacy (UR5) as well as data integrity mechanism (UR7), with an overall score of at least 91%. The requirements for incentive allocation (UR12) and co-development procedures (UR8) still perform well with scores around 73%. Users often request technical features in their requirements because they may lack the necessary skills and resources to handle them within the consortium. This is underlined by the fact that the most strongly agreed upon topic (deep blue) is data privacy (56,5%), whereas the least strongly agreed upon topic is collaboration aspects (8,5%).

4.3 Provider Requirements

The provider GRs delineate the governance responsibilities typically undertaken by a service provider (see Fig. 5). They play a crucial role in facilitating access to specific technologies, knowledge, or infrastructural capabilities and may operate

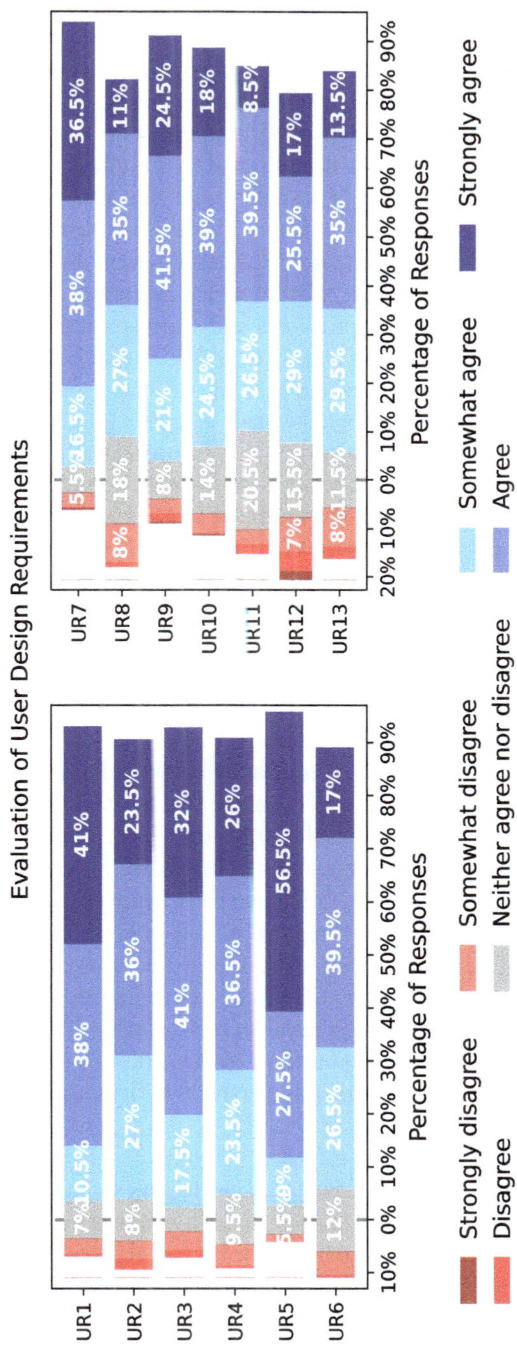

Fig. 4 Evaluation results of GRs from a user perspective with a 7-point Likert scale

under contractual, subscription-based, or pay-per-use models. In our case, the same organization that uses the blockchain also provides the service for it.

Our first GR (**PR1**) comprises the standardization of processes considering technological and organizational aspects to improve collaboration between the participating actors [33]. Furthermore, compliance with recent legislation such as the General Data Protection Regulation (GDPR) or the Supply Chain Due Diligence Act [12] that need to be adhered for the specific use case environment [35]. Standardization of procedures, such as onboarding or auditing, improves transparency and strengthens trust within the consortium [8]. *"Standardized containerized applications are required, which simplifies the maintenance and deployment processes without needing new experts or administrators"*, EI8 mentioned and pointed out that a decentralized system without standardized processes and structures cannot be successful. A decentralized consortium requires centralized and decentralized mechanisms (**PR2**) for implementing specific processes. An example of centralized execution would be chain code development, which should be made available transparently. On the other hand, the deployment of updates on the network is a decentralized measure, since no participant has the rights to change chain code or smart contracts of another participant. Another critical GR within decentralized blockchain environments (**PR3**) is the management of certificates. *"If someone says that they want to join, they would have to be verified through a specific process and then approved by the appropriate authority"* (EI11). The network is based on a permissioned blockchain; in this sense, certificates and authorized users must be shared with the consortium to reduce fraud [67]. Blockchain experts pointed out that the duration of certificates plays a particularly important role and that an incorrect extension can have serious consequences, such as an internal company system failure.

Next, **PR4** outlines the demand for uniform interface provision and logging mechanisms to enable data exchange. This is accompanied by the definition of a standardized data model that is identical for all participants [31]. In this regard, organizations should be included to prevent business-critical data from being entered on the blockchain [65]. If sensitive data are contained on the network, additional protection mechanisms must be identified and implemented to ensure confidentiality and privacy (**PR5**). The coffee supply chain stakeholders interviewed in particular called for an additional encryption option to facilitate collaboration with certain partners. As already described in the user requirements section, the provider perspective also requires incentives (**PR6**) to provide technology capabilities in terms of infrastructure, hardware, and software. From this perspective, it is essential to ensure the coverage of costs [3, 30, 57].

The decentralized technological infrastructure hinders the automated deployment of updates on the blockchain, so the focus on testing in the field or within test environments should be enhanced, ensuring a high matured quality (**PR7**) [61, 62]. Furthermore, the immutability and persistence of the data entered on the blockchain require measures, especially in a production environment, that allow corrections such back-up functions (**PR8**) on the network [28]. Some experts have noted that, in an industrial environment and with human involvement, there is always a possibility of erroneous entries, thus making amendments a necessity. Taking into account our

ID	Requirement	Description	Expression Measure
PR1	**Process standardization**	Definition and implementation of standardized processes for using the system, e.g., uniform on-boarding, documentations or auditing. Additionally, processes for compliance and legal standards need to be considered and outlined for the specific use case application.	Organizational
PR2	**Decentralization vs. Centralization**	A fully decentralized ecosystem (technological and organizational) requires dynamic and transparent mechanisms for decision-making. At this stage, the consortium has to decide whether to operate specific processes centralized (e.g., chain code development) or decentralized (e.g., blockchain updates).	Organizational
PR3	**Certificate management**	Certificates and keys need to be documented by the consortium and the users. An overview of authorized users should be made available to the consortium.	Organizational
PR4	**Form of data exchange**	The consortium requires an interface provision and logging to enable data exchange. The users should use a uniformed (standardized) data model for accessing the blockchain to improve collaboration with other participants.	Technical
PR5	**Confidentiality and privacy**	Putting sensitive data on the blockchain could be a risk for the companies, they should be able to choose which data they disclose.	Technical
PR6	**Incentive allocation**	In addition to the incentives to use the network, the system should provide incentives to provide the technological capabilities on business level (cost coverage).	Organizational
PR7	**Quality assured**	The decentralized implementation and associated complicated implementation of updates requires a strong focus on testing. A faulty blockchain significantly impairs the security of the network.	Organizational /Technical
PR8	**Corrective measures**	Identification and implementation of corrective measures (e.g., back up functions) to restore wrong entered data sets and information without compromising integrity of the network.	Technical
PR9	**Long-time scalability**	Build technological components and prevent mechanisms that reduce the blockchain usage to enable scalability over the long term. It is still unclear how lifecycles of specific blockchain applications look like, therefore the weighting of scalability needs to be set individually.	Technical
PR10	**Risk management**	Risk management in a fully decentralized consortium relates to both the technology and the participating players. It requires processes that identify stakeholder-related risks and how to deal with them. Furthermore, the technology also provides risks, such as entry of sensitive data or failure of a blockchain node.	Organizational /Technical
PR11	**Data authenticity and transparency**	Ensuring transparency for authorized participants and ensuring authenticity through various validation mechanisms (e.g., data validation by downstream supply chain participants or third-party audits).	Technical

Fig. 5 Requirements catalog from a provider perspective

stakeholder interests, a blockchain-based supply chain consortium should aim to achieve long-term relationships. Thus, scalability (**PR9**) plays a crucial role in the building of technological components and preventing mechanisms that reduce the use of blockchain [2]. At this point, theory and practice agree, it is still unclear how the life cycles of specific blockchain applications will evolve [30, 62].

Blockchain also poses specific technological (smart contract attacks or failures) and organizational (key loss or expiration of the certificate) risks that must be considered for a governance strategy. Therefore, internal risk managements (**PR10**) have to be expanded by processes and mechanisms that include blockchain and inter-organizational collaboration [8]. Our last GR covers the authenticity and transparency of the data flows (**PR11**). Here, validation mechanisms are required, such as downstream verification by supply chain participants or third-party audits that ensure the integrity of entered data [34].

4.4 Provider Evaluation

Our experts from the focus group (FG1-5) mentioned the practical relevance of our requirements and the need for prioritization when operating the requirements. "In some of our projects, we have found that there isn't much expertise or support out there for consortia with a very high degree of decentralization" (FG3). "We find the division into user and provider requirements very successful, as one of the two sides is very often neglected" (FG1). In general, experts agreed that our research recognized the most important aspects of a successful governance structure, but that an application in a virtual environment or field tests would provide new insights into the control and regulation of decentralized consortia. "It would be really exciting to see how these requirements can be implemented and used in a virtual governance lab" (FG4). Finally, we conducted a quantitative survey with our experts. With the results of this study, we could recognize a high confirmation of the feasibility and accessibility. In addition, most of the participants highlighted our high level of completeness, clarity, and understandability, which is essential to designing requirements as an artifact. We adopted a participatory approach in developing our GRs, and applicability is a high priority, as confirmed by the participants.

5 Discussion and Conclusion

This article addresses the importance of designing a governance strategy for blockchain-based (private permissioned) supply chain consortia. To this end, we derive 13 GRs from the user's perspective and 11 GRs from the provider's perspective validated by a two-sided evaluation strategy.

The GRs proposed in this article offer new insights by integrating perspectives from both users and providers, which have not been extensively explored in the existing literature. These GRs emphasize the importance of aligning user-friendly system accessibility with robust provider infrastructure management, ensuring that both ends of the blockchain network are effectively governed. This approach takes into account the results of the research agenda suggested by Beck et al. [3] and aspects of decision problems in blockchain consortia provided by Ziolkowski et al. [66] incorporating decision rights and responsibilities. Additionally, the GRs address both technical and organizational aspects, building on the approach of Laatikainen et al. [23] by incorporating comprehensive governance mechanisms that span the entire lifecycle of blockchain networks, including roles, incentives, membership criteria and communication protocols. Our results emphasize the need for standardized certification management to ensure interoperability, aligning with Zavolokina et al. [62] on governance and value creation. Furthermore, the focus on data privacy and security mechanisms considers the governance attributes of Yue et al. [60] on the critical importance of these factors within blockchain consortia. Our emphasis on multi-layered governance resonates with Rikken et al. [45]'s classification of governance layers and stages, providing user and provider needs to manage both technical and organizational aspects of blockchain networks.

The identified GRs face implementation challenges, including the need for all stakeholders to adhere to standardized processes and effectively manage the technological complexities of blockchain integration. Potential barriers to real-world application include varying levels of technological capability among stakeholders and resistance to change, as the decentralized nature of governance can complicate the achievement of consensus and the maintenance of accountability. As blockchain technology rapidly evolves, our GRs will need to adapt by incorporating more advanced security measures and automated compliance checks to keep pace with recent vulnerabilities and regulatory standards. Furthermore, advances in artificial intelligence and machine learning could enhance decision-making processes within blockchain consortia, allowing for more efficient and dynamic governance structures that can respond quickly to changing conditions and stakeholder needs [22].

This research lays the foundation for a governance strategy for blockchain-based (private permissioned) supply chain consortia, operating without a central service provider or authority. The focus on the coffee supply chain could limit the generalizability of the findings, as the specific challenges and dynamics of this industry may not fully represent those in other sectors. Therefore, future research could explore other industries to validate and potentially expand the applicability of the GRs.

Considering automation in supply chains, effective governance of decentralized blockchain-based consortia can significantly advance transparency, security, and efficiency. Blockchain can streamline transaction tracking and verification, automate compliance through smart contracts, and facilitate real-time data sharing, enhancing operational efficiency, and reducing manual interventions.

Finally, we extend the existing body of knowledge toward governance in private permissioned blockchains in supply chain environments without a central authority by providing a set of requirements that are necessary to develop a governance strategy within a specific environment.

Acknowledgements This work has been developed in the project InKryBa and is partly funded by the DZ-Bank-Stiftung under grant number FRFMM-788/2022. Furthermore, we acknowledge funding for Project LIONS as part of dtec.bw. dtec.bw is funded by the European Commission under NextGenerationEU.

References

1. Androulaki, E., Barger, A., Bortnikov, V., Muralidharan, S., Cachin, C., Christidis, K., De Caro, A., Enyeart, D., Murthy, C., Ferris, C., Laventman, G., Manevich, Y., Nguyen, B., Sethi, M., Singh, G., Smith, K., Sorniotti, A., Stathakopoulou, C., Vukolić, M., Cocco, S.W., & Yellick, J. (2018). Hyperledger fabric: A distributed operating system for permissioned blockchains. In *Proceedings of the 13th EuroSys Conference, EuroSys 2018*. https://doi.org/10.1145/3190508.3190538
2. Balcerzak, A. P., Nica, E., Rogalska, E., Poliak, M., Klieštik, T., & Sabie, O. M. (2022). Blockchain technology and smart contracts in decentralized governance systems. *Administrative Sciences, 12*, 96. https://doi.org/10.3390/ADMSCI12030096
3. Beck, R., Müller-Bloch, C., & King, J. (2018). Governance in the blockchain economy: A framework and research agenda. *Journal of the Association for Information Systems*
4. Brennan, N. M., Subramaniam, N., & Van Staden, C. J. (2019). Corporate governance implications of disruptive technology: An overview
5. vom Brocke, J., Simons, A., Niehaves, B., Riemer, K., Plattfaut, R., & Cleven, A. (2009). Reconstructing the giant: On the importance of rigour in documenting the literature search process. In *European Conference on Information Systems* (pp. 2206–2217)
6. Bryman, A. (2006). Integrating quantitative and qualitative research: How is it done? *Qualitative Research, 6*(1), 97–113.
7. Crosby, M., Pattanayak, P., Verma, S., Kalyanaraman, V., et al. (2016). Blockchain technology: Beyond bitcoin. Applied. *Innovation, 2*(6–10), 71.
8. De Filippi, P., Mannan, M., & Reijers, W. (2020). Blockchain as a confidence machine: The problem of trust & challenges of governance. *Technology in Society*, 101284. https://doi.org/10.1016/J.TECHSOC.2020.101284
9. Di Pierro, M. (2017). What is the blockchain? *Computing in Science & Engineering, 19*(5), 92–95.
10. Ertz, M., & Boily, É. (2019). The rise of the digital economy: Thoughts on blockchain technology and cryptocurrencies for the collaborative economy. *International Journal of Innovation Studies, 3*(4), 84–93.
11. Fatorachian, H., & Kazemi, H. (2021). Impact of industry 4.0 on supply chain performance. *Production Planning & Control, 32*(1), 63–81.
12. Federal Ministry of Labour and Social Affairs: BMAS - Supply Chain Act. (2021). https://www.bmas.de/EN/Europe-and-the-World/International/Supply-Chain-Act/supply-chain-act.html
13. Greiner, M., Seidenfad, K., Langewisch, C., Hofmann, A., & Lechner, U. (2024). The digital product passport: Enabling interoperable information flows through blockchain consortia for sustainability. In *International Conference on Innovations for Community Services* (pp. 377–396). Springer
14. Hacker, J., Miscione, G., Felder, T., & Schwabe, G. (2023). Commit or not? How blockchain consortia form and develop. *California Management Revie*, 110–131.
15. Halaburda, H., & Mueller-Bloch, C. (2020). Toward a multidimensional conceptualization of decentralization in blockchain governance: Commentary on "two sides of the same coin? Decentralized versus proprietary blockchains and the performance of digital currencies" by cennamo, marchesi, and meyer. *Academy of Management Discoveries, 6*(4), 712–714.

16. Hevner, A. R., March, S. T., Park, J., & Ram, S. (2004). Design science in information systems research. *MIS Quarterly*. https://doi.org/10.2307/25148625
17. Hofman, D., DuPont, Q., Walch, A., & Beschastnikh, I. (2021). Blockchain governance: De facto (X)or designed? In *Building decentralized trust: Multidisciplinary perspectives on the design of blockchains and distributed ledgers* (pp. 21–33). https://doi.org/10.1007/978-3-030-54414-0_2/FIGURES/2
18. Hoiss, T., Seidenfad, K., & Lechner, U. (2021). Blockchain service operations-a structured approach to operate a blockchain solution. In *2021 IEEE International Conference on Decentralized Applications and Infrastructures (DAPPS)* (pp. 11–19). IEEE.
19. Jain, G., Shrivastava, A., Paul, J., & Batra, R. (2022). Blockchain for SME clusters: An ideation using the framework of Ostrom commons governance. *Information Systems Frontier, 4*, 1125–1143. https://doi.org/10.1007/S10796-022-10288-Z
20. Jensen, T., Hedman, J., & Henningsson, S. (2019). How tradelens delivers business value with blockchain technology. *MIS Quarterly Executiv, 4*, 221–243. https://doi.org/10.17705/2msqe.00018
21. Katina, P. F., Keating, C. B., Sisti, J. A., & Gheorghe, A. V. (2019). Blockchain governance. *International Journal of Critical Infrastructure, 2*, 121–135. https://doi.org/10.1504/IJCIS.2019.098835
22. Klare, M., Verlande, L., Greiner, M., & Lechner, U. (2022). How blockchain and artificial intelligence influence digital sovereignty. In *European, Mediterranean, and Middle Eastern Conference on Information Systems* (pp. 3–16). Springer.
23. Laatikainen, G., Li, M., & Abrahamsson, P. (2023). A system-based view of blockchain governance. *Information and Software Technology*, 107149. https://doi.org/10.1016/J.INFSOF.2023.107149
24. Lacity, M. C. (2018). Addressing key challenges to making enterprise blockchain applications a reality. *MIS Quarterly Executiv*.
25. Lamken, D., Wagner, T., Hoiss, T., Seidenfad, K., Hermann, A., Kus, M., & Lechner, U. (2021). Design patterns and framework for blockchain integration in supply chains. In *2021 IEEE International Conference on Blockchain and Cryptocurrency (ICBC)* (pp. 1–3). IEEE.
26. Laurier, W., Schwaiger, W. S., & Polovina, S. (2020). Traditional accounting with decentralised ledger technology. In *CEUR Workshop Proceeding* (pp. 202–208).
27. Li, Z., Kang, J., Yu, R., Ye, D., Deng, Q., & Zhang, Y. (2018). Consortium blockchain for secure energy trading in industrial internet of things. *IEEE Transactions on Industrial Informatics*, 3690–3700. https://doi.org/10.1109/TII.2017.2786307
28. Liang, W., Fan, Y., Li, K. C., Zhang, D., & Gaudiot, J. L. (2020). Secure data storage and recovery in industrial blockchain network environments. *IEEE Transactions on Industrial Informatics*, 6543–6552. https://doi.org/10.1109/TII.2020.2966069
29. Lindman, J., Tuunainen, V. K., & Rossi M. (2017). Opportunities and risks of blockchain technologies – A research agenda. In *Hawaii International Conference on System Sciences 2017 (HICSS-50)*.
30. Liu, Y., Lu, Q., Yu, G., Paik, H. Y., & Zhu, L. (2022). Defining blockchain governance principles: A comprehensive framework. *Information Systems*, 102090. https://doi.org/10.1016/J.IS.2022.102090
31. Liu, Y., Lu, Q., Zhu, L., Paik, H. Y., & Staples, M. (2023). A systematic literature review on blockchain governance. *Journal of Systems and Software, 197*, Article 111576.
32. López-Pintado, O., García-Bañuelos, L., Dumas, M., Weber, I., & Ponomarev, A. (2019). Caterpillar: A business process execution engine on the Ethereum blockchain. *Software - Practice and Experience*, 1162–1193. https://doi.org/10.1002/spe.2702
33. Lumineau, F., Wang, W., & Schilke, O. (2021). Blockchain governance-A new way of organizing collaborations? *Organization Science*, 500–521.
34. Mackey, T. K., Shah, N., Miyachi, K., Short, J., & Clauson, K. (2019). A framework proposal for blockchain-based scientific publishing using shared governance. *Frontiers in Blockchai*, 486144. https://doi.org/10.3389/FBLOC.2019.00019/BIBTEX

35. Mahmud, H., Islam, A. K., Naqvi, B., & Mäntymäki, M. (2022). *Toward a GDPR compliant blockchain governance framework*. Lecture notes in computer science (including subseries Lecture notes in artificial intelligence and lecture notes in bioinformatics (pp. 471–484). https://doi.org/10.1007/978-3-031-15342
36. Miehle, D., Henze, D., Seitz, A., Luckow, A., & Bruegge, B. (2019). PartChain: A decentralized traceability application for multi-tier supply chain networks in the automotive industry. In *2019 IEEE International Conference on Decentralized Applications and Infrastructures (DAPPCON)* (pp. 140–145). IEEE. https://doi.org/10.1109/DAPPCON.2019.00027
37. Narayanaswami, C., Nooyi, R., Govindaswamy, S. R., & Viswanathan, R. (2019). Blockchain anchored supply chain automation. *IBM Journal of Research and Development, 63*(2/3), 7–1.
38. Nitsche, B. (2021). Exploring the potentials of automation in logistics and supply chain management: Paving the way for autonomous supply chains.
39. Ostrom, E. (1990). Governing the commons: The evolution of institutions for collective action. *Governing the Commons*. https://doi.org/10.1017/CBO9780511807763
40. Pelt, R. v., Jansen, S., Baars, D., & Overbeek, S. (2021). Defining blockchain governance: A framework for analysis and comparison. *Information Systems Manageme, 1*, 21–41. https://doi.org/10.1080/10580530.2020.1720046
41. Pereira, J., Tavalaei, M. M., & Ozalp, H. (2019). Blockchain-based platforms: Decentralized infrastructures and its boundary conditions. *Technological Forecasting and Social Change, 146*, 94–102.
42. Poux, P., & Filippi, P. D. (2020). Blockchains for the governance of common goods. In *Proceedings of the 1st International Workshop on Distributed Infrastructure* (pp. 7–12). https://doi.org/10.1145/3428662.3428793
43. Pytel, N., Zeiß, C., & Winkelmann, A. (2023). Enabling UTXO-based backwards and fordwards traceability. In *ECIS 2023 Research Paper* (pp. 5–11)
44. Reijers, W., Wuisman, I., Mannan, M., De Filippi, P., Wray, C., Rae-Looi, V., Cubillos Vélez, A., & Orgad, L. (2021). Now the code runs itself: On-chain and off-chain governance of blockchain technologies. *Top*, 821–831. https://doi.org/10.1007/S11245-018-9626-5/METRICS
45. Rikken, O., Janssen, M., & Kwee, Z. (2019). Governance challenges of blockchain and decentralized autonomous organizations. *Information Polity, 24*(4), 397–417.
46. Seidenfad, K., Greiner, M., Biermann, J., Dannenberg, D., Keineke, S., & Lechner, U. (2024). Greenhouse gas emissions as commons: A community service approach with blockchain on the edge. In *International Conference on Innovations for Community Services* (pp. 351–376). Springer.
47. Seidenfad, K., Greiner, M., Biermann, J., & Lechner, U. (2023). Carbonedge: Collaborative blockchain-based monitoring, reporting, and verification of greenhouse gas emissions on the edge. In *International Conference on Innovations for Community Services* (pp. 123–147). Springer.
48. Shrimali, B., & Patel, H. B. (2022). Blockchain state-of-the-art: Architecture, use cases, consensus, challenges and opportunities. *Journal of King Saud University - Computer and Information Science*. https://doi.org/10.1016/J.JKSUCI.2021.08.005
49. Sonnenberg, C., & vom Brocke, J. (2012). Evaluations in the science of the artificial – Reconsidering the build-evaluate pattern in design science research (pp. 381–397). https://doi.org/10.1007/978-3-642-29863-9_28
50. Spinuzzi, C. (2005). The methodology of participatory design. *Society for Technical Communication*.
51. Strauss, A., & Corbin, J. (1998). *Basics of qualitative research techniques*. Sage publications.
52. Tomitza, C., Schaschek, M., Straub, L., & Winkelmann, A. (2023). What is the minimum to trust AI?—A requirement analysis for (generative) AI-based texts. In *Wirtschaftsinformatik 2023 Proceedings*.
53. Venable, J., Pries-Heje, J., & Baskerville, R. (2016). FEDS: A framework for evaluation in design science research. *European Journal of Information System*. https://doi.org/10.1057/ejis.2014.36

54. Viguerie, C., Ciriello, R.F., & Zavolokina, L. (2024). Formative archetypes in enterprise blockchain governance: Exploring the dynamics of participant dominance and platform openness. In *57th Hawaii International Conference on System Sciences*.
55. Weber, I., Xu, X., Riveret, R., Governatori, G., Ponomarev, A., & Mendling, J. (2016). *Untrusted business process monitoring and execution using blockchain*. Lecture notes in computer science (including subseries lecture notes in artificial intelligence and lecture notes in bioinformatics) (pp. 329–347). https://doi.org/10.1007/978-3-319-45348-4_19
56. Webster, J., & Watson, R.T. (2002). Analyzing the past to prepare for the future: Writing a literature review. *MIS Quarterly*, xiii–xxiii.
57. Weill, P. (2004). Don't just lead, govern: How top-performing firms govern it. *MIS Quarterly Executive, 3*(1), 1–17.
58. Xu, X., Weber, I., Staples, M., Zhu, L., Bosch, J., Bass, L., Pautasso, C., & Rimba, P.: A taxonomy of blockchain-based systems for architecture design. In *2017 IEEE International Conference on Software Architecture (ICSA)* (pp. 243–252). IEEE.
59. Yaga, D., Mell, P., Roby, N. & Scarfone, K. (2019). Blockchain technology overview. arXiv:1906.11078
60. Yue, K. B., Kallempudi, P., Sha, K., Wei, W., & Liu, X.(2021). Governance attributes of consortium blockchain applications. In *Twenty-Seventh Americas Conference on Information Systems, Montreal*.
61. Zachariadis, M., Hileman, G., & Scott, S. V. (2019). Governance and control in distributed ledgers: Understanding the challenges facing blockchain technology in financial services. *Information and Organizatio*, 105–117. https://doi.org/10.1016/J.INFOANDORG.2019.03.001
62. Zavolokina, L., Ziolkowski, R., Bauer, I., & Schwabe, G. (2020). Management, governance and value creation in a blockchain consortium. *MIS Quarterly Executive, 19*(1), 1–17.
63. Zeiss, C., Straub, L., Schaschek, M., & Winkelmann, A. (2024). The obscure world of digital assets - design principles for user-centered platforms. In *ECIS 2024 Proceedings* (Vol. 4, pp. 1–16). https://aisel.aisnet.org/ecis2024/track16_fintech/track16_fintech/4
64. Zeiß, C., Straub, L., Hahn, V., Lang, K., Schaschek, M., Tomitza, C., & Winkelmann, A. (2024). Designing for banking resilience: A DeFi e-learning solution (Vol. 14621, pp. 325–338). Springer. https://doi.org/10.1007/978-3-031-61175-9_22
65. Zhang, R., Xue, R., & Liu, L. (2019). Security and privacy on blockchain. *ACM Computing Survey*. https://doi.org/10.1145/3316481
66. Ziolkowski, R., Miscione, G., & Schwabe, G. (2020). Decision problems in blockchain governance: Old wine in new bottles or walking in someone else's shoes? *Journal of Management Information Systems, 37*(2), 316–348.
67. Zutshi, A., Grilo, A., & Nodehi, T. (2021). The value proposition of blockchain technologies and its impact on Digital Platforms. *Computers & Industrial Engineering*, 107187. https://doi.org/10.1016/J.CIE.2021.107187

How to Achieve Hyperautomation? Towards a Maturity Model for SMEs

Christoph Tomitza, Lisa Straub, Ulvi Ibrahimli, Pascal Rützel, Christian Zeiß, Willy Kögler, and Axel Winkelmann

Abstract Companies have pursued automation for years. Small and medium-sized enterprises (SMEs) are still far from achieving complete hyperautomation of their entire company or individual areas of their business. There is uncertainty surrounding the causes and strategies for achieving a fully networked and autonomous process chain. In a DSR process, we aim to develop a tool that assists companies in recognizing the opportunities of hyperautomation, advancing their company step by step, and identifying current weaknesses. First, we analyze the problem space through focus groups with German SME partners. We extend the knowledge base through structured literature analysis to develop a comprehensive overview of hyperautomation barriers. Building on this, we aim to establish a success model before developing a maturity model as a second artifact as well as a canvas tool for evaluation. In this way, we support companies on their way to hyperautomated business processes.

C. Tomitza (✉) · L. Straub · U. Ibrahimli · P. Rützel · C. Zeiß · W. Kögler · A. Winkelmann
Julius-Maximilians-Universität Würzburg, Würzburg, Germany
e-mail: christoph.tomitza@uni-wuerzburg.de

L. Straub
e-mail: lisa.straub@uni-wuerzburg.de

U. Ibrahimli
e-mail: ulvi.ibrahimli@uni-wuerzburg.de

P. Rützel
e-mail: pascal.ruetzel@uni-wuerzburg.de

C. Zeiß
e-mail: christian.zeiss@uni-wuerzburg.de

W. Kögler
e-mail: willy.koegler@uni-wuerzburg.de

A. Winkelmann
e-mail: axel.winkelmann@uni-wuerzburg.de

C. M. Flath et al. (eds.), *Artificial Intelligence, Data, and Decision-Making*, Lecture Notes in Information Systems and Organisation 82,
https://doi.org/10.1007/978-3-032-08480-4_15

1 Introduction

A click, a short command, or a tiny gesture triggers a chain of processes that operate autonomously, achieving the desired result without additional human intervention [12, 17]. That is the ultimate goal behind a one-trigger process. It is a development becoming increasingly tangible with emerging technologies such as artificial intelligence, big data, robotics process automation (RPA), and the Internet of Things (IoT) to raise productivity [16, 22]. Therefore, our research deals with how companies can increasingly develop in the direction of hyperautomation to establish complete process handling without human involvement. The challenge is to create comprehensive end-to-end automation by linking complementary technologies to optimize business processes [16, 24]. Despite this, there is still a long way to go to achieve this goal, especially in small and medium-sized enterprises (SMEs). Automation technologies pose numerous challenges that often overwhelm SMEs [16, 18]. They are at a competitive disadvantage to large companies because they lack the necessary resources. Failure to experiment with automation or new technologies can threaten their very existence. SMEs also have fewer IT resources than large companies. Technological innovations promise enormous potential and enable the combination of intelligent systems that meet complex requirements, incorporate human expertise, and contribute to complete automation as a merged unit [12, 17]. SMEs should embrace hyperautomation to be able to withstand the pressure of competition. This study delves into the imperative for SMEs to embrace hyperautomation, focusing on the barriers that hinder its adoption.

Employing a design science research (DSR) approach, we encapsulate barriers for SMEs when adopting hyperautomation. The research project aims to develop success and maturity models for SMEs, bringing them closer to the goal of hyperautomation. An associated canvas tool for SMEs is also being developed to make it easier to implement the findings and evaluate the scientific results. Our study contributes to the scholarly discussion of SMEs' challenges in adopting hyperautomation and sheds light on the intricacies involved in the adoption process. By identifying and analyzing these challenges, we provide valuable insights that can inform strategies for overcoming them. This paper unfolds as follows: Sect. 2 draws on previous research and highlights the current state of SMEs and automation. In Sect. 3, we outline the research design and present the previous and future steps of our work before Sect. 4 focuses on the currently identified barriers and results. In Chap. 5, we discuss our existing findings and point out future research steps and the limitations of our work.

2 Hyperautomation in SMEs

For centuries, the prospect of automation has sparked intrigue and concern among people. Automation transpires when a machine, represented as capital, takes over the execution of one or more tasks within a workflow that is traditionally performed by human labor [6]. This shift leads to increased productivity, a crucial determinant of long-term economic growth and the average standard of living [1].

The impact of this transition to automated business processes has not gone unnoticed in academia. There is an ongoing discourse in IS scholarship concerning the merits of automation and its business applications alongside challenges faced, particularly by SMEs, in adopting automation technologies [6, 30]. The extant literature documents process automation use cases in numerous business areas like human resource management, production, sales [28], marketing, and finance [33] alongside the associated challenges [3, 31, 32]. Yet researchers also find that such automation only pays off for processes that are structured, repetitive, and rule-based. But [24] explains that not all processes are simple and rule-based; many are complex, requiring intelligent decision-making and optimization. Scaling such processes often necessitates hyperautomation, as a single tool may not suffice [6, 16]. Hyperautomation involves the coordinated use of Artificial Intelligence, Machine Learning, RPA, and Business Process Management [12, 17]. It enables faster task execution with fewer errors, coverage of decision-making processes, and the automation of knowledge work. However, the current literature lacks a comprehensive understanding of the challenges faced by SMEs and how they can transition to businesses with hyperautomated processes. Therefore, this paper sets out to establish a foundational understanding of the hyperautomation landscape, exploring the barriers that arise for SMEs.

3 Research Design

We aim to develop a maturity model for SMEs to reach hyperautomation. Our approach (see Fig. 1) adheres to the DSR method according to [27]. The outcome of this research-in-progress paper highlighted in Sect. 4 serves as the starting point for our research project.

Problem Identification and First Evaluation. We first conducted a workshop involving six focus groups with $n = 33$ participants to unveil the current issues in SMEs with hyperautomation. Participants included chief executive officers and employees from German SMEs as well as researchers specializing in information systems and business psychology to ensure diverse perspectives on barriers, challenges, and facilitators of hyperautomation. We conducted internal workshops with all authors to analyze and consolidate the unstructured results.

Furthermore, we perform a structured literature review following vom [5] to explore the current state of academic research. This literature review augmented and scientifically reinforced the barriers identified from the workshop results. Our search string (*"Hyperautomation" OR "Hyper automation" OR "Digital Process Automation" OR "Cognitive Automation" OR "Intelligent Automation" OR "Intelligent Process Automation" OR "Integrated Automation Platform"*) focuses on hyperautomation and related terms [3, 8, 22] to gain more insights about barriers and challenges. Using the search strings, we analyzed the publications of the four databases

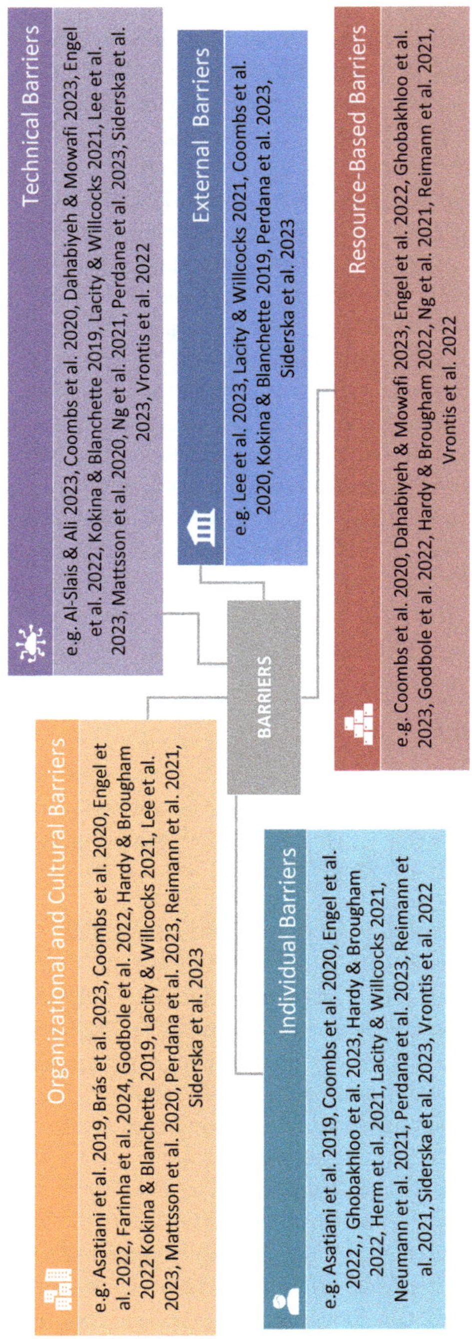

Fig. 1 Research design following [27]

AIS eLibrary, EBSCOhost, ScienceDirect, and Web of Science. Our analysis focused on publications that used or presented technically advanced automation methods or contained basic information, thus minimizing the need for additional exclusion criteria. The keyword search results in $n = 626$ publications. After removing duplicates and conducting the title ($n = 106$), abstract ($n = 25$), and full-text analysis, we obtained $n = 14$ relevant papers. Subsequently, the finalization of forward and backward searches extended the literature pool to $n = 23$ publications.

After the data collection, we conducted internal workshops with all authors and substantiated and linked the derived barriers with the findings of the structured literature research. Finally, we are going to evaluate our barriers in qualitative interviews with experts and workers according to [27].

Design and Second Evaluation. In the first workshop, we gather enablers for hyperautomation. We use these, the previous results, and another literature analysis to develop a hyperautomation success model as our first artifact. It identifies fields of action that need to be addressed in SMEs to reach the one-trigger process. To ensure a robust artifact, we are going to conduct a second ex-ante evaluation with expert interviews.

Construction and Third Evaluation. In this phase, we transfer the core elements of the success model into the maturity model and derive dimensions as well as sub-categories. We elaborate on associated measurements from previous literature sources and examine further elements through workshops and interview studies with SMEs. Because it is relevant for SMEs to have a practical tool to help them with hyperautomation, we also transfer the maturity model to a canvas tool. To ensure the quality, we conduct an ex-post evaluation with focus groups.

Usage and Fourth Evaluation. The maturity model and the canvas are then utilized under real conditions in companies. Therefore, we ensure that our results work in practice and are valid. We also use it to evaluate the maturity model for its viability by interviewing users of our model and tool. Finally, we integrate and analyze the evaluation results. Should new information emerge or fundamental changes to the model be deemed necessary, we initiate another cycle, incorporating the acquired knowledge into the existing artifacts from previous cycles. This iterative process ensures that our model remains adaptable and reflective of the dynamic hyperautomation landscape in SMEs.

4 Barriers to Hyperautomation

The barriers derived from the previous research process are presented below; these were identified with SMEs focusing on hyperautomation. We group all barriers into five main areas shown in Fig. 2. All the listed barriers came up in the workshops and were underpinned and confirmed by the relevant literature.

Organizational and Cultural Barriers. Current approaches are less user-centered and more technologically focused [19]. As a result, employees in SMEs fall by the wayside and resist the automation approaches [18]. An established culture

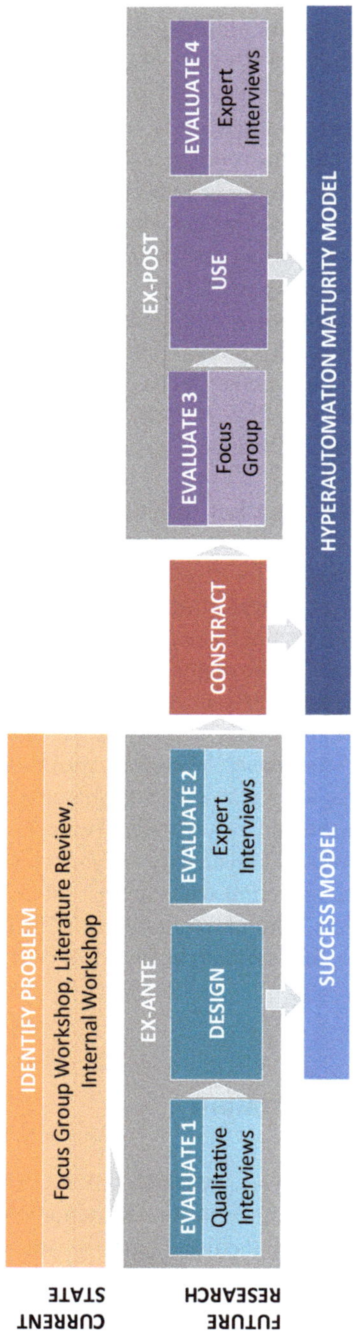

Fig. 2 Identified barriers

of dealing with critique, good communication [16], job redefinition [26], and clear automation strategies [4, 9] are necessary. Digitalization decisions are often short-term, and companies must be more open to innovation, especially in SMEs. This also results in inadequate change management concerning hyperautomation [13, 23]. A lack of interest, commitment, and misconception at the management level hinder progress towards hyperautomation [18]. Additionally, fear of making wrong decisions and unrealistic goals also challenge effective adoption [8, 11]. Clear overview [4], process maps, and standardized processes as well as trainings [4, 21] are missing in companies. For SMEs, many of these points are based on the size of the company. Also, there are ethical and moral aspects as well as the dangers of technology over-reliance hindering hyperautomation [6, 29].

Technical Barriers. Data is a crucial factor and plays a significant role in hyperautomation for SMEs [7, 16]. Its consistency [15, 21], availability [15, 18] quality, [18, 26], and completeness [8] is necessary. Incompatible systems [6, 18] and infrastructure that do not support integration are also challenging [19, 26]. Maintenance and logistics problems represent further challenges for SMEs [6]. There is a lack of system transparency [19, 31] and the technology is not yet sufficient to map the desired complexity [6] or exhibit security risks [2, 23]. On the other hand, the increasing complexity of technologies [15, 31] and difficulties towards standardization [6] are documented as barriers.

Individual Barriers. At the employee level, barriers are emerging in the area of acceptance of new routines and technologies [6, 31], which also leads to hindrance of the change process [13, 16]. Lack of trust in technical support or systems [8, 14] and inadequate human-machine interaction [6] are mentioned as barriers for SMEs to hyperautomation. Employees are also concerned about losing their jobs [20, 26], impending changes, technological competition [13] and the fear of being overwhelmed [10, 31].

Resource-Based Barriers. The workshop reveals knowledge, time, employees, and budget as central issues for SMEs to reach hyperautomation. Missing knowledge about potential starting points [7, 21], process management, and technical implementations [25, 31] is a central issue for SMEs [10, 13]. Therefore, integration is perceived as a challenge [8]. Furthermore, SMEs see the upcoming shortage of skilled workers as critical [18]. Automation costs are perceived as very high [10, 31]. The subsequent maintenance costs are also feared [16]. Another barrier is limited time that employees usually have for change in their day-to-day work and investments only show positive effects too late [6].

External Barriers. The external barriers affecting SMEs include trends, legal requirements [6], privacy and security issues [6, 26], office politics, and compliance regulations [15]. The unpredictable economic situation and customers' fear of technology pose additional challenges for SMEs in reaching hyperautomation. This is accompanied by technology acceptance, the desire for a human touch, and fears that good processes will deteriorate [16, 18]. There is also a lack of partnerships and networks to compensate for a shortage of expertise within the company [16]. Lastly, the work with outsourcing one's data, using bad advisors, or choosing the wrong partners reveals as barriers [16].

5 Conclusion

During the DSR process, we delve into the barriers that challenge SMEs in transitioning into hyperautomated businesses. Our findings are categorized into five barrier areas: organization and culture, technology, individuals, resources, and external influences. Although the results are preliminary, they motivate a scholarly discussion on sources of the challenges that both scholars and practitioners need to consider. Analyzing these challenges, we aim to provide actionable recommendations as our research progresses, assist SMEs in navigating hyperautomation, and unlock its potential benefits by developing a maturity model. Furthermore, we contribute to the areas of business process automation and SME change management in IS. We want to advance research in hyperautomation to support SME's further technology development. As a limitation, it should be noted that the conclusions were drawn from interviews with German SMEs. This is countered by the consideration and enrichment of international literature research. We also acknowledge the potential for future research and call for a standardized definition of the various terms related to hyperautomation, such as those discussed by Park [22] and Bornet et al. [3], as well as related concepts. This will help create a clear distinction between terminologies and in the elaboration of the individual barrier areas and encourage an international perspective on thematic priorities for generalization. Although SMEs are currently far from being hyperautomated businesses, this is a target state that companies should aim for to remain competitive in the long term. Achieving this goal will require collaboration between academia and industry, and research can play a pivotal role in facilitating this transition.

Acknowledgements This work has been developed in the project Hyko and is partly funded by the Bavarian Ministry of Economic Affairs, Regional Development and Energy enabled by the European Regional Development Fund (ERDF) under grant number 1.2-StMWK-F.4-UFR-002. The authors are responsible for the content of this publication.

References

1. Agrawal, A., Gans, J. S., & Goldfarb, A. (2023). Do we want less automation? *Science, 381*(6654), 155–158.
2. Al-Slais, Y., & Ali, M. (2023). Robotic process automation and intelligent automation security challenges: A review. In *2023 International Conference on Cyber Management and Engineering (CyMaEn)* (pp. 71–77). IEEE.
3. Bornet, P., Barkin, I., & Wirtz, J. (2021). *Intelligent automation: Welcome to the world of hyperautomation: Learn how to harness artificial intelligence to boost business & make our world more human*. World Scientific.
4. Bras, J. C., Pereira, R. F., Moro, S., Bianchi, I. S., & Ribeiro, R. (2023). Understanding how intelligent process automation impacts business continuity: Mapping IEEE/2755:2020 and ISO/22301:2019. *IEEE Access, 11*, 134239–134258.

5. Brocke, J. V., Simons, A., Niehaves, B., Niehaves, B., Reimer, K., Plattfaut, R., & Cleven, A. (2009). Reconstructing the giant: On the importance of rigour in documenting the literature search process. In *ECIS 2009 Proceedings, Verona* (pp. 2206–2217).
6. Coombs, C., Hislop, D., Taneva, S. K., & Barnard, S. (2020). The strategic impacts of intelligent automation for knowledge and service work: An interdisciplinary review. *Journal of Strategic Information Systems, 29*, 1–30.
7. Dahabiyeh, L., & Mowafi, O. (2023). Challenges of using RPA in auditing: A socio-technical systems approach. *Intelligent Systems in Accounting, Finance and Management, 30*(2), 76–86.
8. Engel, C., Ebel, P., & Leimeister, J. M. (2022). Cognitive automation. *Electronic Markets, 32*, 339–350.
9. Farinha, D., Pereira, R., & Almeida, R. (2024). A framework to support robotic process automation. *Journal of Information Technology 39*(1), 149–166.
10. Ghobakhloo, M., Asadi, S., Iranmanesh, M., Foroughi, B., Mubarak, M. F., & Yadegaridehkordi, E. (2023). Intelligent automation implementation and corporate sustainability performance: The enabling role of corporate social responsibility strategy. *Technology in Society, 74*, Article 102301.
11. Godbole, M., Syed, R., & Bandara, W. (2022). Exploring the nexus between process complexity and intelligent automation. In *PACIS 2022 Proceedings* (Vol. 23).
12. Haleem, A., Javaid, M., Singh, R. P., Rab, S., & Suman, R. (2021). Hyperautomation for the enhancement of automation in industries. *Sensors International, 2*, Article 100124.
13. Hardy, S., & Brougham, D. (2022). Intelligent automation in New Zealand: Adoption scale, impacts, barriers and enablers *New Zealand Journal of Human Resources Management, 22*(1), 15–31.
14. Herm, L.-V., Janiesch, C., Reijers, H. A., & Seubert, F. (2021). From symbolic RPA to intelligent RPA: Challenges for developing and operating intelligent software robots. In *Business Process Management: 19th International Conference, BPM 2021, Rome, Italy, September 06–10, 2021, Proceedings 19* (pp. 289–305).
15. Kokina, J., & Blanchette, S. (2019). Early evidence of digital labor in accounting: Innovation with robotic process automation. *International Journal of Accounting Information Systems, 35*, Article 100431.
16. Lacity, M., & Willcocks, L. (2021). Becoming strategic with intelligent automation. *MIS Quarterly Executive*, **20**, 1–14. https://standards.ieee.org/
17. Lasso-Rodriguez, G., & Winkler, K. (2020). Hyperautomation to fulfil jobs rather than executing tasks: the BPM manager robot vs human case. *Romanian Journal of Information Technology & Automatic Control/Revista Română de Informatică şi Automatică, 30*(3).
18. Lee, M. C., Scheepers, H., Lui, A. K., & Ngai, E. W. (2023). The implementation of artificial intelligence in organizations: A systematic literature review. *Information and Management, 60*.
19. Mattsson, S., Fast-Berglund, Å, Li, D., & Thorvald, P. (2020). Forming a cognitive automation strategy for operator 4.0 in complex assembly. *Computers & Industrial Engineering, 139*, 105360.
20. Neumann, W. P., Winkelhaus, S., Grosse, E. H., & Glock, C. H. (2021). Industry 4.0 and the human factor-a systems framework and analysis methodology for successful development. *International Journal of Production Economics, 233*, 1–16.
21. Ng, K. K., Chen, C.-H., Lee, C., Jiao, J. R , & Yang, Z.-X. (2021). A systematic literature review on intelligent automation: Aligning concepts from theory, practice, and future perspectives. *Advanced Engineering Informatics, 47*, Article 101246.
22. Park, S. C. (2018). The fourth industrial revolution and implications for innovative cluster policies. *AI and Society, 33*, 433–445.
23. Perdana, A., Lee, W. E., & Kim, C. M. (2023). Prototyping and implementing robotic process automation in accounting firms: Benefits, challenges and opportunities to audit automation. *International Journal of Accounting Information Systems, 51*, 1–23.
24. Ray, S., Tornbohm, C., Kerremans, M., & Miers, D. (2019). Move beyond rpa to deliver hyperautomation. *Gartner*, 1–16.

25. Reiman, A., Kaivo-oja, J., Parviainen, E., Takala, E.-P., & Lauraeus, T. (2021). Human factors and ergonomics in manufacturing in the industry 4.0 context-a scoping review. *Technology in Society, 65*, 1–9.
26. Siderska, J., Aunimo, L., Süße, T., von Stamm, J., Kedziora, D., & Aini, S. N. B. M. (2023). Towards intelligent automation (IA): Literature review on the evolution of Robotic Process Automation (RPA), its challenges, and future trends. *Engineering Management in Production and Services, 15*, 90–103.
27. Sonnenberg, C., & vom Brocke, J. (2012). Evaluations in the science of the artificial - reconsidering the build-evaluate pattern in design science research. In K. Peffers, M. Rothenberger, & B. Kuechler (Eds.), *Design science research in information systems. Advances in theory and practice* (pp. 381–397). Springer.
28. Tomitza, C., Ibrahimli, U., & Herm, L.-V. (2024). AI-based methods of dynamic pricing in e-commerce: A systematization of literature. In *ECIS 2024 Proceedings* (Vol. 4, pp. 1–16).
29. Tomitza, C., Schaschek, M., Straub, L., & Winkelmann, A. (2023). What is the minimum to trust AI?–A requirement analysis for (generative) AI-based texts. In *Wirtschaftsinformatik 2023 Proceedings* (Vol. 7).
30. Van der Aalst, W. M., Bichler, M., & Heinzl, A. (2018). Robotic process automation.
31. Vrontis, D., Christofi, M., Pereira, V., Tarba, S., Makrides, A., & Trichina, E. (2022). Artificial intelligence, robotics, advanced technologies and human resource management: A systematic review. *The International Journal of Human Resource Management, 33*, 1237–1266.
32. Zeiß, C., Straub, L., Hahn, V., Lang, K., Schaschek, M., Tomitza, C., & Winkelmann, A. (2024). *Designing for banking resilience: A DeFi e-learning solution* (Vol. 14621, pp. 325–338). Cham: Springer.
33. Zeiß, C., Straub, L., Schaschek, M., & Winkelmann, A. (2024). The obscure world of digital assets - design principles for user-centered platforms. In *ECIS 2024 Proceedings* (Vol. 4, pp. 1–16).

Multiple-Criteria Decisions for Information Security—A Case Study of Volkswagen Financial Services AG

Laura Bauer, Stephan Kuehnel, Ilja Nastjuk, Leonard Nake, and Heiko Seidel

Abstract Companies today seek to protect their information systems from security breaches by the implementation of effective security measures. The decision which measures to choose mostly relies on the information at hand. Business processes turn out to be a valuable source of information for the identification of decision criteria. Based on this, we developed a practical and innovative multiple-criteria procedure model. It builds on the Analytic Hierarchy Process and is applied it to a single case study of the Volkswagen Financial Services AG.

1 Introduction

As every business today relies on the use of information systems (IS), the reliability of its information security (InfoSec) measures is highly relevant for them [1, 2]. Security breaches might cause severe consequences in terms of liability claims or damage to the corporate image [2]. Therefore, companies seek to protect their IS (e.g., business processes, data, etc.) from such breaches [1]. InfoSec is already anchored in European law, such as the Digital Operational Resilience Act (DORA), a replacement of the IT

L. Bauer (✉) · S. Kuehnel · L. Nake
Martin Luther University, Halle (Saale), Germany
e-mail: laura.bauer@wiwi.uni-halle.de

S. Kuehnel
e-mail: stephan.kuehnel@wiwi.uni-halle.de

L. Nake
e-mail: leonard.nake@wiwi.uni-halle.de

I. Nastjuk
Georg August University, Göttingen, Germany
e-mail: ilja.nastjuk@wiwi.uni-goettingen.de

H. Seidel
Volkswagen Financial Services AG, Braunschweig, Germany
e-mail: heiko.seidel@vwfs.com

C. M. Flath et al. (eds.), *Artificial Intelligence, Data, and Decision-Making*, Lecture Notes in Information Systems and Organisation 82,
https://doi.org/10.1007/978-3-032-08480-4_16

Security Act, to ensure resilience of the finance sector as critical infrastructure [3], or the General Data Protection Regulation [4]. Although this already prescribes a certain security standard, there is no indication on how to assess or choose the proper security measures. Still, the decision of which measures to deploy is one of the highest priorities for any IT department [1, 5]. The objective of every Chief Information Security Officer (CISO) is, therefore, to invest the available InfoSec budget most effectively [6]. Thus, InfoSec includes "technology, processes, and people" [7, p. 572] and information governance topics [8].

Throughout many scientists' research on decisions of InfoSec measures, it turns out that the core of decision-making relies on the information at hand [9, 10]. However, due to a growing digitization, information systems become increasingly complex, so the amount of information contributing to a decision, is rapidly growing [10, 11]. In this regard, especially business processes serve as valuable sources for the identification of decision criteria [12]. The impact of business processes on a company's performance and the strong influence of InfoSec on the operation of business processes are two indicators of this [13]. For InfoSec decisions, economic methods focusing on monetary criteria are still dominant, while qualitative and non-monetary criteria are mainly not considered [14]. Especially financial metrics, such as the Return on Security Invest, are often applied in practice but present the challenge that many criteria relevant for an InfoSec decision cannot be monetized [15, 16]. As a result, it shows that monetary decision methods do not sufficiently reflect a thorough assessment of InfoSec measures.Therefore, [15] and [17] argue that experts should focus on multiple criteria influencing a business's performance instead of simply comparing costs and benefits. Based on business processes, these criteria can be derived and the influence of InfoSec on a company's performance becomes visible [18].

For this purpose, we developed a procedure model for process-oriented multiple-criteria decision-making (MCDM). The model is based on an adapted decision method and decision hierarchy of [19] Analytic Hierarchy Process (AHP). AHP enables MCDM of decision problems using a hierarchy of three levels: objective, criteria, and alternatives. In this study, we focus on business processes and identify non-monetary (e.g., 'data quality') and monetary (e.g., 'employee expenses') process dimensions as criteria and consider InfoSec measures as alternatives. We apply our model to a single case study of a vehicle leasing process with Volkswagen Financial Services AG (VWFS). VWFS faced the decision to implement an Intrusion Detection System (IDS) and had to choose between a Network Intrusion Detection System (NIDS) and a Security Information and Event Management (SIEM) system based on IDS.

Our paper's **research objective** is to develop and apply a process-oriented multiple-criteria procedure model for information security measures based on a single case study of VWFS. We therefore used a four-step research approach, including a domain analysis, a moderated focus group (MFG), a single case study, and a moderated reconvened focus group (MRFG) [20–23]. The approach builds on both science and practice in the development and application of the procedure model. Our research contributions are threefold. First, we show how multiple criteria can be derived from business processes. Second, we provide an innovative procedure model for InfoSec measures. Third, we illustrate findings from our case study that can be applied to other cases.

We structured our paper as follows. Chapter 2 discusses the theoretical background. We explain the single case study in Chap. 3. Chapter 4 shows the structure and application of the procedure model. In Chap. 5 we discuss our implications as well as limitations and future research. We conclude our paper in Chap. 6.

2 Theoretical Background

As economically efficient investments and implementations of InfoSec measures have been relevant for a while, several research streams exist for InfoSec decision-making [24]. Most researchers differentiate between three dominant streams: Game Theory, Risk and Return, and Behavioral approaches [11, 24–26]. Despite this multitude of research streams, scientists, e.g., [11, 14, 15, 27], still criticize the lack of variety of criteria for InfoSec decision-making, as they do not take sufficient account of the context in which decisions are made. Accordingly, the application of only one research stream when deciding about an InfoSec measure could automatically lead to the neglect of other important criteria, as well as poor results of the decision process [5]. Therefore, a well-balanced and multi-dimensional model for security measures that adapts to the complex world of InfoSec is needed [17].

Considering that, it is important to be aware of the strong impact of InfoSec measures on the flow and performance of business processes [2]. Security measures require companies to make significant investments, financially and in terms of business operations. This can severely impact the efficiency of business processes as these might become more time-consuming and complex [16, 28]. Business processes allow the impact of IS, especially information technology (IT), on a company to be measured [18]. This can be done by looking at the business process performance and comparing inputs and outputs. It is precisely this business process performance that ultimately has an impact on the performance of the entire company [18]. Accordingly, key figures can be derived from business processes, which should be used as a foundation for InfoSec's decision-making [17].

MCDM addresses this need and that of multi-dimensionality by incorporating multiple criteria and alternatives into a decision problem [29, 30]. Thus, MCDM not only focuses on monetary criteria but also uses the numerous non-monetary criteria. This helps to take a broader perspective when assessing InfoSec investments [30, 31]. Since there is insufficient data for many criteria, especially for non-monetary or qualitative criteria, MCDM must benefit from the knowledge of experts. Yet, their information is characterized by subjectivity [32]. This subjectivity is counterbalanced in MCDM by weighting and comparing the individual criteria and alternatives against each other [32, 33]. As for the number of experts to be consulted for a decision, both group and individual decisions can be made [34].

Our research lies in the field of information systems, where the most widespread MCDM theory is AHP [35–37]. The AHP theory by [19] was developed to break down complex multiple-criteria decision problems into a decision hierarchy. AHP is based on pairwise comparisons. These are conducted by individuals or groups on a consistent scale at the hierarchy levels of 'criteria' and 'alternatives' [38]. Decisions are based on a priority vector, ranking alternatives and criteria based on relevance [38]. Especially the challenge of assessing intangible and subjective information is addressed by using linguistic terms [36]. These terms are backed by numbers on a scale from one to nine [38]. Finally, a reciprocal decision matrix produces scientifically quantifiable results [39]. AHP offers several advantages. It is analytical by structuring complex problems in hierarchies, it is useful in the aggregation of group weightings [34], it offers proof for the reliability of its results by using the Consistency Ratio (CR) [35], and it is widely used in IS research, e.g., [37, 40, 41].

3 Single Case Study

We use a single case study to apply [19] AHP theory to the case of InfoSec measures. Case studies examine complex contemporary problems and apply them in a real-world context "[…] such as organizational and managerial processes." [42, p. 93]. In addition, *single* case studies are helpful in examining typical scenarios that can also be adapted to other cases [20]. They are applied when the findings are particularly informative for the field of interest [42]. Since these requirements suit our case, we use a single case study of VWFS to develop our process-oriented multiple-criteria procedure model.

3.1 Use Case and Business Process

VWFS was founded in 1994 and has its headquarters in Germany. The company manages all of Volkswagen's financial services worldwide. Its focus is on mobility services, such as the sale of Volkswagen Group brands in terms of leasing or insurance and mobility solutions [43]. We chose VWFS since their business model is highly process-oriented. In addition, the company operates with many personal data of their business customers and partners. The process of a *'New vehicle leasing business'* served as assessment foundation for our procedure model. The interfaces between the sub-processes, as well as the various process participants, enable an extended assessment of InfoSec measures and provide useful feedback. VWFS models the leasing process at the highest level as a value chain comprising several sub-processes [44]. We adopted this modeling in our paper (see Fig. 1). Both the value chain and the sub-processes have been modeled by us with the SAP Signavio Process Transformation Suite [45].

Fig. 1 Process landscape of the vehicle leasing value chain

The business process *'New vehicle leasing business'* represents a leasing process offered by a salesperson for a vehicle. The aim is to provide business customers with a vehicle at a monthly rate to promote vehicle sales. It describes the process from a customer request for a leasing contract to the customer's credit rating, the preparation of a quotation, the handover of the leasing contract, and the delivery of the vehicle to the customer. Although the entire leasing process works with sensitive data, the successive sub-processes *'Edit rating request (Leasing)'* and *'Conclude contract'* are of particular interest due to the system interfaces, the credit rating of the customer as well as the contract that is developed. This leads to an increased data exchange between VWFS and the salesperson of the VWFS dealership. We therefore focus on the description of these sub-processes in the following and modeled their business process (see Fig. 2).

After offering a vehicle in combination with a desired payment method, the sub-process *'Edit rating request (Leasing)'* follows. Its aim is to check and decide on the leasing creditworthiness and is operated via a leasing system by the VWFS AG. Based on the data record received electronically, including the customer's self-disclosure, a transaction is created. Subsequently, necessary data for the rating are prepared by an expert with high expertise and objectivity. If the rating is negative, the whole leasing process ends. If the rating is positive, the leasing operation is sent to the salesperson in the dealership. Based on this, the *'Conclude contract'* sub-process follows. Here, the salesperson contacts the business customer to provide they with the information obtained and to arrange an appointment to conclude the leasing contract. The salesperson then again checks the quotation and customer data for the operation before the contract is signed on both sides. The contract is digitized and sent as a contract application to the VWFS AG. After receiving the contract application documents in digitized form, the documents required are checked for validity. Once the vehicle invoice has been received, the whole business process ends with the delivery of the vehicle.

3.2 Data Collection

We applied a four-step research approach (see Fig. 3) to build the procedure model. The **first step** is described in Sect. 2, where the theoretical background is discussed based on a domain analysis following [21].

As we also wanted to draw on expert knowledge to generate data for the decision, the assessment was directed to a focus group of eight experts from VWFS's Information Security Department. Complex decision problems benefit from group

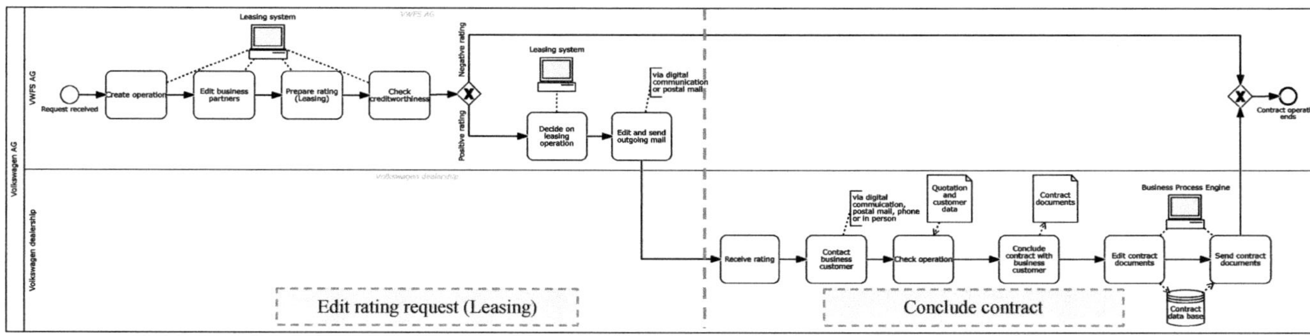

Fig. 2 Sub-processes of 'Edit rating request (Leasing)' and 'Conclude contract'

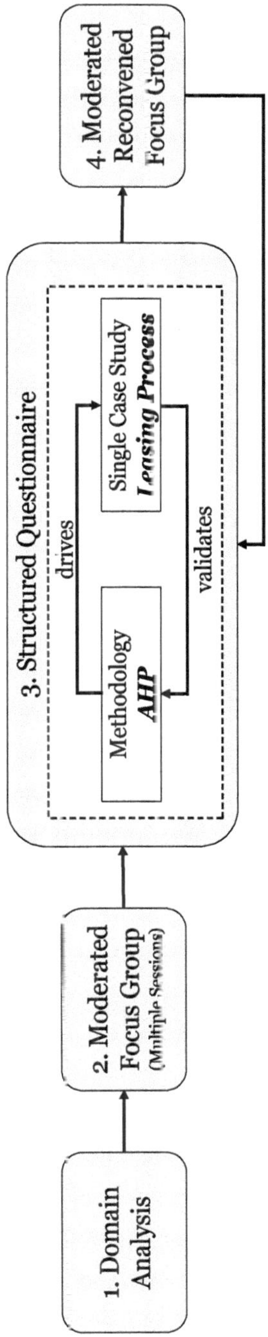

Fig. 3 The four steps of our research approach

assessments as they require a variety of different expertise [46]. The topic of group sizes for decision-making has been discussed intensively in the literature, e.g., [41, 47, 48]. Smaller group sizes are particularly suitable for making complex decisions that require a certain expertise of the participants [48]. In this context, Swim's rule of thumb recommends a group size of seven for good decision quality and group consistency [47]. Existing research in high-quality journals chooses group sizes between six and eight for the application of AHP in case studies, e.g., [41, 49]. Therefore, we also used eight experienced participants for our group decision. The experts had an average of 11.38 years of work experience. They worked in the business unit (*absolute number of people*) of Information Security (*6*), IT Services (*1*), and IT Compliance (*1*). Their professional titles (*absolute number of people*) are CISO (*1*), Information Security Officer (*5*), IT Compliance Officer (*1*), and Project Manager (*1*).

Consequently in **step two** of the research approach, we conducted a MFG [22] consisting of multiple sessions with the same experts (n = 8) in which we discussed the case study, i.e., the business process, as well as the objective and alternatives of the decision problem. Thereupon, the focus group analyzed the business process and defined process dimensions, which served as decision criteria for the assessment. In **step three**, the decision hierarchy and underlying AHP theory were explained to the focus group experts to prepare them for the structured questionnaire of our case study (Access to the questionnaire: https://cloud.uni-halle.de/s/IS66jtcGL Iot2UC). For this, each expert performed the decision procedure individually and anonymously. In **step four**, the results of the decision problem were calculated and presented to the experts as part of a MRFG. MRFGs reunite the experts of preceding focus groups, which allows them to discuss newly gained knowledge and to give feedback [23]. Due to the iterative nature of the data collection process, feedback from the MRFG led to some adjustments to be made in the procedure model. Finally, an assessment of the adjusted model with the questionnaire was performed a second time, as well as the MRFG. Thus, the process was completed and the procedure model was finished.

4 Structure and Application of the Procedure Model

The procedure model and decision hierarchy are divided into four levels (see Fig. 4). As we already identified the business process for the case study, we discussed the assessment objective, which was named 'Identification of the optimal information security measure for the leasing process', in the MFG (**step two** of our research approach).

Subsequently, the process dimensions of the leasing process were identified. Therefore, we applied [50] systematic approach and conducted multiple focus group sessions. At the beginning, generic factors of the single case for a goal-oriented process were discussed within the group based on the participants' expertise. These were then assigned and grouped to first-order concepts, second-order themes, and

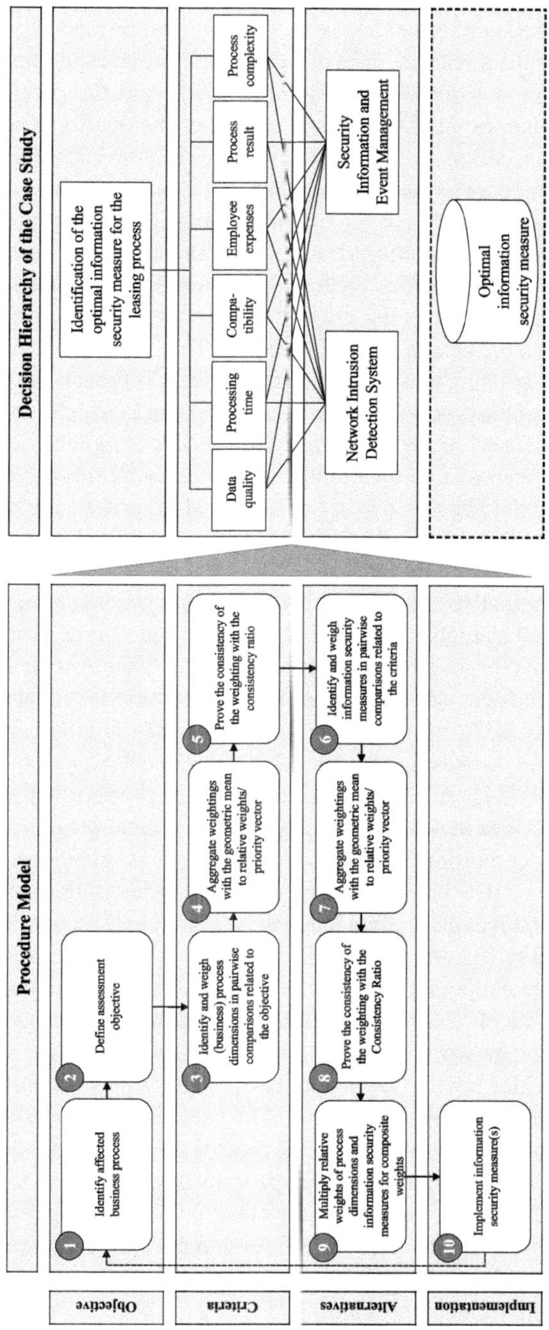

Fig. 4 Structure of the procedure model

aggregate process dimensions. At the beginning of each session, the previous results were presented, reviewed, and supplemented to reach a consensus within the group. Finally, in the last iteration, no changes or additions were made by the VWFS experts. They identified six relevant dimensions as well as corresponding definitions to serve as criteria for our decision problem, derived from the previously established concepts and themes: (1) Data quality describes the quality of data required for the initiation or execution of the process. This can be measured using the key figures accuracy, completeness, and consistency, (2) Processing time describes the time between process start and process end or a changed time of process start, (3) Process compatibility (Compatibility) describes the interaction or compatibility of different processes of a company as well as their joint or coordinated application, (4) Employee expenses describes the effort that must be made by employees of a company to ensure that the process can be executed. This can be done in the form of relocating existing or creating new employee resources, (5) Process result describes the operational scope of the process outcome as to the extent to which certain products and services can be offered or restricted, and (6) Process complexity describes the complexity of a process based on the number of process activities or the number of process branches. It should be clarified at this point that the criteria are individual for each business process. Therefore, other criteria should be applied when evaluating a different decision problem.

For the level of alternatives, it must be stated that our procedure model requires the prerequisite that all available alternatives of InfoSec measures meet at least the minimum requirements for securing the business process. Therefore, in the decision-making procedure, we focus on identifying the InfoSec measures that comply best with the business process. According to the focus group, two alternatives were available for this decision in the leasing process, a NIDS and a SIEM system. Both found on the concept of IDS [51]. An IDS describes an active process that monitors and detects malicious activities in networks and systems to protect sensitive data against attacks and resulting compromise or misuse [52, 53]. It is, therefore, particularly useful to implement an IDS in the leasing process to protect the sensitive data of customers. Both alternatives use pattern languages to analyze threats, allowing attack identification scalability [52–54]. The performance of NIDS and SIEM, therefore, depends on their exact configuration. Otherwise, due to a large amount of network traffic in a company, the efficiency of attack identification decreases [51].

A NIDS is based on network packages that use patterns of known threats or the identification of activities not corresponding to the regular network traffic to match anomalies in regular network operations [52]. The greatest advantage of NIDS is its focus on detecting malicious network traffic. It thereby operates particularly efficient [52]. Unlike NIDS, SIEM systems use threat patterns based on event logs for attack identification [53]. They seek to minimize the effort involved in log reviews as well as to identify new threat patterns [51, 54, 55]. In doing so, they gather and analyze data from a multitude of data sources, such as applications, IT infrastructure, and networks, with the help of machine learning [53, 55].

After building the procedure model and decision hierarchy, the structured assessment of the decision problem begins (**step three** of our research approach). The experts (n = 8) used the structured questionnaire, based on AHP, to compare and weigh the criteria and alternatives, focusing on the objective of the decision hierarchy. On the second level of the hierarchy, the criteria are weighted by each expert individually in reciprocal matrices using pairwise comparisons. The result is a priority vector of the decision criteria for each expert [6]. For these comparisons, Saaty (2008) provided a numerical scale with associated definitions. This scale indicates the extent to which one element, i.e., criterion or alternative, is more important than another.

Due to length restrictions, we, unfortunately, cannot describe all formulas of our calculations in-depth and refer for this purpose to the well-known works of, e.g., [34] or [56]. However, for the aggregation of the weightings of all eight experts among the six criteria, we apply the geometric mean. According to Saaty (2008), the geometric mean provides a higher significance than the often-used arithmetic mean. We, therefore, first aggregated the individual weightings to one overall comparison, determined the geometric mean, and then calculated the relative weight among the criteria $w_c^{[r]}$. The relative weights build the priority vector which indicates the relative importance of the individual elements. This vector from the level of criteria is additionally used to weigh the elements in the level below, i.e., the alternatives [38, 39]. The overall pairwise comparisons, the geometric mean, and the priority vector with its relative weights can be seen in Table 1.

As mentioned in the theoretical background, proving the consistency of the expert's weighting is one of the key advantages of AHP [35]. Since our criteria are based on subjective weightings and these weightings might not be entirely consistent, proving the consistency using the CR is particularly important [57]. Here, we only refer to the consistency of the criteria weighting, as consistency of the alternative weighting is inevitable with a number of two. To determine the CR for our criteria, we first need to calculate the consistency index (CI) (see (1)), with λMax being the major or principal eigenvalue of our overall ranking and n as the number of criteria considered in the decision hierarchy. Finally, the CR is obtained by comparing the calculated CI = 0.074 with the corresponding number of a set of numbers from average random consistency indices (RI) (see (2)).

Table 1 Overall comparison and ranking of the criteria

Overall ranking	DQ	PT	CO	EE	PR	PC	Geometric mean	Relative weight $w_c^{[r]}$
DQ	1.000	3.022	4.139	2.048	0.381	2.063	1.649	0.243
PT	0.331	1.000	2.605	2.169	0.561	2.290	1.157	0.171
CO	0.242	0.384	1.000	1.292	0.463	0.977	0.615	0.091
EE	0.488	0.461	0.774	1.000	0.517	1.149	0.685	0.101
PR	2.627	1.783	2.159	1.933	1.000	4.095	2.076	0.306
PC	0.485	0.437	1.024	0.871	0.244	1.000	0.599	0.088
Sum	5.172	7.086	11.701	9.312	3.166	11.574	6.781	1.000

Note DQ = Data quality, PT = Processing time, CO = Compatibility, EE = Employee expenses, PR = Process result, PC = Process compatibility

$$CI = \frac{(\lambda Max - n)}{(n - 1)} \tag{1}$$

$$CR = \frac{CI}{RI} \tag{2}$$

Thereby, RI depends on the number of criteria n (see Table 2). Based on the consistency of the criteria, of which the acceptable level according to Saaty (2006) must not exceed 0.1, for our case study we obtain a consistency of CR = 0.06.

On the third level, the alternatives are also listed in reciprocal matrices and are weighted by the experts. For this, the extent to which an alternative is preferred over another alternative, with regard to the criteria listed above, is considered [6, 37]. As with the criteria, a priority vector is calculated for the alternatives (see Table 3). This is done similarly to the calculation of the criteria. We first aggregated the individual judgments to an overall comparison, determined the geometric mean, and calculated the relative weights of the alternatives, i.e., the priority vector. It becomes clear that SIEM is preferred over NIDS, especially with regard to the criterion 'employee expenses'. To receive the composite weights of the alternatives $w_a^{[c]}$, the priority vector of an alternative is multiplied by the priority vector of the upper criteria [40]. Consequently, the relative weights alongside the path are multiplied to receive the final composite weight for each alternative [40].

After each criterion and alternative were compared in pairs and the relative importance, as well as the composite weights, were calculated, the result of the decision is available. Accordingly, the priority ranking identifies SIEM as this case's dominant and optimal solution. SIEM should thus be implemented as an InfoSec measure in the leasing process. SIEM achieves a composite weight of $w_{SIEM}^{[c]}$= 0.586, which is significantly higher than NIDS with a composite weight of $w_{NIDS}^{[c]}$= 0.414. As seen

Table 2 Random Consistency Indices (RI), following [56]

n	1	2	3	4	5	6	7	8	9	10
RI	0	0	0.52	0.89	1.11	1.25	1.35	1.40	1.45	1.49

Note n = Number of criteria, RI = Numbers from average random consistency indices

Table 3 Overall priority vectors and composite weights for the alternatives

Priority vector	DQ	PT	CO	EE	PR	PC	Composite weight $w_a^{[c]}$
NIDS	0.457	0.494	0.457	0.259	0.383	0.381	0.414
SIEM	0.543	0.506	0.543	0.741	0.617	0.619	0.586
SUM	1.000	1.000	1.000	1.000	1.000	1.000	1.000

Note DQ = Data quality, PT = Processing time, CO = Compatibility, EE = Employee expenses, PR = Process result, PC = Process compatibility, NIDS = Network Intrusion Detection System, SIEM = Security Information and Event Management in Table 1, the criteria *process result* was given the highest relative weight [0.306] and thus represents the most critical dimension in the vehicle leasing process. This is followed in descending order by *data quality* [0.243], *processing time* [0.171], *employee expenses* [0.101], *compatibility* [0.091], and *process complexity* [0.088].

5 Discussion

The procedure model and its results should finally be discussed for their contribution to the research objective [58, 59]. For this study's implications and limitations, we refer to the results of the MRFGs, i.e., **step four** of our research approach. Here, we benefit from the different levels the experts work on, as they are distributed from strategic to operational ones.

Models for MCDM are generally very rare in InfoSec research. In this study, we present a multiple-criteria procedure model that is aligned with a company's business processes that serve as source of information. Consequently, we address our research objective by developing and applying a procedure model based on a case study of VWFS. To guarantee scientific rigor, we adhere to the specifications of the AHP theory by [19]. This ensures that our procedure model is comprehensible and can also be applied to other companies. From the application of our generic model, it can be deduced that it is particularly suitable for companies that are under high pressure to ensure InfoSec. This applies above all to business sectors of critical infrastructures, e.g. healthcare, finance, and energy. Within these, the model is very effective for companies or departments that possess a high degree of process orientation from which criteria can be derived.

Beyond that, our procedure model offers several *implications for theory and practice*, which additionally contribute to our research objective. First, to the best of our knowledge, our model builds on a new idea of MCDM by deriving information (i.e., process dimensions) from business processes. This leads us to take a new process-oriented view when assessing InfoSec measures and it allows us to examine multiple, both monetary and non-monetary, criteria. Therefore, we avoid the widespread practice of basing investment decisions mostly on monetary criteria, see [27]. Our MRFGs further confirmed this insight. When discussing the results of the procedure model, the experts questioned whether a valid assessment of an InfoSec investment decision based on purely quantitative or monetary criteria was possible at all. Due to our focus on business processes, we also examined the object that is most affected by the implementation of new InfoSec measures. Combined with our structured examination, this helped us prevent important criteria from being left out. This was also emphasized by an expert during the MRFG well: "The procedure model enables assessments relating to the context of the company and business process. A specific business model is assessed in terms of its InfoSec measures, which is interesting considering that the leasing process is a business model itself".

Second, by applying a four-step research approach and due to the several sources of feedback, we achieved a broad perspective as well as findings that are of great interest to practitioners and scientists. In general, the clear structure and comprehensibility are key benefits of our model for the process-oriented assessment of InfoSec measures. This was also noted in the MRFGs. Exemplary explanations and transparency in the decision-making procedure additionally supported these advantages and emphasized the user-friendliness of our model. One participant of the MRFGs summarized this by saying: "With this model, for the first time, we have a viable possibility to compare security investments and not just rely on our gut feeling when making a decision".

Third, in terms of the results of the IDS decision problem, we could derive from Table 1 that the criteria 'process result' and 'data quality' are the most relevant process dimensions for the vehicle leasing process. This also aligns with other studies, e.g., [18]. However, our study also demonstrated that criteria emphasized previously, e.g., [2, 28], such as 'process complexity', was classified as less relevant considering the leasing process. For the alternatives, we identified the SIEM system as the optimal IDS in this case (see Table 3). However, the result of our procedure model of course depends on the criteria considered. For the VWFS experts, only the six criteria listed in Sect. 4 were relevant for the business process. If other experts consider other criteria as important, for example the implementation costs of the InfoSec measures, this could change the assessment result and a decision could be made for a NIDS. This demonstrates the flexibility of our procedure model. The criteria and associated definitions of the dimensions from this case can be used or they can be adapted if required for different decision contexts.

Apart from the contributions, our study was also subject to some *limitations*. Among other things, the selection of participants is quite crucial for process-oriented MCDM. When assessing InfoSec investments based on business processes one should mostly consult InfoSec experts. Thereby, small groups of experts are particularly suitable for complex decisions but also require a lot of expertise [48]. Some may still criticize the small sample size of our case study. However, considering Swim's rule of thumb [47] and related high-quality papers from journals, e.g., [41, 49], our sample of eight participants is to be sufficient. Furtherly, it should be considered to assign different weights to the assessments of different experts. The statement of a CISO should possibly be given more weight in the assessment.

Another challenge to our MCDM approach might be the problem of scalability of criteria and alternatives [35]. If additional criteria or alternatives are added to the decision problem after this has already been fully assessed, it requires a whole new run of pairwise comparisons at the level where an element is added. Obviously, this causes additional effort for the experts involved. Scientists should, therefore, work on adapting the model so that only selective adjustments need to be made in the decision process when adding individual elements. In this context, the effectiveness of the model under changing InfoSec conditions, e.g. after a security breach, should be tested. Regarding this, the security goals, confidentiality; integrity; and availability [60], were also not part of the case study, discussing them specifically in future research may still provide new insights regarding the model's outcomes or effectiveness though.

Further research should also identify and prioritize dimensions for specific business processes or industries, e.g., in the form of a criteria catalog. This would support companies and especially the InfoSec department to work more efficiently. When quick decisions are required, one could simply apply the catalog. In addition, process dimensions could also be allocated on a smaller scale, e.g., for individual process activities. Many activities occur repeatedly in business processes so the process dimension could be derived in part automatically.

6 Conclusion

With our study, we developed an innovative process-oriented MCDM procedure model for InfoSec measures based on the AHP theory by [19]. We demonstrated its applicability with the single case of *'New vehicle leasing business'* of VWFS. In doing so, we responded to the complex world of InfoSec, in which a sole monetization of InfoSec measures reaches its limits. For this reason, we considered, in particular, qualitative criteria for decision-making and built the model around business processes as key drivers and foundation for a company's performance.

Acknowledgements The project on which this study is based was funded by the German Federal Ministry of Education and Research under grant number 16KIS1331. The responsibility for the content of this publication lies with the authors.

References

1. Cavusoglu, H., Cavusoglu, H., Son, J.-Y., & Benbasat, I. (2015). Institutional Pressures in Security Management: Direct and Indirect Influences on Organizational Investment in Information Security Control Resources. *Information & Management, 52*(4), 385–400.
2. Weishäupl, E., Yasasin, E., & Schryen, G. (2015b). IT Security Investments Through the Lens of the Resource-Based View: A New Theoretical Model and Literature Review. In *Proceedings of the European Conference on Information Systems.* AISeL.
3. BMI (Bundesministerium des Inneren und für Heimat). (2021). Stellungnahme Betreff: Stellungnahme der Deutschen Kreditwirtschaft zum Entwurf einer zweiten Verordnung zur Änderung der BSI-Kritisverordnung, https://www.bmi.bund.de/SharedDocs/gesetzgebungsverfahren/DE/Downloads/stellungnahmen/bsi-kritisverordnung/deutsche-kreditwirtschaft.pdf?__blob=publicationFile&v=1. Accessed: 13.06.2024.
4. General Data Protection Regulation. (2021). Art. 32 GDPR security of processing, https://dsgvo-gesetz.de/art-32-dsgvo/. Accessed: 20.03.2024.
5. Niedzela, L., Nake, L., & Matschak, T. (2022). Categories of Approaches for IT Security Investment Decisions: A Systematic Literature Review. In *Proceedings of the International Workshop on Current Compliance Issues in Information Systems Research (CIISR), International Conference on Wirtschaftsinformatik.* AISeL.
6. Bodin, L. D., Gordon, L. A., & Loeb, M. P. (2005). Evaluating Information Security Investments Using the Analytic Hierarchy Process. *Communications of the ACM, 48*(2), 78–83.
7. Zafar, H., & Clark, J. G. (2009). Current State of Information Security Research in IS. *Communications of the Association for Information Systems, 24*(1), 571–596.
8. von Solms, B. (2006). Information Security—The Fourth Wave'. *Computers & Security, 25*(3), 165–168.

9. Mithas, S., Tafti, A., & Mitchell, W. (2013). How a Firm's Competitive Environment and Digital Strategic Posture Influence Digital Business Strategy. *MIS Quarterly, 37*(2), 511–536.
10. Wanner, J., Heinrich, K., Janiesch, C., & Zschech, P. (2020). How much AI Do You Require? Decision Factors for Adopting AI Technology. In *Proceedings of the International Conference on Information Systems.* AISeL.
11. Li, H., Yoo, S., & Kettinger, W. (2019). The Changing Tides of Investments and Strategies and Their Impacts on Security Breaches. In *Proceedings of the International Conference on Information Systems.* AISeL.
12. Kühnel, S., & Zasada, A. (2018). An Approach Toward the Economic Assessment of Business Process Compliance. In *Proceedings of Advances in Conceptual Modeling—ER 2018 Workshops.* Xi'an.
13. Kühnel, S., Sackmann, S., Trang, S., Nastjuk, I., Matschak, T., Niedzela, L., & Nake, L. (2021). Towards a Business Process-Based Economic Evaluation and Selection of IT Security Measures. In *Proceedings of the International Workshop on Current Compliance Issues in Information Systems Research (CIISR), International Conference on Wirtschaftsinformatik.* AISel.
14. Heidt, M., Gerlach, J. P., & Buxmann, P. (2019). A Holistic View on Organizational IT Security: The Influence of Contextual Aspects During IT Security Decisions. In *Proceedings of the Hawaii International Conference on System Sciences.* AISeL.
15. Shao, X., Siponen, M., & Liu, F. (2020). Shall We Follow? Impact of Reputation Concern on Information Security Managers' Investment Decisions. *Computers & Security, 97*, 1–10.
16. Weishäupl, E., Yasasin, E., & Schryen, G. (2018). Information Security Investments: An Exploratory Multiple Case Study on Decision-Making, Evaluation and Learning. *Computers & Security, 77*, 807–823.
17. van Looy, A., & Shafagatova, A. (2016). Business Process Performance Measurement: A Structured Literature Review of Indicators, Measures and Metrics. *Springerplus, 5*(1), 2–24.
18. Melville, N., Kraemer, K. L., & Gurbaxani, V. (2004). Information Technology and Organizational Performance: An Integrative Model of IT Business Value. *MIS Quarterly, 28*(2), 282–322.
19. Saaty, T. L. (1980). *The Analytic Hierarchy Process.* McGraw Hill.
20. Eisenhardt, K. M. (1989). Building Theories from Case Study Research. *The Academy of Management Review, 14*(4), 532–550.
21. March, S. T., & Smith, G. F. (1995). Design and Natural Science Research on Information Technology. *Decision Support Systems, 15*(4), 251–266.
22. Morgan, D. L. (1997). *Focus Groups as Qualitative Research* (2nd ed.). SAGE Publications, Inc.
23. Morgan, D., Fellows, C., & Guevara, H. (2008). Emergent Approaches to Focus Group Research. In S. Hesse-Bibeer (Ed.), *Handbook of Emergent Methods* (pp. 189–205). Guildford Press.
24. Weishäupl, E., Yasasin, E., & Schryen, G. (2015a). A Multi-Theoretical Literature Review on Information Security Investments Using the Resource-Based View and the Organizational Learning Theory. In *Proceedings of the International Conference on Information Systems.* AISeL.
25. Niedzela, L., Kuehnel, S., Nastjuk, I., Matschak, T., Sackmann, S., & Trang, S. (2023). A Qualitative Study on Acceptance Factors of Economic Approaches on IT Security Investment Decisions. In *Proceedings of the Americas Conference on Information Systems.* AISeL.
26. Shao, X., Siponen, M., & Pahnila, S. (2019). To Calculate or to Follow Others: How do Information Security Managers Make Investment Decisions?. In *Proceedings of the Hawaii International Conference on System Sciences.* AISeL.
27. Schatz, D., & Bashroush, R. (2017). Economic Valuation for Information Security Investment: A Systematic Literature Review. *Information Systems Frontiers, 19*(5), 1205–1228.
28. Sonnenschein, R., Loske, A., & Buxmann, P. (2017). The Role of Top Managers' IT Security Awareness in Organizational IT Security Management. In *Proceedings of the International Conference on Information Systems.* AISeL.

29. Chen, P.-C., Chern, C.-C., Chen, C.-Y., & Tzeng, G.-H. (2013). IT Portfolio Investment Evaluation on ECommerce Solution Alternatives. In *Proceedings of the Pacific Asia Conference on Information Systems*, AISeL.
30. Huang, K. Y., & Huang, Y. C. (2014). An Efficient Multi-Criteria Decision-Making Approach Based on Hybridizing Data Mining Techniques. In *Proceedings of the Pacific Asia Conference on Information Systems*. AISeL.
31. Perçin, S. (2008). Fuzzy Multi-Criteria Risk-Benefit Analysis of Business Process Outsourcing (BPO). *Information Management & Computer Security, 16*(3), 213–234.
32. Sheen, J. N. (2010). Information Security Investment Decision by Fuzzy Economics. In *Proceedings of the International Conference on Information Sciences and Interaction Sciences*. AISeL.
33. Peng, Y., Zhang, Y., Kou, G., & Shi, Y. (2012). A Multicriteria Decision Making Approach for Estimating the Number of Clusters in a Data Set. *Public Library of Science ONE, 7*(7), 1–9.
34. Ssebuggwawo, D., Hoppenbrouwers, S. & Proper, E. (2009). Group Decision Making in Collaborative Modeling—Aggregating Individual Preferences with AHP. In *Proceedings of the SIKS Conference in Enterprise Information Systems (EIS)*.
35. Achimugu, P., Selamat, A., Ibrahim, R., & Mahrin, M. N. (2014). A Systematic Literature Review of Software Requirements Prioritization Research. *Information and Software Technology, 56*(6), 568–585.
36. Lee, Y.-C., Tang, H., & Sugumaran, V. (2012). A Deployment Model for Cloud Computing using the Analytic Hierarchy Process and BCOR Analysis. In *Proceedings of Americas Conference on Information Systems*. AISeL.
37. Mayer, J. H., Quick, R., & Friedrich, C. (2018). Towards a More Situated IS Design by Prioritizing Use Situations. In *Proceedings of the European Conference on Information Systems*. AISeL.
38. Saaty, T. L. (2006). The Analytic Network Process. In T. L. Saaty, & L. G. Vargas (Eds.), *Decision Making with the Analytic Network Process* (pp. 1–26). Springer.
39. Saaty, T. L. (2008). Decision Making with the Analytic Hierarchy Process. *International Journal of Services Sciences (IJSSCI), 1*(1), 83–98.
40. Benlian, A. (2010). Which Type of Software Model is First Choice? An AHP-based Comparison of Traditional, Open-Source, and On-Demand Office Suites on the Fulfillment of Evaluation Criteria. In *Proceedings of the European Conference on Information Systems*. AISeL.
41. Lai, V. S., Wong, B. K., & Cheung, W. (2002). Group Decision Making in a Multiple Criteria Environment: A Case Using the AHP in Software Selection. *European Journal of Operational Research, 137*(1), 134–144.
42. Yin, R. K. (2012). Case Study Research: Design and Methods. *German Journal of Research in Human Resource Management, 26*(1), 93–95.
43. Volkswagen Financial Services AG. (2024). Volkswagen Financial Services, https://www.vwfs.com/companies/volkswagen-financial-services-ag.html. Accessed: 25.03.2024.
44. SAP Signavio Process Manager. (2024). Modeling Notations: Value Chains, https://help.sap.com/docs/signavio-process-manager?locale=en-US. Accessed: 20.03.2024.
45. SAP Signavio: Academic and Research Alliances. (2024). https://www.signavio.com/academic-and-research-alliances/. Accessed: 20.03.2024.
46. Saaty, T. L. (1989). Group Decision Making and the AHP. In B. L. Golden, E. A. Wasil, & P. T. Harker (Eds.), *The Analytic Hierarchy Process: Applications and Studies* (pp. 59–67).
47. Swim, L. K. (2001) Improving Decision Quality in the Analytic Hierarchy Process Implementation Through Knowledge Management Strategies [Online], Durham, North Carolina, USA, Bell & Howell. Available at https://search.proquest.com/openview/8a953e88bca2619509653bb6f921283a/1?pq-origsite=gscholar&cbl=18750&diss=y
48. Tsyganok, V. V., Kadenko, S. V., & Andriichuk, O. V. (2012). Significance of Expert Competence Consideration in Group Decision Making Using AHP. *International Journal of Production Research, 50*(17), 4785–4792.
49. Sarker, S., Munson, C. L., Sarker, S., & Chakraborty, S. (2009). Assessing the Relative Contribution of the Facets of Agility to Distributed Systems Development Success: An Analytic Hierarchy Process approach. *European Journal of Information Systems, 18*(4), 285–299.

50. Gioia, D. A., Corley, K. G., & Hamilton, A. L. (2013). Seeking Qualitative Rigor in Inductive Research. *Organizational Research Methods, 16*(1), 15–31.
51. Kiennert, C., Ismail, Z., Debar, H., & Leneutre, J. (2018). A Survey on Game-Theoretic Approaches for Intrusion Detection and Response Optimization. *ACM Computing Surveys, 51*(5), 1–31.
52. Aldarwbi, M. Y., Lashkari, A. H., & Ghorbani, A. A. (2022). The Sound of Intrusion: A Novel Network Intrusion Detection System. *Computers and Electrical Engineering, 104*, 1–12.
53. Kim, J., & Kwon, H.-Y. (2022). Threat Classification Model for Security Information Event Management Focusing on Model Efficiency. *Computers & Security, 120*, 1–19.
54. Yang, L., Manadhata, P., Horne, W., Rao, P., & Ganapathy, V. (2012). Fast Submatch Extraction using OBDDs. In *Proceedings of the ACM/IEEE Symposium on Architecture for Networking and Communications Systems (ANCS)*, (pp 163–174).
55. Rosa, L., Cruz, T., Borges de Freitas, M. de, Quitério, P., Henriques, J., Caldeira, F., Monteiro, E., & Simões, P. (2021). Intrusion and Anomaly Detection for the Next-Generation of Industrial Automation and Control Systems. *Future Generation Computer Systems, 119*, 50–67.
56. Saaty, T. L., & Vargas, L. G. (2012). *Models, Methods, Concepts & Applications of the Analytic Hierarchy Process* (2nd ed.). Springer.
57. Katarne, R., & Negi, J. (2014). Consistency in the Analytic Hierarchy Process: A Framework for Automobile Steering Technology. *International Journal of Engineering Research & Technology (IJERT), 3*(5), 559–564.
58. Gregor, S., & Hevner, A. R. (2013). Positioning and Presenting Design Science Research for Maximum Impact. *MIS Quarterly, 37*(2), 337–355.
59. Peffers, K., Tuunanen, T., Rothenberger, M. A., & Chatterjee, S. (2007). A Design Science Research Methodology for Information Systems Research. *Journal of Management Information Systems, 24*(3), 45–77.
60. BSI (Bundesamt für Sicherheit in der Informationstechnik). (2022). Lerneinheit 4.1: Grundlegende Definitionen—Lerneinheit 4.1, https://www.bsi.bund.de/DE/Themen/Unternehmen-und-Organisationen/Standards-und-Zertifizierung/IT-Grundschutz/Zertifizierte-Informationssicherheit/IT-Grundschutzschulung/Online-Kurs-IT-Grundschutz/Lektion_4_Schutzbedarfsfeststellung/4_01_Definitionen.html. Accessed: 12.06.2024.

What Challenges the Productization of Software? An Organizational Transformation Perspective

Mathias Eggert, Hans Peter Rauer, and Alexander Becker

Abstract Successful software companies typically shift their organization from developing customer-specific software solutions to releasing standardized product software. This shift is called productization. It affects many internal processes and customers' expectations. Particularly, the role-specific challenges and conflicts of software productization are mostly unattended in IS research, which motivates this paper. Based on Organizational Role Theory, the paper sheds light on the role-specific conflicts associated with changing role expectations. A case study, based on the productization transformation process of one business unit within a software company, enabled the identification of role expectations and transformation challenges. A problematization approach is employed to identify challenges of software productization from literature and our case, thereby uncovering new challenges. These are then discussed in the broader context of Organizational Role Theory.

1 Motivation

Software companies that develop custom software for individual customers may find that these projects have significant reuse potential. In order to fully exploit this potential, software products are created with the intention of addressing a larger customer base. This transformation process is called productization [1–3]. This transition means challenging and questioning the established assumptions and paradigms of the prior project-based single-customer business in several ways [4–6]. For instance, customer centricity previously entailed focusing on a single customer

M. Eggert · A. Becker
Aachen University of Applied Sciences, Aachen, Germany
e-mail: eggert@fh-aachen.de

A. Becker
e-mail: alexander.becker@alumni.fh-aachen.de

H. P. Rauer (✉)
Bielefeld University of Applied Sciences and Arts, Bielefeld, Germany
e-mail: hrauer@hsbi.de

C. M. Flath et al. (eds.), *Artificial Intelligence, Data, and Decision-Making*, Lecture Notes in Information Systems and Organisation 82,
https://doi.org/10.1007/978-3-032-08480-4_17

and then listening to many. The underlying assumption here is, that customers can directly voice their requirements. Hence, the new role product management is appointed [7, 8]. The role is concerned, among other things, with the management of multiple customers' expectations [4, 9–15] and is closely intertwined with other customer-facing business functions, such as sales, marketing, and support—at times even superseding them [4, 5, 15]. This disruptive constellation makes it an organizational challenge to transform to a product-centric organization [16]. The challenges of other business functions that support product management remain unclear. While some insights are provided regarding the challenges of the product owner [6], other functions are neglected [16]. This growth journey is one that many organizations, both growing and startup-based, are likely to encounter. Against this background, we have formulated the following research question: *What role-specific challenges and conflicts are perceived through the transformation from a project-centric to product-centric software development organization?*

To be able to answer this research question, we conducted a case study and investigated the case of one business unit of a large German software company, which is in the transition from a project-centric *one-release-delivery* to a product-centric software development consisting usually of many recurrent releases [2]. Investigating this case enabled three research contributions. First, we draw on Organizational Role Theory [17] to create an understanding of organizational roles in the context of productization. Secondly, we elucidate the roles and role-specific challenges that emerge during software productization and assess their significance. Thirdly, to the best of our knowledge, no prior research has directly documented the transformation process from a project-centric to a product-centric software development organization, thereby enhancing the body of knowledge on software productization transformation. From a practical standpoint, the findings facilitate the ability of companies to anticipate and address role-specific challenges and conflicts proactively, thereby enhancing the transformation process from its inception.

The paper is structured as follows. The next section provides an overview about relevant literature on software product management and introduces the Organizational Role Theory, followed by a description of the research gap and relevant studies in the field. Section 3 provides details about the applied case study research method. Section 4 contains the results of the case study, which we discuss in Sect. 5. An outlook on further research closes the article.

2 Foundations

2.1 *Software Product Management*

The concept of software product management was first coined in 1997 [18–20]. As proposed by Ebert et al. [14], software product management is a discipline that oversees the entirety of a product's lifecycle, from inception to market release and customer delivery. Its objective is to generate the greatest possible value for a company.

In software product management, the fundamental principles of general product management are adapted to an IT organization, and the role of the product manager is defined. This individual is accountable for the outcome of a software product [7, 8]. A software product differs from other products in that it is an intangible product that can be easily extended and copied [21]. For instance, changes to the software are possible and necessary after its sale by providing updates [3]. Furthermore, the frequency of releases is higher compared to other products [1]. The responsibilities of a product manager include defining the product, managing requirements, and planning the release of the software, which involves internal and external stakeholders [1, 22]. Consequently, the main activities of a product manager comprise requirements management, release planning, product planning, and portfolio management [23, 24].

2.2 *Organizational Role Theory and Research Paradigm*

This study is situated within the interpretivist paradigm, wherein the social phenomenon of organizational change is perceived through the subjective experiences of interviews. We used Organizational Role Theory to examine how our interviewees perceive their individual challenges and act in their roles [25]. It describes the relationships and possible conflicts between roles within "social systems that are preplanned, task-oriented, and hierarchical" [26]. It views individuals as social beings who adapt to the prevailing work practices, which are essential for their current role within an organization [27]. The interaction of persons is characterized as a relationship between various role transmitters, who send expectations to various role receivers and can even exert pressure to act in accordance with the received role. The transmission process is influenced by personality factors and interrelationship factors. Finally, the role transmitter assesses the work results of the role receiver and sets role expectations (c.f. Fig. 1). The role receiver usually acts conformationally [17].

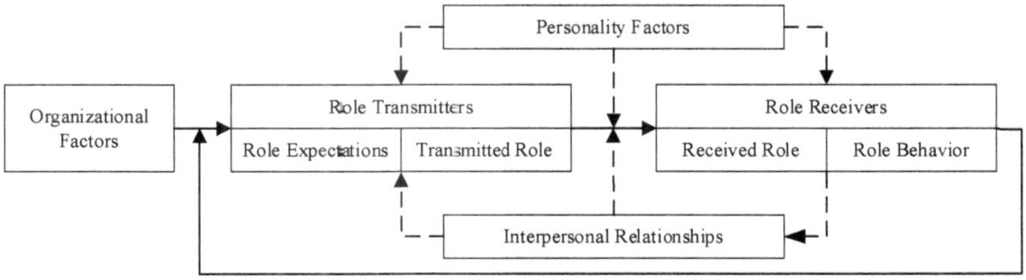

Fig. 1 Concepts of organizational role theory. *Adapted from Katz* et al. [17]

There are four potential areas for problems [26]. The first is *role conflict* (also known as *role malintegration*), which occurs when received roles of a person contradict each other. The second is *role discontinuity* which arises when a sequence of roles is poorly integrated, such as working in sales one day and engineering the next. Third, *role ambiguity* is also a common issue, where expectations are incomplete or insufficient [26]. Fourth, *role overload* occurs when a role faces too many expectations [26].

In line with Ghobadi et al. [28] and Venkatesh et al. [29], software development involves specific roles such as Product Development, e.g., software developers, or Project Managers, who ensure that customer requirements are addressed in the final product. These roles align with the Organizational Role Theory [28]. The role **product management** [4] is responsible for managing all customer requirements and is deciding whether to modify the standardized software product. This role also acts as a role transmitter and expects the delivery of a software release while adhering to time and budget constraints. This impacts the **product development** role (role receiver). The software company expects the **customer management** role (role receiver), who is in direct contact with existing customers, to represent the switch to a software productization albeit it has only decreased influence. This investigation focuses on the expectations and experiences of the three roles and potential challenges and conflicts that may arise against the background of Organizational Role Theory.

2.3 Software Productization Challenges

To provide an overview of existing research on role implications of software productization, we screened software product management literature and worked out the objective (best practice, challenges, and overview). Several articles deal with providing an overview of software product management topics [e.g., 12, 14]. For example, Ebert and Brinkkemper [14] provide a report on experiences to introduce the role of the product manager. They identify software product management challenges for the product manager as well as general challenges. Wagenblatt [5] and Kristinsdottir et al. [6] focus on challenges of specific roles. Wagenblatt [5] reports about challenges of the product manager role, while Kristinsdottir et al. [6] focus on challenges of the product owner role. Springer and Miler [4] deal with challenges for product managers but also mention challenges that are not specific to that role. They then identify five problem areas [30]. Kittlaus and Fricker [15] investigate tasks of a product manager and indicate how they can be completed in the best possible way. Moe et al. [31] identify challenges of software product managers in agile organizations. Finally, Olsson et al. [32] cast a glance on challenges induced by generative AI solutions.

In total, we identified ten different challenges associated with software productization (c.f. Table 1). The most frequently mentioned challenge is creating a consistent product roadmap that outlines the next features to be developed. Such roadmaps serve as a crucial reference point for customers, enabling them to anticipate forthcoming changes to the product. Second, the introduction of the new role of the software product manager appears to give rise to organizational difficulties, as in numerous instances the role is not adequately defined and the responsibilities and objectives are not clearly delineated [4, 30]. Third, the internal communication of the product strategy is identified as a challenge for the product manager. For instance, it is necessary for teams to be aligned around shared objectives [30]. Consequently, new reporting lines must be established, and decisions must be synchronized with a greater number of stakeholders. Fourth, the management and prioritization of requirements encompasses communication with customers, as well as the derivation and prioritization of requirements for a large customer base with experiments or A/B tests and the analysis of customer data [31, 32]. Both approaches are fundamentally different to the direct, dialog-oriented elicitation methods of a project-oriented style. Moreover, data-centricity and AI offer a new impetus for software product management, providing a foundation for developing new product features [32].

Regarding the above-mentioned challenges it is still unclear, which of the three aforementioned roles is affected and what the organizational repercussions of the introduction of the new role software product manager are. To reveal these, we examine the transformation towards product-centricity as it happens in the following sections.

Table 1 Software productization challenges

Task/Challenge	Freq	Rank	[4]	[15]	[14]	[30]	[12]	[5]	[6]	[31]	[32]
Product planning	7	1	X	X	X	X	X			X	X
Introducing the role product man	5	2	X	X	X		X	X			
Internal communication	5	2	X	X	X	X			X		
Requirements management	5	2	X	X	X					X	X
Product development	4	5	X			X	X				X
Customer man	4	5		X		X	X			X	
Human resources management	4	5	X	X	X					X	
Administration	3	8			X			X		X	
Enterprise strategy	3	8	X					X		X	
Expectation man	3	8	X			X			X		

3 Research Design

The research question is answered by conducting a case study and interviews [33], whose analysis follows Vogelsang et al. [34]. We decided to conduct semi-structured interviews to elicit different aspects of real phenomena [33]. We prepared an interview guide to structure the interviews and make the results comparable. A semi-structured interview method allows the interviewer to deviate from the guide to better suit the individual setting of the interviewees. After developing the guide, we established inclusion criteria [35] that employees had to meet in order to be eligible for the interview. First, interviewees should have at least five years of work experience in their respective roles to ensure that they know their roles. Second, the employees must know what the concept of product-oriented software development is, which ensures that all interview participants understand how their activities will change in the future and what challenges may arise in their role because of the change. Third, the interviewees must give their consent that the information and challenges they mention may be used in the context of this work.

In order to find interview participants, we applied the stratified sampling approach with respect to their respective roles [35]. All selected employees were approached and informed about the objective of the study and the protection of anonymity as well as the voluntary nature of their participation. At the beginning of the interview, each employee's consent was first obtained to ensure that the interview could be recorded, and the information obtained could be used in the context of this work. After collecting the interviewee's demographics, we gave the participants a brief introduction to the topic, as well as an explanation about the purpose of the interview. In the main part of the interview, the role-non-specific and role-specific questions were asked. The interview transcripts were analyzed using qualitative content analysis [36]. In the context of this work, the procedure of inductive category formation was chosen, which belongs to the analysis technique of summarization and aims at creating a system of categories that abstractly represent the analysis material [35, 36]. We worked inductively, which means that there was no predefined system of categories. Each statement that an employee made about a role-specific challenge was analyzed. In addition, the level of abstraction of the categories were determined. In the next step, the abstraction level of the statements was raised so that suitable categories could subsequently be formed. Subsequently, the following challenges were examined to see whether they fell under the categories already formed or whether a new category had to be formed. According to Mayring [36], once the majority of the statements has been worked through, a revision examines the categories and decides whether the categories are close to the goal of the analysis and whether the previously established level of abstraction is met. After each challenge was assigned to a category, main categories were formed to summarize categories on a higher level of abstraction. In order to compare the importance of the identified challenges, we used the following indicators [34]. The *interview frequency* indicates how many different experts mentioned a challenge that belongs to the respective category. *Statement frequency* indicates the total number of statements of a challenge belonging to a category. *Relevance* is the most suitable indicator for ranking the categories according to their importance, as it best reflects the opinions of the employees in the weighting of the challenges. Four values were determined to rank the relevance of a statement (*0: no rating; 1: low relevance; 2: medium relevance; 3: high relevance*) (Table 2).

The investigated company operates as a software manufacturer in the field of logistics. In total, it has more than 1000 employees and receives a revenue of above 100 Mio. €. The selected business unit has been conducting individual projects in which agile project teams implemented customer's specific requirements. This resulted in several slightly different systems over the years. Now, the previously customer-controlled software development is to be replaced by a standard product that can be adapted to the customer-specific logistics processes through configuration. As a result, customer-specific code fragments are largely eliminated, and the product manager defines the upcoming features of the product by means of a product roadmap. The main source for data collection of this case study is the conduction of 13 expert interviews (M1–M13) with employees with different job profiles (provided in Table 3). All interviewees have at least five years of work experience with M10 being the only exception. However, we opted to include M10 to provide a product

Table 2 Interviewee demographics

ID	Profile	Gender	Age	Practical experience	Years, employed	Interview duration
M1	Operative Product Owner (OPO)	Female	34	9	9	33:03
M2	Documenter (DOK)	Female	43	15	10	21:02
M3	Product manager (PM)	Male	32	15	8	33:54
M4	Sales manager (SM)	Male	59	34	21	38:20
M5	Support (S)	Male	56	26	21	33:32
M6	Business Consultant (BC)	Male	34	8	2/3	42:24
M7	Developer (DEV)	Male	24	6	6	32:59
M8	Marketing Expert (M)	Male	45	12	3	36:33
M9	UX-Designer (UX)	Female	27	6	6	22:42
M10	Controller (C)	Female	25	1,33	1,33	29:43
M11	Tactical Product Owner (TPO)	Male	42	15	10	38:54
M12	Head of Business Development (HoB)	Male	37	12	1,5	52:12
M13	Project manager (PRM)	Male	29	9	6	35:28

controlling perspective to the case. All interviews were conducted over a period of two weeks in early 2023.

All interviewees have a specific job profile, e.g., Tactical Product Owner (TPO), which is a part of the company's organizational chart. According to Organizational Role Theory, each employee belongs to one of the three previously mentioned roles (cf. Section 2.2). The Product Management role includes all job profiles (PM, OPO, TPO, HoB, C) that work on the product and its roadmap in a non-technical capacity but are not in direct customer contact. This role does not implement requirements from individual customers. Instead, the Customer Management role includes all job profiles (BC, SM, M, S, PRM) that directly interact with existing or potential customers. Prior to the transition to standardized product software, this role was primarily responsible for identifying new requirements that were closely aligned with customer needs. Finally, the Product Development role includes job profiles that focus on technical aspects such as development (DEV), user experience (UX), and documentation (DOK). However, the job profiles in this role do not have a say in the prioritization of features.

4 Role-Specific Software Productization Challenges

Based on the interviews, four categories of challenges were derived: Requirements and Customer Management, Product Planning and Development, Marketing and Sales, as well as Communication and Organization. A total of 254 codes categorized into16 challenges were identified. The summarized results are provided in Table 3 (sorted by relevance). The left side of the table lists the created categories and challenges. In addition, the table contains both the interview and statement frequency (int. and stat. frq.) as well as the associated relevance (rel.) of each challenge. The right side of the table lists the affected roles. We focus only the most relevant challenges with a relevance score above the median of 22,5.

Expectation management—In product-oriented software development, a single customer must understand that only those features are implemented that are consistent with the product roadmap (M3, M11, M10, M13). Developing a new feature is more time-consuming in the product-based approach: "*You think much longer about what you do, how you do it*" (M3). As the feature is released to all customers of the product, more effort is spent for the design and development, which significantly lengthens the release cycle (M7). This creates major challenges for the role Customer Management who manage the customer's expectations. For example, M6 stated that "*Product-oriented software development [...] leads to the fact that not all customer wishes are fulfilled [...], you then say 'no' to requirements and that does not always make the customer happy and will also not be pleasant for us business consultants*" (M6). M13 said that customer satisfaction could decrease as a result, "*You teach them that certain concepts are no longer tailor-made and also take even longer [...] this could also lead to problems with customer satisfaction*" (M13). While M6 and M13 related the challenge to the role of the business consultant and the project manager,

Table 3 Role-specific software productization challenges

Category and Challenge	Metrics			Roles affected												
Role	Int. frq	Stat. frq	Relevance	Product Management					Product Dev			Customer Management				
Interviewees				M3	M1	M11	M12	M10	M7	M9	M2	M8	M4	M5	M6	M13
Requirements and customer management																
Expectation management	10	19	39	x	x	x			x	x					x	x
Requirement elicitation & prio	9	17	36	x												x
Requirement standardization	6	7	18	x	x	x			x	x					x	x
Product planning and development																
Product development	10	38	60						x	x				x	x	
Product standardization	9	19	39	x	x	x			x	x	x				x	x
Product strategy development	11	16	29	x									x		x	x
Business case creation	10	15	19	x			x	x								x
Configurability determination	5	5	11	x		x									x	
Marketing and sales																
Marketing and sales transform	8	14	25	x	x	x	x					x	x			

(continued)

Table 3 (continued)

Category and Challenge	Metrics			Roles affected												
Role	Int. frq	Stat. frq	Relevance	Product Management					Product Dev			Customer Management				
Interviewees				M3	M1	M11	M12	M10	M7	M9	M2	M8	M4	M5	M6	M13
Market strategy	8	12	19	x			x					x	x			
Sell standard product	7	8	15										x			x
Communication and organization																
Internal communication	12	43	66	x	x	x	x	x	x	x	x	x	x	x	x	x
Administration	9	22	43	x	x	x	x	x	x	x				x	x	x
New role familiarizing	7	8	20	x	x	x			x	x			x			x
Mindset Change	6	7	17	x	x	x	x	x	x	x	x	x	x	x	x	x
Project vs. product prioritization	3	4	8	x			x									x

M1 directed the challenge to the product team: *"we will say 'no' to some things and that will be messy"* (M1).

Requirement elicitation and prioritization—Previously, requirements were elicited directly from the customer within a project (M7). With the product-based approach, the requirements for new features come increasingly from the internal stakeholders and potential customers at the market (M1). It is no longer exclusively implemented what the existing customer expresses in the project, but the product manager determines in which direction the product and its features develop (M3, M10, M11, M13). M1 stated that it will be a challenge for the product manager to identify those requirements, that potential customers have: *"For me, the product manager is the one, who […] keeps an eye on the market. […] 'What requirements do potential customers have in general that we could perhaps still implement to be able to place our product there? That is an important product management task for me, and I would even classify that as relatively difficult"* (M1). It is more important to understand the basic problem of the requirement during the requirements elicitation and not to focus on the customer's proposed solution (M6). In addition, challenges with the prioritization of requirements were mentioned. M3 said, *"the challenge […] is […] to distinguish what is sustainable […]. Or we just must look that we are always on the latest technology […] Weighing that against each other [is] hard to quantify: 'what is more important now?'"* (M3). The challenge of prioritization is to estimate the added value of a requirement: "*[…] is this just a perceived priority on the market or is it an actual priority"* (M3).

Product development—The interviewees frequently mentioned that releasing new features in the product to all customers, they must be implemented more error-free and efficiently than in the project-oriented organization (M7, M10). M7 cited the following for his role as a developer: *"[…] we have to be much more disciplined in our approach […] to just avoid that half-baked [features] get into the product"* (M7). UX designers need to create cleaner designs for new features (M7, M10). However, since old features will also be implemented in the new standard product, it will become a challenge for the roles of the developer and the UX designer to validate them (M6, M7, M9). For the UX designers, this means that they must redesign old, possibly custom, system designs (M6, M7). According to M7, this challenge means that old features, which are transferred to the new system, must be reintegrated: *"reimplementing custom stuff and accommodating it in the new architecture"* (M7).

Product standardization—This challenge comprises the identification of customer types and their standard processes as well as the migration of existing customers to the new and standardized product. M1 mentioned that it is not possible to define standard processes that work for all customers. Rather, types of customers that are similar in their processes need to be identified (M1).

In addition, it is difficult to move existing customers from their prior, customized solution to the standard product (M1, M10, M13). M13 described this as a technical and social challenge: *"The move alone will be huge […] On the technical side, to bring this over the stage at all […] and to tell [the customers] that we are moving them back to a standard product, whereby also expenditures, which they have made in the past, actually become invalid, [which] will be a very big problem"* (M13).

Furthermore, the challenge of maintaining discipline, keeping the standard product as free of customer specifications as possible, and making sure that every feature in the product is relevant to the entire customer base was mentioned (M5, M7).

Product strategy development—The product manager develops a product roadmap that specifies what features will be implemented (M7, M11, M12). *"I would see the creation of a product roadmap [...] a heavy challenge for the product manager"* (M11). Here, capacities must be considered, and requirements of potential customers, existing customers, and internal stakeholders need to be aligned. The product manager then decides which features to implement and when (M2, M11).

In addition to creating the product roadmap, the product manager is also responsible for developing a product vision (M3, M5). M3 said, *"the hardest part is building a vision where all [stakeholders] are reflected in and that really addresses all the individual strategies"*. It is important to work continuously on this scope to ensure the product features match the customer needs (M12). Furthermore, M3 mentioned the challenge of not losing the sight of the customer: *"the most difficult thing is always to balance how much I look at the product without ignoring the individuality of the customer"* (M12). It is difficult to efficiently make decisions for the product (M3). *" How can you efficiently, make these decisions [...] how can you run this efficiently?"* (M3).

Marketing and sales transformation—As a result of the company's change from developing an individualized software to developing a standard product, the established marketing, and sales processes change (M1). *"Sales will definitely be a big challenge, because they will have to adapt their service catalog"* (M1). To do so, new license models and sales strategies are required (M10).

The Customer Management roles, e.g., sales and marketing, must create new sales arguments since the old ones can no longer be used (M1, M3, M10). M1 expressed that the *"unique selling point [...] 'We can do and implement anything you want, we can do anything' [had to be cut] back a lot because that just doesn't match anymore"*. In addition, according to M3, it is a great challenge to find ways to differentiate from competitors when selling a standard product. However, the sales processes of the company *"have to be more standardized. Standardizing that won't be easy either."* (M4).

Internal communication—The most frequently mentioned challenge is the increase of communication within the different teams (M3, M4, M6, M9, M10). M3 mentioned, *"you have to communicate internally very, very much. You think much longer about what you do, how you do it, [which is] among the biggest challenges"*. It is important to note that this challenge is faced by everyone without exception. *"Due to the increased communication, it could also happen that the communication channels are more confusing than before [...] certain channels, such as for teams, are flooded and coordination processes take even longer"* (M10). To this end, M3 mentioned the task of developing governance mechanisms to reduce coordination efforts. Another challenge is the communication of the newly introduced roles of product manager and operative and tactical product owner (M1, M10).

Another challenge is the navigation of internal conflicts. They primarily stem from the impending shift in decision-making authority concerning the implementation of product features. The Customer Management role will no longer wield the same level of control over future features. Specifically, project managers will need to grapple with situations where the Product Management roles, responsible for determining future features, may decline their requests (M12).

Administration—To ensure that every employee in the company understands the new tasks, new roles are defined (M1, M10, M11, M12). In addition, developers face the challenge of formulating programming guidelines, so that a certain quality standard is maintained, and the source code remains readable for all developers (M7, M10).

5 Discussion

The goal of this paper is to identify role-specific challenges in software productization. To identify these, we conducted 13 expert interviews, which led to 16 challenges, ranked by frequency. In this section, using a problematization approach, we compare the prescribed challenges from literature (c.f. Table 1) with those from our case (c.f. Table 3). During the analysis, we identify the organizational role theory as a suitable theoretical lens and applied it to theorize about the possible reasons. Each element of each Tables 1 and 3 is prioritized by using the standard competition ranking by frequency.

Literature identifies the product planning as the most important challenge software product managers face (Table 1, rank 1). In contrast, our interviewees M2, M3, M5, M7, M11, and M12 perceive it as less challenging (Table 3, rank 6). This may be attributed to the fact that our case company is still deeply engaged with other, rather operational tasks, such as internal communication, which may lead to an underestimation of such strategic challenges.

Secondly, literature identifies the introducing of the role product manager and internal communication (Table 1, both rank 2). These two challenges are closely interrelated, as both pertain to the introduction of the new role and its impact within the transformed company. Consequently, internal communication was frequently referenced by interviewees from the case company (M3, M4, M6, M9, M10), indicating that it remains closely associated with the new internal structure (Table 3, rank 1). With respect to Organizational Role Theory, we see these challenges connected to the *role ambiguity* of the product management role [5, 11, 15]. It arises from an unclear role definition and insufficient communication of the role to all employees within the organization [4]. Four participants in our interviews reiterated this and found creating and communicating a clear role definition to be a challenge. This is also backed by other sources. Maglyas et al. [13] investigate the implications of an ambiguous role definition and conclude that product managers lack autonomy and tend to rely on the support of top management to implement changes to the product.

Thirdly, the management of requirements is importantly featured as a challenge in literature on software product management (Table 1, rank 2). In contrast, the interviewees M1, M3, M7, M10, M11 and M13 reflect on this topic as well, but prioritize it much lower (Table 3, rank 5). This discrepancy can be attributed to the fact that the complexity of gathering requirements in the new setting is still underestimated in the case company. This is likely due to the fact that nearly all customized requirements were created within a custom-made software solution until recently. This presents a challenge for Customer Management roles who are still in close contact with the customer but whose influence has diminished. Precisely, their whole role is inverted from role transmitter (issuing new requirement from customers) to a mere role receiver that configures pre-built solutions at the customers without the decision-making power on the implementation of product features. Previously, this role was always able to decide independently which features should be included in the respective customer system. This was possible because these features were not released for other customers. Thus, almost everything that the customer explicitly requested was implemented in the customer project. With the introduction of the new concept, decisions about new features are made by the Product Management roles, so the Customer Management roles no longer have any decision-making power about new functionalities. This change represents the *role discontinuity* between the tasks before and after the organizational change. We explain the first appearance of this conflict with the exclusive documentation of the transformation to a product-oriented software development organization that is visible during a brief snapshot in time.

Fourth, behind the aforementioned challenges, literature ranks the development of the software product (Table 1, rank 4). Our case company, in contrast, ranks this as second most important challenge (Table 3, rank 2) as they deem it difficult to develop the software disciplined and flexible enough for various customers. This was identified as a challenge in this study, but not mentioned in other studies. It refers to the role of the Product Developer and describes the establishment of a new system architecture during the change. The case company is moving from its previous monolithic system architecture to a service-oriented software architecture. This introduces new onboarding challenges that affect the product developer's role as new opportunities and constraints emerge. We consequently interpretate this additional effort as *role overload* which hits the Product Developer role with operational and strategic development tasks.

Two new challenges, though interconnected, were revealed in the interviews. Our interviewees found it difficult to standardize a product that was previously customer-tailored and is now subject to deconstruction. At the same time, they found this transformation difficult to sell and market, i.e., to find new sales concepts. Both of these challenges are both technical and social in nature and have not been covered by existing literature (see Table 1).

This work is based on interviews within a single business unit within one single case company. As such, all challenges are company-specific and may be influenced by personality factors, which may limit the generalizability of the findings. However, the phenomenon of shifting to a product-centric organization is rarely observed, which explains the discrete nature of this single case study. Despite our exhaustive search, the applicability of AI in the context of software productization remains elusive. Our findings yielded only one source, namely Olsen et al. [30], which posits that AI can yield new digital offerings and revenue streams. Furthermore, the use of AI will transform the role of a software product manager from eliciting requirements to conducting experiments and analyzing users' data for hypothesis testing.

This paper sheds light on role-specific challenges associated with the change process towards software productization. We found these challenges especially in situations, where role transmitters and role receivers changed in the course of the transition. What at the first glance seemed to be a challenge in software product management, turned out to be situations with deficient communication lines and changed hierarchies. In this context, we found Organizational Role Theory a suitable frame to interpretate those challenges. We were able to show that each of the three previously identified roles is affected by one problem that can be portrayed in the light of the theory: *role overload* influences the role of Product Development, *role ambiguity* characterizes the role of Product Management and *role discontinuity* affects the Customer Management role. However, the potential of this theory is not yet exhausted, and we could well imagine using it to examine other concepts, e.g., role behavior, role expectations and intrapersonal relationships (cf. Fig. 1).

Furthermore, we employed the technique of problematization. By comparing the challenges that were prescribed by authoritative literature in such a situation (Table 1) to the challenges that were actually reported in the interviews (Table 3), we found that our newly productized company tends to underestimate the strategic planning in favor of its internal reorganization and changes to the product.

Finally, the identification and analysis of additional comparable cases, coupled with the inclusion of further expert interviews conducted within the context of a larger comparative case study, would enhance the generalizability of the findings presented in this work.

References

1. van de Weerd, I., Brinkkemper, S., Nieuwenhuis, R., Versendaal, J., & Bijlsma, L. (2006). Towards a Reference Framework for Software Product Management. In Glinz, M. (Ed.) *Proceedings/14th IEEE International Requirements Engineering Conference, RE '06* (pp. 319–322). IEEE Computer Society. https://doi.org/10.1109/RE.2006.66
2. Artz, P., van de Weerd, I., Brinkkemper, S., & Fieggen, J. (2010). Productization: *Transforming from Developing Customer-Specific Software to Product Software.* In 1st ICSOB Conference. Springer. https://doi.org/10.1007/978-3-642-13633-7_8
3. Xu, L., & Brinkkemper, S. (2007). Concepts of Product Software. *European Journal of Information Systems, 16*, 531–541. https://doi.org/10.1057/palgrave.ejis.3000703
4. Springer, O., Miler, J.: A comprehensive overview of software product management challenges. Empir Software Eng, vol. 27 (2022). https://doi.org/10.1007/s10664-022-10134-5
5. Wagenblatt, T. (2019). Software Product Management. *Finding the Right Balance for YourProduct Inc*. Springer.
6. Kristinsdottir, S., Larusdottir, M., & Cajander, Å. (2016). Responsibilities and Challenges of Product Owners at Spotify—An Exploratory Case Study. In *6th International Conference on Human-Centered Software Engineering, HCSE* (Vol. 9856, pp. 3–16). Springer. https://doi.org/10.1007/978-3-319-44902-9_1
7. Maedche, A., Botzenhardt, A., & Neer, L. (2012). *Software for people: Fundamentals, Trends and Best Practices.* Springer.

8. Ebert, C. (2014). Software Product Management. *IEEE Software, 31*, 21–24. https://doi.org/10.1109/MS.2014.72
9. Maglyas, A., Nikula, U., Smolander, K.: Comparison of Software Product Management Practices in SMEs and Large Enterprises. In: Cusumano, M.A., Iyer, B., Venkatraman, N. (eds.) Software Business. Third International Conference, ICSOB 2012, Cambridge, MA, USA, June 18–20, 2012. Proceedings. SpringerLink Bücher, vol. 114, pp. 15–26. Springer Berlin Heidelberg, Berlin, Heidelberg (2012). https://doi.org/10.1007/978-3-642-30746-1_2
10. Maglyas, A., Nikula, U., & Smolander, K. (2012). Lean Solutions to Software Product Management Problems. *IEEE Software, 29*, 40–46. https://doi.org/10.1109/ms.2012.108
11. Maglyas, A., Nikula, U., & Smolander, K. (2012, September 24–28). *What Do Practitioners Mean When they Talk About Product Management?* In Heimdahl, M. (Ed.) 2012 20th IEEE International Requirements Engineering Conference (RE 2012). Chicago, Illinois, USA (pp. 261–266). IEEE, Piscataway, NJ. https://doi.org/10.1109/RE.2012.6345812
12. Maglyas, A., Nikula, U., Smolander, K., & Fricker, S. A. (2017). Core Software Product Management Activities. *Journal of Advances in Management Research, 14*, 23–45. https://doi.org/10.1108/JAMR-03-2016-0022
13. Maglyas, A., Nikula, U., & Smolander, K. (2013). What are the Roles of Software Product Managers? An Empirical Investigation. *Journal of Systems and Software, 86*, 3071–3090. https://doi.org/10.1016/j.jss.2013.07.045
14. Ebert, C., & Brinkkemper, S. (2014). Software Product Management—An Industry Evaluation. *Journal of Systems and Software, 95*, 10–18. https://doi.org/10.1016/j.jss.2013.12.042
15. Kittlaus, H. -B., & Fricker, S. A. (2017). *Software Product Management*. The ISPMA-Compliant Study Guide and Handbook. Springer Berlin Heidelberg.
16. Dver, A. S. (2007). *Software Product Management Essentials. A Practical Guide for Small and Mid-Sized Companies*. Anclote Press.
17. Katz, D., & Kahn, R. L. (1966). *The Social Psychology of Organizations*. Wiley.
18. Kilpi, T. (1997, April 8–9). Choosing a SCM-Tool: A Framework and Evaluation. In Ebert, J. (Ed.) *Proceedings/8th Conference on Software Engineering Environments* (pp. 164–172), Cottbus, Germany. IEEE Computer Society Press, Los Alamitos, Calif. https://doi.org/10.1109/SEE.1997.591828
19. Kilpi, T. (1997, March 17–19). New Challenges for Version Control and Configuration Management: A Framework and Evaluation. In *Proceedings/First Euromicro Conference on Software Maintenance and Reengineering* (pp. 33–41), Berlin, Germany. IEEE Computer Society Press, Los Alamitos, Calif. https://doi.org/10.1109/CSMR.1997.583000
20. Kilpi, T. (1997). Product management Challenge to Software Change Process: Preliminary Results from three SMEs Experiment. *Software Process: Improve Practice, 3*, 165–175. https://doi.org/10.1002/(SICI)1099-1670(199709)3:3%3c165::AID-SPIP79%3e3.0.CO;2-6
21. Fricker, S. A. (2012). Software Product Management. In Maedche, A., Botzenhardt, A., & Neer, L. (Eds.), *Software for People. Management for professionals* (pp. 53–81). Springer. https://doi.org/10.1007/978-3-642-31371-4_4
22. Gorchels, L. (2000). *The Product Manager's Handbook. The Complete Product Management Resource*. NTC Business Books.
23. van de Weerd, I., Brinkkemper, S., Nieuwenhuis, R., Versendaal, J., & Bijlsma, L. (2006). *On the Creation of a Reference Framework for Software Product Management: Validation and Tool Support*. In International Workshop on Software Product Management (IWSPM'06—RE'06 Workshop) (pp. 3–12). IEEE. https://doi.org/10.1109/IWSPM.2006.6
24. Condon, D. (2002). *Software Product Management: Managing Software Development from Idea to Product to Marketing to Sales*. Aspatore.
25. Merton, R. K. (1957). The Role-Set: Problems in Sociological Theory. *The British Journal of Sociology, 8*, 106. https://doi.org/10.2307/587363
26. Biddle, B. J. (1986). Recent Developments in Role Theory. *Annual Review of Sociology, 12*, 67–92. https://doi.org/10.1146/annurev.so.12.080186.000435
27. Solomon, M. R., Surprenant, C., Czepiel, J. A., & Gutman, E. G. (1985). A Role Theory Perspective on Dyadic Interactions: The Service Encounter. *Journal of Marketing, 49*, 99–111. https://doi.org/10.1177/002224298504900110

28. Ghobadi, S., & Mathiassen, L. (2016). Perceived Barriers to Effective Knowledge Sharing in Agile Software Teams. *Information Systems Journal, 26*, 95–125. https://doi.org/10.1111/isj.12053
29. Venkatesh, V., Thong, J. Y. L., Chan, F. K. Y., Hoehle, H., & Spohrer, K. (2020). How Agile Software Development Methods Reduce Work Exhaustion: Insights on Role Perceptions and Organizational Skills. *Information Systems Journal, 30*, 733–761. https://doi.org/10.1111/isj.12282
30. Springer, O., Miler, J., & Wróbel, M. (2023). Strategies for Dealing With Software Product Management Challenges. *IEEE Access, 11*, 55797–55813. https://doi.org/10.1109/ACCESS.2023.3282605
31. Moe, N. B., Berntzen, M., Barbala, A., & Stray, V. (2024). Software Product Management in Large-Scale Agile. In Šmite, D., Guerra, E., Wang, X., Marchesi, M., & Gregory, P. (Eds.), *Agile Processes in Software Engineering and Extreme Programming 25th. Lecture Notes in Business Information Processing* (Vol. 512, pp. 53–69). Springer International Pu [S.l.]. https://doi.org/10.1007/978-3-031-61154-4_4
32. Olsson, H. H., & Bosch, J. (2023, November 27–29). Strategic Digital Product Management in the Age of AI. In Hyrynsalmi, S., Münch, J., Smolander, K., & Melegati, J. (Eds.), *Software Business*. 14th International Conference, ICSOB 2023, Lahti, Finland: proceedings. Lecture Notes in Business Information Processing (Vol. 500, pp. 344–359). Springer. https://doi.org/10.1007/978-3-031-53227-6_24
33. Brinkmann, S., & Kvale, S. (2018). *Doing Interviews*. Sage.
34. Vogelsang, K., Steinhüser, M., & Hoppe, U. (2013). *A Qualitative Approach to Examine Technology Acceptance International Conference on Information Systems (ICIS)*.
35. Robinson, O. C. (2014). Sampling in Interview-Based Qualitative Research: A Theoretical and Practical Guide. *Qualitative Research in Psychology, 11*, 25–41. https://doi.org/10.1080/14780887.2013.801543
36. Mayring, P. (2015). *Qualitative Inhaltsanalyse. Grundlagen und Techniken*. Beltz.

Part III
Data Science & Business Analytics

A Multivocal Literature Review on Privacy and Fairness in Federated Learning

Beatrice Balbierer, Lukas Heinlein, Domenique Zipperling, and Niklas Kühl

Abstract Federated Learning presents a way to revolutionize AI applications by eliminating the necessity for data sharing. Yet, research has shown that information can still be extracted during training, making additional privacy-preserving measures such as differential privacy imperative. To implement real-world federated learning applications, fairness, ranging from a fair distribution of performance to non-discriminative behavior, must be considered. Particularly in high-risk applications (e.g. healthcare), avoiding the repetition of past discriminatory errors is paramount. As recent research has demonstrated an inherent tension between privacy and fairness, we conduct a multivocal literature review to examine the current methods to integrate privacy and fairness in federated learning. Our analyses illustrate that the relationship between privacy and fairness has been neglected, posing a critical risk for real-world applications. We highlight the need to explore the relationship between privacy, fairness, and performance, advocating for the creation of integrated federated learning frameworks.

1 Introduction

In today's digital age, the increasing availability of data offers unprecedented opportunities for innovation, particularly for machine learning (ML) [1]. However, utilization remains a challenge as data is usually not stored centrally, but distributed across data owners, i.e., clients, like edge devices or organizations [2–4]. Yet, storing data centrally is infeasible due to privacy and intellectual property (IP) exposure risks [5]. Federated Learning (FL) can inherently mitigate these privacy risks by avoiding the centralization of sensitive data [6, 7]. To harness all data, clients utilize their data to

B. Balbierer · L. Heinlein · D. Zipperling (✉) · N. Kühl
University of Bayreuth, Bayreuth, Germany
e-mail: domenique.zipperlin@uni-bayreuth.de

D. Zipperling · N. Kühl
Fraunhofer FIT, Bayreuth, Germany

C. M. Flath et al. (eds.), *Artificial Intelligence, Data, and Decision-Making*, Lecture Notes in Information Systems and Organisation 82,
https://doi.org/10.1007/978-3-032-08480-4_18

train an ML model locally and only transfer model updates to a central server, aggregating these updates to a final model [8]. By not sharing raw data, FL has opened up new possibilities for ML applications for edge devices [9] or more sensitive domains such as healthcare [10]. Although the centralization of data is avoided, the risk of information leakage remains as shared updates can be analyzed to extract information about the training data, thereby posing a privacy and/or IP exposure risk [11, 12]. Additionally, aggregating multiple local model updates into a single final model that is then utilized by all clients can lead to unequal performance across clients or disparate outcomes for underrepresented social groups [13]. This is a common issue when dealing with machine learning models based on historical data, often referred to as algorithmic fairness [14, 15]. Applications of FL in healthcare illustrate the importance of privacy and fairness quite vividly as patient data, due to its sensitive nature, must be kept private. Additionally, the application's performance, e.g., detection of skin cancer [16], should neither vary across hospitals nor ethnic groups as it is not the case among physicians [17]. Unfortunately, achieving both objectives simultaneously is not trivial and measures to ensure privacy may negatively affect efforts to ensure fairness [18]. While privacy has been a focus within FL research for quite some time, less focus has been on fairness demonstrated by the lack of fairness aspects in recent surveys regarding current challenges in FL [7, 19, 20].

With our research, we want to explore current methods that enhance privacy or foster fairness in FL while especially focusing on efforts to fuse the two as they contribute to the development of FL systems that are both technologically sophisticated and ethically sound. To evaluate the current methods, we will explore the following research question (RQ).

1.1 What Are Current Methods that Ensure Privacy and Fairness in Federated Learning Independently and Together?

Using a multivocal literature review (MLR), based on Kitchenham und Charters [21] guidelines for conducting a structured literature review, extended by the inclusion of gray literature as suggested by Garousi et al. [22], we assess current methods for privacy and fairness in FL. Choosing an MLR instead of a strategic literature approach allows us to capture literature that is not formally published and thereby might capture emerging research topics, which is especially relevant when analyzing the current body of knowledge in fast-evolving fields like ML and FL.

Our findings highlight that research is centered around avoiding data leakage and ensuring data integrity while fostering fairness regarding performance across clients (client fairness) and social groups (group fairness). The identified literature demonstrates that the relationship between privacy and fairness has been neglected. Furthermore, we find that over half of the identified literature does not focus on certain domains or explicit applications but rather on developing new methods. Therefore, the results of our work encourage and call for research at the intersection of privacy and fairness with a focus on real-world applications [23].

2 Conceptual Background

The conceptual background provides a basic understanding of FL and its relation to privacy and fairness. Therefore, this chapter explores the mechanisms of FL, while defining the terms of privacy and fairness more closely.

FL is an innovative paradigm for enabling decentralized training of ML models [8]. Training takes place on distributed devices or clients, eliminating the need for centralized storage of raw data. Thereby, FL protects privacy as the data remains on individual clients contributing to the improvement of the model by sharing model updates [6]. As a result, FL facilitates the cross-company use of AI and improves data access without disclosing personal data, which is crucial for exploiting the full potential of AI in the industrial sector [24]. This not only improves data protection but also enables flexible adaptation to the different operating conditions of different companies. The typical process includes initializing a global model, distribution to devices or clients, independent training with local data, aggregation of updates, and iterative refinement of the model. FL is used in areas such as healthcare, finance, and edge computing to address privacy concerns while enabling collaborative model building. This approach represents a technical advance and marks a shift toward decentralized, privacy-centric ML methods [25]. Although FL avoids sharing raw data, privacy concerns are not muted. Privacy within information systems is usually connected to information and definitions "typically include some form of control over the potential secondary uses of one's personal information" [26]. Various attacks such as membership inference attacks can affect the control over potential use by extracting information about the training data based on the shared model updates, thereby compromising privacy [12]. This is often referred to as data leakage [27, 28].

While privacy has been a focus within FL research for quite some time, less focus has been on fairness which is demonstrated by the lack of fairness aspect in a recent survey regarding the current state and challenges in FL [7, 19, 20]. Yet, fairness is crucial when designing inclusive and efficient FL applications [15]. To address this challenge, Su et al. [29] emphasize the importance of two key dimensions of fairness: group and client fairness. Client fairness focuses on equal distribution of performance and fair compensation for clients' contribution of data or computational resources. Group fairness refers to debates about algorithmic fairness and the mitigation of biases towards underrepresented social groups.

3 Method

Our study aims to provide a comprehensive overview of the current methods to ensure fairness and privacy in FL applications and to identify future research directions. Therefore, we conducted a multivocal literature review (MLR) following Kitchenham and Charters [21] guidelines for academic literature (AL), supplemented by the inclusion of gray literature (GL) to ensure a more holistic perspective by including not formally published literature. As recommended by Garousi et al. [22] including gray literature is especially useful to identify emerging research topics. As the field of FL and ML in general evolves rapidly, including gray literature is important to capture all relevant topics. Choosing an MLR facilitates the identification of a significant number of relevant articles and the development of a concise dataset, supporting the identification of further research needs.

For AL, we screened eight databases covering various interdisciplinary fields using the search string, "Federated Learning" AND (Priva* OR Fair*), yielding 2,746 hits. We defined inclusion and exclusion criteria (Table 1) and performed a two-step title screening, assessing the relevance and contextual contribution of the articles individually and then collectively. In addition, a stop criterion was defined to include only the first eight pages of a database if it does not offer an export function. To enhance the relevance of the publications in our database, we analyzed the citation rates of the articles using the importance of citations as described by Kladroba et al. [30]. Specifically, for articles published until 2022, a minimum of three citations is required, while works from 2023 must have at least one citation.

The papers underwent relevance evaluation by the author team using a 1-to-5 Likert scale, where 5 indicates high relevance, 3 denotes neutrality, and 1 reflects irrelevance.

A rating of 5 was assigned to papers that made a direct and significant contribution to the field of research. A rating of 4 implied that the paper contained relevant

Table 1 Inclusion and exclusion criteria

Inclusion criteria	Exclusion criteria
Availability of the full text	Brief mention of the research content without significant contribution to the existing knowledge
Publication before 2024	The mere outline of the research question without in-depth analysis or discussion
Paper's relevance to the research question	Privacy-preserving methods and fairness examinations unrelated to federated learning approaches
	Federated learning is employed as the methodology for ensuring the preservation of privacy
	Papers published at MDPI due to concerns regarding the peer-review process

information but was less central. A score of 3 indicated general relevance but without direct contribution to the core of the research. Only papers scoring 4 or above were included in the dataset. Any disagreements were resolved through discussion, leading to 62 relevant AL items. Regarding the GL, the identical search terms and stop criterion were used in Google, Google Scholar, and arXiv to ensure consistency in our methodology. We choose the sources in alignment with the methodology and other papers performing an MLR [31]. The preliminary search yielded 488 GL items of GL. However, these were subject to a rigorous evaluation process, employing the same inclusion and exclusion criteria used for AL. Following this evaluation, only eleven GL items were deemed relevant and of sufficient quality to be included in the final dataset. Furthermore, snowballing was performed and evaluated using the previously defined criteria, with the object of exhausting all literature sources. This yielded 38 additional relevant papers, bringing the total number of items in our final dataset to 133 (see Fig. 1).

Our research aims to examine current methods in the area of privacy and fairness in the context of FL. To this end, a two-stage analysis process was undertaken to provide a comprehensive overview of these issues. The first phase focused on privacy

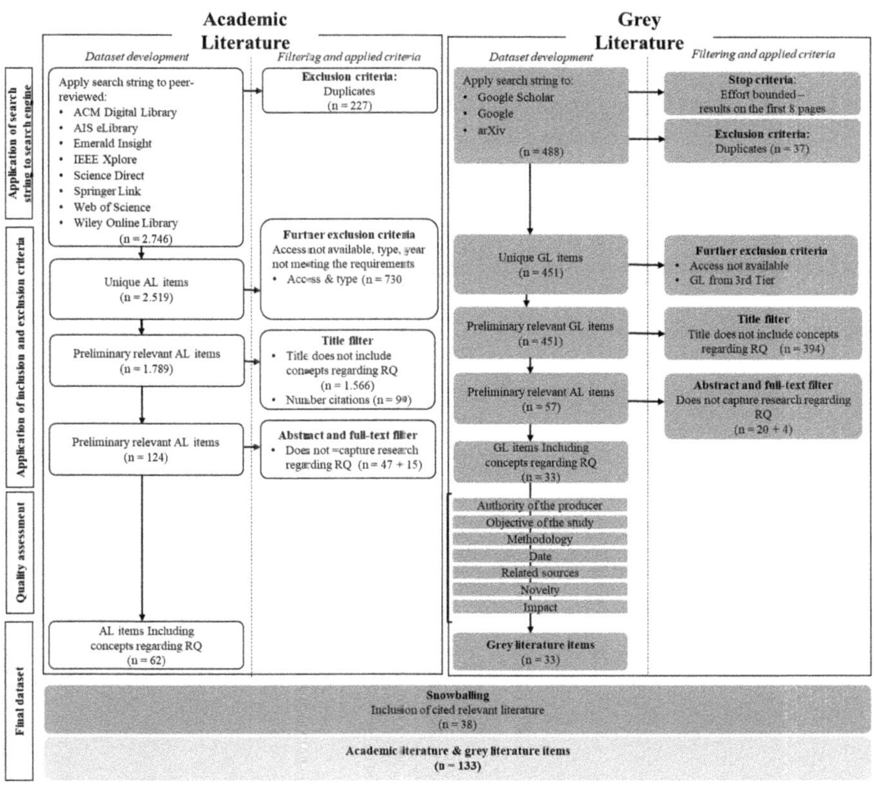

Fig. 1 Search and selection process

in the context of FL, followed by a detailed consideration of fairness approaches in this area. Each section of the analysis presents the technologies identified and their interrelationships with other technologies. The goal is to provide a comprehensive overview of the most common approaches and techniques, thereby deepening the understanding of these key areas.

4 Results

To capture the current state of research on fairness and privacy in FL, we examine the characteristics of the identified literature. We analyze the distribution concerning literature classification and investigate specific sub-dimensions of fairness and privacy. Our goal is to pinpoint where recent research has concentrated its efforts and thereby identify which dimensions, sub-dimensions, and cross-dimensional inquiries have been neglected.

4.1 Characteristics of the Included Publications

A review of eleven databases was conducted to identify relevant literature on privacy and fairness. A total of 45 significant papers were found in Web of Science, 15 in IEEE Xplore, 8 in ScienceDirect, 7 in ACM Digital Library, 5 in SpringerLink, and 4 in Wiley Online Library. ArXiv had the highest number of publications in the field of GL with 24 entries, followed by Google Scholar (23) and Google (2). Analyzing the thematic distribution of articles, there is a strong overrepresentation in the privacy dimension, with 98 articles addressing privacy concerns and only 24 articles discussing fairness issues. Privacy research is predominantly associated with AL (70%), while fairness research is almost equally split between AL and GL. Only 11 papers examine both privacy and fairness simultaneously (four from AL and seven from GL). We identified two sub-dimensions for each dimension: data leakage and data integrity for privacy, and client and group fairness for fairness. Data leakage has attracted the most attention, with 72 papers addressing it alone and another 35 in combination with data integrity. Data integrity specifically is addressed in two papers. Fairness research focuses on emphasizing client fairness (23 papers) while group fairness is addressed in eight papers. Four papers address both dimensions of fairness. Cross-dimensional research is scarce, with eleven articles addressing at least one privacy and one fairness dimension simultaneously. No literature was identified that covers both dimensions of privacy and both dimensions of fairness simultaneously (Fig. 2).

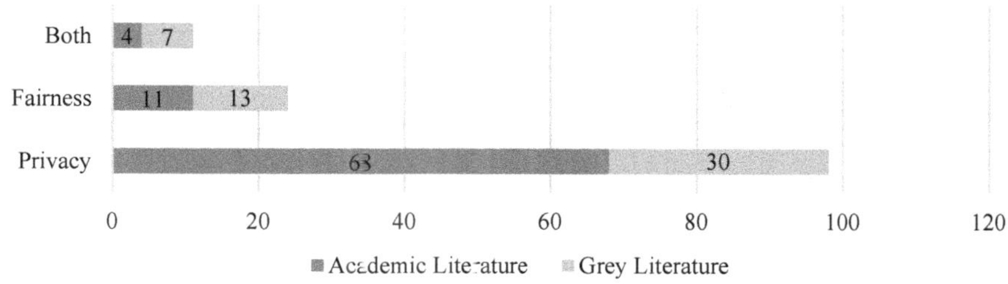

Fig. 2 Thematic distribution of publications

4.2 *Overview of Methods to Address Privacy and Fairness in Federated Learning*

After describing the characteristics of the included literature, we will overview different methods to ensure privacy or fairness, including brief descriptions. We will also illustrate how these methods are combined to achieve various objectives within or across dimensions. Figure 3 shows the number of papers focusing on one or both dimensions and the specific sub-dimensions they address. Additionally, the figure provides insight into the applications: the first number shows the papers that are domain-unspecific, and the second shows those focusing on domain-specific applications. A detailed description of the domains is provided in Sect. 4.3.

Methods used to ensure privacy. Preventing data leaks and maintaining system integrity are crucial challenges in the field of FL. A variety of different methods are used to protect user data from disclosure by anonymization or encrypting. The most common techniques include Differential Privacy (DP) with 56 papers, Homomorphic Encryption (HE) with 34 papers, and Secure Multi-Party Computation (SMPC) with 17 papers. DP adds noise to the actual dataset thereby enabling the extraction of aggregated or static information from a data set while protecting the privacy of individuals [32] addressing privacy concerns in industries like healthcare. Exemplarily, DP is employed in Label DP [33] or combination with stochastic gradient descent for secure aggregation. Label DP is used in classification tasks obscuring the direct link between features and their labels while DP for secure aggregation preserves the privacy of model updates when shared with a server for model aggregation [34]. HE prevents data leakage by enabling computations to be performed directly on encrypted data without prior decryption or reduction in the liability of the result [35]. 17 papers are identified combining DP with HE providing two levels of privacy: a user and a model-based level. Another approach is to combine HE with secret sharing [36]. Secret sharing divides information into several parts, called shares. The shares themselves do not reveal any insights and the information can only be reconstructed by combining a certain number of shares. Thereby, greater flexibility and scalability are offered as new shares can be added and removed without changing the entire system while increasing data security. SMPC enables multiple users to pool their data and perform computations without disclosing their private information to each

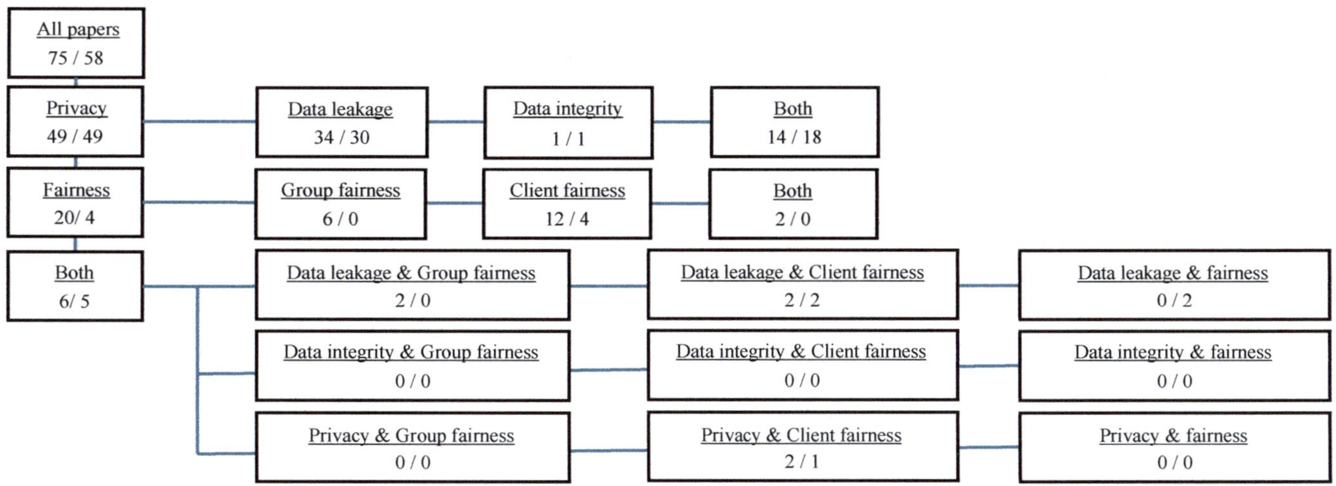

Fig. 3 Overview of the identified literature grouped by (sub-) dimensions and whether there is a focus on an application domain (e.g., healthcare). For each (sub-) dimension, the first number represents the number of papers without focusing on an application domain (domain-unspecific), while the second number represents the number of papers with an application domain (domain-specific)

other while cryptographic techniques ensure the correctness of the final result [37]. All identified papers consistently use SMPC in conjunction with DP enhancing both privacy preservation and data usability. SMPC enables secure computation, while DP adds noise to the data to ensure user anonymity [38]. Another layer of security can be provided by applying HE to a combination of SMPC and DP, as introduced by seven identified papers. The combination of these three methods results in a robust data protection system that ensures the secure exchange and analysis of information while maintaining privacy [39]. Yang et al. [40] and Maurya und Prakash [41] introduce specialized approaches that use a particular form of SMPC called secure aggregation to complement the application of DP and HE.

Secure aggregation is specifically designed for the aggregation of FL systems, while SMPC has a much broader application area [42]. Smahi et al. [43] propose an approach that emphasizes privacy protection to ensure data integrity. The approach primarily focuses on using FL to protect privacy while utilizing BC and zero-knowledge proofs (ZKPs) as sub-elements. Thereby, model updates are stored securely in an immutable and transparent manner while keeping the actual data confidential. BC-based systems therefore generally represent a technological advance, as these decentralized ledger technologies contribute significantly to the transparency and reliability of digital transactions and foster trust in decentralized processes [44].

Our analysis of the literature shows that BC, complemented by other techniques, is oftentimes utilized to address data leakage as well as data integrity [45]. The Federated Visual Learning System, known as FedVisionBC, mitigates issues such as single point of failure, model poisoning, and membership inference attacks [46]. Consensus protocols such as Delegated Proof of Stake and Proof of Authority strengthen the security mechanisms and trustworthiness of decentralized systems [47, 48]. Recent advancements in secure FL for IoT and edge computing include the integration of Learning with Errors encryption and Consistent Hashing Algorithm for secure data computations [49] and a model parameter aggregation protocol that ensures data privacy on user devices introduced by Eltaras et al. [50] Verifiable Privacy-Preserving Federated Learning for edge computing systems uses HE and combines Distributed Selective Stochastic Gradient Descent with the Paillier cryptosystem to achieve efficient distributed encryption [51]. Dynamic Successive Verification Mechanisms use HE thereby enhancing security and privacy through dynamic verification and encryption [52]. This protocol, based on Boneh-Lynn-Shacham signatures and multi-party security, verifies the integrity of client-uploaded parameters and the correctness of server-aggregated results. Additionally, approximate homomorphic Cheon-Kim-Kim-Song encryption protects client data privacy [53].

Methods used to achieve fairness. In the area of FL, there are a variety of research efforts to improve both fairness and accuracy. A wide range of innovative approaches and technologies are being explored, including developing personalized models, innovative aggregation methods, and asynchronous mechanisms. The papers mainly present use cases related to inter-hospital collaboration and learning from histopathology images [4, 54, 55]. Client fairness in FL aims to evenly distribute benefits among clients, focusing on equitable performance distribution, resource-driven participation, collaboration incentives, trust assessment, and reducing bias through algorithmic fairness. A key approach involves crafting personalized models tailored to the unique needs and data profiles of each client, essential for fostering more equitable and impactful outcomes. Innovative aggregation methods, such as the use of double momentum gradients, can enable more efficient and equitable integration of contributions from various clients [56]. Asynchronous mechanisms address the variability in client availability and computing power by allowing clients to submit updates on their schedules without the need for synchronized communication. This approach leads to more efficient resource utilization and ensures fairer participation among clients [57]. Another approach uses incentivization mechanisms, such as reverse auctions and trust assessments, to promote efficiency and ensure a fair distribution of resources [58]. Proportional Fair FL adjusts weights dynamically addressing the challenge of unequal starting conditions of clients [4]. Multi-gradient descent and adaptive accuracy control mechanisms enhance the efficiency and fairness of the methods used by allowing models to learn in different directions and dynamically adjust learning rates and other parameters to achieve optimal results under varying conditions [59].

Group fairness is addressed by five articles from GL and one from AL introducing six different approaches: FedGFT [60], cCFLVvis [61], Fair-Fate [62], multiparty calculation [63], FedMinMax [64], and FedFB [65]. These approaches aim to reduce systematic discrimination towards certain population groups. Fair-Fate adjusts the weighting of clients based on their contribution to the overall model, providing a fairer distribution of performance results across subgroups defined by sensitive characteristics [62]. In contrast, FedGFT is designed to achieve global fairness by regulating an objective function that balances individual performance and collective benefits [60]. This approach promotes demographic fairness and mitigates the Matthew effect [66]. Techniques such as dynamic reweighting and adaptive accuracy checks can promote a more even distribution of performance, creating a more inclusive and equitable learning environment [55]. Two identified papers cover both, client and group fairness. Fair Hypernetworks [67] adjust the parameters of a target network based on various fairness criteria. They are trained to minimize discrimination and promote fair decisions between different groups, aiming to balance model performance and fairness [68]. Dynamic Q Fairness Federated Learning Algorithm with Reinforcement Learning [69] combines FL with reinforcement learning methods to improve both fairness and efficiency. The algorithm uses a dynamic Q-function to make optimal decisions for model updates and resource allocations, while continuously adapting to changing conditions [70]. This maximizes the overall performance of the federated learning system while ensuring that all participating devices are treated fairly [71].

Methods to address privacy and fairness. Eleven papers were identified that consider both privacy and fairness in their analysis. The papers present a variety of methods to improve fairness, privacy, and efficiency in FL, covering the use of cryptographic methods, as well as the development of specific algorithms and frameworks. You et al. [72] and Ratnayake et al. [73] cover data leakage and client fairness. While Ratnayake et al. [73] present a review that examines and extends the existing taxonomy of fairness approaches in FL and analyzes the implementations of different methodological groups, the other three papers discuss distinct methodological approaches. You et al. [72] introduce the FedACC framework, a server-led approach for controlling the global model accuracy. It ensures the validity of client gradients, and measures the cumulative contributions of new clients, while only granting access to a model if the accuracy matches their contributions. Utilizing differential privacy adds a layer of privacy. Annapareddy et al. [74] address both fairness dimensions (group and client fairness) while additionally considering data leakage by introducing the FedFa using a double momentum mechanism to process non-IID data. The server aggregates client information by considering both historical gradient information and quantity information about client accuracy and participation frequency. An appropriate weight is determined for each client based on this information. Furthermore, Rückel et al. [75] cover both dimensions of privacy (data leakage and integrity) while addressing client fairness by introducing a BC-based architecture for FL systems that combines ZKPs, local DP, and BC to create a fair, and manipulation-proof FL environment. This system allows clients to verify the integrity of each other's model training, promoting fair compensation. The novel use of ZKPs ensures both accurate model inferences and fairness throughout the training process.

4.3 Overview of Application Domains and Technology-Focused Research

While identifying methods to ensure group and client fairness, and data integrity, and mitigate data leakage is important, it's crucial to analyze their application to specific use cases. About 60% of the literature focuses on theoretical and initial empirical evidence without specifying an explicit domain. The applied research is mainly centered around healthcare, IoT, and edge devices. The aggregated data shows that Healthcare (8 privacy, 1 fairness, 1 both), IoT & Edge Computing (15 privacy, 0 fairness, 2 both), and Big Data & Cloud Computing (6 privacy, 2 fairness) are frequently discussed in terms of privacy concerns. Privacy research is almost equally divided between domain-specific and domain-unspecific studies, while fairness research is mostly domain-unspecific. Categories such as Cyber-Physical & Autonomous Systems (3 privacy, 1 both), Finance (4 privacy, 1 both), Industry & Communication (7 privacy), and Energy Sector (1 fairness) show broader applications. Mobility & Traffic (2 privacy) and Multimedia & Visual Detection (4 privacy) also focus more on privacy. This indicates a need for more application-specific fairness studies to match the developed state of privacy research. Future research should bridge this gap by developing and validating theoretical frameworks in practical applications across various sectors.

5 Discussion

Using a multivocal literature review, we identified 133 papers surrounding privacy and/or fairness in federated learning. The results show a clear focus of research on privacy (98) and demonstrate the lack of focus on fusing privacy and fairness concerns as only 11 papers were identified that look at (minimum) one privacy and one fairness dimension simultaneously. When it comes to privacy, there were three core methods identified: differential privacy, homomorphic encryption, and secure multi-party computation. Interestingly, the identified research regarding privacy also focuses on security with an emphasis on the integrity of data (35 papers). Here, one or multiple mentioned technologies are combined with blockchain technology. Research on fairness (24 papers) is mostly centered around client fairness (16 papers) while six papers focus on group fairness and only four papers consider both dimensions. Additionally, almost half of the research on privacy focuses more on the implementation of methods in real-world applications. In contrast, only 17% of research regarding fairness focuses on specific domains. Especially research on group fairness has no connection to specific domains, indicating that research on (group) fairness in FL is mostly abstract and still in its infancy as literature focuses on the development of methods rather than their implementation in the real world.

The lack of fairness-centered research, especially group fairness, is concerning in light of newly passed legalization like the AI Act [76] calling for the detection and mitigation of biases during the development and deployment of machine learning-based applications. Furthermore, as current legislation on privacy laws like the General Data Protection Regulation (GDPR) [23] put high demands on the privacy of data combined with known trade-offs between dimensions, e.g., anonymization for privacy vs. ensuring group fairness, research must focus on the interplay between different methods (77, 78). Therefore, we call for the development of a holistic FL framework considering the dependencies across dimensions.

To achieve this goal, we propose the following research directions. Firstly, we call for interdisciplinary research incorporating technical, ethical, legal, and social considerations into the design and deployment of FL applications. Initial research must extend the knowledge of trade-offs between the dimensions on an empirical level. Inspired by [18] we propose to analyze the interplay between two sub-dimensions, and how they impact each other. Furthermore, we are interested in how they could influence model accuracy in a controlled environment. To keep complexity managed, future research should focus first on understanding relationships between two sub-dimensions more deeply. In the next step, research should push toward understanding the dependencies between data leakage, data integrity, client fairness, and group fairness. Additionally, research should focus on implementations in real-world scenarios thereby leaving the laboratory-like evaluation. Here, a design science research approach could help identify suitable design requirements, principles, and features which is especially true for fairness concerns.

Furthermore, we want to highlight a neglected aspect of the privacy-preservation debate in FL: the right to be forgotten, a key component of data privacy laws. Despite some integration efforts into FL, our findings indicate it has been overlooked in current discussions. Ignoring such a crucial right could hinder the real-world application of FL. Additionally, we advocate for a life-cycle-centric approach to ensure group fairness. Fairness must be considered holistically, not just during model training [79]. Furthermore, focusing on additional fairness dimensions will help to gain a holistic perspective. A prominent candidate could be informational fairness [80]. Lastly, we highlight a managerial challenge in ensuring group fairness in FL. Group fairness relies on a normative definition that influences the choice of fairness metrics and is already challenging in centralized ML applications [81, 82]. How independent clients, such as organizations or companies, can agree on a single definition of fairness and its metric remains a major challenge for FL to become practical.

6 Conclusion

This paper provides a comprehensive overview of the methods currently presented and discussed for ensuring privacy and fairness in federated learning systems. For this purpose, an extensive multivocal literature review was conducted to highlight recent research efforts, summarize methods to ensure privacy and fairness and identify research directions. Subsequently, we identified sub-dimensions on which privacy and fairness research has been focused: data leakage, data integrity, client fairness, and group fairness. This was followed by a detailed discussion of methods in each (sub-)dimension and whether there have been efforts to combine them. Furthermore, application areas are discussed illustrating that the focus of research has been on applying federated learning in healthcare. Here, ensuring privacy and fairness are paramount for real-world applications. We discussed the challenges of integrating privacy and fairness in federated learning to identify further research avenues for future research. Among them is more research in the trade-off between multiple dimensions, implementing them in more real-world scenarios while utilizing the design science research paradigm. Furthermore, missing components such as unlearning or informational fairness were proposed to illustrate further research directions. Yet, our research is still limited as it only provided a superficial analysis of methods. In future work, the collected data can be used to create a more detailed picture of methods, their precise intentions as well as their technological readiness. Nevertheless, we hope our findings will serve as a valuable roadmap towards fairer and more private applications for federated learning.

References

1. Courville, A., Bengio, Y., & Goodfellow, I. (2018). *Deep Learning. Das umfassende Handbuch: Grundlagen, aktuelle Verfahren und Algorithmen, neue Forschungsansätze.* mitp Verlag.
2. Zheng, G., Kong, L., & Brintrup, A. (2023). Federated Machine Learning for Privacy Preserving, Collective Supply Chain Risk Prediction. *International Journal of Production Research, 61*, 8115–8132. https://doi.org/10.1080/00207543.2022.2164628
3. Wang, K.I.-K., Zhou, X., Liang, W., et al. (2022). Federated Transfer Learning Based Cross-Domain Prediction for Smart Manufacturing. *IEEE Trans Ind Inf, 18*, 4088–4096. https://doi.org/10.1109/TII.2021.3088057
4. Hosseini, S. M., Sikaroudi, M., Babaie, M., et al. (2023). Proportionally Fair Hospital Collaborations in Federated Learning of Histopathology Images. *IEEE Transactions on Medical Imaging, 42*, 1982–1995. https://doi.org/10.1109/TMI.2023.3234450
5. Wieringa, J., Kannan, P. K., Ma, X., et al. (2021). Data Analytics in a Privacy-Concerned World. *Journal of Business Research, 122*, 915–925. https://doi.org/10.1016/j.jbusres.2019.05.005
6. Mothukuri, V., Parizi, R. M., Pouriyeh, S., et al. (2021). A Survey on Security and Privacy of Federated Learning. *Future Generation Computer Systems, 115*, 619–640. https://doi.org/10.1016/j.future.2020.10.007
7. Wen, J., Zhang, Z., Lan, Y., et al. (2023). A Survey on Federated Learning: Challenges and Applications. *International Journal of Machine Learning and Cybernetics, 14*, 513–535. https://doi.org/10.1007/s13042-022-01647-y
8. McMahan, H. B., Moore, E., Ramage, D. et al. (2016). Communication-Efficient Learning of Deep Networks from Decentralized Data. In *Proceedings of the 20th International Conference on Artificial Intelligence and Statistics (AISTATS).*
9. Saylam, B., & İncel, Ö. D. (2023). *Federated Learning on Edge Sensing Devices: A Review.*
10. Joshi, M., Pal, A., & Sankarasubbu, M. (2022). Federated Learning for Healthcare Domain—Pipeline, Applications and Challenges. *ACM Trans Comput Healthcare, 3*, 1–36. https://doi.org/10.1145/3533708
11. Wei, K., Li, J., Ding, M., et al. (2020). Federated Learning With Differential Privacy: Algorithms and Performance Analysis. *IEEE Transactions on Information Forensics and Security, 15*, 3454–3469. https://doi.org/10.1109/TIFS.2020.2988575
12. Zhang, J., Zhang, J., & Chen, J., et al. (2020). GAN Enhanced Membership Inference: A Passive Local Attack in Federated Learning. In *ICC 2020–2020 IEEE International Conference on Communications (ICC)* (pp. 1–6). IEEE.
13. Su, C., Yu, G., & Wang, J. et al. (2024). Multi-Dimensional Fair Federated Learning. *AAAI, 38*, 15083–15090. https://doi.org/10.1609/aaai.v38i13.29430
14. Ledford, H. (2019). Millions of Black People Affected by Racial Bias in Health-Care Algorithms. *Nature, 574*, 608–609. https://doi.org/10.1038/d41586-019-03228-6
15. Shi, Y., Yu, H., & Leung, C. (2021). *Towards Fairness-Aware Federated Learning.*
16. Kumar, A., Satheesha, T. Y., Ahmed, S. T., et al. (2024). Trained Neural Networking Framework Based Skin Cancer Diagnosis and Categorization Using Grey Wolf Optimization. *Science and Reports, 14*, 9388. https://doi.org/10.1038/s41598-024-59979-4
17. Fahmy, L. M., Schreidah, C. M., & Geskin, L. J. (2023). Racial and Ethnic Disparities in the Perception of Respect from Physicians Among Skin Cancer Patients in the United States. *JAAD International, 11*, 78–82. https://doi.org/10.1016/j.jdin.2023.01.009
18. Gu, X., Tianqing, Z., Li, J., et al. (2022). Privacy, Accuracy, and Model Fairness Trade-Offs in Federated Learning. *Computers & Security, 122*, Article 102907. https://doi.org/10.1016/j.cose.2022.102907
19. Guo, J., Peng, J., & Bao, F. (2024). Current Challenges in Federated Learning: A Review. In Zhang, Y., Qi, L., & Liu, Q. et al. (Eds.), *Proceedings of the 13th International Conference on Computer Engineering and Networks* (Vol. 1127, pp. 32–38). Springer Nature Singapore.
20. Guendouzi, B. S., Ouchani, S. E. L., & Assaad, H. et al. (2023). A systematic review of federated learning: Challenges, aggregation methods, and development tools. *Journal of Network and Computer Applications, 220*, 103714. https://doi.org/10.1016/j.jnca.2023.103714

21. Kitchenham, B., & Charters, S. (2007). *Guidelines for performing Systematic Literature Reviews in Software Engineering.*
22. Garousi, V., Felderer, M., & Mäntylä, M. V. (2019). Guidelines for Including Grey Literature and Conducting Multivocal Literature Reviews in Software Engineering. *Information and Software Technology, 106*, 101–121. https://doi.org/10.1016/j.infsof.2018.09.006
23. General Data Protection Regulation: GDPR. (2024).
24. Feuerriegel, S., Hartmann, J., Janiesch C., et al. (2024). Generative AI. Bus Inf. *Systems Engineering, 66*, 111–126. https://doi.org/10.1007/s12599-023-00834-7
25. Rieke, N., Hancox, J., Li, W., et al. (2020). The Future of Digital Health with Federated Learning. *NPJ Digital Medicine, 3*, 119. https://doi.org/10.1038/s41746-020-00323-1
26. Bélanger, C. (2011). Privacy in the Digital Age: A Review of Information Privacy Research in Information Systems. *MIS Quarterly, 35*, 1017. https://doi.org/10.2307/41409971
27. Wang, Z., Song, M., & Zhang, Z. et al. (2019). Beyond Inferring Class Representatives: User-Level Privacy Leakage From Federated Learning. In *IEEE INFOCOM 2019—IEEE Conference on Computer Communications* (pp. 2512–2520). IEEE.
28. Ren, H., Deng, J., & Xie, X. (2022). GRNN: Generative Regression Neural Network—A Data Leakage Attack for Federated Learning. *ACM Transactions on Intelligent Systems and Technology, 13*, 1–24. https://doi.org/10.1145/3510032
29. Su, C., Yu, G., & Wang, J. et al. (2023). *Multi-dimensional Fair Federated Learning.*
30. Kladroba, A., Buchmann, T., & Friz, K., et al. (2021). *Indikatoren für die Messung von Forschung, Entwicklung und Innovation.* Springer Fachmedien Wiesbaden.
31. Paez, A. (2017). Gray Literature: An Important Resource in Systematic Reviews. *Journal of Evidence-Based Medicine, 10*, 233–240. https://doi.org/10.1111/jebm.12266
32. Li, Y., Huang, C. –W., & Wang, S. et al. (2023). *Privacy-preserving Federated Primal-dual Learning for Non-convex and Non-smooth Problems with Model Sparsification.*
33. Tang, H., Zhao, Z., & Liu, D., et al. (2023). *Edge-assisted U-Shaped Split Federated Learning with Privacy-preserving for Internet of Things.*
34. Ghazi, B., Golowich, N., & Kumar, R., et al. (2021). *Deep Learning with Label Differential Privacy.*
35. Lloret-Talavera, G., Jorda, M., & Servat, H., et al. (2021). *Enabling Homomorphically Encrypted Inference for Large DNN Models.* https://doi.org/10.48550/arXiv.2103.16139
36. Shi, Z., Yang, Z., Hassan, A., et al. (2023). A Privacy Preserving Federated Learning Scheme Using Homomorphic Encryption and Secret Sharing. *Telecommunication Systems, 82*, 419–433. https://doi.org/10.1007/s11235-022-00982-3
37. Zhu, H. (2020). *On the Relationship Between (secure) Multi-Party Computation and (Secure) Federated Learning.*
38. Abaoud, M., Almuqrin, M. A., & Khan, M. F. (2023). Advancing Federated Learning Through Novel Mechanism for Privacy Preservation in Healthcare Applications. *IEEE Access, 11*, 83562–83579. https://doi.org/10.1109/ACCESS.2023.3301162
39. Kadhe, S. R., Ludwig, H., & Baracaldo, N. et al. (2023). *Privacy-Preserving Federated Learning over Vertically and Horizontally Partitioned Data for Financial Anomaly Detection.*
40. Yang, Q., Huang, A., Fan, L., et al. (2023). Federated Learning with Privacy-Preserving and Model IP-Right-Protection. *Machine Intelligence Research, 20*, 19–37. https://doi.org/10.1007/s11633-022-1343-2
41. Maurya, J., & Prakash, S. (2023). Privacy Preservation in Federated Learning, its Attacks and Defenses using SMC-GAN. In *2023 Third International Conference on Secure Cyber Computing and Communication (ICSCCC)* (pp. 55–60). IEEE.
42. Bonawitz, K., Ivanov, V., & Kreuter, B. et al. (2016). *Practical Secure Aggregation for Federated Learning on User-Held Data.*
43. Smahi, A., Li, H., Yang, Y., et al. (2023). BV-ICVs: A Privacy-Preserving and Verifiable Federated Learning Framework for V2X Environments Using Blockchain and zkSNARKs. *Journal of King Saud University—Computer and Information Sciences, 35*, Article 101542. https://doi.org/10.1016/j.jksuci.2023.03.020

44. Hayati, H., Murguia, C., & van de Wouw, N. (2022). *Privacy-Preserving Federated Learning via System Immersion and Random Matrix Encryption.*
45. Kalapaaking, A. P., Khalil, I., & Yi, X. (2023). *Blockchain-Based Federated Learning With SMPC Model Verification Against Poisoning Attack for Healthcare Systems.*
46. Zhang, J., Zhou, J., Guo, J., et al. (2023). Visual Object Detection for Privacy-Preserving Federated Learning. *IEEE Access, 11*, 33324–33335. https://doi.org/10.1109/ACCESS.2023.3263533
47. Fang, C., Guo, Y., Ma, J., et al. (2022). A Privacy-Preserving and Verifiable Federated Learning Method Based on Blockchain. *Computer Communications, 186*, 1–11. https://doi.org/10.1016/j.comcom.2022.01.002
48. Ullah, I., Deng, X., Pei, X., et al. (2023). A Verifiable and Privacy-Preserving Blockchain-Based Federated Learning Approach. *Peer-to-Peer Networking and Applications, 16*, 2256–2270. https://doi.org/10.1007/s12083-023-01531-8
49. Ren, Y., Li, Y., Feng, G., et al. (2022). Privacy-Enhanced and Verification-Traceable Aggregation for Federated Learning. *IEEE Internet of Things Journal, 9*, 24933–24948. https://doi.org/10.1109/JIOT.2022.3194930
50. Eltaras, T., Sabry, F., Labda, W., et al. (2023). Efficient Verifiable Protocol for Privacy-Preserving Aggregation in Federated Learning. *IEEE Transactions on Information Forensics and Security, 18*, 2977–2990. https://doi.org/10.1109/TIFS.2023.3273914
51. Zhang, J., Liu, Y., & Di, W. et al. (2023). VPFL: A verifiable Privacy-Preserving Federated Learning Scheme for Edge Computing Systems. *Digital Communications and Networks, 9*, 981–989. https://doi.org/10.1016/j.dcan.2022.05.010
52. Gao, H., He, N., & Gao, T. (2023). SVeriFL: Successive Verifiable Federated Learning with Privacy-Preserving. *Information Sciences, 622*, 98–114. https://doi.org/10.1016/j.ins.2022.11.124
53. Ma, J., Naas, S.-A., Sigg, S., et al. (2022). Privacy-Preserving Federated Learning Based on Multi-Key Homomorphic Encryption. *Int J of Intelligent Sys, 37*, 5880–5901. https://doi.org/10.1002/int.22818
54. Li, T., Sanjabi, M., & Beirami, A. et al. (2019). *Fair Resource Allocation in Federated Learning.*
55. Zhao, Z., & Joshi, G. (2022). A Dynamic Reweighting Strategy For Fair Federated Learning. In *ICASSP 2022–2022 IEEE International Conference on Acoustics, Speech and Signal Processing (ICASSP)* (pp. 8772–8776). IEEE
56. Huang, W., Li, T., Wang, D., et al. (2022). Fairness and Accuracy in Horizontal Federated Learning. *Information Sciences, 589*, 170–185. https://doi.org/10.1016/j.ins.2021.12.102
57. Gu, W., & Zhang, Y. (2023). FedEem: A Fairness-based Asynchronous Federated Learning Mechanism. *Journal of Cloud Computing, 12*. https://doi.org/10.1186/s13677-023-00535-2
58. Pan, C., Xu, J., & Yu, Y. et al. (2023). *Towards Fair Graph Federated Learning via Incentive Mechanisms.*
59. Fu, A., Zhang, X., & Xiong, N. et al. (2020). *VFL: A Verifiable Federated Learning with Privacy-Preserving for Big Data in Industrial IoT.*
60. Wang, G., Payani, A., & Lee, M. et al. (2023). *Mitigating Group Bias in Federated Learning: Beyond Local Fairness.*
61. Huang, L., Cui, W., & Zhu, B. et al. (2023). Visually Analysing the Fairness of Clustered Federated Learning with Non-IID Data. In *2023 International Joint Conference on Neural Networks (IJCNN)* (pp. 1–10). IEEE.
62. Salazar, T., Fernandes, M., & Araújo, H. et al. FAIR-FATE: Fair Federated Learning with Momentum. Computational Science—ICCS 14073, 524–538. https://doi.org/10.1007/978-3-031-35995-8_37
63. Pentyala, S., Neophytou, N., & Nascimento, A. et al. (2022). *PrivFairFL: Privacy-Preserving Group Fairness in Federated Learning.*
64. Papadaki, A., Martinez, N., & Bertran, M. et al. (2022). *Minimax Demographic Group Fairness in Federated Learning.*
65. Zeng, Y., Chen, H., & Lee, K. (2021). *Improving Fairness via Federated Learning.*

66. Gao, J., Huang, C., & Tang, M. et al. (2023). *EFFL: Egalitarian Fairness in Federated Learning for Mitigating Matthew Effect*
67. Carey, A. N., Du, W., Wu, X. (2022). Robust Personalized Federated Learning under Demographic Fairness Heterogeneity. In Tsumoto, S. (Ed.), *Proceedings, 2022 IEEE International Conference on Big Data: December 17–December 20* (pp. 1425–1434), 2022, Osaka, Japan. IEEE, [Piscataway, New Jersey].
68. Qu, J., Faney, T., & Wang, Z. et al. (2022). *HMOE: Hypernetwork-based Mixture of Experts for Domain Generalization.*
69. Chen, W., Junping, D., & Shao, Y. et al. (2023). *Dynamic Fair Federated Learning Based on Reinforcement Learning*
70. Cao, M., Zhao, M., Zhang, T., et al. (2024). FedQL: Q-Learning Guided Aggregation for Federated Learning. Springer VerlagIn K. Li, Z. Tari, & H. Wu (Eds.), *Algorithms and Architectures for Parallel Processing: 23rd International Conference, ICA3PP 2023, Tianjin, China, October 20–22, 2023, Proceedings, Part I* (Vol. 14487, pp. 263–282). Singapore.
71. Woo, J., Joshi, G., & Chi, Y. (2023). *The Blessing of Heterogeneity in Federated Q-Learning: Linear Speedup and Beyond.*
72. You, X., Liu, X., Lin, X., et al. (2023). Accuracy Degrading: Toward Participation-Fair Federated Learning. *IEEE Internet of Things Journal, 10*, 10291–10306. https://doi.org/10.1109/JIOT.2023.3238038
73. Ratnayake, H., Chen, L., & Ding, X. (2023). A Review of Federated Learning: Taxonomy, Privacy and Future Directions. *Journal of Intelligent Information System, 61*, 923–949. https://doi.org/10.1007/s10844-023-00797-x
74. Annapareddy, N., Preston, J., & Fox, J. (2023). *Fairness and Privacy in Federated Learning and Their Implications in Healthcare*
75. Rückel, T., Sedlmeir, J., & Hofmann, P. (2022). Fairness, Integrity, and Privacy in a Scalable Blockchain-Based Federated Learning System. *Computer Networks, 202*, Article 108621. https://doi.org/10.1016/j.comnet.2021.108621
76. EU Artificial Intelligence Act. (2024).
77. Kusner, M. J., Loftus, J. R., & Russell, C. et al. (2017). *Counterfactual Fairness.*
78. Dwork, C., Hardt, M., & Pitassi, T. et al. (2011). *Fairness Through Awareness.*
79. Deck, L., Schomäcker, A., & Speith, T. et al. (2024). *Mapping the Potential of Explainable AI for Fairness Along the AI Lifecycle*
80. Schoeffer, J., Kuehl, N., & Machowski, Y. (2022). “There Is Not Enough Information”: On the Effects of Explanations on Perceptions of Informational Fairness and Trustworthiness in Automated Decision-Making. *2022 ACM Conference on Fairness, Accountability, and Transparency* (pp. 1616–1628). ACM.
81. Franklin, J. S., Bhanot, K., & Ghalwash, M. et al. (2022). An Ontology for Fairness Metrics. In Conitzer, V., Tasioulas, J., Scheutz, M. et al. (Eds.) *Proceedings of the 2022 AAAI/ACM Conference on AI, Ethics, and Society* (pp. 265–275). ACM.
82. Saleiro, P., Kuester, B., & Hinkson, L. et al. (2018). *Aequitas: A Bias and Fairness Audit Toolkit.*

Age Ain't Just a Number: Exploring the Volume vs. Age Dilemma for Textual Data to Enhance Decision Making

Lukas Hägele, Mathias Klier, Andreas Obermeier, and Torben Widmann

Abstract The common belief that more data leads to better results often leads to all available data being used to derive the best possible decision. However, the age of data can strongly affect data-driven decision making. Consequently, the desire for larger data volume and at the same time contemporary data leads to the "volume vs. age" dilemma, which has not yet been sufficiently researched. In this work, we rigorously investigate the "volume vs. age" dilemma for textual data using four experiments with real-world data containing customer reviews from the Yelp platform. Contributing to theory and practice, we show that more data is not always better, as the effect of data age can outweigh the effect of data volume, resulting in overall poorer performance. Moreover, we demonstrate that different aspects within textual data can exhibit different temporal effects and that considering these effects when selecting training data can clearly outperform existing practices.

1 Introduction

The rapid proliferation of data and the expanding realm of data analytics have reshaped the landscape of decision making across various domains [1–3]. In today's data-driven world, organizations recognize the pivotal role of data as a cornerstone for achieving competitive advantage [4–6]. Data fuels the generation of insights along with better products or services, as in the case of the movie streaming platform Netflix,

L. Hägele (✉) · M. Klier · A. Obermeier · T. Widmann
University of Ulm, Institute of Business Analytics, Ulm, Germany
e-mail: lukas.haegele@uni-ulm.de

M. Klier
e-mail: mathias.klier@uni-ulm.de

A. Obermeier
e-mail: andreas.obermeier@uni-ulm.de

T. Widmann
e-mail: torben.widmann@uni-ulm.de

C. M. Flath et al. (eds.), *Artificial Intelligence, Data, and Decision-Making*, Lecture Notes in Information Systems and Organisation 82,
https://doi.org/10.1007/978-3-032-08480-4_19

which has achieved tremendous success due to its advanced analytics capabilities and recommender system [7, 8]. Among the different types of data, unstructured textual data play a particularly prominent role, as vast volumes of textual data are generated every day, encompassing sources as diverse as customer reviews, social media, news articles, and more [9–11]. This influx of unstructured textual data has become a goldmine for data analytics, fostering the development of more sophisticated models and leading to success stories such as ChatGPT [12–14]. A critical success factor for models such as GPT is the vast volume of training data that the algorithms use [12, 13], strengthening the common belief in the data-driven paradigm that *more data leads to better results*.

But is this common belief generally valid? Often, all available data is used to derive decisions, without considering the data age, i.e., the time since the data was recorded. However, the quality and validity of data can change over time [15, 16]. Such temporal effects can include, for instance, data becoming outdated or changes in the distribution of the input data and their relation to the output data (concept drift) [16–18]. An example is the age of customer reviews, which relates to their relevance to the current state of products/services and users and is highly correlated with the helpfulness to users [19, 20]. Indeed, data age is a linchpin in the efficacy of data-driven models and can strongly affect derived decisions [21–23]. Overall, there exists an inherent contradiction between the desire for larger data volume and the imperative of using contemporary data. We refer to this interplay of the opposing facets, data volume and data age, as the "volume vs. age" dilemma.

Both the influence of data volume and data age have been studied individually in the literature, and insightful results have been obtained for both effects. However, the complex interplay between the need to leverage large data volumes and the imperative of using contemporary data has not been adequately explored—indeed, for the context of textual data, it has not been researched at all. To fill this research gap, we thus investigate the dilemma explicitly for unstructured textual data, using the case of a recommender system based on textual customer reviews. Moreover, we are the first to study the interplay of data volume and data age conducting analyses at the aspect-level—a perspective especially important for textual data. The results reveal that more data is not always better and that handling the "volume vs. age" dilemma for textual data requires a nuanced, aspect-level view, paving the way for more sophisticated training data selection strategies that can significantly outperform existing practices.

2 Related Work

According to the common belief in the data-driven paradigm that *more data leads to better results*, as much (training) data as possible should be used for decision making [24–26]. To better understand the impact of data volume on the performance of data-driven methods, many studies have investigated this relationship experimentally. While in some cases, even relatively small data volumes can yield satisfactory results [27], the literature generally indicates that increasing data volume further improves performance, while the marginal benefit of using more data decreases [28–30]. Further literature [31–34] also emphasizes that more data can lead to better performance, while identifying different factors that influence this effect, such as the representation of original distributions, diverse data sources, model complexity, and proper data cleaning. Taken together, these studies provide further insights into the common belief that *more data leads to better results*. They argue that the marginal benefit of more data decreases as data volume increases and that the effect of data volume should be evaluated in conjunction with other critical factors.

Indeed, various data characteristics can have diverse (negative) effects on data-driven decision making [35–37]. One of the characteristics to be considered is data age, which refers to the time since the data was recorded. Due to the corresponding temporal effects such as obsolescence or concept drift, several studies have examined the impact of data age on the performance of data-driven methods. As data can evolve over time, predictions of models using data that is not contemporary anymore experience fluctuations [15, 38]. Resulting negative effects of data age are particularly evident in unstructured textual data. Several studies concluded from experiments that models perform worse the older the used training data was for cases like recommender systems [39], sentiment classification [40], large language models [22, 23], and text classification [41]. The studies highlight the critical impact data age can have on the performance of data-driven methods due to changes in the data over time.

Both data volume and data age have emerged as critical drivers of effective decision making. However, the complex interaction of data volume and data characteristics like age, has rarely been addressed in the literature. Only a few studies (e.g., [42, 43]) consider the quality of data in conjunction with data volume, but do not consider data age. Thus, there is paucity of research focusing on the intertwined nature with data age. The study by Pessemier et al. [44] stands out as an exception. They particularly investigate recommender system performance when gradually increasing data volume by successively adding data of higher age. They demonstrate that using older data may initially increase performance but can actually decrease recommendation accuracy as the data used is drawn from further back in time.

The "volume vs. age" dilemma has received very little attention in the literature. Pessemier et al. [44] examined this dilemma but consider only structured data in terms of user ratings, leaving the impact for unstructured text data unexplored. Furthermore, existing studies that focus on the impact of data age consider temporal effects only in the context of an entire instance, e.g., an entire customer review. As a result, they lack the granularity to differentiate between temporal effects of different features within an instance. For the example of a customer review, the information about the location of a restaurant in a customer review may still be valid while the information about the quality of the food may not be, if these aspects age at different rates (cf. [45, 46]). Thus, there is a compelling need to explore the "volume vs. age" dilemma in more detail, focusing explicitly on textual data and taking into account the nuanced effects of different aspects within textual data—both uncharted territory in the current body of literature.

3 Design and Realization of the Experiments

In this section, we present our methodological approach to study the "volume vs. age" dilemma. First, we outline the design of the experiments. Then, we describe the realization of the experiments by elucidating the used textual data and describing the model for data-driven decision making as well as the employed evaluation metrics.

3.1 Experimental Design

In the following, we outline the design of the experiments conducted to investigate the effects of volume and age of textual data. To rigorously study these effects, a data-driven model that constitutes our experimental basis is used to leverage available training data to provide predictions for decision making. In our experiments, we then systematically vary the training data for this model regarding data volume and data age and monitor the resulting performance of the model's predictions on recent and static test data. Our study unfolds across four distinct experiments, each designed to investigate specific facets of the "volume vs. age" dilemma. We commence with two experiments on the effects of data volume and data age, respectively. Then, we elucidate our experimental design for both data volume and data age to capture the "volume vs. age" dilemma. Finally, we conclude with the design of an experiment allowing a more nuanced investigation of the dilemma by differentiating specific aspects within the textual data (e.g., comments regarding *Food* or *Location* in customer reviews).

Experiment (A)—Studying the Data Volume Effect. Our first experiment focuses on the isolated effect of data volume. To study this effect, we iteratively increase the amount of training data (data volume), while the training data is randomly selected from the entire training data corpus to abstract from temporal (data age) effects (Fig. 1 (A)). More precisely, we vary the proportion of training data used from the training data corpus in 10% increments from 10% to 100% and evaluate the models' corresponding performance on the test dataset. By selecting the training data randomly, we are able to isolate the volume effect and exclude any potential temporal effects stemming from the age of the training data in a first step.

Experiment (B)—Studying the Data Age Effect. Our second experiment aims to isolate the effect of data age. To systematically analyze this effect, we adopt a controlled approach that has already been used in previous studies [17, 23]. As illustrated in Fig. 1 (B), we construct a series of equally sized training datasets (hereafter referred to as data chunks) from the training data corpus, each containing the same quantity of data instances N_{Chunk} to abstract from potential effects of varying data volume. Moreover, the series of data chunks is constructed to contain training data of increasing age, such that the first data chunk contains the N_{Chunk} most recent and the last chunk the least recent N_{Chunk} data instances of the training data corpus. By selecting data chunks of the same size for training, we are able to isolate the temporal effect and exclude any potential effects due to data volume.

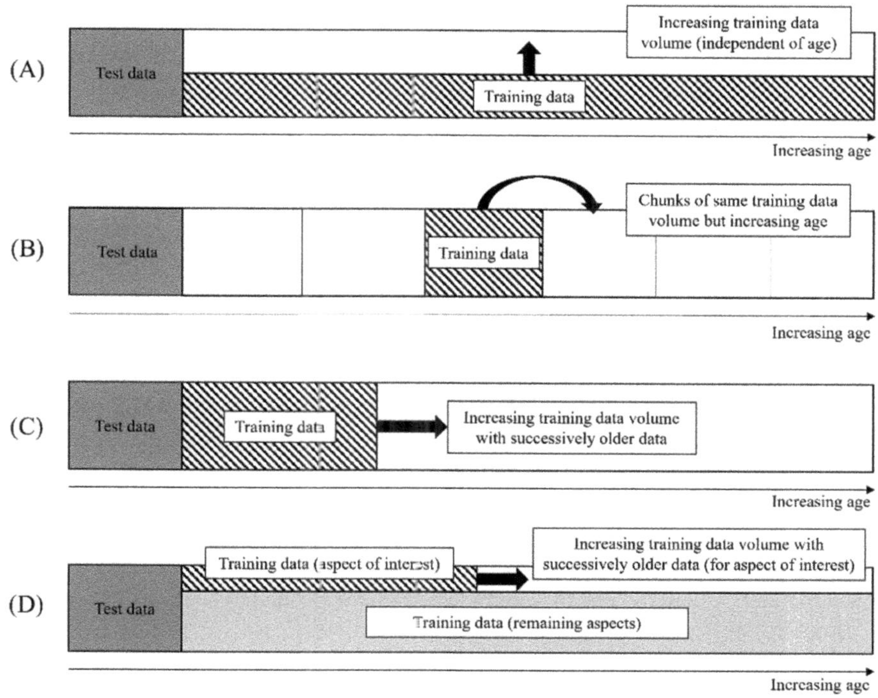

Fig. 1 Schematic illustration of the experiments. (A): Increasing data volume by random and age independent sampling. (B): Increasing age of data with same volume. (C): Increasing data by successively adding older data. (D): Increasing data for the aspect of interest

Experiment (C)—Studying the "Volume vs. Age" Dilemma. With this pivotal experiment, we aim to get an integrated view considering both data volume and data age to be able to rigorously study the "volume vs. age" dilemma (Fig. 1 (C)). Thereby, the volume of the training data used is gradually increased by successively adding older data. More precisely, the first training dataset contains the 10% most recent data instances of the training data corpus. Then, the volume of the training data is successively increased by the next 10% most recent remaining data instances. Evaluating the performance of the models trained based on these training datasets on the test dataset, we aim to gain deeper insights into the interplay of data volume and data age, thereby contributing new knowledge regarding the "volume vs. age" dilemma.

Experiment (D)—Studying the "Volume vs. Age" Dilemma at Aspect-Level. According to literature (cf. [45, 46]), different features of data can age at different rates and their durability is not uniform (cf. Section 2). In the case of customer reviews, for instance, information regarding the aspect *Food* may be subject to different temporal effects than information regarding the aspect *Location*. In our fourth experiment, we aim at more fine-grained insights regarding the interplay of data volume and data age conducting analyses at the aspect-level. More precisely, we conduct Experiment (C) by differentiating specific aspects within the data (e.g., comments regarding *Food* or *Location* in a customer review), as illustrated in Fig. 1 (D). Hence, for the aspect under observation, the volume of the training data used is gradually increased by successively adding older data, while the data regarding all other aspects remains constant (using the whole training data corpus). Thus, we are able to investigate the "volume vs. age" dilemma for each single aspect.

3.2 Realization of the Experiments

Customer reviews serve as paramount example of impactful textual data. By providing valuable, detailed insights into products and services [47], customer reviews have been shown to support consumers in making purchasing decisions [48–50]. The contained wealth of information makes them a prime asset for data-driven decision making. Recommender systems are a common and highly relevant field of application leveraging textual data [51] to derive personalized recommendations [52, 53]. For the realization of our experiments, we thus use the case of a recommender system for restaurants based on customer reviews.

Dataset. We select a publicly available real-world dataset from Yelp, a leading customer review platform [54]. It contains customer reviews of users sharing their insights about various aspects of restaurants. From this massive dataset, we use customer reviews regarding restaurants in the state of Florida, USA, from the beginning of 2009 to the end of 2019. We choose our test data to contain all customer reviews from the most recent six months, i.e., from July first to December 31st, 2019. This test data is static in all our experiments to rigorously compare the performance of our model when the training data is varied. Customer reviews that are not contained in the test data (i.e., those created before July 2019) constitute the whole training data corpus. To enhance the reliability of our analyses, we employ a 10-core test dataset, a well-known preprocessing technique [55, 56] so that the dataset exclusively contains customer reviews of users that generated at least ten customer reviews in the test dataset. The resulting dataset comprises 58,128 customer reviews, with a test set containing 9220 and a training data corpus encompassing 48,908 customer reviews.

Model for Data-Driven Decision Making and Evaluation Metrics. To make recommendations, we use the well-known explicit factor model of Zhang et al. [57], a common and decisive model with far-reaching impact. To avoid bias from the structured ratings that can influence the effect of the dilemma for textual data, we adapt the model of Zhang et al. [57] so that the recommendations only depend on the information contained in the customer reviews. The adapted model keeps using the textual customer reviews in the form of aspect-sentiment tuples, e.g., for the exemplary review sentence, *I liked the food, however, the staff was rude*, the resulting aspect-sentiment tuples correspond to (*Food*, positive) and (*Staff*, negative). Hereby, each aspect pertains to a particular feature of the reviewed restaurant and each sentiment reflects the sentiment polarity expressed in the associated text. The aspect-sentiment tuples serve as the foundation for the creation of characteristic profiles for both customers and restaurants. Finally, to yield a recommendation, the model bases its decision on the match between the customer and restaurant profiles. In this line, the model calculates a ranking score, quantifying the match in terms of the similarity between customer and restaurant profiles. To extract the required aspect-sentiment tuples from the customer reviews, we use a state-of-the-art language model for aspect-based sentiment analysis [58] based on transformer models [59]. We further employ a standard clustering approach [60, 61] to group the extracted aspects based on GloVe embedding vectors [62], resulting in a total of 24 distinct aspect classes such as *Food*, *Service*, and *Location* (hereafter just referred to as aspects).

The review-based recommender system generates a ranking score for the relevance of each recommendation [63]. In line with a widely adopted approach to differentiate between relevant and non-relevant recommendations [64], a restaurant is considered relevant for a specific customer if the associated rating is 3 or higher, while otherwise deemed as non-relevant. To differentiate between both classes, the Area Under the Curve (AUC) of the Receiver Operating Characteristic (ROC) curve and Mean Average Precision (MAP) have proven to be robust and comprehensive evaluation metrics (cf. [64–66]). The AUC is used to evaluate a recommender system's overall separation performance without directly considering the ranking order of recommendations [63]. The MAP assesses the precision of a recommender system at various recall levels by considering the presence of relevant restaurants and their positions in the ranking [67], thus reasonably complementing the AUC.

4 Results

In this section, we first present the results of the isolated effects of data volume and data age, respectively. Then, we take an integrated view considering both data volume and data age and conclude with our fine-grained analysis differentiating specific aspects within the data.

4.1 The Data Volume Effect

In Experiment (A), we iteratively increase the volume of training data from 10% to 100% of the entire training data corpus in 10% increments, while the respective training data is randomly selected to abstract from temporal effects. The left side of Fig. 2 depicts the performance of the trained models on the test datasets with respect to both evaluation metrics employed (AUC and MAP). The results show that increasing data volume goes along with an increase in model performance. Indeed, the performance curves for AUC and MAP show a similar progression and are monotonically increasing. Especially for smaller data volumes, using more data considerably improves model performance. As the data volume continues to increase, the marginal benefit of using more data slightly decreases. Thus, the observed effect that more data increases performance is less evident as more data is available.

4.2 The Data Age Effect

In Experiment (B), we analyze model performance for a series of data chunks containing training data of increasing age but same size to abstract from volume effects. We chose each data chunk to contain $N_{Chunk} = 6{,}000$ customer reviews. This choice leads to a sufficient number of data chunks to follow the course of the resulting performance curves as data age increases, while ensuring that the number of customer reviews in each chunk is large enough to yield meaningful model outputs. Indeed, model performance shows a negative trend as the age of the training data increases (Fig. 2). Thereby, in line with Experiment (A), the performance curves for AUC and MAP exhibit a very similar shape. Despite some fluctuations, the performance curves for both evaluation metrics drop sharply when older data chunks are used.

4.3 The "Volume vs. Age" Dilemma

Integrating the effects of data volume and data age, Experiment (C) focuses on the "volume vs. age" dilemma. The results of the experiment are shown in Fig. 3 in separate plots for both evaluation measures. By including the curves of Experiment (A), we highlight the difference between increasing the data volume by successively adding older data (Experiment (C)) in contrast to adding randomly selected data (Experiment (A)). The results of Experiment (C) reveal that, for both evaluation metrics, performance initially increases rapidly when increasing data volume by successively adding older data (dashed lines in Fig. 3). This trend, however, diminishes quickly as the data volume is further increased with continuously less recent data. In fact, there exists a tipping point when the performance is even decreasing. Thus, when using more and more but less recent data, we do not only observe a reduction in the marginal benefit of increased data volume, but actually a decline in performance. Comparing the results of Experiment (C) with those of Experiment (A) reveals, that except for the last point in each curve (representing the use of all training data and thus coincides), selecting data by age clearly outperforms selecting data randomly. It is noticeable that the performance curve for selecting the data by age starts higher, rises more steeply at the beginning and shows a tipping point that is not observed when selecting data randomly. Based on 20 experimental runs, the Wilcoxon signed-rank test [68] shows that the best possible performance is significantly higher when selecting training data based on age instead of random ($p < 0.05$ for AUC, $p < 0.01$ for MAP).

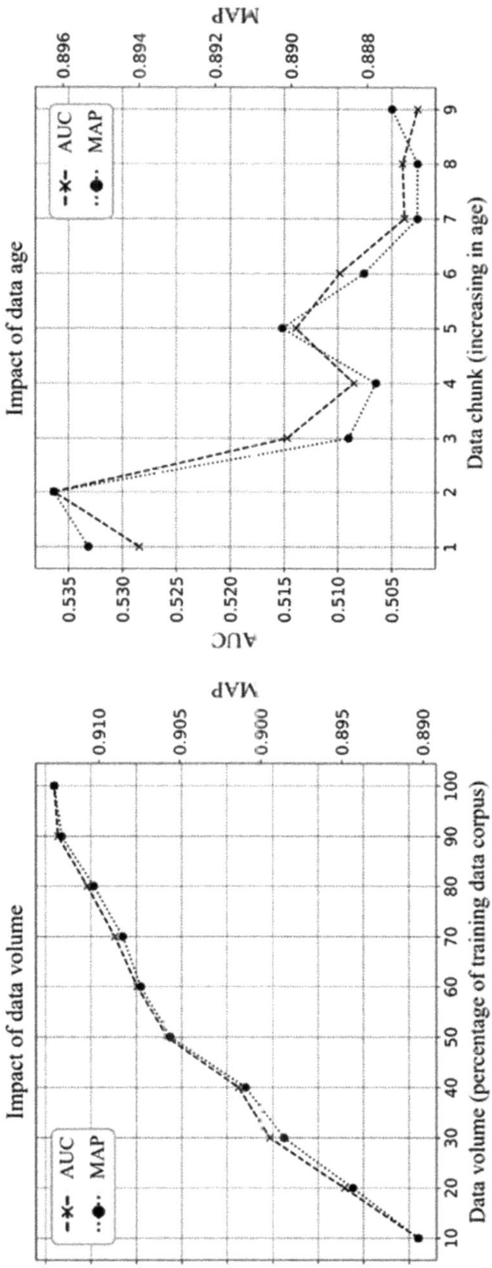

Fig. 2 Results of Experiment (A) (left) and Experiment (B) (right) for AUC and MAP

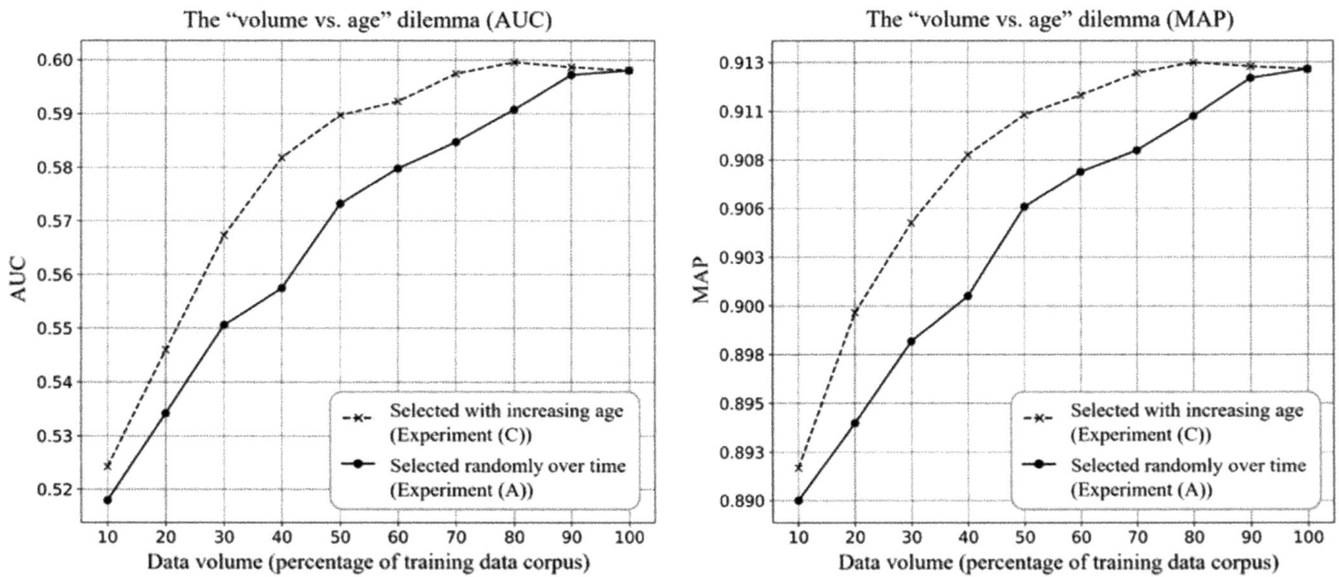

Fig. 3 Results of Experiment (C) for AUC (left) and MAP (right)

4.4 The "Volume vs. Age" Dilemma at Aspect Level

To gain more fine-grained insights into the "volume vs. age" dilemma, Experiment (D) differentiates specific aspects within the textual data. Thereby, we consider five (clusters of similar) aspects—*Food*, *Drinks*, *Service*, *Location and Ambience*, and *Price*—and analyze model performance when gradually increasing the volume of the training data used by successively adding older data for the aspect under observation (data for all other aspects is kept constant). As remarkably seen in Fig. 4, the respective curves for each aspect differ strongly in their progression and show different trajectories when the associated data volume is increased gradually. For instance, adding more older data for the aspect *Food* decreases the performance rather monotonically. The same holds for the aspect *Price*. On the other hand, for the aspect *Drinks*, the model performance increases as the data volume is increased up to a certain point. The curves for the aspects *Service* and *Location and Ambience* show no clear trends.

Consequently, these in-depth insights regarding the interplay of data volume and data age on the aspect-level give rise to leverage the training data sampling on the aspect-level. In this context, we use the observed results from Experiment (D) and use only the most recent 20 percent of data for *Food* and *Price*, as a strong decrease in model performance is observed when more older data is added for these aspects. For the remaining aspects, we use all data, since for these aspects the addition of more old

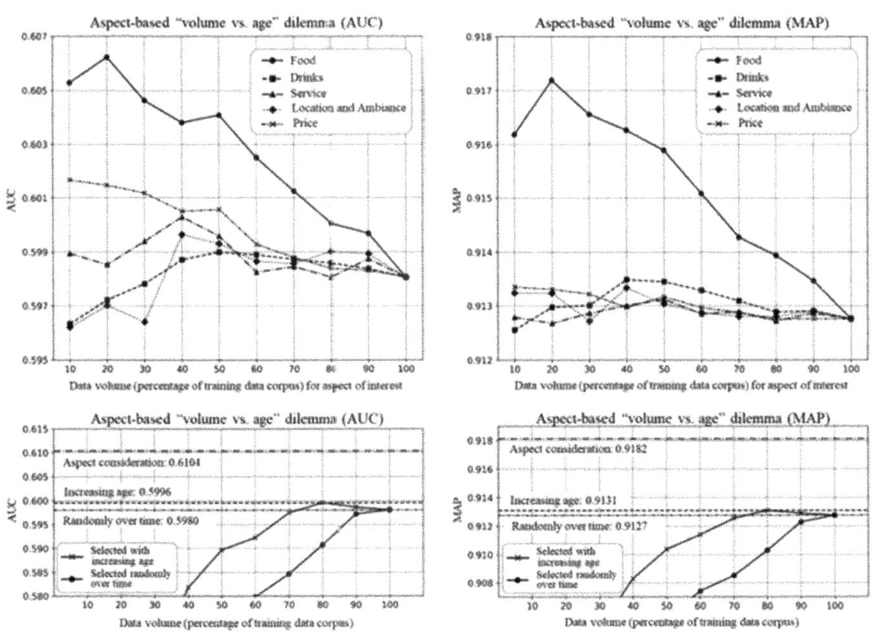

Fig. 4 Results of Experiment (D) (upper Figures) and a resulting aspect-based filtering of data (lower Figures) for AUC (left) and MAP (right)

data does not lead to a clear decrease in model performance. The results using this filtering strategy are also presented in the lower part of Fig. 4. The achieved performance when using the aspect-based training data filter noticeably exceeds the performance when using all training data and also exceeds the best performance achieved in Experiment (C), i.e., the optimal trade-off of the "volume vs. age" dilemma for our experiment without aspect-based consideration. To show that the aspect-based selection of data was not a chance hit, we randomly varied the filters for each aspect by $\pm 10\%$ for 20 different experimental runs. Here, the Wilcoxon signed-rank test shows significant outperformance for both evaluation metrics ($p < 0.01$ for AUC and MAP), underscoring the robustness of this aspect-based training data selection.

5 Discussion and Conclusion

5.1 *Implications for Theory and Practice*

Our experiments yield novel insights that challenge conventional assumptions about the advantages of more extensive data volumes in data-driven decision making. Contrary to the common belief that *more data leads to better results*, our findings highlight the interplay between data volume and data age and their impact on the performance of data-driven decision making. Our major contribution is twofold. First, we contribute to theory and practice by rigorously examining the "volume vs. age" dilemma for unstructured data, highlighting that more data is not always better. Second, we are the first to provide in-depth insights regarding the "volume vs. age" dilemma conducting analyses at the aspect-level. The results reveal that handling this dilemma for textual data requires a more differentiated, aspect-level view, paving the way for more sophisticated selection strategies for training data that can significantly outperform existing practices.

Before delving into the "volume vs. age" dilemma, we examine the isolated effects of increasing data volume and increasing data age, respectively. In line with existing literature, we find that excluding any potential temporal effects stemming from data age, more data indeed leads to better results (cf. [25, 26]) while the marginal benefit of using more data decreases with increasing data volume (cf. [28, 29]). When isolating the effect of data age, our results reveal that using older data leads to worse performance (cf. [23, 41]). Taken together, the Experiments (A) and (B) demonstrate the dichotomy of data volume and data age, resulting in the "volume vs. age" dilemma.

Integrating the effects of data volume and data age, Experiment (C) focuses on the "volume vs. age" dilemma. The results show that more data is not always better, as the age of the data is a very critical factor. In fact, there can exist a tipping point where increasing data volume leads to poorer performance. While performance initially increases as data volume increases by adding less recent data, the marginal benefit decreases. Performance can even decline despite an increase in data volume. Thus, the "volume vs. age" dilemma can not only lead to a reduction of the marginal benefit of increasing data volume but can even cancel it out. Thereby, our experiments show that the diminishing marginal benefit may not be solely due to a saturation regarding data volume—as indicated by Chen et al. [28]—but also due to the age of the data. Consequently, in some cases, less data can yield better results. For this reason, temporal effects, such as outdated data or concept drift, emerge as critical factors. Thus, practitioners should carefully consider whether less recent data is actually helpful and contributes to performance. Summing up, both facets of the dilemma—data volume and data age—need to be weighted in terms of their potential to improve decision making.

Differentiating specific aspects within the textual data, Experiment (D) allows a more nuanced analysis of the "volume vs. age" dilemma. The results show that aspects within the textual customer reviews can exhibit different effects and influence performance differently. For some aspects, additional data positively contributes to performance while hindering the performance for others. For instance, with respect to the aspect *Location*, performance improves when increasing data volume regarding this aspect. Regarding the aspect *Food*, however, performance decreases when adding less recent data. Thus, our findings advocate for a nuanced consideration of data on individual aspects within textual data. As our study shows, differentiating aspects and incorporating the respective insights into the selection of training data can leverage performance and outperform any data selection strategy not considering the aspect-level.

Different features of data can age at different rates (cf. [45, 46]), which is also true for textual data and the underlying aspects. When using textual data, temporal effects should be considered at the aspect-level. A systematic evaluation of aspects—and in particular the effect of their age—can guide decision makers as to whether the performance of data-driven decision making benefits or suffers from the inclusion of more but less recent data. Data selection should therefore be tailored to the specific effects at the aspect-level. Ultimately, our results argue in favor of moving away from undifferentiated data selection strategies and taking a closer look at the underlying data. Indeed, a nuanced, aspect-driven analysis and selection of input data paves the way for improving the performance of data-driven decision making.

5.2 *Limitations and Future Work*

While our study provides first valuable insights into the "volume vs. age" dilemma, there are limitations that warrant acknowledgement and open avenues for future research. First, this primary exploratory study is dedicated to one application area of data-driven decision making and is based on a single dataset and a single model. Thus, future research should expand this scope and investigate the "volume vs. age" dilemma for other datasets, data-driven tasks, and models. Moreover, as the observed effects may differ between different application areas, it is crucial to expand the significance and generalizability of our findings by ruling out possible confounding variables and working in a hypothesis-driven manner with different datasets. Second, this study was the first to examine the "volume vs. age" dilemma at a more granular level and found that the five clusters of similar aspects within textual customer reviews have different effects. However, we do not yet differentiate between the individual aspects but considered five clusters. Thus, future research should explore the intricate landscape of textual data by meticulously investigating the "volume vs. age" dilemma at the level of individual aspects to gain insight into even more nuanced effects and ultimately understand how different aspects contribute to overall performance in different contexts.

Other promising directions for future research involve the design of data quality metrics to be able to assess age-related effects of data, such as currency [46] and concept drift [69], particularly at the aspect-level of textual data. Integrating such metrics into the decision making calculus of machine learning methods (cf. [70, 71]) seems to be a promising way to tackle the "volume vs. age" dilemma. Indeed, by incorporating fine-grained age-related effects, future research has the potential to support data-driven decision making with more robust tools for navigating the dynamics in an ever-changing environment.

5.3 Conclusion

In the field of data-driven decision making, the common belief that *more data leads to better results* usually leads to all available data being used to derive the best possible decisions. However, the age of data can strongly affect the decisions derived from it. Consequently, the desire for larger data volume and at the same time contemporary data leads to the "volume vs. age" dilemma, which has not yet been sufficiently researched. In this paper, we rigorously investigate the "volume vs. age" dilemma for textual data using four experiments with real-world data containing customer reviews from the Yelp platform. We contribute to theory and practice in two ways. First, our results show that more data is not always better. In fact, there can be a tipping point where increasing data volume by adding less recent data worsen the results. Second, we are the first to delve deeper into the "volume vs. age" dilemma not only for textual data but also conducting analyses at the aspect-level. The results show that effectively dealing with the "volume vs. age" dilemma for textual data requires a differentiated view at the aspect-level, which paves the way for more sophisticated training data selection strategies that can significantly outperform existing practices. Overall, the age of data is not just a number, but a critical factor for data-driven decision making.

Acknowledgements Funded by the Deutsche Forschungsgemeinschaft (DFG, German Research Foun-dation)—494840328.

References

1. Loebbecke, C., & Picot, A. (2015). Reflections on societal and business model transformation arising from digitization and big data analytics: A research agenda. *The Journal of Strategic Information Systems, 24*(3), 149–157.
2. Awan, U., Shamim, S., Khan, Z., Zia, N. U., Shariq, S. M., & Khan, M. N. (2021). Big data analytics capability and decision-making: The role of data-driven insight on circular economy performance. *Technological Forecasting and Social Change, 168*, 120766.
3. Dubey, R., Gunasekaran, A., Childe, S. J., Papadopoulos, T., Luo, Z., Wamba, S. F., & Roubaud, D. (2019). Can big data and predictive analytics improve social and environmental sustainability? *Technological Forecasting and Social Change, 144*, 534–545.
4. Hagiu, A., & Wright, J. (2020). When data creates competitive advantage. *Harvard Business Review, 98*, 94–101.
5. Sandeep, S. R., Ahamad, S., Saxena, D., Srivastava, K., Jaiswal, S., & Bora, A. (2022). To understand the relationship between machine learning and artificial intelligence in large and diversified business organisations. *Materials Today: Proceedings, 56*(4), 2082–2086.
6. Vassakis, K., Petrakis, E., & Kopanakis, I. (2018). *Big data analytics: Applications, prospects and challenges, in 'Mobile big data—A roadmap from models to technologies', 3–20*. Springer.
7. Davenport, T., & Harris, J. (2017). *Competing on analytics: Updated, with a new introduction, the new science of winning*. Harvard Business Press.
8. Rataul, P., Tisch, D. G., & Peter, Z. (2018). *Netflix. Dynamic capabilities for global success.* SAGE Publications: SAGE Business Cases Originals.
9. Egger, R., & Gokce, E. (2022) *Natural language processing (NLP): An introduction, in 'applied data science in tourism'* (pp. 307–334). Springer International Publishing.
10. Gandomi, A., & Haider, M. (2015). Beyond the hype: Big data concepts, methods, and analytics. *International Journal of Information Management, 35*(2), 137–144.
11. Weitzenboeck, E. M., Lison, P., Cyndecka, M., & Langford, M. (2022). The GDPR and unstructured data: Is anonymization possible? *International Data Privacy Law, 12*(3), 184–206.
12. Kalla, D., & Smith, N. (2023). Study and analysis of chat GPT and its impact on different fields of study. *International Journal of Innovative Science and Research Technology, 8*(3), 827–833.
13. Lund, B. D., & Wang, T. (2023). Chatting about ChatGPT: How may AI and GPT impact academia and libraries? *Library Hi Tech News, 40*(3), 26–29.
14. Deng, J., & Lin, Y. (2022). The benefits and challenges of ChatGPT: An overview. *Frontiers in Computing and Intelligent Systems, 2*(2), 81–83.
15. Bennin, K. E., Ali, N., bin Borstler, J., & Yu, X. (2020). Revisiting the impact of concept drift on just-in-time quality assurance. In *2020 IEEE 20th international conference on software quality, reliability and security (QRS)*. IEEE.
16. Spruit, M., & van der Linden, V. (2019). *BIDQI: The Business Impacts of Data Quality Interdependencies Model.'*, *Technical Report Series* UU-CS-2019, *001*, 1–25.
17. Agarwal, O., & Nenkova, A. (2022). Temporal effects on pre-trained models for language processing tasks. *Transactions of the Association for Computational Linguistics, 10*, 904–921.
18. Leysen, J. (2023). Exploring unlearning methods to ensure the privacy, security, and usability of recommender systems. In *Proceedings of the 17th ACM conference on recommender systems.* ACM.
19. Luo, L., Duan, S., Shang, S., & Pan, Y. (2021). What makes a helpful online review? Empirical evidence on the effects of review and reviewer characteristics. *Online Information Review, 45*(3), 614–632.
20. Meng, Y., Yang, N., Qian, Z., & Zhang, G. (2021). What makes an online review more helpful: An interpretation framework using XGBoost and SHAP values. *Journal of Theoretical and Applied Electronic Commerce Research, 16*(3), 466–490.
21. Raza, S., & Ding, C. (2022). News recommender system: A review of recent progress, challenges, and opportunities. *Artificial Intelligence Review, 55*(1), 749–800.

22. Lazaridou, A., Kuncoro, A., Gribovskaya, E., Agrawal, D., Liska, A., Terzi, T., Gimenez, M., de Masson d'Autume, C., Kocisky, T., Ruder, S., Yogatama, D., Cao, K., Young, S., & Blunsom, P. (2021). Mind the gap: Assessing temporal generalization in neural language models. In *'Advances in neural information processing systems' (NeurIPS)*. Virtual Event.
23. Röttger, P., & Pierrehumbert, J. (2021). Temporal adaptation of BERT and performance on downstream document classification: Insights from social media. In *Findings of the Association for computational linguistics: EMNLP 2021* (pp. 2400–2412). Association for Computational Linguistics.
24. Prusa, J., Khoshgoftaar, T. M. & Seliya, N. (2015), The effect of dataset size on training tweet sentiment classifiers, *in* '2015 IEEE 14th international conference on machine learning and applications (ICMLA)', IEEE, 96–102.
25. Lei, S., Zhang, H., & Su, S. (2019). *How training data affect the accuracy and robustness of neural networks for image classification.* ICLR.
26. Barbedo, J. G. A. (2018). Impact of dataset size and variety on the effectiveness of deep learning and transfer learning for plant disease classification. *Computers and Electronics in Agriculture, 153*, 46–53.
27. Fang, Y., Wang, J., Ou, X., Ying, H., Hu, C., Zhang, Z., & Hu, W. (2021). The impact of training sample size on deep learning-based organ auto-segmentation for head-and-neck patients. *Physics in Medicine and Biology, 66*(18), 185012.
28. Chen, H., Xiong, F., Wu, D., Zheng, L., Peng, A., Hong, X., Tang, B., Lu, H., Shi, H., & Zheng, H. (2017). Assessing impacts of data volume and data set balance in using deep learning approach to human activity recognition. In *2017 IEEE international conference on Bioinformatics and biomedicine (BIBM)* (pp. 1160–1165). IEEE.
29. Sun, C., Shrivastava, A., Singh, S., & Gupta, A. (2017). Revisiting unreasonable effectiveness of data in deep learning era. In *2017 IEEE international conference on computer vision (ICCV)* (pp. 843–852). IEEE.
30. Durden, J. M., Hosking, B., Bett, B. J., Cline, D., & Ruhl, H. A. (2021). Automated classification of fauna in seabed photographs: The impact of training and validation dataset size, with considerations for the class imbalance. *Progress in Oceanography, 196*, 102612.
31. Althnian, A., AlSaeed, D., Al-Baity, H., Samha, A., Dris, A. B., Alzakari, N., Abou Elwafa, A., & Kurdi, H. (2021). Impact of dataset size on classification performance: An empirical evaluation in the medical domain. *Applied Sciences, 11*(2), 796.
32. Langenkämper, D., van Kevelaer, R., Purser, A., & Nattkemper, T. W. (2020). Gear-induced concept drift in marine images and its effect on deep learning classification. *Frontiers in Marine Science, 7*, 538862.
33. Simmonds, E. G., Jarvis, S. G., Henrys, P. A., Isaac, N. J. B., & O'Hara, R. B. (2020). Is more data always better? A simulation study of benefits and limitations of integrated distribution models. *Ecography, 43*(10), 1413–1422.
34. Zhu, X., Vondrick, C., Fowlkes, C. C., & Ramanan, D. (2016). Do we need more training data? *International Journal of Computer Vision, 119*(1), 76–92.
35. Janssen, M., Brous, P., Estevez, E., Barbosa, L. S., & Janowski, T. (2020). Data governance: Organizing data for trustworthy artificial intelligence. *Government Information Quarterly, 37*(3).
36. Helfert, M., Ge, M. (2018). Perspectives of big data quality in smart service ecosystems (quality of design and quality of conformance). *Journal of Information Technology Management, 10*(4), 72–83.
37. Heinrich, B., Hopf, M., Lohninger, D., Schiller, A., & Szubartowicz, M. (2021). Data quality in recommender systems: The impact of completeness of item content data on prediction accuracy of recommender systems. *Electronic Markets, 31*(2), 389–409.
38. Kabir, M. A., Keung, J. W., Bennin, K. E., & Zhang, M. (2019). Assessing the significant impact of concept drift in software defect prediction. In *2019 IEEE 43rd annual computer software and applications conference (COMPSAC)* (pp. 53–58). IEEE.
39. Zheng, G., & Horace, H. S. I. (2013). Effectiveness of the data generated on different time in latent factor model. In *Proceedings of the 7th ACM conference on recommender systems* (pp. 327–330).

40. Lukes, J., & Søgaard, A. (2018). Sentiment analysis under temporal shift. In *Proceedings of the 9th workshop on computational approaches to subjectivity, sentiment and social media analysis* (pp. 65–71). Association for Computational Linguistics.
41. Alkhalifa, R., Kochkina, E., & Zubiaga, A. (2023). Building for tomorrow: Assessing the temporal persistence of text classifiers. *Information Processing & Management, 60*(2), 103200.
42. Luca, A. R., Ursuleanu, T. F., Gheorghe, L., Grigorovici, R., Iancu, S., Hlusneac, M., & Grigorovici, A. (2022). Impact of quality, type and volume of data used by deep learning models in the analysis of medical images. *Informatics in Medicine Unlocked, 29*, 100911.
43. Roccetti, M., Delnevo, G., Casini, L., & Cappiello, G. (2019). Is bigger always better? A controversial journey to the center of machine learning design, with uses and misuses of big data for predicting water meter failures. *Journal of Big Data, 6*(1), 1–23.
44. De Pessemier, T., Dooms, S., Deryckere, T., & Martens, L. (2010). Time dependency of data quality for collaborative filtering algorithms. In *Proceedings of the fourth ACM conference on recommender systems* (pp. 281–284). ACM.
45. Heinrich, B., & Klier, M. (2015). Metric-based data quality assessment—Developing and evaluating a probability-based currency metric. *Decision Support Systems, 72*, 82–96.
46. Klier, M., Moestue, L., Obermeier, A., & Widmann, T. (2021). Event-driven assessment of currency of wiki articles: A novel probability-based metric. In *International conference on information systems*. TX.
47. Mudambi, S. M., & Schuffm, D. (2010) What makes a helpful online review? A study of customer reviews on Amazon.com. *MIS Quarterly, 34*(1), 185–200.
48. Dellarocas, C. (2003). The digitization of word of mouth: Promise and challenges of online feedback mechanisms. *Management Science, 49*(10), 1407–1424.
49. Chevalier, J. A., & Mayzlin, D. (2006). The effect of word of mouth on sales: Online book reviews. *Journal of Marketing Research, 43*(3), 345–354.
50. Zhu, F., & Zhang, X. (2010). Impact of online consumer reviews on sales: The moderating role of product and consumer characteristics. *Journal of Marketing, 74*(2), 133–148.
51. Kanwal, S., Nawaz, S., Malik, M. K., & Nawaz, Z. (2021). A review of text-based recommendation systems. *IEEE Access, 9*, 31638–31661.
52. Chen, L., Chen, G., & Wang, F. (2015). Recommender systems based on user reviews: The state of the art. *User Modeling and User-Adapted Interaction, 25*(2), 99–154.
53. McAuley, J., & Leskovec, J. (2013). Hidden factors and hidden topics. In *Proceedings of the 7th ACM conference on recommender systems*. ACM.
54. Yelp Inc. (2023), *Yelp Open Dataset*. Retrieved March 12, 2024, from https://www.yelp.com/dataset
55. Cheng, Z., Ding, Y., Zhu, L., & Kankanhalli, M. (2018). Aspect-aware latent factor model. In *Proceedings of the 2018 world wide web conference* (pp. 639–648).
56. He, X., Liao, L., Zhang, H., Nie, L., Hu, X., & Chua, T.-S. (2017). Neural collaborative filtering. In *Proceedings of the 26th international conference on world wide web*.
57. Zhang, Y., Lai, G., Zhang, M., Zhang, Y., Liu, Y., & Ma, S. (2014). Explicit factor models for explainable recommendation based on phrase-level sentiment analysis. In *Proceedings of the 37th international ACM SIGIR conference on research & development in information retrieval* (pp. 83–92).
58. Yang, H., Zeng, B., Yang, J., Song, Y., & Xu, R. (2021). A multi-task learning model for chinese-oriented aspect polarity classification and aspect term extraction. *Neurocomputing, 419*, 344–356.
59. Devlin, J., Chang, M.-W., Lee, K., & Toutanova, K. (2019). BERT: Pre-training of deep bidirectional transformers for language understanding. In *Proceedings of north American chapter of the association for computational linguistics: Human language technologies (NAACL-HLT) 2019* (pp. 4171–4186).
60. Mohammed, S. M., Jacksi, K., & Zeebaree, S. R. M. (2020). Glove word embedding and DBSCAN algorithms for semantic document clustering. In *2020 international conference on advanced science and engineering (ICOASE)* (pp. 1–6). IEEE.

61. Reimers, N., & Gurevych, I. (2019). Sentence-BERT: Sentence Embeddings using Siamese BERT-networks. In *Empirical methods in natural language processing and international joint conference on natural language processing* (pp. 3982–3992).
62. Pennington, J., Socher, R., & Manning, C. (2014). Glove: Global vectors for word Representation. In *Proceedings of the 2014 conference on empirical methods in natural language processing (EMNLP): Association for Computational Linguistics* (pp. 1532–1543).
63. Lü, L., Medo, M., Yeung, C. H., Zhang, Y.-C., Zhang, Z.-K., & Zhou, T. (2012). Recommender systems. *Physics Reports, 519*(1), 1–49.
64. Karatzoglou, A., Baltrunas, L., & Shi, Y. (2013). Learning to rank for recommender systems. In *Proceedings of the 7th ACM conference on recommender systems* (pp. 493–494). ACM.
65. Bellogin, A., Castells, P., & Cantador, I. (2011). Precision-oriented evaluation of recommender systems. In *Proceedings of the fifth ACM conference on recommender systems* (pp. 333–336). ACM.
66. Ying, H., Zhuang, F., Zhang, F., Liu, Y., Xu, G., Xie, X., Xiong, H., & Wu, J. (2018). Sequential recommender system based on hierarchical attention network. *IJCAI, International Joint Conference on Artificial Intelligence*, 3926–3932.
67. Yue, Y., Finley, T., Radlinski, F., & Joachims, T. (2007). A support vector method for optimizing average precision. In *Proceedings of the 30th annual international ACM SIGIR conference on research and development in information retrieval* (pp. 333–336). ACM.
68. Wilcoxon, F. (1945). Individual comparisons by ranking methods. *Biometrics Bulletin, 1*(6).
69. Agrahari, S., & Singh, A. K. (2022). Concept drift detection in data stream mining: A literature review. *Journal of King Saud University—Computer and Information Sciences, 34*(10), 9523–9540.
70. Hristova, D. (2014). Considering currency in decision trees in the context of big data. In *International conference on interaction sciences.*
71. Firouzian, I., Zahedi, M., & Hassanpour, H. (2019). Investigation of the effect of concept drift on data-aware remaining time prediction of business processes. *International Journal of Nonlinear Analysis and Applications, 10*(2), 153–166.

Assessing Value Creation of Analytics Projects in SMEs

Benedict Langer and Felix Pütterich

Abstract In an era where data is a crucial resource, small and medium-sized enterprises (SMEs) must harness analytics to remain competitive. This research paper synthesizes existing studies on analytics value for SMEs, resulting in a comprehensive model that outlines key aspects of value creation. The model covers enabling capabilities, main risks, core profiting business functions, and impact on firm performance. Transactional, transformational, strategic, and informational value creation types are identified. Given resource constraints, SMEs are encouraged to initiate pilot projects in distinct business functions, aided by cost-effective, user-friendly cloud solutions. A proposed scoring framework further aids in assessing and prioritizing business analytics projects, enabling informed decisions and resource allocation for sustainable competitiveness in the data-driven future.

Keywords Data · Analytics · Value · Literature review · Assessment

1 Introduction

Within the turbulent and competitive global environment, organizations are required to adapt more rapidly to dynamic business scenarios [7]. Through the use of analytics, firms can optimize operational efficiency, agility and performance [65]. Analytics, in a business context often referred to as business analytics (BA), is becoming a key differentiator between high and low performers [18, 20]. One study found that firms using data-driven decision-making were, on average, 5 % more productive and 6 % more profitable than their competitors [39]. A broader awareness of analytics has been developed in recent years and is reflected by an increased spending on analytical tools and applications [12].

B. Langer (✉) · F. Pütterich
Technical University of Munich, TUM School of Management, Munich, Germany
e-mail: benedict.langer@tum.de

F. Pütterich
e-mail: felix.puetterich@tum.de

C. M. Flath et al. (eds.), *Artificial Intelligence, Data, and Decision-Making*, Lecture Notes in Information Systems and Organisation 82,
https://doi.org/10.1007/978-3-032-08480-4_20

The upward trend of data & analytics adoption, however, does not seem to translate to small and medium-sized enterprises (SMEs). SMEs amount for 99.8 % of enterprises in the European economy, cumulatively accounting for 52.6 % of the total economic output [17]. Yet, according to a study by the Organization for Economic Co-operation and Development (OECD) in the European Union, data analytics is adopted by 33 % of large firms, 19 % of medium-sized companies, and only 10 % of small organizations [8]. Although they perform significantly better when using data-driven processes [43], and although financial barriers have been lowered by recent progress [41], many SMEs still refrain from adopting BA [7]. Demonstrating the business potential of analytics for SMEs and enhancing the adoption rate of analytical tools requires future attention from scholars as research is still primarily focused on large organizations [65]. A literature review on business intelligence and analytics in SMEs from 2000 until 2018 gave insights into analytics solutions in SMEs, yet only a few studies specifically discussed the benefits of analytics for SMEs [32]. Mikalef et al. [41] proposed that additional research is required to understand the different mechanisms and processes to derive value from the application of analytics in businesses. This study attends to the research gap by concentrating on the following research questions:

RQ1: *How does analytics create value for SMEs?*
RQ2: *How can SMEs assess the value created by analytics projects?*

To further the understanding of value created through analytics, especially for SMEs, a systematic literature review (SLR) was conducted. The SLR was supported by multiple expert interviews, synthesizing and extending the findings with a practical perspective. To address the first research question, a comprehensive theoretical model was developed, illustrating five aspects of value creation through analytics in SMEs. Enabling capabilities, main risks, value creation types, main profiting business functions and the influence on firm performance were investigated in detail. The theoretical model was then adapted into a scoring framework that allows assessment and comparison of value created by analytics projects. The proposed framework answers the second research question and hypothesizes a tool for SMEs to compare fulfilled requirements and benefits associated with their BA initiatives.

2 Background

Previous research suggests great benefits from analytics [51, 65]. It has been portrayed as a key performance driver and differentiator in competition [18, 43]. Scholars in the field of information systems have begun to describe the different dimensions of business value created by analytics. Various frameworks have been developed, highlighting impacting factors such as information quality or leadership support and categorizing different types of analytics value. Ji-fan Ren et al. [29] categorized business value into transformational, transactional, and strategic value, emphasizing the importance of information and system quality. Fosso Wamba et al. [19] found a positive correlation between information quality, business value, and firm performance. Raguseo and Vitari [54] demonstrated that analytics significantly influences a firm's financial performance through various value dimensions. Côrte-Real et al. [13] showed that analytics enhances knowledge management, business processes, and agility, leading to competitive advantages. Seddon et al. [58] developed the so called Business Analytics Success Model (BASM), which identifies key drivers for creating business value, including strong leadership and aligning projects with capabilities.

The literature provides evidence that analytics generates value and increases performance [13, 20, 33], yet value assessment and necessary capabilities are not addressed in detail. Additionally, extant literature on analytics explores its value mostly in larger organizations, while the specific challenges faced by SMEs require further investigation [52]. Some studies have started to address this issue and examine the value creation process in SMEs from different partial perspectives. Gauzelin and Bentz [21] found that analytics tools improve decision-making and profitability in SMEs. Scholz et al. [57] highlighted benefits like better decision-making, and financial savings. Llave [33] proposed an iterative investment strategy for SMEs and developed a high-level framework for BA value creation tailored for SMEs. In general, research on specific benefits and a comprehensive model of business value creation in SMEs is still lacking [32, 65]. To the best of the current knowledge, no researcher has yet developed a framework to evaluate and compare different analytics projects. Based on the necessity for SMEs to take action regarding analytics implementation, this study shall aid in understanding and assessing the business value created by analytics projects in SMEs.

The resource-based view (RBV) is a key framework for understanding how firms create competitive advantages by efficiently utilizing resources [3]. Valuable, rare, inimitable, and non-substitutable resources are linked to greater business value and higher firm performance [40]. As analytics can play a crucial role in creating and utilizing such resources [61], the RBV has been chosen as a foundational layer for this study.

3 Method

A systematic literature review (SLR) according to vom Brocke et al. [62] was selected as the main research method. The general approach of an SLR has been proven useful to identify relevant articles and then gather, analyze, and most importantly aggregate the data critically to gain a deeper understanding of research carried out on a specific topic over time [48]. The herein applied research process followed a defined methodological sequence and was divided into the five key steps: (i) conceptualization, (ii) search, (iii) selection, (iv) analysis, and (v) synthesis [31].

3.1 Data Collection

The *conceptualization* of the topic was performed based on existing literature, the RBV and exploratory discussions with experts from academia and practice. The research was organized into three distinct domains: (i) "`value`" (with keywords: success, value, success benefit, performance and advantage), (ii) "`SME`" (with keywords: SME, small enterprise and small business) and (iii) "`analytics`" (with keywords: business analytics, data analytics, business intelligence, and big data). For the *search*, the source-neutral, interdisciplinary, large scientific database Scopus was queried. The three domains with their keywords were combined into two search terms: "`SME AND analytics`" as well as "`analytics AND value`". In November 2023 a total of 3,229 articles matching the search terms in their title were identified. A *selection* was executed to ensure that only relevant articles were included in the study. In the first step, the search results were reduced to only include studies published between 2012–2023 and papers written in English. Only peer-reviewed studies were considered to increase quality of the results [7]. Duplicates were identified and excluded. In the second phase, a title and subsequent abstract screening of the remaining 1387 articles was performed. Most of the excluded articles either covered peripheral areas or too specific topics [31]. 91 articles remained for a full text assessment. Two inclusion criteria were evaluated: (i) the research focuses on the value and benefits of analytics or (ii) the research is directly related to the usage of analytics in SMEs. In this analysis step, each article was examined to identify the core themes and objectives. All papers that covered analytics or SMEs only as a secondary topic were eliminated. Final elimination and backward search lead to a total inclusion of 52 research papers for the analysis.

3.2 Data Analysis

The *analysis* of the extracted literature was based on inductive category development proposed by Gioia et al. [22]. The aim was to aggregate extracted research, to generate additional insights and to close research gaps. In the first step, open coding was performed to capture all relevant concepts from current research. To connect the different concepts, related codes are linked to higher order themes in axial coding [22]. The 2nd-order themes are further distilled into aggregate dimensions [22]. A data structure emerges from the full set of 1st-order concepts, 2nd-order themes, and aggregate dimensions, which describes the analysis progress and provides a representation of the analyzed content [22]. This procedure was supported by a concept-centered unit matrix outlined by Webster and Watson [64]. After a thorough review of the articles, 56 concepts were identified and then clustered into 24 themes and 5 distinct dimensions. Afterwards a saturation analysis was performed to ensure exhaustiveness of the SLR. This was reached after 40 of the analyzed 52 articles.

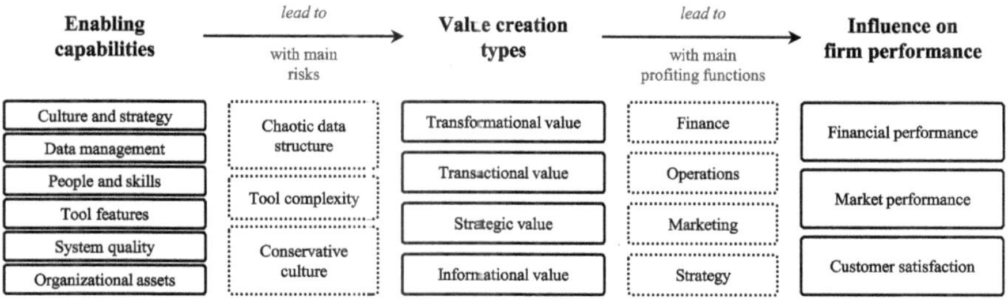

Fig. 1 Analytics value creation model for SMEs

3.3 *Data Synthesis*

In the *synthesis* phase, the SLR data structure was augmented by eight semi-structured expert interviews to gain deeper practical insights into the discovered model and constructs. One tool provider with experience working with SMEs, four CEOs of SMEs and three consultants with experience in SMEs were interviewed. This allowed for a differentiated perspective on the value of analytical tools. The interviews were subjected a deductive investigation [38]. While the deductive approach was initially employed to guide the examination based on the results of the SLR, the nature of semi-structured interviews allowed for flexibility to unexpected insights and gave interviewees the opportunity to share valuable thoughts [42]. Some categories were refined or adapted to enhance the overall depth and practicality of the results.

4 Findings and Resulting Model

The model displayed in Fig. 1 summarizes the SLR findings and provides a holistic picture of different aspects of value creation. The forthcoming sections report in detail on the aggregate dimensions found in the analysis: Enabling capabilities for value creation, specific risks and challenges, different value creation types, main profiting business functions, and the effect of on firm performance.

4.1 *Enabling Capabilities*

Numerous researchers identified a variety of capabilities aimed at enabling value creation through the application of analytics. The literature reveals six essential dimensions.

Culture and strategy build the basis for analytics success. Active management support is a crucial value enabler, as it ensures the allocation of resources and drives adoption [45, 68]. A data-driven culture further promotes use of the technology [66].

To overcome resistance in SMEs, effective change management is necessary, emphasizing the benefits and involving employees [10]. Strategic alignment of analytics initiatives with business objectives ensures collaboration, reduced complexity, and enhanced processes [10, 63, 66].

High-quality *data management* has a positive impact on analytics use, information quality and value [25, 67]. Data availability is a prerequisite for analytics [19], especially as the lack of necessary data can be a significant barrier for SMEs [45]. Enhancing and managing data quality is also vital for value creation of analytics [60, 68]. Consistent data processing and formatting are critical to ensure data quality and integrity [66, 68]. Data currency, or the timeliness of information, is essential for the quality of the subsequent decision-making [67].

While technology is important, it is *people and skills* that ultimately enable the success of analytics [15]. Analytical skills and experience in using BA tools are vital for accessing the technology's potential and gaining a competitive edge [27]. To maintain their competitiveness, SMEs should consider up-skilling and training [7, 9]. Clear leadership and a skilled (in business and analytics) decision-maker are essential for interpreting outputs and taking appropriate actions [26, 68]. Successful use of BA tools additionally requires effective collaboration between business and IT [27, 49].

Tool features also contribute to value creation. Functionality, architecture and the IT environment are key criteria for tool selection [49]. Usability is vital for enhancing tool usage and value creation [36], especially in SMEs [63]. Cloud solutions offer SMEs opportunities to leverage analytics, as they are cost-effective, user-friendly and easy to implement and scale [12, 32].

Overall *system quality* is a crucial factor in information systems and analytics adoption [29, 67]. System quality is influenced by multiple factors. Adaptability and flexibility minimize implementation risks and increase scalability [2, 66]. Compatibility and integrability of a tool ensure information flow and quality [2, 14]. Accessibility allows easy data and results extraction [66].

Adequate *organizational assets* need to be available for the success of an BA projects [36, 66], especially for SMEs which often face strong resource constraints [12]. Financial resources are arguably the main asset for any technology adoption. Evaluating various cost dimensions, including hardware, software, infrastructure, and human costs, is necessary [33]. Starting with pilot projects is recommended for SMEs, allowing them to gradually invest and create benefits [33, 63]. SMEs also face difficulties in acquiring suitable human capital for BA utilization [7]. Training [66] and user-friendly tools with minimal implementation effort can help mitigate missing skills [12]. Cloud solutions can augment the often lacking IT infrastructure in SMEs [45] by offering lower internal system requirements and usage-based pricing [32].

4.2 Main Risks

Different risks can diminish generated value and hinder an efficient use of BA. This is particularly dangerous for SMEs as they often cannot afford failure of technological projects [12]. A risk mitigation strategy is essential to ensure the success of analytics projects. Three significant risks for SMEs emerged from the literature.

Chaotic data structure and governance hinder the success of analytics projects. Associated challenges in data management are critical to address to ensure the success of analytics initiatives [49]. The main risks are inconsistent data quality [9, 49], complicated data processing as well as limited data security [10]. To mitigate the risks, organizations should establish robust data preparation processes [9].

High tool complexity is another barrier for SMEs. Analytics can only create value in the long term if users fully understand the functionality and appropriate handling of the system [10]. Otherwise, employees will refrain from using the tool due to its high complexity and unknown features [58].

SMEs often face a *conservative firm culture* containing cultural barriers and intrinsic conservatism, resulting in low utilization of analytics [7] and a stronger resistance to change [12]. Moreover, SME managers, while experienced in their markets, often lack data-driven knowledge [49]. Limited managerial support and knowledge, coupled with competing projects, also hinder BA adoption [46].

4.3 Value Creation Types

Extant literature describes four distinct types of analytics value creation. The use of BA delivers transformational, transactional, informational and strategic value, which are ultimately transformed into performance [23, 54].

Transformational value is defined as benefits through "changes in a firm's structure and capacity" [23]. There are three major components of transformational value in the analytics domain. Firstly, BA tools directly and indirectly enhance overall organizational capabilities such as collaboration or knowledge [4, 21, 37]. Analytics also helps to identify and develop innovation in business models and products [10, 59, 61]. Combined with improvements in market understanding [28, 46, 47], these factors collectively facilitate the transition to a data-driven enterprise.

Analytics generates *transactional value*, by facilitating operational advantages [19, 23]. Techniques like process mining scan for automation potential and improve operational processes [41] Errors and waste can be minimized by detecting anomalies and improving resource management [46]. Analytics helps achieve higher cost efficiency through tracking prices, predicting resource availability and reducing procurement costs [41, 49]. BA enhances the return on assets and general profitability by analyzing sales, optimizing revenue generation and improving customer analysis [1, 16].

Strategic value has been defined as "benefits to the organization at a strategic level" [23]. In analytics, strategic value is mainly comprised of enhanced decision-support by creating transparency, providing option assessment and delivering actionable recommendations [44, 50]. Improvements to decision-making in turn supports strategic planning and market positioning [24, 41]. BA also helps companies make quicker decisions by identifying emerging trends and threats, thus increasing agility. This is crucial for SMEs to compete effectively in a dynamic environment [21].

Informational value of analytics focuses on the benefit from improved information. Information quality adds value by providing data in better formats, with higher accuracy or higher completeness [19, 29, 54]. BA also helps facilitate faster and easier access to information [32, 49]. Finally, analytics can generate additional information as basis for further analyses [13, 63].

4.4 Main Profiting Business Functions

The value creation happens through applications of analytics on a hands-on level. With BA, companies can develop strategic and operational capabilities to stay ahead of the competition. Especially SMEs can benefit from these advantages as they need to survive in an increasingly competitive environment. Four business functions that particularly profit from BA have emerged from the SLR.

By applying analytics in the *finance* department, the firm can achieve increased budgeting efficiency through transparency and forecasting [21, 35, 56], better accounting quality by use of anomaly detection and automation [56] and enhanced analytical fraud detection [53]. Richins et al. [55] predict that around 94 % of accounting and auditing processes will be automated by 2025.

Analytics support the *operations* unit by enabling transparency and productivity. The literature identifies quality assurance through classification or prediction [28, 46, 51, 59] and better planning in supply chain [28, 51, 59] as high value use cases. Optimal use of raw materials by means of historical analyses and forecasting [10, 51] as well as more efficient and flexible production through transparency and prediction [11, 46] conclude the main value drivers.

Firms can align their *marketing* activities through the analysis of customer, sales and external market data [49, 63]. External analyses help react to emerging market opportunities [16, 41, 52]. Companies use customer data to enable e.g. individually targeted marketing [16, 28]. Sales data explorations can be used to evaluate sales channels [34] or to forecast demands and facilitate resource allocation or strategy development [46].

In the *strategy* division, analytics enables enhanced risk analysis and strategy adaption [11] Efficient forecasting algorithms facilitate better decision-making and allow for correct allocation of resources [47]. Integration of internal and external data sources allows for a better market understanding subsequently adding value through transparency of market potential and business environment changes [13, 49].

4.5 *Influence on Firm Performance*

Analytics can create valuable and rare resources through data-driven insights. According to the RBV this provides a competitive advantage that should lead to a performance increase [3]. Multiple scholars have empirically studied the influence of analytics on firm performance. Ji-fan Ren et al. [29] and Fosso Wamba [20] pioneered the examination of the link between analytics and firm performance.

A firm's *financial performance* pertains to its capacity to augment sales, profitability, and return on investment. Previous studies showed a correlation between BA adoption and financial performance [20, 29, 54]. This also holds true for smaller enterprises [37].

Market performance, the firm's capacity to acquire and retain market share, also correlates with the use of BA [20, 29]. Maroufkhani et al. [37] also observed this relationship in SMEs. Raguseo and Vitari [54] additionally found that market performance does not significantly affect financial performance.

Generally, *customer satisfaction* is defined as the degree to which products and services meet or exceed customer expectations. Leveraging BA, firms can provide more value to customers, better align with consumer needs, and enhance customer retention [61]. The improved customer experience and loyalty contributes to a firm's financial performance [54, 59].

5 Proposed Assessment Framework

To assess value created by specific projects, a scoring model is derived. Scoring models are a well-suited and easily applicable evaluation method based on transparently pre-determined factors [5]. Two rating scales are introduced in this study to comprehensively assess and compare different BA projects.

For the evaluation of the identified required *capabilities*, each category is assessed with three questions on a 5-point Likert scale. The items are derived from the data structure's subcategories. The scale allows to quantify subjective responses and obtain an assessment of views or preferences [30]. Each question is answered for a specific project. The higher the score, the better the fulfillment of the project's capability requirements. The questions and scale are depicted in Table 1.

Assessment of the determined *value* types follows a similar process with three questions per type on a 5-point Likert scale. The explicit items are depicted in Table 2. Aiding the assessment of the value factors, the respondents can rank the four value creation types by importance. This prioritization ensures that each dimension receives the necessary emphasis based on its strategic significance. The points of the most important dimension are doubled, while those of the second are increased by 50 %, those of the third remain stable and the points of the last dimension are halved.

Table 1 Analytics capability assessment scheme

			Low				High
Data management	DM1	How would you rate the availability of the project's required data?	0	1	2	3	4
	DM2	How would you rate the quality of the project's required data?	0	1	2	3	4
	DM3	How would you rate the currency of the project's required data?	0	1	2	3	4
People and skills	PS1	How would you rate the domain and analytic skills and experience of the project's user group?	0	1	2	3	4
	PS2	How would you rate the domain and leadership skills and experience of project's management?	0	1	2	3	4
	PS3	How would you rate the project's involvement of and alignment with the IT department?	0	1	2	3	4
Tool features	TF1	How would you rate the functional fit of project's tool(s)?	0	1	2	3	4
	TF2	How would you rate the usability of the project's tool(s)?	0	1	2	3	4
	TF3	How would you rate the accessibility of the project's tool(s)?	0	1	2	3	4
System quality	SQ1	How would you rate the ability to integrate the project's tool(s) into the system landscape?	0	1	2	3	4
	SQ2	How would you rate the flexibility and scalability of the project's tool?	0	1	2	3	4
	SQ3	How would you rate performance and reliability of the systems landscape?	0	1	2	3	4
Organizational assets	OA1	How would you rate the availability of required financial resources to execute the project?	0	1	2	3	4
	OA2	How would you rate the availability of required personnel to execute the project?	0	1	2	3	4
	OA3	How would you rate the availability of required IT infrastructure effort to execute the project?	0	1	2	3	4

Table 2 Analytics value assessment scheme

			Low				High
Tranformational value	TfV1	How would you rate the expectation to increase employee productivity?	0	1	2	3	4
	TfV2	How would you rate the expectation to develop new business models?	0	1	2	3	4
	TfV3	How would you rate the expectation to improve product or service quality?	0	1	2	3	4
Transactional value	TaV1	How would you rate the expectation to improve and optimize operational processes?	0	1	2	3	4
	TaV2	How would you rate the expectation to generate financial savings	0	1	2	3	4
	TaV3	How would you rate the expectation to increase revenue and return on assets?	0	1	2	3	4
Strategic value	SV1	How would you rate the expectation to improve decision-making?	0	1	2	3	4
	SV2	How would you rate the expectation to improve reaction time and agility?	0	1	2	3	4
	SV3	How would you rate the expectation to gain better market and competition understanding?	0	1	2	3	4
Informational value	IV1	How would you rate the expectation to gain access to data and information?	0	1	2	3	4
	IV2	How would you rate the expectation to generate additional knowledge?	0	1	2	3	4
	IV3	How would you rate the expectation to enhance information quality?	0	1	2	3	4

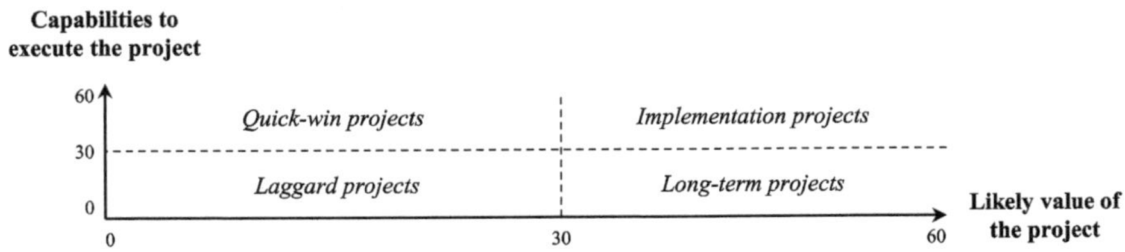

Fig. 2 Analytics capability-value scoring matrix

The overall project assessment is based on the accumulated points. 60 points represent the highest score for the capability and value scale respectively. The scores can be illustrated in the matrix displayed in Fig. 2 which allows for a visual comparison of BA projects. Grounded in the scoring matrix, analytics project can be differentiated into four groups. Projects with less than 30 points on the value scale and more than 30 points on the capability scale are defined as *quick-win projects*. The prerequisites for quick-wins are already in place, thus requiring relatively little implementation effort while providing lower value. *Laggard projects* require a lot of work and do not deliver much value. Those projects are characterized by less than 30 points on the value scale and less than 30 points on the capability scale. Projects that yield substantial value but lack necessary capabilities are classified as *long-term projects*. These endeavors often demand significant time and resources, however, they also provide substantial value. *Implementation projects* are the shining stars among initiatives, as their requirements are in place and they deliver substantial value. Those projects have a score of 30 or higher on the value scale and a capability score of 30 or higher as well.

Based on the comparison enabled by the assessment framework, companies can select BA projects that are particularly suited for the available capabilities and offer the highest value, thus maximizing the impact of their BA initiatives.

6 Discussion

The following discusses the main findings of the proposed model and assessment framework. Synthesized with the expert opinions, implications and limitations are outlined.

6.1 About the Value Creation Model

Extant literature tends to deal either with business value creation through analytics or with its required capabilities and success factors. This papers emergent value creation model combines both to deliver a holistic picture of analytics value creation.

This research aggregates existing enabling capabilities and expands beyond the initially identified factors of people and technology. While earlier perspectives, such as Seddon et al. [58], primarily emphasized these two dimensions, a more comprehensive understanding has emerged, encompassing organizational culture and specific technical requirements in terms of data and systems. This expanded view has been supported by empirical evidence from the interviews. High data quality was consistently underscored as pivotal for accurate outcomes and value delivery. Furthermore, system integration was highlighted as crucial for the correct application of analytics. The cultivation of a data-driven culture was identified as instrumental in driving BA adoption, emphasizing the importance of organizational aspects. Analytical skills and a competent workforce were reiterated as critical success factors. Particularly for SMEs, the challenge of resource constraints emerged as a significant hurdle, echoing concerns raised in the SLR. The evolving and nuanced understanding of BA capabilities offers a more comprehensive perspective for both research and practical application, enhancing the ability to unlock and leverage the full potential of analytics for organizational success.

Different types of BA value creation have been extensively explored in literature, highlighting dimensions such as transformational, transactional, strategic, and informational value [23, 54]. These dimensions, although not mutually exclusive, collectively offer a comprehensive view of BA's value creation. Aggregated in the SLR, each dimension contributes distinct insights into the impact of analytics solutions. The interviews synthesized the the literature-based value creation model and led to a better understanding of practical analytics applications. They also emphasized untapped opportunities for enhancing the effectiveness and impact of analytics initiatives. The resulting model can provide a starting point for value creation in an era of artificial intelligence, machine learning, and big data processing. It has been proven a successful tool to qualitatively guide workshops and interviews.

6.2 About the Value Assessment Framework

The proposed scoring model offers scholars and practitioners an initial approach to quantitatively apply the value creation model. This was lacking both in extant literature and in industry according to the interviews. Three interviewees stated that the financial dimension is most important when evaluating analytics use cases. In this context, it was highlighted that qualitative characteristics support the adoption, but the financial benefits are the ultimate reason to start a project. Other interviewees argued in the contrary direction. They stressed that SMEs should rather focus on a qualitative assessment and on the understanding of the solutions, instead of forcing a viable business case from the beginning. For another interviewee, fast scenario analyses and time savings through enhanced decision-making were the key drivers to start a BA project.

Ultimately, neither the SLR nor the interviews provided a clear guide to evaluate different analytics projects. The created framework can thus be seen as a first step towards achieving this. Even if the dimensions emerged from the literature review, the factors and scoring questions have to be empirically validated in future research and provide an expandable basis for further research. A validated and appropriate weighting of the different aspects is also a crucial next step. Additionally, a more differentiated view on costs and risks could give these important dimensions more prominence. However, the created scoring framework can already help SMEs compare various BA projects. By refining this model to their needs and priorities, firms can further benefit from it and select analytics projects with the highest value and lowest failure probability.

7 Conclusion

This paper aggregates and syntheses research on how analytics can effectively generate value for SMEs. The resulting model creates a holistic picture of value creation and shows that firms need very specific capabilities to create business value. Efforts must be made to ensure the seamless integration of BA into the existing system, minimizing any potential challenges or disruptions. Employees with analytics experience as well as a data-driven culture and management support ensure the success of BA. As SMEs often struggle with limited financial, human and IT-related resources, small pilot projects in a distinct unit are discovered as a suitable measure to introduce the technology and minimize the failure rate. Cloud solutions with high usability and low deployment costs can facilitate value creation and increase adoption within the company. Transactional, transformational, strategic, and informational value were identified to drive business benefits and lead to numerous enhancements, e.g. in the firm's finance, operations, marketing, and strategy unit. The proposed scoring framework contributes towards assessing and prioritizing BA projects. With the framework, firms can conduct a first check to assess different options, eliminate high-effort projects or identify quick wins. As analytics gains additional importance for SMEs, the results of this study can assist in making informed decisions and effectively prioritize their initiatives in the future.

Despite the contributions of this study, further empirical research and validation of the proposed models is necessary. The wide range of characteristics among SMEs could potentially limit the extent to which the recommendations can be applied universally. Vitari and Raguseo [61] stress a particular applicability of analytics tools in the manufacturing sector and Bhardwaj et al. [6] mentions that the firm size has a significant impact on SME readiness for analytics. A further differentiation between sectors or sizes could be an additional interesting research direction. Pilot projects were identified to be an excellent approach to showcase the benefits of BA on a smaller scale. Further research should explore which use cases are particularly suited in a small business environment.

The ongoing technological advancements such as the rise of artificial intelligence have the potential to uncover additional BA use cases and serve as a catalyst for generating value in this domain. The move to cloud applications further strengthens the BA market and will make analytical solutions more affordable and easy to implement. By developing a clear adoption strategy for data and analytics and strategically aligning the projects with their business needs, SMEs can fully exploit the growing benefits, drive business value in the long term and maintain their competitive edge.

References

1. Aboud, A., & Robinson, B. (2022). Fraudulent financial reporting and data analytics: An explanatory study from Ireland. *Accounting Research Journal, 35*(1), 21–36. https://doi.org/10.1108/ARJ-04-2020-0079
2. Akter, S., Fosso Wamba, S., Gunasekaran, A., Dubey, R., & Childe, S. J. (2016). How to improve firm performance using big data analytics capability and business strategy alignment? *International Journal of Production Economics, 182*, 113–131. https://doi.org/10.1016/j.ijpe.2016.08.018
3. Barney, J. B., Ketchen, D. J., Wright, M., Barney, J. B., David J. Ketchen, J., & Wright, M. (2011). The future of resource-based theory: Revitalization or decline? *Journal of Management, 37*(5), 1299–1315. https://doi.org/10.1177/0149206310391805
4. Barton, D., & Court, D. (2012). Making advanced analytics work for you. *Harvard Business Review*, 78–83. https://hbr.org/2012/10/making-advanced-analytics-work-for-you
5. Becker, W., & Weber, J. (1984). Scoring-modelle, 345–359.
6. Bhardwaj, S. (2022). Data analytics in small and medium enterprises (SME). *Information Resources Management Journal, 35*(2), 1–18. https://doi.org/10.4018/irmj.291691
7. Bhardwaj, S., Behl, A., & Pereira, V. (2023). Proposing an integrative data-analytics framework for micro, small and medium enterprises: A systematic review substantiated by evidence from two case studies. *Annals of Operations Research*. https://doi.org/10.1007/s10479-023-05186-9
8. Bianchini, M., & Michalkova, V. (2019) Data analytics in SMEs. OECD SME and Entrepreneurship Papers (15). https://doi.org/10.1787/1de6c6a7-en, https://www.oecd-ilibrary.org/content/paper/1de6c6a7-en
9. Brinch, M., Gunasekaran, A., & Fosso Wamba, S. (2021). Firm-level capabilities towards big data value creation. *Journal of Business Research, 131*, 539–548. https://doi.org/10.1016/j.jbusres.2020.07.036
10. Britzelmaier, B., Graue, C., & Sterk, M. (2020). Big data in SMEs - findings of an empirical study. *Global Business and Economics Review, 22*, 115–134. https://doi.org/10.1504/GBER.2020.105034
11. Choi, T. M., Chan, H. K., & Yue, X. (2017). Recent development in big data analytics for business operations and risk management. *IEEE Transactions on Cybernetics, 47*(1), 81–92. https://doi.org/10.1109/TCYB.2015.2507599
12. Coleman, S., Göb, R., Manco, G., Pievatolo, A., Tort-Martorell, X., & Reis, M. S. (2016). How can SMEs benefit from big data? Challenges and a path forward. *Quality and Reliability Engineering International, 32*(6), 2151–2164. https://doi.org/10.1002/qre.2008
13. Côrte-Real, N., Oliveira, T., & Ruivo, P. (2017). Assessing business value of Big Data Analytics in European firms. *Journal of Business Research, 70*, 379–390. https://doi.org/10.1016/j.jbusres.2016.08.011
14. Cosic, R., Shanks, G., & Maynard, S. B. (2015). A business analytics capability framework. *Australasian Journal of Information Systems, 19*. https://doi.org/10.3127/ajis.v19i0.1150
15. Davenport, T. H., Competing on analytics: The new science of winning (2006). https://www.researchgate.net/publication/7327312_Competing_on_Analytics

16. Dong, J. Q., & Yang, C. H. (2020). Business value of big data analytics: A systems-theoretic approach and empirical test. *Information & Management, 57*(1), 103–124. https://doi.org/10.1016/j.im.2018.11.001
17. Eurostat: Key figures on European business. (2022). https://ec.europa.eu/eurostat/documents/15216629/15230677/KS-06-22-075-EN-N.pdf/930f2188-48cb-ef84-678e-e6f96682b072?t=1672841155329
18. Ferraris, A., Mazzoleni, A., Devalle, A., & Couturier, J. (2019). Big data analytics capabilities and knowledge management: Impact on firm performance. *Management Decision, 57*(8), 1923–1936. https://doi.org/10.1108/md-07-2018-0825
19. Fosso Wamba, S., Akter, S., Trinchera, L., & de Bourmont, M. (2019). Turning information quality into firm performance in the big data economy. *Management Decision, 57*(8), 1756–1783. https://doi.org/10.1108/MD-04-2018-0394
20. Fosso Wamba, S., Gunasekaran, A., Akter, S., Ji-fan Ren, S., Dubey, R., & Childe, S. J. (2017). Big data analytics and firm performance: Effects of dynamic capabilities. *Journal of Business Research, 70*, 356–365. https://doi.org/10.1016/j.jbusres.2016.08.009
21. Gauzelin, S., & Bentz, H. (2017). An examination of the impact of business intelligence systems on organizational decision making and performance: The case of France. *Journal of Intelligence Studies in Business, 7*(2). https://doi.org/10.37380/jisib.v7i2.238
22. Gioia, D. A., Corley, K. G., & Hamilton, A. L. (2012). Seeking qualitative rigor in inductive research. *Organizational Research Methods, 16*(1), 15–31. https://doi.org/10.1177/1094428112452151
23. Gregor, S., Martin, M., Fernandez, W., Stern, S., & Vitale, M. (2006). The transformational dimension in the realization of business value from information technology. *The Journal of Strategic Information Systems, 15*(3), 249–270. https://doi.org/10.1016/j.jsis.2006.04.001
24. Guarda, T., Santos, M., Pinto, F., Augusto, M., & Silva, C. (2013). Business intelligence as a competitive advantage for SMEs. *International Journal of Trade, Economics and Finance*, 187–190. https://doi.org/10.7763/IJTEF.2013.V4.283
25. Hajiheydari, N., Delgosha, M. S., Wang, Y., & Olya, H. (2021). Exploring the paths to big data analytics implementation success in banking and financial service: An integrated approach. *Industrial Management & Data Systems, 121*(12), 2498–2529. https://doi.org/10.1108/imds-04-2021-0209
26. Janssen, M., van der Voort, H., & Wahyudi, A. (2017). Factors influencing big data decision-making quality. *Journal of Business Research, 70*, 338–345. https://doi.org/10.1016/j.jbusres.2016.08.007
27. Janyapoon, S., Liangrokapart, J., & Tan, A. (2021). Critical success factors of business intelligence implementation in Thai hospitals. *International Journal of Healthcare Information Systems and Informatics, 16*(4), 1–21. https://doi.org/10.4018/IJHISI.20211001.oa19
28. Jeble, S., Kumari, S., & Patil, Y. (2018). Role of big data in decision making. *Operations and Supply Chain Management: An International Journal*, 36–44. https://doi.org/10.31387/oscm0300198
29. Ji-fan Ren, S., Fosso Wamba, S., Akter, S., Dubey, R., & Childe, S. J. (2017). Modelling quality dynamics, business value and firm performance in a big data analytics environment. *International Journal of Production Research, 55*(17), 1–16. https://doi.org/10.1080/00207543.2016.1154209
30. Joshi, A., Kale, S., Chandel, S., & Pal, D. (2015). Likert scale: Explored and explained. *British Journal of Applied Science & Technology, 7*(4), 396–403. https://doi.org/10.9734/bjast/2015/14975
31. Kitchenham, B. (2004). *Procedures for Performing Systematic Reviews*. Computer Science Department, Keele University.
32. Llave, M. R. (2019). A review of business intelligence and analytics in small and medium-sized enterprises. *International Journal of Business Intelligence Research, 10*(1), 19–41. https://doi.org/10.4018/IJBIR.2019010102
33. Llave, M. R., Hustad, E., & Olsen, D. (2018). Creating value from business intelligence and analytics in SMEs: Insights from experts. In *Americas Conference on Information Systems 2018*.

34. Lu, J., Cairns, L., & Smith, L. (2021). Data science in the business environment: Customer analytics case studies in SMEs. *Journal of Modelling in Management, 16*(2), 689–713. https://doi.org/10.1108/JM2-11-2019-0274
35. Lueg, R., & Lu, S. (2013). How to improve efficiency in budgeting: The case of business intelligence in SMEs. *European Journal of Management, 13*(2), 109–120. https://doi.org/10.18374/ejm-13-2.13
36. Maroufkhani, P., Iranmanesh, M., & Ghobakhloo, M. (2023). Determinants of big data analytics adoption in small and medium-sized enterprises (SMEs). *Industrial Management & Data Systems, 123*(1), 278–301. https://doi.org/10.1108/IMDS-11-2021-0695
37. Maroufkhani, P., Wan Ismail, W. K., & Ghobakhloo, M. (2020). Big data analytics adoption model for small and medium enterprises. *Journal of Science and Technology Policy Management, 11*(4), 483–513. https://doi.org/10.1108/JSTPM-02-2020-0018
38. Mayring, P. (2000). Qualitative content analysis. *Forum Qualitative Sozialforschung/Forum Qualitative Social Research, 1*(2). https://doi.org/10.17169/fqs-1.2.1089
39. Mcafee, A., & Brynjolfsson, E. (2012). Big data: The management revolution. *Harvard Business Review, 90*(10), 60–68.
40. Melville, K. (2004). Gurbaxani: Review: Information technology and organizational performance: An integrative model of IT business value. *MIS Quarterly, 28*(2), 283. https://doi.org/10.2307/25148636
41. Mikalef, P., Krogstie, J., Pappas, I. O., & Pavlou, P. (2020). Exploring the relationship between big data analytics capability and competitive performance: The mediating roles of dynamic and operational capabilities. *Information & Management, 57*(2), 103–169. https://doi.org/10.1016/j.im.2019.05.004
42. Newcomer, K. E., Hatry, H. P., & Wholey, J. S. (2015). *Handbook of practical program evaluation*. Wiley. https://doi.org/10 1002/9781119171386
43. O'Connor, C., & Kelly, S. (2017). Facilitating knowledge management through filtered big data: SME competitiveness in an Agri-food sector. *Journal of Knowledge Management, 21*(1), 156–179. https://doi.org/10.1108/JKM-08-2016-0357
44. Olszak, C., & Mach-Król, M. (2018). A conceptual framework for assessing an organization's readiness to adopt big data. *Sustainability, 10*(10), 3734. https://doi.org/10.3390/su10103734
45. Olszak, C. M., & Ziemba, E. (2012). Critical success factors for implementing business intelligence systems in small and medium enterprises on the example of upper Silesia, Poland. *Interdisciplinary Journal of Information, Knowledge, and Management, 7*, 129–150. https://doi.org/10.28945/1584
46. Omar, Y. M., Minoufekr, M., Plapper, P. (2019). Business analytics in manufacturing: Current trends, challenges and pathway to market leadership. *Operations Research Perspectives, 6*, 100–127. https://doi.org/10.1016/j.orp.2019.100127
47. Özemre, M., & Kabadurmus, O. (2020). A big data analytics based methodology for strategic decision making. *Journal of Enterprise Information Management, 33*(6), 1467–1490. https://doi.org/10.1108/JEIM-08-2019-0222
48. Page, M. J., McKenzie, J. E., Bossuyt, P. M., Boutron, I., Hoffmann, T. C., Mulrow, C. D., Shamseer, L., Tetzlaff, J. M., Akl, E. A., Brennan, S. E., Chou, R., Glanville, J., Grimshaw, J. M., Hróbjartsson, A., Lalu, M. M., Li, T., Loder, E. W., Mayo-Wilson, E., McDonald, S., âŁ¦ Moher, D. (2021). The PRISMA 2020 statement: An updated guideline for reporting systematic reviews. *BMJ*. https://doi.org/10.1136/bmj.n71
49. Papachristodoulou, E., Koutsaki, M., & Kirkos, E. (2017). Business intelligence and SMEs: Bridging the gap. *Journal of Intelligence Studies in Business, 7*(1). https://doi.org/10.37380/jisib.v7i1.216
50. Popovič, A., Hackney, R., Coelho, P. S., & Jaklič, J. (2012). Towards business intelligence systems success: Effects of maturity and culture on analytical decision making. *Decision Support Systems, 54*(1), 729–739. https://doi.org/10.1016/j.dss.2012.08.017
51. Popovič, A., Hackney, R., Tassabehji, R., & Castelli, M. (2018). The impact of big data analytics on firms' high value business performance. *Information Systems Frontiers, 20*(2), 209–222. https://doi.org/10.1007/s10796-016-9720-4

52. Popovič, A., Puklavec, B., & Oliveira, T. (2019). Justifying business intelligence systems adoption in SMEs. *Industrial Management & Data Systems, 119*(1), 210–228. https://doi.org/10.1108/IMDS-02-2018-0085
53. Raghavan, P., & Gayar, N. E. (2019). Fraud detection using machine learning and deep learning. In *2019 International Conference on Computational Intelligence and Knowledge Economy (ICCIKE)* (pp. 334–339). https://doi.org/10.1109/ICCIKE47802.2019.9004231
54. Raguseo, E., & Vitari, C. (2018). Investments in big data analytics and firm performance: An empirical investigation of direct and mediating effects. *International Journal of Production Research, 56*(15), 5206–5221. https://doi.org/10.1080/00207543.2018.1427900
55. Richins, G., Stapleton, A., Stratopoulos, T. C., & Wong, C. (2017). Big data analytics: Opportunity or threat for the accounting profession? *Journal of Information Systems, 31*(3), 63–79. https://doi.org/10.2308/isys-51805
56. Saleh, I., Marei, Y., Ayoush, M., & Afifa, M. M. A. (2023). Big data analytics and financial reporting quality: Qualitative evidence from Canada. *Journal of Financial Reporting and Accounting, 21*(1), 83–104. https://doi.org/10.1108/jfra-12-2021-0489
57. Scholz, P., Schieder, C., Kurze, C., Gluchowski, P., & Böhringer, M. (2010). Benefits and challenges of business intelligence adoption in small and medium-sized enterprises. In *ECIS 2010 Proceedings*.
58. Seddon, P. B., Constantinidis, D., Tamm, T., & Dod, H. (2017). How does business analytics contribute to business value? *Information Systems Journal, 27*(3), 237–269. https://doi.org/10.1111/isj.12101
59. Segarra, L. L., Almalki, H., Elabd, J., Gonzalez, J., Marczewski, M., Alrasheed, M., & Rabelo, L. (2016). A framework for boosting revenue incorporating big data. *Journal of Innovation Management, 4*(1), 39–68. https://doi.org/10.24840/2183-0606_004.001_0005
60. Vidgen, R., Shaw, S., & Grant, D. B. (2017). Management challenges in creating value from business analytics. *European Journal of Operational Research, 261*(2), 626–639. https://doi.org/10.1016/j.ejor.2017.02.023
61. Vitari, C., & Raguseo, E. (2020). Big data analytics business value and firm performance: Linking with environmental context. *International Journal of Production Research, 58*(18), 5456–5476. https://doi.org/10.1080/00207543.2019.1660822
62. vom Brocke, J., Simons, A., Niehaves, B., Riemer, K., Plattfaut, R., & Cleven, A. (2009). Reconstructing the giant: On the importance of Rigour in documenting the literature search process. In *ECIS 2009 Proceedings*.
63. Wang, S., & Wang, H. (2020). Big data for small and medium-sized enterprises (SME): A knowledge management model. *Journal of Knowledge Management, 24*(4), 881–897. https://doi.org/10.1108/JKM-02-2020-0081
64. Webster, J., & Watson, R. T. (2002). Analyzing the past to prepare for the future: Writing a literature review. *MIS Quaterly, 26*(2), 8–23.
65. Wee, M., Scheepers, H., & Tian, X. (2022). Understanding the processes of how small and medium enterprises derive value from business intelligence and analytics. *Australasian Journal of Information Systems, 26*. https://doi.org/10.3127/ajis.v26i0.2969
66. Williams, R. A., Sheikh, N. J., Duman, G. M., & Kongar, E. (2022). Critical success factors of business intelligence systems implementation. *IEEE Engineering Management Review, 50*(4), 88–97. https://doi.org/10.1109/EMR.2022.3197096
67. Wixom, B. H., & Todd, P. A. (2005). A theoretical integration of user satisfaction and technology acceptance. *Information Systems Research, 16*(1), 85–102. https://doi.org/10.1287/isre.1050.0042
68. Yeoh, W., & Koronios, A. (2010). Critical success factors for business intelligence systems. *Journal of Computer Information Systems, 50*(3), 23–32.

On Optimal Covariance Matrix Shrinkage Levels in Forecast Combination

Thomas Setzer and Marco Fuchs

Abstract Forecast combination is an established technique to improve forecast accuracy and enterprise planning, where a key research question is (still) how to weight individual forecasts. One common but largely unsuccessful approach is to learn weights that minimize the mean squared error (MSE) on known observations, usually from (instable) sample covariance matrices of past errors. These weights are then shrunk to mitigate over-fitting and avoid high errors when using the weights in novel forecasts. This can be done by shrinking the sample covariance matrix to a less flexible matrix, e.g. the unit diagonal matrix, where even formulas for the shrinkage level minimizing the expected deviation between the shrunk and the true covariance matrix exist. We provide analyses with synthetic error data showing that such shrink-levels generally do not lead to MSE-minimizing weights and argue that adjusted shrinkage criteria or machine-learning-based shrinkage tuning is advised to successfully apply such approaches in forecast combination.

Keywords Forecast combination · Error covariance matrix · Matrix shrinkage · Selection of target covariance matrix

1 Introduction and Related Literature

Business forecasting is crucial in the field of information systems, as accurate forecasts are fundamental to many decision-making processes in organizations. Information systems are designed to collect, store, process, and distribute information, and their effectiveness is enhanced by integrating accurate forecasting models. To this end, an expanding array of statistical learning-, machine learning- and forecast support system-based methods has emerged to provide reliable forecasts. One well-established technique to leverage information from a multitude of individual

T. Setzer · M. Fuchs (✉)
Catholic University Eichstätt-Ingolstadt, Ingolstadt School of Management, Ingolstadt, Germany
e-mail: marco.fuchs@ku.de

T. Setzer
e-mail: thomas.setzer@ku.de

C. M. Flath et al. (eds.), *Artificial Intelligence, Data, and Decision-Making*, Lecture Notes in Information Systems and Organisation 82,
https://doi.org/10.1007/978-3-032-08480-4_21

forecasts is forecast combination. A substantial body of empirical research has found that, on average, a linear combination of individual forecasts outperforms a single "best forecast" [7, 15, 16, 18, 25, 31]. For instance, automated forecast combinations can improve the accuracy of demand forecasts, leading to better inventory control and reduced stockouts [10, 28, 29]. Also, forecast combinations can enhance budgeting, financial planning, and risk assessment [2, 14].

However, the effectiveness of forecast combinations depends on the quality of the combination weights. There are two main approaches to determining weights. First, using fixed weights such as the simple average or subset-average, where the latter discards forecasters with poor performance. Second, fitting weights to training data to minimize some loss function like the mean squared error (MSE), as first proposed in [1] and coined "Optimal Weights (OW)".

However, it has been empirically shown that OW are usually dominated by predefined, fixed weights [3, 15, 17, 25]. This so-called "forecast combination puzzle" [26] is largely attributed to overfitting [4–6, 23]. Learning weights from (finite) training samples introduces estimation uncertainty, particularly due to challenges in estimating the forecasters' error covariance matrix from which the weightings are then derived [30]. This estimation error increases the out-of-sample error and quickly overwhelms potential performance gains due to learning weightings from data.

There are two possible approaches to address this estimation uncertainty. First, the stabilization of the estimated OWs, e.g., by shrinking them towards simple average weights [4, 22, 27]. Second, one can enhance the robustness of the covariance matrix estimation itself, allowing subsequent weighting schemes to benefit from reduced estimation errors. This paper will address the latter approach.

Proposals emerged to manipulate the sample covariance matrix to enhance the robustness of the weights derived therefrom. For instance, [1] and [19] argue that correlations between forecasters cannot be reliably estimated when many forecasts are combined and only few training samples are available. They consequently propose to disregard correlations, implying that the sample covariance matrix should be treated as if it were a diagonal matrix.

The first paper to propose a more nuanced transformation of the sample covariance matrix in the context of forecast combinations stems from [8]. They develop a Bayesian approach where the prior implies exchangeability between forecasters. The output of their method is a shrunk sample covariance matrix for which any differences among forecasters (in variances or pairwise covariances) are reduced. One general drawback of this method is that the number of degrees of freedom of the target matrix and the shrinkage intensity must be specified by the user, to whom the task-specific error structure and optimal shrinkage intensity are typically unknown.

Almost two decades later, [13] build on the Steinian shrinkage principle and propose to estimate the covariance matrix by an optimally weighted average of two estimators: the sample covariance matrix and a structured Target T (e.g. an estimator for which no or fewer parameters need to be estimated from training data). They derive a closed-form solution for the optimal weight of the structured target, a.k.a shrinkage intensity, aiming to minimize the estimation error of the covariance matrix for a given training set. This formula is also known as Ledoit-Wolf lemma.

The method has been applied in a wide range of fields as diverse as Finance [12], Chemistry [11] or Genetics [9] but was only recently applied to forecast combination by [20].

In their study, [20] applied the Ledoit-Wolf lemma in forecast combination and evaluated its performance relative to other combination methods, specifically those using cross-validation-tuned shrinkage levels to adjust learned weights toward equal weights. The results were mixed; different methods resulted in the lowest out-of-sample Root Mean Squared Error (RMSE) depending on the scenario. However, the authors do not analyze and/or explain these differences in performance in depth. In particular, they did not systematically investigate the roots of these differences or the impact of the misfit between the chosen target matrix and the (true) data structure.

In our work, we address this unresolved issue by providing the first study to systematically analyze and evaluate [13]'s lemma for the optimal shrinkage intensity in forecast combination.

Our contributions are twofold: First, we show that the application of Steinian shrinkage to the sample covariance matrix can reduce the out-of-sample error of a forecast combination. Second, we demonstrate that although the lemma-based estimation of the optimal shrinkage intensity minimizes the estimation error of the covariance matrix, it does not necessarily result in well-estimated optimal weights (OWs). Instead, we establish that selecting an appropriate shrinkage target is crucial for the method's correct functioning and for the learned weights to achieve strong out-of-sample performance.

Our key finding is that the formula should only be used when there is high certainty about the fit of the target matrix. Otherwise, the learned weights tend to be overfitted and also biased towards an incorrect target structure, resulting in high out-of-sample errors. Consequently, this work motivates further research on data-driven methods for determining or verifying suitable target matrices, as well as the development of more advanced tuning procedures as suggested in this paper's outlook.

The remainder of the paper is organized as follows. In Sect. 2, we outline concepts of forecast combination and introduce Steinian matrix shrinkage together with notation. In Sect. 3, we analyze the MSE of a forecast combination when applying Steinian shrinkage to error covariance matrices and its dependence on targets and shrinkage levels. Finally, in Sect. 4 we conclude by highlighting challenges revealed in this article and give an outlook to further research on Steinian Shrinkage in forecast combination.

2 Forecast Combination and Error Covariance Matrix Shrinkage

In this section we first introduce the general concept of forecast combination, before we introduce the learning of combination weights from error covariance structures estimated on past error observations. We then introduce Steinian shrinkage of estimated covariance matrices to regularize learned weights, i.e., to mitigate the problem of overfitted weights that tend to lead to high errors with novel forecasts if left unshrunk.

We start by introducing some notation. Let $f = (f_1, \ldots, f_k)$ denote a vector of k point forecasts provided by k forecasters (or statistical models), where an individual forecaster is indexed by $i \in \{1, \ldots, k\}$. It is usually assumed that the forecasts are efficient, i.e., that errors of the forecasters approximately follow a multivariate normal distribution with mean zero. We therefore model the error structure of the k forecasters as $e \sim \mathcal{N}_k(0, \Sigma)$ with error covariance matrix $\Sigma \in \mathbb{R}^{k\times k}$.

A combined forecast using weights $w \in \mathbb{R}^k$ with $\sum_{i=1}^{k} w_i = 1$ can be computed as $f'w$, with f' indicating the transpose of f. While the weights w can be set in advance, in a data-agnostic fashion (e.g. simple average weights), such fix weights obviously do not necessarily minimize the error, e.g., the mean squared error (MSE), on future forecasts. Therefore, a key aim of forecast combination research is to estimate weights with lower MSE on future forecasts from training data. Next, the OW approach introduced in Sect. 1 is discussed in detail.

2.1 *Learned Weights from Observed Error Covariances*

OW as proposed by [1] minimize the MSE of a combination of two forecasts. Its multivariate generalization is introduced for instance in [19].

With ι indicating a vector of k 1's, and Σ^{-1} indicating the inverse of error matrix Σ, OW are computed in (1).

$$w = \frac{\Sigma^{-1}\iota}{\iota'\Sigma^{-1}\iota} \tag{1}$$

However, Σ is generally unknown and estimated from the training error matrix $E \in \mathbb{R}^{n\times k}$ (n observed errors for each of the k forecasters) as $\hat{\Sigma}$. This results in OW estimates $\hat{w}$ shown in (2).

$$\hat{w} = \frac{\hat{\Sigma}^{-1}\iota}{\iota'\hat{\Sigma}^{-1}\iota} \tag{2}$$

Therewith, $\hat{w}$ and the combined forecast $f'\hat{w}$ are subject to uncertainty and prone to overfitting randomness in the training data. This impacts the MSE of the combined forecast on unseen data, where then rather extreme and misfit weights often lead to higher errors than expected.

The reason is that $\hat{w}$ are sensitive to even small changes in the elements in $\hat{\Sigma}$ [8]. These elements are, however, subject to uncertainty and randomness in the observed error vectors used for estimating $\hat{\Sigma}$. Hence, the predictive quality of estimated OW crucially relies on $\hat{\Sigma}$ being a sound estimate of the true Σ.

In forecast combination, the common choice of $\hat{\Sigma}$ is the sample covariance matrix of observed errors $\hat{\Sigma} = \frac{1}{n}E'E$, Σ's maximum likelihood estimator, as the sample covariance matrix is an unbiased estimate of Σ (its expected value is equal to Σ), $Bias(\hat{\Sigma}) = 0$ by construction. However, as the estimate $\hat{\Sigma}$ requires the determination of $(k^2 + k)/2$ parameters, it is also well known to be an unstable estimate of Σ, i.e. its variance is high unless the training error matrix E is large, which is often not the case in forecast combination.

The high sampling-based variance of the estimated values in $\hat{\Sigma}$ often leads to extreme, highly overfit weights derived from $\hat{\Sigma}$, resulting in high forecast errors on unseen data [30, 32].

Therefore, estimators for Σ are required with lower variance at the cost of increased bias, i.e., estimates that better solve the bias–variance trade-off in approximating Σ. An intuitive and natural target is therefore the derivation of a $\hat{\Sigma}$ estimate with minimum overall distance to Σ, usually measured by the Frobenius norm (the root of the sum of squared element-wise differences) of $\hat{\Sigma}$ with regard to Σ as defined in (3).

$$FN(\hat{\Sigma}) = \|\hat{\Sigma} - \Sigma\|_F = \sqrt{\sum_{i=1}^{k}\sum_{j=1}^{k} |(\hat{\Sigma}_{ij} - \Sigma_{ij})|^2} \tag{3}$$

Schäfer and Strimmer [21] have shown that $FN(\hat{\Sigma})$ can further be decomposed into a bias component related to the expected fit to the data (systematic deviation from expected values) and a variance component resulting from estimation uncertainty. The bias-variance trade-off related to the estimation of Σ from E (the formula that needs to be minimized in order to minimize the Frobenius norm) is depicted in (4).

$$FN(\hat{\Sigma}) = Bias(\hat{\Sigma})^2 + Var(\hat{\Sigma}) \tag{4}$$

An approach to solve this trade-off is Steinian shrinkage introduced next.

2.2 Steinian Matrix Shrinkage

The Stein Theorem developed by [24] states that one can reduce the expected $FN(\hat{\Sigma})$ by trading in bias in exchange for a reduction in variance. This can be done by linearly shrinking $\hat{\Sigma}$ towards a more structured target T. With $\lambda \in [0, 1]$ being the shrinkage intensity, the shrunk covariance matrix estimate $\hat{\Sigma}_S$ is derived in (5).

$$\hat{\Sigma}_S = \lambda T + (1 - \lambda)\hat{\Sigma} \tag{5}$$

Consider, for instance, the identity matrix $\mathbf{I}_k$ as target T. As the variance component results from over-sensitivity to the training data (overfitting), $\mathbf{I}_k$ clearly has a variance of 0, as no parameter is estimated from the training data. However, it is characterized by an increased bias as compared to the maximum likelihood estimate $\hat{\Sigma}$, as the expected fit to the data is lower.

Therefore, $\hat{\Sigma}$ and $\mathbf{I}_k$ are extremes, with $\mathbf{I}_k$ having no variance but high bias, whereas $\hat{\Sigma}$ has high variance but low bias. Steinian shrinkage suggests that by combining both extremes through a weighted average rather than selecting one extreme, one obtains a regularized estimator $\hat{\Sigma}_S^*$ that outperforms the individual estimators both in terms of accuracy and statistical efficiency.

To apply Steinian shrinkage, two decisions are to be made. First, which shrinkage level λ^* optimizes the bias–variance trade-off given $\hat{\Sigma}$ and T? Second which structured estimator T is suitable given the context of the estimation problem? As will be shown later in our analysis, the key challenge is that the decisions cannot be answered in isolation, as the goal is to find the combination of target and shrinkage level that collectively minimizes the MSE of a combined forecast.

Schäfer and Strimmer [21] answer the first question given a fixed shrinkage target. They provide a list of commonly employed shrinkage targets and build upon an analytical result of [13] to derive a data-driven estimate of the shrinkage level $\hat{\lambda}^*$ minimizing the expected Frobenius norm in (3) for a fixed T from their list. We note that $\hat{\lambda}^*$ can be computed solely with the sample error data. Details on how to understand and proof $\hat{\lambda}^*$ are provided in [21].

Table 1 specifies the six shrinkage targets T in [21] by their respective values t_{ij} at row i and column j along with the number of parameters to be estimated, and the estimators of the optimal shrinkage intensity $\hat{\lambda}^*$.

The second question, the choice T, remains open. In principle, the choice of the target should reflect the true structure of the data generation process. This is because on the one hand the bias induced by shrinkage depends on how closely the target T matches the true matrix Σ. On the other hand, a target with more flexibility increases the variance of the shrunk covariance estimate due to overfitting. Common suggestions are to use domain knowledge to make a good guess for the proper target matrix, and no data-driven approaches have been proposed so far.

Targets A, B and C, are low-dimensional, with zero parameters to be estimated for A (identity matrix), one for B (common variance), and two for C (common (co)variance). All three targets yield related effects on estimated OW as they implicitly assume that all forecasters can be treated interchangeably. As λ increases, the OW $\hat{w}$ converge gradually, until for $\lambda = 1$, the combined forecast becomes a simple averaging.

While D maintains differences in forecasters accuracy (variances remain unchanged), it sets all off-diagonal elements of $\hat{\Sigma}$ to zero, therefore assuming independence of forecasters' errors. For $\lambda = 1$, the combined forecast relies solely on each forecaster's relative training-set accuracy.

Unlike D, E presumes that the errors of all forecasters are perfectly positively correlated. This strong assumption is relaxed in F, where a constant correlation $\bar{r}$ of forecast errors is assumed and estimated from the data.

We note that the flexibility of a target to capture structure of the sample covariance matrix increases from A with 0 estimated parameters to F with $p + 1$ estimated parameters, and that more flexibility reduces bias but increases sampling-based variance. Hence, there is clearly a further bias–variance trade-off to be solved when selecting T.

Table 1 Commonly used shrinkage targets T and associated estimators of optimal shrinkage

Target A: "diagonal, unit variance"	**Target B**: "diagonal, common variance"
0 estimated parameters	1 estimated parameter: v
$t_{ij} = \begin{cases} 1 & \text{if } i = j \\ 0 & \text{if } i \neq j \end{cases}$	$t_{ij} = \begin{cases} v = \text{avg}(s_{ii}) & \text{if } i = j \\ 0 & \text{if } i \neq j \end{cases}$
$\hat{\lambda}^* = \frac{\sum_{i \neq j} \hat{\text{Var}}(s_{ij}) + \sum_i \hat{\text{Var}}(s_{ii})}{\sum_{i \neq j} s_{ij}^2 + \sum_i (s_{ii} - 1)^2}$	$\hat{\lambda}^* = \frac{\sum_{i \neq j} \hat{\text{Var}}(s_{ij}) + \sum_i \hat{\text{Var}}(s_{ii})}{\sum_{i \neq j} s_{ij}^2 + \sum_i (s_{ii} - v)^2}$
Target C: "common (co)variance"	**Target D**: "diagonal, unequal variance"
2 estimated parameters: v, c	p estimated parameters: s_{ii}
$t_{ij} = \begin{cases} v = \text{avg}(s_{ii}) & \text{if } i = j \\ c = \text{avg}(s_{ij}) & \text{if } i \neq j \end{cases}$	$t_{ij} = \begin{cases} s_{ii} & \text{if } i = j \\ 0 & \text{if } i \neq j \end{cases}$
$\hat{\lambda}^* = \frac{\sum_{i \neq j} \hat{\text{Var}}(s_{ij}) + \sum_i \hat{\text{Var}}(s_{ii})}{\sum_{i \neq j} (s_{ij} - c)^2 + \sum_i (s_{ii} - v)^2}$	$\hat{\lambda}^* = \frac{\sum_{i \neq j} \hat{\text{Var}}(s_{ij})}{\sum_{i \neq j} (s_{ij}^2)}$
Target E: "perfect positive correlation"	**Target F**: "constant correlation"
p estimated parameters: s_{ii}	$p + 1$ estimated parameters: $s_{ii}, \bar{r}$
$t_{ij} = \begin{cases} s_{ii} & \text{if } i = j \\ \sqrt{s_{ii} s_{jj}} & \text{if } i \neq j \end{cases}$	$t_{ij} = \begin{cases} s_{ii} & \text{if } i = j \\ \bar{r}\sqrt{s_{ii} s_{jj}} & \text{if } i \neq j \end{cases}$
$\hat{\lambda}^* = \frac{\sum_{i \neq j} \hat{\text{Var}}(s_{ij}) - f_{ij}}{\sum_{i \neq j} (s_{ij} - \sqrt{s_{ii} s_{jj}})^2}$	$\hat{\lambda}^* = \frac{\sum_{i \neq j} \hat{\text{Var}}(s_{ij}) - \bar{r} f_{ij}}{\sum_{i \neq j} (s_{ij} - \bar{r}\sqrt{s_{ii} s_{jj}})^2}$
with $f_{ij} = \frac{1}{2}\{\sqrt{\frac{s_{jj}}{s_{ii}}} \hat{\text{Cov}}(s_{ii}, s_{ij}) + \sqrt{\frac{s_{ii}}{s_{jj}}} \hat{\text{Cov}}(s_{jj}, s_{ij})\}$	

Abbrev.: v: average sample variance; c: average sample covariance; $\bar{r}$: average sample correlation
$\hat{\lambda}^*$ *Source* [21]

Next, we will develop an understanding of how Steinian Shrinkage operates within the field of forecast combination.

3 Analysis of Sigma-Optimal Shrinkage

We start with generating six scenarios (Scenario A, …, Scenario F), where the error samples within each scenario align with one of the six target matrices (A to F). Per scenario, we analyze the lemma-based shrinkage levels designed to minimize

$FN(\hat{\Sigma}_S)$ when shrinking the respective sample covariance matrices to one of the six targets, and whether these also minimize the MSE of the corresponding OW-based forecast combination.

3.1 Example Shrinkage with Different Targets

For our analysis we generate error samples with $k = 5$ forecasters by drawing 20·5 train error observations from a multivariate normal distribution parameterized with Σ_A corresponding to scenario A, Σ_B corresponding to scenario B, etc. This process is repeated to create 100 independently drawn training error sets per scenario. Similarly, a single large test set of 5M observations is drawn per scenario.

Next, we estimate $\hat{\Sigma}$ per training sample and shrink it in increments of 0.01 towards the six targets to obtain 6·101 different shrunken covariance matrices $\hat{\Sigma}_S$ per sample. As this is done for each of the training samples, this results in the consideration of 6·101·100 covariance matrices per scenario. For each sample we also calculate the optimal shrinkage intensity $\hat{\lambda}^*$ per target using the formulas in Table 1.

Figure 1 shows example outcomes with Scenario C (first row) and F (second row), whereby the outcomes are averaged across the 100 training samples per scenario. The plots on the left-hand side show the curves of $FN(\hat{\Sigma}_S)$ over shrinkage intensity λ. In addition, the mean estimated optimal shrinkage intensity $\hat{\lambda}^*$ corresponding to each target is labeled as a point; the first and third quartiles of $\hat{\lambda}^*$'s empirical distribution over the 100 training samples are indicated by triangles.

The right-hand plots show the mean curves of the out-of-sample error MSE($\hat{\Sigma}_S$) over λ, derived by computing $\hat{w}$ using (2) per shrunk matrix $\hat{\Sigma}_S$, and determine the MSE with the combined forecast $f'\hat{w}$ on the large test set corresponding to this scenario. Like in the left plots, mean $\hat{\lambda}^*$ as well as its first and third quartiles are shown.

In both scenarios, per target $\hat{\lambda}^*$ mostly corresponds well to the minima of the $FN(\hat{\Sigma}_S)$ curves as $\hat{\lambda}^*$ minimizes the expected $FN(\hat{\Sigma}_S)$ with a given error sample.

Regarding the forecast error curves over shrinkage, one observes that for all targets, MSE($\hat{\Sigma}_S$) is reduced when applying appropriate shrinkage to $\hat{\Sigma}$ in both scenarios. However, one also observes that (i) $\hat{\lambda}^*$ often deviates strongly from the minimum of the corresponding MSE($\hat{\Sigma}_S$) curve, and (ii) that the choice of the target has a crucial impact on the MSE of a forecast combination.

In Scenario C we observe too short shrinkage towards targets A, B and D, targets wrongly assuming independent errors of the forecasters (as in scenario C, Σ generates positively correlated errors), such that stronger shrinkage would heavily increase bias. We further observe that targets C and F, both having the flexibility to learn the structure of Σ, behave differently. While full shrinkage to C is optimal here as solely variance of $\hat{\Sigma}$ is then reduced, shrinkage towards F, with more degrees of freedom and higher flexibility than C, leads to much higher MSE out-of-sample with

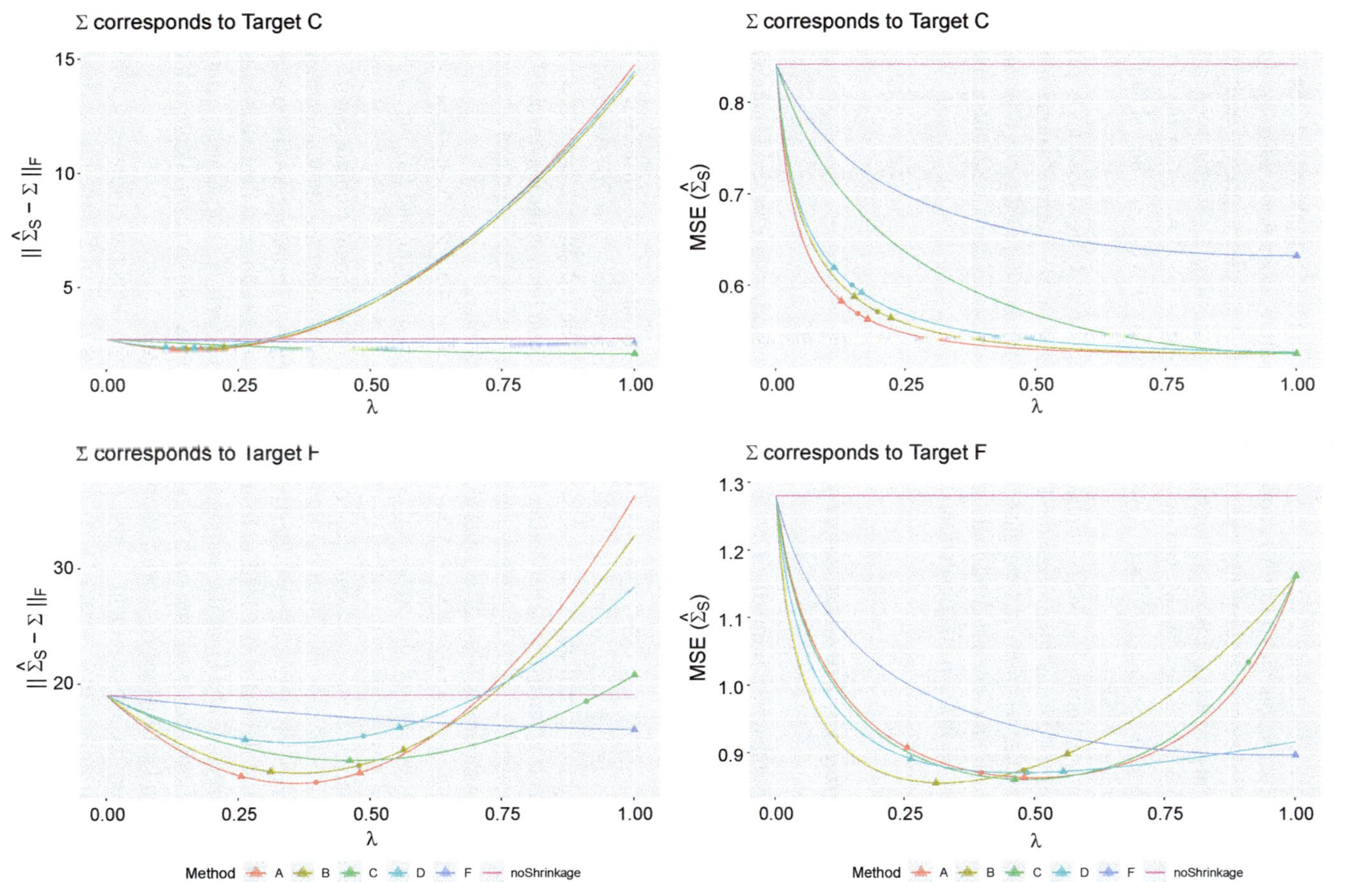

Fig. 1 $FN(\hat{\Sigma}_S)$ (left) and MSE$(\hat{\Sigma}_S)$ (right) in Scenario C (top) and Scenario F (bottom), together with $\hat{\lambda}^*$'s mean value (point) and its first and third quartile (triangles) when shrinking to targets A–F

a combined forecast; that is due to overfitting and insufficient variance reduction with such a flexible target.

In scenario F, we also observe a very interesting behavior. Shrinkage to F, the only target with sufficient flexibility to capture Σ's structure, does not lead to minimal MSE. This is because of the many estimated parameters and the respective high level of uncertainty, making this target highly prone to overfitting $\hat{\Sigma}$. In this scenario, a target matrix too inflexible to capture the true structure in Σ is in fact the better choice. We also see that shrinkage towards A minimizes $FN(\hat{\Sigma}_S)$, while shrinkage to B minimizes MSE.

In summary, finding the MSE-minimizing weights strongly depends on the target chosen, and the $\hat{\lambda}^*$ that minimizes the Frobenius norm of $\hat{\Sigma}_S$, perhaps surprisingly, doesn't translate to optimized weights $\hat{w}$ and the minimization of the out-of-sample MSE of a resulting forecast combination. A better understanding of these phenomena will be derived in the next subsection.

3.2 Sigma Vs. Forecast Error Curves

To gain insights why minimizing $FN(\hat{\Sigma}_S)$ does not optimize weights $\hat{w}$ and hence the out-of-sample MSE of a forecast combination, we consider a novel scenario, where Σ corresponds to a linear combination of Targets C and D, i.e., with $\Sigma = a\Sigma_C + (1-a)\Sigma_D$, $a \in [0, 1]$. Figure 2 depicts six covariance matrices with different a.

Figure 3 shows the developments of different quantities over shrinkage of the Σ matrices in Fig. 2. Like in Fig. 1, 100 training errors sets ($n = 20$) were drawn per multivariate distribution parameterized with Σ. The red (blue) curves show the developments when using target matrix C (D). The solid lines in the upper row show the development of $FN(\hat{\Sigma}_S)$ when shrinking towards C or D. The mean $\hat{\lambda}^*$ across all training set draws from Σ is labeled by a point symbol.

To further analyse the $FN(\hat{\Sigma}_S)$ curves, we note that $FN(\hat{\Sigma}_S)$ is the root of the sum of (i) the sum of the squared deviations of the diagonal and (ii) the sum of the squared deviations of the off-diagonal elements. The curves of the L_2-norms of the diagonal-element deviations (dashed lines) and off-diagonal element deviations (dotted lines) are also shown in the figure. These components are shown separately as their curves provide a better understanding of (wrong) shrinkage levels later on.

For $a = 0$, the share of $FN(\hat{\Sigma}_S)$ from the off-diagonal elements decreases with λ for both targets C and D, as the assumptions of both targets (C: constant covariance, D: zero covariance) hold true with regard to the true Σ and thus shrinkage reduces variance and estimation error without increasing bias.

However, the development of the L_2-norm of the diagonal component differs between shrinkage to C versus D. As only the assumption of D (unequal variance) holds true, the $FN(\hat{\Sigma}_S)$ driven by the diagonal elements stays constant for D. Conversely, shrinking towards C under the false assumption of equal variances drives the bias component. The induced bias quickly overtakes the variance-reducing effect

a = 0

1.00	0.00	0.00	0.00	0.00
0.00	1.25	0.00	0.00	0.00
0.00	0.00	1.50	0.00	0.00
0.00	0.00	0.00	1.75	0.00
0.00	0.00	0.00	0.00	[illegible]

a = 0.2

0.94	0.10	0.10	0.10	0.10
0.10	1.14	0.10	0.10	0.10
0.10	0.10	1.34	0.10	0.10
0.10	0.10	0.10	1.54	0.10
0.10	0.10	0.10	0.10	[illegible]

a = 0.4

0.88	0.20	0.20	0.20	0.20
0.20	1.03	0.20	0.20	0.20
0.20	0.20	1.18	0.20	0.20
0.20	0.20	0.20	1.33	0.20
0.20	0.20	0.20	0.20	[illegible]

a = 0.6

0.82	0.30	0.30	0.30	0.30
0.30	0.92	0.30	0.30	0.30
0.30	0.30	1.02	0.30	0.30
0.30	0.30	0.30	1.12	0.30
0.30	0.30	0.30	0.30	2.42

a = 0.8

0.76	0.40	0.40	0.40	0.40
0.40	0.81	0.40	0.40	0.40
0.40	0.40	0.86	0.40	0.40
0.40	0.40	0.40	0.91	0.40
0.40	0.40	0.40	0.40	1.56

a = 1

0.70	0.50	0.50	0.50	0.50
0.50	0.70	0.50	0.50	0.50
0.50	0.50	0.70	0.50	0.50
0.50	0.50	0.50	0.70	0.50
0.50	0.50	0.50	0.50	0.70

Fig. 2 Covariance matrices utilized in the scenario depicted in Fig. 3. With $a = 0$, Σ corresponds to Target D: "diagonal, unequal variance", whereas $a = 1$, Σ corresponds to Target C: "common (co)variance". The four intermediate Σ matrices represent linear combinations of targets C and D

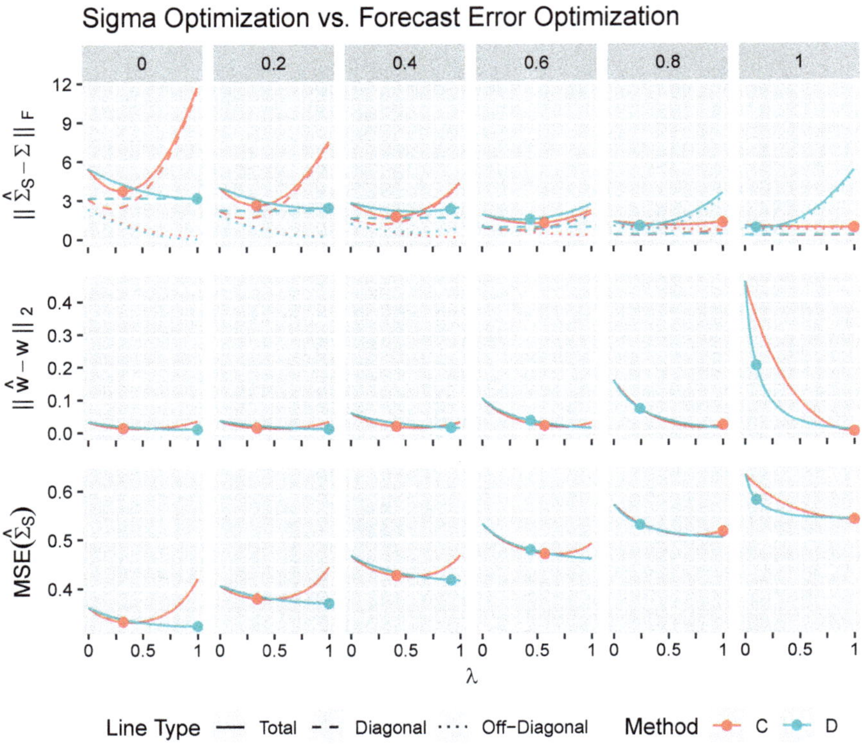

Fig. 3 $FN(\hat{\Sigma}_S)$ (top row), $\|w - \hat{w}\|_2$ (L_2 deviations of estimated and optimal weights, intermediate row) and MSE($\hat{\Sigma}$) (bottom row) with Σ as a linear combination of target C and D when shrinking towards C or D

of shrinkage to C, such that the lemma-based optimal shrinkage intensity towards Target C is low, while we obtain full shrinkage to Target D.

Overall, $\hat{\lambda}^*$ effectively solves the bias–variance trade-off related to $FN(\hat{\Sigma}_S)$ for both targets. This translates to well-estimated weights $\hat{w}$ which minimize the out-of-sample MSE as shown in the intermediate and lower rows of the figure.

The intermediate row shows the deviation over shrinkage of the in-sample learned weights and the truly optimal (population) weights in terms of the L_2-norm of the weight differences, denoted as $\|w - \hat{w}\|_2$. This quantity is important, as the estimated weights $\hat{w}$ serve as the link between Σ-estimation and the subsequent out-of-sample performance of the resulting forecast combination.

We observe how $\hat{\lambda}^*$ translates to a certain estimation accuracy of w, which ultimately determines the decisive out-of-sample MSE shown in the bottom row where we observe out-of-sample MSE optimal shrinkage.

With $a = 0.2$ a similar behavior can be observed, whereby the narrower range of the diagonal elements of Σ reduces the variance in the estimation of the diagonal elements when shrinking to target D, while the bias induced by shrinking to target C is notably reduced (dashed lines).

However, the curves with $a = 0.4$ to $a = 1$ illustrate why the minimization of the Frobenius norm does not always optimize the learned weights $\hat{w}$ and hence the out-of-sample MSE. As the off-diagonal elements in Σ gradually increase towards 0.5, the bias induced by target D on the off-diagonal components rises (dotted lines). This escalation stems from the growing disparity between the true covariances in Σ and the target's covariance of 0.

$\hat{\lambda}^*$ adjusts to this dynamic, aiming to resolve the bias–variance-trade-off with respect to the $FN(\hat{\Sigma}_S)$ minimization. Consequently, $\hat{\lambda}^*$ suggests lower shrinkage levels for target D, particularly evident in the scenario where $a = 1$. However, the adjustment of $\hat{\lambda}^*$ translates to under-shrinkage in estimating w, resulting in sub-optimal out-of-sample MSE outcomes.

The reason for this discrepancy is that from the point of forecast combination, Σ_D suggests that all forecasters are exchangeable due to identical variance and covariance patterns. In the quest for optimal weights $\hat{w}$, all that matters is that this property aligns with the shrinkage target. Shrinking towards D would indeed achieve this objective, as it would ensure that all forecasters exhibit a similar variance (albeit distorted by some estimation error) and equal covariances of 0. However, the focus of $\hat{\lambda}^*$ on the absolute values of $\hat{\Sigma}$, rather than its relative properties, prevents this alignment from being fully utilized, resulting in an overall sub-optimal forecast combination.

4 Conclusion and Outlook

Shrinking an error sample covariance matrix to a less flexible target matrix and subsequently deriving weights from this shrunk matrix, rather than the instable sample covariance matrix itself, enhances the accuracy of a combined forecast. The benefits associated with this shrinkage heavily rely on making appropriate selections for both the shrinkage target and a suitable shrinkage intensity. However, determining how to make these selections remains an unresolved issue.

Our findings indicate that a target matrix must strike a balance. On the one hand, it must be sufficiently flexible to capture the true error covariance structure to some extend; otherwise the induced bias prevents sufficient shrinkage. On the other hand, excessive flexibility should be avoided to prevent overfitting of the weights.

As in practical settings the true covariance matrix is unknown and might have a more complex structure, arguably most target candidates will have, in some respects, inappropriate levels of flexibility with respects to certain characteristics of the covariance matrix. For example, there could be distinct groups of forecasters with similar within-group correlations but dissimilar between-group correlations. Additionally, a matrix might accurately capture the diagonal structure while inadequately representing the off-diagonal elements, or vice versa.

Our analyses demonstrate that the shrinkage level, which minimizes the Frobenius norm between estimated and true covariance matrices, does not necessarily translate to optimal weights that minimize the MSE of combined forecasts.

Considering the true (yet unknown) structure of the covariance matrix and the chosen target matrix, the deviations from MSE-optimal shrinkage are quite substantial.

The aim of this study was to systematically analyze the inherent challenges associated with shrinking covariance matrices in forecast combination, laying the groundwork for the systematic development of suitable shrinkage methods and criteria in future research.

While there are several open directions that can be followed, our future research will aim at providing further insights into the relationships of targets, their flexibility, and optimal shrinkage intensities. Additionally, we will investigate the effectiveness of machine learning-based tuning procedures, such as nested cross-validation, in selecting targets and tuning shrinkage levels.

The study's limitations encompass several factors: it assumes efficient individual forecasts with errors distributed as multivariate normal, and it does not account for structural breaks, thus assuming homoscedasticity. Additionally, the study does not address block-structured matrices, which are required for specific combination techniques such as shrinkage towards the subset average.

References

1. Bates, J. M., & Granger, C. W. (1969). The combination of forecasts. *Journal of the Operational Research Society, 20*(4), 451–468.
2. Baumeister, C., & Kilian, L. (2015). Forecasting the real price of oil in a changing world: A forecast combination approach. *Journal of Business & Economic Statistics, 33*(3), 338–351.
3. Blanc, S. M., & Setzer, T. (2016). When to choose the simple average in forecast combination. *Journal of Business Research, 69*(10), 3951–3962.
4. Blanc, S. M., & Setzer, T. (2020). Bias-variance trade-off and shrinkage of weights in forecast combination. *Management Science, 66*(12), 5720–5737.
5. Chan, F., & Pauwels, L. L. (2018). Some theoretical results on forecast combinations. *International Journal of Forecasting, 34*(1), 64–74.
6. Claeskens, G., Magnus, J. R., Vasnev, A. L., & Wang, W. (2016). The forecast combination puzzle: A simple theoretical explanation. *International Journal of Forecasting, 32*(3), 754–762.
7. Clemen, R. T. (1989). Combining forecasts: A review and annotated bibliography. *International Journal of Forecasting, 5*(4), 559–583.
8. Clemen, R. T., & Winkler, R. L. (1986). Combining economic forecasts. *Journal of Business & Economic Statistics, 4*(1), 39–46.
9. Endelman, J. B., Jannink, J. L. (2012). Shrinkage estimation of the realized relationship matrix. *G3: Genes|Genomes|Genetics, 2*(11), 1405–1413.
10. Fildes, R., Goodwin, P., Lawrence, M., & Nikolopoulos, K. (2009). Effective forecasting and judgmental adjustments: An empirical evaluation and strategies for improvement in supply-chain planning. *International Journal of Forecasting, 25*(1), 3–23.
11. Guo, S. M., He, J., Monnier, N., Sun, G., Wohland, T., & Bathe, M. (2012). Bayesian approach to the analysis of fluorescence correlation spectroscopy data II: Application to simulated and in vitro data. *Analytical Chemistry, 84*(9), 3880–3888.

12. Ledoit, O., & Wolf, M. (2003a). Honey, I shrunk the sample covariance matrix. UPF economics and business working paper (691).
13. Ledoit, O., & Wolf, M. (2003). Improved estimation of the covariance matrix of stock returns with an application to portfolio selection. *Journal of Empirical Finance, 10*(5), 603–621.
14. Lee, A. C., Lee, J. C., & Lee, C. F. (2009). *Financial analysis, planning and forecasting: Theory and application*. World Scientific Publishing Company.
15. Makridakis, S., & Hibon, M. (2000). The m3-competition: Results, conclusions and implications. *International Journal of Forecasting, 16*(4), 451–476.
16. Makridakis, S., Spiliotis, E., & Assimakopoulos, V. (2018). The m4 competition: Results, findings, conclusion and way forward. *International Journal of Forecasting, 34*(4), 802–808.
17. Makridakis, S., Spiliotis, E., & Assimakopoulos, V. (2020). The m4 competition: 100,000 time series and 61 forecasting methods. *International Journal of Forecasting, 36*(1), 54–74.
18. Marcellino, M. (2004). Forecast pooling for European macroeconomic variables. *Oxford Bulletin of Economics and Statistics, 66*(1), 91–112.
19. Newbold, P., & Granger, C. W. (1974). Experience with forecasting univariate time series and the combination of forecasts. *Journal of the Royal Statistical Society: Series A (General), 137*(2), 131–146.
20. Roccazzella, F., Gambetti, P., & Vrins, F. (2022). Optimal and robust combination of forecasts via constrained optimization and shrinkage. *International Journal of Forecasting, 38*(1), 97–116.
21. Schäfer, J., & Strimmer, K. (2005). A shrinkage approach to large-scale covariance matrix estimation and implications for functional genomics. *Statistical Applications in Genetics and Molecular Biology, 4*(1).
22. Schulz, F., Setzer, T., & Balla, N. (2022). Linear hybrid shrinkage of weights for forecast selection and combination. In *Proceedings of the 55th Hawaii International Conference on System Sciences*.
23. Smith, J., & Wallis, K. F. (2009). A simple explanation of the forecast combination puzzle. *Oxford Bulletin of Economics and Statistics, 71*(3), 331–355.
24. Stein, C. (1956). Inadmissibility of the usual estimator for the mean of a multivariate normal distribution. In *Proceedings of the Third Berkeley Symposium on Mathematical Statistics and Probability, Volume 1: Contributions to the Theory of Statistics* (Vol. 3, pp. 197–207). University of California Press.
25. Stock, J. H., Watson, M. W. (1998). A comparison of linear and nonlinear univariate models for forecasting macroeconomic time series.
26. Stock, J. H., & Watson, M. W. (2004). Combination forecasts of output growth in a seven-country data set. *Journal of Forecasting, 23*(6), 405–430.
27. Stock, J. H., & Watson, M. W (2012). Generalized shrinkage methods for forecasting using many predictors. *Journal of Business & Economic Statistics, 30*(4), 481–493.
28. Syntetos, A. A., Boylan, J. E., & Disney, S. M. (2009). Forecasting for inventory planning: A 50-year review. *Journal of the Operational Research Society, 60*(sup1), S149–S160.
29. Syntetos, A. A., Babai, Z., Boylan, J. E., Kolassa, S., & Nikolopoulos, K. (2016). Supply chain forecasting: Theory, practice, their gap and the future. *European Journal of Operational Research, 252*(1), 1–26.
30. Timmermann, A. (2006). *Forecast combinations. Handbook of economic forecasting* (Vol. 1, pp. 135–196).
31. Wang, X., Hyndman, R. J., Li, F., & Kang, Y. (2023). Forecast combinations: An over 50-year review. *International Journal of Forecasting, 39*(4), 1518–1547.
32. Winkler, R. L., & Makridakis, S. (1983). The combination of forecasts. *Journal of the Royal Statistical Society: Series A (General), 146*(2), 150–157.

Reinforcement Learning for Integration of Autonomous On-Demand Services with Conventional Public Transport

Robert Janus, Dominik Theilen, Abdumalik Mamatkulov, Di Zhang, and Bastian Amberg

Abstract This paper introduces a novel automated decision-making system for integrating autonomous Mobility-on-Demand (AMOD) services with conventional public transport systems, focusing on two main optimization tasks: vehicle order matching (VOM) and vehicle relocation (RE). In VOM, the system decides which active orders are serviced by AMOD vehicles, assigns idle vehicles to these orders and decides which direct or combined routes with existing public transport should be executed. RE focuses on moving idle vehicles to better locations to boost network efficiency and ensure vehicles are optimally positioned for present and upcoming needs. Implemented in a Reinforcement Learning framework, this paper compares Q-Learning (QL) and Deep Reinforcement Learning (DRL) approaches to enhance operational efficiency in urban transport. The evaluation, conducted with real-world data from New York City, demonstrates that Reinforcement Learning significantly outperforms automated non-learning approaches, highlighting its suitability for enhancing AMOD services and their integration with existing public transportation systems.

R. Janus (✉) · D. Theilen · A. Mamatkulov · D. Zhang · B. Amberg (✉)
Freie Universität Berlin, Department of Information Systems, Berlin, Germany
e-mail: robert.janus@fu-berlin.de

B. Amberg
e-mail: bastian.amberg@fu-berlin.de

D. Theilen
e-mail: dominik.theilen@fu-berlin.de

A. Mamatkulov
e-mail: abdumalik.mamatkulov@fu-berlin.de

D. Zhang
e-mail: di.zhang@fu-berlin.de

C. M. Flath et al. (eds.), *Artificial Intelligence, Data, and Decision-Making*, Lecture Notes in Information Systems and Organisation 82,
https://doi.org/10.1007/978-3-032-08480-4_22

1 Introduction

The transition from motorized individual transport to public transportation marks a significant, climate-positive transformation that is already being advanced in various places [1]. This process has progressed further in city centers, thanks to well-developed public transport infrastructure. In contrast, suburban areas continue to rely on private vehicles or Mobility-on-Demand (MOD) services such as Uber/Bolt [2, 3], indicating a disparity in the advancement of sustainable mobility solutions across different urban environments. The use of autonomous vehicles in public transport is currently being investigated in numerous pilot projects (see, e.g., in Germany [4, 5]). Enhancing the conventional line-based public transportation system by incorporating (electric) autonomous Mobility-on-Demand (AMOD) services not only facilitates the creation of integrated travel chains combining AMOD and existing public transport networks but also allows for more direct and shorter routes exclusively via AMOD. This innovation promises to increase public transport's efficiency and effectiveness [6–10], significantly contributing to the transformation of the current transportation ecosystem [11, 12]. In this way, public transport providers can potentially replace less profitable line services with AMOD services and also make public transport more attractive to passengers by offering faster travel times, especially in peripheral locations and at off-peak times.

The integration of AMOD services into public transport brings many challenges. In this work, we focus on automatic decision-making for public transportation companies during operation. We examine how a fleet of AMOD vehicles can be coordinated in real-time to efficiently meet individual travel needs and create a travel chain with conventional public transportation: First, the dynamics of travel requests (orders) from passengers must be taken into account. Orders may vary depending on the time of day, day of the week, and season. For all orders, the starting location, destination, and dispatching time must be processed, where in large cities, this can result in hundreds of thousands of data entries per day. Second, the final position after ordering an AMOD vehicle plays an important role in reducing the idling rate of the vehicles and completing further orders. Therefore, continuous planning of vehicle orders based on travel requests data and implementing vehicle repositioning when necessary are needed to optimize positions of AMOD vehicles. Third, passengers should immediately receive feedback on whether their ride request has been accepted or not, necessitating real-time execution with low response times. This feature is crucial for enhancing user experience, ensuring passengers can make informed decisions about their travel plans without unnecessary delays. In summary, automatic decision-making requires considering existing public transport networks, real-time travel requests, real-time AMOD vehicle positions, and the implementation of the optimization tasks vehicle order matching (VOM) and vehicle relocation (RE). VOM encompasses three sub-tasks: order dispatching to determine which orders can be served, assigning specific vehicles to orders, and deciding whether to use direct routes (service directly from origin to destination) or combined routes with public transportation. RE focuses on positioning idle vehicles in locations where they can best meet future demand, optimizing the overall efficiency of the transport network.

To address real-time order processing, dynamic solution approaches, such as Reinforcement Learning, are extensively discussed in the literature for improving MOD services [13–16]. However, the integration of MOD services with existing public transport is only superficially addressed in the literature [13, 17]. For example, [13] consider the combination of taxi services and Metro, but only from the perspective of a taxi company and taking into account a simplified public transport network. To support the integration of AMOD services into public transport, based on existing literature [13, 14, 18, 19], we propose a self-learning automated decision-making system based on reinforcement learning techniques: a Q-Learning-based algorithm (QL) and a Deep Reinforcement Learning (DRL)-based algorithm. According to the starting/end point of the orders, the algorithm generates a direct route and multiple combined routes linked with the existing public transport network at transfer points (station to transfer from AMOD to conventional public transport). In each time period, the agent (an idle vehicle) will undertake one of three actions: (1) accept a suitable order based on its location, (2) remain idle, or (3) execute vehicle relocation to better position itself for future orders.

To improve the accessibility and efficiency of public transportation, we consider the perspective of two stakeholders: passengers and public transport companies. Thus, the research question is how to coordinate a fleet of AMOD vehicles so that individual travel requests can be efficiently served for both the passenger and the public transport company. The created multi-criteria optimization framework is subsequently tested on real data from New York City. The paper proceeds with the current state of research, explaining the Reinforcement Learning based automated decision-making framework and presents the results of the experiments, followed by the conclusion and outlook.

2 State of the Research

A selection of pivotal papers about automated decision-making for (autonomous) on-demand services, subjected to comparative analysis on multiple dimensions, are systematically presented in Table 1, highlighting the nuanced differences and similarities among the studies. Differences can be articulated from three perspectives: the content level of the problem considered, the included optimization tasks, and the type of the solution method to fulfill these tasks.

On the content level, two different problems are considered. Most studies focus solely on MOD services like taxis or Uber, while only a few [13, 17] investigate a coupling with existing public transportation services, but from the perspective of a private MOD operator. None of these studies deal explicitly with AMOD services. Regarding the optimization task, we distinguish between VOM and RE. Most studies

Table 1 Tabular comparison of state of the art approaches to solve MOD problems

Paper	Content		Optimization task		Method		
	MOD	MOD & PT	VOM	RE	Exact Method	QL	DRL
[20–23]	X		X		X		
[14, 16, 24]	X		X				X
[18]	X		X	X			X
[15]	X			X			X
[13]		X	X			X	
[17]		X		X	X		
This work		X	X	X		X	X

focus on optimizing one of these tasks, especially VOM. Only [18] optimizes both tasks in a combined solution approach. This is because RE poses an optimization challenge, where the ideal strategy is either cost or time-efficient, which conflicts with optimal VOM due to the negative impacts of empty rides.

On the level of solution methods, two approaches are commonly used: Exact methods and Reinforcement Learning. Reinforcement Learning is further divided into QL and DRL techniques. Exact methods such as Branch-and-Cut [25] are valued for delivering optimal solutions but are limited by excessive computational demands, especially for complex issues, as highlighted by [20, 21]. They are generally applicable only to smaller problems or as components of larger systems, rendering them ineffective for the dynamic challenges addressed in this paper. On the other hand, studies by [13–16] highlight Reinforcement Learning's effectiveness in traffic management and planning, capable of optimizing long-term outcomes like matching vehicles with passengers in real-time. Reinforcement Learning excels in dynamic scheduling, improving metrics such as reduced passenger wait times, balanced bus loads, and shorter travel durations. However, its decision-making process lacks transparency, posing challenges to interpretability. [13] applies QL to enhance taxi platform profits by integrating with the New York subway, viewing it as an advanced MOD problem. They offer pertinent findings on combining MOD services with public transport, which is applicable to our study. Their approach creates direct and combined routes for each order, evaluated through a state-value function and profitability. They then employ a bipartite allocation model to optimally assign vehicles to orders, demonstrating superior performance over baseline models. In contrast, [14] unveiled the DRL based CVNet framework for optimizing VOM in ride-sharing services. They closely mirror [13]'s strategy but diverge significantly in the computation of the state-value function, where [14] adopt the Double Deep Q-Networks (DDQN) approach to estimate the state-values from the current state, showcasing enhanced efficiency against numerous reinforcement learning models, including those grounded in QL and other DRL approaches. [18] propose the V1D3 Framework, which integrates a DRL algorithm for optimizing value functions to synergize VOM and RE. Their approach allows for the repositioning of vehicles who have been idling for a certain period, selecting a subset of potential locations for each vehicle and stochastically deciding their destinations based on the weighted, discounted state-values of new locations.

To the best of our knowledge, this is the first work that addresses the integration of (A)MOD services into the existing public transportation system, taking into account the perspective of public transport companies and passengers, and optimizing both VOM and RE. Furthermore, this work compares different Reinforcement Learning approaches.

3 Methodology

This section describes the proposed framework for automated decision-making, starting with the considered objectives in the first step, the influence and use of Reinforcement Learning in the second step, and a description of the entire system in the third step.

3.1 Objectives and Target Criteria

In this study, we address a complex multi-criteria optimization problem focusing on passenger transportation efficiency and cost efficiency for public transport companies. For each time interval during operation, the optimization tasks consist of dispatching idle vehicles to pick up active orders (VOM) and carrying out vehicle relocations (RE). Considering the perspectives of both stakeholders, the two objectives are: (1) maximizing total time savings for passengers in comparison to using public transport without AMOD services, thereby enhancing service quality and user satisfaction; (2) minimizing operational costs without passenger transportation, i.e. minimizing idling costs, which arises from idling for orders and carrying out relocation tasks without passengers. This balancing act requires a sophisticated approach to solution development.

To compare solution approaches, we consider evaluation criteria that cover both perspectives. From the passengers' perspective, the time savings compared to using only public transportation without AMOD services are considered. From the perspective of public transportation companies, the number of accepted orders per day, the idling rate (the proportion of time when no orders were served), the proportion of combined routes, and the spatial distribution of vehicles are evaluated.

3.2 Use of Reinforcement Learning

To accurately model and solve the dynamic dispatching and vehicle relocation problem, we employ a model based Markov Decision Process (MDP) similar to [13] and [18]. The MDP facilitates a comprehensive representation of the sequential decision-making environment, where each decision impacts future states and choices. Within this framework, vehicles are conceptualized as agents, governed by a central policy π that maps observed environmental states to actions. These actions encompass the selection of orders and the determination of transportation modes—either direct routes or the aforementioned combined routes. The components of the MDP are defined as follows:

State ($s \in S$) :Combination of the current time interval and a vehicle's location, capturing the temporal dynamics and operational context of the dispatching process.
Action ($a \in A$): Actions include serving orders in a direct route, initiating a combined route, remaining idle or executing relocation. The choice of action is influenced by the need to optimize both time savings for passengers and cost efficiency for operators.
Reward (r): Either way the time reduction in seconds in case of a route or idling cost for idling or relocation.
State transition probability ($P^a_{s,s_{next}}$): The probability of transitioning from a state s to the next state s_{next} is determined through simulation of the learned policy.

To solve the MDP, a policy π_i must be found for a vehicle i that maximizes the expected cumulative reward $E_{\pi_i}[J^i_t | S = s^i_t]$ in each time interval t, where $J^i_t = \sum_{t'=t}^{T} r^i_{t'}$, T is the termination time, $r^i_{t'}$ is the reward for vehicle i in interval t', and s^i_t is the state of vehicle i in interval t.

From the framework's perspective, the objective function is max $E_\pi[\sum_{i \in V} J^i_t | S = s_t]$ with the state s_t and the set of vehicles V. Assuming the independence of the vehicles [26], the function can be approximated by max $\sum_{i \in V} E_{\pi_i}[J^i_t | S = s^i_t]$. To simplify the problem, it is assumed that all vehicles share the same policy π, hence $E_{\pi_i}[J^i_t | S = s^i_t] \approx Q_\pi(s^i_t, a^i_t)$, where $Q_\pi(s^i_t, a^i_t)$ represents the Q-value of action a^i_t in state s^i_t. Assuming the independence of actions and states of the vehicles, the objective function of the MDP can be approximated by max $\sum_{i \in V} Q_\pi(s^i_t, a^i_t)$. The objective function indicates that in each interval t, actions a_t must be performed by the vehicles to maximize the sum of the Q-values. The Q-function $Q_\pi(s_t, a_t)$ can be approximated by $r(s_t, a_t) + V_\pi(s_{next})$ with $r(s_t, a_t)$ as the reward for action a_t, s_{next} as the state after performing the action, and $V_\pi(s_t)$ as the state-value function. To limit the influence of future rewards, the discount factor $\gamma' = \gamma^{\frac{t_{next}-t}{\gamma_{weight}}}$ is introduced, where γ is the discount rate and γ_{weight} is the discount weight, which weights the influence of the time difference $t_{next} - t$. Thus, the Q-value of an action a_t in state s_t is approximated by $r(s_t, a_t) + \gamma' V_\pi(s_{next})$ (cf. [13]).

The optimal selection of actions by the agents in the VOM is described by [13] as a simplified integer problem. For efficiency reasons, we transformed this into the

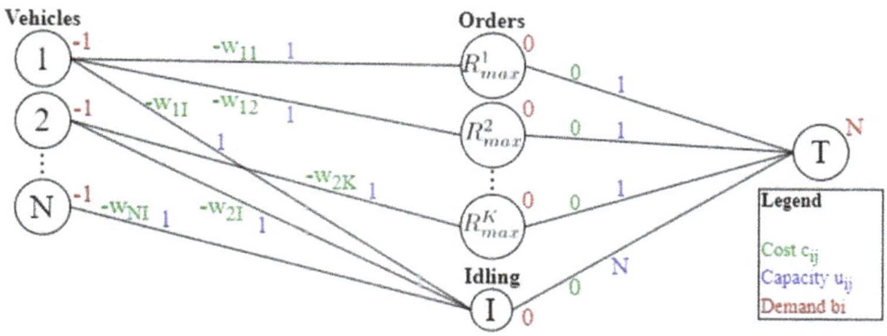

Fig. 1 Network view of the created minimum-cost flow problem **P1** for VOM

Minimum-Cost Flow problem **P1**, which is graphically described by Fig. 1. The network is composed of nodes and edges, with nodes encompassing vehicles, actions and a helper node T. Formulated as a standard Min-Cost-Flow problem, edges connecting vehicles to actions indicate possible matches, whereas edges between actions and T ensure that each vehicle is allocated and that each order is serviced by only one vehicle.

Actions include both the routes R^k_{max} with the highest weight w_{ik} for each order $k \in \{1, .., K\}$, as well as a central idling action I. Since not all orders can be served by all vehicles, there are only edges between compatible vehicle order matches. The weight w_{ij} of vehicle i and action j is determined by the Q-value (state value) of the state s [13], where r is the direct reward, represented by the time savings from fulfilling the order or idling cost when idling, and $\gamma' V(s_{next})$, the indirect expected future reward represented as the discounted state value of the next state:

$$w_{ij} = Q(s^i, j) = r + \gamma' V(s_{next}). \tag{1}$$

For RE, we adhere to the methodology proposed by [18]. Vehicles that have not accepted an order for a certain period C are repositioned. The probability that a specific location l is selected for repositioning based on the current position i is described by

$$p(s^i, s^l) = \frac{w(l)}{\sum_{h \in O(s^i)} w(h)}, \; w(x) = \gamma'(|V_{min}(s^i)| + V(s^x) + 1) \tag{2}$$

Various alternative locations $l \in O(s^i)$ based on current state s^i within a specified radius are evaluated, with the selection of the new position being made through weighted randomness, guided by the state value of next state s^l. $|V_{min}(s^i)|$ describes the magnitude of the minimal state value from all locations l and is added to all state values $V(s^l)$ to avoid negative values for the calculation. The sum is then multiplied by the discount factor γ', which decreases as the travel time $t_l - t_i$ of the route increases. This ensures that more distant destinations are selected less frequently than closer ones, to reduce the higher idling costs.This strategy aims to optimize the positioning of vehicles to more effectively meet anticipated demands. [18] utilize exponential functions for weight calculations. Given the significantly higher state values that can arise in the MDP we are considering, we have adapted this to use linear functions instead. This adjustment ensures our model's applicability and responsiveness to a wider range of state values.

The state value function learns by feeding back the observed results of the VOM into it after each iteration, with the goal of finding an almost optimal policy π. Thus, each implemented vehicle order match can be viewed as a transition $[s, a, s_{next}, r]$, where the state value function can be updated according to the Temporal Difference Rule [19]:

$$V(s) = V(s) + \alpha(r + \gamma' V(s_{next}) - V(s)) \tag{3}$$

Here, α describes the learning rate parameter, and γ' the discount factor. The goal of the training phase is for the state value function to eventually not change significantly, which would mean that an optimal policy π has been found. However, this is not always the case, which is why it is recommended to limit the duration of the training from the outset. Since the described MDP is model-based, policy-function approximating methods are excluded. Instead, two types of value-function approximations are used to implement the state value function: tabular QL and a DRL approach.

Q-Learning: QL describes a dynamic programming method in which the state-value function is represented by a state-value table, where the state-values contained in the cells are updated in each iteration through the Temporal Difference Rule. As [13] use QL, we have largely adopted their approach. In their model, they consider a table with cells for all combinations of zones and time intervals, corresponding to the state-space S. To cope with the magnitudes of the state-values caused by the extended problem setting in our work, we integrated a parameter to limit these to $\pm V_{max}$. A disadvantage of the QL method lies in the discretization of the state-space. Predefined discrete intervals for space and time must be used, which can limit the course of the solution process.

Deep Reinforcement Learning: In DRL, deep neural networks enhance the reinforcement learning process, with various approaches differing significantly. To ensure comparability with the Q-Learning method by [13], we use Double Deep Q-Networks (DDQN), which approximate state values through regression [14, 18]. DDQN employs two networks: the Main Network predicts state values, while the Target Network evaluates these predictions. The Main Network's weights are adjusted via backpropagation using Mean-Squared Temporal-Difference Error, and periodically synchronized with the Target Network to stabilize the solution process [14]. We adopt the approach of [18], combining offline training with online learning. During offline policy evaluation, networks with the same architecture as those used online are trained on historical order trajectories over various time intervals $\mathcal{E}$. In the online mode, the weights of the online networks (ω) are combined with those of the offline networks ($1 - \omega$) using a weighted average to enhance learning stability. The time intervals $\mathcal{E}$ are determined through a dynamic programming method by [27], identifying order changes over time. With time components integrated into the networks, only the zone information is needed as input. Zones are discretized spaces. [18] originally used a multilayer hexagonal grid for location quantization, but we employ numerical IDs of the zones as input instead of continuous coordinates for practicality, with the disadvantage of losing some information about the proximity of zones to each other.

3.3 Automated Decision-Making System

To solve the initially described problem (see Sect. 3.1), the developed MDP is integrated into an automated decision-making system similar to that in [13]. The system makes decisions, observes the effects, and subsequently adjusts its policy accordingly (see Fig. 2). For the experiments, the system operates on a simulation of reality. However, the system also supports online processing, where the simulation would be replaced by the real environment. It operates iteratively in seven stages for each considered time interval, i.e., in this work, for each minute of the day. After collecting active orders (1), for each order, a direct route and possible combination routes with existing public transport network are generated (2). The underlying public transport network is generated in a pre-processing step, with the fastest routes for all pairs of stations (at different time intervals) being stored to reduce computational effort. For combined routes, we focus on the First-Mile problem, similar to [13]. Thus, only the journey from the starting point to a transfer point in the network can be serviced by AMOD services. The challenge in generating combined routes lies in the combinatorial complexity, where [13] consider all possible pairs of stations in a simplified public transport network as potential combination routes. To maximize the capacity utilization of the existing public transportation infrastructure and to keep AMOD trips short, we adjusted this process by only considering stations at the start and end points of an order that represent the nearest station on a line. In a hypothetical public transport network of 300 stations and 20 lines, this reduces the set of possible combination routes from 300^2 to 20^2.

In the next stage (3), pairs of possible actions (routes and idling) and idling vehicles are formed. The challenge here lies in the correct weighting of the pairs, where the state-value function from the reinforcement learning process is responsible for that. In the following stage (4), the vehicle order matches are determined. Here, we have reformulated the integer problem described by [13] into the Minimum-Cost Flow problem **P1**, to then solve it efficiently and optimally through the Network Simplex Algorithm. The resulting vehicle order matches, however, are identical to the approach used by [13]. In stage (5), the central difference between the framework according to [13] and this work lies in the repositioning of long-idling vehicles. This is performed analogously to the method outlined in [18], where only vehicles that have not been assigned for a specific period, in this case, over 2 min, are repositioned. The destination is determined through weighted random selection based on the state value function, ensuring that vehicle deployment optimally aligns with predicted demand patterns and enhances the system's overall efficiency. In the next stage (6), the

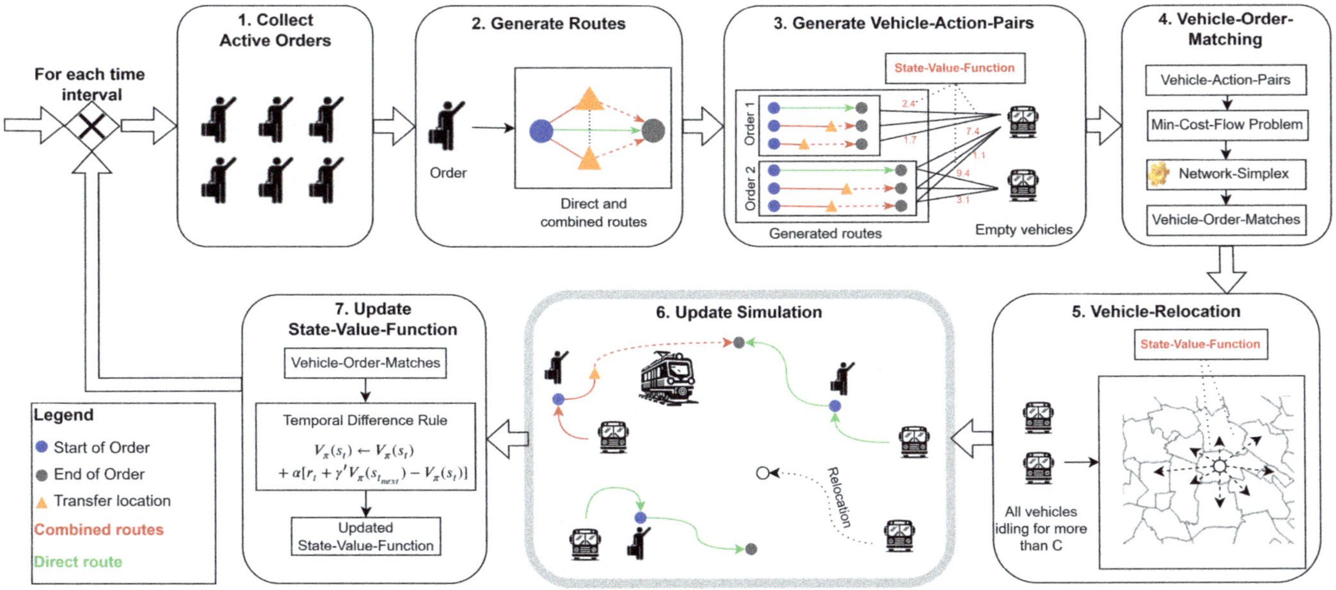

Fig. 2 This illustration depicts the iterative multi-step process of the automated decision-making system. The structure is similar to [13], with the addition of Stage 5 (RE). In practical application, Stage 6 would include real world movements of AMOD vehicles and passengers

Table 2 Created software artifacts for automated decision-making

Artifact	Underlying methodology	Supported tasks
BL	Baseline, non-learning approach	VOM
QL	Approach based on Q-Learning	VOM
QLRE	QL with relocation	VOM and RE
DRL	Approach based on Deep Reinforcement Learning	VOM
DRLRE	DRL with relocation	VOM and RE

calculated vehicle order matches and repositioning are embedded into the simulation, allowing them to proceed to the next iteration. In a real-world deployment of the system, this stage would be eliminated. In such a case, the decisions made by the system would be sent to the actual vehicles. The rest of the system would not need to be altered for real-world application. Subsequently, in stage (7), the state value function is updated as described in the previous section.

4 Experiments

In order to test the proposed automatic decision-making system, different QL- and DRL-based software artifacts were implemented (see Table 2). In addition, a baseline approach (BL) was created, which works according to the proposed framework, but without learning components. It works like a myopic system that finds the best possible solution for each time interval without taking possible future developments into account.

The artifacts were tested in various scenarios, with different numbers of orders and vehicles serving these orders. In the following, we present two series of experiments: (1) all artifacts are compared on an order dataset that contains only 5% of the original data, (2) the artifacts BL, QL, and QLRE are compared on the full dataset, where the influence of the number of vehicles is examined in more detail.

The artifacts were tested with real data from New York City. As order dataset, the NYC High Volume For-Hire dataset from the period of July 10 to July 31, 2023, which contains an average of 600,000 orders per day, was used.[1] Thus, the experiments covered all of NYC (excluding Staten Island), whereas the Yellow Cab dataset often used in the literature (e.g., by [13]) is mainly limited to Manhattan and the airports. For the public transportation network, only the NYC Metro network was considered, as bus lines offer significantly lower capacity, which might be further strained by the new AMOD services. The framework was implemented in Python, with the Network Simplex Algorithm using the ortools library (C++) and the Deep Neural Networks for the DRL/DRLRE artifacts implemented with PyTorch. Testing

[1] TLC trip record data: https://www.nyc.gov/site/tlc/about/tlc-trip-record-data.page.

Table 3 Average waiting times[4] on transfer points over the day

12:00 a.m.–6:30 a.m.	6:30 a.m.–9:30 a.m.	9:30 a.m.–3:30 p.m.	3:30 p.m.–8:00 p.m.	8:00 p.m.–12:00 a.m.
10 min	2.5 min	5 min	2.5 min	7.5 min

was conducted on an Intel Core i7 13700k with 32GB RAM. Each artefact was trained on two weeks of the data set. After this training, the test phase, which included the following week of the dataset, was carried out.

4.1 Parameter Settings

There are several parameters to emulate the operational environment of the proposed automatic decision-making system and to influence its behavior. We distinguish between procedural parameters, which are generally used for Reinforcement Learning, and operational parameters for controlling the results related to the target criteria mentioned in Sect. 3.1. Parameters were set through sensitivity analyses, labelled by *(min. value; max. value; number of tests)*, with the following values applicable for the scenario with 2000 vehicles and a full order dataset.

Procedural parameters: Key parameters for each Reinforcement Learning method include the learning rate α and the discount rate γ. The discount rate was set to 0.95, as in [13], while for the learning rate, a value of 0.01 *(0.001; 0.02; 8)* was used to achieve good results with less training. We added a limitation of the state-value expressions V_{max} to ± 1000 *(30; 10000; 12)*, to limit the influence of extremely good or bad zones. For the QL, the state-value table was divided into intervals of 30 min, using the NYC Taxi Zones for the zones.[2] Relevant for the DDQN method (used in DRL/RE) are additionally a synchronization rate between Main and Target Network (every 60 iterations) and the hyperparameter $\omega = 0.4$ (we refer to [18] for further explanations).

Operational parameters: Waiting times on transfer points for combined routes depend on the time of day, as described in Table 3. Entry and exit times into and out of the metro system are set at 2 min each, as in [13].

Table 4 describes further parameters that are already used in the literature. In addition, we introduce idling costs (5 per iteration) *(1; 60; 15)*, which penalize not serving orders to make less frequented zones less attractive. For RE, we consider a relocation radius (10km) *(1; 20; 9)*, and a maximum idling duration (2.5 min) [18]. Further, a discount factor for direct routes was introduced (0.5) *(0.1; 1; 18)* to control the proportion of direct routes in the solutions.

[2] NYC Taxi Zones: https://data.cityofnewyork.us/Transportation/NYC-Taxi-Zones/d3c5-ddgc.

Table 4 Further operational parameters of the framework (see [13] for detailed descriptions)

Vehicle speed	Walking speed	L_1	L_2	L_S	Order expiry duration	Pickup distance threshold
6.33 m/sec	1 m/sec	0	30 min	60	2 min	1900 m

Table 5 Evaluation criteria for 100 autonomous vehicles and 5% of the dataset

Evaluation criteria	BL	QL	QLRE	DRL	DRLRE
Time savings per vehicle per hour (in minutes)	56	64	62	48	34
Accepted orders per day	4380	4620	5621	6998	5778
Proportion combined routes	31%	35%	30%	34%	35%
Idling rate (incl. RE)	47%	52%	45% (29%)	39%	50% (26%)

4.2 Results

In the first series of experiments, 100 vehicles and 5% of the dataset were used. Table 5 compares all evaluation criteria. It clearly shows that the BL performance can be improved by QL/DRL approaches. Furthermore, QLRE performs better (or similarly) than all other artifacts in every evaluation criterion. The results of QL/QLRE and DRL/DRLRE are indifferent. Using QL/QLRE, the calculation of one iteration described by Fig. 2 takes up to two seconds, depending on the model's size. DRL/DRLRE requires up to 30 s. For this reason, the following tests focus on QL/QLRE.

In the second series of experiments, the entire dataset was considered. Table 6 shows the results for 100 and 2000 vehicles. When using 100 vehicles, QL and QLRE perform significantly better than BL, but no significant difference can be seen between QL and QLRE. It is obvious that with a higher number of vehicles, considerably more orders can be served. For this case, QLRE, i.e., the simultaneous

Table 6 Evaluation criteria for 100 and 2000 autonomous vehicles and 100% of the dataset

	100 vehicles			2000 vehicles		
Evaluation criteria	BL	QL	QLRE	BL	QL	QLRE
Time savings per vehicle per hour (in minutes)	120	163	157	58	25	104
Accepted orders per day	5971	8425	8211	60144	26459	141353
Proportion combined routes	38%	56%	57%	39%	49%	56%
Idling rate (incl. RE)	12%	11%	12% (3%)	55%	84%	27% (16%)

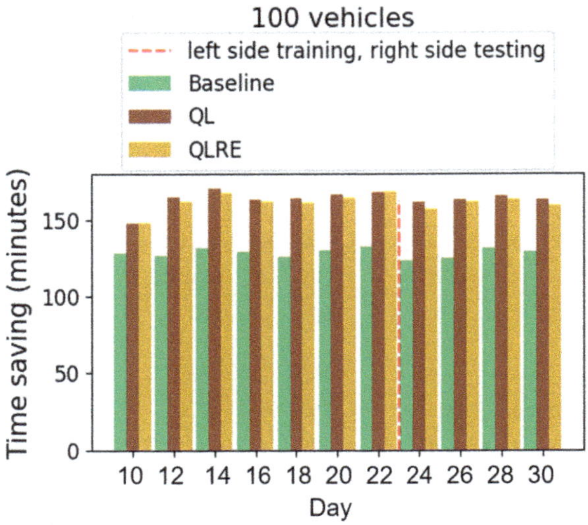

Fig. 3 Criterion "Time saving per vehicle per hour" for 100 vehicles

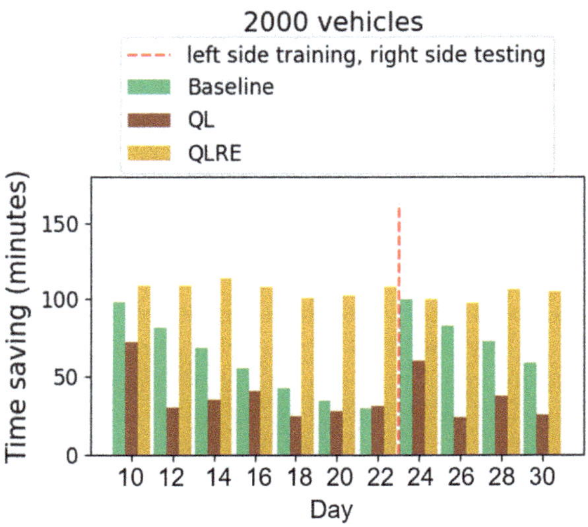

Fig. 4 Criterion "Time saving per vehicle per hour" for 2000 vehicles

consideration of VOM and RE, shows a significant positive impact on the overall performance.

Figures 3 and 4 provide further details for evaluating *time savings per vehicle per hour* (the time that passengers can save compared to using the conventional public transport network alone). QL and QLRE show a clear learning curve in Fig. 3, which extends over approx. five days and after which an increase in performance of 15% compared to the initial value is recorded. Figure 4 shows the same evaluation criterion for 2000 vehicles, where QLRE performs significantly better than QL and BL.

From a passenger perspective, the average time saved per accepted order is 36.5 min compared to a trip using only public transport (with median, upper quartile, and lower quartile of 31.32, 49.00, and 17.91 min), according to the QLRE model.

4.3 Evaluation

We demonstrated that the proposed QLRE approach performs very well, especially with many vehicles. However, it requires intensive parameter tuning. Settings that work well for smaller datasets do not necessarily scale. Idling cost, learning rate, and direct trip discount factor significantly impact the results. For example, the balance between idle costs and discount factor is essential. Both high and low idle costs reduce passengers' time savings. A low discount factor increases accepted orders but reduces time savings.

Furthermore, the results indicate that the DRL approach is less computationally efficient than a comparable QL approach. Nonetheless, the DRL approach still holds potential for enhancement, although it is generally more difficult to apply due to its higher complexity. For instance, the method proposed by [18] leverages additional information regarding the spatial proximity of zones in the process. The proposed approaches can be applied to other cities' public transport systems, but need to be re-trained for each city to adapt to its unique characteristics and customer patterns. Parameters such as the vehicle speed-based relocation radius need adjustment for new conditions.

5 Conclusion and Outlook

We developed an automated decision-making system that enables the coupling of AMOD services with regular public transport. The system is designed to make two types of decisions while considering the perspective of passengers and public transport companies: how to allocate available vehicles to currently active orders (VOM), and how to reposition idle vehicles so that they can serve future demand (RE). According to the current state of the art, Reinforcement Learning is used to tackle the dynamics in passenger demand.

The proposed framework iteratively solves the two optimization tasks VOM and RE, and systematically enhances the optimization through Reinforcement Learning by integrating experiences to predict travel requests. It implements two types of Reinforcement Learning: Q-Learning (QL) similar to [13], and Deep Reinforcement Learning (DRL) similar to [18].

The experiments yield three central insights. First, QL/DRL approaches are superior to a basic approach (BL) that supports decision-making without taking possible future developments into account. Second, the simultaneous consideration of VOM and RE leads to an improvement in the results across all considered target criteria.

Third, the pursued QL approaches proved to be more suitable for the problem at hand. The longer runtime of the DRL method, especially in larger problem cases, is an obstacle to its use.

From a methodological point of view, the framework could be easily implemented in real scenarios. In stage 6 of the framework, the simulation would need to be replaced with actual vehicles that are controlled by the system's commands. At the same time, an infrastructure for collecting orders would need to be provided. Since AMOD services are intended to be integrated into the public transport offering anyway, it would be conceivable to use existing public transport route planning apps for this purpose. Here, orders would be generated through passengers' route requests, with passengers then being directly shown whether an autonomous vehicle could take them to the next station.

Possible improvements to the DRL approach were identified for future work. In addition, possible extensions arise in four areas. First, on the algorithmic level, runtime could be significantly reduced if concurrency along with multithreading were employed, esp. in stages 2, 3 of the framework. Second, the problem statement could be expanded by integrating further aspects such as the Last-Mile problem or Ride Pooling. Third, different datasets that offer potential for AMOD services could be used, e.g., car commuter data. Fourthly, the impact of the properties of the public transport network could be analyzed.

References

1. European Commission: Sustainable transport (last access 2025-03-27). https://transport.ec.europa.eu/transport-themes/sustainable-transport_en
2. Bian, Z., & Liu, X. (2019). Mechanism design for first-mile ridesharing based on personalized requirements part i: Theoretical analysis in generalized scenarios. *Transportation Research Part B: Methodological, 120*, 147–171. https://doi.org/10.1016/j.trb.2018.12.009
3. Wang, H. (2019). Routing and scheduling for a last-mile transportation system. *Transportation Science, 53*, 131–147. https://doi.org/10.1287/trsc.2017.0753
4. Verband Deutscher Verkehrsunternehmen: Autonome Shuttle-Bus-Projekte in Deutschland (last access 2025-03-27). https://www.vdv.de/liste-autonome-shuttle-bus-projekte.aspx
5. Bundesministerium für Digitales und Verkehr: AVF-Projekte (last access 2025-03-27). https://bmdv.bund.de/DE/Themen/Digitales/Automatisiertes-und-vernetztes-Fahren/AVF-Forschungsprogramm/Projekte/avf-projekte.html
6. de Séjournet, A., Rombaut, E., & Vanhaverbeke, L. (2023). Cost analysis of autonomous shuttle services as a complement to public transport. *Transportation Research Procedia, 72*, 2323–2330. https://doi.org/10.1016/j.trpro.2023.11.723
7. Zuniga-Garcia, N., Gurumurthy, K. M., Yahia, C. N., Kockelman, K. M., & Machemehl, R. B. (2022) Integrating shared mobility services with public transit in areas of low demand. *Journal of Public Transportation, 24*. https://doi.org/10.1016/j.jpubtr.2022.100032
8. Qiao, S., & Yeh, A. G. O. (2023). Is ride-hailing competing or complementing public transport? a perspective from affordability. *Transportation Research Part D: Transport and Environment, 114*. https://doi.org/10.1016/j.trd.2022.103533
9. Shen, Y., Zhang, H., & Zhao, J. (2018). Integrating shared autonomous vehicle in public transportation system: A supply-side simulation of the first-mile service in singapore. *Transportation Research Part A: Policy and Practice, 113*, 125–136. https://doi.org/10.1016/j.tra.2018.04.004

10. McDonald, M., Stam, D., Salucci, M.V., Graindorge, M., Nair, S., Graindorge, T., Malhene, N., Portouli, E., Karaseitanidis, I., Amditis, A., Raptis, O., Karaberi, C., Vollichard, P., Guala, L., Sechi, F., Koskela, G., Murgoitio, J., Izaguirre, M., Inclán, A., Pérez, J. M. (2018). *Evaluation of automated road transport systems in cities* (pp. 81–207). Elsevier. https://doi.org/10.1016/B978-0-12-812993-7.00003-6
11. Polzin, S. E. (2016). *Implications to public transportation of emerging technologies*. Tech. rep.: University of Florida.
12. Machek, E. (2017). *Low-speed automated shuttles foundational research*. US Department of Transportation: Tech. rep.
13. Feng, S., Duan, P., Ke, J., & Yang, H. (2022). Coordinating ride-sourcing and public transport services with a reinforcement learning approach. *Transportation Research Part C: Emerging Technologies, 138*. https://doi.org/10.1016/j.trc.2022.103611
14. Tang, X., Qin, Z., Zhang, F., Wang, Z., Xu, Z., Ma, Y., Zhu, H., & Ye, J. (2019). *A deep value-network based approach for multi-driver order dispatching* (pp. 1780–1790). Association for Computing Machinery. https://doi.org/10.1145/3292500.3330724
15. Jiao, Y., Tang, X., Qin, Z., Li, S., Zhang, F., Zhu, H., & Ye, J. (2021). *Real-world ride-hailing vehicle repositioning using deep reinforcement learning*. https://doi.org/10.48550/arXiv.2103.04555
16. Wang, Z., Qin, Z., Tang, X., Ye, J., & Zhu, H. (2018). *Deep reinforcement learning with knowledge transfer for online rides order dispatching* (pp. 617–626). Institute of Electrical and Electronics Engineers Inc. https://doi.org/10.1109/ICDM.2018.00077
17. Ma, T. Y., Rasulkhani, S., Chow, J. Y., & Klein, S. (2019). A dynamic ridesharing dispatch and idle vehicle repositioning strategy with integrated transit transfers. *Transportation Research Part E: Logistics and Transportation Review, 128*, 417–442. https://doi.org/10.1016/j.tre.2019.07.002
18. Tang, X., Zhang, F., Qin, Z., Wang, Y., Shi, D., Song, B., Tong, Y., Zhu, H., & Ye, J. (2021). *Value function is all you need: A unified learning framework for ride hailing platforms* (pp. 3605–3615). Association for Computing Machinery. https://doi.org/10.1145/3447548.3467096
19. Samuel, A. L. (1959). Some studies in machine learning using the game of checkers. *IBM Journal of Research and Development, 3*(3), 210–229. https://doi.org/10.1147/rd.33.0210
20. Ho, S. C., Szeto, W. Y., Kuo, Y. H., Leung, J. M., Petering, M., & Tou, T. W. (2018). A survey of dial-a-ride problems: Literature review and recent developments. *Transportation Research Part B: Methodological, 111*, 395–421. https://doi.org/10.1016/j.trb.2018.02.001
21. Mourad, A., Puchinger, J., & Chu, C. (2019). A survey of models and algorithms for optimizing shared mobility. *Transportation Research Part B: Methodological, 123*, 323–346. https://doi.org/10.1016/j.trb.2019.02.003
22. Martins, L., Torre, R., Corlu, C. G., Juan, A., & Masmoudi, M. (2021). Optimizing ride-sharing operations in smart sustainable cities: Challenges and the need for agile algorithms. *Computers and Industrial Engineering, 153*. https://doi.org/10.1016/j.cie.2020.107080
23. Chen, W., Mes, M., Schutten, M., & Quint, J. (2019). A ride-sharing problem with meeting points and return restrictions. *Transportation Science, 53*, 401–426. https://doi.org/10.1287/trsc.2018.0832
24. Shi, J., Gao, Y., Wang, W., Yu, N., & Ioannou, P. A. (2020). Operating electric vehicle fleet for ride-hailing services with reinforcement learning. *IEEE Transactions on Intelligent Transportation Systems, 21*, 4822–4834. https://doi.org/10.1109/TITS.2019.2947408
25. Cordeau, J. F., & Laporte, G. (2007). The dial-a-ride problem (darp): Models and algorithms. *Annals OR, 153*, 29–46. https://doi.org/10.1007/s10479-007-0170-8
26. Xu, Z., Li, Z., Guan, Q., Zhang, D., Li, Q., Nan, J., Liu, C., Bian, W., & Ye, J. (2018). Large-scale order dispatch in on-demand ride-hailing platforms: A learning and planning approach. In *Proceedings of the 24th ACM SIGKDD International Conference on Knowledge Discovery & Data Mining, KDD '18* (pp. 905–913). New York, NY, USA: Association for Computing Machinery. https://doi.org/10.1145/3219819.3219824
27. Truong, C., Oudre, L., & Vayatis, N. (2020). Selective review of offline change point detection methods. *Signal Processing, 167*. https://doi.org/10.1016/j.sigpro.2019.107299

Spatio-temporal Pricing and Fleet Management under Mixed Autonomy

Ignacio Úbeda and Gunther Gust

Abstract Mobility-on-Demand services will soon have the opportunity to integrate autonomous vehicles into their operations. During the transition towards full automation, MoD systems will operate a mixed fleet, where human-driven (HVs) and autonomous vehicles (AVs) coexist. In such scenarios, the AVs fully complies with the operator's decisions while HVs must be incentivized through wages–i.e. the size and locational distribution of the human fleet is impacted by the wage decisions of the operator. In this paper, we present a data-driven information system to manage such mixed fleets. The system decides on trip prices, relocation of AVs, and wages of the HVs. Thereby, it takes into account the effect of wage decisions on the behavior of HVs. Validation of the system is conducted through a case study based on observed trip demand data in New York City. Our study demonstrates the importance of accounting for wage-dependent HVs' supply in this new scenario.

1 Introduction and Related Work

Mobility-on-Demand (MoD) platforms, such as Uber and Lyft, have been widely deployed during the past decade and have become the new status quo in cities. In comparison to conventional human-driven vehicles (HVs), the advent of autonomous vehicles (AVs) is going to provide additional advantages for these platforms [23]. First, unlike human drivers, AVs fully comply with the platform's dispatching and relocation decisions. Second, AVs can provide continuous service regardless of the time of day. Third, platform operators avoid wage cost for the human drivers, which is estimated as 75% of the total per mile cost [9]. Given these benefits, both Uber and Lyft have declared that incorporating autonomous vehicles is key for the future of

I. Úbeda (✉) · G. Gust
Center for Artificial Intelligence and Data Science (CAIDAS), University of Würzburg, Würzburg, Germany
e-mail: ignacio.ubeda@uni-wuerzburg.de
URL: https://www.wiwi.uni-wuerzburg.de/wiki/

G. Gust
e-mail: gunther.gust@uni-wuerzburg.de

C. M. Flath et al. (eds.), *Artificial Intelligence, Data, and Decision-Making*, Lecture Notes in Information Systems and Organisation 82,
https://doi.org/10.1007/978-3-032-08480-4_23

Table 1 Scope of related work

	Operational decisions	Mixed Autonomy	Spatial Pricing	Temporal Pricing	Wage-dep. supply	Wage-dep. relocation
[23]	✓	✓				
[22]	✓	✓				✓
[12, 18, 19]	✓		✓	✓		
[4, 10]	✓		✓	✓	✓	✓
[6, 14, 16]	✓			✓	✓	
[1, 20, 21]		✓	✓		✓	✓
[7]		✓			✓	✓
[13, 24]		✓			✓	
[3, 5, 25]			✓		✓	
Our Project	✓	✓	✓	✓	✓	✓
This RIP	✓	✓	✓	✓	✓	

their companies [11, 15]. Nevertheless, AVs will be gradually introduced and adopted in the market [8]. During the transition towards full automation, MoD platforms will operate under *mixed autonomy*, i.e., in a system where HVs and AVs coexist.

Operating such mixed fleets is challenging due to the complex problem characteristics. In particular, there are four levers available to consider. First, to take into account the fluctuating nature of ride demand, the platform operator should set prices that vary across time and space. Second, to adjust vehicle supply, the operator may relocate AVs to the most desirable locations. Third, by differentiating wages across time and space, the operator can encourage human drivers to start (or stop) working at certain hours or at certain locations, and, forth, the operator may use wage-differentiation to incentivize human drivers to relocate to more profitable locations.

Given its complexity, approaches to solve the underlying decision problem do not yet exist. In Table 1, we review related work with regard to the individual problem characteristics. There is a group of research focused on mixed autonomy [1, 20, 21] that has addressed the mentioned characteristics assuming that the transportation system has reached a steady-state equilibrium (i.e. state variables do not change in time). However, these models are not suitable for operational decision-making in markets that present abrupt changes (e.g. number of riders and drivers) within a short time frame because they may not have enough time to balance back into equilibrium [14]. Regarding the operational problem, none of the related approaches takes into account all key characteristics of the mixed-autonomous setting—its solution is still open for research.

In this research project, we aim to provide an information system (IS) that closes this gap. While at the end of the project, the IS will take into account all problem characteristics, this research-in-progress (RIP) paper presents preliminary results. In particular, the IS models spatio-temporal pricing, AV relocation, as well as wage-based working incentives for human drivers. We demonstrate the associated benefits with a real-world study based on observed taxi trips in New York City.

2 Data-driven Information System for Fleet Management

To solve the decision problem of the platform operator, we develop the IS in Fig. 1. The system consists of a data base, a predictor, and a controller. Since we're interested in the operational problem and characterizing the decisions, it adapts the principle of model predictive control (MPC), which works as follows. First, the predictor fetches past data on transportation demand in different zones of the city. Using machine learning, it generates predictions of future ride demand. The predictions are then forwarded to the controller, which then collects information on the current location and status (on-trip, relocating, or idle) of the vehicles in the city. Using the predictions and vehicle status information, the controller then decides about prices, wages, and relocation of AVs by solving an optimization problem for a discrete planning horizon T. The decisions for the first time step are then communicated to the vehicles in the city. Then, the vehicles perform corresponding transportation and relocation tasks, remain idle, enter or leave the system. This results in a new state of vehicles, which is communicated to the data base and the controller, and the process repeats for the next timestep.

2.1 *Controller: Model and Assumptions*

We consider the transportation network as a graph $G = (Z, E)$ where Z is the set of nodes (zones) and E is a set of directed edges. We discretize the time horizon T into intervals of fixed length (e.g. 5 minutes) that we denote with t. The travel time for edge $(i, j) \in E$ is denoted as $\tau_{ij} \in \mathbb{Z}_+$ and represents the number of time steps t to reach zone j from zone i. We assume the operator can estimate the short-term potential origin-destination (i, j) demand through historical data, which we denote by $\overline{D}_{ij,t}$. We use the cumulative distribution of the riders' willingness to pay, which is denoted by $F(\cdot)$, to account for price-dependent demand. That is, when the operator sets a price $p_{i,t}$ for zone i[1], the realized demand is given by: $D_{ij,t}(p_{i,t}) = \overline{D}_{ij,t}F(p_{i,t})$.

Each type of vehicle $v \in \{a, h\}$ (AVs and HVs, respectively) can be in one of three statuses: idle (I), relocating (R), or on-trip (O). Let $n_{i,t}^{I,v} \geq 0$ be the number of idle vehicles of type $v \in \{a, h\}$ in zone i at time step t, $n_{ij,t}^{R,v} \geq 0$ and $n_{ij,t}^{O,v} \geq 0$ be the number of vehicles of type $v \in \{a, h\}$ assigned for relocation and on-trip along edge (i, j) at time step t, respectively. We assume that only idle vehicles can be

---

[1] We use origin-based pricing instead of origin-destination pricing. This is consistent with the research and industry practice where a surge multiplier is based on the trip's origin [1, 20].

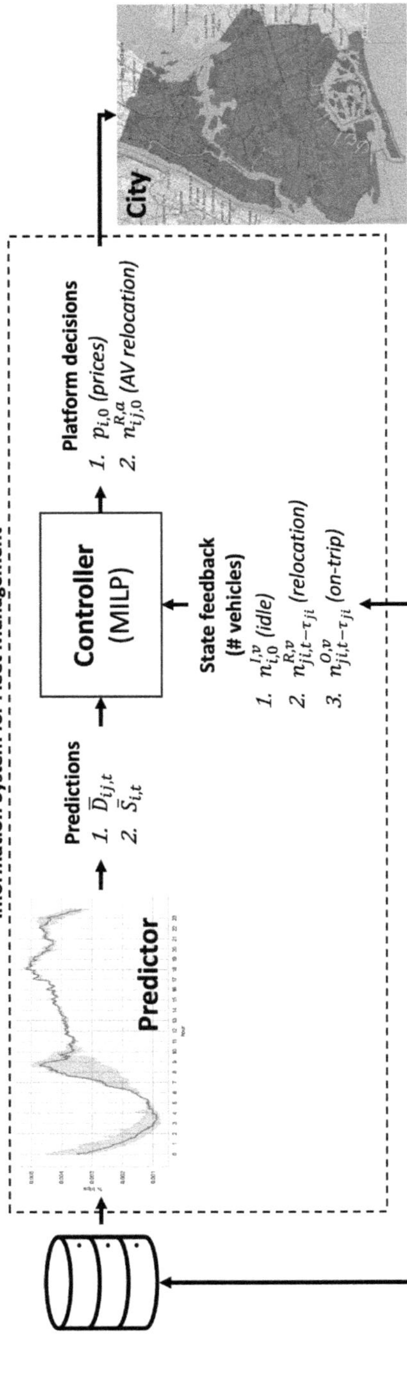

Fig. 1 Components of the information system and data flow

assigned for relocation or on-trip (vehicles that remain idle are modeled as vehicles relocating to the same zone, i.e. $n_{ii,t}^{R,v}$, $v \in \{a, h\}$) and ride-sharing is not possible. Furthermore, passengers can only be matched to vehicles located in the same zone. Human vehicles will receive a compensation $c_{ij,t} = w_{i,t}(p_{i,t})\tau_{ij}$ for serving a (i, j) trip where $w_{i,t}(p_{i,t}) = \delta p_{i,t}$. On the other hand, AVs have a fixed per-time cost c^{AV}, which is only incurred if the vehicle is relocating or on-trip.

To account for wage-dependent HVs' supply, we make use of two functions, U^{in} and U^{out} [14], which represent the proportion of HVs that enter and leave the market, respectively. In particular, let $\overline{S}_{i,t}$ be the number of HVs that are willing to enter the market in zone i at time t, which can be estimated using historical data (e.g. registered drivers in the platform). The number of HVs that enter the market on zone i at time t, $A_{i,t}$, is such that: $A_{i,t}(p_{i,t}) = \overline{S}_{i,t}U^{in}(w_{i,t}(p_{i,t}))$. Where $\frac{\partial U^{in}}{\partial w} \geq 0$ because higher wages will attract more drivers to enter the system. Similarly, idle drivers can decide to leave the market because of low earnings. Therefore, the number of HVs that leave the market on zone i at time t, $E_{i,t}$, is given by: $E_{i,t}(p_{i,t}) = n_{i,t}^{I,h}U^{out}(w_{i,t}(p_{i,t}))$. Where $\frac{\partial U^{out}}{\partial w} \leq 0$ because more drivers leave as they face lower wages.

Unmatched vehicles can remain idle or relocate to another zone. The relocation decisions for AVs are made by the operator, while HVs relocate on their own. The relocation of HVs is given by a probability matrix $\mathbb{P}_{ij,t}$. Similar to [4], we assume that the relocation matrix depends on the potential demand of the destination zone and the time to reach it (but not on the operator's decisions). In that regard, the operator only incurs a cost for relocating the AVs fleet but not the HVs. Under this setting, the central operator decides spatio-temporal prices $p_{i,t}$ and the relocation flows of AVs $n_{ij,t}^{R,a}$ aiming to maximize performance.[2]

2.2 Controller: Decision Problem

The operator solves the optimization model presented in Eq. (1–1g). The objective function in (1a) represents profit, defined as revenue from served trips minus cost (served trips and relocation of AVs fleet). Constraints (1b)–(1d) model the matching procedure, where on-trip vehicles are limited by the trip demand (1b) and the number of available vehicles for each type (1c) and (1d). Constraints (1e) and (1f) correspond to the flow conservation for HVs and AVs, respectively. Lastly, constraint (1g) models HVs' relocation, where unmatched vehicles are distributed for relocation by multiplying them with the probability matrix $\mathbb{P}_{ij,t}$.

The model of Eq. (1–1g) is non-linear due to the price-demand and wage-supply functions and the product of decision variables in the objective function. In practice, the operator must select a price from a discrete set of available price levels $p^m, m \in M$. To do so, we reformulate the operator's decision with a variable $q_{i,t}^m \in \{0, 1\}$ such that $p_{i,t} = \sum_m p^m q_{i,t}^m$ and we impose that only one price level

[2] Profit in this case, but other relevant metrics can be used as well.

p^m is selected. After this reformulation, Eq. (1–1g) can be linearized[3] via piece-wise functions and the multiplication of binary and continuous variables [2]. With this, Eq. (1–1g) is transformed into a MILP and can be solved with commercial optimization softwares (e.g. Gurobi).

$$\max_{\mathbf{p},\mathbf{n}^{\mathbf{I}},\mathbf{n}^{\mathbf{O}},\mathbf{n}^{\mathbf{R}}} \Big(\sum_{t\in T}\sum_{(i,j)\in E} p_{i,t}\,\tau_{ij}\,(n_{ij,t}^{O,h}+n_{ij,t}^{O,a})\Big) - \Big(\sum_{t\in T}\sum_{(i,j)\in E} \tau_{ij}\,(w_{i,t}(p_{i,t})\,n_{ij,t}^{O,h}+c^{AV}\,n_{ij,t}^{O,a})\Big) - \Big(\sum_{t\in T}\sum_{(i,j)\in E} \tau_{ij}\,c^{AV}\,n_{ij,t}^{R,a}\Big) \tag{1a}$$

s. t.

$$(n_{ij,t}^{O,h}+n_{ij,t}^{O,a}) \le D_{ij,t}(p_{i,t}), \qquad \forall i,j\in Z, t\in T \tag{1b}$$

$$\sum_{j\in Z} n_{ij,t}^{O,h} \le \left(n_{i,t}^{I,h}+A_{i,t}(p_{i,t})-E_{i,t}(p_{i,t})\right), \qquad \forall i\in Z, t\in T \tag{1c}$$

$$\sum_{j\in Z}\left(n_{ij,t}^{O,a}+n_{ij,t}^{R,a}\right) \le n_{i,t}^{I,a}, \qquad \forall i\in Z, t\in T \tag{1d}$$

$$n_{i,t+1}^{I,h} = n_{i,t}^{I,h}+A_{i,t}(p_{i,t})-E_{i,t}(p_{i,t})+\sum_{j\in Z}\left(n_{ji,t-\tau_{ji}}^{R,h}-n_{ij,t}^{R,h}\right) + \sum_{j\in Z}\left(n_{ji,t-\tau_{ji}}^{O,h}-n_{ij,t}^{O,h}\right), \qquad \forall i\in Z, t\in T \tag{1e}$$

$$n_{i,t+1}^{I,a} = n_{i,t}^{I,a}+\sum_{j\in Z}\left(n_{ji,t-\tau_{ji}}^{R,a}-n_{ij,t}^{R,a}\right)+\sum_{j\in Z}\left(n_{ji,t-\tau_{ji}}^{O,a}-n_{ij,t}^{O,a}\right), \qquad \forall i\in Z, t\in T \tag{1f}$$

$$n_{ij,t}^{R,h} = \mathbb{P}_{ij,t}\left(n_{i,t}^{I,h}+A_{i,t}(p_{i,t})-E_{i,t}(p_{i,t})-\sum_{j\in Z} n_{ij,t}^{O,h}\right), \qquad \forall i,j\in Z, t\in T \tag{1g}$$

Equation (1–1g) Optimization model solved by the Controller.

---

[3] Linearizations are omitted due to space constraints.

3 Results and Discussion

We perform a case study simulating a weekday in New York City using TLC trip record data [17]. The city is divided into hexagons of around 0.74 km^2 and the top 10 zones are selected, based on the volume of trips. The duration of a time step t is set to 5 min and the planning horizon for the controller is 25 min, i.e. for an entire day, the optimization problem of Eq. (1) is solved 288 times, each with a look-ahead of 5 steps in a rolling-window manner. A simulator of the city is created to account for the feedback loop presented in Fig. 1. We compare the performance of two different controllers: one that accounts for wage-dependent HVs' supply and one that does not (the latter is used as a baseline). In particular, the baseline considers that $A_{i,t}(p_{i,t}) = E_{i,t}(p_{i,t}) = 0,\ \forall i \in Z, t \in T$ in Eq. (1). Nevertheless, in the simulator, HVs can enter or leave the system regardless of the controller type.

The difference in profit is presented in Fig. 2 at several AVs fleet sizes and cost ratios between AVs and HVs. Specifically, the cost ratio is such that c^{AV} ranges from the minimum (0.5) to the maximum (1.5) potential HVs wage level. Accounting for wage-dependent HVs' supply always leads to an increase in profit. As expected, the improvement decreases as more AVs are included in the system because they gradually replace HVs. However, this holds only when AVs are cheaper than HVs. Conversely, when the AVs fleet is expensive (1.5) the increase in profit remains relatively constant because AVs are used only as a backup fleet. In such a situation, accounting for wage-dependent HVs's supply is crucial for improving the performance of the operator.

The reasons for this improvement can be understood by analyzing the share of ride demand that is served and the utilization of HVs. Figure 3 displays these metrics for the two types of controllers. In panel (a), we observe that by adjusting the wages, the wage-dependent controller consistently achieves a higher utilization of HVs across

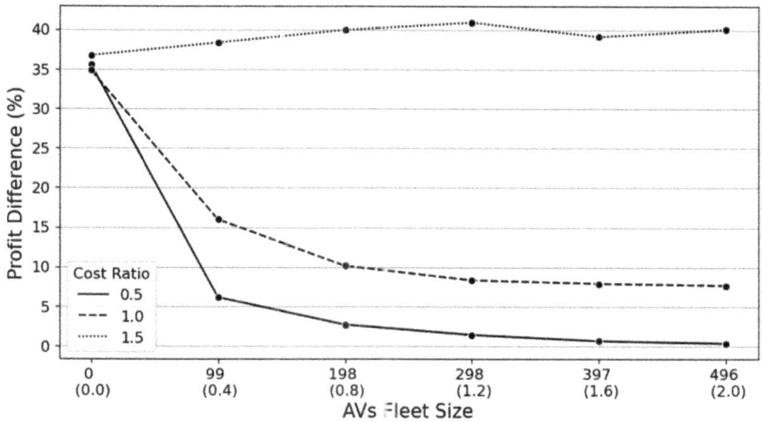

Fig. 2 Relative difference of profit for various AVs fleet sizes and cost ratios. In parenthesis, the ratio between AVs fleet size and median potential demand (at each time step)

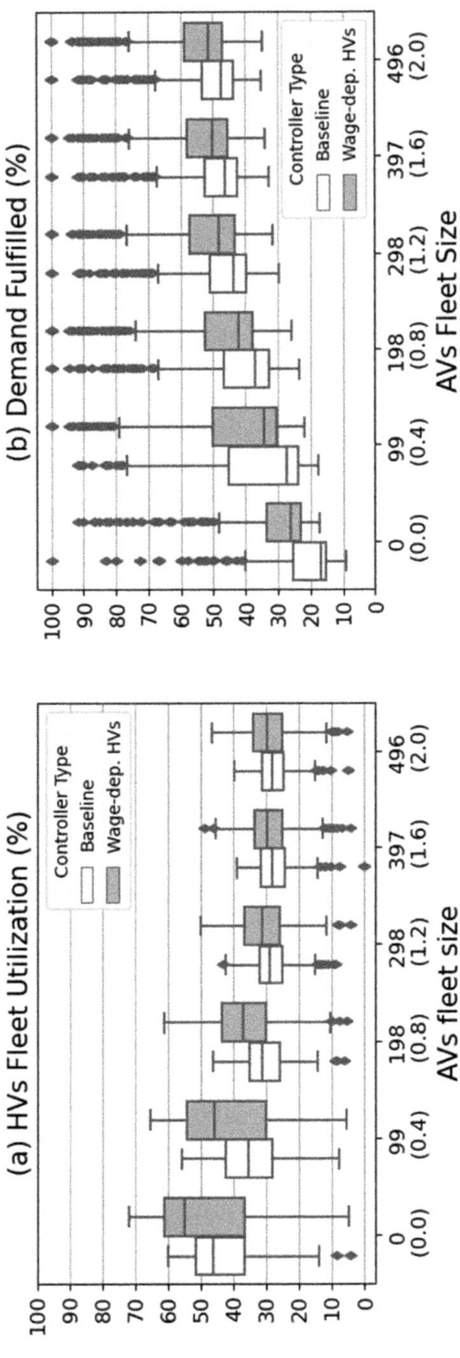

Fig. 3 **a** HV fleet utilization, and **b** fulfilled ride demand (for cost ratio = 1.0)

all fleet sizes. The controller deliberately incentivizes HVs to enter (and exit) the market in undersupplied (and oversupplied) zones. Thereby, the controller is also able to serve the ride demand at higher degrees, as displayed in panel (b). Eventually, this results in higher revenues and higher profits. Overall, the results support the contribution of this paper. The IS that is able to take into acount wage-incentives achieves consistent advantages across all scenarios.

4 Conclusion

We have developed an IS for managing mixed, human and autonomous fleets. Our real-world case study demonstrates the relevance of acknowledging that HVs are not controlled by the operator but incentivized through wages. Next, we focus on extending the IS to also take into account that human drivers relocate depending on wage incentives. For research, we thereby contribute by solving the novel and complex problem of managing mixed fleets. For management and policy, we intend to use the proposed system to understand how AVs will affect human drivers. We thereby aim to determine necessary policies and regulations to better prepare for the advent of autonomous mobility.

References

1. Ao, D., Gao, J., Lai, Z., & Li, S. (2024). Regulating transportation network companies with a mixture of autonomous vehicles and for-hire human drivers. *Transportation Research Part A: Policy and Practice, 180*, Article 103975.
2. Asghari, M., Fathollahi-Fard, A. M., Mirzapour Al-E-Hashem, S. M. J., & Dulebenets, M. A. (2022). Transformation and linearization techniques in optimization: A state-of-the-art survey. *Mathematics, 10*(2), 283.
3. Bimpikis, K., Candogan, O., & Saban, D. (2019). Spatial pricing in ride-sharing networks. *Operations Research, 67*(3), 744–769.
4. Chen, C., Yao, F., Mo, D., Zhu J., & Chen, X. M. (2021). Spatial-temporal pricing for ride-sourcing platform with reinforcement learning. *Transportation Research Part C: Emerging Technologies, 130*, Article 103272.
5. Chen, X., Chen, C., & Xie, W. (2019). Optimal spatial pricing for an on-demand ride-sourcing service platform. *Available at SSRN 3464228.*
6. Chen, X. M., Zheng, H., Ke, J., & Yang, H. (2020). Dynamic optimization strategies for on-demand ride services platform: Surge pricing, commission rate, and incentives. *Transportation Research Part B: Methodological, 138*, 23–45. Elsevier.
7. Chen, Z., Miao, Y., Ke, J., & He, Q.-C. (2024). Operations and regulations for a ride-sourcing market with a mixed fleet of human drivers and autonomous vehicles. *Transportation Research Part C: Emerging Technologies, 160*, Article 104519.
8. Grush, B., & Niles, J. (2018). *The end of driving: Transportation systems and public policy planning for autonomous vehicles*. Elsevier.
9. Henao, A., & Marshall, W. E. (2019). An analysis of the individual economics of ride-hailing drivers. *Transportation Research Part A: Policy and Practice, 130*, 440–451.

10. Huang, J., Huang, L., Liu, M., Li, H., Tan, Q., Ma, X., Cui, J., & Huang, D.-S. (2022). Deep reinforcement learning-based trajectory pricing on ride-hailing platforms. *ACM Transactions on Intelligent Systems and Technology (TIST), 13*(3), 1–19.
11. Hur, K. (2022). Lyft plans to build a hybrid network of autonomous and driver vehicles, co-founder says. Retrieved March 07, 2024, from https://www.cnbc.com/2022/06/07/lyft-plans-to-build-a-hybrid-network-of-autonomous-and-driver-vehicles-co-founder-says.html
12. Lai, Z., & Li, S. (2023). *Spatiotemporal pricing and fleet management of autonomous mobility-on-demand networks: A decomposition and dynamic programming approach with bounded optimality gap*. IEEE Transactions on Intelligent Transportation Systems. IEEE.
13. Mo, D., Chen, X. M., & Zhang, J. (2022). Modeling and managing mixed on-demand ride services of human-driven vehicles and autonomous vehicles. *Transportation Research Part B: Methodological, 157*, 80–119.
14. Nourinejad, M., & Ramezani, M. (2020). Ride-Sourcing modeling and pricing in non-equilibrium two-sided markets. *Transportation Research Part B: Methodological, 132*, 340–357.
15. Shetty, S. (2020). Uber's self-driving cars are a key to its path to profitability. Retrieved March 07, 2024, from https://www.cnbc.com/2020/01/28/ubers-self-driving-cars-are-a-key-to-its-path-to-profitability.html
16. Song, J., Cho, Y. J., Kang, M. H., & Hwang, K. Y. (2020). An application of reinforced learning-based dynamic pricing for improvement of ridesharing platform service in Seoul. *Electronics, 9*(11), 1818. MDPI.
17. TLC Trip Record Data. Retrieved March 07, 2024, from https://www.nyc.gov/site/tlc/about/tlc-trip-record-data.page
18. Turan, B., Pedarsani, R., & Alizadeh, M. (2020). Dynamic pricing and fleet management for electric autonomous mobility on demand systems. *Transportation Research Part C: Emerging Technologies, 121*, 102829. Elsevier.
19. Wang, A., & Turan, B. (2022). Multi-Agent Reinforcement Learning for Dynamic Pricing and Fleet Management in Autonomous Mobility-On-Demand Systems. In *Proceedings of the International Foundation for Telemetering.*
20. Wang, Z., Ke, J., & Li, S. (2024). Planning and operation of ride-hailing networks with a mixture of level-4 autonomous vehicles and for-hire human drivers. *Transportation Research Part C: Emerging Technologies, 160*, Article 104541.
21. Wei, Q., Pedarsani, R., & Coogan, S. (2020). Mixed autonomy in ride-sharing networks. *IEEE Transactions on Control of Network Systems, 7*(4), 1940–1950. IEEE.
22. Xie, J., Liu, Y., & Chen, N. (2023). *Two-sided deep reinforcement learning for dynamic mobility-on-demand management with mixed autonomy*. INFORMS: Transportation Science.
23. Yang, K., Tsao, M. W., Xu, X., & Pavone, M. (2021). Real-time control of mixed fleets in mobility-on-demand systems. In *2021 IEEE International Intelligent Transportation Systems Conference (ITSC)* (pp. 3570–3577). IEEE.
24. Ye, A., Zhou, Q., Liu, X., Zhang, Y., Tao, Z., Li, J., Bell, M. G. H., Bhattacharjya, J., Ben, S., & Chen, X. (2022). Modeling and managing an on-demand meal delivery system with mixed autonomy. In *2022 IEEE 25th International Conference on Intelligent Transportation Systems (ITSC)*, 2007–2012. IEEE.
25. Zha, L., Yin, Y., & Xu, Z. (2018). Geometric matching and spatial pricing in ride-sourcing markets. *Transportation Research Part C: Emerging Technologies, 92*, 58–75.

Unveiling Green Facades: Exploring the Confluence of Greenwashing and Fake News

Marvin Motz, Tobias Kölbel, and Anuja Hariharan

Abstract In the global pursuit of sustainability, the role of private sector capital is pivotal, necessitating a shift in financial flows towards sustainable initiatives. However, the proliferation of greenwashing undermines trust among investors and consumers alike. The detection and mitigation of greenwashing demand robust automated systems. Nonetheless, this endeavor is challenging due to ambiguous definitions, limited availability of high-quality data, and the qualitative nature of sustainability claims. In contrast, the field of fake news detection, facing similar obstacles, has undergone substantial methodological evolution. Employing a systematic mapping approach, we link existing types of greenwashing and fake news, unveiling similarities and distinctions. Our findings contribute to the linking of these two fields by establishing the conceptual foundation to transfer methodological advancements, such as detection algorithms, from fake news literature to the realm of greenwashing. Furthermore, we outline promising research avenues in the domains of greenwashing, fake news and their intersection.

1 Introduction

Addressing climate change and advancing sustainability necessitates substantial investments both now and in the future, surpassing the financial capacity of the public sector alone [23]. Mobilizing private sector capital, involving investors and consumers, becomes essential for channeling sufficient financial resources toward sustainable initiatives [14]. Despite encouraging trends in both the capital market [13] and consumer segments [59], the phenomenon of greenwashing emerges as a

M. Motz (✉) · T. Kölbel · A. Hariharan
Karlsruhe Institute of Technology, ISM, Karlsruhe, Germany
e-mail: marvin.motz@kit.edu

T. Kölbel
e-mail: tobias.koelbel@kit.edu

A. Hariharan
e-mail: anuja.hariharan@kit.edu

C. M. Flath et al. (eds.), *Artificial Intelligence, Data, and Decision-Making*, Lecture Notes in Information Systems and Organisation 82,
https://doi.org/10.1007/978-3-032-08480-4_24

barrier to achieving these goals [11, 15, 71]. Given the early stages of greenwashing detection literature, this work aims to link the more advanced fake news research with the greenwashing literature. By providing a conceptual basis, we enable future research to transfer established findings, such as detection methods, from the realm of fake news to greenwashing.

Greenwashing, the deceptive practice of presenting an overly positive image of an organization's sustainability performance [34], erodes trust among investors and consumers, hindering overall progress towards sustainability [19, 65, 71]. Some (in)famous examples include the "save the towel movement" in the hotel industry [43] or the Volkswagen emission controlling testing procedures in 2015 [26]. The detrimental consequences extend to potential stakeholders, consumers, and society at large, outweighing any short-term gains for existing stakeholders [71]. While greenwashing is not a novel phenomenon [34], its escalation in recent years poses a critical challenge [48]. Particularly, in both Europe and the Americas, the banking and financial services sectors saw a 70% increase in the number of climate-related greenwashing incidents in 2023, compared to the year prior [48].

Addressing greenwashing and its widespread repercussions necessitates the development of automated detection systems [42]. However, this is a complex effort due to the absence of standardization, transparency, and accessible data [18, 22]. Presently, the main data sources are self-published data by businesses (e.g., sustainability reports, estimated emissions) or third-party ratings from data vendors (e.g., MSCI, LSEG). The qualitative nature of sustainability claims makes their objective assessment and detection of greenwashing even more difficult [53]. Therefore, there is a critical need to develop methods capable of navigating the absence of an objective ground truth and working with available data sources.

Furthermore, there are different types of greenwashing that also necessitate different detection methods. For instance, an algorithm designed to detect *empty green claims*, which are "statements that organizations are realistically unable to carry out" ([58], p. 28), is unlikely to effectively detect more subtle types of greenwashing such as visuals used for *misleading* [8]. An example for this behavior is a company adopting a green color palette for its corporate design without improving their actual sustainability efforts.

Nevertheless, researchers have started to develop concepts and methods for greenwashing detection. The methods found in literature tackle two different steps of the process. The initial step focuses on detecting claims associated with sustainability in different types of text (e.g., business reports, Twitter posts), a task already known for its complexity, as evidenced by the breadth of existing approaches [4, 30, 31, 41, 61, 68, 70].

The second step involves evaluating these claims for greenwashing practices, an area where research is still evolving. For instance, [35] employ a partial least squares structural equation model to identify greenwashing in sustainability reports, while [42] use linguistic cues to discern deceptive environmental statements in tweets. Notably, [42]'s method circumvents the need for a ground truth, thereby advancing greenwashing detection literature where obtaining a reliable ground truth is burdensome or even impossible. Furthermore, [42] also created the link between greenwashing and fake news. However, they do not discuss the various types of greenwashing [58] and their relation to the different types of fake news. Fake news, again being a broad term, usually covering different forms of mis- and disinformation [66]. Similar to the greenwashing phenomenon, there are however, a multitude of different types of fake news that can vary substantially, for example, in terms of veracity, intent, or medium. A *photo manipulation* [62], for instance, is very different in all three of these dimensions from *citizen journalism* [12]. Given this multitude of different forms of fake news and greenwashing, a transfer of existing methods is not trivial and first needs a conceptual linkage that we aim to contribute with this study.

Given the early stage of greenwashing detection research, a pragmatic approach involves delving into related fields to identify possible solutions that can be further developed and adapted. Given the more evolved literature on fake news detection [44, 57, 72], our study focuses on establishing a connection between different types of greenwashing and fake news by examining the formal classification and conceptualization of both phenomena, leaving the actual transfer of detection methods for future work. Hence, we pose the following research question:

What types of greenwashing can be matched to established concepts from the fake news literature?

To address this question and consolidate the ongoing discourse, we conduct a literature-based analysis following the three-step approach of a systematic mapping study by [45]. Systematic mapping studies differ from systematic reviews (see e.g. [6, 69]) in various aspects [28, 45]: The research goal is more general, the search terms are derived from a whole topic area instead of specific topics, the search is less stringent and an assessment based on the quality of the underlying papers is typically not a requisite. The results of a mapping study is a collection of papers that are aggregated in different categorizations. In this study we aim to find different types of fake news and greenwashing in order to map them to each other. Our research goal is thus exploratory in nature and results in a categorization of these types and the corresponding articles. Therefore, we consider the use of the systematic mapping study method appropriate in this context

We contribute to the greenwashing detection literature by offering a formal conceptualization of the interplay between fake news and greenwashing. We aim to systematize the deceiving techniques used and provide a clearer picture of when and where it occurs. This endeavor not only facilitates future research in selecting applicable fake news detection methods as a starting point for greenwashing detection but also provides the necessary conceptual foundation and rationale for doing so. Additionally, we contribute to the greenwashing and fake news literature by offering promising research avenues that warrant exploration in the future and by proposing *smearing* and *adversarial attack* as two new types of greenwashing.

2 Research Design

Our approach to map the greenwashing and fake news methods involves establishing a connection between these two phenomena through a comparative analysis of the different forms of misleading in both fields. To ensure rigor and transparency, we align our analysis with the systematic mapping approach, and adopt the three-step procedure (planning, conducting, reporting) suggested by [45].

To address our overarching research question, we break it down into the following three standalone questions, to adopt a more systematic approach in the search phase of our study:

RQ1: What types of fake news are established in literature?
RQ2: What types of greenwashing are established in literature?
RQ3: Which types of greenwashing have a counterpart in fake news literature?

As indicated by these questions, we aim to find a representative list of types of fake news and greenwashing for subsequent comparison. Therefore, we need to conduct two separate searches, one for the fake news literature and one for the greenwashing literature, in preparation for the mapping. We focus our review on publications within the fields of information systems (IS), finance, business, and sustainability, with a specific emphasis on secondary and tertiary sources that cover multiple conceptualizations simultaneously. First, we refine our search topic by incorporating related terms for fake news, namely information disorder, disinformation, misinformation and malinformation [66]. Although greenwashing is inherently specialized, it is occasionally referred to as greenwash in literature [34]. Next, we construct a search phrase that incorporates the topic-related terms along with the descriptors of typology, taxonomy, and categorization to guide our search towards the secondary and tertiary literature.

For our search strategy we initiated a search across reputable databases, including Web of Science, Scopus, AISeL, Emerald and Wiley. These databases are recognized for hosting high-quality research as well as the most recent publications in the related disciplines. Employing the search string "(fake news OR information disorder OR disinformation OR misinformation OR malinformation) AND (typolog* OR taxonom* OR categor*)" on titles, we focus exclusively on articles published post January 1, 2010, given the novelty of the topic in tandem with advancements in digital technologies fostering fake news. This initial search yielded 25 publications (as of November 11, 2023), with one duplicate. Conducting an initial screening based on titles, abstracts, and keywords, we retained nine papers covering various forms of single or multiple types of fake news. Subsequently, we expanded our database search using forward and backward search to further enrich our sample. This resulted in 19 articles that contribute to a comprehensive understanding and collection of fake news categories. Replicating this process for the greenwashing literature, utilizing the search string "(greenwash*) AND (typolog* OR taxonom* OR categor*)", we initially identified four articles post duplicate removal. Augmenting our findings through the forward and backward search expanded our data set to 16 articles.

Table 1 Information disorder matrix, based on [66]

	True	False
Good intent	True information	Misinformation
Harmful intent	Malinformation	Disinformation

Two independent researchers conducted the data extraction and classification process. After one researcher finalized a first version of the extraction and classification, the second researcher reviewed the results and a consensus meeting was held to clarify open discussion points. Fitting our research goals, we use topic-specific classification, starting with the overarching concepts of disinformation, misinformation, and malinformation [24, 42, 66]. We populate these categories by adding corresponding types of fake news extracted from the reviewed literature. This step also includes consolidating possible differences in definitions or naming conventions. In the second step we extract the contents of the identified greenwashing literature, synthesise the information and draw comparisons between the types of greenwashing and fake news.

3 Results

Our analysis aligns with the overarching conceptualization of disinformation, misinformation, and malinformation in contemporary literature [24, 42, 66]. In a bipartite distinction, the validity is characterized as true and false and the intention as good intention or harmful intention. True information denotes valid information devoid of harmful intent, whereas malinformation is typically accurate but disseminated with an intention to harm. Disinformation and misinformation entail false information, with harmful intent in the former and an absence of harmful intent in the latter. Table 1 illustrates this 2×2 matrix.

Our categorization of various fake news examples into these three broader classifications of disinformation, informed by related literature [37, 42, 46, 62, 72], is presented in Table 2 as a response to *RQ1*. Similarly, Table 3 answers *RQ2* and shows the conceptualizations that we extracted from the greenwashing literature. Finally, Fig. 1 illustrates which types of greenwashing we were able to map to the existing fake news literature thus solving *RQ3*.

In the following, we describe the different conceptualizations of greenwashing and fake news to create a common understanding and to substantiate the mapping between the various types of greenwashing and fake news. For the sake of parsimony we only provide enough explanation to understand our rationale for the categorization and mapping. For more elaborate definitions and examples we encourage the reader to consult the literature cited in Tables 2 and 3.

Table 2 Aggregation of extant types of fake news and related literature. Names printed in bolt have corresponding types of greenwashing

Information disorder	Fake news types	Articles
Disinformation	**News fabrication/Deceptive news/False news**	[24, 50, 62, 66, 72]
	Imposter content	[24]
	Hoax	[40, 50]
	Photo manipulation	[24, 62]
	Opinion spam	[25]
Misinformation	Conspiracy theory	[1, 64]
	Satire/ Humorous fakes/ Parody	[2, 24, 40, 50, 62]
	Pseudosience	[21]
	Misreporting	[40]
	Citizen journalism	[12, 40]
Malinformation	**Cherry-picking**	[3]
	Rumor	[49, 56]
	Trolling	[5, 56]
	Clickbait/ False connection	[24, 37]
	Sensationalism	[39, 40]
	Hidden advertising/ Propaganda	[40, 62]

3.1 Disinformation Conceptualizations

For the disinformation category we found two types of fake news that have counterparts in the greenwashing literature. *News fabrication* constitutes information that has no factual basis but is intentionally created to mislead and obfuscated to imitate legitimate sources [50]. Clearly corresponding types of greenwashing are *sin of fibbing* [63] or *empty green claims and policies* [47] the only difference lies in the topic of sustainability in the case of greenwashing, while no such restriction is made in the case of fake news. Decoupling practices, such as *structure/activities decoupling* or *means/end decoupling*, as well as *cheap talk, sin of no proof* and *implied superiority* can also be matched to this type of fake news if we assume a company to deliberately engage in these methods. They describe scenarios where claims about goals or activities are stated even though the company is in reality unable or unwilling to fulfill these claims [34, 63].

For the rest of the disinformation category, we did not find any matching types of greenwashing in extant literature. *Imposter content* refers to content distributed under misuse of the name or logo of often reputable journalists or organizations without their consent [24]. A related type from the greenwashing literature is *astroturf lobbying* [32]. In both instances, the apparent source of the information is altered to create more trust with the audience. The difference is that the source in the *astroturf lobbying* case is aware of what they are doing and often receive funding for it, whereas in the case of *imposter content*, the source is often not even aware that their reputation is impermissibly used.

Hoaxes are similar to less problematic issues such as practical jokes, but tend to be more serious and elaborate fabrications that can also be aimed at causing harm [50].

Photo manipulation [62] can be another strong form of disinformation. It is the intentional manipulation and alteration of visual media with the aim to deceive the audience. The advancements in generative artificial intelligence that greatly facilitate the creation of made up visuals makes this form of fake news one of the growing threats for information credibility in the future.

Opinion spam is mainly found in online retailing in the form of fake reviews for products or brands [25].

3.2 Misinformation Conceptualizations

We did not map any types of greenwashing to misinformation. In Sect. 3.5 we go into more detail about the rational behind this decision. *Conspiracy theories* simplify reality with often obscure rationals. They intentionally leave room for uncertainty that allows their supporters to ignore evidence against their theories [64].

Satire, humorous fakes and *parody* are types of misinformation that use humor and exaggerations as a means to transport information. This can lead to inaccurate statements or stories, however, the authors do not try to disguise as serious news outlets but are usually clear about their intent to entertain rather than to accurately inform [50].

As the name suggests, *pseudoscience* describes a type of fake news that is closely connected to the realm of science. However, the information provided here is unreliable and not rooted in scientific principles. Although there is usually no intention to harm or deceive, followers often try to convince others of their views [21].

Misreporting illustrates the archetype of misinformation. False information is spread unintentionally, often from otherwise reputable sources [40].

Citizen journalism is the reporting of news worthy events trough the lens of non-professionals. It often lags the rigor and stylistic form of professional journalism which can lead to incorrect or biased reporting [12].

3.3 Malinformation Conceptualizations

For the malinformation category we found suitable types of greenwashing in extant literature for *Cherry-picking*, which refers to the deliberate passing on of information that is helpful to a particular position, while omitting facts that support opposing arguments [3]. *Selective disclosure, sin of hidden trade-off, sin of vagueness, sin of irrelevance, sin of lesser of two evils* and *incomplete comparisons* are related types from the greenwashing literature. All of these methods have in common that critical information is kept from the recipients that would be necessary to form an unbiased opinion about the content [34, 63].

For the remaining types, there are no greenwashing counterparts available in the existing literature. However, for *rumors* and *trolling* we propose two new types of greenwashing in Sect. 3.5.

Rumors have an unclear level of truthfulness when they start out but might turn out true, false, or, as it is often the case, somewhere in between. While rumors can also develop without intent, they can be spread deliberately with either the intent to harm an opposing side or to promote the spreaders' own interests [49].

Trolling is mainly present online and describes offensive messages usually disseminated to provoke conflict in communities. The motivation behind it can be amusement for the "troll" or weakening of an opposing side or community [5].

False connection or clickbait describes a disconnect between (often attention-grabbing) headlines or visuals and the actual content [37].

Sensationalism is used to manipulate audiences' opinion on a specific matter. It is often connected to alarming headlines to trigger human instincts. One-sided reporting, implied information and divisive information are typical characteristics of sensationalism [39].

Hidden advertising describes the practice of producing seemingly informative and unbiased content with the hidden goal of advertising, e.g., a product or company. Even though the information is often true, it can be biased, and by disguising the actual source and masquerading as unbiased content, attempts are made to deceive the audience and create (unwarranted) trust [62]. *Propaganda* is similar to *hidden advertising*, however, here the motives are often political instead of financial [40].

3.4 Other Types of Greenwashing

Our analysis indicates that multiple forms of greenwashing can be attributed to a corresponding form of fake news, underlining the connection between these two deception types. Nevertheless, instances arise where a close connection is not apparent.

Misleading [8, 36, 58] uses written text and visual communication to create a skewed image. While it may fit the *fabricated news* type, given its often strategic and persistently built narrative, we argue that it goes one step further and therefore falls in a category of its own.

The *Halo effect* [34, 51] describes how an audience can infer a positive overall image of a product or company based on individual communicated attributes. While this effect can of course also be misused, e.g. through *cherry-picking*, it can also occur without malicious intent on the part of the company, as it is mainly based on a human behavioral bias. For types like *pooling* [11], *costly state falsification* [20],

Table 3 Aggregation of extant types of greenwashing and related literature. Names in bold have corresponding types of fake news. Newly proposed types of greenwashing are labeled with *

Greenwashing type	Articles
Sin of fibbing/Empty green claims and policies	[47, 63]
Structure/Activities decoupling	[34, 38, 58]
Means/End decoupling	[7, 34, 58]
Cheap talk/Sin of no proof/Implied superiority	[16, 34, 58, 60, 63]
Astroturf lobbying	[32, 34]
Selective disclosure/Sin of hidden trade-off/ Sin of vagueness/Sin of irrelevance	[33, 34, 58, 63]
Incomplete comparisons	[34, 55, 58]
Sin of lesser of two evils	[58, 63]
Misleading	[8, 36, 58]
Halo effect	[34, 51, 58]
Pooling	[11, 34]
Costly state falsification	[20, 58]
Sin of worshipping false labels	[58, 63]
Deceptive manipulation	[58]
Smearing	*
Adversarial attack	*

sin of worshipping false labels [63], and *deceptive manipulation* [58], no matching types were identified in the fake news literature. Here, the main difference lies in the greater emphasis on underlying actions as opposed to mere communication. Investigating whether these deceptive methods manifest in other contexts from a fake news perspective requires further exploration.

3.5 Further Observations

While our analysis reveals connections between many types of greenwashing and fake news, distinctions between the two fields surface. Notably, a primary difference involves the higher dependence on underlying actions and often more future-oriented claims in greenwashing instances compared to types usually regarded in the fake news literature. For example, a *decoupling* claim, such as promising to reduce emissions to zero, may be made sincerely and with good intent. However, if the company fails to fulfill this commitment, the claim transforms into greenwashing. In such cases, the determination of intent becomes crucial, distinguishing between disinformation (i.e., intent-driven false news) and misinformation (i.e., unintentional misreporting).

Types of Greenwashing / Fake News	News Fabrication / Deceptive News / False news	Imposter content	Cherry-picking	Trolling	Rumor
Sin of fibbing/ Empty green claims and policies	X				
Structure/ Activities decoupling	X				
Means/ End decoupling	X				
Cheap talk	X				
Sin of no proof	X				
Implied superiority	X				
Astroturf lobbying		X			
Selective disclosure			X		
Sin of hidden trade-off			X		
Sin of vagueness			X		
Sin of irrelevance			X		
Sin of lesser of two evils			X		
Incomplete comparisons			X		
Smearing				X	
Adversarial attack					X

Fig. 1 Mapping between types of fake news and greenwashing based on existing literature

However, given the competences and resources of especially large companies that should enable them to prevent most unwanted mishaps [67], we would argue to lean towards assuming intent rather than unawareness, when in doubt. This also explains the lack of greenwashing types from the misinformation category in our mapping.

Recognizing that real-world claims often fall between complete falsity and absolute truth [37] and that discerning the intent behind a claim or action is often challenging, especially for external observers [72], it is clear that extracted types do not necessarily have definite boundaries and neither need to be mutually exclusive in reality. For example, a claim that is untrue and issued with intent to harm or deceive is usually declared as *fabricated news*, however, if the intent is determined as insufficient, one might instead label it as *misreporting*. Furthermore, a *rumor* might also be labeled as *fabricated news* or both, depending on the level of truth that it inherits. These ambiguities present opportunity for future research in the fake news literature. A more unified taxonomy is needed along with clear definitions and naming of the various types. Furthermore, the practical problem of identifying intent remains an open question to be addressed. Future research might look at practices in criminal law [10, 17], where there exists a similar problem in deciding between intent and negligence, to find solutions to this conundrum.

Figure 1 shows that most types of greenwashing can be categorized into only three types of fake news. We argue that this is mainly due to the focus of the greenwashing literature currently being on corporate communications, whereas the fake news literature covers a broader spectrum, including, for example, the political and individual spheres. We contend that given the high reputational risk associated with the spread of fake news and greenwashing, companies could be limiting themselves to methods where they can defend themselves by claiming to not have disseminated any lies (i.e., *cherry-picking* and *astroturf-lobbying*) or by denying intent (i.e., *fabricated news*).

Similarly, the literature predominantly examines companies that improve their own image to appear greener, however, there are instances also where an opposing side is denigrated to achieve a similar objective [52]. Expanding the focus beyond corporations as primary practitioners of greenwashing presents another promising research avenue. When regarding *trolling* and *smearing* from the fake news types some examples come to mind that we call *smearing* and *adversarial attack*. A prominent example for *smearing* is Elon Musk twittering on May 18, 2022 that "ESG is a scam." and that "It has been weaponized by phony social justice warriors." after Tesla was removed from the S&P 500 ESG index [27]. This behavior is very similar, for example, to former President Donald Trump's fake news trolling campaigns on Twitter [9]. The *adversarial attack* shows, for example, in proponents of combustion engines who give bad press to electric vehicles by calculating their total emissions less favorably than generally accepted [29]. Since we were not able to find these forms of deception in existing greenwashing literature, we did not list any exemplary sources for these cases in Table 3. Notably, in both examples it is not an organization engaging in the greenwashing behavior but third parties (albeit with varying degrees of association) that carry out the greenwashing. We are convinced that more examples and forms of greenwashing can be found by future studies by further exploring the connection between the fake news and greenwashing literature.

4 Discussion

Our findings have several implications for researchers and practitioners in the field of Information Systems (IS). The primary motivation behind this study was to establish a conceptual foundation that facilitates the transfer of methodologies from fake news detection to greenwashing detection. By leveraging existing reviews (e.g., [54]) and approaches targeting specific types of fake news (e.g., [50]), our mapping now enables this methodological transfer. Conducting a literature review that categorizes existing fake news detection approaches based on the type of fake news they aim to detect would further enhance this transferability to greenwashing detection.

Promising technologies for these applications include Natural Language Processing for analyzing text-based communications and Computer Vision for image-based content. The recent advancements in Transformers, such as GPT-4, show significant promise in handling a wide variety of fake news and greenwashing types. Additionally, given the diverse nature of greenwashing and its communication channels, a comprehensive research avenue would be to integrate multiple methods and data sources. This could include analyzing corporate reports, social media activity, and advertisements at the same time to create a more holistic assessment of a company's greenwashing tendencies. Following these research avenue can further enhance the contribution of the IS field towards more transparent and sustainable economy in the future.

Beyond detection, our study has implications for the conceptual frameworks of fake news and greenwashing. Although various taxonomies and categorizations exist for both fields, there is no widely agreed-upon comprehensive overview. Considering their close relationship, it would be beneficial to include greenwashing within fake news taxonomies. Both fields are continuously evolving, with new forms of deception emerging. For instance, AI-generated hallucinations could be considered a new type of fake news. Future research should continuously explore new forms of fake news and greenwashing, developing a more comprehensive and conclusive framework to categorize these diverse phenomena.

5 Conclusion

This study bridges the gap between greenwashing and fake news literature by providing a conceptual mapping between different types of fake news and greenwashing. This linkage facilitates the transfer of existing detection methodologies from fake news to greenwashing. Our systematic mapping demonstrates that many types of greenwashing can be linked to fake news, allowing the adaptation of techniques such as Natural Language Processing (NLP) and Computer Vision used in fake news detection to identify deceptive sustainability communications. Furthermore, we show that both the fake news and greenwashing literature needs to be extended continuously since new types of both phenomenons keep emerging.

Greenwashing presents a significant challenge, in sustainable finance. It undermines the ability of investors and consumers to discern and support companies genuinely committed to sustainability initiatives. Yet, the identification of greenwashing instances remains a formidable challenge and often still requires labor-intensive manual investigation. Improving and finding new ways for greenwashing detection thus leads to more transparency and accountability in the market.

References

1. Ahmed, W., Vidal-Alaball, J., Downing, J., & Seguí, F. L. (2020). Covid-19 and the 5g conspiracy theory: Social network analysis of twitter data. *Journal of Medical Internet Research, 22*, e19458.
2. Allcott, H., & Gentzkow, M. (2017). Social media and fake news in the 2016 election. *Journal of Economic Perspectives, 31*, 211–236.
3. Asudeh, A., Jagadish, H. V., Wu, Y. W., & Yu, C. (2020). On detecting cherry-picked trendlines. In*Proceedings of the VLDB Endowment, VLDB Endowment* (Vol. 13, pp. 939–952).

4. Bingler, J. A., Kraus, M., Leippold, M., & Webersinke, N. (2022). Cheap talk and cherry-picking: What climateBert has to say on corporate climate risk disclosures. *Finance Research Letters, 47*, 102776.
5. Bishop, J .(2015). The psychology of trolling and lurking: The role of defriending and gamification for increasing participation in online communities using seductive narratives (pp. 162–179). IGI Global
6. Brocke, J. V., Simons, A., Niehaves, B., Reimer, K., Plattfaut, R., & Cleven, A. (2009). Reconstructing the giant: On the importance of rigour in documenting the literature search process. In *ECIS 2009 Proceedings*.
7. Bromley, P., & Powell, W. W. (2012). From smoke and mirrors to walking the talk: Decoupling in the contemporary world. *Academy of Management Annals, 6*, 483–530.
8. Cervellon, M. C., & Shammas, L. (2013). The value of sustainable luxury in mature markets: A customer-based approach. *Source: The Journal of Corporate Citizenship*, 90–101
9. Cillizza, C. (2018). Donald trump, internet troll.
10. Dam, C. V. (2013). Intention and negligence. In *European Tort Law*. Oxford University Press.
11. Delmas, M. A., & Burbano, V. C. (2011). The drivers of greenwashing. *California Management Review, 54*, 64–87.
12. Downie, L., & Schudson, M. (2009). The reconstruction of American journalism. *Columbia Journalism Review*.
13. ETFGI. (2022). Report on global ESG ETF inflows.
14. EU. (2018). Final report 2018 by the high-level expert group on sustainable finance - financing a sustainable European economy.
15. EU. (2023). Proposal for a directive of the European parliament and of the council on substantiation and communication of explicit environmental claims (green claims directive)
16. Farrell, J., & Rabin, M. (1996). Cheap talk. *Journal of Economic Perspectives, 10*, 103–118.
17. Fletcher, G. P. (2019). Intention vs. negligence. In *The grammar of criminal law: Volume two: International criminal law*. Oxford University Press
18. Gatti, L., Seele, P., & Rademacher, L. (2019). Grey zone in – greenwash out. A review of greenwashing research and implications for the voluntary-mandatory transition of CSR. *International Journal of Corporate Social Responsibility, 4*, 1–5
19. Gatti, L., Pizzetti, M., & Seele, P. (2021). Green lies and their effect on intention to invest. *Journal of Business Research, 127*, 228–240.
20. Hamilton, S. F., & Zilberman, D. (2006). Green markets, eco-certification, and equilibrium fraud. *Journal of Environmental Economics and Management, 52*, 627–644.
21. Hansson, S. O. (2017). Science denial as a form of pseudoscience. *Studies in History and Philosophy of Science Part A, 63*, 39–47.
22. In, S. Y., & Schumacher, K. (2021). Carbonwashing: A new type of carbon data-related ESG greenwashing, working Paper.
23. IPCC. (2022). Sixth assessment report - mitigation of climate change.
24. Ireton, C., & Posetti, J. (2018). Journalism, 'fake news' & disinformation: Handbook for journalism education and training. UNESCO.
25. Jindal, N., & Liu, B. (2008). Opinion spam and analysis.
26. Jung, J. C., & Sharon, E. (2019). The Volkswagen emissions scandal and its aftermath. *Global Business and Organizational Excellence, 38*, 6–15.
27. Kerber, R.,& Jin, H. (2022). Tesla cut from s&p 500 ESG index, and Elon Musk tweets his fury.
28. Kitchenham, B. A., Budgen, D., & Brereton, O. P. (2010). The value of mapping studies-a participant-observer case study. In *14th International Conference on Evaluation and Assessment in Software Engineering*.
29. Lienert, P. (2021). When do electric vehicles become cleaner than gasoline cars?
30. Luccioni, A., & Palacios, H. (2019). Using natural language processing to analyze financial climate disclosures. In *Proceedings of the 36th International Conference on Machine Learning, Long Beach, California, European Language Resources Association (ELRA)*.

31. Luccioni, A., Baylor, E., & Duchene, N. (2020). Analyzing sustainability reports using natural language processing. In *Tackling Climate Change with Machine Learning workshop at NeurIPS 2020*.
32. Lyon, T. P., & Maxwell, J. W. (2004). Astroturf: Interest group lobbying and corporate strategy. *Journal of Economics and Management Strategy, 13*, 561–597.
33. Lyon, T. P., & Maxwell, J. W. (2011). Greenwash: Corporate environmental disclosure under threat of audit. *Journal of Economics and Management Strategy, 20*, 3–41.
34. Lyon, T. P., & Montgomery, A. W. (2015). The means and end of greenwash. *Organization and Environment, 28*, 223–249.
35. Makrenko, I., Makarenko, S., & Rubanov, P. (2023). Greenwashing detection and impact on responsible business and investment: Case of ukrainian companies (agriculture leaders). In *Springer Proceedings in Business and Economics* (pp. 129–145). Springer Nature.
36. Matejek, S., & Gössling, T. (2014). Beyond legitimacy: A case study in BP's "green lashing." *Journal of Business Ethics, 120*, 571–584.
37. Meel, P., & Vishwakarma, D. K. (2020). Fake news, rumor, information pollution in social media and web: A contemporary survey of state-of-the-arts, challenges and opportunities. *Expert Systems with Applications, 153*, 112986.
38. Meyer, J. W., & Rowan, B. (1977). Institutionalized organizations: Formal structure as myth and ceremony. *The American Journal of Sociology, 83*, 340–363.
39. Molek-Kozakowska, K. (2013). Towards a pragma-linguistic framework for the study of sensationalism in news headlines. *Discourse and Communication, 7*, 173–197.
40. Molina, M. D., Sundar, S. S., Le, T., & Lee, D. (2021). "Fake news" is not simply false information: A concept explication and taxonomy of online content. *American Behavioral Scientist, 65*, 180–212.
41. Moodaley, W., & Telukdarie, A. (2023). A conceptual framework for subdomain specific pre-training of large language models for green claim detection. *European Journal of Sustainable Development, 12*, 319.
42. Oppong-Tawiah, D., & Webster, J. (2023). Corporate sustainability communication as 'Fake News': Firms' greenwashing on twitter. *Sustainability Switzerland, 15*, 6683.
43. Orange, E., & Cohen, A. M. (2010). From eco-friendly to eco-intelligent. *The Futurist, 44*(5), 28.
44. Oshikawa, R., Qian, J., & Wang, W. Y. (2018). A survey on natural language processing for fake news detection. In *Proceedings of the 12th Language Resources and Evaluation Conference*.
45. Petersen, K., Vakkalanka, S., & Kuzniarz, L. (2015). Guidelines for conducting systematic mapping studies in software engineering: An update. *Information and Software Technology, 64*, 1–18.
46. Rahmanian, E. (2023). Fake news: a classification proposal and a future research agenda. *Spanish Journal of Marketing, 27*, 60–78.
47. Ramus, C. A., & Montiel, I. (2005). When are corporate environmental policies a form of greenwashing? *Business and Society, 44*, 377–414.
48. RepRisk. (2023). On the rise: Navigating the wave of greenwashing and social washing.
49. Rojecki, A., & Meraz, S. (2016). Rumors and factitious informational blends: The role of the web in speculative politics. *New Media and Society, 18*, 25–43.
50. Rubin, V. L., Chen, Y., & Conroy, N. J. (2015). Deception detection for news: Three types of fakes. *Proceedings of the Association for Information Science and Technology, 52*, 1–4.
51. Russo, J. E., Metcalf, B. L., & Stephens, D. (1981). Identifying misleading advertising. *Journal of Consumer Research, 8*, 119–131.
52. Samoilenko, S. A., & Cook, J. (2023). Developing an ad hominem typology for classifying climate misinformation. *Climate Policy, 24*(1), 138–151.
53. Seele, P., & Gatti, L. (2017). Greenwashing revisited: In search of a typology and accusation-based definition incorporating legitimacy strategies. *Business Strategy and the Environment, 26*, 239–252.
54. Shah, M. N., & Ganatra, A. (2022). A systematic literature review and existing challenges toward fake news detection models. *Social Network Analysis and Mining, 12*(1), 168. https://doi.org/10.1007/s13278-022-00995-5

55. Shimp, T. A. (1978). Do incomplete comparisons mislead. *Journal of Advertising Research, 18*, 21–27.
56. Shin, J., Jian, L., Driscoll, K. & Bar, F. (2018). The diffusion of misinformation on social media: Temporal pattern, message, and source. *Computers in Human Behavior, 83*, 278–287.
57. Shu, K., Sliva, A., Wang, S., Tang, J., & Liu, H. (2017). Fake news detection on social media: A data mining perspective. *ACM SIGKDD Explorations Newsletter, 19*, 22–36.
58. Siano, A., Vollero, A., Conte, F., & Amabile, S. (2017). "more than words": Expanding the taxonomy of greenwashing after the Volkswagen scandal. *Journal of Business Research, 71*, 27–37.
59. Simon-Kucher. (2022). Sustainability study 2022
60. Snyder, R. (1989). Misleading characteristics of implied-superiority claims. *Journal of Advertising, 18*, 54–61.
61. Stammbach, D., Zurich, E., Webersinke, N., Bingler, J. A., Kraus, M., & Leippold, M. (2023). Environmental claim detection. In *Proceedings of the 61st Annual Meeting of the Association for Computational Linguistics, Short Papers* (Vol. 2, pp. 1051–1066).
62. Tandoc, E. C., Lim, Z. W., & Ling, R. (2018). Defining "Fake News": A typology of scholarly definitions. *Digital Journalism 6*, 137–153.
63. TerraChoice. (2010). The sins of greenwashing: Home and family edition.
64. Vicario, M. D., Bessi, A., Zollo, F., Petroni, F., Scala, A., Caldarelli, G., Stanley, H. E., & Quattrociocchi, W. (2016). The spreading of misinformation online. *Proceedings of the National Academy of Sciences of the United States of America, 113*, 554–559.
65. Wang, H., Ma, B., & Bai, R. (2020). The spillover effect of greenwashing behaviours: An experimental approach. *Marketing Intelligence and Planning, 38*, 283–295.
66. Wardle, C., & Derakhshan, H. (2017). Information disorder: Toward an interdisciplinary framework for research and policy making.
67. Watkins, M., & Bazerman, M. (2003). Predictable surprises: The disasters you should have seen coming. *Harvard Business Review, 81*, 72–85.
68. Webersinke, N., Kraus, M., Bingler, J. A., & Leippold, M. (2022). Climatebert: A pretrained language model for climate-related text.
69. Webster, J., & Watson, R. T. (2002). Analyzing the past to prepare for the future: Writing a literature review. *MIS Quarterly, 26*, xiii–xxiii.
70. Woloszyn, V., Kobti, J., & Schmitt, V. (2021). Towards automatic green claim detection. In *ACM International Conference Proceeding Series, Association for Computing Machinery* (pp. 28–34).
71. Yang, Z., Nguyen, T. T. H., Nguyen, H. N., Nguyen, T. T. N., & Cao, T. T. (2020). Greenwashing behaviours: Causes, taxonomy and consequences based on a systematic literature review. *Journal of Business Economics and Management, 21*, 1486–1507.
72. Zhou, X., & Zafarani, R. (2020). A survey of fake news: Fundamental theories, detection methods, and opportunities. *ACM Computing Surveys, 53*, 1–40.

Using Materialised Ontology-Based Data Access (MOBDA) for the Harmonisation of Trace Data from Enterprise Collaboration Systems

Lucas Schlömer, Martin Just, and Petra Schubert

Abstract Recent changes in the workplace have led to a significant increase in the use of enterprise collaboration software. The adoption of collaboration software is not always straightforward, and its interpretive flexibility can easily lead to its uncontrolled and heterogeneous use. If we are to improve this situation, we need to understand the actual practices of users. However, there are no readily available analysis tools for the (longitudinal) analysis of collaborative work processes. Users leave behind traces when they interact with the software. These traces are a by-product, and their examination has great potential for uncovering how collaboration processes are carried out. In its current form, however, this data is not suited for analysis. For this reason, we developed a novel approach for the collection, transformation and harmonisation of trace data. Using Design Science Research, we developed and successfully evaluated a software prototype.

1 Introduction

In this paper, we present a novel approach for the collection, harmonisation and interpretation of digital trace data from Enterprise Collaboration Systems. Our work contributes to (Social) Collaboration Analytics [45], which comprises methods and techniques to better understand collaborative work processes and aims to turn trace data into actionable insights.

The digital support of collaborative work has gained increasing importance over the last years, not least due to the home office imperative during the COVID-19

L. Schlömer · M. Just (✉) · P. Schubert
Center for Enterprise Information Research, University of Koblenz, Koblenz, Germany
e-mail: martinjust@uni-koblenz.de

L. Schlömer
e-mail: lucschloemer@uni-koblenz.de

P. Schubert
e-mail: schubert@uni-koblenz.de

C. M. Flath et al. (eds.), *Artificial Intelligence, Data, and Decision-Making*, Lecture Notes in Information Systems and Organisation 82,
https://doi.org/10.1007/978-3-032-08480-4_25

pandemic [16]. In particular, knowledge workers [24] rely on Enterprise Collaboration Systems (ECS), which support them in their communication (e. g. in chat and online meetings), cooperation (e. g. in joint workspaces), coordination of work (e. g. through calendars and task lists) as well as in the joint creation of content [54]. Collaborative work is multi-faceted and supported by many different collaboration tools that provide digital workspaces, digital environments, which are used by different kinds of workgroups [19] for communication, cooperation, coordination and the (joint) generation of content [3]. The literature in the field of Computer Supported Cooperative Work (CSCW) contains many classifications of collaborative work. These include, among others, the *synchronicity* of work [28], different *types* of work [15] and *areas* of collaborative work [44]. The literature also contains comprehensive descriptive models that focus on the *functional aspects* of collaboration software for particular use cases and collaboration scenarios, e. g. the socio-technical classification model of CSCW and groupware [10], the APERTO model [37] or the IRECS model [43]. Some of these models have been used for in-depth studies of *software usage* carried out to develop *metrics and scales* for the classification of network relations, workspaces and collaborative processes.

Collaboration software is characterised by its interpretative flexibility [13], which leaves the choice of concrete use in the hands of the users. Studies show that the way employees use collaboration software—their user interactions [33]—differ substantially even among people in the same workgroup [35]. Additionally, understanding the whole gamut of digitally supported collaborative work requires collecting traces from all involved software products often developed by different software vendors (e. g. Microsoft Teams/SharePoint/Yammer/Exchange, Atlassian Confluence/Jira, HCL Connections/Domino, Zoom).

Along with the increasing importance of this software type comes a growing interest in the development of business intelligence solutions for collaboration analytics, e. g. *social network analysis (SNA)* [53] and *social process mining (SPM)* [6]. However, even though SPM, the application of process mining [51] techniques to ECS trace data, seems like a suitable approach to explore sequences of work, researchers in this field are struggling with the ad hoc nature of collaborative work and the lack of adequate trace data [30]. The data in the event logs of collaboration systems are of inadequate data quality [1], the records are often incomplete (missing attributes), the information is at different granularity levels and the need for a multi-system analysis is limited by *heterogeneous log formats* [7].

These problems are not surprising as digital traces are *observational data* "that result from observing a social system without intervening in some way" [41, p. 13]. They are a by-product of the actions that employees perform in collaboration software and are not designed for research but to ensure the proper functionality of the system (e. g. for auditability). As a consequence, this type of data is not readily available and has to be (intricately) prepared for research before it can be used. The correct interpretation of the traces requires a detailed understanding of the collaborative activity that was actually performed. Against this backdrop, novel analytics approaches are needed that rely on *data preparation methods* for the collection, transformation and harmonisation of trace data to build expedient business intelligence solutions.

Accordingly, our **research question** is: How can we collect, transform and harmonise the digital traces from multiple heterogeneous collaboration systems in a joint data storage and create an analysis method for the continuous and longitudinal analysis of collaborative work processes that translates the queries of the analyst into the language (vocabulary) of the heterogeneous backend systems?

To address this question, we investigated the nature of trace data in collaboration software products and developed an approach for the harmonisation of the event data. We also looked for ways of visualising the collected data that support the interpretation and theorisation about the user activities expressed in the traces. The developed approach makes use of Materialised Ontology Based Data Access (MOBDA), a Semantic Web technology [49]. With the help of the graph database Neo4j, we developed a MOBDA prototype for examining and understanding the digital support of joint work in organisations. The underlying method is intended to enable data scientists to support user organisations with the examination of their use of collaboration software, potentially identifying improper use and missing functionality with the ultimate goal of improving the *digital support* of *groupwork*.

In the remainder of the paper, we describe (2) the background and related work and (3) our research design. The main section presents (4) the MOBDA approach, prototype development and evaluation. We (5) conclude with our contribution, limitations and future research directions.

2 Background and Related Work

In our work, we address research interests from Information Systems (IS) research with a technology solution from the Web and Data Sciences. Our phenomenon of interest is the *digital support of collaborative work* in organisations. In the following sections, we review related work.

IS Research on Collaboration Analytics (CA). *Collaboration Analytics* is the term used for the methods and techniques for analysing and visualising the digital traces (user activities and content) that accrue when users interact with collaboration software. CA is performed on the data that is created in and generated by ECS. Schwade and Schubert define Social Collaboration Analytics as "the approach for analysing and displaying collaboration activity of users in socially-enabled collaboration systems" [46, p. 2].

The literature contains a large number of studies on CA with different focus topics. Some studies examine system usage, e. g. looking at different types of user actions [2], classification of collaborative actions [38] or metrics for collaborative actions [23]. Another area of interest is user participation, with a focus on the identification of user types, e. g. lurkers, contributors and uploaders [36], promoters and super promoters [52], creators, contributors and consumers [47] or lead users [42]. Other studies examine the nature of use, e. g. knowledge worker roles [24], user typology and hierarchy [18] or general user roles [25]. Another area of interest is group workspaces and their characteristics, e. g. in the form of an ESN group typology [39], workspace types [3] or types of social support [26]. There is also a body of literature on the effect of formal hierarchies on social networking behaviour (e. g. [5, 32, 34]).

It is important to note that most of these studies are very specialised **in-depth** studies that were performed **one time** on a particular set of data. The work presented in this paper has a different purpose: We aim to develop a business intelligence method and prototype for the recurring long-term analysis of collaborative work in organisations.

Technologies for Collaboration Analytics from Web and Data Sciences. As mentioned in the introduction, one key challenge of CA is the heterogeneity of the event logs that need to be collected from *multiple* sources because of the large range of "media tools" [27]. To address this issue, we draw on the idea of ontologies. Gruber [22, p. 908] defines an ontology as "an explicit specification of a conceptualization". It provides a shared abstract and simplified view on a part of the world that is to be represented. The concepts and their interrelations need to be provided in a machine-readable format [22]. For our solution, we use publicly available ontologies, the *Social Documents Ontology*[1] (SocDOnt) and the *Collaborative Actions on Documents Ontology*[2] (ColActDOnt). SocDOnt [54] provides a structure for *content data* in ECS. It was extended into ColActDOnt [29], which provides a description of *transactional data* (events). Both ontologies reuse concepts from Social Media ontologies, such as SIOC [9] and FOAF [31].

Over the years, there have been attempts to use Web technology for CA. In 2020, Schwade and Schubert suggested a novel approach for harmonising data from cross-platform digital workspaces using ontology-based data access (OBDA) [48]. The authors created a repository for cross-system event logs and used emerging technology for building a *semantic data lake*, in which queries are formed with the concept of *OBDA*. "Ontology-based Data Access is a novel approach for developing information systems where an ontology defines a high-level global schema of already existing data sources and provides a vocabulary for user queries" [20, p. 858]. It allows end users and applications to query a database through a high-level ontology and provides a vocabulary for user queries [8, 11, 20, 21, 55]. The first attempt to realise a semantic layer using Ontop was promising, but due to the large number of databases and, more importantly, records in the event logs, Schubert and Schwade found that schema-on-read was not a viable option for analysing transactional data. Executing trivial queries can take many minutes or, in the worst case, lead to memory overflows, even if systems with extensive resources are used. Overall, the prototypical implementation showed that the combination of a data lake and a (real-time) semantic layer is not a suitable solution for analysing collaborative activities.

In the approach described in this paper, we reuse the idea of ontology-based data access (ODBA) and use it in combination with data materialisation [11, 20]. In a materialised approach, the ontology as well as the data from the source systems (in ontological form) are stored in a graph-based database in order to reduce query

---

[1] w3id.org.

[2] w3id.org/ColActDOnt.

times and enable advanced analyses (e. g. SNA), which are natively provided by some graph databases.

3 Research Design

We applied Design Science Research (DSR) according to Vaishnavi et al. [50] as our research methodology. DSR is focused on the creation of knowledge through the design and evaluation of innovative artefacts, which is in line with our research objective, the development of a method and a prototype for the generation and analysis of ECS trace data.

The DSR research process was divided into the following steps: (1) investigation of event logs in commercial collaboration software products, (2) identification of a suitable (graph) database for our harmonised log, (3) development of a method for materialised ontology-based data access (MOBDA), (4) data extraction, transformation and harmonisation from an operational collaboration system and, with this data, (5) evaluation of the novel MOBDA approach using scales and metrics from prior studies. In this paper, we focus on the evaluation phase in which we performed a study with existing classifications from the literature.

4 Development of the Novel MOBDA Method

In the following subsections, we explain the key idea behind MOBDA and describe the evaluation process.

4.1 Materialised Ontology-Based Data Access (MOBDA)

To implement a prototype, the approach of materialised ontology-based data access with a graph database was selected. Neo4j[3] was chosen as a graph database [4]. The implementation followed a similar process as described by Cysneiros and Salgado [11], Elbattah et al. [14] and Figueres-Esteban et al. [17]. Both, Elbattah et al. [14] and Figueres-Esteban et al. [17] start with an exploration of the data sources and a selection of an ontology. For the evaluation of our prototype, we used an operational instance of HCL Connections,[4] which is an ECS with a broad spectrum of modules such as blogs, forums, wikis, files and tasks. The ColActDOnt was selected for the harmonisation of the source data [29]. The ontology was used to derive a schema for the graph. All 54 *classes* of the ontology were created as individual nodes with a

[3] neo4j.com.

[4] hcl-software.com/connections.

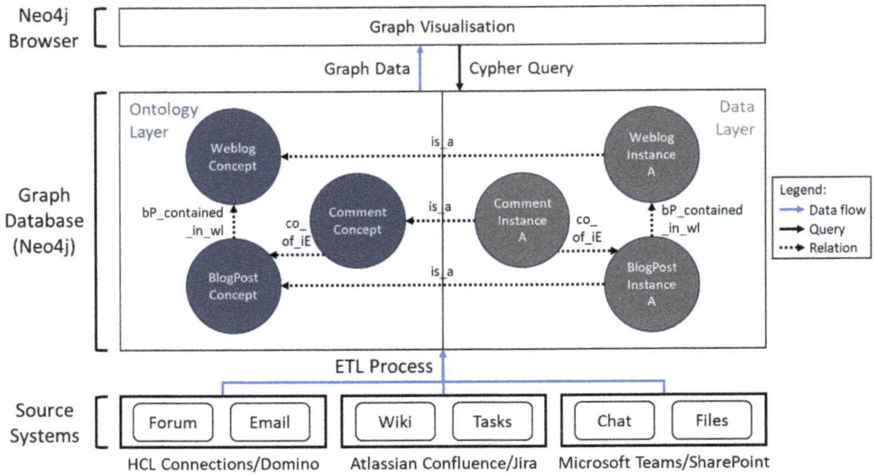

Fig. 1 The architecture of the MOBDA prototype

corresponding type (called "label" in Neo4j). The 108 *object properties* were defined as relations between nodes and the *data properties* were added as properties to the nodes. The derived schema is stored as the *ontology layer* and is used as a blueprint for materialising the concrete nodes and relations of the *data layer* (Fig. 1). To relate the data from the source system to the concepts of the ontology, and therefore to the schema, a mapping is required. Every class and property of the ontology is mapped to the corresponding set of data from the source system [11, 14, 17]. This is vital for integrating the data from the source system into the graph correctly. [11]. The mappings are stored in the form of SQL queries, which are used for the data extraction and mapping lists [11]. The mapping for *BlogPosts*, for example, contains SQL queries to retrieve all information on the nodes, attributes and relations from the source system and mapping lists that relate this data to their corresponding elements defined by the ontology.

Figure 1 shows the architecture of the MOBDA prototype, which comprises three main elements: The source systems, the Neo4j database and the Neo4j browser. A MOBDA application was developed using Python to perform the ETL (extract, transform, load) process that ingests the data into the graph database. This MOBDA application utilises a database connector to extract data from the source system. The extracted data is pre-processed using Pandas data frames[5] and transformed into a suitable format for the NeoInterface[6] import library. Cypher (the native query language of Neo4j) scripts were developed with which the import library constructs the graph from the data frames. The scripts include queries to create the ontology and data layer in the graph. At first, the ontology layer was created with its nodes and relations. Following the examples from the literature, all nodes of the data layer

[5] Pypi.org/project/pandas.

[6] github.com/GSK-Biostatistics/neointerface.

were imported and all relations among the data objects were created. To create a graph similar to the one described by Cysneiros and Salgado [11], the nodes of the data and ontology layer were connected with "is_a" relations. Thus, a node of the data layer can be connected to more than one node of the ontology layer and thus reflect inheritance.

4.2 Data Visualisation and Analysis

The MOBDA database contains the aggregated linked data (the knowledge graph) of selected data from the source systems. This provides the analyst with a powerful tool to query the data, to examine the interactions of users in their collaborative work and to use the derived knowledge to make informed decisions. The Neo4j database provides native graph visualisations of the nodes and relations. We were able to use this functionality to test and evaluate our application. We selected three SNA studies from the literature in an attempt to use existing classifications and to replicate some of the findings [25, 40, 45].

For the evaluation, we purposefully selected the data from **three workspaces**, which we are familiar with and which represent workspace types identified by [40]: an information forum (**InfForum**), a community of practice (**PracticeCom**) and a project team (**ProjTeam**). The *InfForum* has 135 members and was used to provide information, material (files) and the possibility to pose questions to its members for a limited time (9 months) in 2021. The *PracticeCom* is still in use and hosts a joint university-industry research collaboration between researchers and practitioners with 93 members. The *ProjTeam* is used for group coordination and discussion of ideas in a joint DFG project of two research groups and has 11 members.

For the evaluation of our prototype, we use **12 types** from the **classifications** of three studies. The types are explained in the next sections (highlighted in ***bold and italics***).

The **Hacker study** [25] provided us with **5 types**. The authors performed a cluster analysis on a Yammer dataset provided by Deloitte Australia and identified 9 different **user roles**. On extraction, the event data had been anonymised by the user organisation and contained account data (hierarchical position) and event records (posts, comments, follows, @mentions) of employees with attributes regarding the who, how, when, where and what of the recorded event. The dataset had been enriched with organisational data and meta-information about the content of a message (indicative keywords and character length). The Hacker study investigates public channels with a focus on communication.

For our evaluation, we are using private (closed) workspaces, which are communication-focused but include functional elements for coordination (tasks) and content creation (wiki) as well. We designed our evaluation study to best match the conditions of the Hacker study. We assign the following names to users: ***power users*** to users with outstanding level of activity, ***conversation starters*** to users who contribute an intellectual entity (the root item of a social document according to our ontology), ***focused information sharers*** to users with a large number of unsolicited file sharing (attachment), ***sporadic users*** to users that create a small number of sporadic replies (intellectual components but not entities), ***team members*** to users who only rarely contribute intellectual content but occasionally provide awareness markers (like, @mention, reaction).

The remaining user roles are not used in our evaluation for the following reasons: *well-connected helpers* are a specific role in open channels of enterprise social networks (and we analysed specific workspaces). With the help of our ontology, two roles can be reliably directly identified: *task coordinators* with task events and *chat users* with instant messaging events, so both of these types were not included in the analysis. Finally, the identification of *offline experts* is outside the scope of our study.

The **Schwade study** [45] of **user types** provided us with the next **3 types**, creator, contributor and consumer, which we used to distinguish the degree of the intellectual contributions of users. ***Consumers*** are users who only perform read events, ***contributors*** add items to existing entities (e. g. edit, recommend, tag) and ***creators*** create intellectual entities (e. g. new posts/pages, upload files). To be assigned to the categories, a predefined threshold (three events) must be reached.

The **Riemer study** [40] provided **4 types**. The authors interpreted 350 workspaces in a large ESN platform (based on Yammer) containing anonymised meta-data with 683,733 interactions by 40,304 users. The available event types were: post, reply, notification, mention and like. The authors analysed their data set iterating between deriving and calculating metrics and testing the derived metrics by using them to cluster the groups. For the final cluster analysis, a 3D cluster containing the following three metrics was used: *Distribution* of activity is measured by the Gini coefficient, which measures how evenly activity is distributed among all users. Thread *reciprocity* reflects the interaction and response rate on posts. The reciprocity is increased for each reply (which is not a like) on the original post. *Density* shows the degree of direct connectedness between members of a group. Since our evaluation is focussed on content creation and does not consider the relationships between accounts, we are only using *distribution* and *reciprocity* for the evaluation of the MOBDA application.

The final cluster analysis of the Riemer study led to **4 workspace archetypes**, which were described as follows: The first type, ***broadcast stream***, has an uneven distribution of activity, a low density and low reciprocity. The main pattern of this archetype is a small number of active users "broadcasting" information for a large number of mostly reading users. The second type is the ***information forum***. Here, we have an even distribution with a low density and reciprocity. In such workspaces, users post information or request help from other users but do not interact a lot. In contrast, the third type, the ***community of practice***, has an uneven distribution of activity with a high reciprocity. A typical example of this archetype is a core group of very active users who initiate and lead a discussion around a particular topic and a large group of users who follow the discussions and only occasionally participate. Due to the low density, the users are not closely connected. Finally, the fourth type, ***project team***, has an even distribution and high density and reciprocity, which is

```
MATCH (gws:GroupWorkspace {TITLE: 'Name of InfForum'})-
[rspacecontainer:space_contains_container]-(container)-[rcontainerblog:blog_post_contained_in_weblog]-
(blog:BlogPost)-[ritemevent:event_affects_item]-(ev:Event)-
[reventaccount:event_performed_by_account]-(acc:Account)
WHERE ev.ACTION <> "UNDEFINED"
RETURN gws, rspacecontainer, container, rcontainerblog, blog, ritemevent, ev, reventaccount, acc
```

Fig. 2 Example query for the blog module in the information forum

typical for a small team working on a joint project interacting and communicating on a regular basis.

Whilst two of the input studies were based on an analysis of *large data sets* by means of SNA, our evaluation was performed *visually* based on the graphical output of the Cypher queries. We analysed patterns in a *small data sample* of 3 selected workspaces. We only included event data for the *blog* and *forum* modules because these are the functions available in Yammer channels.

Figure 2 shows a query that was used to create a graph visualisation. Similar queries were used for each workspace and their respective blog and forum module. In these queries, data concerning the blog or forum, the related events and the users (accounts) who performed the events are retrieved. For the visual analysis, read events were excluded from the primary analysis and the visualisations to focus on active contributions to information exchange and to reduce the number of nodes for better readability.

In the following, the three workspaces are described, analysed and classified based on the data in their Forums and Blogs. The analysis is supported by Fig. 3 containing the node types and their quantity and by Fig. 4 showing the graph visualisations organised by workspace and module.

We begin our analysis with the **Forum** module and compare the findings for the three workspaces.

In the Information Forum (**InfForum**), the moderator of this workspace can be clearly identified as a ***power user*** (Hacker study) in the middle of the graph (Fig. 4, bottom left), accompanied by 33 conversation starters with few contributing events. Most accounts, especially the ones with only read events, have the ***consumers*** role. This low interaction with rather even distribution matches the workspace archetype ***information forum***.

The Community of Practice (**PracticeCom**) is the **second workspace** (Figs. 3 and 4, bottom centre). Most forum entries were only enriched by their creator. The distribution of activity is rather even, reflecting a *group of core users* who direct the conversation and provide content, which is consumed by the members. As a consequence, this workspace fits the description of an ***information forum***.

The third workspace (Figs. 3 and 4, bottom right) is a Project Team (**ProjTeam**). Here, the forum module shows a relatively high number of forum entries and events per account. Further analysis of the events shows little interaction concerning the

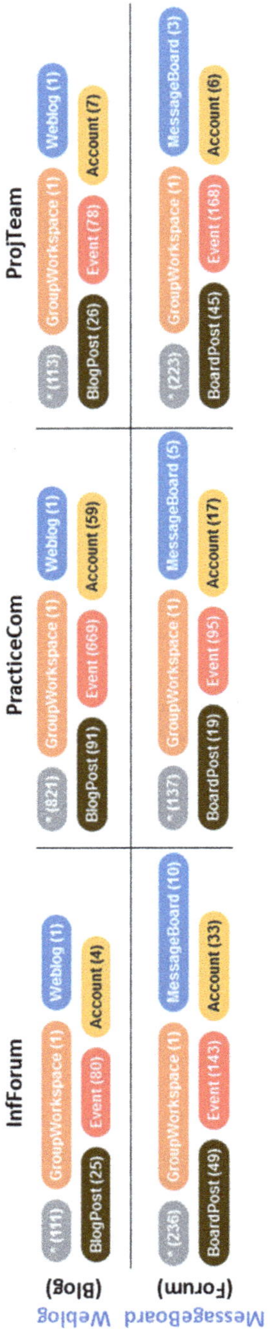

Fig. 3 Labels and node quantities in two selected modules of the three workspaces

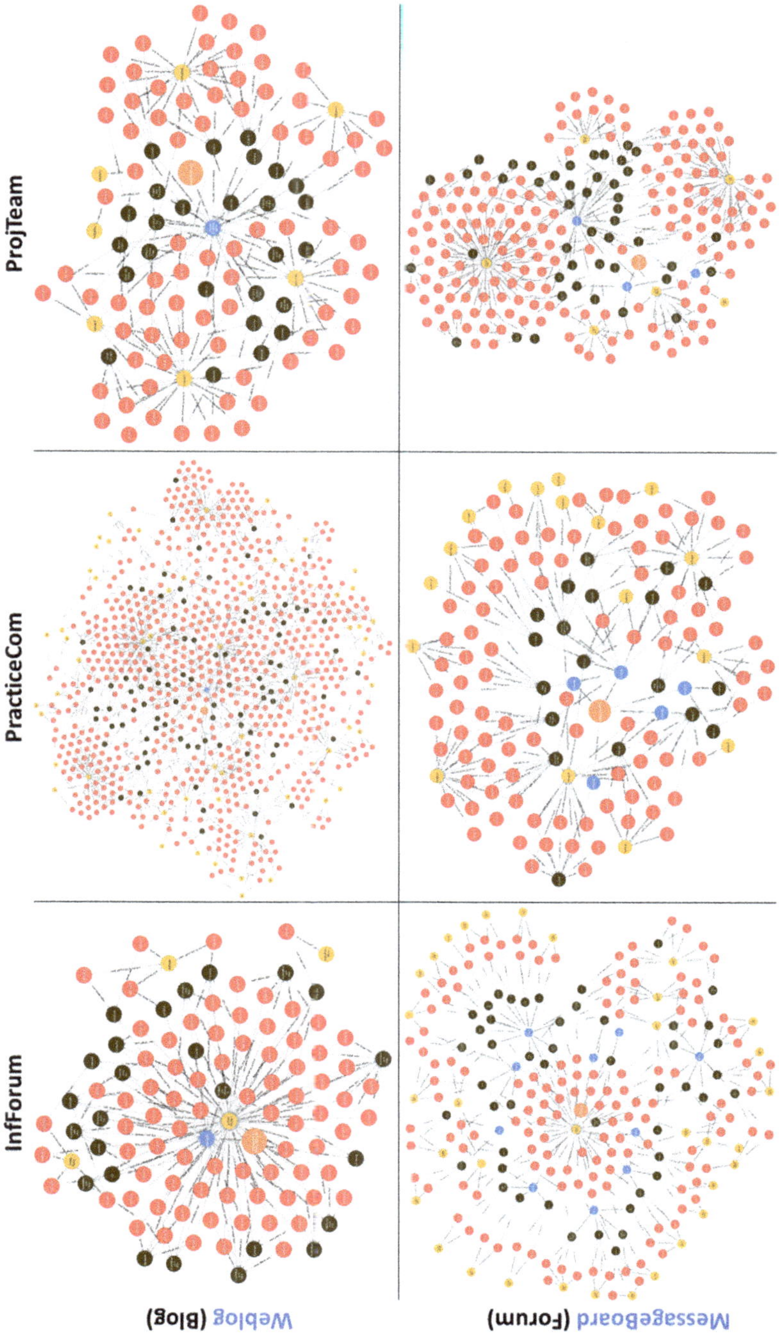

Fig. 4 Relations between accounts, events and entries in two modules of the workspaces

forum entries of other accounts. Similar to the other forums, the rather even ***distribution of activity***, low level of interaction but a rather high number of accounts consuming content, indicates an ***information forum***.

We continue the analysis with the **Blog** module. The **InfForum** workspace is visualised in the top left of Figs. 3 and 4. Especially the single ***power user*** in the middle of the graph who is performing 80 percent of all contributing events is noticeable.

The blogs module of the **PracticeCom** workspace (Figs. 3 and 4, top centre) shows a large number of nodes and relations, making this workspaces module the largest and most active in the analysis. The visualisation (top centre) shows several ***power users***, who are performing the majority of events, one of them even 93 of 669 events. In contrast to the previous workspaces, the number of likes (380) and tags (75) of all events (669) and the ratio of active accounts is higher indicating a higher level of interactivity.

The workspace is clearly used for information exchange, since some ***power users*** are providing the majority of the input and a high number of users only interact with this content. Due to the uneven distribution of activity and the high ***reciprocity*** the workspace matches a ***community of practice***. This pattern shows a kind of one-sided information pipeline filled by one ***power user*** and consumed by a silent majority. This uneven distribution of activity with low reciprocity fits the workspace archetype ***broadcast stream*** (Riemer study).

The workspace analysis concludes with the blog of the **ProjTeam** workspace (Figs. 3 and 4, top right). The visualisation shows a high degree of reciprocity and interaction due to relatively high numbers of tags and likes between blogs of different accounts showing interaction among the accounts. The visualisation suggests that the workspace is used by a small group of very actively collaborating users. Furthermore, the more active part of this group (***power users***) are core project members, while the less active ones are the team leaders discussing and making decisions. These observations confirm the ***project team*** type.

A summary of the data of all six modules is provided in the following two tables. Table 1 shows the figures for the **Forum** module.

The **visual** analysis showed that the *user roles are closely linked to the functional module* and thus the *type of work* that is carried out. Especially the **blogs** component of all 3 workspaces was used distinctively and led to the identification of different workspace types. **All forums**, however, show the characteristics of ***information forums***. In summary, we were able to successfully confirm the Riemer workspaces in our data set collected from a different software product (HCL Connections instead of Yammer).

Table 2 contains the values for the **Blog**. The row "graph elements" shows the node quantities (with and without READ events). The three following rows show the numbers for the concepts from the literature [25, 40, 47].

The visual analysis showed that the *user roles are closely linked to the functional module* and thus the *type of work* that is carried out. Especially the **blogs** component of all 3 workspaces was used distinctively and led to the identification of different workspace types. **All forums**, however, show the characteristics of ***information forums***. In summary, we were able to successfully confirm the Riemer workspaces

Table 1 Analysis overview—**Forum**

	Descriptions	InfForum	PracticeCom	ProjTeam
Graph elements (+ read events)	Nodes	236	137	223
	Forum entries	49	19	45
	Events	143 + 4006	95 + 780	168 + 943
	Accounts	33 + 95	17 + 48	6 + 8
User roles (Hacker & Riemer, 2021)	Power users	1	0	2
	Conversation starters	33	17	5
	Team members	4	17	1
Workspace types (Riemer et al., 2020)	Active users	33/128	17/65	6/14
	Activity distribution	rather even	rather even	even
	Reciprocity	low	low	low
	Workspace archetype	information forum	information forum	information forum
User types (Schwade, 2021)	Creators	4	2	4
	Contributors	2	6	1
	Consumers	122	57	9

Table 2 Analysis overview—**Blog**

	Descriptions	InfForum	PracticeCom	ProjTeam
Graph elements (+ read events)	Nodes	111	821	113
	Blog entries	25	91	26
	Events	80 + 2160	669 + 3176	78 + 353
	Accounts	4 + 134	59 + 51	7 + 5
User roles (Hacker & Riemer, 2021)	Power users	1	5	4
	Conversation starters	4	18	6
	Team members	4	33	5
Workspace types (Riemer et al., 2020)	Active users	4/138	59/110	7/12
	Activity distribution	uneven	uneven	even
	Reciprocity	low	high	high
	Workspace archetype	broadcast stream	community of practice	project team
User types (Schwade, 2021)	Creators	1	10	4
	Contributors	0	23	1
	Consumers	137	77	7

in our data set collected from a different software product (HCL Connections instead of Yammer).

5 Conclusions and Future Research

MOBDA is a novel method, which aims at providing insights into the use of collaboration software in organisations. The resulting database provides a data warehouse of harmonised trace data from multiple heterogenous event logs. It combines the research interests from IS Research with a solution from the academic field of Web and Data Science. Design Science Research was applied for developing the MOBDA method and the prototype. This paper focuses on the evaluation of the method by applying it to previous work of other authors. The source code of the MOBDA application is publicly available on GitHub.[7]

With the MOBDA prototype, we are able to solve some of the problems that have prevented researchers from using ECS trace data for analysis: (1) On data import, we are using an ontology to harmonise the format of the aggregated event log from *different* software products and we (2) provide data analysts with a stable vocabulary (ColActDOnt) for the data queries. As a consequence, a data analyst only needs to know the data structure and vocabulary of the ontology. Our current prototype contains more than five million events and has a remarkably better performance than the solution based on a data lake and a (real-time) semantic layer proposed by Schwade and Schubert [48]. We chose a (3) materialisation approach, in which data is extracted, transformed and permanently stored in a graph database. The database is performant and shows good response times even for big data. It also provides us with a tool for the generation of (4) graph visualisations, which we used for our visual, in-depth evaluation. The database acts as a harmonised central data warehouse and it is possible to export selected data sets from the graph database and import them into other tools (e. g. process mining tools or BI tools).

There are, however, some limitations and open issues. (1) We need to set up a mapping table ("adaptor") for each collaboration software product. While this is a time-consuming task it only needs to be done once for each source system. (2) In this study we have only used the prototype to analyse a subset of the data. We are currently looking for ways to run platform-level analyses (based on all data). This will then allow us to perform replication studies [12] for studies similar to the three that were used for the evaluation of our prototype in this paper. We need to do this because, with the inclusion of more data, (3) the graphs are too complex for humans to interpret. The study of the three workspaces was only performed to evaluate the general functionality of the prototype. Our future vision is to create a knowledge graph for the entire Enterprise Collaboration Platform (the portfolio of all collaboration software).

References

1. Altendeitering, M., & Tomczyk, M. (2022). A Functional Taxonomy of Data Quality Tools: Insights from A Functional Taxonomy of Data Quality Tools: Insights from Science and Practice Science and Practice. Wirtschaftsinformatik 2022.
2. Appelt, W. (2001). What Groupware Functionality Do Users Really Use? Analysis of the Usage of the BSCW System. *9th Euromicro Workshop on Parallel and Distributed Processing, PDP 2001*, 337–341. https://doi.org/10.1109/EMPDP.2001.905060
3. Bahles, S., Schwade, F., & Schubert, P. (2022). A Workspace Typology for Enterprise Collaboration Systems. *Procedia Computer Science, 196*, 296–304. https://doi.org/10.1016/j.procs.2021.12.017

[7] w3id.org/CEIR/MOBDA.

4. Barmpis, K., & Kolovos, D. S. (2014). Evaluation of Contemporary Graph Databases for Efficient Persistence of Large-Scale Models. *Journal of Object Technology, 13*(3), 1–26. https://doi.org/10.5381/jot.2014.13.3.a3
5. Behrendt, S., Klier, M., Klier, J., Richter, A., & Wiesneth, K. (2015). The Impact of Formal Hierarchies on Enterprise Social Networking Behavior. In *36th International Conference on Information Systems*, 1–19.
6. Blatt, J., Delfmann, P., & Schubert, P. (2023). Event Abstraction for Enterprise Collaboration Systems to Support Social Process Mining. *ArXiv Preprint, 2308*(04396), 1–8.
7. Blatt, J., Delfmann, P., Schwade, F., & Schubert, P. (2021). Log Shifting for Enterprise Collaboration Systems: A Supervised Event Abstraction Approach (Extended Abstract). In *International Conference on Process Mining (ICPM).*
8. Calvanese, D., Giacomo, G. D., Lembo, D., Lenzerini, M., & Rosati, R. (2017). Ontology-Based Data Access and Integration. *Encyclopedia of Database Systems.* https://doi.org/10.1007/978-1-4899-7993-3
9. Champin, P. A., & Passant, A. (2010). SIOC in Action Representing the Dynamics of Online Communities. In *6th International Conference on Semantic Systems, January*, 1–7. https://doi.org/10.1145/1839707.1839722
10. Cruz, A., Correia, A., Paredes, H., Fonseca, B., Morgado, L., & Martins, P. (2012). Towards an Overarching Classification Model of CSCW and Groupware: A Socio-Technical Perspective. *Lecture Notes in Computer Science, 7493 LNCS*(September), 41–56. https://doi.org/10.1007/978-3-642-33284-5_4
11. Cysneiros, N. C., & Salgado, A. C. (2016). Including Hierarchical Navigation in a Graph Database Query Language with an OBDA Approach. In *2016 IEEE 32nd International Conference on Data Engineering Workshops, ICDEW 2016*, 109–114. https://doi.org/10.1109/ICDEW.2016.7495627
12. Dennis, A., & Valacich, J. (2014). A Replication Manifesto. *AIS Transactions on Replication Research, 1*, 1–4.
13. Doherty, N. F., Coombs, C. R., & Loan-Clarke, J. (2006). A Re-conceptualization of the Interpretive Flexibility of Information Technologies: Redressing the Balance Between the Social and the Technical. *European Journal of Information Systems, 15*(6), 569–582. https://doi.org/10.1057/palgrave.ejis.3000653
14. Elbattah, M., Roushdy, M., Aref, M., & Salem, A. B. M. (2015). Large-Scale Ontology Storage and Query Using Graph Database-Oriented Approach: The Case of Freebase. In *2015 IEEE 7th International Conference on Intelligent Computing and Information Systems, ICICIS 2015*, 39–43. https://doi.org/10.1109/IntelCIS.2015.7397191
15. Ellis, C. A., Gibbs, S. J., & Rein, G. (1991). Groupware: Some Issues and Experiences. *Communications of the ACM, 34*(1), 39–58.
16. Ferreira, J., Claver, P., Pereira, P., & Thomaz, S. (2020). Remote Working and the Platform of the Future. In *Boston Consulting Group* (Issue October).
17. Figueres-Esteban, M., Hughes, P., El Rashidy, R. A. H., & van Gulijk, C. (2018). Manifestation of Ontologies in Graph Databases for Big Data Risk Analysis. In *Safety and Reliability - Safe Societies in a Changing World—Proceedings of the 28th International European Safety and Reliability Conference, ESREL 2018, January 2019*, 3189–3194. https://doi.org/10.1201/978 1351174664-399
18. Frank, L., Schmidt, M., Gimpel, H., Schoch, M., Schmidt, M., & Schoch, M. (2017). Emergent User Roles of a Digital Workplace: A Network Analysis Based on Trace Data. In *38th International Conference on Information Systems (ICIS), 4801*, 1–18.
19. Gerbl, J., & Williams, S. P. (2023). Identifying workgroup dimensions and their implications for the design of digital workspaces. In *CENTERIS—Conference on ENTERprise Information Systems 2023.*
20. Gomez, S. A., & Fillottrani, P. R. (2018). *Towards a Framework for Ontology-Based Data Access : Materialization of OWL Ontologies From Relational Databases* (pp. 857–866).
21. Gomez, S. A., & Fillottrani, P. R. (2020). Materialization of OWL Ontologies from Relational Databases: A Practical Approach. *25th Argentine Congress of Computer Science, CACIC 2019*

Río Cuarto, Argentina, October 14–18, 2019 Revised Selected Papers, 1184. https://doi.org/10.1007/978-3-030-48325-8
22. Gruber, T. R. (1995). Toward Principles for the Design of Ontologies Used for Knowledge Sharing. *International Journal of Human-Computer Studies, 43*(5–6), 907–928.
23. Hacker, J., Bodendorf, F., & Lorenz, P. (2016). A Framework to Analyze Enterprise Social Network Data. In M. Atzmueller, O. Samia, & T. Roth-Berghöfer (Eds.), *Enterprise Big Data Engineering, Analytics, and Management* (pp. 84–107). IGI Global.
24. Hacker, J., Bodendorf, F., & Lorenz, P. (2017). Helper, Sharer or Seeker?—A Concept to Determine Knowledge Worker Roles in Enterprise Social Networks. In *13th International Conference on Wirtschaftsinformatik*, 668–682.
25. Hacker, J., & Riemer, K. (2021). Identification of User Roles in Enterprise Social Networks: Method Development and Application. *Business & Information Systems Engineering, 63*(4), 367–387. https://doi.org/10.1007/s12599-020-00648-x
26. Henry, M. S., Parry, D. A., & Roux, D. B. le. (2023). *We're in This Together: Visible Social Support Actions in Virtual Teams Using Enterprise Social Media.* Preprint. https://osf.io/preprints/mediarxiv/nsevg
27. Hüllmann, J. A. (2022). Media Choice in the Digital Era: A Replication Study Using Digital Traces. In *35th Bled EConference*, 277–294.
28. Johansen, R. (1988). *Groupware: Computer Support for Business Teams.* The Free Press.
29. Just, M., & Schubert, P. (2023). Collaborative Actions on Documents Ontology (ColActDOnt). *Procedia Computer Science, 219*, 294–302. https://doi.org/10.1016/j.procs.2023.01.293
30. Just, M., Schubert, P., Blatt, J., & Delfmann, P. (2023). Data Preprocessing for Cross-System Analysis: The DaProXSA Approach. In *Conference on ENTERprise Information Systems 2023*, 1–10.
31. Kalemi, E., & Martiri, E. (2011). FOAF-Academic ontology: A Vocabulary for the academic community. In *3rd IEEE International Conference on Intelligent Networking and Collaborative Systems, INCoS 2011*, 440–445. https://doi.org/10.1109/INCoS.2011.94
32. Klier, J., Klier, M., Richter, A., & Wiesneth, K. (2017). Two Sides of the Same Coin?- The Effects of Hierarchy Inside and Outside Enterprise Social Networks. In *Thirty Eighth International Conference on Information Systems*, 1–19.
33. Leno, V., Polyvyanyy, A., Dumas, M., La Rosa, M., & Maggi, F. M. (2021). Robotic Process Mining: Vision and Challenges. *Business and Information Systems Engineering, 63*(3), 301–314. https://doi.org/10.1007/s12599-020-00641-4
34. Meske, C., Kissmer, T., & Stieglitz, S. (2020). Bridging Formal Barriers in Digital Work Environments—Investigating Technology-Enabled Interactions Across Organizational Hierarchies. *Telematics and Informatics, 48*, 1–14.
35. Mosen, J., Williams, S. P., & Schubert, P. (2023). Work Practice Diversity in Enterprise Collaboration Systems: An Analysis of Social Documents. *Conference on ENTERprise Information Systems, 2023*, 1–8.
36. Muller, M., Ehrlich, K., Matthews, T., Perer, A., Ronen, I., & Guy, I. (2012). Diversity among Enterprise Online Communities: Collaborating, Teaming, and Innovating Through Social Media. In *Proceedings of the SIGCHI Conference on Human Factors in Computing Systems*, 2815–2824.
37. Richter, A., Behrendt, S., & Koch, M. (2012). APERTO: A Framework for Selection, Introduction, and Optimization of Corporate Social Software. In *Sprouts: Working Papers on Information Systems* (Vol. 12, Issue 1).
38. Richter, A., Heidemann, J., Klier, M., & Behrendt, S. (2013). Success Measurement of Enterprise Social Networks. In *Proceedings 11th International Conference on Wirtschaftsinformatik, August*, 1–15.
39. Riemer, K., Lee, L. L., Kjaer, C., & Haeffner, A. (2018). Metrics Selection for Group Type Identification in Enterprise Social Network (ESN) Analytics. In *Australasian Conference on Information Systems (ACIS)*, 1–12.
40. Riemer, K., Lee, L. L., Kjaer, C., & Haeffner, A. (2020). Identification of Enterprise Social Network (ESN) Group Archetypes in ESN Analytics. *Australasian Journal of Information Systems, 24*, 1–20.

41. Salganik, M. J. (2019). *Bit by Bit: Social Research in the Digital Age*. Princeton University Press.
42. Schmid, I., Wörner, J., & Leist, S. (2022). Automated Identification of Different Lead Users Regarding the Innovation Process. *Electronic Markets, 32*(2), 945–970. https://doi.org/10.1007/s12525-022-00568-6
43. Schubert, P. (2023). IRECS Framework: Identification of Requirements for Enterprise Collaboration Systems. In *International Conference on ENTERprise Information Systems*, 1–9.
44. Schubert, P., & Williams, S. P. (2022). Enterprise Collaboration Platform Configurations: an Empirical Study. In *European Conference on Computer-Supported Cooperative Work*, 1–17.
45. Schwade, F. (2021). Social Collaboration Analytics Framework: A Framework for Providing Business Intelligence on Collaboration in the Digital Workplace. *Decision Support Systems, 148*, Article 113587.
46. Schwade, F., & Schubert, P. (2017). Social Collaboration Analytics for Enterprise Collaboration Systems: Providing Business Intelligence on Collaboration Activities. In *Hawaii International Conference on System Sciences*, 401–410.
47. Schwade, F., & Schubert, P. (2019). Developing a User Typology for the Analysis of Participation in Enterprise Collaboration Systems. In *52nd Hawaii International Conference on System Sciences*, 460–469.
48. Schwade, F., & Schubert, P. (2020). A Semantic Data Lake for Harmonizing Data from Cross-Platform Digital Workspaces using Ontology-Based Data Access. In *Americas Conference on Information Systems*.
49. Skjæveland, M. G., Giese, M. Hovland, D., Lian, E. H., & Waaler, A. (2015). Engineering Ontology-Based Access to Real-World Data Sources. *Journal of Web Semantics, 33*, 112–140. https://doi.org/10.1016/j.websem.2015.03.002
50. Vaishnavi, V., Kuechler, B., & Petter, S. (2017). Design Science Research in Information Systems. *Association for Information Systems*, 1–66.
51. van der Aalst, W. M. P. (2016). Process Mining: Data Science in Action. In *Process Mining: Data Science in Action* (2nd ed.). Springer.
52. van Osch, W., Bulgurcu, B., & Kane, G. (2016). Classifying Enterprise Social Media Users: A Mixed-Method Study of Organizational Social Media Use. In *2016 International Conference on Information Systems, ICIS 2016*, 1–17
53. Wasserman, S., & Faust, K. (1994). *Social Network Analysis: Methods and Applications*. Cambridge University Press.
54. Williams, S. P., Mosen, J., & Schubert, P. (2020). The Structure of Social Documents. In *53rd Hawaii International Conference on System Sciences*, 2825–2834.
55. Xiao, G., Calvanese, D., Kontchakov, R., Lembo, D., Poggi, A., Rosati, R., & Zakharyaschev, M. (2018). *Ontology-Based Data Access: A Survey* (pp. 5511–5519).

Part IV
Digital Markets, Platforms & Data Spaces

Business Model Types for Data Trustees

Anzelika Lipovetskaja, Seyyid Ahmed Ciftci, Julia Schweihoff, Christian Janiesch, and Frederik Möller

Abstract EU regulations and business result in a growing awareness of the benefits of inter-organizational data sharing. However, data sharing is often hindered by obstacles such as potential data misappropriation and perceived risks that outweigh possible benefits. One mitigation strategy is using a data trustee—a neutral data intermediary—that addresses these challenges and ensures secure and trusted data sharing. These data trustees uphold the rights of the data provider and give the data user legal assurance and clarity about what they are allowed to do with the data they obtain. Data trustees are still a novel phenomenon, and only a few are operating in the market. In our paper, we shed explore the characteristics of data trustees through a business model lens.

1 Introduction

Sharing data between organizations can be a powerful engine for business model (BM) innovation [41]. Data has developed from a mere business necessity to a strategic asset [20]. Subsequently, it seems sensible for organizations to tear down

A. Lipovetskaja · F. Möller
Fraunhofer ISST, Dortmund, Germany
e-mail: anzelika.lipovetskaja@isst.fraunhofer.de

F. Möller
e-mail: Frederik.Moeller@tu-braunschweig.de

A. Lipovetskaja · J. Schweihoff · F. Möller
TU Braunschweig, Braunschweig, Germany
e-mail: julia.schweihoff@tu-dortmund.de

S. A. Ciftci (✉) · J. Schweihoff · C. Janiesch
TU Dortmund University, Dortmund, Germany
e-mail: seyyid.ciftci@tu-dortmund.de

C. Janiesch
e-mail: christian.janiesch@tu-dortmund.de

C. M. Flath et al. (eds.), *Artificial Intelligence, Data, and Decision-Making*, Lecture Notes in Information Systems and Organisation 82,
https://doi.org/10.1007/978-3-032-08480-4_26

their data silos and engage with potential complementors in generating new value. Using a pool of shared data is often perceived as a major driver for competitive diversification [11]. From a business perspective, data sharing is a potential success factor and advantage for companies, and depending on their relative value, they contribute to different mechanisms of achieving competitive advantages [18]. Yet, most organizations have significant concerns when sharing data rooted in a distrust of the data user or data intermediaries and a sense of loss of control over their data [10, 17].

Against this background, a relatively new type of data intermediary—the data trustee—has emerged as a mediating agent organizing data sharing on behalf of a data provider with a distinct focus on upholding their data sovereignty [34]. For instance, the Bundesdruckerei [4] operates the CenTrust Data Platform, which offers multiple services for data providers, such as anonymization, pseudonymization, and a highly secure data infrastructure. Another example is the neutral data trustee TÜV Rheinland [39], who operates the Trusted Data Center to manage automobile data flows and make them accessible to fleet operators.

New EU legislation, such as the Data Governance Act (DGA) or the Data Act (DA), provides a legal framework for data sharing in the EU [16], making the data trustee ever more relevant. For instance, The DGA underlines the need for trust in data sharing as "necessary to increase trust in data sharing by establishing appropriate mechanisms for control by data subjects and data holders over data that relates to them" but also the need for data intermediation services as they are "expected to play a key role in the data economy, in particular in supporting and promoting voluntary data sharing practices" [9]. Subsequently, the data trustee is at the verge of becoming a highly valuable data intermediary both for addressing organizations' concerns about data sharing and orchestrating data intermediation services.

Data trustees require business models gaining them long-term success—an aspect that the current literature does not focus on. Stachon et al. [34], identified several characteristics of data trustee BMs on an abstract level and carved out three BM types: for-profit, non-profit, and governmental. In our paper, we use these three BM types as a starting point and explore the characteristics of each of them in detail. This results in the research question: "What are the characteristics of common business model types for data trustees?".

In response, we analyzed the broad landscape of data trustees currently operating in the market with the aim of creating a shared understanding of the building blocks and components of data trustee BM types. We used the taxonomy of Stachon et al. [34] as the starting point for analyzing and structuring the acquired information of data trustees and extended it with the BM perspective using the V4 model of Al-Debei and Avison [1]. The V4 model—as opposed to more detailed business model ontologies such as the Business Model Canvas (BMC)—gives us the freedom to explore data trustee building blocks in a proven frame of reference without the constraints of too many predefined elements.

The remainder of the paper is structured as follows: First, we outline and characterize the data trustee concept, followed by a definition of a business concept and the V4 model. Then, we illustrate our research approach and present our findings.

Finally, we provide an evaluation of the contribution to research and practice, as well as discuss the limitations and a future research outlook.

2 Theoretical Foundation

2.1 Data Trustees

Data intermediaries facilitate data sharing in socio-technical data sharing networks—so-called data ecosystems—and can be instantiated in a variety of ways, i.e., as data marketplaces, service providers, or data trustees [15, 23]. Depending on the specifics of the data ecosystems, data intermediaries can be adjusted and serve a variety of purposes [31]. Janssen and Singh [13] define the data intermediary as a mediator between data providers and data users. There are different opinions in the literature as to whether and how data intermediaries and data trustees are different. Some publications see data intermediaries and data trustees as equivalent terms [22], while others see data trustees as a category of data intermediaries [6, 29]. In this paper, we adopt the understanding that data trustees are an instance of data intermediaries.

Companies still hesitate to share their data. A prominent reason for this is the lack of trust regarding data security and handling of (sensitive) data and losing control of their data [10, 14, 24]. Trust is characterized by "*the willingness of an entity (i.e., the trustor) to become vulnerable to another entity (i.e., the trustee). In taking this risk, the trustor presumes that the trustee will act in a way that is conducive to the trustor's welfare despite the trustee's actions being outside the trustor's control*" [45, p. 250]. The dual nature of data sharing complicates data trust. Not only does the data provider have concerns regarding the use of their data, but the data user must be assured as well that the data they receive is eligible for use. To accommodate legal, organizational, and ethical requirements *data trustees* can provide appropriate governance structures and facilitate "*a relationship between trustor and trustee in which the trustor relies on the trustee based on a given criterion*" [44, p. 2].

The Open Data Institute defines a data trustee as "*a legal structure that provides independent stewardship of data*" and Radovesic et al. [28] consider data trustees as a "*relatively new type of data governance model.*" Carovano and Finck [6] see a data trustee as a provider of "*fiduciary data stewardship on behalf of data subjects.*" There is no standard definition for data trustees, but there are characteristic attributes that can be used to differentiate the construct [2, 34]. To realize its full potential as a data trustee, it is necessary to be perceived as trustworthy [3]. The data trustee's responsibilities include the transfer, management, and processing of data for the involved parties. Another core function is compliance with legal regulations (e.g., data protection) [22, 28]. Depending on the use case, the data trustee establishes trust-promoting mechanisms that also have a value-creating function [2]. Data trustees act as neutral authorities with the purpose of securely regulating the access and use of the data available. This means that data trustees are loyal to the data providers and data users without having conflicts of interest or further dependencies on the actors [22]. They can anonymize data, for example, and track all data requests [28].

2.2 Business Models

BMs are a "conceptual instrument" that outlines the financial and organizational structure of a company [39, p. 14]. A BM describes how a company "creates and delivers value to customers" [54, p. 173]. Typically, BMs cover a range of ontological elements, spanning from value proposition, customer segments and relationships, cost structure and profit model to key resources and activities [1, 21, 26, 38]. The increased value of data spurred new types of BM, such as data-driven BMs and data-sharing BMs [5, 12, 32]. In particular, the design of BM for the shared use of data is a relatively new topic area [32], which means that the design of BM for data sharing, especially for data trustees, has received little attention in the literature to date.

To address the growing design options for business models and the resulting complexity and uncertainty, appropriate instruments for analyzing the core logic and value creation activities of the business model can be used [30]. There are various ways in which BMs can be described conceptually in the literature [36]. These include the BMC [25], the VISOR model [8], and the V^4 model [1]. The BMC, which classifies a business model according to nine essential building blocks, is a conceptualization tool for business models that is equally accepted and widespread in both research and practice. All the elements can be categorized into the four V^4 business model dimensions. The four-dimensional categories are especially suitable for mapping data-driven business models where the key resource and central role in the value architecture is data [35].

The V^4 model comprises four interdependent dimensions for systematizing a BM. The *value proposition* reflects the products and services as well as all value-creating elements, including the addressed market segments and their preferences. The *value architecture* presents a holistic overview of the organizational structures. In addition to resources and core competencies, tangible and intangible organizational assets are included. The *value network* includes both inter-organizational and cross-company collaborations involving multiple stakeholders. The positioning of the organization and its relationships with each other in the value network is examined in more detail. *Value finance* refers to cost structures, income streams, and pricing methods [1].

We define data trustees as data-driven business models and use the more compact representation of the V^4 model to conceptualize the business models. This allows us to ensure that our work is in the conceptual scope of business models but is more freely operationalized than it would be in the more detailed BMC.

3 Research Design

To address the research question and to provide a comprehensive overview of data trustee BMs, we conducted an initial review of all the available information in the field and developed a six-phased research approach.

Phase (1)—Review Scientific and Gray Literature: At this point of our research, we screened the available literature and conducted a narrative review [27]. This was necessary, since the academic literature on data trustees is in its infancy and a systematic review is, hence, impractical. After the initial screening, we opted to only include the few papers we found (e.g., [34] or [19]) and delay a systematic review until the body of literature is more mature. We enriched the body of data by screening the web for gray literature (e.g., [33] or [2]).

Phase (2)—Public Data Analysis: Consequently, we turned to publicly available data on data trustees on the market. In BM research, this is a sensible strategy since many organizations provide ample information about their BMs—what *they do* and sometimes what *they charge for* it—transparently [37]. For this purpose, we searched databases like Crunchbase and Google Search using keywords such as "data trustee", the German equivalent "Datentreuhänder", as well as the synonyms "data trust exchange" and "trusted intermediary", especially to find private-sector companies (e.g., *Data Trustee GmbH* or *TÜV Rheinland*). Due to the novelty of the phenomenon and to examine the broadest possible range of data trustees, all actors available in the initial screening of the companies' websites that matched the searched keywords were included. The number resulted in 47 available organizations, mainly located in European countries, for example Germany, Austria, or USA, e.g., *Yale University Open Data Access*, as well as Canada, e.g., *Data Sentinel.*

Phase (3)—Iterative Data Analysis: We constructed and analyzed the database by continuously matching and evaluating the examples collected by two authors with the definition of a data trustee from Stachon et al. [34]. From the initial sample of 47 data trustees, we had to exclude a few because of a lack of information (e.g., *bitsabout.me* or *TÜV Süd*). Nor could we include data trustees that are out of business, as they did not have a viable stand-alone BM (e.g., *LunaDNA* or *DataCoup*). The final database encompassed 34 data trustees, whose information was acquired primarily from their websites or blogs, as well as reports on the companies in newspapers.

Phase (4)—Classification: For a systematic classification and analysis, all data trustees were categorized according to the dimensions of the taxonomy by Stachon et al. [34]. The selected taxonomy is the only available classification schema of data trustees in the research literature to date. For us, it serves as a basis for the investigation of data trustees, as it can be assumed that similar actors were identified and investigated in accordance with the research design of the taxonomy. Additionally, we added further characteristics that we found to be relevant for BMs but were not covered in the taxonomy (e.g., community building). These are highlighted in bold in Tables 2 and 3.

Phase (5)—Frequency Analysis and Correlation: As a next step, we determined the frequency of occurrences for each characteristic in relation to the total number of all data trustees in the subcategory. The coding was non-exclusive: for example, *Data Trustee GmbH* pseudonymizes, encrypts, and, in some cases, anonymizes personal data. As a result, it is possible to determine which attributes are complied with in the BM in relation to the total number in the target group.

Phase (6)—Characterization of the Business Models: We used the V^4 model to structure the characteristics of the data trustee BMs (see Sect. 2). By classifying the characteristics of the various organizations in the V^4 model, an inductive elaboration of the similarities between the business models was carried out, with the result that all actors were assigned to one of three categories.

4 Findings

4.1 Overview

In Table 1 we summarize and describe our classification of the data trustees BM types.

After classifying, structuring, and expanding the characteristics and dimensions using the taxonomy of Stachon et al. [34], we incorporated them into the V4 model. In this way, similarities and differences between the BM types became apparent. Tables 2 and 3 show the frequency analysis of the three BM types we discuss below.

Some characteristics emerge so frequently that they build the foundation for data trustee BM types. In all BM types, the data trustee is a governance authority at the center of a multi-sided data ecosystem. It is always a neutral, trusted data intermediary in value-creating data-sharing activities. Unsurprisingly, all data trustees—naturally—comply with data protection legislation. A particular instance is sharing

Table 1 Description of the data trustee BM types

BM type	Description
For-Profit Data Trustee	A market-oriented perspective characterizes the BM. With an accent on a financially viable and feasible BM that competes on the market through data trustee value-added services. The customer base predominantly encompasses private-sector companies. A particular focus is on monetization of data providers
Non-Profit Data Trustee	The design of the BM has a societal emphasis, similar to the governmental data trustee, but is differentiated by its diverse customer base, including a focus on financial and customer data, as well as the monetized support services provided. A particular focus is on community building
Governmental Data Trustee	The BM has a distinct social focus, making the data trustee naturally a trustworthy entity that is often funded by the government and maintains partnerships with research institutions and universities. In contrast, the service offering is rather basic and the access to the data and platforms is for free

Table 2 Business model characteristics for the value network and value finance

			For-profit data trustee	Non-profit data trustee	Governmental data trustee
Value Network	Data Provider	Individuals	83%	67%	31%
		For-Profit Organizations	58%	83%	56%
		Governmental Organizations	25%	67%	88%
		Non-Profit Organizations	0%	50%	75%
	Data User	Individuals	25%	33%	6%
		For-Profit Organizations	100%	67%	63%
		Governmental Organizations	50%	100%	94%
		Non-Profit Organizations	33%	67%	88%
Value Finance	Data Sharing Incentives	Received Service	67%	50%	25%
		Social Good	0%	67%	69%
	Revenue Model	Access Fee	33%	0%	0%
		Free	0%	67%	56%
		Service Fee	8%	33%	6%
		Pay-Per-Use	8%	17%	13%
	Revenue Source	Data Provider	50%	33%	0%
		Data User	50%	67%	13%
		Governmental Funding	8%	33%	81%

sensitive data, as 80% of our sample of data trustees work with personal data. Primarily, they organize data sharing via an upload interface or by being manually triggered. On the data's side, data is received by downloading upon request. Next to requesting consent for data sharing and data use, some data trustees provide additional services around consent and identity management so that the users are verified in the stakeholder network.

4.2 *For-Profit Data Trustee Business Model Type*

The private sector data trustees include 12 businesses. The **value network** comprises data providers, with 83% being individuals (e.g., *citizens and company service consumers*) and 58% being other private companies (e.g., *financial, insurance,*

Table 3 Business model characteristics for the value architecture and value proposition

			For-profit data trustee	Non-profit data trustee	Governmental data trustee
Value Architecture	Data Type	Personal Data	92%	83%	75%
		Customer Data	83%	33%	25%
		Financial Data	50%	33%	25%
		Company Data	33%	17%	6%
		Health/**Clinical** Data	25%	83%	81%
		Research Data	17%	67%	63%
		Social Data	8%	0%	38%
		Governmental Data	33%	17%	31%
	Data Source	**Individuals**	58%	67%	63%
		Companies	50%	50%	25%
		Local Data Sources	17%	33%	69%
	Data Security	Encryption	75%	67%	31%
		Anonymization	58%	50%	31%
		Pseudonymization	17%	0%	50%
	Trust Signaling Mechanisms	Trusted Technology	67%	50%	31%
		Domestic Data Center/ **Trust Platform**	58%	100%	56%
		Trusted Certifications & Licenses	42%	33%	25%
		Customer Reputation	33%	0%	6%
		Trustworthy Cooperation Partners	25%	67%	44%
		Governmental Support	0%	17%	38%
		Data Trust Reputation	8%	17%	50%
Value Proposition	Access Authorization Management	Individual Data Provider and/or Data User Consent	67%	67%	69%
		Individual Data Set Consent	33%	50%	25%
		Forwarding Reason	8%	33%	44%

(continued)

Table 3 (continued)

			For-profit data trustee	Non-profit data trustee	Governmental data trustee
	Data Preparation	**Data Storage/ Organization**	58%	50%	44%
		Data Aggregation	50%	17%	44%
		Data Standardization	17%	33%	44%
	Value Added Services	Data Management	67%	33%	38%
		Data Analysis	67%	67%	63%
		Aggregated Data Visualization	58%	50%	56%
		Trained Models	58%	17%	19%
		Client Software or Apps	33%	0%	25%
		Consulting and **Data Support**	8%	33%	19%
		Data Quality Management	42%	0%	38%

healthcare). Data users include for-profit organizations like media groups or fleet operators, public institutions such as universities, non-profits organizations, and individuals like lawyers or tax consultants. Partners often include trust-promoting entities (e.g., *data protection authorities, IDSA*), financial supporters (e.g., *ventures, capital partners*), technology-enabling, or promoting data trustee reputation (e.g., *IBM* or *Microsoft*).

Revenue sources for **value finance** comes equally from data providers and consumers, who pay an access fee. The incentive for data sharing is the service provided by the data trustees.

Within the **value architecture**, for-profit data trustees focus on key industry data types, primarily personal and customer data, followed by company-related and financial data. Consequently, data is usually generated by individuals or companies. Security measures include encryption and anonymization. Mechanisms used to promote trust include trust-enhancing technologies and dedicated platforms. Certifications (e.g., ISO27001) or licenses are common, as well as trust-building customer reputations.

Data trustees' **value proposition** includes regulating data access for data users', but also ensuring monitored and recorded data movements with sufficient transparency. The most common method (67%) is individual tracking, allowing data providers to see which users accessed their data. Alternatively, a general indication can follow so that a publicly available visualization of data access is provided. Among for-profit data trustees, 42% support data providers monetize their data, and offer data management, analysis, and aggregated visualization services.

Illustrative Example: *Data Sentinel* [7] is a for-profit data trustee that provides a platform for especially sensitive data. Companies such as insurance companies, legal firms, and individuals (e.g., consumer data), as well as higher education and the healthcare sector, share data. Among these are sensitive personal information, judicial data, public data sets, and research data. All data is stored centrally at Data Sentinel and comes from various sources such as payment systems, doctors, and company information systems. In order to gain access to the data, the data trustee obtains individual consent for the relevant data set and records and monitors all access so that each data provider can see who has had access to the data at any time. The data trustee provides a comprehensive service for preparing the data, and classification and standardization are conducted. The focus of Data Sentinel is on the automation of compliance, data remediation, and data auditing as a service, among others. The company secures its funding through access fees collected from data consumers and has partnerships with additional capital providers (e.g., *Sentiero Ventures*).

4.3 Governmental Data Trustee Business Model Type

There are 16 governmental data trustees. In the governmental BM **value network**, data is predominantly shared between governmental institutions or non-profit organizations, such as research institutions, government authorities, and universities.

Value finance incentivizes data sharing through trustees in value-generating input for public welfare and social good. Government funding and subsidies ensure the financing of the data trustee, while the access to the platform and services is free.

Data security is a key aspect of the **value architecture**, involving pseudonymization. Data sources include local storages (e.g., doctors, hospitals) or individuals. Common data types are health, clinical study, often linked to personal records, and research data. This architecture includes mechanisms to build trust among network actors, primarily through secure platforms or data centers, while public data trustees rely on their reputation for trust.

The **value proposition** of governmental data trustees covers data storage, organization, standardization, and aggregation. Trustees regulate access by obtaining individual consent from data providers and users or by specifying the data transfer purpose. While value-added services are less extensive than those of for-profit trustees, emphasis is placed on data analysis and aggregated visualization.

Illustrative Example: The *Bundesdruckerei* [4] has established the CenTrust platform, which is a neutral, intermediary, privacy-compliant data trustee. The primary purpose is to position itself as a trust service that shares pseudonymized (e.g., health data), anonymized, and encrypted data. Other data types include customer data, judicial data, and governmental or research data. As the platform is government financed, it is used as a vehicle to promote trust in its reputation and credibility as a German governmental organization with a platform that is DGA-compliant.

4.4 Non-Profit Data Trustee Business Model Type

There are six non-profit data trustees. Unlike the governmental model, their **value network** includes for-profit organizations, public organizations, and individuals (e.g., social enterprises, charities, co-operatives, initiatives, research institutions) who share data. Notably, 67% of non-profit trustees emphasize community building.

Within **value finance**, data is consumed mainly by public entities. While the primary motivation for data sharing is social good, the trustees' services add appeal. Access to data is free in 67% of cases, though some BMs charge service fees or Pay-Per-Use fees for supportive activities and services. Revenue comes from data users, providers, and government funding, with data users often being billed if fees apply.

The **value architecture** covers personal, financial, health, and research data from individuals, companies, and local repositories. Data security is ensured through encryption or anonymization. Trust is built through proprietary platforms or domestic data centers and represent the most significant trust-building mechanism. Additional trust-building efforts include partnerships and technologies.

In the **value proposition**, non-profit trustees regulate access via agreements with data providers or consumers, individual authorizations, or specifying the data users' reasons for access. They offer basic data storage, organization, and also data standardization, along with data analysis, management, and consulting services.

Illustrative Example: The non-profit organization *Vivli* [40] is an independent, global platform for the sharing of data and data analysis. The focus is on individual patient data from clinical studies. The data trustee acts as a neutral broker between the data users and emphasizes mechanisms that promote the data-sharing community. The company anonymizes data from clinical studies and focuses on data security. Access to data on the Vivli Platform is free, but Vivli Service charges data users exclusive access to its secure research environment. The social focus of the company is to propose only fundamental services of data management, aggregated data visualization, and data analysis.

5 Discussion and Limitations

The three data trustee BM types, non-profit, for-profit, and governmental, provided a starting point for examining the viability of data trustee BMs. With our research, we contribute an empirical underpinning to these BM types by evaluating organizations in the market. For practical implementation, we provide a framework that can be used for orientation as well as to develop, position, and establish data trust models within the data ecosystem to ensure secure and sovereign data sharing.

Although the general function of data trustees remains the same across the BM types, we found that the BM types differ according to the objective and purpose they pursue. For-profit data trustees naturally differentiate themselves from the other two models. In fact, their focus is to develop a viable, market-ready BM to operate as a data trustee while still generating revenue and separating themselves from the competitive environment with the services they offer. By contrast, the other two data trustee BM types focus on the social component as an incentive for data sharing. Consequently, governmental data trustees emphasize other fundamental characteristics, for example, health data, government funding, or free access to data trustee platforms and services. Non-profit data trustees operate in-between and have characteristics of both other types. Although their BM is driven more by social incentives and, thus, the design leans more towards governmental data trustees, they can be still classified as a distinct type of data trustee. Financing, for example, is ensured by many sources, while the model is usually provided for free. In some cases, financing options such as service fees and pay-per-use are also available. Table 4 provides a summary of our findings across the four dimensions of the V^4 model and the three data trustee BM types.

It is important to note that the success of data trustees in the market is not solely based on their main features of security and transparency but also on the services they provide. However, individuals who use data trustees to protect their personal data and incidentally sell data are the main data providers for most non-governmental organizations. However, the services offered by data trustees are mainly aimed at other organizations that use the acquired data. These services include the preparation, analysis, and visualization of big data, as well as the training of AI models, which is essential in all market sectors today.

Furthermore, for-profit and non-profit organizations must ensure the security of their platforms through advanced technologies and security certificates. In contrast, governmental data trustees rely on their reputation as a secure source. Nevertheless, it is typically transparent which security technologies are used in these organizations.

The novelty of the topic implies that the current documented structure for the data trustee BM could already find other alternatives in the near future. This is a limitation on highly innovative topics that are subject to rapid, dynamic developments: data trustees may soon undergo BM developments, or newer approaches to BMs may enter the market and shift the current picture we developed. Further, the collection and structuring of data from publicly available sources is naturally subject to bias by the participating authors.

6 Contributions and Outlook

In this paper, we address the question of archetypical BM for data trustees. With our research, we expanded this novel thematic area of data intermediation and contribute concrete knowledge through observations from practice. We detail BM types for-profit, non-profit, and governmental data trustees and discusses their specificities.

Our research can provide a starting point for further research. We only showed a selection of characteristics for the three identified BM types. The characteristics can be analyzed more deeply in future studies and explored with new methods.

Table 4 Overview and classification of the data trustee business model types

<table>
<tr><th></th><th>For-profit data trustee</th><th>Non-profit data trustee</th><th>Governmental data trustee</th></tr>
<tr><td rowspan="2">Value Network</td><td>The consuming entities are other companies, while the data is provided by individuals or privately owned companies</td><td>Data providers are very diverse, mainly companies, but also individuals and public organizations
Support community building</td><td>Tend to share data between the public entities but also between non-profit and private businesses</td></tr>
<tr><td colspan="3">• Stakeholders who are interested in data sharing
• Data trustee acts as a governance authority—a neutral, trusted data intermediary
• Data can be transferred through a download, or via request from the data provider to the data trustee and provided to the data receiver through an upload or by being manually triggered</td></tr>
<tr><td rowspan="3">Value Architecture</td><td rowspan="2">Share data that will benefit their network participants the most-personal data, customer data or financial data
Rely primarily on trust-promoting technologies and provide support with (e.g., blockchain technologies, encrypted connections or SaaS)
Certifications or licenses (e.g., ISO27001) are also a trust mechanism</td><td>Customer and/or financial data</td><td>Data sources are besides individuals also local data providers (e.g., doctors or hospitals)
Natural reputation that fosters trust and confidence</td></tr>
<tr><td colspan="2">Primarily health and clinical data or research data
Focused on the societal intent as a trust mechanism
Partnerships are intended to promote trust (e.g., university and public institutions or research institutes)</td></tr>
<tr><td colspan="3">• Sharing of sensitive data—personal data
• Place emphasis on establishing a trust-enhancing platform or data center</td></tr>
</table>

(continued)

Table 4 (continued)

	For-profit data trustee	Non-profit data trustee	Governmental data trustee
Value Finance	Are primarily driven by financial goals and aim to generate revenue by offering a wider range of services and charging access fees for data users or/and data provider Support monetization of data provider	Demand compensation (e.g., service fee) if support services are used Diverse sources of income (e.g., data user, government, fees)	Often governmentally funded Few services, but they are free of charge
		Grant free access to their data and/or platforms Incentives for data sharing are socially driven	
Value Proposition	Offer several services and provide additional microservices (e.g. data banking) Services range from data management to data analysis and the use of AI models. In addition, they often offer their own software or apps to supplement the services or to provide continuous access to the data	Differentiate themselves by also offering consulting services and support	Incorporate data quality management
		Have the same services that are predominantly offered, such as data analysis, aggregated data visualization, or data management In some cases, access to the data requires a specific, legitimate reason that must be specified by the data user in order to obtain the data	
	• Compliance with data protection legislation (e.g., GDPR) • Consent management • Identity management		
Sample	Data Sentinel, Data Trustee GmbH, idento.one, TÜV Rheinland, IBM & Mastercard—Truata, DRACOON, Apheris, Polypoly, itsmydata, Complero, ODE Infinity, DataVillage	Mydex, Data for Good Platform, JoinData, MIDATA Genossenschaft, Project Data Sphere Initiative, Vivli	Nortal—Vertrauensstelle nach § 299 SGB V, Westdeutsche Biobank Essen, Bundesdruckerei Plattform CenTrust, THS Greifswald, Racoon, Greater London Authority/London DataStore, World Data Exchange/digi.me, Findata, Clinical Study Data Request Program, Consumer Data Research Centre, Data and Analytics Facility for National Infrastructure, Djust Connect, Grampian Data Safe Haven, OpenSafely, The Genomic Data Commons/National Cancer Institute, Yale University Open Data Access

For instance, we focus on empirically exploring BM types, which could be used for theorizing using methods such as qualitative comparative analysis or cluster analysis. Particularly, it could be interesting to extend the underlying database with qualitative interview data, which could provide richer insights into the practice of data trustees.

In addition, in the process, we noticed that the employed taxonomy of Stachon et al. [34] could potentially be further refined and used as a coding scheme to cluster archetypes of data trustees, eventually hinting at furthermore fine-granular BMs or even novel BM (sub-)types. In addition, case studies based on BM types are also conceivable to work out in detail how BMs for data trustees can be developed. This would allow us to make data trustee BM more usable for the industry. Lastly, the processes for data sharing among the data trustees have not yet been scrutinized in a structured fashion. The derivation of process patterns for sharing, brokering, and using data could assist in building trust in these novel intermediary services and better operationalize the services with the data providers and consumers—potentially leading to even further BM for data trustees.

Acknowledgements This research and development project is funded by the German Federal Ministry of Education and Research (BMBF) within the "Richtlinie zur Förderung von Projekten zur Erforschung oder Entwicklung praxisrelevanter Lösungsaspekte ('Bausteine') für Datentreuhandmodelle" (Funding No. 16DTM201A/B) and financed by the European Union—NextGenerationEU. The authors are responsible for the contents of this publication

References

1. Al-Debei, M. M., & Avison, D. (2010). Developing a Unified Framework of the Business Model Concept. *European Journal of Information Systems, 19*(3), 359–376.
2. Blankertz, A., & Specht, L. (2024). Wie eine Regulierung für Datentreuhänder aussehen sollte, Policy Brief, Eine Regulierung für Datenbtreuhänder, Stiftung Neue Verantwortung, https://www.stiftung-nv.de/sites/default/files/regulierung_fuer_datentreuhaender.pdf, last acecessed 2024/03/12.
3. Blankertz, A., & Specht, L. (2024). What Regulation for Data Trusts Should Look Like, Policy Brief, On Regulation for Data Trusts, Stiftung Neue Verantwortung, https://www.stiftung-nv.de/sites/default/files/regulation_for_data_trusts_0.pdf, last accessed 2024/03/12.
4. Bundesdruckerei: Datentreuhänder: Datentreuhänder-Plattforn mit Vertrauensstellendienst on demand. https://www.bundesdruckerei-gmbh.de/de/loesungen/datentreuhaender, last accessed 2024/03/08.
5. Bärenfänger, R., & Otto, B. (2015). Proposing a Capability Perspective on Digital Business Models. In D. Aveiro & A. Caetano (Eds.), *2015 IEEE 17th Conference on Business Informatics (CBI). 13–16 July 2015* (pp. 17–25). IEEE.
6. Carovano, G., & Finck, M. (2023). Regulating Data Intermediaries: The Impact of the Data Governance Act on the EU's Data Economy. *Computer Law & Security Review, 50*, Article 105830.
7. Data Sentinel. (2024). Data Sentinel-Homepage, https://www.data-sentinel.com/, last accessed 2024/03/03.
8. El Sawy, O. A., & Pereira, F. (2013). *Business Modelling in the Dynamic Digital Space an Ecosystem Approach.* Springer.

9. European Commission. (2022). Regulation (EU) 2022/868 of the European Parliament and of the Council of 30 May 2022 on European Data Governance and Amending Regulation (EU) 2018/1724 (Data Governance Act). *Official Journal of the European Union.*
10. Fassnacht, M., Benz, C., Heinz, D., Leimstoll, J., & Satzger, G. (2023). Analyzing Barriers to Data Sharing among Private Sector Organizations: Combined Insights from Research and Practice. In *Proceedings of the 56th Hawaii International Conference on System Sciences, Hawaii, USA.*
11. Goasduff, L. (2021). Data Sharing Is a Business Necessity to Accelerate Digital Business. https://www.gartner.com/smarterwithgartner/data-sharing-is-a-business-necessity-toaccelerate-digital-business, last accessed 2024/03/09.
12. Hartmann, P. M., Zaki, M., Feldmann, N., Neely, A. D., & Neely, A. D. (2014). *Big Data for Big Business? A Taxonomy of Data-driven Business Models used by Start-up Firms.* Social Science Research Network.
13. Janssen, H., & Singh, J. (2022). Data intermediary. *Internet Policy Review, 11*(1).
14. Jussen, I., Möller, F., Schweihoff, J., Gieß, A., Giussani, G., & Otto, B. (2024). Issues in Inter-Organizational Data Sharing: Findings from Practice and Research Challenges. *Data & Knowledge Engineering, 150*, Article 102280.
15. Jussen, I., Fassnacht, M., Schweihoff, J., & Möller F. (2024). Reaching for the Stars: Exploring Value Constellations in Inter-Organizational Data Sharing. In *ECIS 2024 Research Papers.*
16. Jussen, I., Schweihoff, J., Dahm, V., Möller, F., & Otto, B. (2023). Data Sharing Fundamentals: Definition and Characteristics. In *Proceedings of the 56th Hawaii International Conference on System Sciences.*
17. Jussen, I., Schweihoff, J., & Möller, F. (2023). Tensions in Inter-Organizational Data Sharing: Findings from Literature and Practice. In *Proceedings of the International Conference on Business Informatics (CBI).*
18. Kugler, P., & Plank, T. (2021). Coping with the Double-Edged Sword of Data-Sharing in Ecosystems. *Technology Innovation Management Review, 11*(11/12), 5–16.
19. Lauf, F., Scheider, S., Friese, J., Kilz, S., Radic, M., & Burmann, A. (2023). Exploring Design Characteristics of Data Trustees in Healthcare—Taxonomy and Archetypes. In *ECIS 2023 Research Papers* (p. 323).
20. Legner, C., Pentek, T., & Otto, B. (2020). Accumulating Design Knowledge with Reference Models: Insights from 12 Years' Research into Data Management. *Journal of the Association for Information Systems, 21*(3), 520–544, 664–810 (2020).
21. Linder, J. C., & Cantrell, S. (2000). *Changing Business Models: Surveying the Landscape* (Working Paper). Accenture Institute for Strategic Change.
22. Micheli, M., Farrell, E., Carballa-Smichowski, B., Posada-Sanchez, M., Signorelli, S., & Vespe, M. (2023). *Mapping the Landscape of Data Intermediaries—Emerging Models for More Inclusive Data Governance.* European Commission, Joint Research Centre Science for Policy Report, Publications Office of the European Union.
23. Oliveira, M. L. S., Barros Lima, G. de F., & Loscio, B. F. (2019). Investigations into Data Ecosystems: A Systematic Mapping Study. *Knowledge and Information Systems, 6*, 589–630.
24. Opriel, S., Möller, F., Burkhardt, U., & Otto, B. (2021). Requirements for Usage Control based Exchange of Sensitive Data in Automotive Supply Chains. In *Proceedings of the 54th Hawaii International Conference on System Sciences.*
25. Osterwalder, A. (2004). *The Business Model Ontology a Proposition in a Design Science Approach.* Doktorarbeit. Université de Lausanne.
26. Osterwalder, A., & Pigneur, Y. (2010). *Business Model Generation: Ein Handbuch für Visionäre, Spielveränderer und Herausforderer.* Campus Verlag.
27. Paré, G., Truder, M.-C., Joana, M., & Kitsiou, S. (2015). Synthesizing Information Systems Knowledge: A Typology of Literature Reviews. *Information & Management, 52*(2), 183–199.
28. Radosevic, N., Duckham, M., Rahaman, M. S., Hoa, S., Williams, K., Hashem, T., & Tao, Y. (2023). Spatial Data Trusts: An Emerging Governance Framework Forsharing Spatial Data. *International Journal of Digital Earth, 16*(1), 1607–1639.

29. Richter, H. (2023). Looking at the Data Governance Act and Beyond: How to Better Integrate Data Intermediaries in the Market Order for Data Sharing. *GRUR International, 72*(5), 458–470.
30. Schoormann, T., Schweihoff, J., Jussen, I., & Möller, F. (2023). Classification Tools for Business Models: Status quo, Comparison, and Agenda. *Electronic Markets, 33*(7), 1–36.
31. Schweihoff, J., Jussen, I., & Möller, F. (2023). Trust Me, I'm an Intermediary! Exploring Data Intermediation Services. In *Proceedings of the 18th International Conference on Wirtschaftsinformatik*.
32. Schweihoff, J., Jussen, I., Dahmns, V., Möller, F., & Otto, B. (2023). How to Share Data Online (fast)—A Taxonomy of Data Sharing Business Models. In *Proceedings of the 56th Hawaii International Conference on System Sciences*.
33. Specht-Riemenschneider, L., & Kerber, W. (2022). *Designing Data Trustees—A Purpose-Based Approach*. Konrad-Adenauer-Stiftung e. V.
34. Stachon, M., Möller, F., Guggenberger, T., Tomczyk, M., & Henning, J.-L.: Understanding Data Trusts. In *ECIS 2023 Research-in-Progress Papers* (p. 36).
35. Strahringer, S., & Wiener, M. (2021). Datengetriebene Geschäftsmodelle: Konzeptuelles Rahmenwerk, Praxisbeispiele und Forschungsausblick. *HMD, 58*, 457–476.
36. Szopinski, D., Massa, L., John, T., Kundisch, D., & Tucci, C. (2022). Modeling Business Models: A Cross-disciplinary Analysis of Business Model Modeling Languages and Directions for Future Research. *Communications of the Association for Information Systems, 51*(1), 774–841.
37. Teece, D. J. (2010). Business Models, Business Strategy and Innovation. *Long Range Planning, 43*(2–3), 172–194.
38. Timmers, P. (1998). Business Models for Electronic Markets. *Electronic Markets, 8*(2), 1–12.
39. TÜV Rheinland. (2023): Prüfdienstleister bietet treuhänderischen Datenschutz für vernetzte Fahrzeuge, https://www.tuv.com/presse/de/meldungen/trusted-data-center. html, last accessed 2024/03/08.
40. Vivli. (2024). Vivli-Homepage, https://vivli.org/, last accessed 2024/03/03.
41. Wixom, B. H., Sebastian, I. M., Gregory, R. W., & Piccoli, G. (2023). Level Up to Strategic Data Sharing: Your data Assets Are Key to Developing New Value for Your Customers and Giving You Clout in Digital Ecosystems. *MIT Sloan Management Review*.

Facing the Multifaceted Impact of Fake Reviews: A Comprehensive Literature Review

Kim Fröhnel, Gabriel Benedikt Thomas Adams, and Rüdiger Zarnekow

Abstract Online reviews became an essential source of knowledge during consumers' online decision-making process. In recent years, the crucial role of online reviews has incentivized fraudsters to game the review system by writing self-promotional fake reviews or bad-mouthing competitors. While detecting fake reviews has become an important task for scholars and practitioners, research on the impact of fake reviews is still limited and distributed across disciplines. Therefore, we conducted a systematic literature review to synthesize empirical and theoretical research findings on the impact of fake reviews. Our findings show that fake reviews are not only a competitive and economic but also a social problem. Moreover, fake reviews undermine the importance of online reviews as quality signals in online decision-making processes. In this paper, we identified research gaps and derived recommendations for future research and practice.

1 Introduction

Today, many platforms offer consumers the opportunity to submit online reviews after a purchase or booking. Online reviews serve as an independent, valuable, and public source of information about a product or service quality [17, 51] and affect consumers expectations [64, 78], online trust-building [37], and decision-making [14, 22]. Moreover, online reviews affect businesses' reputation and their transactions and revenue (e.g., [5, 61]).

K. Fröhnel (✉) · G. B. T. Adams · R. Zarnekow
Information and Communication Management, Technical University of Berlin, Berlin, Germany
e-mail: k.froehnel@tu-berlin.de

G. B. T. Adams
e-mail: g.adams@tu-berlin.de

R. Zarnekow
e-mail: ruediger.zarnekow@tu-berlin.de

C. M. Flath et al. (eds.), *Artificial Intelligence, Data, and Decision-Making*, Lecture Notes in Information Systems and Organisation 82,
https://doi.org/10.1007/978-3-032-08480-4_27

Over the last few years, the power of reviews has increasingly incentivized fraudsters to game the review system by writing or buying fake reviews. Thus, besides the importance of online reviews for building and maintaining trust, the question of reviews' trustworthiness has arisen. According to various former estimates, 10–20% of all online reviews are fake (e.g., [40, 61, 84]). Fraudsters are often driven by financial profit or competition and, thus, generate fake reviews to promote their reputation and products or to discredit competitors [65, 69]. Moreover, the fabrication of fake reviews emerges as a new business model by which people pay for review-posting services. Further, businesses can incentivize fake reviewers through social network sites and refund the item after the review is submitted [34].

If customers rely on fake reviews that do not represent the items' real quality, the purchased product does not meet consumers' needs [51]. As *"[o]nline reviews are only as good as the value they provide to users"* [13, p. 3], the prevalence of fake reviews on platforms means that customers have to think critically about their beliefs and decision-making based on online reviews [40]. In the worst case, online reviews may lose their credibility [94] and be viewed as less helpful by users in the future.

Consequently, the awareness for fake reviews has increasingly become crucial for practitioners and academia. Many studies focus on fake review detection to tackle the review manipulation problem. Although these studies often motivated their approach by fake reviews' impact (e.g., [2, 9, 58], the impact of fake reviews has not been researched thoroughly [110]. The reasons lie in the difficulties in observing and examining the impact of fake information on consumer decisions over time [103], the missing truth about actual manipulation, the lack of a database with the review history dynamics [111], and review manipulations complexity [74, 75]. Further, detection approaches are reactive, require high-quality training data, and are platform-specific [74]. Thus, so far, no detection approach can fully solve the review manipulation problem.

The problem of missing studies on the impact of fake reviews strongly relates to the problem of fake review detection. Nevertheless, some studies focus on fake reviews' impact by trying to circumvent the detection problem using platform-filtered, lab-generated, or bot-generated reviews [33]. Wu et al. [108] and Ansari and Gupta [6] have already conducted a literature review on fake reviews. Still, both literature reviews provide no detailed view of research on fake reviews' impact. Additionally, researchers increasingly focus on fake reviews, and the number of studies steadily increases. To the best of our knowledge, no research explicitly investigates the status quo of research on the impact of fake reviews. To address this gap in the academic literature, we perform a systematic review of the existing empirical and theoretical fake review literature to synthesize and comprehend *(RQ) what is known about the impact of fake reviews?*

The remainder of the paper is structured as follows. Firstly, we define the fake review and impact term and describe our literature search strategy, data extraction, and synthesis in Methodology. In Results, we present our literature review results, including summary statistics, fake reviews' impact, and employed theories. We finish this paper with our discussion, limitations, and theoretical and practical implications in Discussion and Conclusion.

2 Methodology

We conducted a systematic literature review to assess the status quo of research on the impact of fake reviews. Webster and Watson [101] guided our methodology approach. Moreover, we also consider the guidelines by Kraus et al. [50] for literature reviews as independent studies. In this section, we first define the terms fake review and impact used in this work and subsequently present our methodological approach to literature search, extraction, and synthesis.

2.1 Fake Review and Impact Definition

Even though the term fake review has been used in numerous articles in recent years, no unified definition exists [108]. According to the taxonomy by Wu et al. [107], truly fake reviews refer to shameless promotion and malicious slander, meaning fake reviews are often spread to improve reputation or to demote competitors' products or services (e.g., [40, 61, 65]). Further, they mislead consumers in their decision-making [6, 108]. Fake reviews can also be incentivized, e.g., using money or discounts [95, 97].

Following most researchers, we define fake reviews as *promotional and defamatory reviews that try to mislead consumers.*

The term impact can be defined as "*the powerful effect that something has on somebody/something*" [72]. In this paper, we aim to identify fake reviews' impact on different mechanisms and actors that have been examined in the platform economy research. To the best of our knowledge, no uniform taxonomy or classification of the impact term exists. Depending on the context, different types of impact can be distinguished, e.g., economic, technological, socioeconomic, or environmental impact.

2.2 Search Strategy and Inclusion Criteria

Inspired by Kraus et al. [50], we define the following criteria for our keyword-based search. Firstly, we searched the scientific databases Web of Science (WoS), Scopus, AIS eLibrary (AISeL), and IEEE Xplore for scholarly articles. We considered relevant documents on the topic and the prerequisites of all four databases (e.g., number of words, wildcards, and boolean operators) to compose a search string. We then performed a keyword search with our refined search string presented in Fig. 1. Due to the limited number of words in the databases, we focused on neutral keywords and synonyms (e.g., impact and consequence) and not on keywords with negative (e.g., disadvantage) or positive (e.g., advantage) connotations. Our search covers research from 2010 to 2024 (March). We narrowed our search to results focusing on fake reviews and their impact in the context of digital platforms. We assumed the search string would be mentioned in the title, keywords, and abstract. We searched for articles (also early access and review articles) and conference papers to include work-in-progress and peer-reviewed finalized work. To ensure high-quality documents, we excluded, e.g., keynotes and books. Regarding the language, we considered English and German documents.

Further, we conducted a backward and forward search that supplemented our keyword-search results.

2.3 Data Extraction and Literature Synthesis

In Fig. 1 visualizes our search and data extraction process in all four databases and our results in each step. After searching in all four databases and filtering the results based on the aforementioned criteria (year, publication type, title/abstract/keywords, and language), we screened the abstract of 4,216 documents in Step 2. Many articles focus on fake review detection and note the impact of fake reviews only as a motivation for their research (e.g., [2, 10, 18]). Other articles focus on (1) fake news and its impact (e.g., [32, 100]) or (2) fake identities [1]. These articles were not considered in our review.

Based on the abstract, we saved the articles that appear promising in addressing our research objective for full-text screening in Step 3. Afterward, we started our full-text reading process. For all relevant articles, we used tags to structure all findings and mark references that may be interesting for the backward search. Furthermore, we added notes, e.g., about the context or findings, for all relevant articles and tagged duplicates. Step 4 shows that the most relevant articles were found in Scopus (39). Still, as we started our search process with WoS, we deleted 25 duplicates for Scopus (22 WoS and three IEEE Xplore duplicates). Moreover, we excluded two literature reviews; one of them was also a Scopus duplicate. At the end of our data extraction process, we had 25 WoS, three IEEE Xplore, no AISeL, and 14 Scopus results. After our keyword-based search, we read all tagged references for our backward search in Step 6. Through our backward search, we identified twelve relevant articles (ten for WoS, one for IEEE Xplore, and one for Scopus). Finally, we used Google Scholar to check all *cited by* references for our forward search and identified ten new articles (eight for WoS and two for Scopus). We finished our initial data extraction with 64 articles.

We carefully re-read and compared all articles identified from the search and data extraction process for the content analysis. Subsequently, two coders conducted the content analysis and classified the articles concerning the theories employed (e.g., Signaling Theory), the context (e.g., eCommerce), the type of fake reviews (positive/negative), and the impact type. Regarding the impact type, we coded the mentioned impact into two main categories (economic and social impact) with several subcategories each, which we identified during the coding process. The chosen classification is not exclusive. Some aspects may overlap multiple categories to some extent.

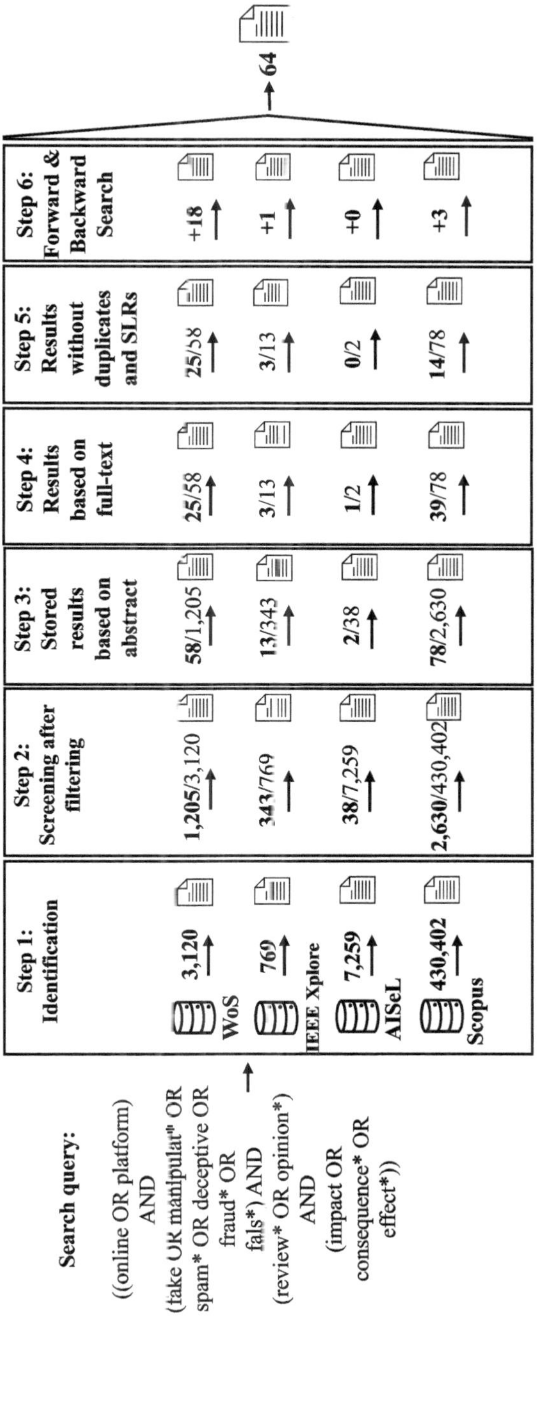

Fig. 1 Search process

3 Results

In the following, we describe our results, starting with a brief overview of our sample, then key findings regarding fake reviews' impact, and ending with employed theories.

3.1 Summary Statistics

Our initial search considered conference and journal articles published between 2010 and 2024 (March). During our backward search, we included the paper of Dellarocas [21], and during our Forward Search, the paper (book chapter) of Román et al. [82] in our sample. Both provide relevant insights into fake reviews' impact. As illustrated in Fig. 2, research on the impact of fake reviews already received attention between 2010 and 2014. The research on the topic become a more notable trend over the years, with an observable upward trend since 2015 and a peak in 2022. Most studies (49) have been published in journal articles, emphasizing fake reviews as a relevant research field. In contrast, the publications in conferences are noticeably limited.

Table 1 visualizes that research on the impact of fake reviews focuses mainly on eCommerce. This fits with Mayzlin et al. [65], who show that fake reviews are common in eCommerce. Furthermore, research on fake reviews' impact on tourism and restaurant platforms plays a significant role. Other contexts include fake reviews' impact, e.g., on reward-based crowdfunding, social network sites, and virtual brand communities. Analyzing the type of fake reviews reveals 26 studies investigating the impact of positive fake reviews, one study investigating exclusively negative fake reviews, and 37 studies considering both positive and negative fake reviews.

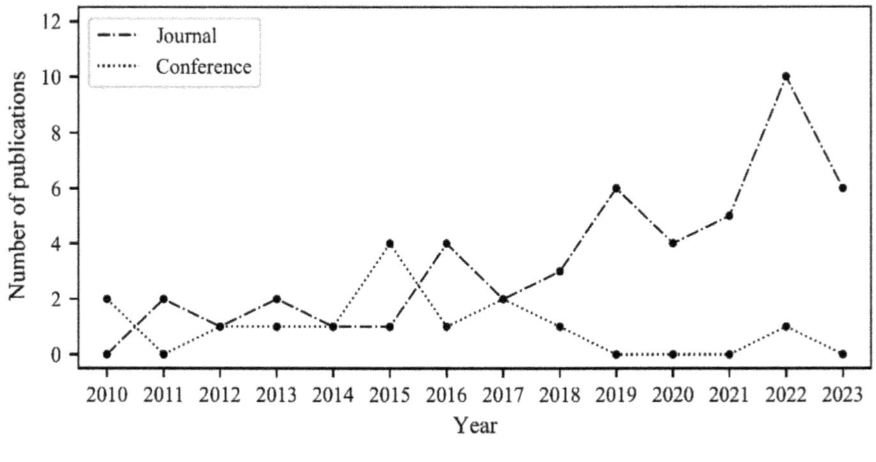

Fig. 2 Number of identified articles ordered by publication date and type

Table 1 Overview of the contexts in which the impact of fake reviews was analyzed; TruongDu Chau et al. [96] focus on two contexts

Context	Source	#	%
eCommerce	[7, 12, 15, 16, 34, 35, 39, 41, 40, 43, 44, 46, 49, 51, 53, 57, 63, 71, 73, 75, 76, 81, 99, 107, 106, 109, 110, 112, 115, 114, 116]	34	53.3
Tourism	[28, 30, 31, 52, 89, 90, 105, 118]	9	13.8
Restaurants	[3, 4, 38, 56, 61, 88, 92, 96, 111]	10	15.4
Others	[21, 24, 48, 60,54, 55, 62, 80, 87, 102, 103, 104]	12	18.5

Regarding the impact, most studies focus on the economic impact of fake reviews, which we describe first. Afterward, we focus on fake reviews' social impact.

3.2 *Economic Impact of Fake Reviews*

Reviews as a Quality Signal. Review systems can be efficient in reducing information asymmetries in online markets. Due to the use of fake reviews, consumers might not overcome information asymmetries as reviews might no longer work as quality signals [15, 35]. Even though consumers are convinced to detect fake reviews, this is often not the case, which can lead to a loss of confidence in the marketplace, and consumers might leave the platform [63]. Further, when fake reviews decrease consumers' trust in reviews, competition within a market can be reduced [63] and developing a lemon market[1] can be a real problem.

Rating Distortion. Truong Du Chau et al. [96] show that fake reviews can successfully promote a target item and lead to an increase in product ranking. Further, fake reviews can contribute to a large dispersion of ratings because their distribution is more extreme compared to legitimate reviews [61]. Fraudsters seem to boost their rating after it declines [38]. Siering and Janze [88] found that after critical health inspection, the average rating increased for restaurants in lower star groups. The authors found indications for an increase in review manipulation that led to these changes. However, He et al. [34] show that fake reviews' effects on the average rating are short-lived. In the long term, the average rating falls significantly after retailers stop recruiting fake reviews and return to pre-promotional levels or lower due to an increase in one-star reviews submitted by unsatisfied customers. Xu et al. [109] investigated the impact of seller-reputation-escalation markets on seller's reputation. These businesses operate as a crowdsourcing marketplace for Taobao stores, where online sellers find individuals who conduct fake transactions to boost their reputation. Compared to genuine reviews, using such services can increase a seller's store reputation at least ten times faster.

[1] E.g., providers of high-quality products or services are pushed out of a market.

Song et al. [90] demonstrate that excluding low-quality reviews (likely fake) can eliminate rating distortions. Further, review distortion caused by fake reviews is more serious than losing information when excluding low-quality reviews.

Purchase Intention and Decisions. The impact of fake reviews on consumers' purchase decisions seems to depend on their perception of review manipulation [117]. When consumers are aware of manipulation tactics, intentionally deleting or hiding reviews is particularly problematic, leading to negative purchase intentions [75]. Jin Ma and Lee [44] found that after respondents were aware that retailers had manipulated positive reviews, their purchase intention decreased considerably. However, when consumers do not perceive fake reviews, they affect purchase decisions positively. Zhuang et al. [118] found that adding positive reviews and deleting or hiding negatives leads to higher purchase intention, especially since the strategy of deleting negative reviews is harder to detect. However, excessive manipulation raises consumer suspicion and negatively affects product performance. Also Kollmer et al. [49] show that an increasing density of deceptive characteristics in reviews increases consumers' suspicion, which decreases their purchase intention. Additionally, consumers who realize review manipulation will not purchase again from that manipulative company or retailer and try to warn others by vindictive complaining [81]. However, consumers' preference for a product can decrease their suspicion of the product's reviews [80].

Sales, Prices, and Manipulation Costs. A higher degree of positive reviews can promote consumers' purchase choices [110] but only to a certain extent because sales decline when a product looks too good and positive reviews do not seem credible. Similarly, Wang et al. [98] found that the short-term manipulation of review quantity positively affects sales, but after a threshold, the effect becomes negative. Review quality manipulation positively affects product sales regardless of the manipulation duration. He et al. [35] found when sellers stop buying fake reviews, sales fall significantly in the long term, even to pre-promotional levels or lower. While Lau et al. [53] found no indications that promotional review spam increases product sales, they found that negative review spam can damage a firm's sales.

In the context of movies, the findings of Ma et al. [62] indicate that the impact of review manipulation in the early stage of a movie's life cycle disappears two weeks after the release. However, the higher number of reviews led to an increase in revenue. Kim et al. [48] show that fake reviews negatively impact box office revenue. Further, in a monopoly eCommerce market where a platform charges sellers transaction fees, fake reviews increase transaction costs for platform users and damage the platform's revenue [15].

Zhao and Zhang [114] show that uncertainty about online reviews significantly affects product price optimization and profit maximization in a competitive online market. In a quality-dominates-fit case (subjective quality evaluation dominates purchasing decisions), two competing retailers lower their prices to compensate consumers for uncertainty about online reviews. On the contrary, in a fit-dominates-quality case (perceived degree of fit dominates purchasing decisions), uncertainty about online reviews encourages both retailers to increase their prices to generate higher profits. Further, Wu and Qiu [106] show that price competition is intensified after manipulation as low-quality sellers raise their prices and high-quality sellers decrease their prices. Thus, consumers can even benefit from high-quality sellers' lowered prices.

Besides possible profits, manipulation costs must also be considered. An increase in sales due to manipulation might lead to more genuine reviews in the future. Thus, fraudsters must invest in more fake reviews, especially low-quality sellers. Overall, sellers face a trade-off between the revenue gain in the current period and further costs for more fake reviews in the future [21].

Fight-backs and Wisdom of Crowds. Park et al. [73, Sect. 1], show that the ratings by others influence a consumer's review generation. Whereas a negative discrepancy (*"worse than what I read"*) leads to negative reviews, a positive discrepancy (*"better than what I read"*) leads to positive reviews. Negative review discrepancy leads to less satisfied consumers who write longer reviews with lower positive emotional intensity, adversely affecting the product's reputation and damaging a business in the long term [56]. Thus, the negative discrepancy can lead to backfiring on firms that generate promotional fake reviews. According to Karabas et al. [46], consumers perceived e-retailers more as trying to unfairly manipulate product reviews once they were exposed to the fact that reviews are not necessarily trustworthy. This leads to fewer positive product reviews. Moreover, consumers reacted least favorably to highly positive or perfect reviews. Zhang et al. [111] found no significant difference in the average rating between before and after review manipulation. A reason might be the wisdom of crowds, meaning consumers' review writing behavior based on positive/negative discrepancy may limit the impact of fake reviews.

In the context of crowdfunding campaigns, Wessel et al. [102, 103] show that after a peak in participation, fake Facebook Likes can backfire as the number of backers' funding declines even to a lower point than before the manipulation.

Further, also firms' fight-backs are possible. Based on a game-theoretical approach, Li et al. [57] show that the manipulation cost (risk cost) and competition intensity are decisive for executing review manipulation, e.g., if the fighter's unit risk cost is moderate, intensified competition triggers fight-backs,low competition intensity does not.

Competition and Prisoner's Dilemma. The findings of Zhang et al. [113] show that if a competitor aggressively solicits fake restaurant reviews, it enhances a restaurant to be more engaged in competition by soliciting more positive fake reviews. According to Dellarocas [21], high-quality firms must invest in online reviews to remain competitive, and low-quality firms must invest to cover up their true low quality. In the presence of rivals, high-quality firms manipulate more when their quality is already better than the quality of their rivals [54]. On the contrary, low-quality firms manipulate much less when their quality is better than the quality of their rivals. Zhang et al. [112] found that firms' competitive review manipulation can increase the value of information and benefit consumers. Nevertheless, the manipulation cost should be high to increase consumers' welfare and ease the prisoner's dilemma. According to Cao [12], the prisoner's dilemma exists when both firms choose manipulation strategies even if they do not gain higher profits. This is more likely for low manipulation costs.

Gössling et al. [30] conducted interviews with accommodation managers. Most of them reported not being involved in manipulation strategies, but few managers actively manipulated reviews. According to these managers, submitting self-promotional reviews is not unethical, whereas submitting negative fake reviews for a competitor is ethically unacceptable. Lappas et al. [52] show that even limited injections of fake hotel reviews can significantly affect the attackers' visibility. From an attacker's perspective, the mixed manipulation strategy (self-promotion and competitors' demotion) is the best strategy [52]. Bad-mouthing competitors can undermine a competitor's product and reduce a competitor's market outcome, especially for unpopular products with more ratings before manipulation [60]. However, due to better visibility, bad-mouthing can also boost the competitor's market outcome [60]. In contrast to Lappas et al. [52], Wu and Qiu [106] show that review manipulation is a self-inhibition mechanism as it does not change the relative ranking of sellers' ratings. Nevertheless, manipulation leads to less dispersion among sellers. According to Cao [12], review manipulation does not always hurt competitors as they can profit from the variance-increasing effect due to less credibility in product reviews, which can lead to increased heterogeneity in consumers' product evaluations.

3.3 *Social Impact of Fake Reviews*

(Social) Welfare, Mental and Physical Health. Product reviews can mislead consumers when they make decisions based on inaccurate quality information, leading to less social welfare [112]. Li et al. [56] show that consumers are increasingly confused by deceptive reviews and might make erroneous purchase decisions. Especially consumers who are naive and unaware of manipulation suffer the most [54, 55]. Owners of small accommodation businesses reported that unjustified reviews affect them personally, e.g., regarding "*emotions of hurt, sadness, irritation, or anger*" [30, p. 491]. 31.5% of surveyed aesthetic plastic surgeons reported mental health issues after defamation, like stress and depression, 10% reported physical health issues, such as sleeplessness and excess alcohol [104].

Informativeness and Membership. In online opinion forums, honest consumer opinions can engage firms to reveal their knowledge of product qualities using manipulation to inflate the true rating (increased informativeness). However, if the manipulation strategy decreases with the true quality of the firm, the forum's informativeness decreases and affects consumers badly [21]. Hu et al. [41] show that manipulation decreases the informativeness of online reviews. Consequently, consumers might discard reviews as products with a higher mean rating do not represent higher quality. Thus, instead of reducing uncertainties, online reviews might enhance uncertainty [41].

The findings of Feng et al. [24] show that hyper reviews positively affect membership (feeling of belonging) and influence (member's participation), whereas defaming reviews hurt membership and influence.

Consumers Trust, Perception, and Decision-making. Consumer trust in reviews significantly decreases when they are aware of a company's involvement in review content manipulation [44]. Their skepticism reduces the review credibility for search products [82]. However, displaying fraudulent reviews increases consumers' trust in the review portal [3, 4].

Shih et al. [87] show that the earlier fake reviews emerge, the more powerful influence they have later on consumers' beliefs and attitudes. Further, Ong et al. [71] found that fake reviews are especially effective for products with fewer real reviews as they significantly increased consumers' quality perceptions.

Moreover, fake reviews influence all dimensions of perceived risk (economic, functional, and time risk), negatively affecting consumer purchase intention [107]. A high proportion of fake reviews can lead to a decrease in consumers' credibility perception and a decrease in sales [99]. Zhao et al. [115] show that consumers update their credibility perception over time based on the similarity between their evaluation and the existing reviews. The existence of fake reviews reduces the effect of subsequent (authentic) reviews because consumers' credibility perception decreases.

Steur et al. [92] show that inconsistent reviews did not always lead to a longer duration in transaction decisions, but inconsistent restaurant reviews with positive texts resulted in faster transaction decisions. Based on an eye-tracking analysis, Chen et al. [16] show that the fixation dwell time and the fixation count for fake comments were not greater than those for real comments. Thus, consumers do not effectively process the content of fake reviews. Ananthakrishnan et al. [4] show that users choose more carefully when displaying suspected fake review information.

3.4 *Employed Theories*

For clustering the most frequently employed theories, we consider the theory and its adaption, the research disciplines of the journal(s)/conference(s) that published the theory and adaption paper, and the research background of the theory papers' author(s). Our clustering can help find an appropriate theory for exploring the impact of fake reviews. It is not exclusive; most theories originally appeared in psychology and have been adopted in other scientific fields later.

Social Psychology Theories focus on understanding human cognition and behavior as well as social interactions and group dynamics (social influence), e.g., how individuals perceive, interpret, and respond to fake reviews as a social stimulus, like the Attribution Theory [36], Cognitive Dissonance Theory [27], Impression Formation Theory [83], Social Comparison Theory [26], Social Influence Theory [47], and Wisdom of Crowds [93].

Information and Communication Theories revolve around the processing and manipulation of information, e.g., how the information contained in fake reviews is transmitted or interpreted, like the Information Theory [86], Information Processing Theory [8, 68], Signaling Theory [91], Interpersonal Deception Theory [11], Information Manipulation Theory [66], and Theory of Source Credibility [67].

Decision-Making and Behavioral Theories explore decision-making processes and behavioral patterns, e.g., to shed light on how fake reviews' content can influence consumer decision-making, like the Behavioral Theory [85], Dual-process Theory [23, 45], Elaboration Likelihood Model [77], Expectancy-disconfirmation Theory [70], Hunt–Vitell Theory of Ethics [42], Prisoner's dilemma [79], Herd Behaviour [19], and the Self-selection Theory [59].

Technology and User Behavior Theories examine the relationship between technology and human behavior, e.g., to explain how individuals' attitudes towards review systems shape their usage intention of such systems, like the Theory of Reasoned Action [29] and the Technology Acceptance Model [20].

4 Discussion and Conclusion

A growing number of scholars investigate the phenomenon of fake reviews; most focus on their detection. Our work provides a comprehensive overview of current knowledge on fake reviews' impact, focusing on the social and economic impact of fake reviews.

Fake reviews can distort online ratings and undermine their effectiveness as a quality signal. If the buyer experience differs from expectations based on fake reviews, this can lead to an increase in negative reviews due to negative discrepancies. Therefore, review manipulation can backfire. In the short term, fake reviews can lead to a better reputation and an increase in sales and revenues to a certain extent; but they can even worsen both in the long term. Especially when consumers are aware of review manipulation, this can negatively affect their purchase intention or repeat purchases. Consumers also become skeptical if a product looks too good or is overly praised. Further, manipulators must consider manipulation costs that can outweigh review manipulations' benefits. The impact of review manipulation on competition depends on various factors, such as the quality of products, manipulation costs, and manipulation strategies of competitors. Companies often face a trade-off decision between their own survival and the power of reputation [30]. Moreover, there is not only competition between hotels, restaurants, or sellers but also between platforms [15].

The social impact of fake reviews includes a decrease in consumer trust, negative effects on their attitude formation process and risk perception, and a decrease in social welfare. Defamation can also lead to mental and physical health issues of attacked actors.

Our approach is not without limitations. The first limitation concerns the literature search process and possible selection bias. This problem should be limited as we searched four databases and included as many studies as possible in our screening process. Moreover, the term fake reviews can be defined differently. For example, incentivized or product testers' reviews can also be included in future analyses. Expanding the term may lead to further results. In principle, a literature review represents the status quo of research. Since research on fake reviews has increased in recent years and will probably increase, our review needs to be continuously expanded.

4.1 Theoretical Implications and Future Research

Combining our findings with the limitations and implications of the identified articles, we derive the following directions for future work.

Most studies focus on the impact of fake reviews on eCommerce platforms, particularly Amazon. The sharing economy is not represented, although fake reviews might appear on sharing platforms [25]. Thus, future work should focus on further platforms and distinguish between reviews on brand-neutral platforms and brand-owner platforms [75]. Future studies should also examine fake reviews in high-risk settings like health care or legal services Ananthakrishnan et al. [3, 82]. Further, except the study of Wokes et al. [104], all studies focus on promotional fake reviews or both positive and negative fake reviews. Thus, future work could focus more on demoting reviews [87, 98] as they can be used strategically to harm competitors (see Sect. 3.2). Moreover, future studies should also consider further manipulation strategies, including incentivization [12] or team manipulation [98]. Additionally, future work could investigate how consumers perceive fake reviews, considering consumer characteristics, previous knowledge, and experience [76, 99]. Moreover, future research should include qualitative data [7, 56], as most studies focus on quantitative data. Lastly, researchers could collaborate with industry partners to build research upon a more clearly labeled dataset.

4.2 Practical Implications

Our findings should continue to motivate researchers and practitioners to pay close attention to fake reviews. The results from our literature review allow us to derive practical implications.

Most mentioned interventions refer to platforms, especially the review systems' design and fake review detection, e.g., focusing on text reviews, splitting the qualitative review component, and offering sorting/filtering options [92], weight reviews differently [111], monitor reviews continually and respond to praise/criticism timely [104, 118], increasing the manipulation cost and make fake reviews costly using credibility mechanisms (e.g., [4, 43]). Further, platforms should implement and improve fake review detection systems [49], display fake reviews or companies' fraudulent activities [3], add the number of filtered reviews [82], choose confrontational strategies like directly respond to reviews [52], impose heavy fines for manipulation, or kick manipulators off the platform [57]. Overall, it is important that the platform increase authentic reviews on their site, e.g., encourage consumers who post honest opinions [87].

Some interventions refer to regulators, e.g., offering education programs about fake review practices for businesses and consumers or rewarding those that detect fake reviews [63, 76]. Further, they should monitor review platforms, introduce regulations to deal with review manipulation [88], and develop consistent guidelines for legitimate reputation management [118].

References

Akhtar, N., Akhtar, M. N., Siddiqi, U. I., Riaz, M., & Zhuang, W. (2020). Unveiling the Effects of Figurative Meanings in Manipulated Online Hotel Reviews on Consumers' Behavioral Intentions. *Asia Pacific Journal of Marketing and Logistics, 32*(8), 1799–1821.

Alsharif, N. (2022). Fake Opinion Detection in an E-Commerce Business Based on A Long-Short Memory Algorithm. *Soft Computing, 26*, 7847–7854.

Ananthakrishnan, U., Li, B., & Smith, M. (2015). A Tangled Web: Evaluating the Impact of Displaying Fraudulent Reviews. In *2015 International Conference on Information Systems (ICIS)*.

Ananthakrishnan, U. M., Li, B., & Smith, M. D. (2020). A Tangled Web: Should Online Review Portals Display Fraudulent Reviews? *Information Systems Research, 31*(3), 950–971.

Anderson, M., & Magruder, J. (2012). Learning From the Crowd: Regression Discontinuity Estimates of the Effects of An Online Review Database. *The Economic Journal, 122*(563), 957–989.

Ansari, S., & Gupta, S. (2021). Review Manipulation: Literature Review, and Future Research Agenda.*Pacific Asia Journal of the Association for Information Systems, 13*(1), 97–121.

Ansari, S., Gupta, S., & Dewangan, J. (2018). Do Customers Perceive Reviews As Manipulated? A Warranting Theory Perspective. In *Proceedings of the 18th International Conference on Electronic Business* (ICEB) (pp. 250–264).

Atkinson, R., & Shiffrin, R. (1968). Human Memory: A Proposed System and Its Control Pro-Cesses. In K. W. Spence & J. T. Spence (Eds.), *Psychology of learning and motivation* (Vol. 2, pp. 89–195). Academic Press.

Birim, S. Ö., Kazancoglu, I., Mangla, S. K., Kahraman, A., Kumar, S., & Kazancoglu, Y. (2022). Detecting Fake Reviews Through Topic Modelling. *Journal of Business Research 149*, 884–900.

Budhi, G. S., Chiong, R., & Wang, Z. (2021). Resampling Imbalanced Data to Detect Fake Reviews Using Machine Learning Classifiers and Textual-Based Features. *Multimedia Tools and Applications, 80*, 13079–13097.

Buller, D. B., & Burgoon, J. K. (1996). Interpersonal Deception Theory. *Communication Theory, 6*(3), 203–242.

Cao, H. (2020). Online Review Manipulation by Asymmetrical Firms: Is a Firm's Manipulation of Online Reviews Always Detrimental To Its Competitor? *Information & Management, 57*(6), Article 103244.

Carbonell, G., Barbu, C.-M., Vorgerd, L., & Brand, M. (2019). The Impact of Emotionality And Trust Cues on The Perceived Trustworthiness of Online Reviews. *Cogent Business & Management, 6*(1), 1586062.

Chakraborty, U. (2019). The Impact of Source Credible Online Reviews On Purchase Intention: The Mediating Roles of Brand Equity Dimensions. *Journal of Research in Interactive Marketing, 13*(2), 142–161.

Chen, L., & Li, Q. (2022). How Does Fake Review Influence E-Commerce Platform Revenue? In *23rd Asia-Pacific Network Operations and Management Symposium (APNOMS)*, IEEE, (pp. 1–4).

Chen, T., Samaranayake, P., Cen, X., Qi, M., & Lan, Y.-C. (2022). The Impact of Online Reviews On Consumers' Purchasing Decisions: Evidence From An Eye-Tracking Study. *Frontiers in Psychology, 13*, 2723.

Cheng, H. K., Fan, W., Guo, P., Huang, H., & Qiu, L. (2020). Can "Gold Medal" Online Sellers Earn Gold? The Impact of Reputation Badges On Sales. *Journal of Management Information Systems, 37*(4), 1099–1127.

Cheng, L.-C., Hu, H.-W., & Wu C.-C. (2021). Spammer Group Detection Using Machine Learning Technology For Observation of New Spammer Behavioral Features. *Journal of Global Information Management (JGIM), 29*(2), 61–76.

Cialdini, R. B. (1993). *Influence: Science and Practice*. Harper Collins.

Davis, F. (1986). *A Technology Acceptance Model for Empirically Testing New End-User Information Systems* (PhD thesis).

Dellarocas, C. (2006). Strategic Manipulation of Internet Opinion Forums: Implications For Consumers And Firms. *Management Science, 52*(10), 1577–1593.

Dellarocas, C., Zhang, X., & Awad, N. F. (2007). Exploring The Value Of Online Product Reviews In Forecasting Sales: The Case Of Motion Pictures. *Journal of Interactive Marketing, 21*(4), 23–45.

Eagly, A. H., & Chaiken, S. (1993). *The Psychology of Attitudes*. Harcourt Brace Jovanovich College Publishers.

Feng, N., Su, Z., Li, D., Zheng, C., & Li, M. (2018). Effects Of Review Spam In A Firm-Initiated Virtual Brand Community: Evidence From Smartphone Customers. *Information & Management, 55*(8), 1061–1070.

Fergusson, A. (2021). 127,183 Airbnb Guest Complaints Expose Scams, Safety Concerns, Infestations & More, https://www.asherfergusson.com/airbnb/ (Accessed April 28, 2023)

Festinger, L. (1954). A Theory Of Social Comparison Processes. *Human Relations, 7*(2), 117–140.

Festinger, L. (1962). *A Theory Of Cognitive Dissonance*. Stanford University Press.

Filieri, R., Alguezaui, S., & McLeay, F. (2015). Why Do Travelers Trust Tripadvisor? Antecedents Of Trust Towards Consumer-Generated Media And Its Influence On Recommendation Adoption And Word Of Mouth. *Tourism Management, 51*, 174–185.

Fishbein, M., & Ajzen, I. (1975). *Belief, Attitude, Intention, and Behavior: An Introduction to Theory and Research* (Vol. 27). Addison-Wesley.

Gössling, S., Hall, C. M., & Andersson, A.-C. (2018). The Manager's Dilemma: A Conceptualization Of Online Review Manipulation Strategies. *Current Issues in Tourism, 21*(5), 484–503.

Gössling, S., Zeiss, H., Hall, C. M., Martin-Rios, C., Ram, Y., & Grøtte, I.-P. (2019). A Cross-Country Comparison Of Accommodation Manager Perspectives On Online Review Manipulation. *Current Issues in Tourism, 22*(14), 1744–1763.

Gupta, A., Kumar, N., Prabhat, P., Gupta, R., Tanwar, S., Sharma, G., Bokoro, P. N., & Sharma, R. (2022). Combating Fake News: Stakeholder Interventions and Potential Solutions. *Ieee Access, 10*, 78268–78289.

He, S., Hollenbeck, B., Overgoor, G., Proserpio, D., & Tosyali, A. (2022a). Detecting Fake-Review Buyers Using Network Structure: Direct Evidence From Amazon. *Proceedings of the National Academy of Sciences, 119*(47), Article e2211932119.

He, S., Hollenbeck, B., & Proserpio, D. (2022b). The Market For Fake Reviews. *Marketing Science, 41*(5), 896–921.

He, S., Hollenbeck, B., & Proserpio, D. (2023). Leveraging Social Media to Buy Fake Reviews. *Communications of the ACM, 66*(10), 98–105.

Heider, F. (1958). *The Psychology Of Interpersonal Relations*. John Wiley & Sons Inc.

Hesse, M., & Teubner, T. (2020). Reputation Portability–Quo Vadis? *Electronic Markets, 30*(2), 331–349.

Hlee, S., Lee, H., Koo, C., & Chung, N. (2021). Fake Reviews Or Not: Exploring The Relationship Between Time Trend And Online Restaurant Reviews. *Telematics and Informatics, 59*, Article 101560.

Hu, N., Bose, I., Gao, Y., & Liu, L. (2011). Manipulation In Digital Word-Of-Mouth: A Reality Check For Book Reviews. *Decision Support Systems, 50*(3), 627–635.

Hu, N., Bose, I., Koh, N. S., & Liu, L. (2012). Manipulation of Online Reviews: An Analysis of Ratings, Readability, And Sentiments. *Decision Support Systems, 52*(3), 674–684.

Hu, N., Liu, L., & Sambamurthy, V. (2011). Fraud Detection In Online Consumer Reviews. *Decision Support Systems, 50*(3), 614–626.

Hunt, S. D., & Vitell, S. (1986). A General Theory Of Marketing Ethics. *Journal of Macromar-Keting, 6*(1), 5–16.

Jabr, W. (2022). Review Credibility As A Safeguard Against Fakery: The Case Of Amazon. *European Journal of Information Systems, 31*(4), 525–545.

Jin Ma, Y., & Lee, H.-H. (2014). Consumer Responses Toward Online Review Manipulation. *Journal of Research in Interactive Marketing, 8*(3), 224–244.

Kahneman, D. (2011). *Thinking, Fast And Slow*. Penguin.

Karabas, I., Kareklas, I., Weber, T., & Muehling, D. D. (2021). The Impact Of Review Valence And Awareness Of Deceptive Practices On Consumers' Responses To Online Product Ratings And Reviews. *Journal of Marketing Communications, 27*(7), 685–715.

Kelman, H. C. (1958). Compliance, Identification, And Internalization Three Processes Of Attitude Change. *Journal of Conflict Resolution, 2*(1), 51–60.

Kim, J. M., Park, K.K.-C., & Mariani, M. M. (2023). Do Online Review Readers React Differently When Exposed To Credible Versus Fake Online Reviews? *Journal of Business Research, 154*, Article 113377.

Kollmer, T., Eckhardt, A., & Reibenspiess, V. (2022). Explaining Consumer Suspicion: Insights of A Vignette Study On Online Product Reviews. *Electronic Markets, 32*, 1221–1238.

Kraus, S., Breier, M., Lim, W. M., Dabi´c, M., Kumar, S., Kanbach, D., Mukherjee, D., Corvel-lo, V., Piñeiro-Chousa, J., & Liguori, E. et al. (2022). Literature Reviews As Independent Studies: Guidelines For Academic Practice. *Review of Managerial Science 16*(8), 2577–2595.

Lappas, T. (2012). Fake reviews: the malicious perspective. *2012 17th International Conference On Application Of Natural Language To Information Systems (NLDB)* (pp. 23–34). Springer-Verlag.

Lappas, T., Sabnis, G., & Valkanas, G. (2016). The Impact Of Fake Reviews On Online Visibility: A Vulnerability Assessment Of The Hotel Industry. *Information Systems Research, 27*(4), 940–961.

Lau, R. Y., Liao, S. S. & Xu, K. (2010). An Empirical Study Of Online Consumer Review Spam: A Design Science Approach. In *Thirty First International Conference on Information Systems (ICIS)*.

Lee, S.-Y., Qiu, L. & Whinston, A. (2014). Manipulation: Online Platforms' Inescapable Fate. In *2014 Thirty Fifth International Conference on Information Systems (ICIS)*.

Lee, S.-Y., Qiu, L. & Whinston, A. (2015). The perils of online manipulation. *In 2015 48th Hawaii International Conference on System Sciences (HICSS)*, IEEE, (pp. 4864–4873).

Li, H., Meng, F., & Pan, B. (2020a). How Does Review Disconfirmation Influence Customer Online Review Behavior? A Mixed-Method Investigation. *International Journal of Contemporary Hospitality Management, 32*(11), 3685–3703.

Li, J., Bian, Y., Liu, C., & Liu, F. (2021). Strategic Manipulation Of Online Information In Duo-Polies: Inducing Fight-Back? *Electronic Commerce Research and Applications, 47*, Article 101052.

Li, J., Wang, X., Yang, L., Zhang, P., & Yang, D. (2020b). Identifying Ground Truth In Opinion Spam: An Empirical Survey Based On Review Psychology. *Applied Intelligence, 50*(11), 3554–3569.

Li, X., & Hitt, L. M. (2008). Self-selection and Information Role Of Online Product Reviews. *Information Systems Research, 19*(4), 456–474.

Liu, Y., & Zhou, W. (2016). Can you really make profit from online rating manipulations? An empirical study. In *IEEE 40th Annual Computer Software and Applications Conference (COMPSAC)*, Vol. 1, IEEE, (pp. 509–518).

Luca, M., & Zervas, G. (2016). Fake It Till You Make It: Reputation, Competition, And Yelp Review Fraud. *Management Science, 62*(12), 3412–3427.
Ma, H., Kim, J. M., & Lee, E. (2019). Analyzing Dynamic Review Manipulation And Its Impact On Movie Box Office Revenue. *Electronic Commerce Research and Applications, 35*, Article 100840.
Malbon, J. (2013). Taking Fake Online Consumer Reviews Seriously. *Journal of Consumer Policy, 36*, 139–157.
Mauri, A. G., & Minazzi, R. (2013). Web Reviews Influence On Expectations And Purchasing Intentions Of Hotel Potential Customers. *International Journal of Hospitality Management, 34*, 99–107.
Mayzlin, D., Dover, Y., & Chevalier, J. (2014). Promotional Reviews: An Empirical Investigation Of Online Review Manipulation. *American Economic Review, 104*(8), 2421–2455.
McCornack, S. A. (1992). Information Manipulation Theory. *Communications Monographs, 59*(1), 1–16.
McGinnies, E. (1973). Initial Attitude, Source Credibility, And Involvement As Factors In Persuasion. *Journal of Experimental Social Psychology, 9*(4), 285–296.
Miller, G. A. (1956). The Magical Number Seven, Plus or Minus Two: Some Limits on Our Capacity For Processing Information. *Psychological Review, 63*(2).
Nie, C., Zheng, Z., & Sarkar, S (2022). Competing With The Sharing Economy: Incumbents'reaction On Review Manipulation. *MIS Quarterly, 46*, 1573–1602.
Oliver, R. L. (1981). Measurement and evaluation of satisfaction processes in retail settings. *Journal of Retailing, 57*(3), 25–48.
Ong, T., Mannino, M., & Gregg, D. (2013). Product Reputation Manipulation: The Impact Of Shill Reviews On Perceived Quality. In *Proceedings of the Nineteenth Americas Conference on Information Systems (AMCIS)*. Citeseer.
Oxford University Press. (2023). Definition of Impact Noun from the Oxford Advanced Learner's Dictionary. Accessed July 28, 2023. https://www.oxfordlearnersdictionaries.com/definition/english/impact_1
Park, Y. J., Joo, J., Polpanumas, C., & Yoon, Y. (2021). "Worse than what i read?" The External Effect of Review Ratings on The Online Review Generation Process: An Empirical Analysis Of Multiple Product Categories Using Amazon.Com Review Data. *Sustainability, 13*(19), 10912.
Paul, H., & Nikolaev, A. (2021). Fake Review Detection On Online E-Commerce Platforms: A Systematic Literature Review. *Data Mining and Knowledge Discovery, 35*(5), 1830–1881.
Peng, L., Cui, G., Zhuang, M., & Li, C. (2016). Consumer Perceptions Of Online Review Deceptions: An Empirical Study In China. *Journal of Consumer Marketing, 33*(4), 269–280.
Petrescu, M., Kitchen, P., Dobre, C., Ben Mrad, S., Milovan-Ciuta, A., Goldring, D., & Fiedler, A. (2022). Innocent Until Proven Guilty: Suspicion Of Deception In Online Reviews. *European Journal of Marketing, 56*(4), 1184–1209.
Petty, R. E., & Cacioppo, J. T. (1986). The Elaboration Likelihood Model Of Persuasion. In *Advances in Experimental Social Psychology*, Vol. 19, (pp. 123–205). Elsevier.
Qazi, A., Tamjidyamcholo, A., Raj, R. G., Hardaker, G., & Standing, C. (2017). Assessing Consumers' Satisfaction And Expectations Through Online Opinions: Expectation And Disconfirmation Approach. *Computers in Human Behavior, 75*, 450–460.
Rapoport, A., Chammah, A. M., & Orwant, C. J. (1965). *Prisoner's Dilemma: A Study in Conflict and Cooperation* (Vol. 165), University of Michigan press.
Ren, J., Ozturk, P., & Luo, S. (2017). Examining Customer Responses To Fake Online Reviews: The Role Of Suspicion And Product Knowledge. In *Internetworked World: 15th Workshop on e-Business, WEB 2016*. (pp. 177–184). Springer.
Román, S., Riquelme, I. P., & Iacobucci, D. (2019). Perceived Deception In Online Consumer Reviews: Antecedents, Consequences, And Moderators. In *Marketing in a digital world* (vol. 16, pp. 141–166). Emerald Publishing Limited.

Román, S., Riquelme, I. P., & Iacobucci, D. (2023). Fake or Credible? Antecedents And Conse-Quences Of Perceived Credibility In Exaggerated Online Reviews. *Journal of Business Research, 156*, Article 113466.
Rozin, P., & Royzman, E. B. (2001). Negativity Bias, Negativity Dominance, And Contagion. *Personality and Social Psychology Review, 5*(4), 296–320.
Schuckert, M., Liu, X., & Law, R. (2016). Insights Into Suspicious Online Ratings: Direct Evidence From Tripadvisor. *Asia Pacific Journal of Tourism Research, 21*(3), 259–272.
Shafir, E., & Tversky, A. (1992). Thinking Through Uncertainty: Nonconsequential Reasoning And Choice. *Cognitive Psychology, 24*(4), 449–474.
Shannon, C. E. (1948). A Mathematical Theory Of Communication. *The Bell System Technical Journal, 27*(3), 379–423.
Shih, C. F., Huang, S. L., & Huang, H. C. (2022). The Dissemination And Impacts Of Deceptive Ewom: A Dynamic Process Perspective. *Behaviour & Information Technology, 42*(8).
Siering, M., & Janze, C. (2019). Information Processing On Online Review Platforms. *Journal of Management Information Systems, 36*(4), 1347–1377.
Sigala, M. (2017). How "Bad" Are You? Justification and Normalisation Of Online Deviant Customer Behaviour. *Information and Communication Technologies in Tourism* (pp. 607–622). Springer.
Song, W., Park, S., & Ryu, D. (2017). Information Quality Of Online Reviews In The Presence Of Potentially Fake Reviews. *Korean Economic Review, 33*, 5–34.
Spence, M. (1973). Job Market Signaling. *The Quarterly Journal of Economics, 87*(3), 355–374.
Steur, A. J., Fritzsche, F., & Seiter, M. (2022). It's All About The Text: An Experimental Investigation Of Inconsistent Reviews On Restaurant Booking Platforms. *Electronic Markets, 32*, 1187–1220.
Surowiecki, J. (2005). *The Wisdom of Crowds*. Anchor.
Tang, H., & Cao, H. (2020). A Review Of Research On Detection Of Fake Commodity Reviews. *Journal of Physics: Conference Series, 1651*(1), Article 012055.
Thakur, R., Hale, D., & Summey, J. H. (2018). What Motivates Consumers To Partake In Cyber Shilling? *Journal of Marketing Theory and Practice, 26*(1–2), 181–195.
Truong Du Chau, X., Toan Nguyen, T., Khiem Tran, V., Quach, S., Thaichon, P., Jo, J., Vo, B., Dieu Tran, Q., & Viet Hung Nguyen, Q. (2024). Towards A Review-Analytics-As- A-Service (Raaas) Framework For Smes: A Case Study On Review Fraud Detection And Understanding. *Australasian Marketing Journal, 32*(1), 76–90.
Wang, C., Li, Y., Luo, X., Ma, Q., Fu, W., & Fu, H. (2018). The Effects Of Money On Fake Rating Behavior In E-Commerce: Electrophysiological Time Course Evidence From Consumers. *Frontiers in Neuroscience, 12*, 156.
Wang, Q., Zhang, W., Li, J., Ma, Z., & Chen, J. (2023). Benefits or Harms? The Effect Of Online Review Manipulation On Sales. *Electronic Commerce Research and Applications, 57*, Article 101224.
Wang, Q., Zhang, W., Li, J., Mai, F., & Ma, Z. (2022). Effect of Online Review Sentiment On Product Sales: The Moderating Role Of Review Credibility Perception. *Computers in Human Behavior, 133*, Article 107272.
Watts, D. J., Rothschild, D. M., & Mobius, M. (2021). Measuring The News And Its Impact On Democracy. *Proceedings of the National Academy of Sciences, 118*(15), Article e1912443118.
Webster, J., & Watson, R. T. (2002). Analyzing The Past To Prepare For The Future: Writing A Literature Review. *MIS Quarterly, 26*(2), 13–23.
Wessel, M., Thies, F., & Benlian, A. (2015). A Lie Never Lives to Be Old: The Effects of Fake Social Information On Consumer Decision-Making In Crowdfunding. In *2015 Twenty-Third European Conference on Information Systems (ECIS)*.
Wessel, M., Thies, F., & Benlian, A. (2016). The Emergence And Effects Of Fake Social Infor-Mation: Evidence From Crowdfunding. *Decision Support Systems, 90*, 75–85.
Wokes, J. E., McLean, N. R., & Boyd, M. (2022). Fake News, Defamation, Online Reviews, And Their Potential Devastating Consequences For Aesthetic Plastic Surgeons. *Aesthetic Surgery Journal, 42*(8), NP546–NP553.

Wu, G., Greene, D., Smyth, B., & Cunningham, P. (2010). Distortion as a Validation Criterion In The Identification Of Suspicious Reviews. In *Proceedings of the first workshop on social media analytics (SOMA)*, (pp. 10–13).

Wu, R., & Qiu, C. (2023). When karma Strikes Back: A Model Of Seller Manipulation Of Consumer Reviews In An Online Marketplace. *Journal of Business Research, 155*, Article 113316.

Wu, S., Wingate, N., Wang, Z., & Liu, Q. (2019). The Influence Of Fake Reviews On Consumer Perceptions Of Risks And Purchase Intentions. *Journal of Marketing Development & Competitiveness, 13*(3), 133–143.

Wu, Y., Ngai, E. W., Wu, P., & Wu, C. (2020). Fake Online Reviews: Literature Review, Synthesis, And Directions For Future Research. *Decision Support Systems, 132*, Article 113280.

Xu, H., Liu, D., Wang, H., & Stavrou, A. (2015). E-commerce Reputation Manipulation: The Emergence Of Reputation-Escalation-As-A-Service. In *Proceedings of the 24th International Conference on World Wide Web* (pp. 1296–1306).

Yin, T., Wang, W., & Shi, W. (2019). A Study On Fraud Reviews: Incentives To Manipulate And Effect On Sales. *China Communications, 16*(3), 165–178.

Zhang, L., Wang, S.-F., Lin, Z.-Z., & Wu, Y. (2019). Online Ballot Stuffing: Influence Of Self-Boosting Manipulation on Rating Dynamics In Online Rating Systems. *Telematics and Informatics, 38*, 1–12.

Zhang, T., Li, G., Cheng, T., & Lai, K. K. (2017). Welfare Economics Of Review Information: Implications For The Online Selling Platform Owner. *International Journal of Production Economics, 184*, 69–79.

Zhang, Z., Li, Y., Li, H., & Zhang, Z. (2022). Restaurants' Motivations To Solicit Fake Reviews: A Competition Perspective. *International Journal of Hospitality Management, 107*, Article 103337.

Zhao, C., & Zhang, Y. (2020). Impacts of Uncertain Online Reviews On Pricing And Profits Of Competitive Retailers. *Kybernetes, 50*(2), 309–332.

Zhao, Y., Yang, S., Narayan, V., & Zhao, Y. (2013). Modeling Consumer Learning From Online Product Reviews. *Marketing Science, 32*([illegible]), 153–169.

Zhong, M., Qu, X., Chen, Y., Liao, S., & Xiao, Q. et al. (2021). Impact Of Factors Of Online De-Ceptive Reviews On Customer Purchase Decision Based On Machine Learning. *Journal of Healthcare Engineering*.

Zhong, M., Yang, H., Zhong, K., Qu, X., & Li, Z. (2023). The Impact Of Online Reviews Manipulation On Consumer Purchase Decision Based On The Perspective Of Consumers' Perception. *Journal of Internet Technology, 24*(7), 1469–1476.

Zhuang, M., Cui, G., & Peng, L. (2018). Manufactured Opinions: The Effect Of Manipulating Online Product Reviews. *Journal of Business Research, 87*, 24–35.

Never Again "The Pizza was Great!"—Developing Design Principles for Dynamic Review Templates

Maximilian Habla, Stefan Napirata, Andrea Wrabel, Alexander Kupfer, and Steffen Zimmermann

Abstract Online review system providers often use review templates to guide reviewers in sharing their product experiences in online consumer reviews. However, there is a huge number of reviews that cover similar product aspects and provide repetitive and less diverse information. To address this issue, we propose to use review templates that dynamically adapt to existing product information in reviews to guide reviewers towards sharing product experiences that have not or only rarely been shared before. Employing the design science research paradigm, we derive design requirements and develop design principles for the design of dynamic review templates. Based on an instantiated dynamic review template following these principles, we show that they successfully guide reviewers towards providing more diverse product information in reviews while maintaining high reviewer engagement. We contribute to research and practice by providing prescriptive design knowledge on dynamic review templates.

Supplementary Information The online version contains supplementary material available at https://doi.org/10.1007/978-3-032-08480-4_28.

M. Habla (✉) · S. Napirata · A. Wrabel · S. Zimmermann
Institute of Business Analytics, Ulm University, Ulm, Germany
e-mail: maximilian.habla@uni-ulm.de

S. Napirata
e-mail: stefan.napirata@uni-ulm.de

A. Wrabel
e-mail: andrea.wrabel@uni-ulm.de

S. Zimmermann
e-mail: steffen.zimmermann@uni-ulm.de

A. Kupfer
Department of Information Systems, Production and Logistics Management, and Research Area Digital Science Center (DiSC), University of Innsbruck, Innsbruck, Austria
e-mail: alexander.kupfer@uibk.ac.at

C. M. Flath et al. (eds.), *Artificial Intelligence, Data, and Decision-Making*, Lecture Notes in Information Systems and Organisation 82,
https://doi.org/10.1007/978-3-032-08480-4_28

1 Introduction

Online consumer reviews ("reviews" in the following) have become a valuable information source for consumers when making product (i.e. a good, a service, or a combination of both) decisions. To effectively support consumers in making an informed product decision, these reviews need to cover a wide range of product aspects and provide diverse product information [1].

A viable approach to promote reviews that address diverse product information is to guide reviewers in their writing process by providing review templates [2, 3]. Hence, it is not surprising that most online review systems implement various forms of review templates to guide their reviewers. Even though these review templates substantially vary in terms of design elements (e.g., one- vs. multidimensional rating scales, one vs. multiple text fields, possibilities to add photos or videos, etc.), we identify a commonality among them that might hinder their effectiveness: To date, all review templates neglect existing product information in reviews. We conjecture this to be the main reason why reviews always tend to cover similar aspects [4–6]. As a consequence, other aspects are not or only rarely addressed, which hinders an online review system's potential to reduce information asymmetries. For instance, reviews stating "the pizza was great!" may overflow, as they present the reviewer's most prominent experience during their restaurant visit, while less obvious details (e.g., the restaurant's payment options) may be underrepresented. As reviews are more effective in reducing information asymmetries, when they cover a wider range of aspects [7] and rarely addressed aspects [1], we provide a solution to this problem. We propose that review templates should dynamically adapt to existing product information in reviews and guide reviewers towards addressing product aspects that have not yet or only rarely been covered.

Following the design science research (DSR) paradigm, we aim to establish a foundation for the design of dynamic review templates (DRTs). For this purpose, we derive two design requirements (DRs) from existing literature. While the first DR targets on the provision of more diverse reviews, the second DR ensures that this does not come at the cost of lower reviewer engagement. Both DRs serve as the basis for developing design principles (DPs) for DRTs. We demonstrate our DPs by translating them into design features (DFs) to instantiate a prototypical DRT. We then evaluate our prototype against one of the foremost review templates globally [8], the Google Maps review template (hereafter "Google template").

Our results indicate that our instantiation successfully guides reviewers to provide more diverse product information in their reviews, while maintaining a high level of reviewer engagement. Hence, the problem of current review templates that fail to guide reviewers to provide diverse product information can be effectively mitigated through the implementation of DRTs following our DPs. This study contributes to existing research on the design of online review systems by providing prescriptive design knowledge in form of actionable DPs on how to design DRTs. In addition, it provides valuable insights and recommendations for online review system providers on how to modify their static review templates to guide reviewers to write more diverse reviews.

2 Related Literature

The majority of existing research on reviews focuses on their economic consequences, such as purchase intentions, sales, etc., (e.g., see [9] for a comprehensive overview). However, there has been a growing interest in understanding how different design elements of online review systems can influence the creation of reviews themselves. Researchers observe that offering monetary incentives to reviewers impacts the length (e.g., [10, 11]) and sentiment [12] of reviews. Further, when the review moderation policies are transparent to reviewers, review length decreases as reviewers are more aware that their review can be filtered out by the online review system [13]. Displaying the existing reviews also has an effect on review creation: review length increases when reviewers encounter disconfirmation with the presented information [14], or decreases when there exists already a high number of reviews [15]. Moreover, providing multidimensional rating scales guide reviewers to address more product aspects in their reviews [16]. While these studies already demonstrate that the design of online review systems can affect review creation, Gutt et al. [2] propose review templates as another promising way to influence review creation. However, we are only aware of one study by Poniatowski et al. [17] that analyzes the impact of review templates. By developing a review template that consists of a rating scale and multiple text fields covering different product aspects, the authors examine how such a template affects the information in the provided reviews. With their template, reviewers write longer reviews and address more product aspects in their reviews.

Even though Poniatowski et al. [17] provide first evidence of the potential of review templates by encouraging reviewers to address multiple product aspects, their review template remains static. That means that their review template does not adapt to existing product information in reviews, which might hinder reviewers from providing diverse product information. To the best of our knowledge, no study has yet considered review templates that dynamically adapt to existing product information in reviews. Hence, it is an open question on how to design DRTs. We aim to address this gap by providing prescriptive design knowledge in form of DPs for the design of DRTs.

3 Methodology

In this paper, we follow the DSR paradigm, which aims to solve an existing problem by developing an artifact and evaluating its utility [18]. In particular, we develop DPs for DRTs that overcome the limitations of static review templates by guiding reviewers to provide more diverse product information in reviews. To do so, we follow the DSR methodology proposed by Peffers et al. [19], which consists of six steps. As a first step, it is necessary to (1) Identify the Problem and Motivate to emphasize the relevance of the study and the value of a potential solution. Thus, we describe the problem and its relevance in the introduction (see Sect. 1) and identify the research gap in the existing literature (see Sect. 2). Based on the stated problem, we (2) Define Objectives of a Solution for an artifact that is better than existing solutions. Thus, we define DRs for DRTs based on existing research. In the (3) Design and Development phase, we translate these DRs into our artifact as DPs towards a design theory following Gregor et al. [20] (see Sect. 4). For (4) Demonstration, we initiate these DPs in form of a prototypical DRT using DFs for the case of writing restaurant reviews (see Sect. 5) and subsequently evaluate them in step (5) Evaluation to prove their value for solving the stated problem (see Sect. 6). Following Venable et al. [21], we conduct an ex-post evaluation of our instantiation in an artificial environment in terms of a controlled online experiment. In this vein, we aim to analyze the utility, effectiveness, efficacy, and usability [21, 22] of our DPs in guiding reviewers to provide more diverse product information in their reviews. Finally, our DSR project involves the (6) Communication of our results with this paper.

4 Development of Design Requirements and Principles

As outlined above, we define DRTs as review templates that dynamically adapt to existing product information in reviews. To obtain design knowledge on how DRTs can effectively support reviewers in the review writing process, we derive two DRs for DRTs based on existing research. These DRs are then translated into our four DPs.

Vallurupalli & Bose [5] observe that reviewers tend to address similar product aspects in their reviews, therefore potentially neglecting other relevant product aspects that might undermine the role of reviews in supporting consumers' informed decision-making [23]. Although repetitive descriptions of certain product aspects may reinforce the evaluation of these aspects, they hinder a comprehensive assessment of the entire product if other aspects remain underrepresented. To address this issue, a review template should be designed to guide reviewers to share diverse product information in their reviews. This leads to our first DR:

DR1: DRTs should guide reviewers towards providing more diverse product information in their reviews.

To provide more diverse product information, reviewers need to address multiple aspects in their reviews. In this context, research by Chen et al. [16] documents that multidimensional rating scales can help reviewers to address multiple aspects. Moreover, Poniatowski et al. [17] find that providing multiple text fields covering different aspects is also an effective means to guide reviewers towards addressing multiple aspects. Hence, we formulate our first DP:

DP1: Provide DRTs with multiple dimensions that guide reviewers to address multiple product aspects in their reviews.

But even though addressing multiple product aspects in reviews is often mandatory to provide more diverse product information, the addressed aspects in reviews are typically unevenly distributed [5]. While some aspects are frequently addressed (e.g., "pizza" in an Italian restaurant), others are only rarely addressed if at all (e.g., "payment options"). This might result in outdated or missing product information. However, Scholz & Dorner [1] report that these rarely addressed product aspects are considered to provide a higher information gain than frequently mentioned product aspects. Thus, DRTs should guide reviewers to also incorporate less frequently addressed aspects or aspects that have not been addressed recently and further guide them to introduce new aspects. This leads to our next DP:

DP2: Provide DRTs with elements that guide reviewers to address product aspects that have rarely and/or not recently been addressed in their reviews.

Moreover, it is a necessary condition that reviewers are willing to review products to cover a wide range of product aspects in their reviews. Thus, the provision of DRTs should not come at the cost of fewer or shorter reviews. As the intention to review strongly correlates with reviewer engagement [24], we define our second DR as follows:

DR2: DRTs should increase reviewers' engagement in review writing.

An important factor that affects reviewer engagement is effort. Burtch et al. [10] and Mudambi & Schuff [25] observe that reviewers tend to write fewer reviews when they perceive their task as demanding. Additionally, tasks that lack enjoyment increase an individual's perceived cognitive effort, leading to decreased engagement [26]. In the context of reviews, Yoo & Gretzel [27] argue that lower engagement results in fewer reviews being written. Hence, we develop our third DP:

DP3: Provide DRTs with elements that reduce reviewers' perceived effort when writing a review.

Further, reviewers might be less engaged in review writing if they perceive that their reviews only have little impact on others. In this context, Rohde et al. [15] find that a high number of existing reviews is negatively correlated with both, the likelihood of writing a review and the length of the review, indicating lower engagement in review writing as well as less product information provided in reviews. Hence, DRTs should emphasize to reviewers that the experiences they provide are unique and help other consumers, producers, or service providers [27]. Highlighting this can trigger altruism, which leads to a higher perceived impact [28]. This results in our final DP:

DP4: Provide DRTs with elements that increase reviewers' perceived impact of review writing.

Table 1 Mapping of design features to design requirements and principles

Design requirements / Principles design features	DR1		DR2	
	DP1	DP2	DP3	DP4
DF1: Five-star Rating Scale	X		X	
DF2: Multiple Topic-Specific Sections	X		X	
DF3: Exemplary Statements	X		X	
DF4: Approval Button	X		X	
DF5: Text Fields	X			X
DF6: Dynamic Sequence		X		X

5 Prototypical Instantiation of Our Design Principles

To demonstrate the proof-of-concept of the DPs outlined in Sect. 4, we now instantiate them into a prototypical DRT. Therefore, we first derive and implement six exemplary DFs that follow our DPs (see Table 1). We demonstrate our instantiated DRT for restaurant reviews, as they encompass a combination of both good aspects (e.g. food and drinks) and service aspects (e.g., waiter's service effort, payment options). However, our instantiation can easily be adjusted to further products.

Like most existing review templates, our instantiation includes a five-star overall rating scale (DF1) that allows for an easy general evaluation of the restaurant visit (DP3). Further, it includes nine topic-specific sections (DF2), such as "food" (see Panel A in Fig. 1). These topic-specific sections aim to guide reviewers towards addressing multiple product aspects across various topics in their review (DP1). We define the sections based on relevant topics for restaurant reviews suggested by Chen et al. [29] and Tian et al. [30] and extend them by topics observed on existing review templates. By implementing topic-specific sections, we also provide a structure for the reviews, which aims to reduce reviewers' perceived cognitive effort (DP3).

For each topic-specific section, our instantiated DRT provides multiple options for reviewers to share their product experiences. More specifically, we include a five-star rating scale for each topic-specific section. After selecting a star rating, up to three exemplary statements are displayed, each covering a single but distinct aspect of the topic (DF3). By presenting exemplary statements, we want to lower reviewers' cognitive effort (DP3) and provide them with ideas about which product aspects could be addressed in their reviews (DP1). Obviously, the statements should fit to the respective topic-specific section and align with a reviewer's chosen star rating. To do so, we apply the following procedure: First, we applied the PyABSA[1] on exemplary statements from existing restaurant reviews to extract the addressed aspects in and the sentiment of each exemplary statement. Second, we employ a topic modeling

[1] PyABSA is a Python-based framework specifically designed for extracting aspects and corresponding sentiments from given textual input. See Yang et al. [31] for details.

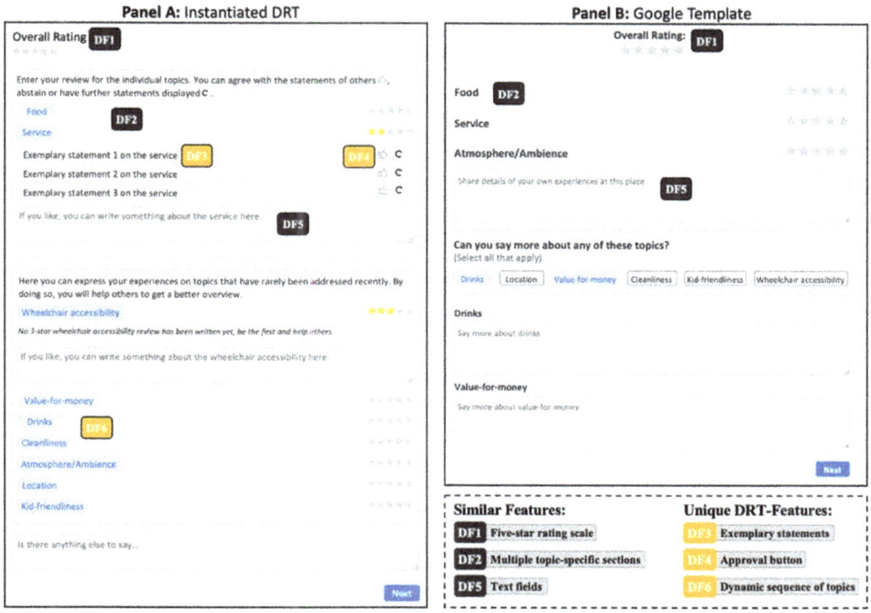

Fig. 1 Instantiated DRT and google template for restaurant reviews

approach using Word2Vec[2] to assign all aspects identified in existing reviews to our predefined topics. For instance, aspects such as "pizza" and "salad" will be assigned to the topic "food". Last, we assign all exemplary statements a topic based on their extracted aspects and a star rating based on their extracted sentiment score. In cases with no exemplary statement for a specific star rating, we display a note encouraging reviewers to be the first to share their experiences and help others.

In addition to the exemplary statements, we also include approval buttons (DF4). These buttons allow reviewers to agree with a statement by simply clicking on the respective button displayed behind them without having to write the same text. This represents another option for reviewers to address multiple product aspects (DP1) with low effort (DP3). In addition, reviewers can reload more statements regarding the specific topic (by clicking on a reload button) if they want to browse through further exemplary statements. Due to the novelty of this DF, our instantiation includes a brief explanation of this functionality. Additionally, each topic-specific section includes a text field (DF5) to give reviewers the possibility to share further (topic-specific) experiences. With this, we aim to increase both the reviewers' perceived impact of their reviews (DP4) and the likelihood of more product aspects being addressed (DP1), as reviewers can share their product experiences that either contradict the information provided by the exemplary statements or address product aspects not yet covered. Please note that all written statements extend the database of exemplary

[2] Word2Vec is a framework that transforms aspects into vectors, mapping their semantic relationships to their distance in a high-dimensional space. See Mikolov et al. [32] for details.

statements that can be displayed to other reviewers. Finally, and in addition to the topic-specific text fields, we add a text field at the end of our instantiation to provide the option to add further product information that cannot be clearly assigned to one of the provided topics.

To guide reviewers towards providing product aspects that are only rarely addressed or have not been addressed recently (DP2), we display the topic-specific sections in a dynamic sequence (DF6). This sequence is determined by considering the existing product information in reviews. In detail, we calculate a relevance score for each topic based on: i) the number of times a topic has already been addressed in existing reviews [7], ii) the time when a topic was last addressed [33], and iii) the sentiment volatility within a topic [34]. The latter is derived by considering the sentiment scores of all statements on a particular topic. The relevance score of a topic increases if it is not frequently addressed, has not been addressed lately, or is highly controversial. This aims at a more balanced coverage of topics, prevents product information from becoming outdated, and gives more attention to controversially addressed topics. The relevance score and therefore the sequence is updated after each review. However—as the most pressing comments of reviewers relate to the most frequently addressed topics (i.e., "food" and "service" in restaurants)—we keep these topics in the upper part and only change the sequence of the remaining topics in its lower part. Nonetheless, the dynamic sequence increases the likelihood that the most relevant topics will be addressed more frequently. Hence, the dynamic feature also makes the note outlined above (i.e., that reviewers can be the first to share their experiences) more likely to be displayed, which amplifies their sense of altruism and consequently increases reviewers' perceived impact of their review (DP4).

6 Experimental Evaluation

We conduct an ex-post evaluation in an artificial environment following Venable et al. [21] by applying a controlled online experiment with a between-subject design.

6.1 Experimental Design

Instantiated vs Competing Artefact. As our goal is to evaluate our DPs, we compare our instantiated DRT with a competing artifact. We opt for the Google template being available in Google Maps as the competing artifact for two reasons. First, the Google template is widely recognized as one of the foremost review templates globally [8]. Second, it incorporates several design features commonly utilized in other well-known online review platforms such as Amazon.com and Booking.com. Hence, it serves as an excellent benchmark for evaluating our DRT.

In Figure 1 shows both, the DRT (Panel A) and the Google template (Panel B). One can observe that both templates have some DFs in common—namely the five-star rating scales (DF1), multiple topic-specific sections (DF2), and text fields (DF5). Moreover, both templates feature an overall star rating and are divided into two sections covering frequently and less frequently addressed topics. However, there also exist notable differences between the templates: The DRT includes star ratings for all topics to propose fitting existing statements (DF3), as well as approval and reload buttons (DF4) for those statements. In contrast, the Google template only provides star ratings for three main topics. Moreover, the Google template includes a text field for the overall rating, while the DRT does not but provides a text field for further comments. Lastly, only the DRT provides a dynamic sequence of topics (DF6), as detailed in Sect. 5.

In our instantiation, we opt for Italian cuisine rather than any cuisine as this only requires extracting exemplary statements from Italian restaurant reviews instead of all potential cuisines. In doing so, our instantiated DRT only displays statements that one would typically expect when reading reviews of Italian restaurants.

Implementation, Pre-Test, and Experimental Procedure. The online experiment including both templates was implemented using the oTree framework [35]. Prior to the main experiment, we performed comprehensive pre-tests with students from a German university and online participants to ensure the comprehensibility of our instantiated DRT and that participants understand the task and questions during the experiment [36]. Online participants (from Germany; at least 18 years old) were recruited via the platform clickworker.com. After starting the experiment, they were instructed to write a review about their last visit to an Italian restaurant and were asked for their demographics and control variables (see next section for details). Participants were then randomly assigned and forwarded to one of the two templates (i.e., our instantiation or the Google template). After completing the task of review writing, we finally asked participants about their perception of the review writing process to investigate the effectiveness of both templates.

To ensure that participants paid full attention to our experiment, we included three attention checks. We informed participants prior to the experiment that failing any attention check would result in exclusion from the experiment without payment. In line with the required payment from clickworker.com, all participants who passed the attention checks and completed the experiment received a payment of 1.60 € as compensation.

Variables. To evaluate our artifact, we measure all criteria mentioned in our DPs. This allows us to examine if our instantiated DRT is effective in addressing our DRs. In the following, we describe how we operationalize the respective DPs and which additional constructs are being evaluated or used as control variables.

DPs 1 and 2 refer to DR1 regarding the guidance of reviewers towards providing more diverse product information in reviews. Thus, we examine the resulting reviews as follows: We gather all information provided in a text field or through statements that were approved by the participant and draw on the PyABSA to identify addressed aspects. Thereafter, we use lemmatization and remove duplicates to ensure that each product aspect is only counted once per participant. Thus, we obtain the *Number of Aspects*. By mapping these aspects to our topics and counting a topic as being addressed when it has received at least a star rating, we obtain the *Number of Topics*. For the Google template the procedure is the same except for the approved exemplary statements.

DPs 3 and 4 refer to DR2 regarding reviewers' engagement in review writing. We assess *Perceived Cognitive Effort* by incorporating three items from Chen [37] and *Perceived Impact* by adapting two items from Yoo & Gretzel [27]. Further, we measure the time participants spent writing the review (*Time Spent*) and calculate how much time participants need to address an aspect (*Time per Aspect*) by dividing the *Number of Aspects* by the *Time Spent*. This indicates the actual effort for reviewers to address a single product aspect. As we are interested in participants' overall perception of our instantiated DRT, we measure the *Usability* of the respective template utilizing two modified items from Hong et al. [38] and Wixom & Todd [39], as well as their *Intention to Use* the template in the future employing an item from Chen [37] and a newly developed item. All items are based on a 7-point Likert scale ranging from 1 = Strongly Disagree to 7 = Strongly Agree.

Prior to the review writing task, we collected several control variables that could affect our results. Thus, we measure participants' familiarity with reading and writing reviews, as this might affect their engagement and written review. We further asked for their age and gender. Finally, as review writing might be more convenient on a desktop computer than on a mobile device, we store the device participants used to complete the experiment.

6.2 Analysis

Data Processing. We recruited a total of 171 participants for our experiment. Of these, 35 were excluded for failing the attention checks. Additionally, seven participants who completed the experiment in less than 100 s were excluded as well as one participant who spent more than twice as much time on the template as any other participant to prevent any bias to the variable *Time Spent* in case the experiment was interrupted. Therefore, our final dataset consists of 128 participants, with 65 belonging to our instantiated DRT and 63 to the Google template, respectively. Before analyzing the data, we check the appropriateness of the sample randomization. Thus, we use a two-sided t-test for the numerical control variable (age), a Wilcoxon rank-sum test for the Likert-scale based control variables and a χ^2-test for the categorical control variables and do not find a significant difference between the two groups. Moreover, we calculate Cronbach's alpha for our main multi-item variables to examine the consistency of our scales [40]. For all our multi-item constructs, Cronbach's alpha is above the recommended value of 0.7 [41].[3]

[3] We provide details on the constructs, their Cronbach's alpha values as well as the extended descriptive statistics in an online appendix available via the following link: https://github.com/DynamicRT/Appendix.

Table 2 Main results

Row	Variables of interest	Instantiated DRT (N = 65)		Google template (N = 63)		Difference in Means
		Mean	SE	Mean	SE	
1	Number of Aspects	7.54	5.00	3.56	2.74	+ 3.98***
2	Number of Topics	7.89	2.05	4.48	1.35	+ 3.41***
3	Perceived Cognitive Effort	2.64	1.20	2.75	1.46	–0.11
4	Perceived Impact	5.72	0.96	5.58	1.04	+ 0.14
5	Time Spent (in seconds)	163	124	147	138	+ 16*
6	Time per Aspect	29.20	28.34	48.11	76.17	–18.91**
7	Usability	5.80	0.90	5.98	0.82	–0.18
8	Intention to Use	4.88	1.38	5.00	1.02	–0.12

Notes $^{*}p < 0.1$, $^{**}p < 0.05$, $^{***}p < 0.01$, statistical significance for differences is based on a one-sided *t*-test (row 1, 2, 5, 6) or a Wilcoxon rank-sum test (row 3, 4, 7, 8)

Main Results. To examine the effectiveness of our instantiated DRT, we test all main variables outlined above for differences between the templates. In this context, we use a nonparametric Wilcoxon rank-sum test for the Likert-scale based variables and a one-sided t-test for all other variables. Table 2 provides the summary statistics for all variables of interest. The last column shows the differences between the two templates and whether this difference is statistically significant.

The first two rows of Table 2 refer to DP1. We observe that significantly more aspects (row 1, $p < 0.01$) as well as more topics[4] (row 2, $p < 0.01$) are addressed when using our instantiated DRT compared to using the Google template. The differences are quite substantial: On average, participants using our instantiated DRT address about 4 (3.3) more aspects (topics) than participants using the Google template. For DP2, we examine the distribution of addressed topics by counting how often each topic is addressed using either template. Figure 2 illustrates the absolute frequency of how often participants addressed the respective nine topics for our instantiation (Panel A) and the Google template (Panel B). The figure indicates that participants address all topics more evenly in our instantiated DRT compared to the Google template. A χ^2-test further indicates that these distributions significantly differ from each other ($p < 0.01$). In addition, this more diverse product information does not come at the cost of lower reviewer engagement. Rows 3–4 display the average values for the item-based constructs referring to DPs 3 and 4. Even though the constructs do not significantly differ between both templates, participants perceive slightly less cognitive effort and slightly higher impact in review writing when using our instantiated DRT. Further, we observe that participants spent more time writing

[4] We count a topic as being addressed when participants at least provide a star rating. For only counting a topic as being addressed when participants either targeted it in the text fields or approved some statement covering this topic, we still observe significantly more topics being addressed with the instantiated DRT compared to the Google template.

the review (row 5, $p < 0.1$) using our instantiated DRT but address aspects more efficiently. Participants need on average 29 s to address an aspect in our instantiated DRT compared to 48 s in the Google template (row 6, $p < 0.05$). Regarding the overall perception of the templates, we do not find a statistically significant difference in *Usability* or *Intention to Use* (rows 7 and 8).

7 Discussion and Conclusion

This paper follows the DSR paradigm to establish DPs for designing DRTs that consider the existing product information in reviews. We derive two DRs based on existing literature and develop four DPs. We instantiate our DPs and demonstrate them in the form of a prototypical DRT for restaurant reviews. This prototypical instantiation is evaluated against the Google template. The evaluation results indicate that our instantiated DRT outperforms the Google template in guiding reviewers towards providing more diverse product information (DR1). Although both templates contain the same topic-specific sections, reviewers address significantly more topics and aspects in their reviews using our instantiation. Furthermore, only rarely or not recently addressed aspects are, on average, covered significantly more often. These findings indicate that current static review templates (like the Google template) fail to guide reviewers towards providing more diverse product information, leading to the situation that mainly similar aspects are addressed in reviews and only a few reviews address other aspects. A dynamic sequence of topic-specific sections and the presentation of exemplary statements can guide reviewers to cover a wide range of product aspects, increasing the effectiveness of online review systems. Further, we observe, that it requires reviewers significantly less time to address one aspect using our instantiated DRT compared to the Google template. This implies that participants not only provide more diverse product information in their reviews, but also do so more efficiently. At the same time, our instantiated DRT does not increase the perceived cognitive effort of reviewers, despite being less familiar compared to the Google template. Hence, our instantiated DRT maintains high reviewer engagement (DR2). In summary, we conclude that DRTs that follow our DPs are significantly better at guiding reviewers to provide more diverse product information in reviews while keeping a high level of reviewer engagement.

We contribute to existing research by extending the knowledge on the design of online review systems in general and review templates in particular and therefore respond to a recent call for research in this area Gutt et al. [2]. As existing research has not yet considered dynamic elements for review templates, we are—to the best of our knowledge—the first to explore DRTs that consider the existing product information in reviews and provide prescriptive design knowledge for the design of such review templates. In line with the DSR contribution framework of Gregor & Hevner [42], the DPs for DRTs represent a Level 2 contribution in terms of a nascent design theory. The instantiation of our DPs further reveals valuable insights to online review system providers: We provide insights on how they can use DRTs to guide reviewers

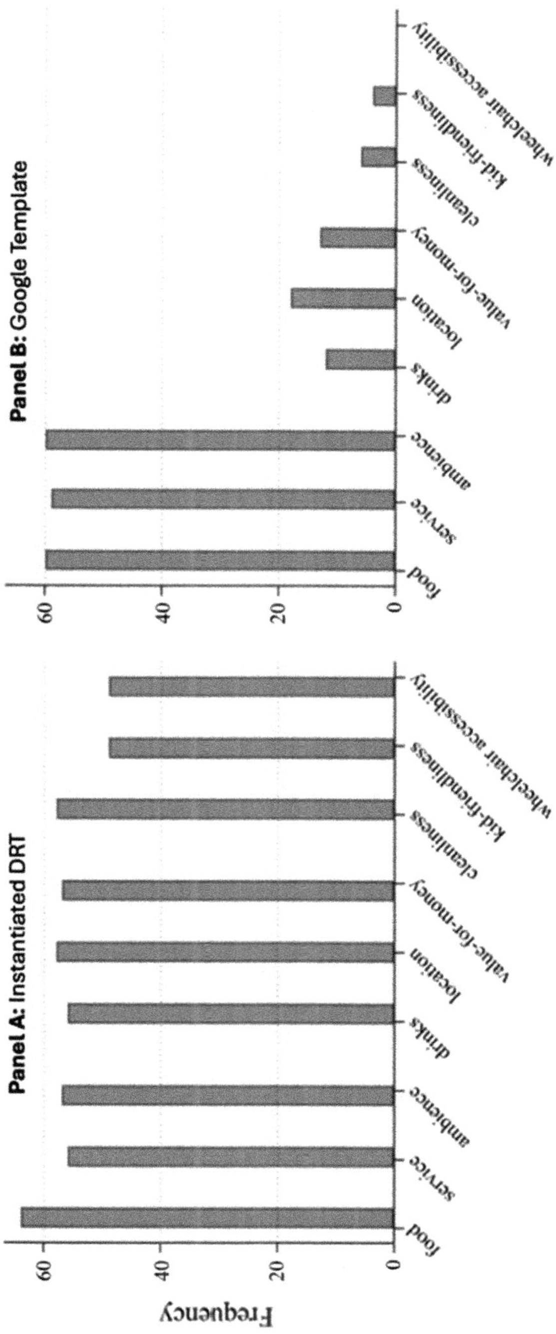

Fig. 2 Distribution of aspects along topics

to provide more diverse product information in their reviews. This can be achieved by displaying exemplary statements from existing reviews with an approval button and adjusting the sequence of topic-specific sections according to their relevance. This more diverse product information helps to reduce the information asymmetry between consumers and businesses leading to more informed product decisions of consumers. Businesses also benefit, as they can expect more comprehensive feedback from reviews due to greater diversity.

While this study is not without limitations, these can be used as fruitful starting points for future research. First and most importantly, although our instantiated DRTs lead to more diverse product information in reviews, future research should analyze whether these reviews also effectively support consumers in making informed product decisions. Second, we develop DPs based on one iteration of the DSR process outlined in Peffers et al. [19]. As a next step, future research should revisit the design and development phases and incorporate evaluation insights to improve and extend our established DPs. Third, we evaluate our instantiated DRT in an artificial environment using an online experiment to write restaurant reviews. In this vein, our evaluation setting does neither fully replicate real-world conditions nor encompass a broad range of products. Therefore, future research could deploy our instantiated DRT on an online review system provider's website and evaluate its applicability to other products. Fourth, our prototypical instantiation represents only one possible design of a DRT. Future research should optimize the design of DRTs by further exploring our DFs, such as optimally adjusting the weights in our metric for the dynamic sequence, or improving how exemplary statements are selected (e.g., based on reviewers' characteristics or their previous reviews). As optimal weights may depend on the product, even AI can be used to determine which information is most relevant and adjust the sequence of topic-specific sections accordingly.

References

1. Scholz, M., & Dorner, V. (2013). The Recipe for the Perfect Review? *Business & Information Systems Engineering, 5*(3), 141–151.
2. Gutt, D., Neumann, J., Zimmermann, S., Kundisch, D., & Chen, J. (2019). Design of Review Systems—A Strategic Instrument to Shape Online Reviewing Behavior and Economic Outcomes. *The Journal of Strategic Information Systems, 28*(2), 104–117.
3. Yin, D., Bond, S. D., & Zhang, H. (2014). Anxious or Angry? Effects of Discrete Emotions on the Perceived Helpfulness of Online Reviews. *MIS Quarterly, 38*(2), 539–560.
4. Guo, Y., Barnes, S. J., & Jia, Q. (2017). Mining Meaning from Online Ratings and Reviews: Tourist Satisfaction Analysis Using Latent Dirichlet Allocation. *Tourism Management, 59*, 467–483.
5. Vallurupalli, V., & Bose, I. (2020). Exploring Thematic Composition of Online Reviews: A Topic Modeling Approach. *Electronic Markets, 30*(4), 791–804.
6. Xianghua, F., Guo, L., Yanyan, G., & Zhiqiang, W. (2013). Multi-aspect Sentiment Analysis for Chinese Online Social Reviews Based on Topic Modeling and HowNet lexicon. *Knowledge-Based Systems, 37*, 186–195.

7. Son, J., Negahban, A., & Chiang, D. T. (2019). Topic Diversity of Online Consumer Reviews and Its Effect on Review Helpfulness. In *Proceeding of the 25th Americas Conference on Information Systems.*
8. Singh, V. (2019). *How Google Reviews Is Crushing TripAdvisor*, https://www.hospitalitynet.org/opinion/4092845.html. Accessed March 26, 2024.
9. Babić Rosario, A., De Valck, K., & Sotgiu, F. (2020). Conceptualizing the Electronic Word-Of-Mouth Process: What We Know and Need to Know About Ewom Creation, Exposure, and Evaluation. *Journal of the Academy of Marketing Science, 48*(3), 422–448.
10. Burtch, G., Hong, Y., Bapna, R., & Griskevicius, V. (2018). Stimulating Online Reviews by Combining Financial Incentives and Social Norms. *Management Science, 64*(5), 2065–2082.
11. Yu, Y., Khern-am-nuai, W., & Pinsonneault, A. (2022). When Paying for Reviews Pays Off: The Case of Performance-Contingent Monetary Rewards. *MIS Quarterly, 46*(1), 609–626.
12. Khern-am-nuai, W., Kannan, K., & Ghasemkhani, H. (2018). Extrinsic versus Intrinsic Rewards for Contributing Reviews in an Online Platform. *Information Systems Research, 29*(4), 871–892.
13. Jiang, L., Ravichandran, T., & Kuruzovich, J. (2023). Review Moderation Transparency and Online Reviews: Evidence from A Natural Experiment. *MIS Quarterly, 47*(4), 1693–1708.
14. Li, H., Meng, F., & Pan, B. (2020). How Does Review Disconfirmation Influence Customer Online Review Behavior? A Mixed-Method Investigation. *International Journal of Contemporary Hospitality Management, 32*(11), 3685–3703.
15. Rohde, C., Kupfer, A., & Zimmermann, S. (2022). Explaining Reviewing Effort: Existing Reviews as Potential Driver. *Electronic Markets, 32*(3), 1169–1185.
16. Chen, P.-Y., Hong, Y., & Liu, Y. (2018). The Value of Multidimensional Rating Systems: Evidence from a Natural Experiment and Randomized Experiments. *Management Science, 64*(10), 4629–4647.
17. Poniatowski, M., Neumann, J., Goerzen, T., & Kundisch, D. (2019). Organizing Their Thoughts—How Online Review Templates Affect The Review Text. In *Proceedings of the 27th European Conference on Information Systems.* Stockholm & Uppsala, Sweden.
18. Hevner, A. R., March, S. T., Park, J., & Ram, S. (2004). Design Science in Information Systems Research. *MIS Quarterly, 28*(1), 75–105.
19. Peffers, K., Tuunanen, T., Rothenberger, M. A., & Chatterjee, S. (2007). A Design Science Research Methodology for Information Systems Research. *Journal of Management Information Systems, 24*(3), 45–77.
20. Gregor, S., Kruse, L., & Seidel, S. (2020). Research Perspectives: The Anatomy of a Design Principle. *Journal of the Association for Information Systems, 21*(6), 1622–1652.
21. Venable, J., Pries-Heje, J., & Baskerville, R. (2012). A Comprehensive Framework for Evaluation in Design Science Research. In *Proceedings of the 7th International Conference on Design Science Research in Information Systems.* Las Vegas, USA.
22. Prat, N., Comyn-Wattiau, I., & Akoka, J. (2015). A Taxonomy of Evaluation Methods for Information Systems Artifacts. *Journal of Management Information Systems, 32*(3), 229–267.
23. Sun, X., Han, M., & Feng, J. (2019). Helpfulness of Online Reviews: Examining Review Informativeness and Classification Thresholds by Search Products and Experience Products. *Decision Support Systems, 124*, Article 113099.
24. Thakur, R. (2018). Customer Engagement and Online Reviews. *Journal of Retailing and Consumer Services, 41*, 48–59.
25. Mudambi, S. M., & Schuff, D. (2010). Research Note: What Makes a Helpful Online Review? A Study of Customer Reviews on Amazon.com. *MIS Quarterly, 34*(1), 185–200.
26. Devine, S., & Otto, A. R. (2022). Information About Task Progress Modulates Cognitive Demand Avoidance. *Cognition* 225.
27. Yoo, K. H., & Gretzel, U. (2008). What Motivates Consumers to Write Online Travel Reviews? *Information Technology & Tourism, 10*(4), 283–295.
28. Hennig-Thurau, T., Gwinner, K. P., Walsh, G., & Gremler, D. D. (2004). Electronic Word-Of-Mouth via Consumer-Opinion Platforms: What Motivates Consumers to Articulate Themselves on the Internet? *Journal of Interactive Marketing, 18*(1), 38–52.

29. Chen, Y., Cramton, P., List, J. A., & Ockenfels, A. (2021). Market Design, Human Behavior, and Management. *Management Science, 67*(9), 5317–5348.
30. Tian, G., Lu, L., & McIntosh, C. (2021). What Factors Affect Consumers' Dining Sentiments and Their Ratings: Evidence from Restaurant Online Review Data. *Food Quality and Preference, 88*, Article 104060.
31. Yang, H., Zhang, C., & Li, K. (2023). PyABSA: A Modularized Framework for Reproducible Aspect-based Sentiment Analysis. In *Proceedings of the 32nd ACM International Conference on Information and Knowledge Management* (pp. 5117–5122). Birmingham, United Kingdom.
32. Mikolov, T., Chen, K., Corrado, G., & Dean, J. (2013). Efficient Estimation of Word Representations in Vector Space. arXiv:1301.3781.
33. Pan, Y., & Zhang, J. Q. (2011). Born Unequal: A Study of the Helpfulness of User-Generated Product Reviews. *Journal of Retailing, 87*(4), 598–612.
34. Leberknight, C. S., Sen, S., & Chiang, M. (2012). On the Volatility of Online Ratings: An Empirical Study. In *E-Life: Web-Enabled Convergence of Commerce, Work, and Social Life* (pp. 77–86). Springer.
35. Chen, D. L., Schonger, M., & Wickens, C. (2016). OTree—An Open-Source Platform For Laboratory, Online, and Field Experiments. *Journal of Behavioral and Experimental Finance, 9*, 88–97.
36. Reynolds, N., & Diamantopoulos, A. (1998). The Effect of Pretest Method on Error Detection Rates: Experimental Evidence. *European Journal of Marketing, 32*(5/6), 480–498.
37. Chen, C.-W. (2017). Five-Star or Thumbs-Up? The Influence of Rating System Types on Users' Perceptions of Information Quality, Cognitive Effort, Enjoyment and Continuance Intention. *Internet Research, 27*(3), 478–494.
38. Hong, W., Thong, J. Y. L., Wong, W. M., & Tam, K. Y. (2002). Determinants of User Acceptance of Digital Libraries: An Empirical Examination of Individual Differences and System Characteristics. *Journal of Management Information Systems, 18*(3), 97–124.
39. Wixom, B. H., & Todd, P. A. (2005). A Theoretical Integration of User Satisfaction and Technology Acceptance. *Information Systems Research, 16*(1), 85–102.
40. Cortina, J. M. (1993). What is Coefficient Alpha? An Examination of Theory and Applications. *Journal of Applied Psychology, 78*(1), 98–104.
41. Hair, J. F., Ringle, C. M., & Sarstedt, M. (2011). PLS-SEM: Indeed a Silver Bullet. *Journal of Marketing Theory and Practice, 19*(2), 139–152.
42. Gregor, S., & Hevner, A. R. (2013). Positioning and Presenting Design Science Research for Maximum Impact. *MIS Quarterly, 37*(2), 337–355.

Platform Disintermediation: A Credence Good Perspective

Robin Christmann and Jürgen Rösch

Abstract This paper extends a well-established credence goods model to digital platforms and disintermediation. Users seek assistance from a digital platform to find the right expert. However, they are not aware of which service type they need, so they consult the expert in the first place. Asymmetric information allows experts to prioritize their profit over the users' needs, as users cannot, even after consumption, detect potential mistreatment. Digital platforms can help users find the right expert and learn about their required service level, mitigating this inefficiency. However, some users with minor quality requirements may systematically bypass the platform to avoid transaction fees. To address the problem of disintermediation, the platform could explore a subscription-based revenue model. However, a transaction-based revenue model potentially increases the number of users on the platform under information asymmetry. This could result in an improved matching algorithm and stronger network effects.

1 Introduction

Disintermediation is a major threat to digital platforms after solving the chicken-and-egg problem. Users may use the platform to find a transaction partner but then conduct transactions outside the platform to avoid transaction fees. This disintermediation, also known as platform leakage, is sometimes compared to shoplifting [1] or showrooming, where consumers get advice in a store but buy online [2]. However, platform disintermediation involves two parties joining the platform and transacting outside it.

R. Christmann
Leibniz-FH, Hannover, Germany
e-mail: christmann@leibniz-fh.de

J. Rösch (✉)
Bauhaus-Universität Weimar, Weimar, Germany
e-mail: juergen.roesch@uni-weimar.de

C. M. Flath et al. (eds.), *Artificial Intelligence, Data, and Decision-Making*, Lecture Notes in Information Systems and Organisation 82,
https://doi.org/10.1007/978-3-032-08480-4_29

To mitigate disintermediation, platforms use strategies like restricting user communication and adding value-added services, such as insurance, to justify fees. Revenue model adjustments, like referral fees or subscriptions and price parity, address fee avoidance and maintain platform utility for standardized transactions. These measures and ethical incentives and sanctions aim to retain users and keep the platform relevant, especially when direct interactions become viable after trust is established [1–4].

Understanding disintermediation requires insight into how platforms create value and what users' risk by circumventing them. One key aspect often overlooked is the role of digital platforms in credence goods markets [5, 6]. Users in these markets need help but cannot determine the precise service required or judge the quality of the service even after consuming it. Experts can diagnose and offer treatment, but their informational advantage may lead to overtreatment, undertreatment, or overcharging, which users cannot detect due to their lack of knowledge [6]. Examples include car or computer repairs, doctor visits, and taxi services, where the expert's superior knowledge may be abused [6].

The credence-good market, especially in the gig economy [7], has not been systematically investigated in the context of platform disintermediation. He, Savin, Goh and Teo [8] model different supplier types in asymmetric information contexts, and Hagiu and Wright [2] highlight information asymmetries as a research frontier. Consumers seeking experts, as defined by Dulleck and Kerschbamer [6], often find help on digital platforms [7]. For instance, Fiverr.com connects users with freelancers for creative jobs, myhammer.com finds handymen, and check24 matches professionals for various tasks. Similarly, health and finance platforms aid users in finding suitable professionals. Even taxi and ride-hailing services have credence good characteristics, where drivers may choose more profitable routes [9].

Markets can address credence goods challenges without experts exploiting information asymmetries. Dulleck and Kerschbamer [6] show that such asymmetries cannot be exploited when conditions like consumer homogeneity, commitment to recommended treatment, and mechanisms like liability or verifiability are met. For some digital platforms, the primary issue is connecting consumers and experts. Consumers face low risks of mistreatment but may experience overpricing or overtreatment for minor treatments. However, experts and platforms might distort services for high-quality treatments, leading to over- or undertreatment or overcharging. Undertreatment can have serious consequences, especially in sensitive sectors like healthcare or car repair.

We aim to close the gap in the existing literature by introducing the digital platform as a new economic agent in the credence goods model of Dulleck and Kerschbamer [6] ("DK-model"). We model a situation where users seek assistance from experts on the platform without knowing what service they need. Consequently, experts may exploit their position by providing unsuitable services or charging for services not rendered [5]. The digital platform acts as an intermediary, helping users diagnose their needs and find the right expert match. This setting allows us to analyze the conditions under which users and experts might bypass the platform and how digital platforms can mitigate disintermediation.

The rest of the paper proceeds as follows: The next section provides an overview of the literature on platform disintermediation. We then introduce the adopted model and discuss its relevance. Following this, we analyze the behavior of consumers and experts with and without the platform. We then discuss the results and draw implications. The paper concludes with a discussion about the limitations of the study.

2 Literature Review

Hagiu and Wright [2] present a comprehensive model on platform leakage, where users bypass the platform for direct transactions to avoid fees. Their model involves a single seller and multiple buyers, with the seller setting prices for both platform and direct transactions, and buyers facing switching costs. The platform structures fees to balance incentivizing usage and minimizing leakage. Hagiu and Wright [2] analyze six strategies, such as additional transaction benefits, referral fees, and price parity, assessing each for effectiveness, impact on profit, and strategic trade-offs. They note that situations with asymmetric information, like car repairs or plumbing, are prone to disintermediation due to the necessary communication between seller and buyer.

Sekar and Siddiq [10] examine the dynamics of information asymmetry and fee structures on digital platforms, particularly with the risk of off-platform transactions. They find that while increased transparency boosts transactions and revenue in a closed platform environment, it may reduce revenue when users can transact off-platform by using the information to mitigate risk. Platforms may respond by raising fees to capitalize on remaining on-platform users. They find that access fees are less profitable without disintermediation. The study highlights the strategic acceptance of some disintermediation to enhance revenue from other users.

He et al. [8] use a Stackelberg-style model to analyze provider behavior under varying information scenarios. In markets with imperfect information, platforms may not attract high-quality providers due to low average service quality. Leakage arises when the risk of bypassing the platform is moderate. The study suggests platforms can deter disintermediation by improving user experience, like reducing waiting times or enhancing overall quality by training lower-quality providers.

Measuring disintermediation empirically is challenging as off-platform transactions are not observable. Gu and Zhu [3] analyze buyer–seller communications for words indicating potential disintermediation. In a field experiment offering enhanced trust signals to some buyers, they find a non-linear trust-disintermediation relationship: initial trust boosts platform value, but excessive trust encourages circumvention.

Gu [11] use a similar approach, leveraging China's ban on Skype as a natural experiment to observe conversations between Chinese freelancers and US clients. They find that potential disintermediation decreases significantly, and platform transactions increase during this period, highlighting the importance of mechanisms preventing off-platform cooperation.

Astashkina et al. [12] and Karacaoglu et al. [13] use geographical distance data for home cleaning platforms in Russia and Europe. While Astashkina et al. [12] find minimal disintermediation, Karacaoglu et al. [13] report significant disintermediation, with the platform potentially selling 24 percent more cleanings without it. One reason for the difference might be that the continuous matching between cleaner and client in Astashkina et al. [12] serve as a countermeasure for disintermediation. Lin et al. [14] also use location data for Airbnb, showing that while disintermediation is an issue, its magnitude is low at five percent. They find that Instant Booking, which reduces host-traveler communication, can reduce disintermediation by nine percent. He et al. [15] observed a decline in third-party sellers' transactions on a Chinese marketplace after the owner began competing with them. Similarly, Farronato et al. [16] cited disintermediation as a reason for reduced transactions on a pet-sitting platform following its acquisition by a competing platform.

Ladd [1] examined disintermediation in platform business models through a practitioner-oriented review, addressing definitions, implications, and solutions. Strategies identified include pricing adjustments, switching revenue models, blocking communication, and enhancing value propositions. Ladd [1] also highlighted how digital platforms address the lemons problem [17] using rating systems, seller information, third-party assessments, and certification.

Our paper connects the literature on platform disintermediation and leakage with credence goods, where consumers cannot judge the quality of a good or service even post-consumption. Dulleck and Kerschbamer [6] identify conditions for efficient credence goods markets: (1) consumers uniformly value solutions, (2) consumers commit to purchasing treatment after diagnosis, (3) experts face liability for inappropriate treatment, and (4) treatments are verifiable to prevent overcharging. Liability or verifiability, along with the first two conditions, is sufficient for market efficiency [6, 18].

3 Baseline Model

3.1 Model Setup

In the following, we apply the basic DK model [6] on credence goods to a scenario where a digital platform facilitates beneficial transactions between parties under asymmetric information, and the provision of this platform service is at risk due to disintermediation. Additionally, we introduce the digital platform as a third maximizing economic agent. Consider platform (dis)intermediation as a strategic game with a single platform (P), n customers (C) and m experts (E), and n and m are large. Information asymmetry exists in this interaction as customers are aware that they require assistance from an expert, but they do not know what type of service or treatment is required. In other words, "the customer knows that he has a problem, but does not know how severe it is" [6 p. 11]. However, the experts can assess the correct type of service at no cost. Each consumer can search for adequate service on or off the platform. The distinct feature of the platform is that it offers to match consumers with the truly required service with a higher probability.

First, consider a single consumer who is unaware of what treatment is needed. Hence, she may receive overtreatment, undertreatment, or adequate treatment, depending on her true type and the provided service. She is also at risk of being overcharged by the expert. Assume that customers are homogenous in the following way: a customer can be one of two types, $\overline{c}$ or $\underline{c}$, and each consumer knows that the probability of being type $\overline{c}$ is $h \in [0; 1]$. Respectively, the type of service provided by the experts can be one of the two types, which we denote as "*treat* $\overline{c}$" or "*treat* $\underline{c}$". We further specify that a consumer of type $\overline{c}$ ($\underline{c}$) requires the service of type $\overline{c}$ ($\underline{c}$). Let the consumer be unable to detect overtreatment, but undertreatment can be detected by her ex-post. This implies that a consumer of the low type $\underline{c}$ will gain utility v independent of the provided treatment, as the service can either be adequate or excessive in quality. A consumer of the high type $\overline{c}$, however, will gain a utility of v if treated adequately with service $\overline{c}$, but receives an utility of zero if undertreated with service $\underline{c}$.. Given the price menus for treatments, the consumer can choose between seeking an expert in the offline market ("*offline*"), via platform services ("*platform*") or to do nothing ("*out*").

For the expert, the type-contingent costs of providing the service are denoted accordingly as $\overline{c}$ and $\underline{c}$, with $\overline{c} > \underline{c} > 0$.. Experts compete for consumers in a Bertrand-fashion and ex-ante announce price menus $(\overline{p}, \underline{p})$ for services of type $\overline{c}$ and $\underline{c}$. As a simplification, we assume that there are always multiple experts active both on the platform and in the offline market. When a consumer meets an expert in the offline market, the expert first provides a diagnosis about the consumer's type. Having received the diagnosis, one can imagine that some consumers may want to see a different expert. Assume that a diagnosis is costly and produces diagnosis cost $d > 0$. Then, if the condition $d > (\overline{c} - \underline{c})(1 - h)$ is satisfied, economies of scope between joint diagnosis and treatment by a single expert are sufficiently high to prevent the consumer from continuing her search after having visited the first expert. We further assume that $v - \overline{c} - d > 0$ always holds, which implies that treatment by the expert is always efficient.

As the third player in the game, the digital platform provides a valuable service to consumers: it provides better matches for its users, i.e. to match consumers on the platform with the correct treatment of experts. Consider that the platform is able to correctly match consumers of type $\overline{c}$ with probability ϕ_H with the required service $\overline{c}$ by an expert. Accordingly, a consumer of type $\underline{c}$ can expect to find a correct match on the platform with probability ϕ_L. This implies that on the platform, experts no longer decide themselves about what type of service is provided but are committed to the identified service by the matching algorithm of the platform. Let this matching accuracy be positively dependent on the number of users on the platform. In other words, the platform successfully generates a positive network effect.[1] The monopolist platform may impose prices t for its service, either upfront (t_1, i.e., a subscription fee) or when the treatment by an expert occurs (t_2, i.e., a transaction fee). The platform may charge the consumer, the expert, or both. Given these specifications, platform matching leads to the following choice of the consumer: either to be treated according to the matching outcome, to disintermediate and execute the transaction outside the platform ("*leave*"), or to do nothing ("*out*"). If a pair of consumers and experts decide to disintermediate, i.e., leave the platform after matching, they evenly split the savings from avoided platform prices. Moreover, we assert that the bargained 'price' upon disintermediation will never make the consumer worse off than exerting search costs d and consulting a different expert.

Furthermore, we assume that all players are risk-neutral, and that all information is common knowledge except for the consumer's true type.

Lastly, we further specify that outside platform matching, neither the liability of the expert nor the verifiability of the true service applies. This produces the risks of undertreatment and overcharging for off-platform consumers. As this paper focuses on platform (dis)intermediation, we assume that a consumer who decides right away to consult an expert only outside the platform is subject to the equilibrium outcome of the DK-model. Figure 1 displays the game tree from the perspective of a single consumer and a single expert.

The game starts with the platform to define its fees, and afterwards experts propose their price menus. Nature then determines the consumer's type, either $\overline{c}$ or $\underline{c}$.. The consumer, in need for treatment, then has three options: consulting an expert offline directly leads to the DK-model outcome, doing nothing ends the game as well, or seeking platform services (subject to subscription fee t_1). On the platform, nature determines the signal about the consumer's true type. The consumer then may either be treated according to the signal (subject to transaction fee t_2), leave the platform and be treated by the expert outside the platform (but prone to the risks of overcharging or undertreatment), or do nothing.

4 Platform Disintermediation

4.1 Stage III: Treatment After Platform Matching

At this last stage of the game, the consumer decides whether to use the expert treatment as suggested by the platform ("treat"), to disintermediate and bargain with the expert outside the platform ("leave") or simply to quit ("out"). Evidently, the latter

[1] Belleflamme and Peitz define a network effect as the impact that an additional user of a service has on the value that other users attach to this service. We assume that the accuracy of the matching algorithm improves with the number of users (consumers, experts), and this increases the valuation (and willingness-to-pay) of users for platform services. The platform then manages such network effects by pricing access to its services and the intensity of usage [19].

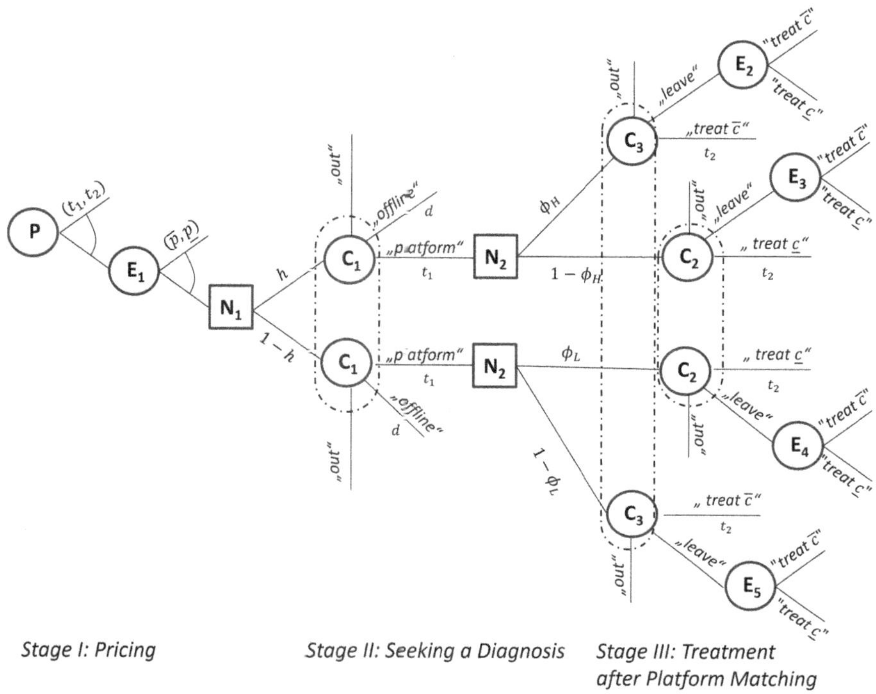

Fig. 1 Game tree for the disintermediation game

option yields zero utility. The gains from disintermediation depend on the expected treatment by the expert (decision nodes E_2 to E_5) and bargained prices. Given the absence of liability and verifiability outside the platform, the expert will always apply the lower treatment $\underline{c}$ and incur the respective costs. If the consumer chooses treatment via the platform, the matching procedure commits the expert to the suggested treatment for the specified prices. Furthermore, Bertrand competition will ensure marginal cost pricing. The gains for the consumer from the choices "leave" and "treat" are type-dependent: while the $\bar{c}$-type consumer is prone both to undertreatment and overcharging, the $\underline{c}$-type consumer is only exposed to overcharging. Thus, a rational consumer has to form beliefs about her true needs.

An important feature of the platform algorithm's ability to match consumers and experts is the potential reduction in information asymmetry: matching serves as an informative signal to the consumer about her true type. Let the belief μ_H be the ex-post probability, i.e. applying Bayesian updating, that the consumer is truly of the $\bar{c}$-type when she observed the signal $\bar{c}$ by the platform. Respectively, consider belief μ_L to describe the ex-post probability that she truly is of the $\underline{c}$-type contingent on receiving the signal $\underline{c}$.

If the platform categorizes her as $\bar{c}$-type consumer, i.e. decision node C_3 is reached, she will receive the certain payoff $v - \bar{c} - t_2$, where t_2 is the transaction fee, when treated via platform services. Note that this means (harmless but costly) overtreatment for the case that she truly was of the low type, and this payoff is certain. The consumer will then decide against platform services only if executing the transaction outside the platform or quitting favors her. For the case of disintermediation, assume that expert and consumer avoid the transaction fee t_2 by the platform and split the gains evenly.[2] However, only the $\underline{c}$-type consumer can expect to be treated efficiently. Thus, a consumer who receives the $\overline{c}$-signal by the platform will stay on the platform if the following condition is met

$$v - \overline{c} - t_2 \geq max\Big[(1 - \mu_H)v - \underline{c} - \min(\frac{t_2}{2}, \mathrm{d})), 0\Big] \tag{1}$$

The right side of the inequality specifies the highest utility out of the two alternatives to treatment via the platform. Rearranging for belief μ_H yields the threshold for choosing strategy "out" over "leave", which gives $\mu_H > 1 - \frac{\underline{c}+\min(\frac{t_2}{2},d)}{v} = \widehat{\mu_H}$. The higher the belief μ_H to be a truly $\overline{c}$-type consumer, the less appealing is disintermediation.

The situation is different if the consumer received the $\underline{c}$-signal, i.e. decision node C_2 is reached. If this signal correctly identifies her type, then she receives a payoff of $v - \underline{c} - t_2$, but if the categorization is wrong, then the consumer is forced to undertreatment on the platform. Then, she receives $-\underline{c} - t_2$. As before, contracting outside the platform generates a utility of zero for the high type, but achieves adequate treatment for the low type while also partly avoiding the transaction fee. Consequently, the decision to stay on the platform contingent on the $\underline{c}$-signal is specified by

$$\mu_L\big(v - \underline{c} - t_2\big) - (1 - \mu_L)\big(\underline{c} + t_2\big) \geq max\Big[(\mu_L v - \underline{c} - \min(\frac{t_2}{2}, \mathrm{d})), 0\Big] \tag{2}$$

The right side of the inequality again provides an indication when choosing strategy "out" over "leave" is the more appealing alternative for the consumer contingent on observing signal $\underline{c}$: rearranging for μ_L gives $\mu_L < \frac{\underline{c}+\min(\frac{t_2}{2},\mathrm{d})}{v} = \widehat{\mu_L}$. Similarly, the higher the belief to be a $\underline{c}$-consumer, the more appealing is disintermediation. The analysis of $\widehat{\mu_H}$ and $\widehat{\mu_L}$ also indicates that platform disintermediation is a more severe problem when the share of $\underline{c}$-types is high, and less so when there are many $\overline{c}$-type consumers in the population.

The conditions (1) and (2) lead to *Corollary 1.*

Corollary 1. *(i) The consumer will use platform services on observing the signal $\overline{c}$if only $t_2 < v - \overline{c}$and her belief adheres to $\mu_H \geq \frac{\overline{c}-\underline{c}+\frac{t_2}{2}}{v}$. (ii) The consumer will always leave the platform on the signal $\underline{c}$when transaction fees exist, i.e. $t_2 > 0$.*

Proof: Proofs will be provided upon request.

[2] Note that search costs d can be regarded as 'threat point' of the consumer in bargaining: she can credibly threaten to consult a different expert if splitting the transaction fee upon disintermediation still makes her worse off.

4.2 Stage II: Seeking a Diagnosis

Consumers at decision node C_1 will decide whether to use platform services, consult an expert offline, or quit. They will use the platform as an intermediator if the improved matching provides a net benefit compared to the individual search for an expert. Bertrand competition will then ensure marginal cost pricing. Given our analysis in Sect. 4.1, we will allow for the following simplifying assumption: a consumer will choose "leave" on signal $\underline{c}$, i.e. $\mu_L > \widehat{\mu_L}$ applies.[3]

We have to distinguish two scenarios: the consumer expects (i) disintermediation to be still feasible after the matching, or (ii) she expects to be committed to the platform.

In the first scenario, where the consumer can choose to leave the platform after matching, *Corollay 1* indicated that consumers who receive the signal $\underline{c}$ will always leave the platform. For consumers who observe $\overline{c}$ this depends on the level of the transaction fee t_2. In the following, let us focus on the interesting case where the consumer stays on the platform only when observing the signal $\overline{c}$, i.e. $t_2 \leq v - \overline{c}$ and $\mu_H \geq \frac{\overline{c} - \underline{c} + \frac{t_2}{2}}{v}$ apply.[4] Then we can write the net utility for the consumer from using the platform service with no commitment, denoted as u_{nc}, as

$$\begin{aligned} u_{nc} = h\left[\phi_H \cdot (v - \overline{c} - t_2) - (1 - \phi_H) \cdot \left(\underline{c} + \frac{t_2}{2}\right)\right] \\ + (1 - h)\left[\phi_L \cdot \left(v - \underline{c} - \frac{t_2}{2}\right) + (1 - \phi_L)(v - \overline{c} - t_2)\right] \end{aligned} \tag{3}$$

In the second scenario, the consumer is committed to the platform, i.e. disintermediation is ruled out by platform design, then the net utility for the consumer from using the platform service, denoted as u_p can be specified as

$$\begin{aligned} u_c = h\left[\phi_H \cdot (v - \overline{c}) - (1 - \phi_H)\underline{c}\right] \\ + (1 - h)\left[\phi_L \cdot (v - \underline{c}) + (1 - \phi_L)(v - \overline{c})\right] - t_2 \end{aligned} \tag{4}$$

When comparing conditions (3) and (4), it is obvious that the only difference is the partly avoided transaction fee through disintermediation.

Corollary 2. *The option to disintermediate always provides a higher expected net utility to the consumer when using platform services except for zero transaction fees.*

Proof. Obvious from the text and therefore omitted.

[3] Note that the threshold $\widehat{\mu_H}$ is not relevant here as the platform will choose fees in a way to keep at least the $\overline{c}$-consumer on the platform.

[4] The other two cases are straightforward: the commitment scenario also includes the case where the consumer always stays on the platform voluntarily. The case where consumers always leave the platform implies, given non-liability and non-verifiability, a digital version of the inefficient lemon market outcome.

Let us now turn to the market for experts outside the platform. Following the DK model, experts will compete in a Bertrand fashion, and prices will equal marginal costs if at least two experts are in the market. Given no verifiability and no liability, experts have no incentive to provide a higher quality than $\underline{c}$, and consumers have similarly no reason to expect a higher quality. With at least two experts active outside the platform by assumption, the market will correspond to a standard lemon market. Experts will provide only quality $\underline{c}$ with price $p_0 = \underline{c}$.[5] In all cases, the market ceases to exist whenever consumers can only expect a negative utility from such a transaction. We thus find that the expected net utility of finding experts outside the platform for the consumer, i.e. the value of the outside option u_0, is given as

$$u_0 = max\big((1-h)v - \underline{c} - d, 0\big) \tag{5}$$

Note that (5) implies that the value of the outside option ceteris paribus is increasing in the probability of being the $\underline{c}$-type. Similarly, the value of the outside option is decreasing with the charged price and search costs.

5 Stage I: Pricing

At the first stage of the game, the platform determines its fees (t_1, t_2) and then "platform experts", observing platform fees, determine their prices $(\overline{p}, \underline{p})$.

Given that experts are committed to the identified service by the matching algorithm of the platform, Bertrand price competition then leads to efficient pricing for each type of treatment. Thus, $\overline{p} = \overline{c}$ and $\underline{p} = \underline{c}$ apply.[6]

For the monopoly platform, the pricing options are as follows: (1) apply a subscription fee on all users or (2) apply a transaction fee without commitment (which effectively applies only for the $\overline{c}$-signal consumers).[7] Although the platform specifies prices at the first stage of the game, it still has to adhere to a participation constraint: as consumers do not know their true type, consumers will only use the platform if their expected gain from platform services at decision nod C_1 is never lower than their outside option.

(1) Subscription fee: Such a fee applies to all users and thus avoids revenue losses due to potential disintermediation. A subscription fee does not preclude the additional use of transaction fees, and disintermediation occurs only for the case of $t_2 > 0$. Given that the platform wants to maximize revenue and, following *Corollary 2*, $u_{nc} \geq u_c$ generally applies, the profit maximizing platform will

[5] See the explanations p. 29 for the case of competition in the credence goods market [6].

[6] Note: Experts cannot use uniform prices, because then specializing only in the $\underline{c}$-type treatment would yield positive profits. This leads to the Bertrand-style price-cutting argument.

[7] Transaction fees with commitment do not provide an alternative solution in our analysis: a subscription fee is identical to a transaction fee under commitment of users. Moreover, when a commitment device is costly, the subscription fee is strictly preferable to the platform.

charge the subscription fee to fulfil $t_1^* = u_{nc} - u_0$ and zero transaction fees. Total profit of the platform for consumers of mass one then is $\pi = t_1^*$.

(2) Transaction fee: This fee applies to consumers with signal $\overline{c}$ directly and disintermediation allows consumers who receive signal $\underline{c}$ to avoid the fee to some extent (although its impact on bargaining remains). This implies that the profit-maximizing transaction fee will be higher than the subscription fee, but the number of paying users is lower. For the optimal transaction fee, a maximizing platform will set t_2 to fulfill $u_{nc}\left(t_2^*\right) - u_0 = 0$. Total profit of the platform then is $\pi = t_2^*(h\phi_H + (1-h)(1-\phi_L)$, as only consumers who receive signal $\overline{c}$ will pay the transaction fee.

Even though platform profits and the number of on-platform transactions may differ between subscription and transaction fees, the number of initial users who use the matching algorithm is identical, i.e., the strength of the network effect is similar in both cases.

5.1 *Beyond the Credence Good Problem*

To see when the two different pricing schemes can have an impact on the network effect (and the platform's profits), consider the following modification to our game: assume that consumers know their true type, i.e. which treatment they really need. How does this affect the outcome of the game?

At first glance, matching services by the platform are no longer relevant for consumers. However, the problem of non-verifiability and non-liability outside the platform remains. Even though consumers know their type, $\overline{c}$-type consumers have to expect undertreatment by the expert: consumers are unable to make payments contingent on the (unobservable) treatment, experts who behave dishonestly make higher profits, and Bertrand competition again leads to the standard lemon market outcome. Evidently, only $\underline{c}$-type consumers are treated efficiently.

The added value of the platform in this modified game is that it guarantees the type of treatment after matching. This makes the platform primarily attractive for the $\overline{c}$-type consumers who will never consult an expert in the outside lemon market. Whether $\underline{c}$-types use the platform depends on the comparison between search costs d and expected platform fees. What is different to the basic game, however, is that the $\underline{c}$-type consumers will never accept a (uniform) subscription fee that applies to $t_1 > d$, as she bears no performance or payment risk in the outside market. This constraint does not apply to transaction fees, as the consumer can always decide to disintermediate and bargain with the expert outside the platform or safely leave the platform and exert search costs in the lemon market. In other words, the number of users on the platform is now sensitive to the price scheme, with potentially many more users under transaction fees.

Let's consider the basic game and this modification as two extreme cases, either complete uncertainty about the treatment required or perfect knowledge of it. We can imagine a real scenario for a matching platform lying in between. Some of its users will have a fairly good idea of what kind of service they need; others will have no idea at all. In such a scenario, charging a transaction fee is likely to lead to more users on the platform. Since the algorithm improves its matching accuracy with the number of users on the platform, and accuracy is valuable to the uninformed users, the platform can generate higher network effects and extract higher profits by applying transaction fees instead of a subscription model.

6 Discussion[8]

Our analysis complements the existing literature on platform disintermediation and leakage by examining how digital platforms create value for users seeking expert assistance. Users consult digital platforms for expert help but do not know what type of treatment they need. Experts can assess and either provide the correct treatment or distort it to their advantage. In these cases, users cannot judge the treatment quality even after receiving it, a phenomenon known as the credence goods problem.

Applying the DK model has the advantage to be able to distinguish different user types but also to take the outside market into consideration. We find that digital platforms might benefit from accepting a certain degree of disintermediation despite providing valuable services. Users needing low-level treatment might bypass platform fees, while those needing high-level treatment will still prefer using the platform, knowing that experts outside the platform typically offer only low-level treatments. This preference ensures the platform remains the better choice for high-quality treatment. Consequently, this leads to fewer transactions on the platform but potentially higher revenue. If more users enhance the matching algorithm through learning-by-doing [20], the platform might accept an optimal level of disintermediation even with a transaction-based fee.

Following the results, digital platforms may need to accept that for some users, the platform does not provide enough value to conduct transactions, even though it generates value for both parties [10, 15]. Digital platforms rely on all users to enhance and maintain network effects, but some transactions will inevitably be lost. We argue that users diagnosed with low-type treatment still contribute to improving the platform's matching algorithm, enhancing the profitability of transactions for high-treatment users. In this context, digital platforms might have an incentive to distort signals, although this requires further investigation with our model.

Applying the DK model to digital platforms illuminates the platform's value generation process. It is well-established that platform services can reduce transaction costs for users as traditional search costs are largely avoided. Beyond cutting transaction costs, the platform can generate added value for users when the outside

---

[8] Note that the results and discussion are still preliminary as model will be developed further based on the feedback of the conference.

market lacks verifiability and liability. In such cases, the platform can improve transparency and guarantee (or enforce) contracted performance. If asymmetric information about the required treatment exists among customers, the platform may facilitate favourable matches and solve the credence good problem. However, when the outside market provides either liability or verifiability, the digital platform's value to users is reduced again to 'cutting transaction costs. This insight is crucial for assessing the profitability of potential platform projects. If the outside market can solve the credence good problem, the platform's potential benefit is lower than if the platform plays a crucial role in overcoming information asymmetry.

Digital platforms may need to adjust their value propositions in response to disintermediation. As Zhu and Iansiti [4] demonstrated, the Chinese platform ZBJ evolved from logo design to trademark registration services because the matchmaking between entrepreneurs and logo designers proved unsustainable. Homejoy, a platform that failed due to disintermediation, exemplifies the problem of an inadequate value proposition after solving the chicken-and-egg problem. Homejoy linked individuals with household services, predominantly cleaning. Still, once a match was established, users saw little benefit in continuing through the platform, undermining Homejoy's transaction-fee-dependent model and leading to its collapse [21]. One approach to address this issue in our model is establishing user commitment to the digital platform, ensuring they remain and receive treatment from suggested experts. Although challenging, Facturee, a Berlin-based startup, has demonstrated its feasibility in B2B. Facturee helps companies create prototypes and small production runs for new products, benefiting producers with improved shop floor utilization and reduced acquisition costs. On the Facturee platform, users and producers do not meet; Facturee manages the entire process from inquiry to delivery and complaint handling, offering a service beyond mere matchmaking.

7 Implications and Conclusion

The extension of the DK model to digital platforms offers insights into platform (dis-) intermediation. First, the platform generates value only when the outside market cannot provide liability or verifiability, indicating platforms are less necessary for symmetrically informed market participants. Second, platforms can design services to meet conditions in credence goods markets and train matching algorithms to identify user types and appropriate experts. Third, platforms must adjust pricing schemes to stimulate on-platform interactions, increase user value, and contain disintermediation risks. Fourth, some disintermediation might be inevitable based on the platform's value proposition and market conditions.

Our model has some limitations. Not every digital platform operates in a credible goods market. Also, the ability of the platform to diagnose problems is crucial. Platforms need to address the problem of credence goods by providing either liability or verifiability. Therefore, the core model presented in this paper is the basis for further development to explore platform disintermediation further. The next step is to integrate network effects into the model explicitly. While the model's logic always applies to offline brokers, the endogenization of network effects will make it even clearer, while the model is particularly well suited to digital platforms.

References

1. Ladd, T. (2022). The Achilles' Heel of the Platform Business Model: Disintermediation. *Business Horizons, 65*(3), 277–289.
2. Hagiu, A., & Wright, J. (2023). Marketplace Leakage. *Management Science.*
3. Gu, G., & Zhu, F. (2021). Trust and Disintermediation: Evidence from an Online Freelance Marketplace. *Management Science, 67*(2), 794–807.
4. Zhu, F., & Iansiti, M. (2019). Why Some Platforms Thrives... and Others Don't What Alibaba, Tencent, and Uber Teach Us about Networks that Flourish. The Five Characteristcs that Make the Difference. *Harvard Business Review, 97*(1), 118–125.
5. Balafoutas, L., & Kerschbamer, R. (2020). Credence Goods in the Literature: What the Past Fifteen Years Have Taught Us About Fraud, Incentives, and the Role of Institutions. *Journal of Behavioral and Experimental Finance, 26*, Article 100285.
6. Dulleck, U., & Kerschbamer, R. (2006). On Doctors, Mechanics, and Computer Specialists: The Economics of Credence Goods. *Journal of Economic Literature, 44*(1), 5–42.
7. Fu, S., et al. (2020). Tell Me What You Want: Disentangling the Impact of Service Specifi-cationOption Repertoires on Service Performance in Gig Economy. In *53rd Annual Hawaii International Conference on System Sciences, HICSS 2020.*
8. He, E. J., et al. (2023). Off-Platform Threats in On-Demand Services. *Manufacturing & Service Operations Management, 25*(2), 775–791.
9. Balafoutas, L., et al. (2013). What Drives Taxi Drivers? A Field Experiment on Fraud in a Market for Credence Goods. *Review of Economic Studies, 80*(3), 876–891.
10. Sekar, S., & Siddiq, A. (2023). *Platform Disintermediation: Information Effects and Pricing Remedies.* Available at SSRN 4378501.
11. Gu, G. Y. (2024). Technology and disintermediation in online marketplaces. *Management Science.*
12. Astashkina, E., et al. (2022). *A Disquieting Lack of Evidence for Disintermediation in a Home-Cleaning Platform.* Available at SSRN.
13. Karacaoglu, N., Li, S., & Stamatopoulos, I. (2022). *Disintermediation Evidence from a Cleaning Platform.* Available at SSRN.
14. Lin, J., Nian, T., & Foutz, N. Z. (2022). *Disintermediation and Its Mitigation in Online Two-sided Platforms: Evidence from Airbnb.*
15. He, S., et al. (2020). Impact of Platform Owner's Entry on Third-Party Stores. *Information Systems Research, 31*(4), 1467–1484.
16. Farronato, C., Fong, J., & Fradkin, A. (2023). Dog Eat Dog: Balancing Network Effects and Differentiation in a Digital Platform Merger. *Management Science.*
17. Akerlof, G. A. (1978). The Market for "Lemons": Quality Uncertainty and the Market Mechanism. *Uncertainty in Economics* (pp. 235–251). Elsevier.
18. Dulleck, U., Kerschbamer, R., & Sutter, M. (2011). The Economics of Credence Goods: An Experiment on the Role of Liability, Verifiability, Reputation, and Competition. *American Economic Review, 101*(2), 526–555.
19. Belleflamme, P., & Peitz, M. (2021). *The Economics of Platforms.* Cambridge University Press.
20. Tirole, J. (2020). *Competition and the Industrial Challenge for the Digital Age.* Paper for IFS Deaton Review on Inequalities in the Twenty-First Century.
21. Iansiti, M., & Lakhani, K. R. (2020). *Competing in the Age of AI: Strategy and Leadership When Algorithms and Networks Run the World.* Harvard Business Press.

The Impact of Transparency in AI Systems on Users' Data-Sharing Intentions: A Scenario-Based Experiment

Julian Rosenberger, Sophie Kuhlemann, Verena Tiefenbeck, Mathias Kraus, and Patrick Zschech

Abstract Artificial Intelligence (AI) systems are frequently employed in online services to provide personalized experiences to users based on large collections of data. However, AI systems can be designed in different ways, with black-box AI systems appearing as complex data-processing engines and white-box AI systems appearing as fully transparent data-processors. As such, it is reasonable to assume that these different design choices also affect user perception and thus their willingness to share data. To this end, we conducted a pre-registered, scenario-based online experiment with 240 participants and investigated how transparent and non-transparent data-processing entities influenced data-sharing intentions. Surprisingly, our results revealed no significant difference in willingness to share data across entities, challenging the notion that transparency increases data-sharing willingness. Furthermore, we found that a general attitude of trust towards AI has a significant positive influence, especially in the transparent AI condition, whereas privacy concerns did not significantly affect data-sharing decisions.

J. Rosenberger (✉) · M. Kraus
Universität Regensburg, Regensburg, Germany
e-mail: julian.rosenberger@ur.de

M. Kraus
e-mail: mathias.kraus@ur.de

S. Kuhlemann · V. Tiefenbeck
Friedrich-Alexander-Universität Erlangen-Nürnberg, Nürnberg, Germany
e-mail: sophie.kuhlemann@fau.de

V. Tiefenbeck
e-mail: verena.tiefenbeck@fau.de

P. Zschech
TU Dresden, Dresden, Germany
e-mail: patrick.zschech@tu-dresden.de

C. M. Flath et al. (eds.), *Artificial Intelligence, Data, and Decision-Making*, Lecture Notes in Information Systems and Organisation 82,
https://doi.org/10.1007/978-3-032-08480-4_30

1 Introduction

Artificial Intelligence (AI) systems are increasingly used in online services to provide a personalized experience to users. However, many AI systems lack transparency regarding how for example individual recommendations are derived, making them appear as black-boxes to users [29, 43, 54]. This lack of transparency may promote user aversion to AI systems, leading to a preference for human involvement in certain cases [11], despite AI's demonstrated superiority in many tasks [10, 25]. Research in the fields of Explainable Artificial Intelligence (XAI) and Interpretable Machine Learning (IML) aims to tackle this aversion towards algorithms by providing insights into the inner workings of AI systems [2, 50]. While XAI tries to provide a glimpse into complex black-box models, IML focuses on developing and applying simpler, clearer models for inherent transparency [46]. Both fields intend to display the outcomes of an AI system in a way that humans can understand. Prior research already suggests that "opening the black-box" [41] by providing explanations of the decision-making processes of an AI system can positively affect users' willingness to engage with the system [22, 29, 43, 53, 62]. However, research shows that factors such as trustworthiness and familiarity of a system influence users' reliance on both, human advisors and AI systems [12, 13, 35, 49].

Despite the reliance of AI systems on user data to provide a personalized experience, there has been little research on how XAI or IML affect users' attitudes on privacy [47]. Privacy studies have shown that when users are faced with the decision to share their data with a service provider, they tend to weigh the costs and benefits of disclosing their data [20]. For instance, it shows that people are more willing to share their personal data if they can see a clear benefit, such as receiving personalized offers [59]. Transparent systems that demonstrate how sharing specific types of personal data can result in more personalized and valuable services thus might have the potential to encourage consumers to share their data for improved experiences. However, providing detailed explanations of data-processing may also make privacy concerns salient to consumers, which could make them less willing to share their personal information [31]. Several studies show that individuals' privacy concerns significantly impact their risk assessment of data-sharing, which ultimately affects their willingness to share their data [14, 19, 36, 42, 55].

This study aims to examine the impact of transparent (white-box AI) and non-transparent (black-box AI) data-processing systems on users' intentions to share data. Building on the insights of prior research suggesting a preference for human decision-making over algorithms [11, 38], we include a human data-processor as a comparative element. Additionally, we are examining how trust factors such as the perceived trustworthiness of different data-processing systems affects users' willingness to share data, based on the research by Chellappa and Sin [12] and Choung et al. [13]. Lastly, we assess the impact of users' privacy concerns within this dynamic. Consequently, we pose the following research questions:

RQ *How does users' willingness to share personal data vary between different data-processing entities, specifically a human expert, a white-box AI system, and a black-box AI system? Furthermore, how do trust in the entity and privacy concerns affect the relationship between data-processing entity and the intention to disclose data?*

To answer our research questions, we conducted a scenario-based experiment in which we presented participants (N = 240) with a fictitious sleep app that aimed to provide tailored advice based on the data entered by the user. Our study contributes to existing AI research on users' adoption of interpretable systems, as well as to privacy research, particularly with respect to data-sharing behavior. In the following section, Sect. 2, we discuss related work from (X)AI and IML research and its connection to trust and privacy concerns and derive our research model. Section 3 summarizes the experimental design followed in our study. In Sect. 4, we present the results of our study. Section 5 discusses our findings and concludes our work.

2 Conceptual Background and Related Work

Many AI systems are characterized by their inability to convey human-interpretable information about how and why they make certain decisions [29, 43, 54], referred to as black-box AI systems [2, 21, 50]. This lack of transparency into the system's decision-making processes can cause people to be hesitant in adopting AI outputs. For example, in the context of healthcare, individuals were shown to feel more confident in understanding the choices made by human healthcare professionals compared to ones made by algorithms. As a result, they typically favor human providers over algorithmic ones [11, 38], even though AI systems have been proven to perform better than humans in various tasks [10, 25]. Additionally, if a human agent is framed as an expert, users are even more likely to depend on human rather than on AI advice: This was demonstrated by Madhavan and Wiegmann [40] in a study in which they examined users' trust in and perceived reliability of human and automated systems based on written descriptions, distinguishing between novices and experts.

Users' tendency to rather rely on human advice than on AI decision-making is commonly known as algorithm aversion and is often attributed to users' desire for perfect predictions and their low tolerance for errors made by an algorithm [17, 18]. However, recent evidence suggests that there are situations in which human actors prefer AI advice, such as the prediction of business or geopolitical events [37]. Furthermore, providing explanations for errors made by a system has been found to positively influence users' perception of the system [22].

Along that line, research in the area of XAI and IML intends to address the potential reluctance towards algorithms by offering insight into the underlying reasoning of a system [46]. Presenting AI systems in an understandable manner has the potential to mitigate the problems associated with their black-box nature while ensuring high predictive accuracy [2, 50]. In recent years, a significant effort within the AI research community has thus been the development of XAI methods to make black-box AI systems more understandable [32, 39, 48]. Despite these advances, concerns persist regarding the adequacy of these explanations for capturing the full complexity of the systems [6, 50, 57]. To address the inherent approximations of XAI methods, white-box AI systems attempt to provide complete transparency and reliable decision-making through intrinsic interpretability [21]. For example, a white-box AI system for diagnosing a specific medical condition might use a transparent decision tree that consists of a series of interpretable if-then rules, allowing for clear tracing of the decision-making process. In contrast, a black-box AI system might employ a complex neural network comprising multiple layers that learn intricate relationships between features, their interactions, and the diagnosis. This multi-layer structure enables the neural network to capture non-linear patterns and high-order interactions, but at the cost of interpretability [58]. However, white-box AI system systems typically face limitations, most notably that they are primarily limited to tabular data [34]. Numerous studies indicate that showing users clarifications can positively impact their perception of the system [22, 29, 43, 53, 62]. Nevertheless, [4, 52] found no such positive effect on users' intention when provided with visual explanations. Previous research has also shown that when humans collaborate with AI, providing explanations can cause users to trust the system too much, leading to "automation bias" [51]. This can result in users accepting incorrect suggestions from the system [7]. In this context, a study by Choung et al. [13] shows that factors, such as the trustworthiness of a system and trust in its functionality, significantly influence users' intention to use a system. Similarly, the results of Chellappa and Sin [12] indicate that familiarity and previous experience, play a significant role in the use of personalization services. These findings are consistent with research on interpersonal trust, which argues that attitudes of trust play an important role in how people rely on each other [35, 49].

Notably, despite the reliance of AI systems on user data, there has been little research on the impact of providing insights to an AI system on the privacy-related behavior of users [47]. Information systems research has explored users' attitudes toward privacy in various contexts such as e-commerce [1, 56], financial services [44], social networks [8], and smartphone applications [24], focusing on users' attitudes towards privacy and its impact on their willingness to participate in e-commerce services [12, 23, 45], as well as their willingness to share personal information with these services [9, 19]. Studies in the context of users' data-sharing behavior suggest that while people consider protecting their personal data important, they often act against their preferences and willingly disclose their data (see [26, 33] for reviews). This contradiction between privacy attitudes and behaviors has been studied extensively and is commonly known as the privacy paradox [44]. Studies revealed that users weigh their sharing intentions based on a cost-benefit analysis of data disclosure [15, 19, 20, 60]. Within this cost-benefit analysis, described as privacy calculus, one of the benefits already studied is personalization [5]. In this context, individuals are found to be more willing to disclose personal information if they receive customized offers in response [59]. However, [31] demonstrates that the tendency to focus on perceived benefits can be reduced by making privacy considerations salient to users by reminding them about risks associated with sharing sensitive data. Numerous studies show that information privacy concerns significantly impact individuals' risk assessment towards information privacy and thus affect their willingness to disclose their data [14, 19, 36, 42, 55].

2.1 Research Model

More in-depth research is needed to investigate the impact of a system's data-processing nature on users' cost-benefit trade-offs when disclosing data, and whether consumers' willingness to share their data changes as a result [47]. Systems that effectively communicate how sharing specific types of personal data can result in more personalized and valuable services may have the potential to motivate consumers to share their data for enhanced experiences [5, 59]. However, transparent systems that provide detailed explanations of data-processing may also raise privacy concerns among consumers, leading them to be less willing to share their personal data [31]. We thus build a research model (see Fig. 1) that, based on previous literature on the "black-box problem" [29, 43, 54] and algorithm aversion [17, 18], distinguishes between human, white-box AI and black-box AI data-processing entities and assesses their impact on users' sharing intentions.

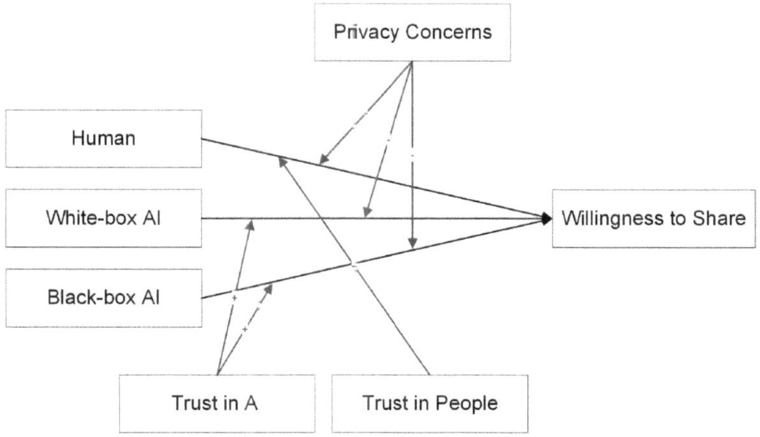

Fig. 1 Research model

As previous research has indicated that users tend to prefer human service providers over algorithmic ones [11, 38], it is reasonable to assume that this notion is also reflected in the privacy-intentions of users as they may perceive human handlers of their personal data as more trustworthy compared to AI systems. Based on this, we hypothesize the following:

H1 a *Users exhibit greater willingness to share personal data when the data is processed by a human entity compared to AI entities.*

However, white-box AI processing, as suggested by Rudin [50], could potentially serve as a mitigator to the concerns related to the black-box nature of common AI systems. Based on this assumption, we derive the following hypothesis in the context of users' data-sharing behavior:

H1 b *Users exhibit greater willingness to share personal data when the data is processed by a white-box AI entity compared to a black-box AI entity.*

Additionally, prior work suggests that factors such as the trustworthiness of a system and trust in its functionality significantly determine users' intention to use a system [12, 13, 35]. We assume that the intention to engage with a system is closely related to user data-sharing, as interactions with AI systems often involve sharing personal data (e.g., sharing location data with map apps or entering health information into a symptom management app). Thus, we expect trust to have a moderating effect on the relationship between AI system and data-sharing willingness:

H2 a *Trust in AI will moderate the relationship between the AI groups and users' willingness to share personal data. Specifically, when trust in AI is high, participants in the white-box AI and black-box AI conditions will show a higher willingness to share data.*

Likewise, we assume that the same moderating effect occurs for the human condition, as literature on interpersonal trust indicates that trust plays a relevant role in how much people rely on each other [35, 49]. Thus, we hypothesize:

H2 b *Trust in people will moderate the relationship between the human group and users' willingness to share personal data. Specifically, when trust in people is high, participants in the human condition will show a higher willingness to share data.*

Finally, we build on research by Dinev and Hart [19], Li et al. [36], Malhotra et al. [42], and Son and Kim [55] suggesting that privacy concerns are a relevant determinant in users' privacy-related decision-making and argue that the relationship between entity and willingness to disclose data is influenced by the individual's concern about their privacy:

H3 *Privacy concerns will moderate the relationship between the human, white-box AI, and black-box AI groups and users' willingness to share sensitive health-related data. Specifically, when privacy concerns are high, participants in all conditions will show a lower willingness to share data.*

3 Methods

3.1 Experimental Design

We tested our hypotheses by conducting an online experiment based on a pre-registered scenario-based experiment with 240 participants.[1] For our study, we chose an environment where subjects could quickly familiarize themselves with the topic and understand the underlying relationships without requiring in-depth knowledge. Specifically, our experiment is a use case related to healthy living and well-being, in which we refer to the dynamics between health and lifestyle factors and sleep. Participants were introduced to a mock-up of SleepOptima, a hypothetical sleep app that aims to provide tailored advice based on user data input. To assess the effects of different data-processing entities on users' data-sharing behavior, we randomly assigned participants to one of three treatment groups representative of the different entities: a human expert, a white-box AI system, and a black-box AI system.

Each condition was presented with identically structured text modules containing detailed explanations of the data-processing techniques used by the respective entity within SleepOptima. In the human condition, it was clarified based on Madhavan and Wiegmann [40] that the expert's recommendation is derived from their acquired knowledge. The white-box and black-box conditions were identical in communicating information about the relevant system and how advice is generated for participants. However, the two groups differed in their clarification of the system's transparency, with the interpretability of the white-box AI being presented in contrast to the lack of interpretability of the black-box AI. To emphasize the different analytical approaches of the individual data-processing entities, we also provided visual aids to participants. For the human group, we used an image of a medical expert to emphasize the human element in data-processing. Based on [21, 50], we chose a decision tree to symbolize the transparent and structured nature of the white-box AI. In contrast, for the black-box AI, a neural network illustration was used to depict the complexity and opacity of its processes. For a detailed presentation of the textual and visual treatments, refer to our online appendix.[2]

3.2 Measurement and Scales

To capture participants' willingness to share their data, we used a 7-point Likert scale—from 1 ("Strongly Unwilling") to 7 ("Strongly Willing")—across seven data categories relevant to the SleepOptima app. The categories range from demographics, over physical and mental status until questions about sexual activities. Each category

[1] Pre-registration link: https://doi.org/10.17605/OSF.IO/U6FN7. The experimental procedure received ethical clearance by the German Association for Experimental Economic Research (No. o3RhQZKR).

[2] Link to online appendix: https://doi.org/10.17605/OSF.IO/8W6G3.

consisted of two items and by calculating the average scores of these 14 items, we derived a continuous measure of each participant's willingness to share sensitive health-related data. In addition, we measured trust in the processing entity and privacy concerns using validated scales that we slightly adapted to our context.

Trust in AI was assessed using an adapted scale from [30], tailored to the context of our study comparing human and AI data-processing entities. This adaptation expanded the original scale to a 7-point Likert scale to capture a broad range of Trust in AI and to align it with other scales in our questionnaire. The statements included in this scale explore general trust in AI systems, perceived reliability, and predictability of AI outcomes.

Trust in People was measured by adapting the General Trust Scale from [61] to ensure consistency with other measures. This scale assesses people's general trustworthiness and honesty, exploring beliefs about people's basic honesty, trustworthiness, and goodness.

Privacy Concerns were measured using the Internet Users' Information Privacy Concerns (IUIPC) scale developed by [42], which provides an exploration of online Privacy Concerns. This scale was selected because of its alignment with the digital context of the study and its focus on consumer perspectives on information privacy [28]. Participants rated their agreement on a 7-point Likert scale, addressing issues such as discomfort with online companies requesting personal information and the importance of control over personal information.

By averaging scores across items for each construct, we derived continuous measures of Trust in AI, Trust in People, and Privacy Concerns in order to test our hypotheses. For further details on the scores for the different health-related categories and items, as well as on the operationalization of constructs, see our online appendix.

3.3 Participants

For our study, we recruited 331 participants over two days in October 2023 using Prolific. The study took approximately 6 minutes and 30 seconds to complete, and participants were compensated £ 14,17/hr for their time. To ensure data integrity, three attention checks were incorporated into the survey. The rate of failed attention checks was evenly distributed across all three conditions, and as a result, 91 participants were excluded based on this criterion. The final sample consisted of 240 participants, detailed in Table 1 with their demographic distribution. Our participant sample comprised 122 females (50.8 %), 114 males (47.5 %), one non-binary, and three who preferred not to disclose.

Table 1 Descriptive results of key socio-demographic data of the study sample across treatment groups (Human, White-box AI, Black-box AI)

	Participants		Gender Identity						Age
			Female		Male		Other[†]		
Human	83	34.6%	43	51.8%	37	44.6%	3	3.6%	40.3 ±15.9
White-box AI	81	33.8%	38	46.9%	42	51.9%	1	1.2%	39.4±14.2
Black-box AI	76	31.7%	41	53.9%	35	46.1%	0	0.0%	40.1±15.0

[†] "Other" includes one non-binary participant and those who chose not to disclose their gender

We conducted randomization checks to confirm that all demographic characteristics were equally distributed across the treatment groups. To assess the uniformity of this distribution, we used Fisher's exact test, which showed no significant differences in gender distribution across the groups ($p = 0.820$). Additionally, we performed an Analysis of Variance (ANOVA), to examine age disparities. The results showed that there were no significant differences in the mean age between the groups ($F(2, 235) = 0.079,\ p = 0.924$). These findings suggest that our sample had a balanced representation of demographics across groups.

3.4 Manipulation Check

To check if participants' perceptions aligned with our intended manipulations, we asked them to rate the transparency level of the received treatment on a 7-point Likert scale ranging from 1 "Low Level of Transparency" to 7 "High Level of Transparency" immediately after presenting the manipulation. This manipulation check was conducted before measuring the dependent variable (willingness to share data) to ensure that participants had accurately perceived the intended manipulation. The results showed that the human group ($M = 5.41,\ SD = 1.23$) reported a notably higher level of transparency than the black-box AI group ($M = 3.92,\ SD = 2.11$). The white-box AI group's perception ($M = 5.19,\ SD = 1.21$) was aligned with the human group. An ANOVA confirmed these observations as statistically significant ($F(2, 237) = 20.67,\ p < 0.001$). To examine these differences more closely, we conducted pairwise t-tests with a Bonferroni correction, revealing significant differences between the human and black-box AI groups ($p < 0.001$) and between the black-box AI and white-box AI groups ($p < 0.001$), but no significant difference between the human and white-box AI groups. These results indicate that participants perceived distinct levels of transparency across the different data-processing entities, with the black-box AI being viewed as less transparent than both the human and white-box AI.

4 Results

4.1 Overall Willingness to Share Data

Our findings revealed subtle differences in the willingness to share data across conditions. Participants showed the highest willingness to share data with the black-box AI system ($M = 6.02$, $SD = 0.85$), slightly exceeding the willingness to share with a human expert ($M = 5.85$, $SD = 0.94$) and the white-box AI system ($M = 5.82$, $SD = 1.04$). We opted for regression analysis throughout the paper to quantify group differences, estimate effect sizes, and allow for the inclusion of interaction effects in subsequent analyses. The regression results, with the human group as a natural choice for comparison, revealed no significant differences between conditions (see Table 2). Thus, H1a, proposing greater willingness to share data with a human entity compared to AI entities, is not supported.

Table 2 Simple regression result for Model Willingness to Share

	Model Willingness to Share	
Variable	$B \pm SE$	p
Intercept	5.85±0.11	<0.001***
White-box AI	–0.03±0.15	0.867
Black-box AI	0.17 ±0.15	0.258
R^2	0.008	
R^2_{Adj}	0.000	

Note Ref = Human

Further regression analysis testing H1b, which suggested greater willingness to share data with a white-box AI entity compared to a black-box AI entity, also revealed no significant differences between the two AI conditions ($F(1, 157) = 1.686$, $p = 0.196$). Consequently, H1b cannot be confirmed based on our study's evidence.

4.2 The Role of Trust in Data-Sharing Decisions

We investigated the influence of trust on participants' willingness to disclose personal information across different data-processing entities. We used two regression models (Model Trust in AI for AI conditions and Model Trust in People for the human condition) and analyzed interactions through simple slopes analysis, following [3].

Model Trust in AI. Regression analysis (see Table 3) shows that Trust in AI positively influences willingness to share data in both AI conditions, with a stronger effect in the white-box AI condition ($B = 0.49$, $p < .001$) compared to the black-box AI condition ($B = 0.24$, $p = 0.08$). Trust in AI had no effect in the human expert condition.

Table 3 Multiple regression results for Model Trust in AI and Model Trust in People

Variable	Model Trust in AI $B \pm SE$	Model Trust in AI p	Model Trust in People $B \pm SE$	Model Trust in People p
Intercept	5.84±0.10	<.001***	5.83±0.10	<.001***
White-box AI	–0.02±0.14	0.913	0.00±0.14	0.986
Black-box AI	0.14± 0.15	0.332	0.19±0.15	0.211
Trust †				
Trust in AI	–0.03±0.09	0.712		
Trust in People			0.22±0.11	0.054
Group × **Trust**				
White-box AI × Trust in AI	0.49±0.13	<.001***		
Black-box AI × Trust in AI	0.24±0.14	0.080		
White-box AI × Trust in People			–0.04±0.15	0.773
Black-box AI × Trust in People			–0.22±0.14	0.118
R^2	0.113		0.035	
R^2_{Adj}	0.094		0.014	

Note †Trust is mean-centered; Ref = Human

Simple slopes analysis (see Fig. 2) confirms these results, showing a modest but significant increase in willingness to share data for the black-box AI group ($B = 0.20$, $p = 0.04$) and a more pronounced effect for the white-box AI condition ($B = 0.45$, $p < .001$). The human condition showed negligible impact of Trust in AI ($B = -0.03$, $p = 0.71$). Therefore, we can partially confirm H2a: Trust in AI has a significant positive effect on the willingness to share data in the white-box AI condition, as evidenced by the regression results, and a modest but significant positive effect in the black-box AI condition, as revealed by the simple slope analysis.

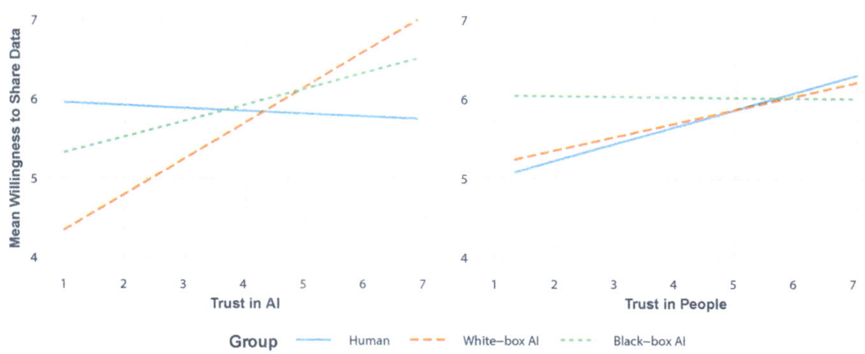

Fig. 2 Simple slopes plots illustrating the relationship between Trust in AI, Trust in People, and Mean Willingness to Share Data for Human, White-box AI, and Black-box AI groups

Model Trust in People. The interaction effect of Trust in People ($B = 0.22$, $p = 0.054$) is shown in Table 3. Simple slopes analysis revealed additional information for the human group ($B = 0.22$, $p = 0.05$) and the white-box AI group ($B = 0.17$, $p = 0.11$). Based on these results, we cannot confirm H2b, as the data do not provide sufficient evidence to conclude that Trust in People significantly impacts data-sharing willingness in the human condition.

4.3 Impact of Privacy Concerns on Willingness to Share Data

Regarding the stated moderating effect of Privacy Concerns on the relationship between data-processing entity and data-sharing intentions, the results of the regression analysis in Table 4 show that Privacy Concerns alone did not significantly predict willingness to share in any condition. This finding suggests that Privacy Concerns did not negatively influence participants' data-sharing behavior, regardless of the data-processing entity involved. Therefore, we cannot confirm H3.

Table 4 Multiple Regression Result for Model Privacy Concerns

	Model Privacy Concerns	
Variable	$B \pm SE$	p
Intercept	5.86±0.11	<.001***
White-box AI	–0.04±0.15	0.789
Black-box AI	0.14±0.15	0.343
Privacy Concerns†	–0.09±0.14	0.536
Group × Privacy Concerns		
White-box AI × Privacy Concerns	–0.16±0.19	0.419
Black-box AI × Privacy Concerns	–0.03±0.18	0.886
R^2	0.030	
R^2_{Adj}	0.009	

Note †Mean-centered; Ref = Human

5 Discussion

Our research explored the influence of different data-processing entities (human expert, white-box AI, and black-box AI) on individuals' willingness to share personal data, considering the moderating effects of trust and privacy concerns. Surprisingly, we found no significant differences in data-sharing willingness across the three conditions, contrary to previous findings on algorithm aversion [17] and algorithm appreciation [37]. However, trust in AI emerged as a critical factor, significantly increasing data-sharing intentions in both white-box and black-box AI systems. Those results are aligned with the findings of Choung et al. [13] stating that factors such as trust in the functionality of an AI system affect users' intentions to use AI. Privacy concerns, on the other hand, did not significantly predict willingness to share data, thus are not in line with broad research previously conducted indicating that information privacy concerns impact individuals' risk assessment towards information privacy and thus affect their willingness to disclose their data [19, 36, 42, 55]

As such, our findings make several important theoretical and practical contributions to the literature on AI transparency, trust, and privacy. First, by showing no significant differences between treatment groups, our results challenge the prevailing academic discourse that argues that the inherent opacity of some AI systems can lead to problems such as a lack of user adoption which should be mitigated by building more transparent systems [2, 46, 50]. Indeed, our results emphasize that providing transparent systems alone is not enough to convince users of AI systems, but that creating trust in AI systems in general may also be beneficial. Finally, by examining users' willingness to share data as our key dependent variable, we provide initial insights into how the nature of the data-processing entity influences individuals' privacy calculus for mobile application services [47]. This contribution enriches the academic discourse on privacy and trust in AI while offering practical guidance for developers on optimizing data-sharing in AI systems based on users' general trust in the system.

However, while our study provides valuable insights, it is important to acknowledge certain limitations. We tested our hypotheses using a mock-up of a fictitious sleep app, which may not fully replicate real-world user experiences. Future studies should explore data-sharing behaviors in more realistic settings. Additionally, our focus on purely human, white-box AI, and black-box AI systems does not account for hybrid systems common in real-world applications [16]. Future research should investigate user perceptions, trust, and interaction strategies for these hybrid systems. Another limitation is that we measured trust only after the experimental manipulation, preventing randomization checks for pre-existing trust levels. Future research should measure trust at multiple time points to control for potential confounding effects. Lastly, our study did not collect comprehensive demographic data (including education, income, profession, and geographical location) and other potentially influential factors like AI experience, literacy, and knowledge. Future research should consider including these variables to provide a more detailed understanding of data-sharing attitudes and behaviors.

In conclusion, our study makes significant contributions to the fields of AI and information privacy by examining the impact of data-processing entities on data-sharing intentions, considering the critical roles of trust and privacy concerns. Our findings offer valuable theoretical insights and practical recommendations for developing AI systems that prioritize transparency, trust, and user privacy. Future research should build upon our work by exploring data-sharing behaviors in different contexts, investigating the effects of hybrid AI systems, and examining the potential negative implications of excessive trust in AI [27]. By continuing to advance our understanding of these complex issues, we can develop AI systems that are not only technologically sophisticated but also ethically responsible and socially beneficial.

Acknowledgements Parts of this research were supported by funding from the Federal Ministry of Education and Research (BMBF) on "White-Box-AI" (Grant 01IS22080). Parts of this research were also supported by the Software Campus 2.0 Program funded by the Federal Ministry of Education and Research (BMBF) and the Bavarian State Ministry of Science and the Arts, in a program coordinated by the Bavarian Research Institute for Digital Transformation (bidt).

References

1. Acquisti, A., & Grossklags, J. (2005). Privacy and rationality in individual decision making. *IEEE Security & Privacy, 3*(1), 26–33.
2. Adadi, A., & Berrada, M. (2018). Peeking inside the black-box: a survey on explainable artificial intelligence (xai). *IEEE Access, 6*, 52138–52160.
3. Aiken, L. S., West, S. G., & Reno, R. R. (1991). *Multiple regression: Testing and interpreting interactions*. Sage
4. Alufaisan, Y., Marusich, L. R., Bakdash, J. Z., Zhou, Y., & Kantarcioglu, M. (2021). Does explainable artificial intelligence improve human decision-making? *Proceedings of the AAAI Conference on Artificial Intelligence, 35*, 6618–6626.
5. Awad, N. F., & Krishnan, M. S. (2006). The personalization privacy paradox: An empirical evaluation of information transparency and the willingness to be profiled online for personalization. *MIS Quarterly*, 13–28.
6. Babic, B., Gerke, S., Evgeniou, T., & Cohen, I. G. (2021). Beware explanations from ai in health care. *Science, 373*(6552), 284–286.
7. Bansal, G., Wu, T., Zhou, J., Fok, R., Nushi, B., Kamar, E., Ribeiro, M. T., & Weld, D. (2021). Does the whole exceed its parts? The effect of ai explanations on complementary team performance. In *Proceedings of the ACM conference on human factors in computing systems* (pp. 1–16).
8. Barnes, S. B. (2006). A privacy paradox: Social networking in the united states. *First Monday*.
9. Belanger, F., Hiller, J. S., & Smith, W. J. (2002). Trustworthiness in electronic commerce: the role of privacy, security, and site attributes. *Journal of Strategic Information Systems, 11*(3–4), 245–270.
10. Brown, N., & Sandholm, T. (2019). Superhuman ai for multiplayer poker. *Science, 365*(6456), 885–890.
11. Cadario, R., Longoni, C., & Morewedge, C. K. (2021). Understanding, explaining, and utilizing medical artificial intelligence. *Nature Human Behaviour, 5*(12), 1636–1642.
12. Chellappa, R. K., & Sin, R. G. (2005). Personalization versus privacy: An empirical examination of the online consumer's dilemma. *Information Technology and Management, 6*, 181–202.
13. Choung, H., David, P., & Ross, A. (2023). Trust in ai and its role in the acceptance of ai technologies. *International Journal of Human-Computer Interaction, 39*(9), 1727–1739.
14. Cichy, P., Salge, T. O., & Kohli, R. (2021). Privacy concerns and data sharing in the internet of things: Mixed methods evidence from connected cars. *MIS Quarterly, 45*(4).
15. Culnan, M. J. (1993). "How did they get my name?": An exploratory investigation of consumer attitudes toward secondary information use. *MIS Q*, 341–363.
16. Dellermann, D., Ebel, P., Söllner, M., & Leimeister, J. M. (2019). Hybrid intelligence. *Business & Information Systems Engineering, 61*(5), 637–643.
17. Dietvorst, B. J., Simmons, J. P., & Massey, C. (2015). Algorithm aversion: People erroneously avoid algorithms after seeing them err. *Journal of Experimental Psychology: General, 144*(1), 114.

18. Dietvorst, B. J., Simmons, J. P., & Massey, C. (2018). Overcoming algorithm aversion: People will use imperfect algorithms if they can (even slightly) modify them. *Management Science, 64*(3), 1155–1170.
19. Dinev, T., & Hart, P. (2006). An extended privacy calculus model for e-commerce transactions. *Information Systems Research, 17*(1), 61–80.
20. Dinev, T., Bellotto, M., Hart, P., Russo, V., Serra, I., & Colautti, C. (2006). Privacy calculus model in e-commerce-a study of italy and the united states. *European Journal of Information Systems, 15*(4), 389–402.
21. Du, M., Liu, N., & Hu, X. (2019). Techniques for interpretable machine learning. *Communications of the ACM, 63*(1), 68–77.
22. Dzindolet, M. T., Peterson, S. A., Pomranky, R. A., Pierce, L. G., & Beck, H. P. (2003). The role of trust in automation reliance. *International Journal of Human-Computer, 58*(6), 697–718.
23. Eastlick, M. A., Lotz, S. L., & Warrington, P. (2006). Understanding online b-to-c relationships: An integrated model of privacy concerns, trust, and commitment. *Journal of Business Research, 59*(8), 877–886.
24. Egelman S, Felt AP, Wagner D (2013) Choice architecture and smartphone privacy: There's a price for that. In *The economics of information security and privacy* (pp. 211–236). Springer.
25. Esteva, A., Kuprel, B., Novoa, R. A., Ko, J., Swetter, S. M., Blau, H. M., & Thrun, S. (2017). Dermatologist-level classification of skin cancer with deep neural networks. *Nature, 542*(7639), 115–118.
26. Gerber, N., Gerber, P., & Volkamer, M. (2018). Explaining the privacy paradox: A systematic review of literature investigating privacy attitude and behavior. *Computers & Security, 77*, 226–261.
27. Greulich, M., Lins, S., Pienta, D., Thatcher, J. B., & Sunyaev, A. (2024). Exploring contrasting effects of trust in organizational security practices and protective structures on employees' security-related precaution taking. *Information Systems Research.*
28. Groß, T. (2021). Validity and reliability of the scale internet users' information privacy concerns (iuipc). *Proceedings on Privacy Enhancing Technologies.*
29. Herlocker, J. L., Konstan, J. A., & Riedl, J. (2000). Explaining collaborative filtering recommendations. In *Proceedings of the ACM conference on computer-supported cooperative work* (pp. 241–250).
30. Hoffman, R. R., Mueller, S. T., Klein, G., & Litman, J. (2023). Measures for explainable ai: Explanation goodness, user satisfaction, mental models, curiosity, trust, and human-ai performance. *Frontiers of Computer Science, 5*(1096), 257.
31. Kehr, F., Kowatsch, T., Wentzel, D., & Fleisch, E. (2015). Blissfully ignorant: The effects of general privacy concerns, general institutional trust, and affect in the privacy calculus. *Information Systems Journal, 25*(6), 607–635.
32. Koh, P. W., & Liang, P. (2017). Understanding black-box predictions via influence functions. In *Proceedings of machine learning research (ICML)* (pp. 1885–1894).
33. Kokolakis, S. (2017). Privacy attitudes and privacy behaviour: A review of current research on the privacy paradox phenomenon. *Computers & Security, 64*, 122–134.
34. Kraus, M., Tschernutter, D., Weinzierl, S., & Zschech, P. (2023). Interpretable generalized additive neural networks. *European Journal of Operational Research.*
35. Lee, J. D., & See, K. A. (2004). Trust in automation: Designing for appropriate reliance. *Human Factors, 46*(1), 50–80.
36. Li, H., Sarathy, R., & Xu, H. (2011). The role of affect and cognition on online consumers' decision to disclose personal information to unfamiliar online vendors. *Decision Support Systems, 51*(3), 434–445.
37. Logg, J. M., Minson, J. A., & Moore, D. A. (2019). Algorithm appreciation: People prefer algorithmic to human judgment. *Organizational Behavior and Human Decision Processes, 151*, 90–103.
38. Longoni, C., Bonezzi, A., & Morewedge, C. K. (2019). Resistance to medical artificial intelligence. *Journal of Consumer Research, 46*(4), 629–650.

39. Lundberg, S. M., & Lee, S. I. (2017). A unified approach to interpreting model predictions. *Advances in Neural Information Processing Systems*, 30.
40. Madhavan, P., & Wiegmann, D. A. (2007). Effects of information source, pedigree, and reliability on operator interaction with decision support systems. *Human Factors, 49*(5), 773–785.
41. Mahmud, H., Islam, A. N., Ahmed, S. I., & Smolander, K. (2022). What influences algorithmic decision-making? a systematic literature review on algorithm aversion. *Technological Forecasting and Social Change,175*, 121390.
42. Malhotra, N. K., Kim, S. S., & Agarwal, J. (2004). Internet users' information privacy concerns (iuipc): The construct, the scale, and a causal model. *Information Systems Research, 15*(4), 336–355.
43. Millecamp, M., Htun, N. N., Conati, C., Verbert, K. (2019). To explain or not to explain: The effects of personal characteristics when explaining music recommendations. In *Proceedings of the international conference on intelligent user interfaces* (pp. 397–407).
44. Norberg, P. A., Horne, D. R., & Horne, D. A. (2007). The privacy paradox: Personal information disclosure intentions versus behaviors. *Journal of Consumer Affairs, 41*(1), 100–126.
45. Pavlou, P. A., Liang, H., & Xue, Y. (2007). Understanding and mitigating uncertainty in online exchange relationships: A principal-agent perspective. *MIS Quarterly*, 105–136.
46. Poursabzi-Sangdeh, F., Goldstein, D. G., Hofman, J. M., Wortman Vaughan, J. W., & Wallach, H. (2021). Manipulating and measuring model interpretability. In *Proceedings from the ACM conference on human factors in computing systems* (pp. 1–52).
47. Rai, A. (2020). Explainable ai: From black box to glass box. *Journal of the Academy of Marketing Science, 48*, 137–141.
48. Ribeiro, M. T., Singh, S., & Guestrin, C. (2016). "Why should i trust you?" explaining the predictions of any classifier. In *Proceedings of the ACM SIGKDD international conference on knowledge discovery and data mining* (pp. 1135–1144).
49. Rotter, J. B. (1967). A new scale for the measurement of interpersonal trust. *Journal of Personality*.
50. Rudin, C. (2019). Stop explaining black box machine learning models for high stakes decisions and use interpretable models instead. *Nature Machine Intelligence, 1*(5), 206–215.
51. Schemmer, M., Kuehl, N., Benz, C., & Satzger, G. (2022). On the influence of explainable ai on automation bias. In *Proceedings of the European Conference on Information Systems (ECIS).*
52. Schrills, T., & Franke, T. (2020). Color for characters-effects of visual explanations of ai on trust and observability. In *Proceedings of the International Conference on Artificial Intelligence in HCI* (pp. 121–135).
53. Shin, D. (2021). The effects of explainability and causability on perception, trust, and acceptance: Implications for explainable ai. *International Journal of Human-Computer Studies, 146*(102), 551.
54. Sinha, R., & Swearingen, K. (2002). The role of transparency in recommender systems. In *Proceedings of the CHI conference extended abstracts on human factors in computing systems* (pp. 830–831)
55. Son, J. Y., & Kim, S. S. (2008). Internet users' information privacy-protective responses: A taxonomy and a nomological model. *MIS Quarterly*, 503–529.
56. Spiekermann, S., Grossklags, J., & Berendt, B. (2001). E-privacy in 2nd generation e-commerce: Privacy preferences versus actual behavior. In *Proceedings of the ACM conference on electronic commerce* (pp. 38–47).
57. Stiglic, G., Kocbek, P., Fijacko, N., Zitnik, M., Verbert, K., & Cilar, L. (2020). Interpretability of machine learning-based prediction models in healthcare. *Wiley Interdisciplinary Reviews-Data Mining and Knowledge Discovery, 10*(5), Article e1379.
58. Tjoa, E., & Guan, C. (2020). A survey on explainable artificial intelligence (xai): Toward medical xai. *IEEE Transactions on Neural Networks and Learning Systems, 32*(11), 4793–4813.
59. White, T. B. (2004). Consumer disclosure and disclosure avoidance: A motivational framework. *Journal of Consumer Psychology, 14*(1–2), 41–51.

60. Xu, H., Teo, H. H., Tan, B. C., & Agarwal, R. (2009). The role of push-pull technology in privacy calculus: the case of location-based services. *Journal of Management Information Systems, 26*(3), 135–174.
61. Yamagishi, T., & Yamagishi, M. (1994). Trust and commitment in the united states and japan. *Motivation and Emotion, 18*, 129–166.
62. Yeomans, M., Shah, A., Mullainathan, S., & Kleinberg, J. (2019). Making sense of recommendations. *Journal of Behavioral Decision Making, 32*(4), 403–414.

GPSR Compliance
The European Union's (EU) General Product Safety Regulation (GPSR) is a set of rules that requires consumer products to be safe and our obligations to ensure this.

If you have any concerns about our products, you can contact us on

ProductSafety@springernature.com

In case Publisher is established outside the EU, the EU authorized representative is:

Springer Nature Customer Service Center GmbH
Europaplatz 3
69115 Heidelberg, Germany

www.ingramcontent.com/pod-product-compliance
Ingram Content Group UK Ltd.
Pitfield, Milton Keynes, MK11 3LW, UK
UKHW021639180926
475650UK00001B/37
9783032084798